PUBLIC OPINION

AND

AMERICAN DEMOCRACY

PUBLIC
OPINION
AND
AMERICAN
DEMOCRACY

V·O·Key, Jr

Alfred·A·Knopf : *New York*

1 9 6 1

L. C. catalog card number: 61-14321

THIS IS A BORZOI BOOK,

PUBLISHED BY ALFRED A. KNOPF, INC.

FIRST EDITION

TO

L. G. K.

PREFACE

DURING the past two decades the study of public opinion, once a major concern of political scientists, has become a preoccupation of sociologists and social psychologists. By the application of the techniques of their trade these specialists have made substantial contributions to the understanding of public opinion. Yet as they have done so, they have also in large measure abstracted public opinion from its governmental setting. We have, consequently, a large body of research findings characterized often by methodological virtuosity and on occasion even by theoretical felicity, whose relevance for the workings of the governmental system is not always apparent.

The object in the preparation of this book was comparatively modest. It was mainly to attempt to place the newer knowledge about public opinion in a political context. Ultimately the achievement of that endeavor requires estimates of how public opinion bears on what government does. The making of such estimates, it must be conceded, encounters formidable problems. Yet our knowledge of the microscopic aspects of public opinion must remain of little avail until the relation of these bits of information to the operation of the political system in the large can be shown. My endeavors in this connection are necessarily tentative and often speculative, but it is hoped that the attempt has resulted in an analysis of some utility to those concerned about the bearing of public opinion on American government.

A combination of circumstances enabled me to undertake this inquiry. McGeorge Bundy, Dean of the Faculty of Arts and Sciences of Harvard University, designated me Ford Research Professor of Government for 1959–60, an arrangement that permitted me to work for an extended period at the Survey Research Center of the University of Michigan. Through the kindness of Professor Angus Campbell, Director of the Center, I was given working facilities and access to the materials accumulated by the Center in its surveys of presidential elections. The availability of these data made it possible to bring empirical data to bear on many of the theoretical questions of interest to students of public opinion. Perhaps for most readers the chief value of the book will rest in its new data from the SRC surveys. Only those who have worked with survey data can appreciate the extent of my obligation to the Survey Research Center. The materials presented here are essentially by-products of its extensive work in the processing of the information recorded on its interview schedules.[1] A visiting scholar, generously granted access to information, may put it to uses that its collectors can view only with uplifted eyebrow. The conventional injunction, therefore, applies with special force: the Survey Research Center should not be taxed with responsibility for what I have done with its data.

To Dean Bundy and Professor Campbell I owe special debts of gratitude. I am also obliged to many others who in one way or another aided me. Professor James K. Pollock, Chairman of the Department of Political Science of the University of Michigan, exerted himself far beyond the call of friendship to make my stay in Ann Arbor both pleasant and productive. Warren E. Miller and Donald E. Stokes, staff members of both the Department of Political Science and the Survey Research Center of the University of Michigan, gave me guidance in the analysis of survey data and aid at many points. Whatever merit the book may have owes much to my research assistant, Nancy W. Men-

---

[1] A word is in order to explain the usages followed in the citation of SRC materials throughout the book. Tables and figures with a source note, "Survey Research Center, University of Michigan, 1952," are drawn from the IBM cards from the Center's 1952 presidential election study. The principal analysis of these materials is Angus Campbell, Gerald Gurin, and Warren E. Miller: *The Voter Decides* (Evanston: Row, Peterson; 1954). Tables and figures with a source note, "Survey Research Center, University of Michigan, 1956," are drawn from data from the Center's 1956 presidential election study. The principal report on this survey is Angus Campbell, Philip E. Converse, Warren E. Miller, and Donald E. Stokes: *The American Voter* (New York: Wiley; 1960). A few tables are also presented from the data of a 1954 survey which has been reported by Angus Campbell and Homer C. Cooper, *Group Differences in Attitudes and Votes* (Ann Arbor: Survey Research Center; 1956). An item occasionally appears from a survey at the time of the 1958 congressional elections the major analysis of which has not appeared.

delsohn; she managed to combine an understanding of the intricacies of IBM machines with an intimate acquaintance with the substance of the SRC materials.

I have had the benefit of the advice of several friends and colleagues who reviewed the manuscript. Oliver Garceau of East Boothbay, Maine, Avery Leiserson of Vanderbilt University, David B. Truman of Columbia University, and Joseph Cooper of Harvard University gave me their comments with the candor borne of friendship. Had I had the wit to take into account all their criticisms, this would have been a better book. I must record my gratitude to them for their help and, of course, absolve them of responsibility for what is written here.

V. O. KEY, JR.

Littauer Center,
Cambridge, Massachusetts

CONTENTS

Part II : *Structural Distribution*

Part III : *Properties*

Part VI : *Conclusions*

PUBLIC OPINION

AND

AMERICAN DEMOCRACY

I

INTRODUCTION

GOVERNMENTS must concern themselves with the opinions of their citizens, if only to provide a basis for repression of disaffection. The persistent curiosity, and anxiety, of rulers about what their subjects say of them and of their actions are chronicled in the histories of secret police. Measures to satisfy such curiosity by soundings of opinion are often only an aspect of political persecution; they may also guide policies of persuasion calculated to convert discontent into cheerful acquiescence. And even in the least democratic regime opinion may influence the direction or tempo of substantive policy. Although a government may be erected on tyranny, to endure it needs the ungrudging support of substantial numbers of its people. If that support does not arise spontaneously, measures will be taken to stimulate it by tactical concessions to public opinion, by the management of opinion, or by both.[1]

1 · Power and Public Opinion

The incubation and gradual spread of the ideas of democracy radically altered expectations about the relations between the views of the citizenry and the acts of its rulers. In early times governments found le-

[1] See Alex Inkeles: *Public Opinion in Soviet Russia* (Cambridge: Harvard University Press; 1950).

gitimacy for their authority in various sources—from divine right on
down—but rarely did they place much store on the consent of the
governed. The citizen's duty was to obey. Gradually over several cen-
turies, from small beginnings in medieval towns to the American and
French Revolutions, these rationalizations of authority were revised
to ground the right to govern in the consent of the governed. The per-
colation of this idea into the mind of man generated an ethical imperative that gave a new color to the relations of governors and governed.
The dynasties of Europe learned from Napoleon that they had to take
into account the wishes of the governed in order to maintain their
power, but the democratic doctrine assumed this to be a condition of
governing rightly. In the nineteenth century the struggles for suffrage
expansion and for parliamentary government led to the establishment
of institutions appropriate to the belief that the mass of the people
should in some way participate in the great decisions of state and
thereby govern themselves. The bundle of ideas, beliefs, and emotions connected with this view had an appeal so universal and so powerful that modern dictatorships took over much of the symbolism, ritual,
and semantics of democracy.

Progressivism and the Efflorescence of Faith in the Public. The ethical
imperative that government heed the opinion of the public has its
origins, thus, in democratic ideology as well as in the practical necessity that governments obtain the support of influential elements in society. The notion of government by public opinion, nourished on
memories of government as exploitation of the mass of men by a few
men, stirred millennial hopes of a lasting popular emancipation. By the
enthronement of public opinion, governors could be brought to heel
and the supposedly idealistic hopes of all men could be realized.
Through the history of American political thought these ideas have
flowed—at times thinly, as disillusionment set in; at times in flood, as
democratic idealism flourished. Democratic hopes and expectations
reached a great peak in the United States in the years before World
War I, when the doughty Progressives fought their battles against
privilege and preached the righteousness of the popular will. To see
that the popular will prevailed, they contrived no end of means to involve the people in the process of government. Not only were officials
to be elected; they were to be subject to recall by the voters. Legislators, long subservient to special interests, were to find themselves subject to a popular veto through a referendum on their acts. Or the
people were to be free to take matters into their own hands and to
initiate legislative action through the new instruments of direct de-

mocracy. The courts, regarded as the sturdiest bastion of the special interests, were to be subjected to the humiliation of a popular review of their constitutional decisions.

Disenchantment: Mr. Lippmann and the Straw Man. This heightened faith in the people proved to be a momentary exaltation, and it was dimmed, if not snuffed out, as Wilsonian idealism declined in the aftermath of World War I. In 1922 Walter Lippmann published his *Public Opinion*, in which he reappraised the function of public opinion in the democratic process. The years of Harding and Coolidge were not times to inspire high hopes in the future of the human race, and in 1925 Mr. Lippmann issued *The Phantom Public*, a volume whose title put more bluntly than did its argument a thesis severely deflating the role of the public.

What Mr. Lippmann did was to destroy a straw man. He did it thoroughly nonetheless. He refuted the more extravagant beliefs about the role of the average man in self-governance by citation of a few cold, hard facts. Whether these beliefs had ever been held save in the autointoxication of political oratory directed to the average man may be doubted. Yet Mr. Lippmann demolished whatever illusion existed that "the public" could be regarded as an omnicompetent and omniscient collectivity equipped to decide the affairs of state. The average person, Mr. Lippmann made clear, had little time for the affairs of state. He exhausted his energies earning a livelihood, and, once home from work, he was likely to take off his shoes and indulge his feet as he looked at the comics rather than to attempt to inform himself on the intricate pros and cons of the weighty matters currently confounding Washington. Even if he were willing to devote his spare time to the study of public issues, the information available to him was both inadequate and unenlightening. The newspapers of that day were no more dedicated to the clarification of public issues than are those of the present. Nor was the amorphous public, even if informed, capable of taking the initiative in any public action.[2]

The New Machiavellians: Barnums and Cabals. Blows from other sources also battered the idyllic vision of the guidance of affairs by the opinions of a virtuous public. In the decades after World War I

[2] It should be remembered that Mr. Lippmann's *Public Opinion* had sprinkled through it a goodly number of insights that the public opinion specialists of a quarter of a century later stumbled on independently and proclaimed as new discoveries.

belief in the ability of propagandists to manipulate public attitudes grew apace. New theories of psychology brought new conceptions of the nature of man, conceptions that made him a nonrational creature of subconscious urges and external suggestion. During World War I itself the propagandists took great strides in the development of their art. The belief that the people could readily be manipulated by the mass media became even more widely held later as radio and television attracted vast audiences. Propagandists and advertising men encouraged the acceptance of the most exaggerated estimates of their powers. Given enough money, they could sell soap, cigarettes, policies, presidential candidates, even monstrous and nonfunctional automobiles. As a group at bottom professionally dedicated to the dissemination of falsehood (we need not blink so obvious a fact), the advertising fraternity had few inhibitions against the propagation of myths that inflated its own capabilities. Eventually the image of public opinion as an irresistible giant yielded to the image of the all-powerful opinion manipulators, engineers of consent and molders of mass opinion.

Obviously no conception of American politics that placed at the apex of power advertising men and public-relations counselors—insecure, ulcer-ridden hucksters—could satisfy for long. A more elegant theory of politics was needed. Mr. C. Wright Mills brought the theoretical evolution full circle in the 1950's as he expounded the role and function of the "power elite." Behind all the constitutional trappings and the self-important activities of most politicians and other front men, he thought he perceived a clique of the big rich, the corporate bosses, the military brass, and a few key politicians. By their consultations and maneuvers this group, if we may caricature Mr. Mills—and he invites caricature—fixes the principal lines of national policy. Behind them trail the lesser men: the press, the radio and TV, and the minor politicians. Then in due course the public tags along.[3]

New Situational Limits to Public Opinion. Without doubt the conditions affecting the relations between government and public opinion have been radically altered during the past half-century. The means for informing and influencing the public have undergone a transformation. With the concentration in large corporations, in labor unions, and in other organizations of the powers of private decision formerly widely dispersed has come a parallel concentration of the power of autonomous political decision into relatively fewer hands. With the growth in range of governmental functions and the increase in their

[3] C. Wright Mills: *The Power Elite* (New York: Oxford University Press; 1956).

complexity, the average man is, or at least is said to be, more and more bewildered, or repelled, by questions of public policy. With the movement of decision to Washington and with the growth in salience of foreign policy questions, matters of public policy are less and less intimately relevant to the experience and knowledge of most people. With the extension of the curtain of secrecy over wider areas, the public is denied information and thereby the opportunity for meaningful criticism of public policy.

Despite all these developments, it is too early to conclude that governments can ignore public opinion or that democratic government amounts only to a hoax, a ritual whose performance serves only to delude the people and thereby to convert them into willing subjects of the powers that be. The most superficial comparison of American public policy in 1900 and in 1960 indicates that there have been changes of no little consequence for the average man. Not all these policy innovations have been willed by a power elite of 100 or 200 persons; nor have they been entirely unconnected with mass sentiment. Unless mass views have some place in the shaping of policy, all the talk about democracy is nonsense. As Lasswell has said, the "open interplay of opinion and policy is the distinguishing mark of popular rule." [4] Yet the sharp definition of the role of public opinion as it affects different kinds of policies under different types of situations presents an analytical problem of extraordinary difficulty. That problem, however, should not lead us to ignore, or to deny, the phenomenon of the conduct of enormous governmental operations in a manner that by and large wins the support of a citizenry of millions and is in the main in accord with their preferences. Given control of the apparatus of authority, to govern is easy; but to govern without heavy reliance on the machinery of coercion is a high art.

2 · Conceptions and Distinctions

Among philosophers, publicists, and spare-time commentators on public affairs, the discussion of public opinion is conducted with style. Aphorisms, epigrams, axioms, and figures embellish the verbal display. One can, with Pascal, christen public opinion the "Queen of the World." One can observe, with the authors of *The Federalist*, that "all government rests on opinion" or, with Hume, that it is "on opinion only that government is founded." One can assert that governments derive their powers from the "consent of the governed" or can picture

[4] Harold D. Lasswell: *Democracy Through Public Opinion* (Menasha, Wis.: Banta; 1941), p. 15.

public opinion as "a giant who is fickle and ignorant yet still has a giant's strength, and may use it with frightful effect." [5]

Such metaphors serve principally to ornament prose rather than to enlighten the reader about the nature of public opinion. Yet the discussion of public opinion becomes murky when meticulous scholars try to define their conceptions and to form distinctions that enable them to make statements that seem to fit the observable realities of the interaction of public opinion and government. This murkiness by no means flows solely from the incomprehensibility of men of learning. To speak with precision of public opinion is a task not unlike coming to grips with the Holy Ghost. Public opinion, Leiserson notes, "has come to refer to a sort of secular idol, and is a 'god-term' to which citizens, scientists, and office-holders alike pay allegiance, partly as an act of faith, partly as a matter of observation, partly as a condition of sanity." [6] Nevertheless, a brief review of some of the conceptions and distinctions that have been developed by scholars in their discussions of the topic should be of value as an aid in orientation.

Public As Organic Entity. Some speculators on public opinion have imagined the public to be a semiorganized entity that in some way or another could move through stages of initiation and debate and reach a recognizable collective decision on an issue. The images of the city-state and of the New England town meeting often color such attempts to form a conception of the reality of public opinion in the modern state. The intricate structure of the nation-state cannot easily be grasped, and some students seek in the processes of opinion formation the equivalent of the citizenry gathered in the town hall or in the market place to discuss, debate, and settle public issues. In its simplest form this analogous thinking personifies the public: "The public expects"; "The public demands"; "Public opinion swept away all opposition." [7] Perhaps a comparable conception is concealed in the assertion that public opinion "is a deeply persuasive organic force," which "articulates and formulates not only the deliberative judgments of the rational elements within the collectivity but the evanescent common will, which somehow integrates and momentarily crystallizes the sporadic sentiments and loyalties of the masses of the population." [8]

[5] Thomas A. Bailey: *The Man in the Street* (New York: Macmillan; 1948), p. 1.

[6] Avery Leiserson: "Notes on the Theory of Opinion Formation," *American Political Science Review*, XLVII (1953), 171.

[7] For a discussion of such fictions and fallacies, see F. H. Allport: "Toward a Science of Public Opinion," *Public Opinion Quarterly*, 1 (January, 1937), 7–23.

[8] Wilhelm Bauer: "Public Opinion," in *Encyclopaedia of the Social Sciences* (New York: Macmillan; 1935), XII, 669–74.

Some observers, in their search for a conception to encompass the public opinion process as a whole, produce statements more complex than the town-meeting analogy but not fundamentally different in kind. An image emerges of a rudimentary organism consisting of individuals and groups linked together by mass communications, which centers its attention on an issue, discusses and deliberates, and in some mysterious way proceeds to a decision. A public becomes a social entity, different from a mob and not the same as a mass. Thus, Young notes that "in terms of stability and degree of institutionalization, . . . a public is a transitory, amorphous, and relatively unstructured association of individuals with certain interests in common." [9] From the conception of the "public" as a social entity it is but a short step to the attempt to identify some pattern of actions or behavior through which the entity travels to reach decision or to form public opinion on an issue. Analysis in such terms is called the study of the dynamics of opinion formation, in contrast with the study of opinion as static (or at a moment in time). On occasion the process is likened to individual action in response to a problem. "Public opinion then becomes a form of group thinking, and the process bears more than an analagous relation to the individual's complete act of thought." [1] Or a sequence of steps is suggested as a standard pattern through which the public moves in the formation of opinion—for example, the rise of an issue, discussion and deliberation, and arrival at a decision.[2]

More is lost than is gained in understanding by the organismic view of the public. Occasionally, in relatively small communities, citizen concern and involvement over an issue may be widespread and community consideration may move in close articulation with the mechanisms of authority to a decision that can realistically be said to be a decision by public opinion. At far rarer intervals great national populations may be swept by a common concern about a momentous issue with a similar result. Yet ordinarily a decision is made not by the public but by officials after greater or a lesser consideration of the opinion of the public or of parts of the public.

Special Publics and the General Public. While the organismic conceptions of the public and of the opinion process may be of more poetic than practical utility, other distinctions developed by students of pub-

[9] Kimball Young: "Comments on the Nature of 'Public' and 'Public Opinion,' " *International Journal of Opinion and Attitude Research*, II (1948), 385.

[1] Carroll D. Clark: "Concept of the Public," *Southwestern Social Science Quarterly*, XIII (1932–3), 311–20.

[2] See W. Phillips Davison: "The Public Opinion Process," *Public Opinion Quarterly*, XXII (1952), 91–106.

lic opinion serve as handy aids to thought on the subject. There is, for example, the distinction between special publics and the general public. At one time it was the custom to speak of "the public." In due course it became evident that on only a few questions did the entire citizenry have an opinion. The notion of special publics was contrived to describe those segments of the public with views about particular issues, problems, or other questions of public concern. In actual politics one issue engages the attention of one subdivision of the population, while another arouses the interest of another group, and a third question involves still another special public. This distinction between general and special publics does, of course, do violence to the basic idea that "the" public shall prevail; it also warps the meaning of the term "public." Yet the usage mirrors the facts of political life and, incidentally, creates a problem for the public opinion theorist. He sometimes copes with the difficulty by the assertion that when the concern of a small special public prevails, it does so with the tacit consent of the general public.

Blumer deals in a different way with the problem created by the existence of special publics. He remarks that public opinion may be "different from the opinion of any of the groups in the public. It can be thought of, perhaps, as a composite opinion formed out of the several opinions that are held in the public; or better, as the central tendency set by the striving of these separate opinions and, consequently, as being shaped by the relative strength and play of opposition among them." [3] Blumer thus brings together the opinions of the special publics into something of a weighted average that takes into account both the numbers holding different kinds of opinions (or no opinion) and the strength of the holders of opinion. Whether this notion has validity, the question of who has what kind of opinion is of basic significance in a consideration of interactions between public and government.

Public and Private Opinion. There are opinions and opinions; their number is as numerous as the kinds of objects about which men have preferences and beliefs. On what range of topics may opinion be considered to be public? Not all opinions of the public, even when widely held within the population, are to be properly regarded as public opinion. It may be assumed that opinions about the desirability of tailfins on Chevrolets are not public opinions, or that preferences for striped or solid white toothpaste fall outside the concern of the student of public

[3] Herbert Blumer: "The Mass, the Public, and Public Opinion," in Bernard Berelson and Morris Janowitz: *Reader in Public Opinion and Communication,* enlarged ed. (Glencoe: Free Press; 1953), pp. 46–8.

opinion. On the other hand, opinion about the length of automobile tailfins may become public opinion if the question becomes one of whether the length of nonfunctional automobile ornamentation has become a public nuisance by its pressure on the available parking acreage. Goldhamer suggests that an opinion is public "if it attaches to an object of public concern."[4] The content of the phrase, "object of public concern," may vary from time to time with the changing scope of governmental action, or it may differ from society to society.

Many American students of public opinion have limited themselves to a narrow range of public opinion; they have tended to regard public opinion as concerned with substantive issues of public policy. That focus results from the basic tenet that public opinion should determine public policy, but it excludes a range of opinions of undoubted political relevance. Opinions about candidates, views about political parties, attitudes about the performance of governments, basic assumptions about what is right and proper in public affairs, and general beliefs and expectations about the place of government in society are also opinions of political relevance, as would be such opinions or states of mind as are embraced by the term "national morale."

Characteristics of Public Opinion. The differentiation between opinions about public objects and about private objects crudely defines the outer limits of the opinion sphere that may be regarded as public. It leaves untouched the question of the characteristics of public opinion. In recent decades considerable scholarly effort has been devoted, principally by social psychologists, to ascertaining the characteristics of public opinion. In an earlier day the practice was to treat the direction of opinion in simple pro and con categories. The majority could be described as for or against, as voting yes or no. The psychometricians have made it clear that a pro-and-con categorization of opinion often conceals wide gradations in opinion. They have contrived scales to measure opinion in its dimension of direction. For example, a division of people who support and oppose government ownership of industry does not provide a useful indication of the nature of public opinion on the question of government policy toward economic activity. Views on economic policy may be arranged along a scale from the extreme left to the extreme right. The opinion of an individual may be located at any one of many points along such a scale. One person may favor governmental ownership of all the means of production; another may be satisfied with a large dose of governmental regulation; still another

---

[4] Herbert Goldhamer: "Public Opinion and Personality," *American Journal of Sociology*, LV (1949–50), 346.

may prefer only the most limited control of the economy; and others may wish to abolish whatever controls exist. The determination of the distribution of the population along such scales measuring the direction of opinion makes possible a more informed estimate of the nature of public opinion, in its dimension of direction, than did earlier and cruder conceptions.

Closely related to the conception of direction of opinion are ideas about the qualities or properties of opinion. Intensity of opinion is one of these qualities. A person may be an extreme conservative or radical on the scale of direction of opinion, but he may care a great deal, a little, or scarcely at all about that opinion; that is, opinions may vary in the intensity with which they are held. Obviously the incidence of opinion intensity within the electorate about an issue or problem is of basic importance for politics. An issue that arouses only opinion of low intensity may receive only the slightest attention, while one that stirs opinions of high intensity among even relatively small numbers of people may be placed high on the governmental agenda. Another quality of opinion of some importance is its stability. An individual, for example, may have a view, expressed on the basis of little or no information, which may readily be changed. On the other hand, an opinion may be so firmly held that it is not easily altered. Issues that relate to opinions of high stability widely held within the population present radically different problems for government than do those matters on which opinion is unstable.

Students of public opinion often differentiate between opinion and custom. Utilizing this distinction, public opinion concerns those issues whose solution is not more or less automatically provided by custom or by the expectations shared predominantly by members of the group. Public opinion, then, concerns live issues. Park said that public opinion emerges when action is in process; it is opinion "before it has been capitalized and, so to speak, funded in the form of dogma, doctrine, or law." [5] The exclusion from public opinion of the settled attitudes of the community unduly narrows the meaning of the term. Governments must pay heed to the mores, the customs, the "funded" or the "standing" opinions quite as much as to the effervescence of today's popular discussion. The distinction between opinion and custom really amounts to a differentiation between qualities of opinions.

Prerequisites for the Existence of Public Opinion. Students of public opinion have also sought to identify those broad conditions under

[5] Robert E. Park: "News and the Power of the Press," *American Journal of Sociology*, XLVII (1941), 1–11.

which public opinion could sensibly be said to exist as a force in government. Democratic theorists that they were, they specified democratic conditions as a prerequisite for even the existence of public opinion. Freedom of speech and discussion, for example, are said to be prerequisites, since it is by public discussion that opinion is formed. Closely associated with this condition is that of the free availability of information about public issues and public questions; those problems handled by government in secrecy can scarcely be a subject of informed public debate.

Opinion theorists almost uniformly place emphasis on the importance of the existence of a consensus on fundamentals as a basis for the settlement of the differences involved in the development of a prevailing opinion on transient issues. Otherwise, government cannot be founded upon public opinion. "There is," says MacIver, "no public opinion unless an area of common ground lies underneath and supports the differences of opinion, finding expression in the traditions and conventions and behavior patterns characteristic of the folk." [6] Similarly, Park argued that there needs to be within the public "a general understanding and a community of interest among all parties sufficient to make discussion possible." [7]

In keeping with this general vein of thought, Lowell sharply restricted the content of the term "public opinion." In his system the views of people generally on public questions of all sorts did not constitute public opinion. For a "real" public opinion to exist, it had to be a community opinion. Thus, when two highwaymen meet a traveler on a dark road and propose to relieve him of his wallet, it would be incorrect to say that a public opinion existed favorable to a redistribution of property. Public opinion, Lowell thought, need not be a unanimous opinion, but it should create an "obligation moral or political on the part of the minority," an obligation, at least under certain conditions, to submit. He laid great stress on the grounds of consensus as a basis for public opinion. "A body of men are politically capable of a public opinion only so far as they are agreed upon the ends and aims of government and upon the principles by which those ends shall be attained." No public opinion could exist in nations with large minorities unwilling to abide by majority decision. Moreover, public opinion could exist only when "the bulk of the people are in a position to determine of their own knowledge or by weighing a substantial part of the facts required for a rational decision," or when the

[6] R. M. MacIver: *Academic Freedom in Our Time* (New York: Columbia University Press; 1955), p. 23. See also Bernard Berelson: "Democratic Theory and Public Opinion," *Public Opinion Quarterly*, XVI (1952), 313–30.

[7] Park: loc. cit., 6.

question involves an issue of "apparent harmony or contradiction with settled convictions."[8]

It seems clear that consensus does not have to prevail for opinions to exist to which governments must accord weight. Yet the emphasis on consensus identifies special problems in governments that accord deference to public opinion. If the public is to project its opinions into public policy, some sectors of the public must be prepared to accept actions distasteful to them. The limits of the general consensus may fix the limits within which widespread participation in public affairs may lead to decisions distasteful yet acceptable to those whose opinions do not prevail.

3 · A Working View of Public Opinion

For purposes of political analysis one need not strain painfully toward the formation of a theoretical representation of an eerie entity called "public opinion." One need not seek to find "the" public embodied in some kind of amorphous social structure that goes through recurring patterns of action as it reaches a decision. "Public opinion" in this discussion may simply be taken to mean those opinions held by private persons which governments find it prudent to heed. Governments may be compelled toward action or inaction by such opinion; in other instances they may ignore it, perhaps at their peril; they may attempt to alter it; or they may divert or pacify it. So defined, opinion may be shared by many or by few people. It may be the veriest whim, or it may be a settled conviction. The opinion may represent a general agreement formed after the widest discussion; it may be far less firmly founded. It may even be contingent opinion—that is, estimates by decision makers of probable responses to actions they consider taking. Whatever the character or distribution of opinion, governments may need to estimate its nature as an incident to many of their actions.[9] Probably any regime needs to heed at least some opinions outside the government; yet the range of opinions that enter into the calculations of governors obviously varies among societies with their political norms and customs.

This view of public opinion resembles the conceptions of several

[8] A. Lawrence Lowell: *Public Opinion and Popular Government* (New York: Longmans, Green; 1913), chs. 1, 2.

[9] The conception of public opinion advanced here, it is cheerfully conceded, is difficult to apply in research. If one is to know what opinions governments heed, one must know the inner thoughts of presidents, congressmen, and other officials. It is even more difficult to know what opinions prudent governments should heed for the sake of the success of their policies or even for their survival.

other commentators. Speier defines, for the purposes of historical analysis, "public opinion" as "opinions on matters of concern to the nation freely and publicly expressed by men outside the government who claim a right that their opinions should influence or determine the actions, personnel, or structure of their government." [1] Wirth observed that the "decisive part of public opinion, then, is the organization of views on issues that exercise an impact upon those who are in a position to make decisions." [2] In the context of a criticism of those pollsters who regard all the responses obtained by their interviewers as public opinion, Blumer remarks that "the character of public opinion in terms of meaningful operation must be sought in the array of views and positions which enter into the consideration of those who have to take action on public opinion." [3]

Virtues and Consequences of a Broad View of Opinion. The adoption of a broad, and somewhat vague, conception of public opinion has consequences for a general survey of the field. While it permits an avoidance of some analytical problems, it also brings within the range of the discussion an extremely wide variety of phenomena. When public opinion is regarded as those opinions that may influence government, it is unnecessary to assume that "the public" exists as any particular sort of loosely structured association or other ghostly sociological entity. On a given question the operative public may consist of a highly structured association, while on another matter opinions may be diffused through a wide public that lacks any special organization. The form of the public concerned about subsidies to maritime shipping could plausibly be expected to differ radically from that of the public concerned about honesty in public office. On one issue the public may consist of one sector of the population; on another, of a quite different sector. Not much overlap would be expected between those deeply interested in policy toward upland game and those concerned about practices in the licensing of plumbers. Or publics may be differentiated by the nature of their involvement in public questions. Almond speaks of the "mass public" and the "attentive public." The mass public, informed by the mass media, pays heed to the tone of discussion of issues and responds by moods of apprehension or complacency. The attentive public, a far smaller group, follows public issues

[1] Hans Speier: "Historical Development of Public Opinion," *American Journal of Sociology,* LV (1949–50), 376.

[2] Louis Wirth: "Consensus and Mass Communication," *American Sociological Review,* XIII (1948), 1–15.

[3] Herbert Blumer: "Public Opinion and Public Opinion Polling," *American Sociological Review,* XIII (1948), 545.

in an analytical manner, is relatively well informed, and constitutes a critical audience for the discussion of public affairs.[4]

To emphasize, in the definition of opinion, relevance for government is to bring opinions with widely varying properties or qualities within our range of concern. Lowell limited opinion to "the acceptance of one among two or more inconsistent views which are capable of being accepted by a rational mind as true."[5] By "opinion" Young means "a belief or conviction more verifiable and stronger in intensity than a mere hunch or impression but less strong than truly verifiable or positive knowledge."[6] Under the present conception no such restricted view of opinion is necessary. Lightly held views and transient anxieties, prejudices, preferences, demands, and convictions all have their relevance for governmental action. Nor need the common distinction between opinion and the mores exclude a set of attitudes from our range of interest. Some students of public opinion conclude that they need to concern themselves only with those contentious issues about which opinion is in process of formation and that settled matters —the mores, the enduring attitudes, the customs—are beyond their purview. Although these distinctions between types of citizen outlook are analytically useful, governments must take both kinds of views into account. The prescriptions of custom may control particular actions; particular actions may aim to modify custom, an objective best undertaken after reflection about the probable public response.

These comments on the qualities of "opinion" bring within the limits of that term a considerable range of views—from whim to conviction to custom—but the term acquires an even broader connotation by mention of the objects about which opinion may be considered "public." The most common assumption is that public opinion concerns issues of substantive policy; yet our emphasis on opinions to which governments need to pay heed requires attention to opinions about many objects other than issues. Indeed, a contented—or discontented—people may have opinions that are most relevant politically but in the main about matters other than concrete issues. They may be exercised about economic conditions; they may have anxieties about the threat of war. In either case their views may not be, at least for most people, centered sharply on well-defined policy issues. Or people may have images of institutions or expectations about institutional performance or evaluations of public personnel—all questions

[4] Gabriel Almond: "Public Opinion and National Security Policy," *Public Opinion Quarterly*, XX (1956), 371–8.
[5] A. Lawrence Lowell: *Public Opinion in War and Peace* (Cambridge: Harvard University Press; 1923), p. 12.
[6] Young: loc. cit., 387.

of the most direct relevance for governmental actions though not formulated as policy issues.

Although all regimes must pay heed to the opinions of their peoples, obviously in democratic orders opinion plays a different role than in dictatorial states. When the doctrine prevails that citizens have a right to be heard and governments have a duty to hear, private opinion may have an impact on most major public actions. For the maximum participation of the public (or the publics) a practice of disclosure or notice of prospective actions and of announcement of the considerations underlying actions must be followed. Freedom of association and freedom of expression of opinion on public matters need also to exist. For these reasons, public opinion is sometimes regarded as that opinion communicated to the government. Yet, in practice, governments may (and often do) give weight to latent opinion; in advance of action, they need to estimate the kinds of opinions that may be expressed if a given course is followed or proposed. Hence, communication of views to the government is not essential to transform opinion into public opinion, although communication may be the general rule.

The Plan of Analysis. The chapters that follow will treat those aspects of public opinion and the processes of its formation and expression that are of major concern to government, with primary attention to American government. The chapters of Part I will be concerned with the simple *distribution of opinions.* That is, they will treat the typical forms that opinions of the population take when they are distributed along attitude scales. In one instance, for example, the opinions of most people may cluster closely together on an attitude scale, a condition indicative of widespread popular agreement on a question. But in another instance the opinion distribution may be marked by a clear bipolarization. Obviously these different types of distribution create radically different opinion contexts for governmental action.

Another group of chapters will deal with what we may call the *structural distribution of opinions.* Opinions about issues or about other political objects may be distributed among different kinds and sorts of people in differing ways. In the geographical distribution of opinions the bases are found for sectional differences within politics. In the differential incidence of opinions among occupations and classes are found the bases for other kinds of political tensions.

A third part of the analysis will concern the *properties of opinion.* Far more information is available on the distribution of opinions than about their properties. Yet the properties of opinion are of prime importance in the governing process. On some questions opinions may be so lightly held by the citizenry that they have only the slightest impact upon public action. In other instances even a small part of the population may hold a position so tenaciously that it may block, if not direct, public action. The chapters on the properties of opinion will summarize the available information, scant though it is, on these characteristics of public attitudes.

For an understanding of the place of opinion in the governing process, some knowledge of the processes of formation of opinion is essential. Hence another cluster of chapters will treat the *formation of opinion*. The scheme of analysis will be to treat some of the principal agencies and institutions influential in the formation of attitudes and opinion—the family, the school, the mass media—and to attempt to delineate their roles and to estimate their strengths and weaknesses as formers of opinion. In truth, all those influences that go to make a person what he is have a hand in the formation of opinion. The analysis will necessarily be selective among these influences, with the object of identifying the sources of influence that seem most immediately significant politically.

Although governments at times may be so sensitive that they can anticipate opinion before they act, opinion commonly gains its influence by being communicated to government. A concluding group of chapters will be concerned with the *linkage of government and opinion*. While the tie between government and opinion often consists of informal communications between citizenry and functionary, there have also developed specialized institutions and procedures whose function is, among other things, to shape, organize, and represent opinion to government. The chief objects of attention in these chapters will be those institutions, such as political parties and pressure groups.

Part I

PATTERNS OF

DISTRIBUTION

OF PRIMARY

significance to government is the pattern of the distribution of public opinion among the citizenry. In its simplest form a distribution of opinion according to its direction may be merely the division of the people into those for and against a proposal, a candidate, or a party. Obviously a government sensitive to public attitudes confronts a different problem when 90 per cent of the people are for and 10 per cent against a proposition than when the division is 50:50. Another kind of situation exists when an issue arises on which 15 per cent are pro, 10 per cent are anti, and 75 per cent are unaware of the question.

While the simple yes-no division is the form most commonly referred to in everyday discourse, the actual distribution of opinion within the public usually takes on a more complex form. Instead of a yes-no dichotomy, attitudes toward a public issue may be ranged along a scale represented by a series of different ways of dealing with the question. For example, assume that the problem of relief for the destitute is at issue. At one extreme some people may hold the view that destitution is a product of shiftlessness or of divine will and that the poor deserve to starve. Further along the scale others may be of the opinion that the destitute should receive from the public treasury the minimum necessary to maintain life. A more liberal attitude would be that they should receive a decent maintenance. And still others might hold that they deserve generous support, for their difficulties are but a consequence of the evil workings of the economic system.

Such gradations in public opinion may be described by the tech-niques that psychologists have developed for measuring, or ranking, attitudes. Psychological scales provide us with estimates of aspects of the character of public opinion not established from its simple division for and against a particular proposition. One of the pioneers in attitude measurement was L. L. Thurstone, who developed the Thurstone scale. In essence his procedure was to prepare a series of statements about an institution—for example, the church—or an issue—for example, pro-hibition. The statements indicated what appeared a priori to be varying degrees of approval or disapproval. They were then submitted to

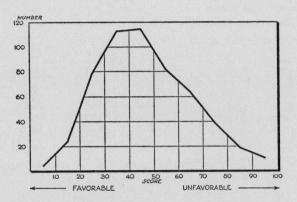

FIGURE I.1. Distribution of University of Texas Students on Scale of Attitudes toward the Negro and Desegre-gation. SOURCE: J. G. Kelley, J. E. Ferson, and W. H. Holtzman: "The Measurement of Attitudes toward the Negro in the South," *Journal of Social Psychology,* XLVIII (1958), 305-17.

several persons, as many as several hundred, with instructions to rank the statements according to degree of approval of the topic of the scale. The ranked list of statements (after the elimination of those whose ranking had varied widely) constituted a scale, which could be administered to subjects to measure their attitude toward the subject of the scale. A person's score on the scale depended upon which state-ments he expressed agreement with.[1]

When the attitudes have been measured (or ranked on a scale), the distribution of attitudes within a group can be pictured in a more revealing fashion than when the only information available consists of the yeas and nays on a single question. To illustrate: A Thurstone-type scale designed to measure attitudes toward the Negro and desegrega-

[1] See L. L. Thurstone and E. J. Chave: *The Measurement of Attitude* (Chi-cago: University of Chicago Press; 1929).

tion was administered to several hundred University of Texas students in 1955 by Kelley, Ferson, and Holtzman. The distribution of students according to their score on the scale took the form appearing in the chart in Figure I.1. Most of them concentrated around the middle of the scale, but a few with views extremely favorable or unfavorable located themselves at the opposite ends of the scale.

It is apparent that attitude scales could serve handily in the description of public opinion. The problems of administering a refined attitude scale to a sample of the national population are such, though, that crude scales are more commonly used. A Fortune Survey *question, asked late in 1940 when the issue of aid to Britain was agitating the country, illustrates the use of a gross sort of scale to ascertain the opinion of a national sample. The* Fortune *pollers asked:*

Which one of these statements comes closest to describing what you would like to see the U.S. do in relation to Great Britain?

1. Declare ourselves allies and send our air force, navy, and army if necessary	7.4%
2. Declare ourselves allies and send our air force and navy but never send an army	3.3
3. See that Britain gets anything she needs except men— even if it's more than half our production and even if we have to give it to her	43.7
4. Continue to sell Britain military supplies up to half our production	27.8
5. Sell food and medical supplies but no fighting equipment	5.9
6. Stop letting her have anything	3.7
7. Don't know	8.2

The psychometricians would not regard this series of statements as a Thurstone-type scale except by courtesy; yet it identified gradations of opinion that would not have been revealed by a yes-no question. If the responses were placed on a curve, they would form a distribution roughly resembling that shown in Figure I.1.[2]

The Likert scale is another technique of attitude measurement. Like the Thurstone scale, it consists of a series of statements about the area of attitude to be measured, but its mode of construction and its technical characteristics differ from that scale. If one were concerned

[2] The point may be made that in the politics of the real world questions are always posed in a yes-no form. Hence, why should we be concerned with gradations of opinion? One answer is that the form of the distribution along a scale determines what question has to be put to obtain a majority.

with, say, attitudes toward public policy about trade unions, he would assemble a series of statements, or items, expressing varying degrees of approval of public regulation of unions. The statements would be so phrased that for about half of them an "agree" response would represent approval of regulation of unions; for the other half of the statements a "disagree" response would represent approval of regulation. For each statement a multiple response would be possible: strongly agree, agree, undecided, disagree, strongly disagree. Each subject would have to check the response that represents his attitude on each statement. A score would then be determined by the assignment of arbitrary weights, such as 1, 2, 3, 4, and 5, to each of the five responses for each statement. By the summation of these weights for the 20 or 25 statements in the scale an individual could be assigned a score.

Many of the analyses in subsequent chapters rest on individual statements of the type employed in the construction of Likert scales. While the administration of a Likert scale to a national sample would be a costly enterprise, individual statements may be administered with alternative responses. Thus, instead of a series of statements expressing varying degrees of approval of government measures to assure the availability of medical care, it is more practicable to ask the respondent in a national sample whether he agrees strongly, agrees but not strongly, is not sure, disagrees, or disagrees strongly with the single proposition: "The government ought to help people get doctors and hospital care at low cost." The distribution of responses among the five alternatives on a single question provides a rough distribution of opinion along a five-point scale.

The Guttman scale now enjoys the widest vogue among the technicians. The manner of its construction is set forth on pages 163–165. It suffices to note at this point that the Guttman scale is a more refined measuring instrument than the other attitude scales mentioned here. Its technical characteristics, however, are such that only quite simple versions of it may be administered to samples of the national population.

All these scales purport to measure direction of attitude. Thus, in our British-aid example a person who wanted to declare ourselves allies and send along the army, navy, and air force would be separated on the scale in the direction toward intervention from the man who wanted to "stop letting her have anything." Or, on a scale of attitude toward business regulation a person who favored nationalization of all industry would occupy a point on a scale remote from the individual who wanted to limit governmental economic endeavor to hydroelectric power and a point even more remote from the person who wanted to sell the TVA to private enterprise. The assumption of the following chapters is that the form of the distribution of public opinion along scales is of basic importance in the description of the context of sentiment within which democratic governments operate.[3]

[3] For an elementary explanation of the types of attitude scaling, see H. H. Remmers: *Introduction to Opinion and Attitude Measurement* (New York: Harper; 1954). Another summary is Bert F. Green: "Attitude Measurement," in Gardner Lindzey, ed.: *Handbook of Social Psychology* (Cambridge: Addison-Wesley; 1954), I, 335–69. A treatise for the technician is Warren S. Torgerson: *Theory and Methods of Scaling* (New York: Wiley; 1958).

2

CONSENSUS

THE CONCEPT of consensus serves as a handy crutch for those who seek to explain the peculiarities of the American political system. Americans can, the theorists tell us, compose their differences because of the existence of a consensus on fundamentals. Commentators on the nature of political orders conclude that an underlying consensus is a prerequisite to the existence of representative government. They may observe that the animosities of conflict are cushioned by the framework of consensus, or that divisive issues may be settled democratically only within the limits of a wider consensus. Or those who dispute a warmly contested issue may, when a decision is reached, happily feel that a consensus has been formed. The magic word "consensus," in short, solves many puzzles, but only infrequently is the term given precise meaning. Even less often are inquiries made about the distribution among the population of whatever attitudes, beliefs, or behaviors constitute consensus. A search for its meaning will indicate the nature of a significant type of distribution of public opinion and will, as such quests invariably do, lead to the discovery that "consensus" has many meanings. However one proceeds to pump concrete content into the nebulous term, he must remember that he is dealing with a pattern of opinion whose importance is that it may condition the behavior of those in positions of public authority.

1 · Government in the Context of Issue Consensus

If any reality is hidden behind the concept of consensus, certain types of distribution of attitudes or opinions should be discoverable within the population. As a first step toward the introduction of concreteness into the idea of consensus, let us turn our back on the ethereal notion of "basic" or "fundamental" consensus and examine opinions on specific issues. In its most uncomplicated form "consensus" means an overwhelming public agreement upon a question of public policy.

If the opinions of the people of the nation are sampled on an issue on which agreement prevails, the opinions will cluster closely together on an attitude scale. Such a distribution of attitude is described as "unimodal." Because of the technical characteristics of devices for attitude measurement, consensus distributions, when plotted, often form a J-curve, or perhaps a double J-curve. Although the marked unimodality of the distribution rather than its J-form constitutes the essence of consensus, that form of curve may be taken as an ideal type of distribution of opinion in consensus. In a J-curve the attitudes of a large proportion of the population cluster closely together on an attitude scale while the dissenters, few in number, scatter in one or the other of the attitudinal directions from the mode to take the form of a J or reverse J. For example, nearly everybody may be for a particular proposition in almost the same degree, but a few extremists, for or against, may be located on the scale at some distance in one direction or the other from the main body of citizens. If the distribution takes a double J-form, as illustrated in Figure 2.1, a heavy concentration will also exist at one point, but the deviants will be dispersed from the mode in both directions along the scale. For example, nearly everybody may be for a proposition while a few extremists who are dead set against it locate themselves in one direction from the mode and a few others who desperately believe that the proposal does not go far enough place themselves in the opposite direction from the mode.[1]

The determination of whether opinion within the national population approximates the form of the J-curve is embarrassed by the limitations of survey procedures. Complex opinion scales can be imposed upon college sophomores or other defenseless subjects but not so readily upon a random sample of the population. Hence, in dealing with national opinion distributions one has to work with rather

---

[1] The J-curve is a type of distribution that recurs in statistical data. Among social psychologists it has gained a special application in the description of a type of distribution of behaviors. See F. H. Allport: "The J-Curve Hypothesis of Conforming Behavior," *Journal of Social Psychology*, V (1934), 141–83.

crude scales or even with yes-no questions that force all shades of
opinion into a dual mold. Whatever its form may be, once data have
been accumulated that indicate the existence of patterns of opinion
consensus within the population the question remains of their significance in the political system. An illuminating approach to that question
is to examine the patterns in their relation to past, present, or prospective governmental action. From that vantage point several functions of
opinion consensus in relation to governmental action may be dis-

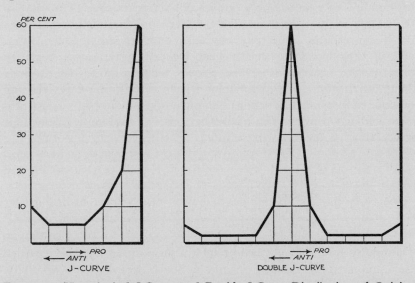

FIGURE 2.1. Hypothetical J-Curve and Double J-Curve Distribution of Opinion.

cerned. On some matters opinion consensus performs a *supportive*
function; that is, opinion underpins existing policy and practice. On
other questions opinion consensus may be *permissive;* that is, widespread public agreement on a question permits government to act
without fear of powerful popular dissent. On still other questions the
movement of opinion may be so closely correlated with governmental
action that as a consensus develops it may be said to be *decisive.*

Supportive Consensus. In some situations the function of opinion
consensus is to support existing policy and detailed actions taken in
accord with that policy. The residue of past discussion and decision
persists in opinion distributions supportive of the going program of
government and often, as a corollary, resistant to the abandonment of
these programs. All this, of course, does not deny that some governmental activities and policies are unfamiliar to many people who have

no opinion about them one way or another. Yet most of the major continuing services, policies, and rules of government are underpinned by opinion distributions that are functionally supportive in the political system.

One of the troubles with the foregoing interpretation is that the data to support it are not copious. Opinion surveyors do not often make extensive studies of settled issues. They manifest no curiosity, for example, about the distribution of the shades of opinion on the basic policy of maintaining a public-school system. Yet even some of the simple yes-no questions of the Gallup poll permit guesses about the form of the supportive consensus underlying specific public policies. For example, beginning in December, 1935, at about the time of the enactment of the Social Security Act, Dr. Gallup's American Institute of Public Opinion (the AIPO) put the following question at intervals to a national sample: "Are you in favor of government old-age pensions for needy persons?" The sample divided, at several times, in the following ways:

	Yes	No
December, 1935	89%	11%
August, 1938	91	9
January, 1939	94	6
November, 1939	90	10

Though by now the approval of such a proposition may be regarded as commonplace, the enactment of the Social Security Act involved a basic shift in public policy, and the state of opinion about it was of interest. Had a more complex measure of opinion been employed to gauge the shades of sentiment on the issue, it would probably have revealed the existence of a J or double-J opinion distribution.[2]

[2] Since in this book extensive use will be made of the findings of sample surveys, a word is in order in their defense. A favorite theme of feature writers and of candidates not doing well in the polls is the absurdity of estimating the state of national opinion on the basis of interviews with two or three thousand persons. The full explanation of the principles of surveys would require more statistical knowledge than most readers of this book are likely to possess. In essence the principle of the process is the same as the random plucking of, say, a thousand beans from a bushel of beans half black and half white. The odds are high that the thousand beans in the sample will be about half black and half white. In the practical operation of sample surveys the interviewing of a random sample of the national population is difficult to achieve. For one thing, we do not have the names and addresses of all people available in such a form that it is really possible to draw by random procedures a couple of thousand names from a hat containing 100,000,000 names. Sampling procedures can only approximate that process. Moreover, when interviewers call at the addresses given to them, they seem never to find some people at home, and a few obstreperous persons refuse to be interviewed. Nevertheless, an approach toward a random sample of the national population can

Similar questions could be used to illustrate the nature of over-whelming support of particular public policies, but no comprehensive census of the constellation of consensus patterns supporting the entire range of governmental activity has been made. Relevant, though, is a sampling of Detroit opinion on a series of governmental activities by Janowitz, Wright, and Delaney. They found that the "outspokenly critical evaluations" of several governmental agencies were shared by only small percentages of the adult population. For each of several administrative authorities these percentages were as follows: [3]

Public schools	16%
Local officials and bureaus	6%
State officials and bureaus	4%
Local police	6%
State police	2%

It is not astonishing that markedly unimodal distributions of supportive opinion are associated with most public policies and serv-ices. These going operations have long since won acceptance. Yet the functional importance of these structures of opinion as a framework within which much of the action of government occurs needs to be recognized. Since widespread support in principle of specified govern-mental activities is tacitly assumed, its significance is often not per-ceived. Sharp curves of supportive opinion mean that proposals to liquidate services or to abandon policies are politically perilous and, hence, that the scope and course of public policy have high predicta-bility. Differences exist over matters of scale, of emphasis, of detail. Acceptance of the principle of social security, for example, makes attacks on the system unfruitful; the burning issues are much narrower than the question of the existence of the program. Consensus on the principle of public education leaves room for debate on details of curriculum, the size of the swimming pool, the magnificence of educational edifices, and the salaries of teachers. The scarcity of genuine pacifists means that the defense establishment does not have to

be achieved. Even when that is done, a sampling error remains that tends to be-come greater as the sample becomes smaller (without reference to the size of the population being sampled). Thus, if a coin is flipped 10 times, the falls will probably depart farther from a division of 50 per cent heads and 50 per cent tails than if it is tossed a thousand times. Withal, the problem in the findings of surveys, given competent administration, is not accuracy. If the sample divides 65:35, the odds are that the national population divides in the same way, plus or minus a few points. The real problem is the significance that should be attributed to the answers people have given to the questions.

[3] Morris Janowitz, Deil Wright, and William Delaney: *Public Administration and the Public—Perspectives toward Government in a Metropolitan Community* (Ann Arbor: Bureau of Government, University of Michigan; 1958), pp. 32–3.

fight for its existence. Thus throughout the range of public activities opinions of approbation both support and color day-to-day governmental action.

If one considers the vicissitudes of the administrators of those operations which from time to time exist without consensual support, the import of supportive opinion distributions becomes readily apparent. Consider the lot of those unfortunate officials whose duty it was to enforce the prohibition of the manufacture and sale of alcoholic beverages. Doubtless, too, the cumulation of individual issues on which supportive consensus prevails contributes to the stability of the political order as a whole. As policy after policy comes to be underpinned by such support, the adaptation of a wider and wider range of government activity to new necessities becomes a matter of detail rather than the occasion for renewal of deep-seated controversy on basic issues.

Permissive Consensus. In another type of relationship between government and opinion a consensual pattern of opinion may be said to be permissive of action. Observers of public opinion have been perturbed by gaps between public opinion and governmental action. On many issues interviewers obtain from heavy majorities of national samples concurrence with views that have not been transmuted into public policy and are not likely to be in the predictable future. If one adheres to the doctrine that majority views, expressed spontaneously without benefit of complete knowledge, should be immediately enacted into statute, the discrepancy may be a cause for unhappiness. On the other hand, existence of general support for a proposition creates what can be termed a "permissive consensus," which is often an antecedent to action once the technical problems have been ironed out and the anxieties of those most immediately concerned quieted. Interpretation of the state of opinion underlying a 90:10 favorable response requires more data than a simple report of agreement and disagreement with the proposition. A 10 per cent dissent may include small pockets of the most determined opposition whose members command controlling points in the governmental mechanism. The 90 per cent concurrence may not include driving clusters of determined leadership, or it may consist largely of persons not strongly attached to their stated position. Yet the existence of a permissive opinion distribution may mean that if the indicated action is taken dissent will not be widespread.

Several illustrations of permissive consensus will indicate the nature of this type of opinion distribution. For over fifteen years prior to the admission of Hawaii as a state in 1959, AIPO polls showed the existence of popular approval of the proposal in the continental

United States. That approval reached a peak shortly before admission, when 72 per cent favored, 9 per cent opposed, and 19 per cent had no opinion. That one in five had no opinion suggests that the question was not one to move the populace deeply. The favorable opinion, though widespread, had no directive power. Southern doubts about a polyglot commonwealth, which coincided with fears that Hawaii's territorial record of Republicanism might be carried into statehood, blocked action for years. Yet the public permissiveness was such that when action was finally taken acceptance was general, though not accompanied by hosannas.

Thus, the consequence of a permissive consensus is not necessarily action tied closely to the development of that consensus. Rather the timing and precise form of the action taken, if it is taken at all, depend on circumstances peculiar to each issue. The press of other matters may divert attention. Small groups may be able to block action. Indeed, those responsible may judge it not in the long-run public interest and may decline to act, usually without fear of public reprisal. Yet the context of public attitudes gives government freedom to act if that is judged desirable. Thus, in 1950, at a moment when congressional leaders were pressing for passage of a universal military training bill, 78 per cent of a national sample questioned by the AIPO gave favorable responses to the inquiry: "In the future do you think every able-bodied young man (who has not already been in the armed forces) should be required to take military or naval training for one year?"; 17 per cent opposed and 5 per cent reported no opinion. For years there had been majorities favorable to the proposition.

The files of opinion surveys, of course, contain many instances of the existence of an approving opinion long before the related statute was enacted. For example, in December, 1943, the AIPO reported 75 per cent favoring legislation to require labor unions to report annually their receipts and expenditures, with 10 per cent opposed and 15 per cent having no opinion. Opinions among union members divided only slightly less favorably. Yet many years were to pass before the principle was transmuted from opinion to law, and no representative or senator suffered for the delay. A census of opinions on policy proposals would uncover many examples of permissive consensus on proposals in the discussion stage. Thus, when in 1954 the AIPO put the question: "At present, people whose permanent home is in Washington, D.C., cannot vote in national elections. Do you think this should be changed so they can vote in national elections?" 80 per cent thought a change in order, 12 per cent opposed, and 8 per cent had no opinion. Nevertheless, in 1960 residents of the District of Columbia still did not vote in national elections.

These illustrations of permissive consensus rest on crude data. The probabilities are that if more refined data were available, opinions on these questions would appear as a J-curve when placed on a graph. Such a form is assumed by the data presented in Figure 2.2, which indicates the distribution of degrees of agreement and disagreement in 1956 with the following proposition: "If cities and towns around the country need help to build more schools, the government in Washington ought to give them the money they need." Well over 50 per cent

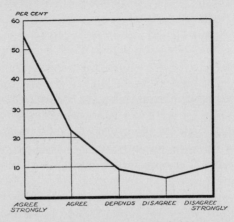

FIGURE 2.2. "If cities and towns around the country need help to build more schools, the government in Washington ought to give them the money they need." DATA SOURCE: Survey Research Center, University of Michigan, 1956. Percentage base excludes those with no opinion.

agreed strongly, while only 10 per cent strongly disagreed; the remainder of the respondents located themselves between these extremes. The conditional phrasing of the question probably in itself reflects something of the spirit of a permissive consensus. If Congress so determines, the people might be saying, the action accords with majority opinion.[4]

[4] Though the array of attitudes on the education question shown in Figure 2.2 is more revealing than the responses to a yes-no question, the side comments of respondents indicate that opinion on even so simple a question has a variety of dimensions. Some respondents seemed to be unable to visualize federal assumption of so formidable a task. A Detroit housewife disagreed: "The government has got so much to do it's pretty hard to pile more on them." A Kansas housewife: "That would be asking too much of the government." Others had some doubts on the details. A Nebraska housewife: "I think they should build schools but not these gymnasiums where they can play basket ball." A California molder: "We have too many schools here in this city now; don't think there could be real need for schools, but if there is, government should help build, but not necessary to make fancy with electricity and water, or past eighth grade; we learned good without

The concept of permissive consensus denotes a political phenomenon whose importance becomes perceptible if one contrasts the position of government when the context of opinion is the reverse—that is, when 80 or 90 per cent oppose an action. When a permissive consensus exists, a government may be relatively free to work out a solution of the issue or it may be free to act or not to act. The permissive consensus is not directive of public action; it merely represents circumstances radically different from the obverse situation of general opposition. Under the latter type of circumstance the odds are that nothing will be done, or at least that those immediately concerned about action will have to set to work educating public opinion.[5]

Consensus of Decision. The permissive consensus, as it has been described, is connected only loosely with the act of governmental decision. Another type of consensus, in form permissive, may be differentiated on the assumption that it is so closely articulated with governmental action as to appear to be decisive if not directive. From time to time truly great public questions are posed whose decision is delayed pending public discussion and the crystallization of opinion; officials appear to be poised for action as they await the development of popular support. A striking example of the consensus of decision consists in the relation between government action and the evolution of public opinion in the period immediately preceding American entry into World War II. The salience of the events of the European war made most of the public aware of the possibility of American involvement in the conflict. The spirited debate led by the Committee to Defend America by Aiding the Allies and by the America First

that." The school-aid question in some way became mingled with foreign policy. The wife of a Minnesota unskilled laborer: "They should build schools instead of sending the money away." A North Carolina housewife: "They help everybody else; they ought to help them too." Others centered on the federal-state problem. An upstate New York utility worker: "I would like to see loans to state governments." A Los Angeles aircraft mechanic: "If the state is wealthy they should finance it; the government should loan some money; some states can afford it, some not." A California metalsmith, in strong disagreement, had an appealing solution: "People with children should pay to educate them, at least pay more school taxes than those with no children."

[5] The obverse of permissive consensus might be called a "negative consensus." A constitutional government operates within boundaries set by consensual limitations which are formalized in constitutional clauses or customs. They may relate either to the scope or the mode of governmental action. The extent of positive understanding and acceptance of these matters through the general population is problematic. Popular negative consensus may also prevail on proposals that are entirely within the realm of the constitutional.

Committee focused general attention on the issue of American foreign policy. The national administration made its sympathies known, but sharp differences existed in leadership echelons about the desirable course of American policy. Moreover, the technique of appraising public sentiment by interviews with small numbers of people had just been invented, and the practitioners of the art happily plied their trade to the accompaniment of the interest and financial support of those concerned.

In June, 1940, the following question was posed: "Which of these two things do you think is the more important for the United States to try to do—to keep out of war ourselves, or to help England win, even at the risk of getting into war?" At this time, shortly after the German invasion of Norway and the Netherlands and the Italian entry into the war, a resounding two-thirds asserted that it was better to keep out of war ourselves. As event piled upon event and as the domestic debate proceeded, the alignment of opinion on the question gradually changed. By January, 1941, when the Lend-Lease bill was under debate, the ratios had reversed themselves: two-thirds then thought it to be more important to help England win even at the risk of getting into war. Opinion hovered around that level until the attack on Pearl Harbor silenced all dissent. Yet the steps in the development of American policy followed closely changes in opinion, and government was more criticized for lagging behind public opinion than for moving ahead of it.

Consensus on an issue of this gravity tends to be more than simply overwhelming agreement upon a question. The process of debate supposedly produces a condition or pattern of opinion that differs from a simple alignment of, say, 70 per cent on this side of the question and 30 per cent on the other. Some change has occurred to reconcile the 30 per cent to the decision (or perhaps some antecedent factors were present which enabled them to accept it once it was made). In somewhat mystical terms, Kallen speaks of the consensual product of the confrontation of opposing ideas or policies: "At the end the initial aggregation of opposed individuals has become an integrated association with organically related members; the opposed interests have molded each other into a mutually sustaining configuration where each has acquired a new character and new values and where all have brought the social process to a stable new level and tempo." [6]

[6] H. M. Kallen: "Consensus," in *Encyclopaedia of the Social Sciences* (New York: Macmillan; 1935) IV, 225–6. The odds are that the consensus of decision occurs far more frequently in relatively small communities than in the nation. In small communities the phenomenon should, at least, be far more readily identifiable.

The process so vividly described by Kallen remains to be clearly perceived within the mass of the people. Yet the process he delineates can be seen in small groups. In legislative assemblies it is plain that discussion and modification of the terms of a proposal may cut new alignments through the group, alter the tone and intensity of conflict, and produce decisions to which all concerned can reconcile themselves. A similar process may occur in the larger public. Perhaps it did so in the debate over aid to Britain, since the realities and perceptions of the involvement of American interest doubtless changed as the debate progressed, and a configuration of opinion thus developed in which the isolationists muttered unhappily but were willing to pay their taxes and to participate in the defense effort even before Pearl Harbor.

Multiple Consensus. The rise of popular consensus on a particular issue may involve the development of simultaneous concurrence by several groups within the public. In the language of political theory, this is called a "concurrent majority." If the line between these groups marks a cleavage, either past or potential over an issue, the effect of multiple consensus is to destroy popular support for those sections of political leadership that might oppose a policy. The movement of opinion within different groups of the population in the stream of events leading to World War II, just discussed, illustrates the growth of a multiple consensus. The gradual shift of opinion from that of a predominant urge to keep out of war to that of willingness to aid England at the risk of war occurred in most major sectors of the population. In a sense, concurrent majorities developed among Democrats and Republicans, among rich and poor, among men and women, and among other classes of people.[7] On some questions governments may hesitate to act without support reaching into all elements of society. The reasons for awaiting such varied support rest on the fear, even the probability, that the resistance of centers of power based on some groups might embarrass the conduct of public policy. A policy supported by a numerical majority that is faced by the determined opposition of organized labor, organized religion, organized business, or some other such center in society may rest on shaky foundations.

The party leaderships are, of course, perpetually in search of issues for exploitation, and consensus across party lines in popular

[7] See the charts showing the trends of opinions in some of these groups in Hadley Cantril: *Gauging Public Opinion* (Princeton: Princeton University Press; 1944), pp. 221–5.

opinion often frustrates leadership elements disposed to capitalize on an issue. Multiple popular consensus among party groups often reflects itself in Congress when majorities of both party groups vote together. In other instances multiple consensus may weaken conflict between party leaders, muffle it, or give it special qualities. In this connection, consider the array of attitudes in Figure 2.3 on the proposition: "The government ought to fire any government worker who is accused of

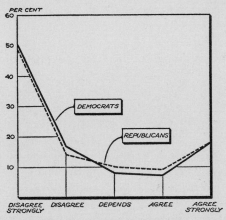

FIGURE 2.3. "The government ought to fire any government worker who is accused of being a communist even though they don't prove it." DATA SOURCE: *Survey Research Center, University of Michigan, 1956.* Percentage base excludes those with no opinion.

being a communist even though they don't prove it." Democrats and Republicans arranged themselves along the attitude scale in almost exactly the same way, about half of each group disagreeing strongly with the proposition and another 15 per cent or so disagreeing but not strongly. Although perhaps the dissenters were too numerous for one to say that a consensus prevailed, the similar distributions of opinion within each party group suggests the difficulty of making a party issue of the matter.

It might be supposed that an overwhelming agreement that exists simultaneously in several groups would envelop the organs of government and make itself felt in public policy. In fact, the mechanisms of government often give differential positions of strength to one shade of opinion or another. The point may be illustrated by Figure 2.4, which shows the distribution of opinion among Democrats and Republicans on this proposal: "If Negroes *are not* getting fair treatment in jobs and housing, the government in Washington should see to it that they do." While agreement on the proposition was perhaps not high enough to qualify as a consensus, substantial proportions of both parties were in agreement. One leg of the Democratic distribution, though, happened to enjoy a special position through the representative system in the House and the Senate; that is, a comparatively small sector of opinion was so located within the institutional system that the leadership which it supported enjoyed powers of obstruction disproportionate to the size of its popular following.

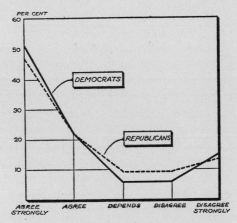

FIGURE 2.4. "If Negroes *are not* getting fair treatment in jobs and housing, the government in Washington should see to it that they do." DATA SOURCE: *Survey Research Center, University of Michigan, 1956.* Percentage base excludes those with no opinion.

2 · Foundations of Consensus

The discussion of opinion consensus in terms of patterns of opinion on particular issues, even though they may be broad issues, does not center squarely on the phenomenon of consensus as it is commonly discerned by political speculators. Nevertheless, consideration of the apparent relationship between opinion consensus on particular issues and governmental action provides us with a clue to the function of one type of consensus in the political system. That type of consensus can be identified from the opinion data, and common-sense judgments can be formed about its functions in the system. Consensus in its more usual meaning raises less manageable problems. Political analysts speak of a "consensus on fundamentals," of "a foundation of consensus," or of a "constitutional consensus." Analyses in such terms usually assume that there exists within a society a general acceptance of fundamental values, a widespread agreement on basic goals, or some common concurrence in the rules of the game which makes it possible to settle the questions that arise from day to day in a manner not intolerable to the losers. The treatment usually ends with some such assertion and stops short of a demonstration of the content of the basic consensus and of its bearing on the way the wheels of government turn as they deal with day-to-day questions.

Negative Aspects of Consensus. The explanation of the capacity to develop consensus on (or acceptable solutions of) working issues as they arise often contains a simple negative component. The political system can handle some current issues because no fundamental issues related to them array the population into irreconcilable camps. Uncritical enthusiasts carry the thought to the point where "basic consensus" seems to be entirely a negative state of affairs. It may thus be said that the area of consensus is that area in which current issues do not run athwart the agreement on fundamentals. Or the contention is made that only in the absence of issues that conflict with the consensus on fundamentals can a constitutional regime be maintained.

When it is put expansively, the argument almost amounts to the proposition that the reason we have no disruptive issues is that we have no disruptive issues. If basic consensus exists within the population, it surely must include positive attitudes as well as the absence of deep-seated disagreements. Yet it must be conceded that the absence of some questions mightily facilitates the conduct of public business. Absence of large enclaves or population groups fundamentally opposed to the regime means that no substantial element of the population on principle resists governmental action whatever its nature. In some nations large enclaves of ethnic minorities have seemed determined not to enter into the negotiation and discussion productive of agreement on the day-to-day issues, fundamental or otherwise. To note the lack of substantial elements in the United States hostile to the regime only creates the problem of explaining the general loyalty to the system. At any rate, the United States does not suffer from the historical accident of including within its borders elements with aspirations of national independence, a negative circumstance of great convenience to government.

Another type of negative explanation of the capacity for achievement of agreement consists in reality of a tacit understanding not to raise issues certain to be disruptive and beyond solution. For example, religious differences seem not to be susceptible to compromise; rather, men are disposed to torture each other in the name of God when they dispute questions of religion. The apparent solution of the matter is to place religious belief and practice beyond the coercive sphere of government by a policy of religious freedom.

Content of the Underlying Consensus. If one sought to identify the positive content of the basic consensus, he would assume that the population is pervaded by beliefs and attitudes which, if measured by attitude scales, would appear as markedly unimodal distributions. These basic attitudes might be thought to exist about both broad and specific questions, such as freedom of speech, procedures in the settlement of legislative controversy, compensation for public confiscation of private property, safety of the person, and judicial procedures. Basic consensus thus might be supposed to prevail with respect to both procedural and substantive matters. An assumption of the doctrine of basic consensus is that the modal popular attitudes on such matters are so articulated with the system of institutions that they limit and guide, within a broad range, governmental action on specific matters.

Trustworthy information is scarce on exactly what basic political attitudes pervade the population. Searching interviews built on ingenious sets of questions would be necessary to obtain the information. Such evidence as exists, though, makes it improbable to suppose that well-organized sets of political beliefs are held by large proportions of the population. In fact, by inference from the kinds of issues that democratic governments manage to settle, Friedrich argues that constitutional democracy involves not agreement but disagreement on fundamentals combined with a capacity to agree upon specific courses of action. Insistence upon agreement on fundamentals, he contends, is "incompatible with constitutional democracy."[8] Certainly when men begin to assert the revealed truth about fundamentals, they seem to be on the road to the repression of dissent from their conception of the fundamentals. However one defines fundamentals—rights of property, freedom, individual liberty, or what not—there can be no doubt that over the past 75 years the United States has coped with question after question that would have been unmanageable within the limits of any rigid and powerfully held consensus on substantive fundamentals. The capacity to solve highly contentious individual issues does not disprove the existence of a mass consensus on "fundamentals," but it suggests that the consensus, if it exists, has a considerable element of flexibility.

If he fails to locate the body of principles supposedly etched into our collective mind, the expositor of the doctrine of basic consensus

[8] Carl J. Friedrich: *The New Image of the Common Man* (Boston: Beacon Press; 1950), ch. 5.

can fall back upon the contention that the characteristic attitudes, beliefs, or behavioral habits of a people, though generally only vaguely political in content, may give tone and color to its politics. This is essentially a variant of the doctrine of national character; the political elements of national character constitute the basic consensus. The expositors of such a thesis, at least tacitly, assume that a substantial proportion of the population holds general attitudes that condition the responses to individual issues as they arise. Moreover, there is an assumption that these attitudes have a considerable degree of stability; that is, that given a knowledge of the modal basic attitudes, the responses to specific issues by Americans, or by Englishmen, or by Egyptians can be roughly forecast. We have caricatures of the authority-loving German, the excitable Frenchman, the optimistic and humanitarian American; yet the analysis necessary to ascertain the frequency of the occurrence of politically relevant basic attitudes and behaviors within national populations has not been made.

The assertion that characteristic features of attitude, belief, or behavior differentiate national populations and color the workings of their political systems has an undeniable plausibility. Yet the identification of those elements of national character that constitute the basic American consensus, or that permit the government to operate as if there were a basic consensus, can be accomplished only by educated intuition.[9] That hazardous task may be approached by the initial observation that the American characteristically manifests an uncommonly high degree of loyalty and satisfaction with things American—an attitude that, on occasion, approaches smugness and, at times, extreme intolerance of matters regarded as un-American. Americans, more than the citizens of most countries, regard their own country as the one that gives them the best chance of leading the kind of life they would like to lead.[1] Similarly, few Americans express a yearning to migrate to a foreign country.[2] These national attachments may

[9] For a review of the literature on national character, see Alex Inkeles and Daniel J. Levinson: "National Character: The Study of Modal Personality and Sociocultural Systems," in Gardner Lindzey, ed.: *Handbook of Social Psychology*, (Cambridge: Addison-Wesley; 1954), II, 977–1020. See also Margaret Mead: "The Study of National Character" in Daniel Lerner and Harold D. Lasswell, eds.: *The Policy Sciences* (Stanford, Calif.: Stanford University Press; 1951), ch. 4.

[1] In a number of UNESCO national sample surveys in 1948 the question was asked: "Which country in the world gives you the best chance of leading the kind of life you would like to lead?" The percentages naming their own country as offering them this chance were: United States, 96; Australia, 83; Britain, 51; Norway, 50; Mexico, 45; France, 43; Netherlands, 31; Italy, 36; Germany, 30. See William Buchanan and Hadley Cantril: *How Nations See Each Other* (Urbana: University of Illinois Press; 1953), p. 30.

[2] In April, 1946, 49 per cent of a national sample of Italians wanted to emigrate. Two per cent of the Americans polled expressed a desire to leave their

express themselves in the most savage hostility toward the alien and the stranger.[3] Or they may be reflected in opinions most intolerant of acts that appear to obstruct the achievement of national purpose.[4] A long history of repression of deviants—anarchists, socialists, communists, atheists, free lovers, nudists, pinks—probably attests also to the existence of some such modal attitude as has been described.

The relevance of this attitude of "Americanism" for the concept of basic consensus may come down to its performance of a screening function in political discussion. To be accorded serious consideration, proposals must not be vulnerable to the charge that they are un-American or alien. In practice, advocates of new policies often go through imposing intellectual contortions to establish the congeniality of their schemes with the American tradition; resisters likewise attempt to tie the alien tag to schemes they dislike. Withal, over the decades proposals that at one time were clearly not the traditional American way have come to be assimilated into the tradition, a result suggestive of elasticity in the fundamental consensus. Yet the strength of the screening device may be suggested by the delays in the adoption of policies long regarded as commonplace in many other countries of the world. It required, for example, the most severe economic depression in American history to bring us to the adoption of measures of social insurance.

Coupled with an ethnocentrism of a peculiar quality there has also been a fairly deep and pervasive concurrence upon the identity of the national friends and, perhaps to a lesser extent, of the national enemies. In the years just before World War II England ranked by far as the European country "liked best" by Americans.[5] Opinion data are not available for earlier periods, but without much doubt a

---

country. In early 1958 the British Institute of Public Opinion reported that 41 per cent of those Britishers polled said that if they were free to do so, they would settle in another country.

[3] In December, 1936, Mr. Gallup reported that 73 per cent of his respondents said yes to the question: "Do you think aliens on relief should be returned to their own countries?"

[4] For example, the AIPO question of October, 1950: "Should Congress pass a law forbidding strikes in industries (plants and factories) that would be important in war time—or should the workers in those industries continue to have the right to go on strike?" Seventy-nine per cent favored prohibition of strikes.

[5] AIPO, June, 1937: "Which of the European countries do you like best?" England, 55 per cent; France, 11 per cent; Germany, 8 per cent; other countries ranged from 4 per cent down. In 1949 the Survey Research Center asked a national sample: "If it came to a showdown between Russia and the United States, which of these countries do you feel would stick with us?" Ninety per cent believed that Canada would "stick with us"; 86 per cent thought the same of England; 70 per cent, of France; 41 per cent, of Italy.—Survey Research Center: *America's Role in World Affairs* (Ann Arbor: Survey Research Center; 1952), p. 81.

similar orientation has prevailed for most of this century. Concurrence
on the identity of the national enemies has probably been less stable
through time and has rested more on the events of the moment than on
the historical and cultural foundations for friendliness toward the
English. The consensus on the external world has certainly not sufficed to settle automatically all questions of foreign policy that arise
from time to time; yet it has sufficed to prevent the country from
being torn asunder by questions of foreign politics. Such questions
may be especially disruptive of national unity, for the partisans of
friendship toward a foreign power, unless their position has a strong
grounding in popular support, are especially vulnerable to the charge
of treason. Advocacy of friendship toward a nation regarded by the
majority as a national enemy is a risky enterprise.

Americans seem characteristically to hold an attitude of suspicion
of authority. Almond observes that the "American tends to 'cut
authority down to his own size,'" that he has a distrust of arbitrary
or traditional authority.[6] Surveys regularly turn up substantial majorities who feel that the labor unions, business corporations, or "the
bosses" have "too much" power. If combinations to grasp arbitrary
power are not plainly visible, we invent them. "Wall Street," the
"trusts," the "labor barons," the "establishment," "Madison Avenue,"
suggest the possibilities. Mr. C. Wright Mills was in a great American
tradition when he wrote of *The Power Elite*. And, if those who
compose American political oratory are informed judges of the expectations of their auditors, it may be supposed that the unhappiness
about power has associated with it an admiration for the "lone hero"
who challenges the wicked holders of power, the interests, the magnates, the bosses, the rings, the oligarchies.[7] Certainly many leaders
who have captured the imagination and loyalties of the masses have
dramatized themselves as gladiators tilting their swords against the
privileged interests in whose existence there seems to be a will to
believe (on occasion with good reason). Paradoxically, structures of
power, though transient, are erected in the name of opposition to
power.

If we have identified an enduring modal attitude, it may bear
significantly on the problem of contriving consensus. Decisions depend on authority, and when authority rests on a consent that distrusts
authority, power is limited. Perhaps centers of leadership based on
unsure foundations of support operate under a special compulsion to

[6] Gabriel Almond: *American People and Foreign Policy* (New York: Harcourt, Brace; 1950), p. 51.
[7] See the reflective comment by G. D. Wiebe: "The Army-McCarthy Hearings and the Public Conscience," *Public Opinion Quarterly*, XXII (1958–9), 490–
502.

seek out grounds of agreement with the minority on specific issues. Coupled with apprehensions about power are, of course, institutional procedures congenial to that attitude. American governmental procedures notoriously encourage delay—not only the delay necessary for full debate, but on occasion a delay of action for years on questions of great import. As delay occurs, popular attitudes do not necessarily remain constant. They may gradually assume a form that permits a settlement of the issue by predominant majorities, if not by universal consent.

Some evidence of the nature of popular attitudes toward power comes from the positions of a national sample regarding the influence of big business corporations and of labor unions in government. The respondents were asked whether they agreed or disagreed with this proposition: "The government ought to see to it that big business corporations don't have much say about how the government is run." The question was then repeated with labor unions as the villain. Slightly more than half the sample agreed with each proposition; on each about one fourth had no opinion. Approximately one sixth disagreed; that is, they thought big business or labor influence ought not to be restrained.[8]

Significant for the present discussion is the fact that those who thought that labor unions ought not to have "much say" were in high degree the same people who thought that big business ought to be kept in its place, as Table 2.1 indicates. Side comments on the question suggested, moreover, that those who disagreed with the statements were often not partisans of either big business or labor unions. The general tenor of the volunteered remarks seemed to be that big business and unions should have their say but that they should not be allowed to push the government around. A Mississippi farmer, for example, disagreed strongly on the labor union question: "They should have a voice; if they don't, it's a bad go." A Kansas banker thought corporations "should have some say about the government" and that unions, too, should "have a voice but not up to the point of dictating." The wife of a Michigan factory worker felt corporations "should have their share of say," as did an Idaho farmer who put it: "They should have their say as much as anybody else."

Perhaps another basic attitude or value is a low level of expecta-

---

[8] The general drift of the findings reported in the text is confirmed by AIPO questions of May, 1960. One question was: "At the present time, which do you think has the most influence on the laws passed in this country—big business or labor?" Forty-three per cent thought big business had the most influence; 34 per cent, labor; 10 per cent thought there was no difference. Then the question was put: "Which do you think should have the most influence?" The percentages were: big business, 14 per cent; labor, 29 per cent; both equal, 46 per cent.

tion of government or, conversely, the expectation that one must lift himself by his own bootstraps. "The American," Almond argues, "is primarily concerned with 'private' values, as distinguished from social-group, political, or religious-moral values." [9] Evidence of the low salience of political means is provided by the responses to an ice-breaking question in a 1954 national survey. It included the inquiry: "What kinds of things do you worry about most?" As they answered off the top of their heads, 80 per cent of the sample defined their worries as personal and family problems: financial anxieties, health

---

TABLE 2.1

RELATION BETWEEN OPINION ON RESTRAINT OF INFLUENCE OF BIG BUSINESS IN
GOVERNMENT AND OPINION ON RESTRAINT OF UNION INFLUENCE [a]

RESTRAIN UNIONS

		RESTRAIN BIG BUSINESS			
	Pro	Depends	Con	No opinion	Total
Pro	34%	2%	7%	7%	50%
Depends	3	2	1	1	7
Con	9	1	6	3	19
No opinion	5	*	2	17	24
Total	51%	5%	16%	28%	100%

[a] The policy statements submitted to the sample for agreement or dis-agreement were: "The government ought to see to it that big business corporations don't have much say about how the government is run," and, "The government ought to see to it that labor unions don't have much say about how the government is run." The entries are the per-centages of the total national sample, 1764, holding the combinations of opinion represented by each cell.
DATA SOURCE: *Survey Research Center, University of Michigan, 1956.*

---

problems, and the like. Spontaneous expressions of anxiety about national and world problems came from only 14 per cent of the sample.[1] The respondents did not take what might be regarded as the next step and worry about what the government was going to do about their problems of finance and health.

The contention that an individualism, a disposition to rely on one's own efforts, is a modal American attitude is embarrassed by the fact that overwhelming majorities of those polled on specific questions often say that the government ought to do this or that. Yet such

[9] Almond: op. cit., p. 48.
[1] Samuel A. Stouffer: *Communism, Conformity, and Civil Liberties* (New York: Doubleday; 1955), ch. 3.

responses probably reflect no lively expectations that the government will do so, nor do they indicate commitments to exertions toward seeing that the government does so. If an individualistic attitude, or perhaps merely a nongovernmental orientation, such as has been described, is an American characteristic, it has an obvious bearing on the processes of arriving at agreement on specific issues. Mass demands upon government—and demands create conflict—are tempered by the underlying low priority upon political means for the achievement of individual objectives.[2]

For most Americans issues of politics are not of central concern, a fact that may contribute to the seeming consensus in American politics. This mass attitude may condition the behavior of elite elements, small in number but with large stakes in public policy. When leadership elements can rally to their support substantial elements of the population with an abiding interest in issues, prospects for abiding conflict are excellent. Moreover, prospects for negotiated agreement among contending leadership blocs may be slight, for leaders in a sense are captives of the emotions of their followers. On the other hand, given only peripheral popular focus on political issues, leadership must clamor for attention, and when attention is aroused it may be only fitful and transient. Rather than being anchored to their following, leadership blocs may be under a compulsion to settle for what they can when they can as they negotiate from points of weakness.

Though a disposition to rely on oneself rather than on government could be an expression of cynicism toward political institutions, it seems in reality to be one facet of the optimism of American character. Almond asserts that there exists "a generally euphoric tendency, that is, the expectation that one can by effort and good will achieve or approximate one's goals." [3] The stereotype of the American as an ebullient and self-confident optimist has some evidential basis.[4]

[2] Richard Centers concluded, from the responses by a 1945 national sample of adult males: "There are no important differences among occupational strata with respect to the rationale for poverty in America. Persons of all strata appear to believe that being poor is the fault of the individual."—"Attitude and Belief in Relation to Occupational Stratification," *Journal of Social Psychology*, XXVII (1948), 159–85.

[3] Almond: op. cit., p. 50.

[4] In 1954 to the question, "On the whole, do you think life will be better for you or worse, in the next few years than it is now?" 63 per cent of a national sample responded in an optimistic vein.—Stouffer, *op. cit.*, pp. 100–3. In 1956 the Survey Research Center checked concurrence with the statement: "I seem to be the kind of person that has more bad luck than good luck." Forty three per cent of a national sample disagreed "a lot"; 35 per cent disagreed a "little"; only 9 per strongly agreed.

A dimension of this optimism relevant for politics is its extension to the prospects for the next generation. The "typical" American entertains hopes that his children have a good chance to be better off than their parents.[5] If this attitude is of some depth, it has significant consequences for the solidarity of groupings in American politics. A rigid class system, with the associated harshness of political conflict, probably can more readily develop when expectations are general that children are frozen in the status of their parents.

Long habituation to democratic rule may generate a disposition to accept or to tolerate the majority view. The experience of achieving agreement thus may enlarge the capacity to do so. Acceptance of an unwanted decision may, to be sure, rest in resignation to the fact that the majority has more spears and dissent is futile. Yet a modal disposition to abide by the majority will may add a quality to the spirit of acceptance as well as enlarge the sheer quantity of acceptance. The capacity of majorities to enforce conformity and, in effect, to enlarge themselves is a matter of common knowledge. Cantril contends that majority opinion induces conformity "when an individual has no clearly structured mental context adequate to interpret a situation and when the majority opinion does not conflict with other frames of reference or ego values."[6] This specification may describe what happens on many foreign policy issues. For many individuals approval of a course of action may be associated with a lack of information, a lack of independent bases for appraisal; the more-or-less informed but diehard isolationist presumably would be unmoved by the mood of the majority. Other evidence points to a tendency to repress private opinions which, if projected into the public arena, would produce conflict. Still other bits of evidence suggest that the tendency toward *pro forma* public conformity or silence is more marked among those whose dispositions move them toward the less prestigeful, and therefore probably the minority, side of an issue.[7]

[5] A Chicago survey in the 1930's, when the future did not look bright for anyone, included the question: "Do you believe the chances are good that your children will have a higher position and be better off than you are?" Affirmative responses were a bit higher than 85 per cent in each of the A, B, C and D income groups.—A. W. Kornhauser: "Analysis of 'Class' Structure of Contemporary American Society: Psychological Bases of Class Divisions," in *Industrial Conflict: A Psychological Interpretation* (Yearbook Society for the Psychological Study of Social Issues; 1939), p. 240. In the 1940's Centers found "small but statistically significant differences" among occupational groups in a national sample with respect to the belief in opportunities for children to rise in the world.—Loc. cit.

[6] *The Psychology of Social Movements* (New York: Wiley; 1941), pp. 74-5.

[7] See Stuart C. Dodd: "On Predicting Elections or Other Public Behavior," *International Journal of Opinion and Attitude Research*, II (1948-9), 494-502.

The American is said to be politically pragmatic. Hence, his reponses to public issues are not fixed in advance by a rigid pattern of belief that produces predictable and firmly held positions on most public questions. Rather, the predominant set of attitudes predisposes the public to judge each question as it arises on its merits and thereby enables men of good will to arrive at a solution *de novo* as the situation demands. There is grave doubt whether any attitude of conscious political pragmatism pervades the American electorate. Yet a set of attitudes and outlooks may prevail which enables political leaders, when they are so disposed, to act as if the electorate had no conscious ideological outlook. Ideology, in the sense of a systematic ordering of specific issues in terms of general beliefs, seems to be limited to a small fraction of the electorate.[8]

Doubtless the reasons for this nonideological orientation of the mass of voters is to be found, if it is to be found, deep in the structure and historic development of American society. Perhaps systematic ideologies widespread through the population, if they are ever widespread, are in part the product of a social structure that sharply differentiates groups of individuals according to rewards and opportunities. Yet whether a pragmatic spirit is widespread within the electorate, some pattern of permissive attitudes, noninvolvement, or substantive beliefs allows government to behave, at least on some questions and at some times, as if the national character were a pragmatic one. And in that sense this trait of the people constitutes an element productive of consensus.

All this evidence on the nature of basic consensus leaves something to be desired. While the data suggest that certain attitudes widely distributed within the population may bear on the way the political system works, to call these beliefs a "consensus on fundamentals" imputes to them a more explicit and ordered content than they seem to possess. The average American manages to get along very well without a burdensome equipment of sophisticated political attitudes; so, too, may the masses of people in almost any stable political system.[9] Characteristics, beliefs, and attitudes attributed to the mass of the people are often only projections of the anxieties, the preferences, or the fantasies of the intellectual analyst. Certainly when a learned

[8] See the revealing analysis by Angus Campbell, Philip Converse, Warren E. Miller, and Donald Stokes: *The American Voter* (New York: Wiley; 1960), chs. 9–10.

[9] H. D. Lasswell and A. Kaplan observe that in a stable social structure "the ideology is non-controversial" and its elaborations are "in the direction of ceremonialization and glorification, not explanation and justification."—*Power and Society* (New Haven: Yale University Press; 1950), pp. 123–4.

observer speaks with confident eloquence about the nature of the mass mind, he should be greeted by an amiable skepticism.[1]

Specific and Basic Consensus. These observations enable us to put in perspective the question of the place of consensus in the political system. From the data it is clear that within the electorate a fairly high degree of agreement, or consensus, prevails on concrete but broad questions of public policy, such as the support of public education or the maintenance of the system of economic security for the aged. This, though, is not the kind of consensus of which the political theorists speak. They are more concerned with a "basic" or "fundamental" consensus, the content of which they do not commonly specify. When one seeks to identify that consensus in the attitudes of people, he is driven toward a quest for information about aspects of national character which, though not always specifically political in their content, might be expected to bear on the way people behave in the political system. Although the data are thin, the probability seems to be that consensus must be found in large measure in these characteristics of the people rather than in strong and widespread attachment to fundamental principles explicitly political in their content. Such evidence as there is, in fact, suggests that popular beliefs in general principles of democracy do not have much bearing on popular attitudes on individual issues that might be subsumed under them. People may concur almost unanimously with glittering generalities, such as "Public officials should be chosen by majority vote," and simultaneously split about 50:50 on the proposition, "In a city referendum, only people who are well informed about the problem being voted on should be allowed to vote." [2] Whatever the characteristics of popular attitude that permit governments to operate as if a basic consensus existed, they do not seem to consist of ideas that amount to a consensus on political fundamentals unless we mean by that phrase nothing more than a popular recognition of the legitimacy of the regime.

---

[1] Other observations about national character are also often deservedly suspect. Thus, an interpretation of some traits of Japanese national character based on the supposed rigid toilet training of Japanese children once enjoyed considerable vogue. Subsequent research found, however, "that the assumption that Japanese children are more rigidly or severely toilet-trained than Western children lacks factual basis."—Muzafer Sherif and Carolyn W. Sherif: *Groups in Harmony and Tension* (New York: Harper; 1953), p. 28.

[2] The example is from a study of Ann Arbor and Tallahassee by James W. Prothro and Charles M. Grigg: "Fundamental Principles of Democracy; Bases of Agreement and Disagreement," *Journal of Politics*, XXII (1960), 276–94.

3 · Carriers and Mechanisms of Basic Consensus

The hypothesis that a consensus on fundamentals pervades the population—which both permits an orderly settlement of specific issues as
they develop and, within broad limits, fixes the terms of their settlement—is most beguiling. Yet the rudimentary information available
strongly indicates that a more complex explanation is required, one that
will take into account the differing roles of sectors of the population in
the political system and their varying baggage of attitudes and values.

Doubtless there exist widely within the population attitudes of
significance for the operation of the political system; we have sought
to identify some of them. Nevertheless, a low degree of political
involvement characterizes most people. Moreover, the content of their
information and the nature of their modal attitudes are not such as to
explain the basic workings of the apparatus of government. Popular
information about even the most elementary aspects of the constitutional system is extremely limited.[3] Appreciation of those subtle
features of the workings of the political system that enable commentators to talk about such abstractions as the "consensus on fundamentals" is certainly even less widely distributed.

Within the population generally the dominant set of attitudes and
expectations may be compatible with a government that operates as if
a consensus on fundamentals existed. Yet to round out the explanation
it is useful to assume that the circles of leadership, the political
activists of the society, constitute what might be called a "political
subculture." Perhaps within this group are to be found in high
degree those beliefs, values, habits of action, and modes of political
life that give the political system its distinctive characteristics. Politicians, lobbyists, officials, party leaders, and influentials may be carriers
of the political culture or holders of the basic consensus on modes
and styles of action, even though they may be sharply divided on the
issues of the day. Among these individuals there may exist a sensitivity
to the problems of the other fellow, a capacity to recognize when it is
futile to fight and more sensible to wait, a disposition to seek out areas
of agreement and to maximize them, a tendency to sweep conflict

[3] NORC (National Opinion Research Center, of the University of Chicago),
November, 1945: "What do you know about the Bill of Rights?" Never heard of
it, 28 per cent; heard but don't know what it is, 36 per cent; know what it is,
21 per cent; confused, 4 per cent; wrong, 5 per cent; part wrong, part right,
3 per cent; don't know, 3 per cent. More searching inquiry would doubtless turn
up a wider popular understanding of particular constitutional principles. For an
example, see pages 135–36.

under the rug, an unprincipled inclination to split the difference or compromise, and a comparatively broad understanding of the place of specific actions for the system as a whole both at the moment and in the stream of time.

To establish whether such qualities exist among the politically active stratum of the population would require more data than are available. Samuel Stouffer's study of the attitudes of people generally and of community leaders at the time of the commotion over communism in the early 1950's provides suggestive data. Community leaders—public officials, party county chairmen, presidents of chambers of commerce, presidents of labor unions, and other community functionaries—rated on the average far higher on a scale of tolerance than did the rank and file of the citizenry. On his scale of willingness to tolerate nonconformists, 66 per cent of the community leaders rated "relatively more tolerant," while only 32 per cent of a cross section of the communities achieved the same rank.[4]

Probably as individuals move into the ranks of leadership—which may include the guiding echelons of many private organizations as well as more formal political institutions—they receive an indoctrination into the mores of the subculture of the political activists. Instances are legion in which the businessman goes to Washington breathing fire and determined "to put a stop to all this foolishness." After his horizons become broadened and he begins to learn the rules of the game, he comes to talk more like a politician than a politician. A similar process occurs on a large scale as men serve on school boards, city councils, party committees, other governing institutions, and committees of private groups that are governmentally oriented.

These observations may seem to distill down to the proposition that the system can operate as though a fundamental consensus prevailed for the reason that a governing elite happens to be imbued with particular values and habits of action. While great significance must be attached to the values, goals, and modes of action of those who devote themselves to the tasks of governing and of leadership, these people do not work in a vacuum. On the American scene it may be supposed that a compatibility exists between the modal expectations, values, opinions, and attitudes of the population generally and the ways of behavior of the political activists. An interaction between the two occurs, with each conditioning the other over the long run but with each fairly closely dependent upon the other over the short run.

This pattern of behaviors among members of the leadership echelons, on the one hand, and between the leadership echelons and the mass of the populace, on the other, may rest not simply on atti-

[4] Stouffer: op. cit., p. 52.

tudes; it may be dependent also on certain kinds of substantive policies and objective circumstances.[5] If the critical points in the system for the maintenance of general consensus and for the gradual accretion to consensus through the settlement of particular issues are in the relationships among the members of the leadership echelons, the allocation of rewards must be such that substantial elements of leadership are not alienated from the etiquette of parliamentary democracy. In short, the system must be such that most men of skill in leadership and management feel on the whole that they get theirs, be it in cash or glory. This, though, may not be enough. The leadership structure exists on a foundation of popular consent, which reflects itself in consensus on specifics as well as in a generalized support of the political system. Its maintenance depends in the long run on the prosecution of policies and practices that do not produce widespread feelings of deprivation or of injustice among the populace.[6] All these are, of course, elements in the puzzle of the fundamental nature of the governing process. As the analysis proceeds, the same kinds of questions will arise again and again.

[5] See the suggestive treatment by David M. Potter: *People of Plenty* (Chicago: University of Chicago Press; 1954).

[6] To establish their validity, these observations require much more systematic evidence than is available, but consider the response to a survey question posed to industrial workers in France and Italy in the fall of 1955. The question was: "In terms of what you see around you, would you say that there is much injustice, or not so much?" The results:

	France	Italy
Much injustice	63%	66%
Not so much	17	17
No opinion	20	17
	100%	100%

Source: Hadley Cantril, *Faith, Hope, and Heresy* (Princeton: Institute for International Social Research; 1957), III-25.

3

CONFLICT

❧ C ONFLICT, to judge from the headlines, is the entirety of politics. The American press, prone as it is to balloon casual differences into small-scale wars, conveys an image of a society ever embroiled in intramural battles. Yet the tempests in officialdom rarely arouse the emotions or even attract the attention of a large part of the citizenry, regardless of the size of the headlines. Popular consensus is more characteristic than conflict, although even on matters on which agreement pervades the population the media may suggest that cleavages are wide and deep. Nevertheless, from time to time issues arise of which substantially the entire population is aware and concerning which people divide. Such popular divisions of opinion parallel cleavages of opinion within the leadership circles of society and may acquire their form and their content from the cues given and the positions taken by leadership cliques. Clusters of popular opinion may form also in response to conditions that affect the population and generate nebulous opinion blocs of approval and disapproval, of discontent and satisfaction; but commonly conflict groupings polarize around divergent points of political leadership, each offering its own diagnosis and its own prescription.

1 · Patterns of Opinion Conflict

Types of Conflict Distributions. When a substantial part of the population is involved in a conflict of opinion, an array of opinions along an attitude scale produces a pattern markedly different from the typical J-distribution of consensus. In statistical terms distributions of opinions in conflict take the form of bimodal or multimodal curves. Characteristically in American politics by the time an issue has been debated sufficiently to activate opinions in most of the population, the alternatives have been so shaped and the opposing camps of leadership so organized that the distribution takes a bimodal form. That pattern in a more or less ideal form, with opinion about evenly divided and nicely arranged along a scale, would look like the curve in Figure 3.1.

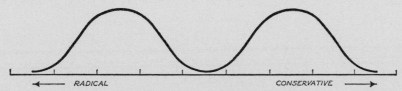

FIGURE 3.1. Bimodal Opinion Distribution

Opinion distributions, to be sure, seldom appear in precisely this form; they may lean this way or that or display other irregularities. The instruments used to measure the opinions of national cross sections are usually too crude to identify the finer gradations of opinion. Nevertheless, at times the bimodal curve may be approximated, and it serves as a useful analytical model.

Logically conflicts of opinion could also be expected to take a multimodal form, with clusters of opinion concentrated at three or more points along a unidimensional scale. Such multimodal distributions, which in ideal form would appear as in Figure 3.2, doubtless are

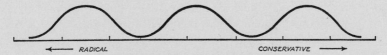

FIGURE 3.2. Multimodal Opinion Distribution

commonplace among relatively thin political elites and perhaps among small and highly informed publics. In the general public, though, the bimodal pattern of attitude is probably far more common. That form may result in part from the types of questions put in opinion surveys which force responses into a bimodal pattern, though the questions generally parallel the actual lines of conflict. The duality of the American party system may also bear on the prevalence of bimodal opinion distributions. By the time an issue attracts wide public attention, it may have become a party issue and have been fitted into the dual-party mold.

For multimodal distributions of opinion to occur, three or more solutions to a problem or viewpoints about it must enjoy considerable public support. That three- or four-sided questions arise so infrequently may be a characteristic of American politics of considerable importance.[1] Achievement of agreement on national purpose may be a more complicated task when the opinion patterns are multimodal. A suggestion of the problem comes from reflection on the period of foreign policy debate when some wanted to attend to China, others thought that efforts should be dedicated to rebuilding western Europe, and still others would have been happier with withdrawal from world affairs.

Examples of Conflict Patterns. If the data were available, an American political history could be written in terms of the successive patterns of conflict in the distribution of public opinion on issues that have rent the Republic. Public opinion sampling is a recent invention, and historical accounts of the epic battles among political leaders are accompanied by no firm knowledge of the extent to which the general public had a concern about the issues or of how it divided. Opinion polls, however, make information available—of varying quality—on the distribution of attitudes on major questions that have agitated the people since about 1935. Examination of a few of these distributions will illustrate the general idea of the bimodality of conflict distributions and indicate as well the divisions on specific issues.

In the 1950's, the era of Eisenhower, a period marked by few dramatic acts of executive initiative in domestic politics, a mixture of consensus and indifference about political issues seemed far more characteristic of the population than did conflict. On only a few questions (within the limits of the available information) did the array of opinions within the population closely approximate the model of more or less symmetrical bimodality. Among the 16 issue propositions used by the Survey Research Center in its study of the 1956 presidential election, the one that yielded a pattern most nearly approximating the conflict model was the following: "The government in Washington should stay out of the question of whether white and colored

---

[1] Technically a distinction may be made between unidimensional issues and multidimensional issues. A multimodal distribution on a unidimensional issue represents only three or more clusterings of opinion differing in degree. Often in politics a multimodal distribution exists primarily because the issue is multidimensional. For example, we might have clusters of opinion along a scale of the degree to which public schools should be supported, which would be unidimensional. When, however, the question of federal participation in finance is introduced, a second dimension is added, which might identify clusters of opinion quite independent of those along the first unidimensional scale.

children go to the same school." [2] Only 10 per cent of the sample had no opinion on this matter; those who had views, as may be seen from Figure 3.3, clustered at the extremes of the scale. Most people had strong opinions either pro or con and those at the midpoint, "not sure, it depends," were few. The distribution could be described as U-shaped. This form is a function of the technique of measurement; if instruments capable of identifying finer gradations of opinion had been employed, the distribution might have more nearly resembled the model bimodal pattern.

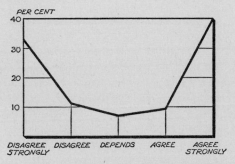

FIGURE 3.3. "The government in Washington should stay out of the question of whether white and colored children go to the same school." DATA SOURCE: *Survey Research Center, University of Michigan, 1956.* Percentage base excludes those with no opinion.

Curves of opinion on other 1956 issues took forms intermediate between patterns of consensus and conflict. In some instances patterns of popular opinion associated with the sharpest congressional conflict approached the consensual form. When these are examined in the light of congressional consideration of the questions concerned, they suggest inferences about the bearing of opinion patterns on behavior within the governing apparatus. Clearly a fairly small popular minority can support a formidable voice within Congress, a voice that often is exercised with the hope that its public support will increase. The converse of this proposition may be that questions of visible import on which action is taken without delay and the accompanying oratorical display tend to be associated with the most marked popular consensus. These notions are relevant in the interpretation of the U-shaped distribution in Figure 3.4, which pictures expressions of agreement and disagreement in 1958 with this proposition: "The government should leave things like electric power and housing for private businessmen to handle." Over 40 per cent of the sample agreed strongly

[2] The text of all 16 propositions is reproduced from the interview schedule in Appendix I.

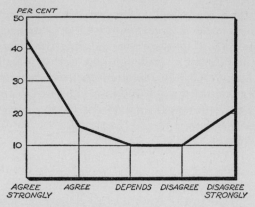

FIGURE 3.4. "The government should leave things like electric power and housing for private businessmen to handle." DATA SOURCE: *Survey Research Center, University of Michigan, 1956.* Percentage base excludes those with no opinion.

with the proposition, while only 21 per cent strongly disagreed. The division appears one-sided, but it sufficed to underpin heated disputes within Congress in the years immediately after 1956 on specific questions of housing and public power.

Another illustration of the U-distribution concerned opinion on the proposition: "The government ought to help people get doctors and hospital care at low cost." Again an asymmetrical peaking of opinion at the two extremes occurred, with 44 per cent of those with opinions agreeing "strongly" while 21 per cent disagreed "strongly" (Figure 3.5). The lack of congruity between the distribution of opinion within the public and the behavior of those with power to

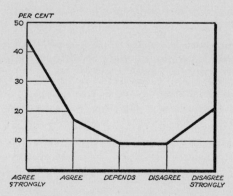

FIGURE 3.5. "The government ought to help people get doctors and hospital care at low cost." DATA SOURCE: *Survey Research Center, University of Michigan, 1956.* Percentage base excludes those with no opinion.

decide is suggested by reflection on this distribution. The minority on this proposition had demonstrated in its activities in the congressional campaign of 1950 and in the presidential campaign of 1952 that it could exert considerable influence. At least a goodly number of politicians felt that they had burned their fingers by advocating compulsory medical insurance, and during the Eisenhower Administration there was no determined effort from the Executive to promote broad action in this field.[3]

Articulation of Conflict Distributions with Governmental Apparatus. Opinion distributions that take the typical conflict form gain political importance only insofar as they affect the behavior of those in control of the governmental apparatus and in other positions of political leadership and influence. The evangel of a simple theory of government by public opinion might say that the views of 51 per cent of the people should be reflected in governmental actions. No such exact articulation can prevail between government and public opinion; but when a conflict pattern prevails, government operates within a matrix of opinion radically different from that created by an opinion distribution of overwhelming consensus.

In the interaction between governmental and leadership levels and the public, bipolarized clusters of opinion form foundations of support for opposing leadership cliques. In turn, oratory and fulminations at the leadership levels maintain cleavages within the public. If the course of events and the tenor of debate gradually produce a consensus in mass opinion, the foundation of popular support for one of the leadership clusters in conflict is weakened, if not destroyed. It may be supposed that, at least on great questions that attract wide public attention, adequate presentation of divergent viewpoints at leadership

[3] An opinion survey on a question of the type mentioned above conceals dimensions of opinion that may be extremely significant in relation to governmental decision. All the alternatives cannot be indicated on the agree-disagree continuum. A Nebraska housewife commented in an aside to her agreement: "I think this should help; lots of children need things that their folks can't do; mainly for the little children." The wife of a Michigan automotive engineer added to her "agree but not strongly": "I'm not in favor of socialized medicine but certainly the sick should be cared for." Others had a word for the aged. Still others looked at the matter ideologically. A Kansas lady, once a registered nurse, agreed and added: "Socialized medicine; it's a good thing." Somewhat incongruously, a California naval officer observed: "Individuals should be responsible for their own medical care." Often the acts of government dodge the broad questions and focus at points at which intersecting opinion dimensions probably provide multiple sources of support. Consider in the medical care field, for example, the medical care of veterans, of aged, or of children. The combination of the friends of veterans and of public medical care may generate far stronger support for action on a narrow front than could be mustered for broad action on medical care.

levels requires the encouragement of an empowering public response. That response, in turn, depends in a measure on the clarity, vigor, and reasonableness with which leaders present various outlooks.

The nature of the support for each extreme in leadership opinion depends somewhat on the composition and distribution of the underlying popular foundation. Given the system of representation, a geographic segregation of divergent opinion clusters tends to produce firm foundations in popular support for viewpoints within the leadership levels. Class and occupational distribution may affect the nature and firmness of the advocacy of differing views within the representative and political apparatus. Those sectors of society most active and most alert politically probably command greater fealty over the long run from their spokesmen than do those groups with only a transient and tangential focus of attention on political matters. In short, the significance of particular bimodal opinion distributions depends in considerable measure on who holds which shade of opinion.[4]

2 · Issue Conflict and Group Conflict

A major frailty in the classical treatments of public opinion came from a disposition to regard the political system as an atomized collection of individuals, each more or less informed about public issues and possessing views about them. This preconception produces a picture of social conflict organized along issue alignments as individuals independently form their opinions. While lines of conflict may thus be shaped, in some degree cleavages that involve the mass public are in terms, not of conflicting attachments to issues, but of loyalties to competing groups. The most inclusive of such groups in our society are the political parties. Though neat distributions of the population may be shown on scales measuring opinions on issues, another important type of conflict is reflected in distributions along a scale of party loyalty.

The content and nature of party attachments are doubtless most diverse among individuals. About all that can be said with assurance is that these attachments vary in their strength and that the voting behavior of individuals differs with the strength and direction of their party identifications. Beyond this, party attachment is to a degree a substitute for opinions on specific issues. In another dimension, party identification is a function of family background and individual social status. A person may, albeit unconsciously, take positions on individual issues as he identifies with parties—positions that may be congruent with what he would wish if he happened to wish. For economy of effort, it

[4] These matters will be explored at length in Chapters 5–8.

makes some sense for people to act in terms of groups rather than in terms of substantive issues. It is simpler to appraise political events and alternatives in terms of "how do they, or will they, affect people like me" than to acquire information on a series of complex issues.

Party identification in some instances has a large component of issue content. Yet among many voters party loyalty seems to be an attitude quite lacking in issue content. In other instances a person's party loyalty may be incongruent with his issue preferences. In short, if we were to apply the language of attitude analysis to party identification, we would probably say that the attitude of loyalty is multidimensional. It has different meanings and serves different functions for different persons.

Conflict patterns in public opinion thus come about in terms partially of substantive issues and partially of party (and other group) loyalties. The two types of cleavage do not invariably coincide; they only approach congruence in degrees that differ from time to time and from issue to issue. To some extent policy differences between the identifiers with the major parties arise from the tendency of parties, by their issue postures, to attract those with similar views. To some extent they are brought about by the capacity of parties to shape the policy views of their adherents. And the incongruencies between party identification and policy outlooks measure the capacity of parties to organize conflict independently of the beliefs of people on substantive issues. Another ingredient also helps to account for the incongruencies. Some people, strong in their party loyalty, seem incapable of perceiving the discrepancies between their issue positions and those of their party.

A Side Excursion into Group Theory. It is possible to estimate the distribution of party loyalties according to their relative strength and to present the results as a bimodal curve after the fashion of the distributions of opinion that conform to the conflict pattern. That exercise, however, does not reveal the qualities of group loyalties that make them different from issue opinions. Group identifications reflect relationships among persons, relationships that are at times influential in the formation and maintenance of issue opinions. To help grasp the place of groups in the organization of political conflict, it may be useful to conduct a side excursion into some of the elements of group theory. Psychologists and sociologists have concerned themselves extensively with the capacity of groups to induce conforming behavior or common outlooks among their members, obviously a topic of basic political importance.

A major subject of study is behavior in primary, or face-to-face, group situations. Under such situations presumably pressures for conformity to group standards would be most marked; people are sensitive to the frowns and silences of their immediate associates. The existence, nature, and extent of these sensitivities have been demonstrated in many experiments. Sherif took advantage of the fact that a stationary pinpoint of light viewed in a quiet dark room seems to the observer to move. When a group watches the pinpoint of light under these conditions, its members arrive at a consensus on the length of the movements of the light, an estimate that differs from that arrived at by isolated individual viewers. The group process generates a common outlook among the members. Further experiments indicated that many individuals introduced to a group with a prearranged estimate of movement adopt the standard of the group.[5]

Asch attacked the question of conformity to group standards by setting up a problem of matching the "length of a given line with one of three unequal lines." A minority of one was placed in the midst of a group whose members had been instructed to respond with the wrong answers. About a third of the experimental subjects yielded to the false majority opinion; two thirds stood by their perceptions against the pressure of the majority. The capacity of the majority to induce concurrence increased, however, with the ambiguity of the situation presented to the subjects. Conversely, the less the ambiguity and the more clearly a subject could see the differences in the length of the lines, the less disposed was he to yield to a majority view divergent from the reality.[6] Other findings suggest that individuals tend to adopt what they perceive to be the standards of their primary groups even when no overt group sanctions are operative.[7] Festinger finds that the capacity of a group to exist depends in part on the magnitude of the change in attitude it attempts to induce in its members; pressure for wide change may disrupt the group. Moreover, its capacity to induce conformity is fixed by the limits of what he calls its "power field," a concept which is more or less equivalent to jurisdiction.[8] Some behaviors are regarded as a proper concern of a group; others are outside its "power field."

Intimate, face-to-face groups have a hand in the shaping of the

[5] Muzafer Sherif: "An Experimental Approach to the Study of Attitudes," *Sociometry*, I (1937), 90–8.

[6] S. E. Asch: "Effects of Group Pressure Upon the Modification and Distortion of Judgments," in H. Guetzkow, ed.: *Groups, Leadership and Men*, (Pittsburgh: Carnegie Press, 1951), pp. 177–90.

[7] Ivan D. Steiner: "Primary Group Influences on Public Opinion," *American Sociological Review*, XIX (1954), 260–7.

[8] Leon Festinger *et al.: Social Pressures in Informal Groups* (New York: Harper; 1950), p. 166.

political attitudes of individuals. In the analysis of large-scale social structures, however, the primary-group concept reaches its explanatory limits quickly, and a more commodious concept is required. To meet that need social theorists adapted the concept of the reference group, a notion originally contrived for other purposes. The idea of the reference group is somewhat recondite, and the doctors differ in their definitions. It need not be a face-to-face group, formal or informal. Sherif and Sherif characterize reference groups "simply as those groups to which the individual relates himself as a part or to which he aspires to relate himself psychologically." [9] Various types of individual attitudes and behaviors—voting, for example—tend to be associated with attitudes toward such remote and nebulous groups as an American political party, which may be regarded, at least for most people, as a reference group. That is, individuals tend to act *as if* they were being subjected to the pressures and sanctions of a primary group, although to regard the extended "reference group" as in the same family of entities as the primary group involves a modicum of poetic license.

The concept of the reference group helps to account for a good deal of electoral behavior; yet for the analysis of behavior in political systems a notion of greater generality may be more appropriate. Even as the concept is used by social psychologists, the term "reference group" produces confusion because of its implication that processes of norm enforcement akin to those of primary groups occur. A concept of *reference symbols* might have broader utility in description of political behavior. A reference symbol could be regarded as a symbol to which an individual relates himself or aspires to relate himself psychologically. Associated with the symbol may be norms, values, standards, approved patterns of behavior, or loyalties that may be adopted by those individuals who relate themselves to the symbol. The reference symbol would include not only reference groups but also other objects of psychological attachment. At the broadest and most nebulous levels are such symbols as the flag, the Constitution, the nation. Political leaders may become reference symbols. A Democrat may not be so much a Democrat as a Wilsonian, a Jacksonian, or a Jeffersonian, though those personages may be assimilated into the party symbol. A Republican may be so attached to the GOP that he would vote for a Chinaman on its ticket; the party may be for him a reference symbol, devoid of issue content, yet a determinant

[9] *Groups in Harmony and in Tension* (New York: Harper; 1953), p. 161. For a review, by the originator of the concept, of the elaborations of the idea of the reference group, see Herbert H. Hyman: "Reflections on Reference Groups," *Public Opinion Quarterly*, XXIV (1960), 383–96.

of voting choice. Or the party symbol may organize sentiment but have no perceptible bearing on behavior.[1] Newspapers, radio commentators, and even abstract principles, for example, the rule of law, may become reference symbols.

As one explores the theory of groups, sooner or later the question of how primary groups and reference groups fit together in the larger political system arises. Primary groups, insofar as they develop or enforce norms about matters of political issue or personality, do not operate in isolation. They are presumably linked in some way to more inclusive reference groups or to reference symbols. The more influential individuals within primary groups may link them to reference groups, to political leadership, to the sources of cues for action by which the attitudes of primary groups are integrated into larger clusters of political attitude and loyalty. It is, of course, unnecessary to assume that all individuals are coupled to these larger clusters through the mediation of primary groups. In many instances they may relate themselves directly to their reference symbols. Nevertheless, the cohesion of a reference group may become more marked as the cohesion of its related primary groups increases.

Still another notion from group theory has some relevance to our problem. Primary groups form norms applicable to the members of the group; they also regulate opinion and behavior toward outsiders by identifying friends and enemies. Newcomb has extended these phenomena to the reference-group concept by conceiving of positive and negative reference groups. A positive reference group "is one in which a person is motivated to be accepted and treated as a member (overtly or symbolically), whereas a negative reference group is one which the person is motivated to oppose or in which he does not want to be treated as a member." These positive and negative notions, as Sherif and Sherif have pointed out, have an immediate relevance for the political system.[2] Presumably these definitions of attitudes toward other groups are fixed in a measure by the positions of groups in the power structure. A person strongly identified with the business

[1] Consider the reply of a Kentucky lady to: "Anything you like about the Democratic party?" "No, I can't say there is. I just go by listening. My husband is a great Democrat but like me, he don't vote. I don't keep up with it. I don't watch it on TV if I can get out of it. I don't understand politics. I guess the only reason I prefer the Democrats is I thought Roosevelt was so great. I liked him. On radio I would listen to him. No TV them days." Replying to: "Anything you like about the Republican party?" "Gosh, I don't know. I wouldn't know what to tell you. As far as that there must be something but I don't know what to tell you. I'm dumb on politics."

[2] "Some Effects of Power Relations in Molding Opinion and Behavior," *Southwestern Social Science Quarterly*, XXXIII (1952-3), 287-96.

community will very probably have reservations about, if not hostility toward, labor unions. A positive attachment to Republicanism may be associated with a negative regard for the Democracy, and so forth.

Party Identification and Conflict Distributions. The foregoing remarks about group theory bear on questions raised in later chapters; at this point they are relevant to a special type of mass distribution of opinion or attitude in conflict form. While bimodal distributions reflective of disagreement on issues occur, attachments to or opinions about political parties—all-encompassing reference symbols—also form bimodal distributions which sometimes coincide with distributions of opinion about substantive issues. Around a single symbol the party organizes loyalties, attitudes, beliefs, and opinions of the most varied content.

Studies by the Survey Research Center in 1948 and at intervals during the 1950's indicate, at least for this period, a high degree of gross stability in party identification. Party identification was determined by responses to this question: "Generally speaking, do you usually think of yourself as a Republican, a Democrat, an independent, or what?" Those who admitted to a party identification were asked: "Would you call yourself a strong (R) (D) or a not very strong (R) (D)?" Those who answered that they were independents were asked: "Do you think of yourself as closer to the Republican or Democratic party?" Those indicating a leaning were denominated independent Republicans or independent Democrats. The results permit the differentiation of persons along a scale of party identification ranging from strong Democratic through independent to strong Republican. When the data were charted (Figure 3.6), a bimodal distribution similar in form to the distributions of opinions on issues about which varying opinions pervade the population resulted. The distribution charted was asymmetrical in reflection of the excess of Democratic over Republican identifiers; presumably if similar data were available for, say, 1908, the imbalance of the distribution would favor the Republican end of the scale.

For our purposes the sense of party identification may be regarded as a public "opinion" or attitude with quite as much bearing upon the workings of the political system as opinions on policies. As has been amply demonstrated by Campbell, Converse, Miller, and Stokes, party identification serves as a point of anchorage for the elector; current issues, candidates, and other factors that impinge upon him may either reinforce or weaken the tie of voting behavior to party identification. Beyond this, as they have also demonstrated, party identification is related to opinions on policy.[3] On the average, strong Democrats differ from weak Democrats, weak Republicans from weak Democrats, and strong Republicans from weak Republicans.

Congruence between policy outlook and party identification comes from the group forces mentioned earlier—that is, the tendency of the party to attract those persons to whom its policy position is

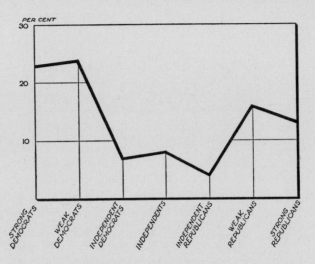

FIGURE 3.6. Distribution of Population According to Party Identification, 1958. DATA SOURCE: *Survey Research Center, University of Michigan, 1958.*

congenial plus the tendency of party adherents to adopt the policy position of their party. Noncongruence between party position and the policy outlook of its adherents flows from nonpolicy factors that may determine party attachment, such as family influence. The net result of all these factors is that considerable similarity in policy attitude characterizes the party groups, although on controversial issues commonly the opinion of the "average" Democrat differs from that of the "average" Republican. These remarks may be illustrated by the stands of Republican and Democratic identifiers in 1956 on this proposition: "The government should leave things like electric power and housing for private businessmen to handle." The two groups of identifiers fell on the scale in the following manner:

[3] See Angus Campbell, Philip E. Converse, Warren E. Miller, and Donald E. Stokes: *The American Voter* (New York: Wiley; 1960), especially ch. 6.

	Republicans	Democrats
Agree strongly; government definitely should	55%	34%
Agree but not very strongly	16	14
Not sure; it depends	9	9
Disagree but not very strongly	8	13
Disagree strongly; government definitely should not	12	30
	100	100
N	490	625

When we arrange in another manner the distribution of opinion on the housing and public power question, another facet of the relation between party identification and policy opinions becomes apparent. Although within parties homogeneity may not be marked, within each issue position the adherents of one or the other of the parties may predominate. In Figure 3.7 attitudes on the power and housing question are shown in a manner indicating the proportions of each issue position

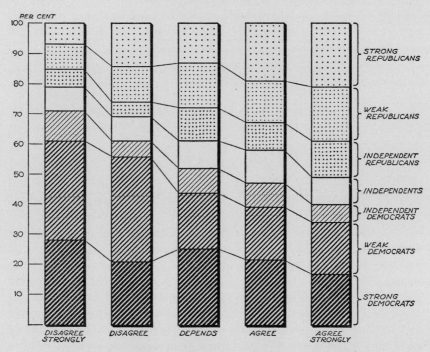

FIGURE 3.7. "The government should leave things like electric power and housing for private businessmen to handle." DATA SOURCE: *Survey Research Center, University of Michigan, 1956.*

composed of partisans of varying kinds. Democrats of one degree or another make up the bulk of those at the pro-public-power end of the scale. Republicans predominate at the free-enterprise extreme though they are reinforced by a substantial number of Democrats. As these patterns are filtered through the representative mechanisms, one party becomes the spokesman for one point of view and the other for the other, although neither party can maintain solidarity within its congressional ranks.

Import for the Political System. The great durability of the clusters of loyalties about the political parties has a deep import for the workings of the political system. That significance may be made apparent by a circuitous route. Individual substantive issues come and go; they flare up and are settled or disappear; they divide the population first this way, then that. Public opinion is not necessarily mercurial, but governments whose composition and tenure depended on the divisions of opinion in the population on the issue of the day would be relatively unstable. When they are based on the more durable attitudes toward parties, a far higher degree of stability may characterize the institutional system.

In the American institutional setting the bimodal pattern of durable party loyalties performs also a supportive role of special significance for minority leadership clusters. Even the vicissitudes of long Democratic rule did not destroy a loyal band of Republican party supporters; nor did the Democrats disappear during the Eisenhower era. A foundation of support persists for a minority leadership and thereby enables it to perform its functions in the system. If support for the minority rested solely on opinions grounded in particular issues, the life of the opposition would be precarious. Given the nature of governments, an opposition with stable popular foundations is a useful piece of equipment to have around.

Primary Groups and Policy Orientations. For many persons the policy position of their party, as they perceive it, may strongly affect their own policy preferences. Cues may emanate from the reference symbol. For many persons, though, influences to conform to a policy position (or perhaps to depart from it) may come from their face-to-face associates, the primary groups to which they belong. Most persons find themselves members of small groups that have at least a mild political relevance. Some individuals doubtless move in informal circles in which the topics of politics are salient and the pressures to conform are high.

The extent to which people form and maintain their policy views and opinions under primary-group influences and the kinds of connections between these groups and the parties could be systematically determined only by the most extensive inquiry. A sliver of evidence, reported in Table 3.1, suggests that many people may derive support

TABLE 3.1

PERCEPTIONS OF THE PARTISANSHIP OF RESPONDENT'S PRIMARY GROUPS IN RELATION TO HIS ISSUE POSITION

RESPONDENT'S POSITION ON FOUR ISSUES	PERCEIVED VOTE OF PRIMARY GROUPS		
	Democratic	Evenly split or nonvoting	Republican
Democratic, no conflict [a]	33%	23%	14%
Democratic, with conflict	20	17	11
Neither Democratic nor Republican	23	33	22
Republican, with conflict	9	10	24
Republican, no conflict	15	17	29
	100%	100%	100%
N	491	427	698

[a] The issue combinations were defined as follows: "Democratic" includes those persons whose positions on the issues were pro-Democratic. Even though a person had an opinion on only one issue, if it was pro-Democratic he placed in this category. The "with conflict" category includes those with views on more issues favoring one party than the other. The middle category includes those either with equal numbers of views in favor of each party or with no opinion on any of the issues. DATA SOURCE: *Survey Research Center, University of Michigan, 1952. For the details on the issues and their grouping, see Angus Campbell* et al.: The Voter Decides *(Evanston: Row, Peterson; 1954), pp. 122–3.*

from their primary-group environment for their policy positions. In 1952 a national sample was asked how their "friends" voted in the presidential election and how their spouse, or, if not married, how their family, voted. The upshot of the analysis was that persons who saw their primary groups so defined as voting Democratic tended themselves to have pro-Democratic views on four selected issues. The assumption may be that their friends and families had policy views resembling their own and that in the interactions of these primary circles a degree of enforcement and reinforcement of opinions occurred. Probably it is correct to picture the political system as one in which a complex network of such group relations fixes and maintains opinions in some systematic relation to the larger components of the system, such as the political parties.[4]

The details of these findings in Table 3.1 show, to be sure, a considerable looseness in the relationships between perceptions of associates' vote and the respondent's policy outlooks. Yet the data probably convey an unduly constricted impression of the attitudinal homogeneity of primary groups. For example, the members of a poker club of southern Democrats who perceived their friends and families as voting Democratic might turn up in this table as persons with Republican views but surrounded by Democrats.

3 · Composition of Conflict

Differences between parties, classes, and other groupings within society endure, though they may wax and wane in intensity with the condition of the times. Conflict groupings over fairly specific policy issues, though, are usually transient. Attitude clusters form in protest, in approval, in resistance, and in advocacy, and they usually disappear in due course. The issue is forgotten or buried, or it is settled with a precipitate onto the body of accumulated consensus. The consideration of these processes for the disposition of conflict would lead one quickly into an examination of the entire process of governance. While that task is beyond our concern at this point, a few conjectures about the bearing of the form of mass-opinion distributions on the composition of conflict are in order.

W-Distributions. Political conflict obviously is settled at the level of political leadership, through the formal and informal mechanisms of government, and not at the levels of mass attitude that we have been describing. Yet presumably actions at the governmental level are conditioned by the distributions of opinions within the mass public, especially on those matters that generate intense opinions among large proportions of the people. In turn, the patterns of attitudes within the general public may be modified as leadership elements engage in debate, negotiation, and compromise.

[4] W. F. Whyte has emphasized that the small group should not be treated as an isolated unit. See his "Small Groups and Large Organizations" in J. H. Rohrer and Muzafer Sherif, eds.: *Social Psychology at the Crossroads* (New York: Harper; 1951), pp. 297–312. See also E. Jackson Baur: "Public Opinion and the Primary Group," *American Sociological Review*, XXV (1960), 208–19. Bernard Berelson *et al.: Voting* (Chicago: University of Chicago Press; 1954), ch. 6, contains a detailed analysis of the relation of primary groups to the act of voting.

In one type of situation the composition of conflict may be affected by characteristics of opinions not suggested by the illustrative examples we have employed. Bimodal distributions of attitudes in divergence may not reveal qualities of opinion that are conducive to the ultimate resolution of the issue. The seeds of reconciliation may be hidden in the opinions arrayed sharply in a conflict pattern whose form is a product of the measurement techniques employed. One type of distribution, though, separates out shades of opinion whose existence may be critical to the resolution of conflict. Analysts of opinion dub this type a "W-distribution" of attitude. A. W. Jones, using more refined measurement techniques than those on which most of our examples rest, found such a distribution of attitude in Akron at a time of especially heated conflict between workers and employers. At each extreme of his attitude scale were peaks created by those individuals firmly attached to the opposing sides of the controversy, but between these extremes was a mode composed of individuals who took a middle position. He concluded that this form of distribution was characteristic of a population in which "there exists both a tendency to conform to a central mode of attitude and a tendency to split to an extraordinary degree." [5] An ideal form of this W-distribution, although not a copy of Jones' Akron curve, appears in Figure 3.8. In the resolution of con-

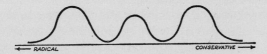

FIGURE 3.8. A W-Distribution

flict the outcome obviously depends on the direction in which those citizens shift who occupy the central position in such a distribution or on their ability to pull to a central position individuals located at the extremes. If the center shifts to the left or to the right, the W-curve might be replaced by a J-curve. If the extremes are pulled to the center, a double J-curve replaces the W.

To the extent that mass attitudes are linked to the operations of the governing apparatus, the existence of the center group in a W-distribution may facilitate the settlement of issues and influence the direction of settlement. Several analyses, for example, suggest that perhaps with respect to business, and in particular big business, something of a W-distribution has prevailed. The central mode consists of individuals characterized by an ambivalence toward business, and its movement toward a pro or con position may depend on the conditions

[5] Alfred Winslow Jones: *Life, Liberty, and Property* (New York: Lippincott; 1941), p. 327.

of the moment or the content of the specific issue conflict. In 1949
Elmo Roper reported from his surveys a "curious sort of verdict"
toward business. He found a mood of approval of the idea of privately
owned business, but mixed with this was a belief that business was "too
greedy" and "apt to overstep its bounds." [6] Presumably differentiated
from this central attitude were those who stood for or against business
without reservation. Fisher and Withey reported a somewhat similar
ambivalence: approval of big business as a productive machine but
negative dispositions toward its "self-perpetuating and self-enhancing
activities in society." [7] Gardner and Rainwater found among what
they call the "middle majority"—white-collar workers, craftsmen,
small-business proprietors, semiskilled and service workers—a respect
for big business mixed with uneasiness about the "beneficence of big
business." Respect for big business is associated with a fear which leads
to reliance on other institutions, government and labor unions, to keep
business in its place.[8]

Information is inadequate on how frequently the W-distribution or
its functional equivalent occurs. Yet when such a pattern of opinion
prevails, those who must decide are encased in a radically different
field of influence than they are when they confront a public sharply
bipolarized. For example, in a study of opinion about President
Roosevelt's proposal to reform the Supreme Court, Roper found a distribution of opinion more or less like the model we have set out. In a
small survey in March–April, 1937, during the discussion of the President's proposal, he found 28 per cent in favor of the proposal; 36 per
cent strongly against. Another 22 per cent did not know what they
thought about the plan, while 14 per cent thought something ought to
be done but believed the President's proposal not to be a good one.[9]
Roper argued that it was from the middle group that converts came
and that their decision on which direction to move eventually settled
the issue.

Some analysts claim to see within the electorate ambivalent
middle groups which, like the central mode of the W-distribution, may
throw their voting strength decisively this way or that. Thus, Saenger,
in a study of the 1944 presidential election in New York City, found
that Republican gains from 1936 to 1944 had been most marked in the

[6] Elmo Roper: "The Public Looks at Business," *Harvard Business Review*,
XXVII (1949), 165–74.

[7] Burton R. Fisher and Stephen B. Withey: *Big Business as the People See It*
(Ann Arbor: Survey Research Center; 1951), pp. 20–1.

[8] Burleigh B. Gardner and Lee Rainwater: "The Mass Image of Big Business,"
Harvard Business Review, XXXIII (1955), no. 6, 61–6.

[9] Elmo Roper: "Neutral Opinion on the Court Proposal," *Public Opinion
Quarterly*, July, 1937, 17–20. See also F. V. Cantwell: "Public Opinion and the
Legislative Process," *American Political Science Review*, XL (1946), 924–35.

medium-income group. He interpreted this to mean that the medium-income group in times of economic distress, as in 1936, leans more toward the lower-income groups, while in times of relative economic security the medium-income category tends to identify with those above it in income.[1] Such a reading of the data imposes a simple scheme upon a complex phenomenon; nevertheless, under some circumstances and on some questions the movements of a central wavering group contribute to the composition of conflict between contrasting extremes.

The theory of the W-distribution resembles this idea of a moderate, judicious, and undecided center which throws its weight first this way, and then that, depending on the circumstances. The existence of such a balancing group is most difficult to establish, although detailed opinion histories might establish that the fortunes of big business, for example, may depend over the long pull on which direction the middle mode of the W-distribution leans as conflict unfolds. Similarly, the legislative status of organized labor may hinge on circumstances that affect the drift of the central cluster of the undecided and indifferent. Repeated checks, with far more refined methods than have been used, would enable us to speak more confidently about whether clusters of opinion similar in function if not in form to those of the central mode in the W-distribution play a recurring role in the composition of conflict. On the basis of the inquiries that have been made one suspects that psychological scales do not capture neatly the reality of popular attitudes on broad and complex questions such as the place of business in society. Many persons may have nebulous sentiments of satisfaction or dissatisfaction, or acceptance or hostility, not readily translated into the verbalism of scales. Yet, as they find expression in the rhetoric of political leaders, these inchoate feelings may under some circumstances govern electoral decision.

Patterns in the Interaction between Leadership and Opinion. From time to time the wavering middle of the W-distribution may affect the composition of conflict, but this interaction is only a special case of a more general pattern of relationships between government and opinion. Those relationships, which are so complex that they can probably never be disentangled into their component elements, probably include several types of interactions. The points of contact in political conflict tend to be principally between the opposing centers of leadership in the formal and informal political apparatus; not often is discussion

[1] G. H. Saenger: "Social Status and Political Behavior," *American Journal of Sociology*, LI (1945), 103–13.

so widespread over a policy question that many men in the street spend much time in argumentation. It is also in the relations between the opposing centers of leadership that the composition or settlement of conflict occurs. In turn, patterns of action at the leadership level affect the distributions of popular opinion which, of course, have repercussions upon the behavior of the governing apparatus. It is probably in this set of complex interactions—among leadership components and between them and clusters of mass opinion—that one must search for the role of public opinion in popular government.

To speak with any confidence on the general nature of these interactions would require data on the flow of pronouncements of leadership clusters and on the changing form of opinion distributions over the life of many issues. And the life history of an issue often has a duration of decades. Without such data we must rely upon more or less tutored conjecture. Ordinarily those questions that precipitate conflict distributions within the general population are issues upon which sharp differences prevail in Congress, in the wider levels of political and nonpolitical leadership, and in the press. The pattern of advocacy and resistance among leadership elements is reflected within the public, and the public response may affect the pattern within the leadership elements. Innovative or retrogressive steps by candidates, by Presidents, or by other centers of leadership may stimulate counteraction by others. If the issue commands widespread attention and concerns nearly everyone, sooner or later public opinion may move toward the bimodal pattern of conflict. Articulate, widely distributed disagreement among the people probably follows rather than precedes division within the political leadership. Yet it is only on a few great issues that this general attention of the public is enlisted.

The form of the distribution of opinion within the public and the intensity of conflict may vary enormously from issue to issue. Some issues raised at leadership levels—school segregation, for example— may arouse deep emotions not easily quieted. Others may stir a transient and surface concern. Moreover, opinion surveyors can identify bimodal distributions within the population on matters about which political leaders are silent, attitude cleavages which have an origin independent of the actions of the moment by political leadership. In the main these are probably issues which, by common consent among the responsibles, are thought to be better left unraised. For example, polls on the Catholic-Protestant dimension will identify a bimodal dispersion of attitude and animosity within the population, but political leaders usually try to avoid arousing the populace on such incendiary matters. Even on questions within the legitimate realm of politics vague and unfocused opinion may develop from conditions (for example, economic deprivation) without much prompting by centers of leadership and agitation; these cleavages within the population, however, remain inchoate until exploited by agencies for the verbalization of sentiment.

The processes of composition of conflict probably involve simultaneous interactions within leadership elements and between such circles and the mass of the public. A pattern that doubtless recurs is that of a resisting leadership structure that finds that its popular support has evaporated. The measures enacted by the innovators over stiff opposition gradually gain acceptance; the pattern of differences within the public is replaced by a curve of consensus; and the band of prominent persons in resistance see that they have lost the battle and subside. Some such sequence of interactions doubtless occurred with respect to many of the innovations of the New Deal period, although the data are lacking to show in detail the course of change in opinion patterns.[2]

In other instances it seems probable that reconciliation occurs first at the level of political leadership, and clusters of public opinion in conflict gradually dissolve because of lack of encouragement from prestigious givers of cues. Thus changes in the form of opinion distributions are preceded by changes in the policy postures of political leadership. It may be that some such sequence of interactions occurred in the great debate over American foreign policy from around 1937 to 1952. Prominent Republican leaders in the 1940's moved away from the traditionally isolationist position of their party. After 1952 few Republican politicians of eminence espoused isolationism, and the followers of the hallowed tradition gradually lost their leadership.

Many variations on these two contrasting patterns occur. One type of sequence may involve a stalemate in the rivalries within the governing circles that persists until the shape of the opinion curve has changed. That change may yield a permissive consensus within the public, and the advocated course of action may then be taken. Or it may make clear that the advocates have been devoting their energies to a losing cause. Perhaps, for example, the debate on the question of federal aid for the support of elementary and secondary education over a period of two or three decades has led from a condition of considerable disagreement toward one permissive of at least certain types of action.

Another sequence may occur that involves a change in the terms of debate among the rival protagonists, a change that facilitates consensus at the popular level by posing a new question. Some such process may have occurred on a limited scale in some localities on the school-

[2] For a suggestive model of the changes in opinion during the life history of an issue, see Berelson: *op. cit.*, pp. 206–12.

integration question. An issue presented as one of white versus black in quite broad terms gradually came to be converted to the question whether a few carefully chosen Negro pupils were to be permitted to enroll in predominantly white schools.

These comments are limited to those great issues of public policy that arouse both widespread attention and concern within the electorate; such issues are few in number. Although evidence is extremely limited to support these hypotheses about interactions within the political elites and about interactions between the political elites and mass opinion, it seems plausible to posit their existence in the American order. At any rate, from the smatterings of evidence available, such an interpretation seems far more plausible than the alternative simplistic views of the role of public opinion. The contention that "public opinion rules," while it no longer enjoys much vogue, tells us nothing about how and under what circumstances opinion makes itself felt. Nor does the thesis that "public opinion is ruled" by the public's betters satisfactorily describe what occurs. The theory of the workings of a democratic order must make a place for mass opinion, but its role needs to be treated as a part of a complex system of interactions within the circles of influence and leadership, and between them and mass opinion.

4

CONCENTRATION

THE DISCUSSION of consensus and conflict patterns of opinion distribution dealt with issues on which most of the population had an opinion of some kind. Under such circumstances mass opinion can be pictured as in conflict or in agreement; hence it is sensible to speak of the existence of an opinion that is public in that it is shared by most people. Many issues of considerable import, though, attract the attention of only a few people, and opinions about them are concentrated in small proportions of the electorate. This type of situation in which awareness and preferences are thus restricted has so patent a significance for the problem of the relationship of government and public opinion that it deserves special attention.

On only a few questions is almost the entire citizenry disposed to express an opinion. Even on the broadest policy propositions many individuals tell interviewers that they have no opinion, and doubtless some of those who express an opinion do so because they either deem it proper to have views or wish to be amiable toward the interviewer. This state of affairs perplexes the romantic democratic theorist; it also requires an addendum to our consideration of the distribution of opinion. Though opinions may be held by only a small proportion of the population on many questions, they may be distributed in miniatures of the patterns that have been made familiar by the preceding chapters. Yet the fact that large proportions of the citizenry have no opinion may create in these situations different interactions between citizenry and government than when awareness and opinion preferences on an issue pervade the population.

A condition markedly different in its consequences for government might be expected to exist when, on the one hand, 75 per cent of the population professes never to have heard of an issue and the remaining 25 per cent is divided about equally pro and con, from that when, on the other hand, the population splits, say, 50:40, with only 10 per cent in complete indifference. For lack of a better term, restriction of opinion to a relatively few may be called a "concentration" of opinion. These contrasts between pervasive and concentrated opinion suggest questions about the qualities of opinion, whether it is based on information, hunch, or reflex, whether it is stable or unstable, whether it is intense or casual. For the moment, however, let us focus attention on the purely quantitative aspect of the situation in which small clusters of opinion holders are surrounded by a majority lacking an opinion.

1 · Opinion and No Opinion

Much discussion of public opinion tacitly assumes a far more general focus of attention on political objects and a far wider distribution of political information among citizens than actually exist. The invention of sampling techniques and their application to the political attitudes of national populations have compelled revision of such suppositions. By these techniques substantial percentages of the population were shown to remain happily unaware even of issues that commanded the attention of Congress for weeks, provided screaming banners for the newspapers, and occupied the time of frenetic newscasters. Disillusioned democrats feared for the survival of the Republic; antidemocrats rejoiced that their gloomiest beliefs had been verified.

Screening Out the "Don't Knows." In the study of public opinion the determination within a national sample of precisely who has and who does not have an opinion is not so easy as it might appear to be. Some types of questions will evoke an expression of agreement or disagreement from almost everyone. Only 6 per cent volunteered that they had no opinion on this question put by the AIPO in 1939: "It has been proposed that the federal government spend three million dollars for clinics to fight cancer. Do you favor this proposal?" Over 90 per cent of those with opinions took a firm stand against cancer and favored the proposal. While the responses could probably be regarded as reflective of a permissive consensus, doubts about the meaning of the responses to such questions were aggravated when high expressions of support were obtained for purely imaginary legislative proposals. The AIPO has attempted to obtain a better gauge of opinion by screening out those who say that they have neither heard nor read about an issue. In August, 1945, for example, when it asked: "Have you heard of the Tennessee Valley Authority—TVA?" 67 per cent of the sample said that they had heard of that institution, which by that time had been a topic of controversy for over a decade. Those who had heard of it were asked: "Will you tell me briefly what it is?" At that point 12 per cent of the total sample admitted that they did not know, and thus the proportion with some familiarity with the TVA was cut down to 55 per cent. (Those who had heard of it had overwhelmingly favorable opinions about it.) Or, in the late 1930's the AIPO put the question: "Have you heard of the Passamaquoddy power project in Maine?" after that New Deal proposal to harness the power of the tides had rocked the halls of Congress and provided grist for the editorial mills. Only 39 per cent of the sample had heard about the project; the Republicans so informed were overwhelmingly against it, and the majority of Democrats were for it.

The "heard or read about" sieve regularly separates out large proportions of the population on questions about specific issues currently receiving a good deal of attention in the press. In May, 1945, a national cross section was asked by the AIPO: "Have you heard or read about the Wagner-Murray-Dingell Bill now up in Congress which would increase the Social Security Tax to 4% for both employers and employees in order to provide more Social Security Benefits?" Only 44 per cent of the sample had heard or read about the bill. Of this number, those with opinions favored the bill in about a 3:2 ratio. In 1954 the AIPO asked: "Have you heard or read anything about the Dixon-Yates proposal?" Thirty-seven per cent said that they had heard or read about it, but a follow-up question made it plain that many of them had not heard or read carefully enough to know what the proposal was about. In January, 1955, the AIPO asked: "Some people say that our present tariffs should be increased. Other people say that the U.S. should establish freer trade with other countries by lowering tariffs. Have you heard or read anything about this?" Fifty-two per cent said yes.[1]

[1] For a tabulation of AIPO questions on which large percentages of the population had no opinion, see Hadley Cantril: *The Psychology of Social Movements* (New York: Wiley; 1941), p. 178. In 1959 a waggish Los Angeles newspaperman got a good deal of mileage out of a telephone survey in which he asked the respondents if they thought "the Mann Act deters or helps the cause of organized labor" and whether it should be repealed; 38 per cent favored repeal, and 10 per

Contrasts between Specific Proposals and General Policy Issues. The assumption of the "heard or read about" test may be that those persons without specific information have no views relevant to the settlement of the particular controversy. That may or may not be a correct assumption. If one inquires about views on general political questions (which may or may not be related to specific current policy proposals), the proportions with no opinions are usually relatively low. The Survey Research Center in its 1956 survey sought judgments on broad policy propositions about which citizens might have an opinion although they might lack information on specific legislation related to it. The interviewers made it clear to the respondent that "different things are important to different people, so we don't expect everyone to have an opinion about all of these" questions. "If you don't have an opinion, just tell me that." Then statements such as the following were read: "The government ought to cut taxes even if it means putting off some important things that need to be done." The respondent was then asked: "Now, would you say you have an opinion on this or not?" On questions of this broad kind most people had opinions. Some of the questions, along with the proportions claiming to have opinions, were as follows:

	Per cent with opinion
"This country would be better off if we just stayed home and did not concern ourselves with problems in other parts of the world."	88
"The government ought to help people get doctors and hospital care at low cost."	88
"The United States should give economic help to to the poorer countries of the world even if they can't pay for it."	85
"The government ought to see to it that big business corporations don't have much to say about how the government is run."	74
"The United States should keep soldiers overseas where they can help countries that are against communism."	82
"The government should leave things like electric power and housing for private businessmen to handle."	73
"The United States should give help to foreign countries even if they are not as much against communism as we are."	74

cent opposed while only 12 per cent had enough information to know that they were being spoofed. The exercise was supposed to demonstrate the uselessness of surveys in the determination of public attitudes. All it demonstrated was that only a fool would ask a question in such a form with the expectation that it would yield anything of utility.

Presumably when governments are concerned about public attitudes, a better test of what those attitudes are comes from a check of the distribution of views on broad questions, such as those cited above, than from an inquiry about opinions on specific bills or acts of which there may be no general awareness. Even on some of these broad issues as many as one fourth concede that they have no opinion, though the question may have been agitated in one form or another for decades. Note the responses on the proposition about the influence of "big business corporations" on government, a question about which it might be supposed that nearly everyone would have an opinion one way or another. Side comments about the questions suggest that the division between those with and those without opinions is not sharp; gradations occur ranging from those with extreme opinions both informed and intense, through those with opinions but no great concern, to those with neither information nor preference.

Other Checks on Opinion Incidence. Other means have been employed in the attempt to separate opinion holders from those without opinions or with only surface opinions. From an examination of polls on foreign-policy questions Martin Kriesberg in 1949 grouped the population into three categories. He estimated that, on the average, about 30 per cent of the population was *unaware* of any given event in American foreign affairs; that is, they cheerfully admitted that they had neither heard nor read about the matter. Another 45 per cent he estimated to be *aware but uninformed;* that is, they may have heard, for example, of the Marshall Plan but either did not know its purpose or thought it meant "just help Europe." Another average 25 per cent he classified as the *informed;* that is, they could, in the instance of the Marshall Plan, give a reasonably accurate statement of its purpose.[2]

Still another treatment of the problem is that of Fisher and Withey in their analysis of attitudes toward big business. They sought to ascertain the "importance, salience or relevance" of the "big business issue." They concluded that at the time of their interviews in October, 1950, this issue had a "high salience" for 25 per cent of their national sample; that is, business size made a difference to this proportion of the people—they were emotionally involved pro or con. For another 50 per cent the issue had a low salience; the respondents had information and opinions but indicated little involvement in the issue. For the remaining 25 per cent the issue had "no salience"; they had no emotional involvement in the matter, and no

[2] Martin Kriesberg: "Dark Areas of Ignorance," in Lester Markel, ed.: *Public Opinion and Foreign Policy* (New York: Harper; 1949), p. 51.

stable opinion was apparent.[3] These figures resemble closely the responses to the 1956 Survey Research Center question cited above on
the influence of business corporations on government, about which
only 74 per cent had an opinion.

2 · Patterns of Concentrated Opinion

The results of a division of the population into those with and without opinions on any given question, be the question narrow or
broad, depend on the criteria employed to draw the line. Nevertheless, it remains useful to visualize the citizenry as divided into those
with and without opinions, those with and without involvement, or
those with and without information on an issue. The bloc with opinions operates in the political process in the context of a much larger
body of citizenry at bottom either unaware of the issue or unconcerned about it. Thus a government disposed to defer to public opinion is confronted by a problem in the case of a concentrated opinion quite different from that it faces when it deals with a question on
which opinions are widely diffused within the population.

Miniature Conflict Patterns. Concentrated distributions of opinion may take the forms of consensus or conflict by now made familiar, but, drawn to the proper scale, the opinion curves would appear
as almost minute figures surrounded by great masses of the uninformed or indifferent. This condition can, and does, prevail on matters of considerable national importance. An extraordinary gap may
exist between the attention given to a controversy in the press and
the actual extent of public involvement. For example, discussion of
the constitutional amendment proposed by former Senator John W.
Bricker, of Ohio, to weaken the President's power in treaty making
consumed a large tonnage of printer's ink, and the disputants developed a high temperature over the issue. Yet the AIPO in October,
1953, reported that 81 per cent of its sample had neither heard nor
read about "Senator Bricker's proposal of an amendment to the Constitution to limit the President's treaty making powers." Those who
had heard or read about the proposal divided (in proportions of the
total sample) into 9 per cent for, 7 per cent against, and 3 per
cent having no opinion. Thus, if we regard only those who had heard
or read about the proposal as having opinions, less than one in five

[3] Burton R. Fisher and Stephen B. Withey: *Big Business as the People See It*
(Ann Arbor: Survey Research Center; 1951), p. 60.

had an opinion, and the great bulk of the population remained both uninformed and uninvolved. The distribution is presented graphically in Figure 4.1.

Another issue, the Taft-Hartley Act, occupied a prominent position in the public prints and in political debate for a much longer time than the Bricker proposal. Although it came to the attention of more people than that proposal, the comparatively high incidence of lack of knowledge about the Taft-Hartley Act is instructive. During the 1952 campaign the Survey Research Center interview schedule included the following question: "Have you heard anything about the Taft-Hartley Law? (If yes) How do you feel about it—do you think it's all right as it is, do you think it should be changed in any way, or don't you have any feelings about it? (If it should be changed) Do you think the law should be changed just a little, changed quite a bit, or do you think it should be completely repealed?" The responses of the national sample to this question, when coded, produced the following distribution of opinion:

Should be repealed	10%
Changed quite a bit in favor of labor	1
Changed a little in favor of labor	2
Left as is	13
Changed a little in favor of management	1
Changed, either amount of change or direction not indicated	16
Don't know what ought to be done	25
Haven't heard of	30
Not ascertained	2
	100%
N	1614

About a year later, in November, 1953, the AIPO released the results of a survey which, although based on different questions, showed a similar picture. The 40 per cent of the respondents who said that they had "followed" the discussion of the Taft-Hartley law were asked: "What action do you, yourself, think Congress should take about the Taft-Hartley law?" The responses fell into the following categories:

Change it, amend it	19%
Leave it as it is	11
Repeal it	3
No opinion	7
	40%
Haven't followed	60%

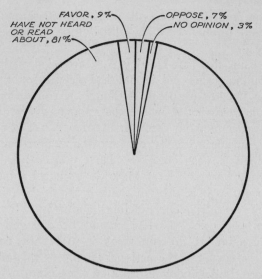

FIGURE 4.1. "Have you heard or read anything about Senator Bricker's proposal of an amendment to the Constitution to limit the President's treaty-making power? (If yes.) Would you favor or oppose this amendment?" *AIPO, October 7, 1953.*

Those who favored changing or amending the act were asked: "Do you think the changes should be in the direction which business leaders want—or do you think the changes should be in the direction which labor leaders want?" The 19 per cent favoring changes divided as follows:

Business	5%
Labor	8
Satisfy both	3
No opinion	3

If these inquires about the Taft-Hartley Act had been in the form of a psychological scale, the results would doubtless appear as some sort of bimodal distribution. Yet the pattern would be that of a miniature conflict pattern in that it would involve only a small part of the electorate.

When data are presented in percentages, as the results of the surveys on the Taft-Hartley Act and on the Bricker Amendment have been, the first reaction may be one of astonishment that so few persons had views on these questions. Yet percentages can conceal as well as reveal. Since at the time of these surveys the total adult population was in the neighborhood of 100 million, each percentage point stood for around a million persons. When the percentages are translated into people, the survey findings could be read to mean that 15 million or so persons had views pro or con on the Bricker Amendment and that 30 million, plus or minus, had sentiments about the Taft-Hartley proposition. With the data put in this fashion, the cause for astonishment may be that so many persons had opinions. And the expectation may be that even when only 10 per cent of the population is concerned about a question public opinion may be a factor to be reckoned with.

The figures on the Bricker Amendment and the Taft-Hartley Act make another point plain, at least by inference. Here were specific issues that gained prominent attention in the press over considerable periods of time and yet had failed to attract the attention of tens of millions of persons. How much smaller must be the sectors of the public with opinions on many issues that students of public affairs would regard as of import for the Republic. Opinion data are lacking on most of the specific issues that concern legislators and executives; if the facts were known, they would surely indicate that attentive publics for most specific questions are much smaller than those that heeded these two widely debated issues. If we think in terms of specific and concrete governmental actions, probably most governmental decisions, even major decisions, are made in the setting of a concentration of opinion about each specific issue. That state of affairs creates its problems for those who place a high value on public action in accord with public opinion.

The Attentive Public, Specific Issues, and Popular Attitudes on General Propositions. These findings that popular preferences on even well-publicized specific issues are limited to relatively small proportions of the electorate have an obvious moral. They point to the existence of a sector of the populace that is especially attentive to public issues and that probably plays a role of basic importance in a regime deferential to public sentiment. That attentive public, which on most issues probably amounts to no more than a fifth of the electorate, will repeatedly command attention in succeeding chapters as we seek to unravel the puzzle of the place of public opinion in governance.

A question about the attentive public that can be raised at this point is whether it functions, in effect, as a representative sample of the entire public. Does it have an outlook peculiar to itself, or does it tend to adopt the opinion that might be taken by the entire public if that public had the time and inclination to inform itself and to develop opinions on specific issues? To that question there can be no satisfactory answer; yet the problem it raises can be approached by indirection. Earlier we saw that quite large proportions of national samples may voice a preference on broadly phrased propositions. On concrete and specific matters requiring some information about particular actions or decisions, many more "don't knows" turn up even though the preference on the broad proposition could logically be extended to apply to the particular matter.

At the core of those who have opinions on broad questions of policy there must be an attentive group whose members would also have preferences on specific legislative proposals calculated to deal with the broad question. If that core of persons could be identified, its opinion on a specific question could be compared with the opinion of the entire public on a related general proposition. The central core of informed people may form a distribution of opinion different in shape from that of the entire population. The latter might express an off-the-cuff opinion in favor of even a foolish proposition, but the central core would be in opposition. Or the opinion of the central core might parallel that of the general population.

On some questions at least, widely diffused opinions about broad policy propositions are distributed in about the same fashion as are the opinions of much smaller and better-informed sectors of the population. It is possible to peel off successive layers of a sample to ascertain whether smaller and smaller, and presumably more sensible and better-informed, blocs of people divide roughly in the same way as the general public. That exercise may be performed with the opinions expressed on a pair of broad questions during the 1956 campaign. Of the respondents to the 1956 survey by the Survey Research Center 72 per cent said that they had an opinion on the following proposition: "The government should leave things like electric power and housing for private businessmen to handle." Those who agreed strongly with the statement outnumbered by about two to one those in strong disagreement. From the group with opinions a segment of less-informed persons may be removed. Those who said they had an opinion included some persons (about 11 per cent of the entire sample) who were unprepared to say whether they thought the government was going too far or not far enough in leaving these matters to private business. When this class is removed from the analysis, the remaining persons, as may be seen in Panel 2 of Figure 4.2, still divide in about the same way, with two persons at the extreme of strong agreement against each one in strong disagreement.

Another group of persons consisted of respondents who were unable to say whether the Democrats or the Republicans would be closer

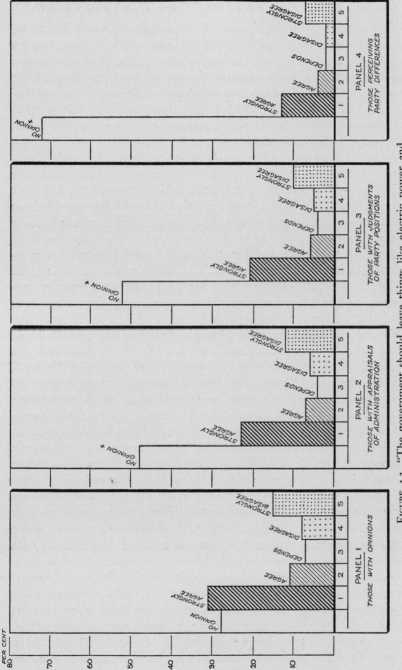

FIGURE 4.2. "The government should leave things like electric power and housing for private businessmen to handle." 1, strongly agree; 2, agree; 3, depends; 4, disagree; 5, strongly disagree. DATA SOURCE: *Survey Research Center, University of Michigan, 1956.*

to what they wanted on this issue. When this group is discarded from the analysis, there still remains (Panel 3) a 2:1 division between the extremes of opinion on the broad question. Still another category of less-informed may be taken out. A considerable number of those willing to make a judgment on the parties (about 18 per cent of the total sample) thought there was no difference between them in their closeness to the respondent's position on the issue. When this group, which by universal agreement would be somewhat deficient in powers of political perception, is removed from the analysis, the residue continues to form (Panel 4) the same sort of distribution with which we began—that is, a 2:1 ratio between the extremes. The final fragment of the sample (28 per cent of the total) forms an opinion distribution of about the same shape as did all those with an opinion.

Another question may be put through a similar step-by-step reduction to see whether the residual distribution retains the general form of the original. Only 10 per cent of the 1956 Survey Research Center sample had no views on this question: "If cities and towns around the country need help to build more schools, the government in Washington ought to give them the money they need." Those who agreed strongly outnumbered those who expressed strong disagreement by about nine to one. When we remove the successive layers—first, those who have not heard what the government is doing or decline to express a view on what it is doing; second, those who have no views on whether the Democrats or Republicans would be closer to what they want on the issue; and, third, those who see no difference between Democrats and Republicans on the question—there remains a distribution in about the same shape as the one based on the opinions of all respondents. If these distributions were charted, they would resemble those in Figure 4.2, although the ratio between the extremes changes somewhat as the sample is reduced. The final residual group, about 30 per cent of the total sample, divides about 6:1 on the extremes of the proposition, in contrast with the 9:1 ratio in the entire sample.

These exercises in successive reduction of the size of the sample are not without significance in the interpretation of the circumstances of a concentration of opinion. The apparent restriction of opinions on many issues to small proportions of the electorate is in part a function of the type of the survey question. One about the Taft-Hartley Act or the Bricker Amendment or some other such specific question may be answered only on the basis of more information than many people have. On the other hand, it requires only a point of view and perhaps some sense of the concrete problem to express an opinion on a general proposition such as the following: "If cities and towns around the country need help to build more schools, the government in Washington ought to give them the money they need." As successive layers of persons less willing to make political judgments were removed from the analysis, a similar predominance of opinion in favor of federal aid remained. Had the inquiry sought a judgment on a particular bill for school aid pending in Congress, doubtless large "don't know" and "no opinion" groups would have been identified despite the existence of substantial agreement on the general proposition.

The import of these data should be made plain. Our procedures have differentiated the better-informed core and successive layers of the less-informed. The similarities in opinion between these groups are more notable than the differences. By other criteria, of course, small population groups could be isolated whose attitudes diverge markedly from those of the generality. Yet it may be of considerable significance that, at least on the issues analyzed, the opinions of the most attentive group resemble those of the group with only a marginal attention to politics. That state of affairs may produce markedly different political results than would be expected when sharp contrasts in opinion and objective characterize the attentive and the inattentive. Our data, though, do not enable us to take the next step and make meaningful observations about the opinions of the attentive and the potential opinions of those who lack an opinion. Perhaps politics is relatively serene when the dominant opinions among the active and the attentive resemble those that would be stirred among the inattentive and uninformed if they should become concerned about public issues.

3 · Government in Accord with Public Opinion

The data of this chapter, though fragmentary, raise an additional broad type of problem in the interactions of government and public opinion. The earlier discussion roughly delineated the types of interrelations between government and opinion when large proportions of the public had views, a concern, or an awareness. On the other hand, when opinion and concern are restricted to only a small part of the citizenry, policy makers work in a radically different context of influence. Precisely what the differences are between the two sets of circumstances, though, is another problem.

Many, if not most, policy decisions by legislatures and by other authorities exercising broad discretion are made under circumstances in which extremely small proportions of the general public have any awareness of the particular issue, much less any understanding of the consequences of decision. A casual review of the major actions of any session of Congress or of a state legislature makes it clear that both the politicians and the technical specialists are taxed to learn the equities of many of the issues dealt with. Probably only at widely separated points in time, and on only a few issues, is mass opinion so pervasively activated that government is compelled to listen most attentively. Since the data on such episodes are scant, speculation about them is reasonably safe. The "first hundred days" of the New Deal, when far-reaching actions were taken in rapid sequence, was probably such a time. Even then opinion coalesced not so much in any informed way on the pro side of New Deal measures as they did around the President whose intimations over the radio that Congressmen were balking would bring a rain of mail onto Capitol Hill. Its general instruction was to do what the President asked. Again, as events unfolded in the preliminaries to World War II, the "don't knows" were few, and government listened intently for indications of the direction of movement of public attitudes as it took those steps it regarded in the national interest. From time to time other questions develop that arouse wide public attention and generate preferences either pro or con in the general public. As the campaign of 1952 began, few people had no views on whether the United States had acted wisely in getting into the Korean War. Yet these episodes and issues are infrequent in the stream of public actions.

If these observations are correct, they throw the problem of government with the consent of the governed into a framework that creates its perplexities for those accustomed to speaking in terms of the public will or of popular consent. On a great many issues no majority will can be said to exist save by a strained interpretation of that concept. Public opinion about a large proportion of the concrete and specific issues that exercise statesmen would fall within our category of concentrated opinions. The task of government becomes, as John Dickinson said, "not to express an imaginary popular will, but to effect adjustments among the various special wills and purposes which at any given time are pressing for realization." [4] Those special wills and purposes are reflected in the small clusters of opinion that develop within the larger uninformed and inattentive public.

We have the reality in which only small proportions of the population share opinions and preferences on many, if not most, specific

[4] "Democratic Realities and Democratic Dogma," *American Political Science Review*, XXIV (1930), 283–309.

issues. What characteristics of the interactions between government and popular opinion can be invoked to convert such a condition into government by or in accord with mass preferences? One type of viewpoint treats broad popular sentiments as indirectly controlling. The argument assumes that vague sentiments of fairness, of justice, of policy propriety, and of community objective are widely held within the public. (The nature of these "opinions" and their distribution must remain nebulous, for the relevant empirical data are sketchy.) Government, the argument continues, tends to be guided by these inchoate popular attitudes as it decides day-to-day questions. Government in such instances may reflect people's opinion better than they know it themselves. Most people may, for example, believe that business corporations should not be granted indefensible privileges, but only a few of them have the slightest notion whether this or that particular measure is in accord with their general views. Their representatives may make the translation for them. Or most people may believe in the principle of progressive taxation, but, as many surveys have shown, the well-to-do would have a much lighter income tax if the system of progression were fixed by mass opinion. Representatives may cut through the fog and speak with greater faithfulness for their constituents than their constituents can speak for themselves.

A weakness in the supposition that nebulous popular sentiments tend to be faithfully translated by government into specific measures is encountered when one tries to locate the popular sanction to assure that translation. How is the broad popular opinion on vague general standards of action to make itself felt in the absence of extensive public information about the related specifics of action? The odds are that the public mobilizes to express its approval, or perhaps more often its disapproval, only by the cumulation of actions that can, in totality, be brought to public attention and understanding. The operation of a democratic order, the linking of public and government, requires an enormous amount of ingenuity and dedication at leadership levels in the explanation and translation of the specifics and technicalities into terms that will capture the attention and understanding of many people. That process has to be accomplished, though, if the popularly understood rules of the game are to be brought into authoritative relation to the actions of government about many of the specifics.

A second line of explanation, which supplements rather than displaces the first, centers attention on the role of the governing groups, the political activists and the political elite. These persons, be they public officials or leaders of private groups, may handle specific problems as they do, not because of a concern about general public standards or of an expectation of public electoral reward or reprisal, but because of their own inner norms and standards. The norms assimilated into the value systems of the politically active may or may not parallel those within the public generally. Probably, though, within a working democratic order the political norms of the community are held in especially explicit form by those professionally dedicated to public affairs.

The significance of the standards held by the governing groups in the determination of lines of action becomes plain enough as one observes state and local jurisdictions led by persons possessed of standards deviant from the national norm. Their brigandage seems unrestrained by whatever general norms of justice or equity may be supposed to permeate the general population. And even in the best-regulated governments the fact that so few people have any information or views about many questions of great importance may help to comprehend the actions of government. A review of any session of Congress or of a state legislature will uncover a goodly number of actions that seem inexplicable to any person who assumes that the people rule in a democracy. As it acts on most issues, a legislature is acting virtually in privacy, though at times its deliberations may paradoxically be emblazoned in the headlines.

To note that opinion on many issues is restricted to small sectors of the population is not to assert that these small blocs of popular opinion are, or may be, ignored by government. Under proper circumstances extremely small numbers of persons can generate sufficient uproar to make life miserable for those in power. They may make themselves distinctly heard as they seek to obtain or, perhaps more commonly, to obstruct action.[5] One of the major problems of popular government consists in the determination of when to yield, and when not to yield, to their demands.

Factors in the disposition of the demands of small opinion blocs, it was suggested, include the general norms of the community and the value standards of governing groups. Another factor, the formal architecture of government, may bear significantly on the disposition of individual questions, at least over the short run. The governmental structure, for example, may channel opinion to those with more or less responsiveness to particular types of demands. A small bloc of opinion may control, or even immobilize, a few legislators, but the remainder of the representative body may be essentially neutral on the question and be able to apply the community standards or at least the general stand-

[5] Several of the Inter-University Case Program studies vividly illustrate the proposition. See 'The Lonesome Train' in Levittown (No. 39, 1958), The Coterminous Boundaries Dispute (No. 33, 1956), The Michigan Athletic Awards Rule (No. 29, 1955), Defending "The Hill" Against Metal Houses (No. 26, 1955), and Moses on the Green (No. 45, 1959). These items were called to my attention by Avery Leiserson.

ards of the remainder of the legislature. A bloc of opinion that is fed to an administrative agency characterized by a spirit of clientelism may trigger a decision formed in an entirely different constellation of standards and influences. The formal structure of government and its internal allocation of jurisdiction may affect the types of opinion that enter effectively into the settlement of particular questions. These observations are but an aspect of David Truman's concept of differentials among groups in their access to government.[6]

A further general point must be remembered as one assays the significance of the absence of opinion or of apparent concern about many concrete issues among large proportions of the population. Judgments on that question could best be made by contrasts among different regimes. In banana republics or camel-tent-and-rug tyrannies, perhaps far less than 1 per cent of the populace may be at all informed or involved in the governing process. If only 10 per cent of the American electorate holds determined views about an issue, 10 million or so people will be concerned. Even that degree of involvement may assure a marked difference in the interactions between rulers and ruled in democratic and nondemocratic orders. At any rate, the analysis points to the pivotal significance in a democratic order of those people who have opinions, of those who attempt to exert influence, and of those who participate actively. In subsequent chapters attention will turn to the identification of these persons and to their location in the structure of the political system.

[6] David B. Truman: *The Governmental Process* (New York: Knopf; 1951), ch. 11.

Part II

STRUCTURAL

DISTRIBUTION

PART I FOCUSED

on a simple but fundamental aspect of public opinion: the principal types of opinion patterns within the nation when individual opinions are arrayed along scales of support and opposition on policy issues. Attention to this aspect of the opinions of the undifferentiated public identifies characteristics of the opinion structure of basic significance for the political process. The relation between the broad patterns of opinion distribution within the public with which we have dealt and the actions of government are matters of central concern in a regime founded on the doctrine of the consent of the governed.

The conceptions of the relations of opinion patterns to governmental action suggested in Part I place the problem of the estimation of the influence of opinion in a new perspective. The anxieties of students about their inability to gauge the effects of opinion rest on an implicit assumption that public opinion is, or, in some way ought to be, positively directive of governmental action. Our analyses suggest that the relationships between government and public opinion must be pictured in varied ways, none of which requires solution of the problem of the precise measurement of the weights of opinion in the governing process. Mass opinion may set general limits, themselves subject to change over time, within which government may act. In some instances opinion may be permissive but not directive of specific action. In others opinion may be, if not directive, virtually determinative of particular acts.

Part II concerns another phase of the distribution of opinion and may give us clues to the relative weights of different kinds of views. The object is broadly to consider who has what kinds of opinions. Our earlier analyses more or less assumed a fluidity and unity within the nation; opinions flowed into our J-curves and bimodal distributions in a frictionless manner. In fact, individuals are anchored at geographical points, in levels of occupational status, among groups of differing levels of political activity, and at other types of points in the political and social structure. The distribution of opinions within the social system in varying patterns may produce differing political consequences. Moreover, the incidence of opinions within the elements of the social system may provide useful indicators of the strains and strengths of the political order. Given the structure of American government, the geographical distribution of attitude may be of controlling importance in the outcome of political controversy and may indicate, too, the skill of government in the management of territorially based cleavages of interest. Similarly, the location of opinions of particular kinds in different classes, occupations, and other such categories may identify the influentials as well as give us indicators of political tension or harmony.

5

GEOGRAPHICAL

DISTRIBUTION

IN ANY REGIME the geographical distribution of opinions, attitudes, and loyalties is likely to be associated with special characteristics or problems of government. Historically, restive provinces on the periphery have been a source of concern for rulers, and in most modern regimes parliaments and presidents must adapt national policies to peculiar regional predilections. In the United States the constitutional structure itself reflects the problem of adjusting policy to geographical preferences. A basic assumption of the federal division of powers is that, within the scope of their jurisdiction, states may act in accord with local opinion however it may differ from that of the remainder of the nation. Thus, federalism may be a means for institutional separation of the modes of an opinion distribution in conflict. In addition, the structure and operating conventions of the national government accord a special strength to geographically concentrated shades of opinion. Through the equal representation of states in the Senate and by virtue of the Senate's working customs, regional opinions gain a negative strength in their capacity to block or delay action, and they also possess a positive bargaining capacity. The geographical basis of representation in the House of Representatives assures a reflection of kinds of opinion that happen to acquire a geographical locus by the distribution of attitudes among congressional districts. The smallness of state legislative districts assures within state representative bodies an even closer approximation of the gradations of opinion that distinguish constituencies.

In American politics the historical salience of place—as contrasted with class, occupation, religion, and other nongeographical categories —colors both intellectual analyses and popular discussions. Our national politics has been regarded as a process of reconciling the conflicting interests and ambitions of the great geographical sections of the country. Beyond the differences of sections are those associated with country, small town, and city, which are projected into government through the geographical system of representation. Metropolis, suburb, small town, and farm are said to have their special viewpoints that come into conflict in legislative bodies as state and national policies are hammered out. Contrasts between northerners and southerners, between easterners and westerners, between village and metropolis are commonly supposed to have declined during the past half-century, and doubtless they have. Within the limits of the available data, the object here is to identify contrasts that remain in the geographical distribution of public opinion and to point to their significance in the governmental process.

As these geographical differentiations of opinion are examined, it should be kept in mind that the foundations of these opinions may not be region or place of residence. A regional outlook may reflect the fact that its population includes, for example, relatively large numbers of industrial workers. Whatever the basis of an opinion, its geographical concentration assures it a special recognition in a political system that employs the single-member district mode of representation. The geographically defined community also may have an independent strength in the formation of opinions. The residents of the Far West, simply by virtue of their living in that area, may acquire an orientation toward national politics that colors their outlook on a range of questions of policy and personnel. The social structure of the small town may in itself impose a homogeneity of attitude not likely to flourish in the metropolis. The life situation of farmers may give their opinions a peculiar cast.

1 · Sectionalism

Discussions of sectionalism in American politics often assume that advocates of sectional causes face each other along regional battle lines that sharply set off westerner and easterner, southerner and northerner, or midwesterner and northeasterner. On the basis of the earlier discussion of opinion measurement and of the kinds of opinion distributions that occur, we should not expect to find region arrayed against region at the opposite ends of attitude scales. Rather, the expectation might be that within each region wide variations in opinion would prevail; only the averages might differ from region to region. A model of what might be expected is, again, provided by the results of the subjection of college students to attitude scales of a more or less refined sort. The administration of Hinckley's Attitude Toward the Negro Scale to a

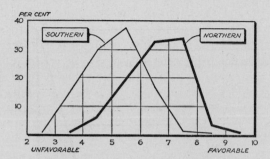

Figure 5.1. Distribution of Southern and Northern Students on Scale of Attitude toward the Negro. Source: V. M. Sims and J. R. Patrick: "Attitude toward the Negro of Northern and Southern College Students," *Journal of Social Psychology*, VII (1936), 192–204.

group of southern students at the University of Alabama and to another group at Ohio University yielded the contrasting distributions shown in Figure 5.1. While the modal attitudes of the two groups differed in "favorableness" toward the Negro, both southern and northern groups included persons with views differing in both directions from the most frequently occurring attitude scores in their group.[1]

On matters on which sectional differences prevail overlapping distributions on the order of those in Figure 5.1 would result from the application of similar measures to the total population. Ordinarily, though, we must be content with cruder measures of national samples. In any case, on few issues would the results look like those in the figure, for in the United States only rarely do wide opinion differences exist between regions.

The South: The Place of the Negro and Other Questions. The South remains the most distinctive region in political opinion; yet its

[1] Verner M. Sims and James R. Patrick: "Attitude toward the Negro of Northern and Southern College Students," *Journal of Social Psychology*, VII (1936), 192–204.

most notable contrast with the rest of the country is in attitudes about national policy toward the Negro. Though the South is often assumed to be conservative on matters of domestic economic policy, its appearance of conservatism results from imperfect representation of its views rather than from a peculiar mass opinion. Even with respect to the Negro the unity of the South varies from aspect to aspect of race policy. Southerners take a far stronger position on school segregation than on such questions as the protection of the economic rights of Negroes.

Southern spokesmen in Congress have been virtually unanimous in

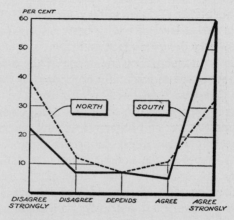

FIGURE 5.2. "The government in Washington should stay out of the question of whether white and colored children go to the same school." DATA SOURCE: *Survey Research Center, University of Michigan, 1956.* Percentage base excludes those with no opinion.

their opposition to school integration. That solidarity is a result of the fact that regional majorities, as they flow through the representative system, appear to be far larger than they actually are. The small southern minority unopposed to integration practically disappears when southern sentiment is filtered through the representative system. Of the southerners questioned by the Survey Research Center in 1956, 22 per cent disagreed strongly with the proposition: "The government in Washington should stay out of the question of whether white and colored children go to the same school"; 59 per cent agreed strongly; another 5 per cent expressed a less-intense agreement.[2] The contrast between southern and nonsouthern opinion distributions on this question appears in Figure 5.2, which incidentally indicates that southern op-

[2] The percentages are not affected materially by the inclusion of Negroes in the southern sample.

ponents of school integration had a sizeable number of allies outside the South.[3]

Southerners show considerably less solidarity about the economic rights of Negroes than they do on the school integration question. Almost as many southerners as nonsoutherners (67 per cent against 71 per cent) expressed agreement in 1956 with the proposition: "If Negroes are not getting fair treatment in jobs and housing, the government in Washington should see to it that they do." The conditional form of the proposition doubtless enabled some persons to agree with it and at the same time to feel that Negroes were already "getting fair treatment." And conceptions of fairness may vary. Nevertheless, the resemblance at this verbal level of equity between the South and the remainder of the country deserves attention.[4]

On domestic economic policy the image of the South that appears in the public prints is one of a soundly conservative region ever ready to ally itself in Congress with northern Republicans. That image itself involves misrepresentation, for some southern Senators and Representatives are conservatives and others are liberals on economic issues, at least as those terms are popularly defined in these days. At the level of mass opinion, however, the conservatism of the South disappears once its opinions are compared with those of the remainder of the country. If southern opinion corresponded to the popular caricature, it would frown on governmental endeavors to maintain employment, it would take a low view of the influence of trade unions, and it would perhaps look with tolerance on the influence of big corporations. In fact, southern opinion on these matters, as is shown in Table 5.1, closely resembles that of the rest of the country. On some questions the South turns out to be a shade more "liberal" than other regions. More southerners than midwesterners, for example, agree that the government "ought to help people get doctors and hospital care at low cost" (68 per cent against 54 per cent), a finding not inconsistent with the specta-

[3] The AIPO in July, 1959, asked: "The U.S. Supreme Court has ruled that racial segregation in the public schools is illegal. This means that all children, no matter what their race, must be allowed to go to the same schools. Do you approve or disapprove of this decision?" In the South 22 per cent approved; in the North 72 per cent. This phrasing of the issue attracted a much higher northern approval than did the 1956 Survey Research Center formulation. Hyman and Sheatsley find some softening of southern opinion toward school integration from 1942 to 1956. See their "Attitudes towards Desegregation," *Scientific American*, December, 1956.

[4] In these tabulations of Survey Research Center data, the South includes those states commonly regarded as border states. For the definition of regions employed in Survey Research Center data, see the map at the front flyleaf of Angus Campbell, Gerald Gurin, and Warren E. Miller: *The Voter Decides* (Evanston: Row, Peterson; 1954).

cle of the late Senator Walter George of Georgia chiding AMA representatives at a Senate hearing about the high cost of medical care and calling to their attention the prospect that their tactics might assure governmental intervention.

Withal, apart from its attitudes on the Negro question, the South takes positions in mass opinion on broad questions of policy remarkably similar to those of the nation. It may still possess some intangible char-

TABLE 5.1

REGION, SOUTH AND NON-SOUTH, IN RELATION TO OPINION ON JOB GUARANTEE, BIG BUSINESS INFLUENCE, UNION INFLUENCE, AND POWER AND HOUSING [a]

OPINION	JOB GUARANTEE		BIG BUSINESS		UNION		POWER AND HOUSING	
	S	N	S	N	S	N	S	N
Agree strongly	53%	46%	55%	52%	50%	51%	43%	43%
Agree but not very strongly	16	14	16	18	16	16	13	16
Not sure; depends	9	7	9	7	8	7	11	9
Disagree but not very strongly	9	13	9	11	13	11	11	11
Disagree strongly	13	20	11	12	13	15	22	21
	100%	100%	100%	100%	100%	100%	100%	100%
N	456	1131	348	924	341	976	332	917

[a] For the text of the issue propositions, see Appendix I.
DATA SOURCE: *Survey Research Center, University of Michigan, 1956.*

acteristics that give its politics a distinctive style. On some specific moral issues, too, it tends to differ.[5] Its people have far lower levels of political participation than do other Americans. Yet on broad substantive issues its opinions have been largely captured by the same forces that prevail over the nation.

[5] A Gallup question of April, 1938, read: "Would you favor lotteries in this state to help pay the cost of government?" The "Yes" replies were: South, 37 per cent; New England, 59 per cent. On sex, though, the Midwest seems to talk, if not act, with a special regional accent. Elmo Roper & Associates put the question: "Do you think it is all right for either or both parties to a marriage to have had previous sexual experience?" Not all right: Midwest, 70 per cent; South, 44 per cent. The pollers add the caution: "No one can tell precisely how the words articulate with the deeds."—*The Public Pulse,* November, 1959. In a May, 1960, AIPO poll 46 per cent of the southerners favored prohibition of the "sale of all beer, wine and liquor throughout the nation"; only 15 per cent in the East took that position. In May, 1959, the AIPO reported results on the question: "If your party nominated a generally well-qualified man for President, and he happened to be a Catholic, would you vote for him?" In the South 53 per cent of the respondents said they would vote for such a nominee; outside the South, 73 per cent.

How can the similarity in opinions between the South and the rest of the country be reconciled with the conservative outlook of many southern Senators and Representatives? The marked differentials in levels of political participation among occupational groups in the South, as compared with the North, probably contribute a part of the explanation. In the South the classes that tend to be conservative approach in their levels of political participation comparable groups outside the South. On the other hand, southern blue-collar workers (both white and black) are far less active in politics than nonsouthern blue-collar workers. In 1956 59 per cent of southern blue-collar workers did

TABLE 5.2

OCCUPATION, SOUTH AND NONSOUTH, IN RELATION TO POLITICAL PARTICIPATION

LEVEL OF PARTICIPATION [a]		OCCUPATION AND REGION					
		White-collar		Blue-collar		Farmers	
		S	N	S	N	S	N
High	4	34%	39%	19%	28%	27%	24%
	3	36	48	22	48	27	61
	2	5	3	8	5	8	0
Low	1	25	10	51	19	38	15
		100%	100%	100%	100%	100%	100%
	N	166	414	203	571	64	100

[a] For an explanation of the content and construction of the index of participation, see Appendix IV.
DATA SOURCE: *Survey Research Center, University of Michigan, 1956.*

not vote in the presidential election; the comparable nonsouthern figure was only 24 per cent. (Table 5.2.) If the blue-collar vote in the South should double, southern conservatives in Congress would probably become less numerous. The bias of the active, as contrasted with the potential, electorate in the South impresses on many southern Representatives outlooks not compatible with what might be expected from the opinion data. Of course, other factors contribute to the conservatism of some southern Representatives. The regional figures conceal the fact that in the South, as elsewhere, opinions are not uniformly spread geographically; southern suburban areas may have views not unlike northern suburbs. These and other such variations are mirrored by the representative system in the South just as they are elsewhere.

The Midwest: Erstwhile Stronghold of Isolationism. The Midwest was long regarded as the stronghold of isolationism. Between World

Wars I and II American foreign policy was supposedly held in check by the disposition of this great region to avoid involvement in the affairs of other parts of the world. Such interpretations probably exaggerated the role of midwestern opinion or rested on an elastic definition of the Midwest. The great spokesmen for the isolationist position included such men as Senator William E. Borah of Idaho and Senator Hiram Johnson of California.[6] Yet within the conventionally defined Midwest opinion surveys during the preliminaries to World War II showed the people of this region to be far more opposed to aid to England and other such measures than were people in other sections of the country.

The impact of World War II in large degree erased regional differences in mass opinion on broad foreign-policy problems. On question after question put by survey organizations during World War II and afterward the Midwest divided in about the same way as did the rest of the country. In 1944, for example, when discussion of America's role in the postwar period was rife, the AIPO put the question: "Do you agree with those people who think that the United States should take an active part in world affairs after the war, or with those people who think we should stay out of world affairs?" Seventy-two per cent of the midwestern sample and 73 per cent of the national cross section agreed that an active American role in world affairs was desirable. Though not all questions produce the same degree of similarity, the region of isolationism has lost its marked contrast with the rest of the country.[7]

Probably on some specific policy questions regional peculiarities exist and will exist, but on the broad question of toleration of, if not zealous support for, American participation in world affairs regional contrasts seem to have disappeared. An attitude measure that bundles up opinions on several questions by Guttman scaling techniques indicates that only a slight residue of the old midwestern isolationism remains. On that scale (Table 5.3) 53 per cent of midwesterners ranked high in willingness to support involvement in international affairs in 1956, in contrast with 59 per cent in the Northeast, not an impressive

[6] Ralph Smuckler has shown that isolationism, as measured by the voting records of Senators and Representatives, formed a broad but not solid band across the northern half of the country.—"The Region of Isolationism," *American Political Science Review*, XLVII (1955), 336–401.

[7] For regional breakdowns of national polls on questions of foreign policy, see Gabriel Almond: *The American People and Foreign Policy* (New York: Harcourt, Brace; 1950), pp. 131–5; W. A. Scott and S. B. Withey: *The United States and the United Nations* (New York: Manhattan; 1958), pp. 129–33; F. W. Williams, "Regional Attitudes on International Cooperation," *Public Opinion Quarterly*, IX (1945), 38–50.

difference.[8] At the other end of the scale, 20 per cent of midwesterners ranked low in internationalism in contrast with 16 per cent of those in the Northeast. If opinion data were available for smaller areas, states and districts would doubtless be found with opinion patterns suppor-

---

TABLE 5.3

REGION IN RELATION TO DISTRIBUTION ALONG SCALE MEASURING ATTITUDES TOWARD AMERICAN INVOLVEMENT IN FOREIGN AFFAIRS [a]

INTERNATIONALISM	MIDWEST	NORTHEAST	FAR WEST	SOUTH
High	53%	59%	58%	56%
Medium	27	25	24	26
Low	20	16	18	18
	100%	100%	100%	100%
N	372	469	177	398

[a] For the items included in the internationalism scale, see Appendix II.
DATA SOURCE: *Survey Research Center, University of Michigan, 1956.*

---

tive of isolationist Representatives and Senators, especially on matters of foreign aid, but they would certainly not all be in the Midwest.[9]

Regional Similarities and Shadings in Differentiation. Save for the special position of the South on the Negro question, the salient characteristic of regional distributions of opinion on many questions in 1952 and 1956 is their similarity. One must search for small differentiations from region to region to account for the appearances of sectionalism that emerge from time to time. Small differences within the public may create marked contrasts in Congress when the popular vote happens to fall in precisely the right manner.

[8] In this tabulation the Midwest was defined as the region from Ohio to Kansas to North Dakota, including these states as corners of the triangle.

[9] Contrary to general belief, the South probably has long had a strain of isolationist sentiment susceptible of activation under appropriate conditions. In 1956 a larger proportion of southerners than of the people of any other region (34 per cent against 22 per cent in the Far West) agreed with this proposition: "This country would be better off if we just stayed home and did not concern ourselves with problems in other parts of the world." The chances are that southern isolationists are especially heavily represented among the region's nonvoters, a factor facilitative of internationalism among southern representatives. Since 1952, without the spur of Democratic presidential leadership, southern representatives have moved away from internationalism. See Charles O. Lerch, Jr.: "Southern Congressmen and the 'New Isolationism,'" *Political Science Quarterly*, LXXV (1960), 321–37.

The Far West, whose population is heavily concentrated in such centers as Los Angeles, San Francisco, Seattle, and Denver, cultivates a style of distinction that reveals itself in shadings in the opinion data. Though that style cannot readily be described, it probably consists of the old western tradition of progressivism reinforced by the New Deal, all fortified by the presence and acceptance on every hand of governmental economic activities on a scale unknown in the East. A more marked concern for civil liberties also seems to characterize the West. Stouffer found from the application of his scale to measure tolerance of deviate political behaviors—such as the making of speeches in favor of government ownership—that the proportions ranked as "more tolerant" ranged from 48 per cent in the West down to 16 per cent in the South.[1] The proportions of "less tolerant" ranged from 13 per cent in the West to 27 per cent in the South. The 1956 Survey Research Center sample confirmed these differences by another question: 61 per cent in the Far West, against 46 per cent in the South, strongly disagreed with the proposition that the "government ought to fire any government worker who is accused of being a communist even though they don't prove it."

The Far West takes a notably more permissive attitude toward government participation in power projects than does the rest of the country. In 1956 42 per cent of the Survey Research Center respondents in the Far West disagreed with the statement that "government should leave things like electric power and housing for private businessmen to handle." Only 28 per cent in the Northeast were so adamant in their doubts about laissez faire. While the West is not populated predominantly by rabid advocates of public ownership, their numbers suffice to give western congressional representation a distinctive coloration. Perhaps strangely, this attitude is mixed with a degree of hardheadedness on taxation. Fewer westerners felt in 1956 that taxes should be cut even if it meant "putting off some important things that need to be done." Only 22 per cent in the Far West accepted this absurdity, as against 38 per cent in the Northeast.[2]

The odds are that the Far West has an attitudinal differentiation on foreign policy that turns attention westward rather than toward Europe, with a corresponding assignment of priority of effort. Though information on the point is scant, in 1952 50 per cent of far westerners in the Survey Research Center sample thought a stronger stand, even to the bombing of Manchuria, was in order in the Korean War, while

[1] *Communism, Conformity, and Civil Liberties* (New York: Doubleday; 1955), p. 112.
[2] For analyses of opinions in the Far West based on the 1952 campaign study by the Survey Research Center, see Alfred de Grazia: *The Western Public* (Stanford: Stanford University Press; 1954).

only 40 per cent of the entire country took so bellicose a stance. Other measures of views on international policy indicate that the pedestals of opinion from which William Borah and Hiram Johnson thundered their isolationism have long since worn away.[3]

Significance of Interregional Consensus. Although on a few vexing questions fairly sharp sectional differences in mass attitudes prevail, the similarities, not the differences, in the distribution of opinions from region to region attract attention. On most broad issues for which the data are available the mass of the people of all sections divide in approximately the same manner. If we were to draw the J-curves of consensus, made familiar in Chapter 2, for each of the sections of the country, they would closely resemble each other on most major issues. Thus, on such questions a concurrent consensus prevails among the geographical regions of the nation. This fact is fundamental for the nature of American politics; and, it must be recognized, the practice of American politics has had something to do with building interregional similarities of attitude. Concurrent interregional consensus on most issues assures that political conflict will occur on lines other than geographical. In the grand architecture of politics the multiplication of issue cleavages along geographical lines threatens national unity; when divisions are nongeographical, the proponents of any major point of view in one region are allied with those having a similar outlook in other sections.

These comments must be reconciled with the fact that a flavor of sectionalism indubitably pervades the discussion of some concrete questions in the councils of government. One phase of such reconciliation consists in the simple fact that the media commonly exaggerate the degree of sectional cleavage that actually prevails. Yet genuine interregional conflict remains. To some extent this is attributable to the magnification of local majorities as they are projected into representative bodies under systems of geographical representation; 51 per cent in popular opinion may become 100 per cent in Congress. By the same token, the popular 49 per cent of today becomes the congressional 100 per cent of tomorrow, so narrow are many of our popular pluralities. Popular differences between geographic areas need not be wide to support marked differences between their representatives.

Another line of reconciliation between sectionalism in Congress and interregional homogeneity of opinion is one for which little

[3] Only 26 per cent in the Far West disagreed in 1956 with the proposition that the United States should give economic aid to the poorer countries "even if they can't pay for it." In the South 33 per cent disagreed (23 per cent "strongly").

evidence is available. Much of our sectionalism is about issues on which probably few people have interest, awareness, or opinion; yet politically influential persons may share a lively sense of sectional concern. Thus, western Senators and Congressmen make common cause in the promotion of silver policy and other mining interests. If we had public opinion data on this issue and on many lesser matters of sectional concern, the chances are that concentrated distributions, as we defined them in Chapter 4, would be found to exist. That is, relatively small numbers of persons would be possessed of an opinion, either pro or con, and they would probably be concentrated geographically. Much sectional conflict may be, in the main, a conflict among relatively narrow political elites who do not enlist much mass support in their respective bailiwicks. Such limited popular involvement may mute sectional conflict. At any rate such an inference might be drawn from contrast with sectional differences on the place of the Negro, a matter on which general involvement of the population seems to mold the behavior of representatives into rigid, rather than muted, patterns of conflict.[4]

2 · Metropolis, City, Town, Countryside

It is common in political discourse to speak of the interests of the metropolitan centers, of the concerns of the smaller cities and towns, and of the individuality of rural America. To a large extent the special orientations of these areas are not the corporate concerns of metropolis, village, or town but are the views of those types of people that predominate within these political units: the workers of the metropolis, the farmers of the countryside, the bourgeoisie of the small towns. Yet the differentials in opinion among places of differing population size and density deserve attention, for the geographical system of representation assures for them special recognition in the governmental process.

These opinions interact with the representative process in a dual fashion. Representatives of geographical areas in which a particular shade of opinion or interest predominates may be relied upon to pro-

---

[4] Another, perhaps extremely significant, fact is that few persons seem to think of politics in sectional terms. In the inquiries by the Survey Research Center in 1952 and in 1956 the respondents were asked: "Is there anything in particular that you like about the Democratic party?" The same questions were asked about the Republican party. As people responded to these open-ended inquiries, few indicated that they saw the political parties as dedicated to the cause of any geographical section. Only three or four comments out of several thousand could be so interpreted.

mote that interest with devotion. On the other hand, interests shared across class and occupational lines within representative units—states or districts—may also be given special emphasis through the geographical system of representation. Opinions on this second type of question —such as, Shall a dam be built in the district?—remain largely unmeasured by opinion surveys. Most of the data bear on the concerns of classes of people whose opinions might be expected to be about the same wherever they live. Yet even on such questions the fact of residence in a metropolis may give a special cast to opinions, a tenor that

TABLE 5.4

SIZE OF PLACE IN RELATION TO OPINION ON JOB-GUARANTEE QUESTION [a]

ISSUE POSITION	METRO [b]	METRO FRINGE [c]	CITIES OVER 50,000 [d]	CITIES 10,000– 50,000	TOWNS 2,500– 10,000	COUNTRY [e]
Agree strongly	58%	46%	53%	34%	47%	46%
Agree but not strongly	13	11	12	16	17	16
Depends	5	6	7	15	5	9
Disagree but not strongly	8	16	11	12	14	11
Disagree strongly	16	21	17	23	17	18
	100%	100%	100%	100%	100%	100%
N	268	171	234	163	295	455

[a] The question was as follows: "The government in Washington ought to see to it that everybody who wants to work can find a job."
[b] The 12 largest cities and their suburbs of 50,000 or more.
[c] Metropolitan fringe consists of the suburbs, with populations of from 2,500 to 50,000, of the 12 metropolitan cities plus some urban fringe and rural suburban territory.
[d] That is, cities over 50,000 not suburban to metropolitan centers.
[e] Includes places under 2,500 not elsewhere classified.
DATA SOURCE: *Survey Research Center, University of Michigan, 1956.*

would be lacking among similar persons resident in small cities. Thus, blue-collar workers in a metropolis may develop outlooks that differ in degree from those of blue-collar workers in towns and small cities.

The detailed evidence on gradations of opinion among places of different population size indicates that even the country is not often set off sharply from the metropolis. Rather, people of all shades of opinion inhabit both the city and the country. The opinion distributions in the two types of areas overlap; only the averages differ.[5] Moreover, on many questions differences in opinion patterns are not related with

[5] For an extensive compilation of poll results comparing farmers with other sectors of the population, see Howard W. Beers: "Rural-Urban Differences: Some Evidence from Opinion Polls," *Rural Sociology*, XVIII (1953), 1–11.

regularity to size of community. For example, the people of villages and countryside are not on all issues the most conservative of population groups. An illustration of the opinion variations among places of different population size appears in Table 5.4, which indicates direction of 1956 opinion on the proposition: "The government in Washington ought to see to it that everybody who wants to work can find a job." The table also serves as a step in the explanation of a means for a more comprehensive comparison between types of communities.

As a preliminary to the presentation of data on other questions, we can by an arithmetical maneuver make the data of Table 5.4 more comprehensible. Let us ignore the differences in strength of opinion on the job-guarantee proposition. Then 71 per cent of the metropolitan sample agrees and 24 per cent disagrees; these figures contrast sharply with the 50 per cent agreement and 35 per cent disagreement in the small cities of 10,000 to 50,000 population. If, taking another step, we use as a single indicator the difference between the percentage that agrees and the percentage that disagrees, we lose some detail but obtain simpler measures of position on the issue. By these operations Table 5.4 can be reduced to the index in the right-hand column below:

	(1) Agree	(2) Disagree	(3) (1)minus(2)
Metropolitan	71	24	47
Metropolitan fringe	57	37	20
Cities over 50,000	65	28	37
Cities, 10,000–50,000	50	35	15
Towns, 2,500–10,000	64	31	33

If we treat several issues in the same manner, we obtain the contrasts in opinion division among places of different size that appear in Table 5.5.

The gradations of opinion among types of communities shown by Table 5.5 fit in part the common suppositions. The metropolitan centers stand at the extreme "liberal" position on each of the domestic issues analyzed. Relatively more people in these centers look approvingly on public enterprise in housing and in power, more regard medical care as a proper subject of governmental action, fewer wish to restrict the influence of unions, and more believe the government should see to it that every one who wants to work can find a job. The table also confounds some political folklore. The stronghold of conservatism, at least on these issues, rests in small cities of from 10,000 to 50,000 population and not in the rural areas. That conservatism, though, is mixed with a sense of fiscal responsibility. Far fewer persons in the small cities agree that taxes should be cut even if it means putting off some important "things that need to be done." In public services the tastes of small cities are simple, but their citizens seem to be more willing to pay for what they want than do metropolitan residents. The thorough control of the politics of these smaller cities by business and professional men is reflected both in popular attitudes and in the generally conservative tendency of Representatives, be they Democratic or Republican, from districts dominated by such communities. Although these small cities account for only about 10 per cent of the na-

TABLE 5.5

INDICES OF OPINION CLEAVAGE IN PLACES OF DIFFERENT SIZE ON SELECTED ISSUES [a]

ISSUE	METRO	CITIES OVER 50,000	TOWNS 2,500– 10,000	COUN- TRY	METRO FRINGE	CITIES 10,000– 50,000
Power and Housing	+17	+21	+23	+28	+39	+43
Union influence	+22	+36	+45	+46	+50	+47
Medical care	+48	+37	+29	+32	+21	+16
Job Guarantee	+47	+37	+33	+33	+20	+15
Cut taxes	−8	−15	−22	−25	−30	−35

[a] The entries, explained in the text, are the differences between the percentage agreeing and the percentage disagreeing with the issue proposition, something of an index of the size of relative pluralities in places of different size. The figure is affected by the proportions of "it depends" responses as well as by the size of the proportions in agreement and in disagreement. In reading the figures the precise form of the question must be kept in mind. For the phrasing of the issue propositions, see Appendix I.

DATA SOURCE: *Survey Research Center, University of Michigan, 1956.*

tional sample, the intensity of their opinions, compounded by their overrepresentation in Congress and in state legislatures, may give them a disproportionate strength in the political process. The hardheaded opinion of the small city represents a strain of politics that probably once was far more typical of America than it now is.

Some common suppositions about the conservatism of the country and of the small towns under 10,000 are in error, at least as measured by opinions on the issues in Table 5.5. In the main people of small towns, of villages, and of the country stand between those of the metropolis and those of the small cities. On other questions places of various sizes would probably arrange themselves in a different order, but the distribution of attitudes on this series of questions indicates that the villages and countryside occupy a middle position. Their swings in attitude over time may contribute to the settlement of conflicts involving the extremes in the small and great cities.

On questions of involvement of the United States in international politics communities arrange themselves in an order different from that prevailing on domestic issues. On a scale designed to measure willingness to see the United States involved in international affairs variations among types of places are not striking, as Table 5.6 shows. While peo-

TABLE 5.6

SIZE OF PLACE IN RELATION TO OPINION DISTRIBUTION ON INTERNATIONALISM SCALE [a]

INTERNATIONALISM	CITIES OVER 50,000	METRO FRINGE	CITIES 10,000– 50,000	METRO	TOWNS 2,500– 10,000	RURAL
High	60%	53%	58%	61%	59%	51%
Medium	27	34	28	22	24	25
Low	13	13	14	17	17	24
	100%	100%	100%	100%	100%	100%
N	217	159	148	223	260	408

[a] See Table 5.4 for definition of place categories.
DATA SOURCE: *Survey Research Center, University of Michigan, 1956.*

ple of all kinds of places rank, on the average, high on the scale, the most marked deviation occurs in the open country and in villages under 2,500, which have relatively about twice as many persons ranking low on the scale of internationalism as do the suburbs. This deviation may not be attributed solely to conditions of rural life, for substantial numbers of metropolitan residents also rank low on the scale. In any case, rural dwellers turn up in relatively large numbers on most questions that seek to tap isolationist attitudes.[6]

Minor Tempests: Rural versus Urban. In American politics several issues of style, morals, and convenience are notorious sources of urban-rural cleavage. The survey data support the popular impressions on these matters. Regularly, for example, the question of daylight-saving time taxes the ingenuity of statesmen for its solution. Farmers, supposedly bound by their way of life to rise early anyway, do not wish

[6] On the average those persons who grew up on farms but were residing in urban places in 1956 ranked lower on the internationalism scale than did their fellow citizens who had not grown up on farms. Substantially more of those who grew up on farms had so few opinions that they could not be placed on the internationalism scale.

to start their day even earlier for the convenience of city dwellers who want more daylight left free for golfing. Mr. Gallup in April, 1957, found the following percentages to favor daylight-saving time: [7]

Farm population	24%
Towns under 10,000	54
Towns 10,000–99,999	54
Cities over 100,000	73

Mr. Gallup also found in 1950 that farmers had little use for the proposal to have all holidays, except Christmas, celebrated on Mondays in order to have a few long week ends. Dwellers in cities of over 100,000 approved the scheme by 58 per cent, but only 37 per cent of the farmers favored it.[8]

Rural concentration of prohibition sentiment has long given battles over policy on the sale of alcoholic beverages the flavor of a conflict between city and country. To some degree at least the urban-rural cleavage on prohibition masks differences in religious doctrine on the liquor question. Yet the conditions of life in small towns and the countryside may generate community opinions less tolerant of deviate behavior than is the impersonal metropolis. Whatever the basis for the attitude differences, their uneven geographical distribution projects the prohibition issue into the governmental mechanism as friction between metropolis and countryside. In February, 1942, the AIPO found the sentiment in favor of national prohibition to be: [9]

	For
Farmers	50%
Towns under 10,000	43
Cities 10,000 to 100,000	31
Cities over 100,000	23

Variations in attitudes toward prohibition are paralleled by, and perhaps connected with, urban-rural differences found by Stouffer by the application of his scale of willingness to tolerate nonconformists.

[7] The figures do not reveal certain urban sources of opposition to daylight-saving time. On occasion an urban utility has made a modest contribution to those campaigning against fast time; to move the clocks up reduces the consumption of electricity for illumination.

[8] What cosmic import to attach to the farmers' views is hard to say. One farmer explained: "My wife's folks are always coming out here as it is, but now, at least, they have to pack up and go home Sunday nights."

[9] Readers may have encountered truly imposing rustic tipplers, but, if we are to believe what people tell interviewers, imbibers are relatively fewer on the farms than in the cities. In 1939 the AIPO asked: "Do you ever drink any alcoholic beverage such as wine, beer, cocktails, highballs?" The yes response among farmers was 43 per cent; the urbanites confessed at the rate of 63 per cent.

Of his sample in the metropolitan areas 14 per cent were rated as "less tolerant"; this proportion increased in smaller cities and in towns under 2,500 and reached 29 per cent in the farm population. Similarly, the proportion rated as "more tolerant" was over twice as great in the metropolitan areas (39 per cent) as among farmers (18 per cent).[1]

Community Size, Social Structure, and Opinion. The fact of variation, or similarity, in the distribution of opinions within metropolitan areas, other urban communities, and the open country alone has its political significance. The further problem remains whether size of community may itself be important in the shaping of opinion. The hypothesis has been suggested that the metropolis—with its neighborhood segregation of income, class, and occupational groupings, with its multiplicity of centers of information and propaganda, and with its *modus vivendi* permitting all kinds of people to live together yet apart—may facilitate the development of diversity in opinion. In contrast, the intimate relations of the small town, the hypothesis goes, may induce a greater homogeneity of opinion, a condition perhaps enforced by the monopolization of the positions of respectability and prestige by a unified and visible norm-setting community leadership. To a degree, the argument is that in smaller communities, lesser peoples without the aid of organizations and opinion-forming centers beholden to them, may be dominated in their views to a higher degree by community leadership.

Such evidence as is available on these plausible arguments relates to voting rather than to policy opinions. Epstein, from an analysis of Wisconsin cities, suggested that the smaller Democratic vote in medium-sized cities, in comparison with that in large cities, might be a function of community size.[2] In a more extended analysis in Michigan, Masters and Wright found that a substantial proportion of the variation in Democratic vote among cities of different sizes could be accounted for by differences in the occupational composition of the cities. Yet laborers in small cities were distinctly less inclined to vote Democratic than were laborers in large cities. Factors present in the larger cities and absent in the smaller ones mobilized workers for the Democrats; the relative absence of labor organization in cities under 10,000 seemed to be the most important of these factors.[3] MacRae, in a correlational analysis

[1] Stouffer: op. cit., p. 112.

[2] "Size of Place and the Two-Party Vote," *Western Political Quarterly*, IX (1956), 138–50.

[3] Nicholas A. Masters and Deil S. Wright: "Trends and Variations in the Two-Party Vote: The Case of Michigan," *American Political Science Review*, LII (1958), 1078–90.

of congressional voting and occupations, arrives at similar general findings. In congressional districts with high percentages of farmers—that is, primarily rural and small-town districts—he found little or no correlation between occupation and vote. In urban districts occupations tended to divide in their voting along the expected party lines.[4] Berelson observed that in Elmira the community norms, more favorable to middle-class and business groups, solidified the middle-class vote, while the workers showed "less political solidarity and more political ambivalence." [5]

TABLE 5.7

PERCENTAGES OF OCCUPATIONAL GROUPS IN METROPOLITAN CENTERS AND IN SMALL CITIES AGREEING STRONGLY WITH SELECTED POLICY PROPOSITIONS

ISSUE	METROPOLITAN		SMALL CITY [a]	
	Blue-collar	White-collar	Blue-collar	White-collar
Union influence	36%	47%	45%	50%
Power and housing	33	43	45	47
Job guarantee	60	51	37	26
Medical care	55	50	42	31

[a] Cities of 10,000–50,000.
DATA SOURCE: *Survey Research Center, University of Michigan, 1956.*

If community pressures in the small town discourage voting dissent from the dominant party, the question remains of whether a similar process operates with respect to policy outlooks. Some evidence indicates that it does. If we single out those persons who "agree strongly" with policy propositions that might be expected to affect white-collar and blue-collar workers differentially, we obtain suggestive contrasts. Table 5.7 shows the percentages of occupational groups in metropolitan centers and in small cities "agreeing strongly" with the indicated policy statements. In each instance blue-collar workers of the small cities differ sharply from their metropolitan brethren, and in each instance that difference moves them toward the position of the white-collar classes of the small cities.[6]

[4] Duncan MacRae, Jr.: "Occupations and the Congressional Vote, 1940–1950," *American Sociological Review*, XX (1955), 332–40.

[5] Bernard Berelson *et al.: Voting* (Chicago: University of Chicago Press; 1954), pp. 56–7. Relevant also is Warren Miller's finding that one-party dominance in counties hampers the minority party in the mobilization of its potential vote; see his "One-Party Politics and the Voter," *American Political Science Review*, L (1956), 707–25. Consistent with the assumption that more interaction occurs among people in small communities are the findings by Stuart C. Dodd in "A Power of Town Size Predicts an Internal Interacting," *Social Forces*, XXXVI (1957), pp. 132–37.

[6] Similar gradations do not appear on every issue. Small-city white-collar people, for example, feel strongly, even more frequently than metropolitan blue-

Whether the facts mean that small-city elites impose upon blue-collar groups their own conservative views one cannot say. Whatever the processes of opinion formation may be, small-city workers tend toward the views of their white-collar fellow citizens and away from the like occupational strata of the metropolis. Table 5.7 may provide a clue to a problem entirely different from that raised in this immediate discussion. At earlier points we have groped toward the identification of leadership groups that set opinion patterns. Perhaps in the professional and business classes of the small cities we can isolate a comparatively small and well-knit elite which, because of its solidarity and the size and nature of the political unit within which it operates, exerts exceptional powers in opinion formation.[7]

3 · Opinion, Geography, and Government

In some degree public opinion consists of responses to public policy; public opinion, in turn, may affect public policy. Actions of government may generate attitudes of resistance or approbation. Those opinions may then influence government as it reverses its action, continues its course unchanged, or modifies its policy. While these interactions occur on all public policies, they are of special interest for those with differential impacts geographically.

Governmental policies may affect classes of persons differentially; a special case of this phenomenon is a differential impact upon the people who happen to reside in geographical subdivisions of the nation. The extreme instance may be a piece of punitive or retributive legislation expressly directed towards the inhabitants of a province. In the United States most federal legislation applies by its terms to all people wherever they live; that fundamental constitutional practice has its profound consequences for public opinion. The region temporarily in ascendance in national politics cannot enact legislation that explicitly discriminates against the people of another region; nor can it take

collar workers, that the government ought to see to it "that big business corporations don't have much to say about how the government is run." This may reflect the greater importance of small business and the professions in smaller places.

[7] The hypothesis that social structure accounts for these differences, though, remains on shaky ground. The processes of equalization of opinion across occupational groups by community pressure do not, for example, seem to operate in so marked a way, as might be expected, in places of less than 10,000. The possibility also remains that the occupational categories in the metropolis and in the cities of from 10,000–50,000 may not be precisely comparable. For example, a higher proportion of skilled craftsmen in the smaller places might be associated with the opinion differential, a possibility that cannot be checked because of the sample size.

measures to enrich the people of a section. Policy national in its terms and uniform in its application discourages the polarization of opinion around sectional centers.

Nevertheless, legislation, by its terms, may be national in its application but, in fact, have a restricted geographical impact. The ancient plaint of agricultural regions producing for the world market against protective tariffs on manufactured goods is illustrative. The resistance of the South to civil-rights legislation, which would apply in form to the entire United States but in fact primarily to the South, provides another illustration. The old-time isolation of the Midwest was a case of a slightly different order: the differential in impact came not so much from different economic interests of regions as from varying beliefs and outlooks. In the actions of government there recurs in many less-obvious ways the possibility of geographical differentiation in the distribution of the fruits and the penalties of public policy.

When government acts in a way that is territorially discriminatory, it stimulates the formation of geographical clusters in opposition to its policies and perhaps of other clusters in support. Within the limits of the data examined, American national policy has been confronted in recent years by only a single marked sectional conflict structure, that with respect to the position of the Negro. On most questions on which information was available in the 1950's practices in national policy had not formed regional points of resistance. Nor did the makers of national policy have to wrestle with pre-existing regional clusters of attitude with a bearing on important national policies. Different kinds of inquiries than those that have been made might identify variations in regional acceptance of national policy—feelings, for example, that in the allocation of the favors at the command of the national government the West had been favored as against the Northeast or vice versa. Yet by and large the truly notable characteristic of American national policy is that it copes so well with the special needs and ambitions of the diverse sections of a country stretched across a continent. Our measures, which indicate roughly similar distributions of opinion within each of the several great regions, provide a rough index of the interaction of governmental policy and public opinion. The total impact of policy produces no sharp regional cleavage save in a single instance.

Undoubtedly the maintenance of interregional consensus has been facilitated by objective developments that make policy national both in form and in reality. Notably the rapid spread of industry into hitherto predominantly agricultural regions has made less possible the pursuit of policies obviously designed to benefit the industrial Northeast at the expense of the rest of the country. The migration of the Negro from the South has been making, and will continue to make, the question of race relations less of a sectional issue.

To a degree geographical differences among metropolitan centers, suburbs, smaller cities, and rural areas have replaced the old sectional lines of politics. Although opinion differences among these types of geographical units are larger than those among geographical sections, the metropolis and country are by no means unified in opposition to one another. Were data available on narrower issues that affect the types of areas in a more direct manner—for example, agricultural price-support policy—areas of sharper conflict might be identifiable. Even so, the metropolis, the small city, and the country exist as geographical foundations for some types of political conflict, both present and potential.

Geographical differentials in opinion have another significance that remains to be noted. Under systems of geographical representation territorial differentials in the distribution of opinion are needed to assure representation of all viewpoints in the governing process. Islands of deviation, though difficult to maintain against the drive of powerful national influences toward uniformity, should be cherished; they provide anchorages for Senators and Representatives able to see that the minority view, even on matters supported by imposing national majorities, can be presented to the end that issues receive a more nearly adequate discussion.

6

OCCUPATION AND CLASS

IN THE ERA of transformation of an agrarian society into an industrial society domestic politics is concerned predominantly with the adjustment of the political system to the new economic arrangements. New centers of power vie against the old and gradually gain both status and legitimacy. New occupations and new institutions arise, which must be assimilated into the political order in a manner conducive to the maintenance of domestic order and tranquillity as well as of a modicum of justice. As the industrial system takes shape, its attendant urbanization and division of labor induce the assumption by government of new functions, debate about which is almost invariably colored by group and class concern. The tasks of political adjustment are most acute during the era of transformation, when old elites, unless they are both nimble and farsighted, may be destroyed.

The maturation of industrialism does not end the political problems of an industrial society. Industrialization creates a complex pattern of differentiation among people: according to function, according to rewards, according to prestige, according to status. The problem persists of ameliorating frictions among these varied kinds of people, of policing those who control the bottlenecks in the system of division of labor, and of coping with new questions born of the dynamism and instability of an industrial order. These frictions have a greater capacity to command attention than do the deprivations of an agrarian or pastoral society. Concentration of workers in factories and in cities permits ready sharing of grievances; the same circumstances facilitate the work of the agitator disposed to exploit discontent. Moreover, the working masses of a pecuniary society are sensitive to interruptions in the flow of income; they lack the shock absorbers of a subsistence society.

Against this background the distribution of opinions among different kinds of people in a democratic industrial order acquires significance. Varying attitudes in the hierarchy of occupations reflect the frictions inevitably associated with an industrial system. To a degree the system of discipline and of incentives necessary to operate an industrial order generates its own peculiar set of political cleavages. The hopes and expectations aroused by a democratic political order, on the other hand, may embarrass the maintenance of the relations essential for the economic order. In the interplay between industrial and political orders the problem may be at one time to maintain sufficient private authority to keep the industrial order running, at another to build up sufficient public authority to restrain the injustices latent within the industrial order.

1 · Occupation and the Direction of Opinion

People differ in status. Some persons, both by their own assessment and by the judgment of their fellows, are accorded a higher position than others. Some enjoy greater influence than others; some command greater rewards, pecuniary and psychological, than others. An incidental function of a politico-economic system is to maintain these inequalities, as well as to mitigate their harshness. Given that painful fact, the differentials and the similarities in the political opinions of persons of various status levels may serve as a useful index of the nature of the management of the political order. To make these contrasts and comparisons raises the practical problem of how to measure status. Levels of income might serve as an index, but American incomes are so distributed that they merge into the same categories persons of different status. Though subjective social class could be used as an indicator, Americans have an attenuated sense of class identification. Occupation remains the most satisfactory index of status, and chief reliance will be placed upon it in this analysis. Popular attitudes rank occupations in a relatively standardized hierarchy in all industrial societies.[1] Occupational rank thus becomes a rough index of subjective sense of status. Moreover, the recurrence of political appeals to the businessman, the professional classes, the workingman, and the farmer reflects the expectation that political conflict may be aroused among occupational groups even though it may not exist at the moment. One of the tasks of a democratic order is to keep tension between occupational categories down to a tolerable level, for the operation of a system whose parts must be nicely integrated requires a considerable degree of cross-occupational consensus.

Domestic Economic Issues. In the American setting, as in other capitalist societies, a major opinion cleavage along occupational lines is on social-welfare policy. Allocation of rewards by the market produces differentials in level, certainty, and continuity of income. These occupational contrasts provide foundations for differing political behaviors and opinions. Those persons less advantaged express their discontent in riots, in prayer, in futile millennial politics, in resignation, or in other ways. One of the triumphs of a democratic order is to direct these discontents into constitutional channels that are so managed as to yield ameliorative action without destroying or seriously disarranging the intricate fabric of the productive system.

We can only surmise the nature of the trends and fluctuations in opinion tensions in the American industrial hierarchy as the system underwent the strains of growth. At times these tensions were doubtless more marked and more bitter than they were in the 1950's. Earlier, too, discontents were probably more lacking in discernible goal. Only gradually did legislation ameliorative of the risks of the industrial order become a possible outcome of political agitation. Political commitments to improve the lot of the workingman were but empty oratory until appropriate administrative, legislative, and constitutional techniques could be devised, and these accomplishments were not the work of a day.

The upshot of evolution in practice and in opinion has been that while cleavages of opinion on social welfare policy remain, they are blunted by a considerable cross-occupational satisfaction with public

[1] See the review of the data on this point by Alex Inkeles and Peter H. Rossi: "National Comparisons of Occupational Prestige," *American Journal of Sociology*, LXI (1956), 329–39. See also Inkeles: "Industrial Man: The Relation of Status to Experience, Perception, and Value," *American Journal of Sociology*, LXVI (1960), 1–31.

policy. The data of Figure 6.1 bundle up a mixed bag of attitudes toward welfare policy. The diagram rests on the 1952 responses of a national sample to the question: "Some people think the national government should do more in trying to deal with such problems as unemployment, education, housing, and so on. Others think that the government is already doing too much. On the whole, would you say that

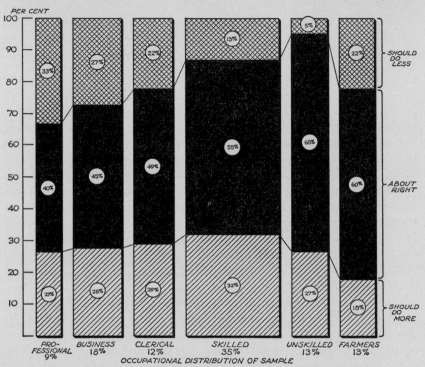

FIGURE 6.1. Distribution, within Occupational Groups, of Responses to the Question: "Some people think the national government should do more in trying to deal with such problems as unemployment, education, housing and so on. Others think that the government is doing too much. On the whole, would you say that what the government has done has been about right, too much, or not enough?" DATA SOURCE: Survey Research Center, University of Michigan, 1952.

what the government has done has been about right, too much, or not enough?" The question was put at a time of high employment and when the Republican candidate was committing his party to acceptance of the major reforms of the New Deal. Nonetheless, contrasts in opinion prevailed. The professional classes included a large contingent of diehards, about a third, who thought the government should do less. Yet similarities among occupational categories were more striking.

About half of each broad occupational group felt that the level of social welfare activity was "about right," which opinion, in the context of the situation, signified their rejection of the retrospective aspirations of the far right of the Republican party. Moreover, those who thought the government ought "to do more" in these welfare fields were relatively about as numerous in the high-status occupations as among workers, a reflection of policy reconciliation across status lines. The mild occupational tension reflected in the figure would probably become less mild under circumstances of economic stringency.[2]

The nature of the cleavage along occupational lines thus depends on the circumstances of the time. It also depends on the nature of the issue. Even in times of economic euphoria the lines may be sharply drawn on some issues. On others economic stress may not markedly increase occupational tensions. Occupational cleavages, in short, are not fixed by a doctrinaire agenda of reform. A specific issue on which occupational differences were quite large in a time of economic prosperity is that of medical care. In so prosperous a year as 1956 occupational differences were great on the proposition: "The government ought to help people get doctors and hospital care at low cost." The values, interests, and exposure of the professional classes to agitation against "socialized medicine" made their opinions markedly different from those of skilled and unskilled workers, as may be seen from Table 6.1. Unskilled workers with opinions concurred with this proposition in the ratio of about 5:1 while professional people divided about 50:50. On issues that raise the possibility of clear and immediate advantage, the industrial working classes tend to have opinions and to express them in the direction that might be expected from the nature of their life circumstances.

Divergencies in opinion among occupational categories, though, have qualities not made apparent by simple contrasts in occupational preferences on bread-and-butter questions. Frictions and tensions are mitigated by cross-occupational consensus on more basic political propositions. Consider in this connection the nature of opinion (also shown in Table 6.1) on the proposition: "The government ought to see to it that big business corporations don't have much say about how the government is run." The expectation might be that occupational lines would be closely paralleled by opinion cleavages on this question or, at any rate, that workers would agree with the proposition in high degree. The fact is, though, that all occupational groups prefer to keep

[2] In Figure 6.1 the occupational categorization conforms to the usual practice of placing respondents in the occupational category to which the head of the household belongs: that is, housewives are assigned to their husbands' occupational groups.

TABLE 6.1

Relation of Occupation to Opinions on Medical Care and on Restraint of
Big Business Influence

Medical Care [a]

	Professional	Business	Clerical	Skilled	Unskilled	Farmers
Agree	38%	45%	49%	56%	65%	61%
Depends	15	9	7	9	8	5
Disagree	41	37	31	23	13	24
No opinion	6	9	13	12	14	10
	100%	100%	100%	100%	100%	100%

RESTRAIN BIG BUSINESS INFLUENCE [b]

	Professional	Business	Clerical	Skilled	Unskilled	Farmers
Agree	53%	48%	52%	56%	42%	54%
Depends	8	8	5	6	3	5
Disagree	23	24	20	13	10	14
No opinion	16	20	23	25	45	27
	100%	100%	100%	100%	100%	100%
N	163	243	169	487	235	180

[a] "The government ought to help people get doctors and hospital care
at low cost."
[b] "The government ought to see to it that big business corporations
don't have much say about how the government is run."
DATA SOURCE: *Survey Research Center, University of Michigan, 1956.*

big business in its place. This is not an attitude of deep hostility toward
big business. It is more in the spirit of: "Big business ought to have a
say about how things go; no more than anybody else; but they ought
not to be allowed to push the government around." [3]

Lack of information, especially among low-status persons, may
also damp tensions among occupational groups. Data on the question of
the influence of big business graphically illustrate the point. Nearly half
the respondents in households headed by unskilled workers had no
opinion on the question. This high incidence of "no opinion" doubtless

[3] A few of the incidental comments by respondents on the big business
question suggest the tenor of attitude. A Nebraska stockman: "They shouldn't
have any more to say than the rest of us." A Connecticut building tradesman: "I
agree for the simple reason that we working people shouldn't go and tell them
(the government) either. We put in a President and Congress and if we have done
wrong in that we have an election." A California skilled worker: "I don't think
the government should be dictated to by big business nor labor either." A Mississippi farmer: "Believe in right, but no more right to tell government how to do,
than farmers or any other group." A Kansas beautician: "Should be treated as well
as someone else." An Ohio skilled worker: "They should have as much say so as
anybody else but not all."

comes in major part from lack of information and from lack of a capacity to understand complex political processes. The potentials of occupational conflict are blunted by inattention to politics by the lower occupational strata. Inattention and lack of understanding of broad issues in the lower occupational reaches also permit the modern counterpart of what in the days of an agrarian politics was termed "hoodwinking the rubes." [4] A defensible generalization might be that the average weight of individuals in the politics of an industrial order declines, by some unknown function, with status in the occupational hierarchy.

While all these data indicate the validity of the supposition that step by step down the scale larger proportions of each occupational level favor measures that would be of direct benefit to them in income and security in the industrial order, the distribution of opinions has its divergencies from common-sense expectations. Cleavages along occupational lines vary in their clarity from time to time with objective conditions and probably with the effectiveness of the rationalizations disseminated by those who enjoy the most prestige and pelf. Occupational boundaries, moreover, do not mark abrupt changes in attitude; opinion categories overlap occupational strata. Further, the dictum that self-interest fixes political opinion must be modified, for the capacity to perceive the bearing of more abstruse policies on self-interest varies widely among occupational groups. And even on measures whose bearing on self-interest is most patent, persons at both ends of the occupational scale, from compassion or restraint, take positions not congruent with the short-run interests associated with their status.[5]

Morale in the Industrial Order. Occupational differentials on welfare issues may reflect only varying degrees of unhappiness about the allocation of rewards of the industrial system. Tensions in the industrial order may also be manifested in attitudes not overtly political, which sooner or later may be transformed into opinions on political issues and on candidates. If over long periods of time measures were available of

[4] Probably people of lesser occupational status and with less education are also more susceptible to demagogic exploitation on noneconomic issues. Thus, the foes of fluoridation of water supplies seem to have relatively greater success among the poor and those with least education. See Thomas F. A. Plant: "Analysis of Voting Behavior on a Fluoridation Referendum," *Public Opinion Quarterly*, XXIII (1959), 213-22.

[5] For suggestive general analyses, see Arthur Kornhauser: "Public Opinion and Social Class," *American Journal of Sociology*, LV (1949-50), 333-45; "Analysis of 'Class' Structure of Contemporary American Society: Psychological Bases of Class Division," in *Industrial Conflict: A Psychological Interpretation* (Yearbook, Society for the Psychological Study of Social Issues; 1939), pp. 230-50.

the prevalence of a sense of general satisfaction with the industrial order among its occupational components, we might have a fever chart of
the basic politics of the system. Though only scattered pieces of information are available, they are of some utility. In October, 1935, *Fortune* asked the question: "Do you believe that in general labor is fairly
or unfairly treated in this country today?" At that time of economic
stress a sense of unfair treatment was common, especially among the
less privileged. The distribution of responses by occupation was as follows:

	Fairly	Unfairly	DK
Proprietors	58.0%	32.4%	9.6%
Salaried persons	56.3	37.1	6.6
Factory labor	39.2	50.5	10.3
Housewives	38.5	45.5	16.0
Farm labor	24.1	62.9	13.0
No employment	26.2	63.8	10.0
TOTAL POPULATION	46.9	42.5	10.6

The responses to a different question in 1956 suggested that at that
time of relatively high prosperity considerably fewer persons were
burning with indignation about the inequities of the economic system.[6]
Though an occupational differential existed, substantial majorities at all
levels felt either "pretty well satisfied" or "more-or-less satisfied" with
the way they were "getting along financially." Almost twice as large a
proportion (Table 6.2) of the unskilled as of the businessmen (22 per
cent against 12 per cent) were "not satisfied at all." Expectations about
future financial circumstances also varied among occupations. Relatively more of those of high-prestige occupations looked forward to
improvement in their financial situation. Of unskilled workers 50 per
cent expected their situation to stay the same, a melancholy statistic.
The data suggest the presence of fairly widespread satisfaction, but
more complete information might isolate even in a time of prosperity
pockets of deep discontent.[7]

Estimates within occupational groups of the opportunity to get
ahead provide further evidence about the state of morale of the order.
The 1952 SRC national sample was asked about its views on "opportunity in America today," whether the average man has a chance to
"get ahead." Remarkably little variation existed in the outlook of different occupational groups, as may be seen in Table 6.3. Prospects for get-

[6] For an analysis intermediate in time to the two items cited, see Richard
Centers and Hadley Cantril: "Income Satisfaction and Income Aspiration," *Journal of Abnormal and Social Psychology*, XLI (1946), 64–9.

[7] Those "not satisfied at all" with their current financial situation constituted
about 18 per cent of the total sample.

TABLE 6.2

OCCUPATION IN RELATION TO CURRENT FINANCIAL SATISFACTION AND TO EXPECTA-
TIONS ABOUT FUTURE FINANCIAL SITUATION

	Pro-fessional	Business	Clerical	Skilled	Un-skilled	Farmers
Satisfaction [a]						
Pretty well satisfied	41%	55%	43%	43%	35%	31%
More or less	41	33	43	39	43	44
Not satisfied	17	12	13	18	22	24
No opinion, NA	1	*	1	*	*	1
	100%	100%	100%	100%	100%	100%
Expectation [b]						
Get better	57%	51%	45%	45%	34%	30%
Stay same	37	37	41	40	50	39
Get worse	4	6	9	8	8	18
No opinion, NA	2	6	5	7	8	13
	100%	100%	100%	100%	100%	100%
N	163	243	170	488	235	181

[a] "We are also interested in how people are getting along financially these days. So far as you and your family are concerned, would you say that you are pretty well satisfied with your present financial situation, more-or-less satisfied, or not satisfied at all?"
[b] "Now looking ahead and thinking about the next few years, do you expect your financial situation will stay about the way it is now, get better, or get worse?"
DATA SOURCE: *Survey Research Center, University of Michigan, 1956.*

ting ahead looked less rosy to the unskilled worker than to the business-man; yet few of either group were so gloomy as to see no opportunity for the "average man." The responses, given the form of the question, could be regarded as estimates of opportunity for the other fellow, no matter how hopeless the respondent's situation might be. However that may be, the gap between the estimates of opportunity and the cold fact of fairly limited occupational mobility may indicate the potency of the American faith in the power of an individual to lift himself by his bootstraps—a faith of not inconsiderable import in the maintenance of the esprit of an industrial order.[8]

These inquiries throw some light on the harmonies and tensions within the industrial system born of satisfaction and dissatisfaction

[8] Consider the thoughtful discussion, based on interviews in depth, of the role of opportunity in the social system by Robert E. Lane: "The Fear of Equality," *American Political Science Review*, LIII (1959), 35–51.

TABLE 6.3

OCCUPATION IN RELATION TO ESTIMATES OF OPPORTUNITY IN AMERICA [a]

	Pro-fessional	Business	Clerical	Skilled	Un-skilled	Farmers
Opportunity, yes	72%	77%	70%	66%	62%	65%
Yes, qualified	16	16	21	21	24	19
Pro-con	2	1	2	2	4	3
No, qualified	8	5	6	6	7	9
Little opportunity, no	2	1	1	5	3	4
	100%	100%	100%	100%	100%	100%
N	106	227	155	462	174	178

[a] "Some people say there's not much opportunity in America, today—that the average man doesn't have much chance to really get ahead. Other say there's plenty of opportunity, and anyone who works hard can go as far as he wants. How do you feel about this?"
DATA SOURCE: *Survey Research Center, University of Michigan, 1952.*

with the allocation of its rewards. Articulation of these attitudes with political opinions and political actions is less than perfect; people will take a great deal in poverty and injustice before they rebel. Yet at some point the tensions that permeate the occupational structure are projected into the political sphere. A basic task of the managers, political and business, of an industrial order is to maintain a modicum of satisfaction at all levels of the occupational hierarchy.[9] All of which is not to say that the ideal world is one in which satisfaction is universal. To maintain the momentum of an industrial order, there must be an optimum admixture of dissatisfaction, tinged with ambition rather than resignation, throughout the industrial hierarchy.

Occupation and Foreign Policy. Occupational peculiarities in attitudes on domestic economic policy are explicable by the readily perceived interests of persons in different walks of life. The presumption might be that outlooks toward questions of foreign policy would have little or no relation to occupational experience. Assembly-line workers, as such, might not plausibly be expected to have a characteristic view about policy toward Formosa, whereas their own experience might

[9] Publicists are prone to emphasize the dangers for an order of dissatisfaction among people of lesser status, a consequence of the fact that in our era dissatisfaction has been more common among such persons. An order may be no less endangered by a sense of dissatisfaction or injustice among persons of high status. Given their role of influence in the system, disaffection on their part may threaten the order more than unhappiness among persons of lower status. He who would govern well should mete out justice to the rich as well as to the poor.

lead them toward firm views about unemployment insurance, accident compensation, and the rights of unions to organize. In fact, however, occupational status is correlated broadly with position on foreign policy. Unskilled workers commonly take a more isolationist position than do professional men, while large proportions of farmers lean toward withdrawal from involvement in affairs abroad. This is not to say that a hod carrier may be an isolationist simply because of his occupation. The finding that large numbers of unskilled workers are isolationists tells us the location of this sentiment in the occupational hierarchy but not necessarily its basis.

Views on foreign policy subsume many opinions and emotions: a dislike of soldiering, a love of the old country, a spirit of parsimony, a suspicion of the stranger, a lack of information, and all their opposites, as well as many other sentiments. This varied composition of outlooks toward policy abroad makes it difficult to measure any general opinion on foreign policy. One never knows precisely how to appraise responses to survey questions in this realm. Nevertheless, differentials in opinions prevail fairly consistently among occupational categories. Whatever the form of the question, the professional and business classes ordinarily include the fewest outright isolationists. The proportions disposed toward withdrawal from the rest of the world are commonly highest among unskilled laborers and farmers, although these contrasts are far more marked on some issues than on others. The differences appeared neatly in the responses (Table 6.4) to the 1954 Survey Research Center question: "Some people think that since the end of the

TABLE 6.4

Occupation of Head of Household in Relation to Respondent's Opinion on U.S. Involvement in World Affairs, 1954 [a]

	Professional, business	Clerical, sales	Skilled	Un-skilled	Farmers
Too much involved	33%	28%	47%	47%	38%
Pro-con, depends	3	*	2	3	8
Not too much involved	56	66	44	36	40
Other responses	8	6	7	14	14
	100%	100%	100%	100%	100%
N	246	102	337	144	104

[a] "Some people think that since the end of the last world war this country has gone too far in concerning itself with problems in other parts of the world. How do you feel about this?"
source: *Angus Campbell and H. C. Cooper: Group Differences in Attitudes and Votes (Ann Arbor: Survey Research Center; 1956), p. 139.*

last world war this country has gone too far in concerning itself with problems in other parts of the world. How do you feel about this?" Unskilled workers were far more likely to respond that the United States had "gone too far" than were business and professional people.[1]

In their responses to another set of questions in 1956 occupational groups revealed contrasts in their outlook toward foreign involvement somewhat similar to those of 1954. Unskilled workers were most disposed toward the view that the country would be better off if we could just stay home and not concern ourselves with problems in other parts of the world; they were least supportive of aid to neutrals who might not be so much against communism as we were; and they least frequently approved the maintenance of troops overseas where they could help "countries that are against communism." These contrasts, which appear in Table 6.5, differ greatly from question to question.

At times the incidence of isolationist sentiments among workers generates in persons of higher-status occupations feelings that by their superior grasp of world affairs they serve the Republic especially well. Better-informed and better-educated, they may better estimate the long-run interests of the country and support public policies beyond the comprehension of the laborer and the farmer—persons of meager

---

TABLE 6.5

OCCUPATION OF HEAD OF HOUSEHOLD IN RELATION TO PERCENTAGES OF RESPONDENTS TAKING THE INTERNATIONALIST POSITION ON SELECTED QUESTIONS [a]

	Professional	Business	Clerical	Skilled	Unskilled	Farmers
Stay home	84%	65%	61%	58%	42%	44%
Aid to neutrals	46 [b]	32 [b]	25	23	23	27
Soldiers overseas	62 [b]	58 [b]	70	59	51	49
Be friendly	73	67	67	65	54	58
Economic aid	53	44	48	39	42	36

[a] Percentage base includes those who said that they had no opinion. For the wording of the issue propositions, see Appendix I.
[b] On these questions there were exceptionally large proportions of "it depends" responses among these groups.
DATA SOURCE: *Survey Research Center, University of Michigan, 1956.*

---

[1] On the same question in October, 1952, far higher proportions than in 1954 in all occupational categories felt that the country had "gone too far" in concerning itself with the rest of the world. At the time of the 1952 survey the Korean incident was still in progress; by 1954 Korea was quiet and the Eisenhower Administration had probably by its policies induced many people to subscribe to a policy of involvement abroad. Opinions on foreign policy may be highly susceptible to the influences of the moment.

information, isolated from the affairs of the world by their occupational and social role, and unable to see the place of the United States in world politics. To a large extent such self-satisfaction is the product of an arithmetical illusion. Support of participation in world affairs occurs, to be sure, far more frequently among professional persons than among blue-collar workers, but there are many more of the latter than of the former. If an internationalist foreign policy depended solely upon the support of professional, business, and other white-collar groups, it would rest on a fragile foundation; at least such would be the case if numbers alone were controlling. Table 6.5 shows, for example, a sharp contrast among occupational groups in their rejection of the proposition that it would be better if we could just stay home. When this table is turned on its side, as in Table 6.6, it becomes clear that each

TABLE 6.6

DISTRIBUTION AMONG OCCUPATIONS OF HOLDERS OF SPECIFIED OPINIONS ON "STAY HOME" QUESTION [a]

HEAD'S OCCUPATION	AGREE	DEPENDS	DISAGREE
Professional, business, clerical	23%	39%	42%
Skilled, unskilled	47	45	40
Farm operators	16	8	8
Others [b]	14	8	10
	100%	100%	100%
N	410	92	953

[a] "This country would be better off if we just stayed home and did not concern ourselves with problems in other parts of the world."
[b] Includes miscellaneous categories such as protective services, unemployed, and retired.
DATA SOURCE: *Survey Research Center, University of Michigan, 1956.*

level of the occupational hierarchy contributes a substantial block of support for the internationalist position. As measured by this question, the internationalists from the blue-collar occupations are about as numerous as are those from the white-collar occupations.[2] Nevertheless, isolationist tendencies among workers create problems for politicians, especially those politicians from working-class districts who are internationalist in their own views. They risk challenge by other politicians

[2] For a suggestive discussion of the significance for the political system of this homogeneity of response across occupational lines, see James C. Davies: "Some Relations Between Events and Attitudes," *American Political Science Review,* XLVI (1952), 777–89.

willing to capitalize upon the isolationist sentiments among their constituents.[3]

The problem of political management created by interoccupational differences in outlooks toward foreign involvement is probably mitigated by the fact that substantial numbers of skilled and unskilled workers declare themselves out of the game on matters of foreign policy. The proportions of "don't know" and "no opinion" answers to questions about such issues increase step by step down the occupational ladder. Probably, too, an acute crisis in external policy is required to command the serious attention of blue-collar workers, for it is evident that many of them do not occupy their time fretting about questions of international politics. Illustrative of the point are the proportions of "no opinion" responses within occupational groups to specified foreign-policy questions shown in Table 6.7.[4]

TABLE 6.7

PERCENTAGE OF RESPONDENTS WITH NO OPINION ON SELECTED FOREIGN POLICY QUESTIONS, BY OCCUPATION OF HEAD OF HOUSEHOLD [a]

	Professional	Business	Clerical	Skilled	Unskilled	Farmers
Stay home	6%	8%	11%	11%	23%	15%
Economic aid	7	12	12	19	26	17
Be friendly	5	9	9	10	18	10
Be tough	10	14	12	19	26	23
Soldiers overseas	13	17	12	20	28	29
Aid to neutrals	15	18	20	29	40	32

[a] For the wording of the issue propositions, see Appendix I.
DATA SOURCE: *Survey Research Center, University of Michigan, 1956.*

---

[3] If one could get to the roots of the matter, occupational differences might turn out to be much sharper on questions of military involvement than on other types of foreign involvement. Thus, marked occupational differences prevailed on the 1952 question whether we did "the right thing in getting into the fighting in Korea." Of farmers, 62 per cent said we had done the "wrong thing"; of unskilled workers, 54 per cent; of the professional group, only 31 per cent.

[4] To some extent interoccupational contrasts in opinion distribution are the product of the mode of calculation. The exclusion of the "don't knows" from the percentage base in most of the tables in the preceding pages enlarges the occupational differences. Thus on the "stay home" proposition, 41 per cent of the unskilled concurred, which figure is reduced to 31 per cent with the inclusion of the "no opinion" group in the percentage base. Moreover, as one contrasts occupational responses, he is left with a lingering curiosity whether the differentials on some questions may be the result to some degree of differences in interviewer rapport with members of lesser occupational groups or of differences among groups in their skill in handling the verbalisms characteristic of interview schedules.

Occupation, Authoritarianism, and Civil Liberties. The isolationism (or nationalism) of workers is paralleled by occupational peculiarities of outlook on such matters as civil liberties and race relations.
The more prestigious occupations usually turn out to be composed in
higher degree of defenders of individual and minority rights than are
the lesser occupations. "Liberalism," as defined by current political
argot, is distributed among occupations in unlike ways on different
types of issues. Blue-collar workers tend to be "liberal" on social-welfare measures, but, on the average, they are less "liberal" on such
questions as school integration.[5]

Stouffer's analysis of tolerance with respect to civil liberties, on
which we have placed reliance in other connections, demonstrates that
marked differences exist among occupational groups in the percentages
that are "more tolerant" as measured by his scale. His "more tolerant"
percentages among male respondents were: [6]

Professional and semi-professional	66%
Proprietors, managers and officials	51
Clerical and sales	49
Manual workers	30
Farmers and farm workers	20

The size of the differences among occupations on issues of civil
liberties depends on what measure of attitude is used. Less striking contrasts than those shown by Stouffer prevail on the question: "The government ought to fire any government worker who is accused of being
a communist even though they don't prove it." While occupational
differences exist on this question, substantial majorities of all groups
stand for due process for the individual. In the side comments on this
question frequent observations to the effect "not guilty until proved
guilty" were made by persons at all status levels. Nevertheless, disagreement with the proposition was highest in the professional group:
80 per cent. Twice as large a proportion of unskilled workers as professionals (26 per cent against 12 per cent) concurred with the statement. See Table 6.8.

[5] For general discussions of the point, see Kornhauser: "Public Opinion and
Social Class"; and Seymour M. Lipset: "Democracy and Working-Class Authoritarianism," *American Sociological Review*, XXIV (1959), 482–501.
[6] Quoted by Lipset: op. cit., p. 486; his treatment includes occupational
breakdowns not presented by Stouffer. Similar findings among college students
have been interpreted as a consequence of a sense of security which may be associated with status. Thus, "college students who are the children of middle-class
parents are more intolerant than college students whose parents are wealthy."—
Hadley Cantril: *The Psychology of Social Movements* (New York: Wiley; 1941),
p. 73.

Another bit of information on occupational attitudes toward civil liberties consists of opinions in the North on this proposition: "The government in Washington should stay out of the question of whether

TABLE 6.8

RELATION OF OCCUPATION TO VIEWS ON FIRING PERSONS ACCUSED OF COMMUNISM [a]

	Pro-fessional	Business	Clerical	Skilled	Un-skilled	Farmers
Agree	12%	23%	19%	24%	26%	33%
Depends	8	8	10	8	7	11
Disagree	80	69	71	68	67	56
	100%	100%	100%	100%	100%	100%
N	152	219	154	426	175	139

[a] "The government ought to fire any government worker who is accused of being a communist even though they don't prove it."
DATA SOURCE: *Survey Research Center, University of Michigan, 1956.*

white and colored children go to the same school." Observe especially in Table 6.9 the percentages within occupational groups in "strong agreement" with the proposition: 55 per cent of the unskilled laborers

TABLE 6.9

OCCUPATION IN RELATION TO OPINION ON SCHOOL SEGREGATION ISSUE, NORTH ONLY [a]

	Pro-fessional	Business	Clerical	Skilled	Un-skilled	Farmers
Agree strongly	22%	31%	43%	45%	55%	30%
Agree	19	18	16	17	14	26
Depends	17	12	7	10	11	6
Disagree	13	12	9	8	7	14
Disagree strongly	29	27	25	20	13	24
	100%	100%	100%	100%	100%	100%
N	119	153	107	343	117	90

[a] "The government in Washington should stay out of the question of whether white and colored children go to the same school."
DATA SOURCE: *Survey Research Center, University of Michigan, 1956.*

in the sample agreed strongly, but only 22 per cent of the professionals. On the other hand, prevalence of strong disagreement—that is, support for governmental intervention—declined step by step down the occupational hierarchy. While the upper occupational groups were by no means alone in their championing of the right of the federal government to intervene in the school segregation question, the brunt of the burden of defense of minority rights evidently fell upon professional, business, and political leadership.

The type of difference just cited has led to the hypothesis that the working class tends to be characterized by a general attitude of authoritarianism, which expresses itself on particular issues as they arise. That hypothesis has gained some support from the fact that larger proportions of lower occupational groups rank high on scales designed to measure authoritarianism. Thus, a Los Angeles County sample yielded the following proportions of authoritarians by occupational groups: professional, 23 per cent; small business, 33 per cent; white-collar, 59 per cent; skilled, 51 per cent; semiskilled, 68 per cent; unskilled, 86 per cent.[7]

Recent analyses throw doubt on whether the conventional authoritarianism scales when applied to a cross section of the population measure anything. The fact seems to be that people of lesser status and education, possessed perhaps of a general amiability and indisposition to wrangle with lady interviewers, agree more readily than do their betters to the kinds of propositions included in scales thought to measure authoritarianism, such as: "What young people need most of all is strict discipline by their parents." When the scale statements are reversed—that is, when the respondent must disagree with the statement to register an authoritarian position—not much of a trace of occupationally related authoritarianism is registered within the general population. Given this property of the measuring instruments, if one is to be a genuine authoritarian by the scales conventionally used, he evidently must be well educated or of upper status.[8]

If these findings are correct, occupational differentials in position on discrete issues may not indicate that an underlying authoritarian syndrome is especially frequent among workers. That differentials in opinion on specific issues exist and that they can be of disturbing practical importance there can be no doubt, but the odds are that their explanation must be sought pragmatically issue by issue rather than in some pervading quality of personality or outlook especially common

[7] W. J. MacKinnon and Richard Centers: "Authoritarianism and Urban Stratification," *American Journal of Sociology*, LXI (1956), 610–20. Other studies locate the peak of authoritarianism in the lower middle class, and the sense of authoritarianism is explained as a result of thwarted aspiration, frustration, and so forth. See Morris Janowitz and Dwaine Marvick: "Authoritarianism and Political Behavior," *Public Opinion Quarterly*, XVII (1953), 185–201.

[8] See Angus Campbell, Philip E. Converse, Warren E. Miller, and Donald E. Stokes: *The American Voter* (New York: Wiley; 1960), pp. 512–15; Gerhard E. Lenski and John C. Leggett: "Caste, Class, and Deference in the Research Interview," *American Journal of Sociology*, LXV (1960), 463–7.

among workers. Thus, regarding views on school segregation in the North the odds are simply that the families of unskilled workers would more frequently be affected by integration than would those of the professional classes.[9] With respect to civil liberties, appropriately phrased questions can locate both ignorance as well as intolerance among lower-status persons. Their attitudes may result in part from their less thorough indoctrination in the values of the culture rather than from their occupation. Moreover, to them due process of law in practice may present a radically different appearance than it does to, say, a lawyer. A major function of the guarantees of civil liberties is to keep competing political elites from putting each other into jail; they need to be more alert about such matters.

2 · Social Class and Opinion

Social class is a staple concept of political analysis. By its powerful impact on modern political thought, Marxism made ubiquitous the image of the political process as a conflict of class against class. But the idea of class friction as a major element of politics long antedated Marx. The rivalries of the haves and the have-nots march through the pages of political analysis, pre-Marxian and post-Marxian, Marxian and non-Marxian. Whether the picture of the political world in the minds of the political theorists matches that in the minds of the mass of the people, though, becomes doubtful as more evidence becomes available about attitudes of the general population. In the United States the sense of identification with social class appears to be weak; the reality of social class as a group with common political concerns seems even weaker. Nevertheless, class has some bearing on political opinions, and the distribution of opinions among classes deserves examination.

Definition of Social Classes. The problem of social class in politics becomes a bit slippery when one attempts to define social classes. One method is to define them by some plausible objective criterion, such as occupation, income, level of education, property ownership, or another similar standard. Political theorists characteristically hold this

---

[9] Social friction is often pictured as conflict between abstractions such as capital and labor. In American practice friction is more likely to occur at points of actual contact which are widely distributed in the social structure and not necessarily concentrated along a few lines of major cleavage. Persons who genuinely hate each other are likely to be separated by short rather than great social distances.

conception of class. The trouble with it is that the persons so grouped are not necessarily aware of their class position. A person obviously proletarian by the objective criteria may neither regard himself as a proletarian nor act politically as such.[1] An alternative mode of demarcation of classes is to discover with what class, if any, people identify. Do they regard themselves as upper, middle, or lower class? How strong is their sense of class identification? If they have a sense of class consciousness, a sense of belonging to one group rather than to another, class takes on political significance.

Technical problems develop as one seeks to discover the sense of class affiliation of people in the mass. What one finds out about American class structure seems to depend upon what one asks. Early surveys seemed to verify the assertion that the United States is one big happy middle-class family. In 1941 the following question was put to a national sample: "To what social class in this country do you feel you belong— middle class, or upper, or lower?" Some persons volunteered that they did not fit into any of these categories; they asserted that they were either upper-middle or lower-middle. The results were:

Upper	4.9%
Upper-middle	10.5
Middle	65.8
Lower-middle	11.1
Lower	7.7

These findings were held to support the proposition that the "overwhelming majority of the American people identify themselves with some category of the great middle class."[2] Editorialists who spoke of the virtues of the great middle class and analysts who hinged their interpretations of American politics on the moderating force of the sensible middle classes found support in this survey.

Concentration of the population in the middle class was later seen to be a consequence of the form of the question. Studies by Richard Centers produced an entirely different pattern of class identification. He put to a national cross section of white males the question: "If you were asked to use one of these four names for your social class, which would you say you belonged in: the middle class, lower class, working

[1] See Morris Rosenberg: "Perceptual Obstacles to Class Consciousness," *Social Forces*, XXXII (1953-4), 22-7. For a discussion of the analytical problems, see W. Lloyd Warner: *Social Class in America, A Manual of Procedure for the Measurement of Social Status* (New York: Harper; 1960).

[2] Hadley Cantril: "Identification with Social and Economic Class," *Journal of Abnormal and Social Psychology*, XXXVIII (1943), 74-80.

class or upper class?" The distribution of the replies in two surveys were:

	July, 1945	February, 1946
Upper class	3%	4%
Middle class	43	36
Working class	51	52
Lower class	1	5
Don't know	2	3

When given the opportunity, a substantial proportion of the middle-class identifiers under the earlier question moved over into the working class, a category probably more acceptable psychologically than lower class.[3]

In 1956 the Survey Research Center took another line on the problem by asking: "There's quite a bit of talk these days about different social classes. Most people say they belong either to the middle class or to the working class. Do you ever think of yourself as being in one of these classes?" The replies were 36 per cent, no; 64 per cent, yes.[4] Those who thought of themselves as being in one of these classes were asked: "Which one?" Then: "Would you say that you are about an average (class selected) person or that you are in the upper part of the (class selected)?" Those who had denied thinking of themselves as being in one of these classes were asked: "Well, if you had to make a choice, would you call yourself middle class or working class?" This was followed by the query about average or upper part of the class. The replies to these questions were distributed as follows:

[3] The figures are from Richard Centers: *The Psychology of Social Classes* (Princeton: Princeton University Press; 1949), p. 77. Centers also found that the distribution of class identifications among women was about the same as that among white males.—"Class Consciousness of the American Woman," *International Journal of Opinion and Attitude Research*, V (1949), 399–408. In another study he neatly demonstrated the dependence in a national sample of class distribution on the wording of the question.—"Nominal Variation and Class Identification: The Working and the Laboring Classes," *Journal of Abnormal and Social Psychology*, XLV (1950), 195–215. Centers' four-class question—middle, lower, working, upper—was used by the Survey Research Center in 1952 with comparable results: upper, 2 per cent; middle, 35 per cent; working, 58 per cent; lower, 2 per cent; with the remainder DK or NA. In a UNESCO survey Centers' question was put in nine countries with results showing far more similarity than might be expected. —William Buchanan and Hadley Cantril: *How Nations See Each Other* (Urbana: University of Illinois Press; 1953), p. 13.

[4] The 36 per cent compares with the 27 per cent who said "don't know" in response to a question put by *Fortune* in 1940: "What word would you use to name the class in America you belong to?" In the 1956 SRC survey some variation existed among occupational groups in the tendency to deny that they thought of themselves as being in one of these classes. Of the male respondents, 50 per cent of the farmers rejected the idea of class membership; 44 per cent of the professionals; 31 per cent of the unskilled.

Upper middle class	7%
Average middle class	29
Upper working class	9
Average working class	52
Don't know	3

These results, although doubtless influenced again by the form of the question, closely resemble Centers' findings.[5]

Studies of small areas by intensive means not readily adaptable to use in a national survey turn up other findings inconsistent with the assumption of the existence of clear and universal identifications with social classes. In Minneapolis Neal Gross used an open-ended inquiry designed to permit the respondent to name his class identification without cue from the interviewer. "Middle class" was the most frequently chosen designation; the number of working-class identifications dropped drastically in comparison with the responses to Centers' four-class question; and considerable proportions either claimed not to know what class they were in or placed themselves in classes with a wide vari-

[5] Some of the comments by respondents to the SRC question suggest the tenuous quality of class identification. A Nebraska farm housewife on class: "I suppose it would be working class as that is about all we do." A North Carolina gift shop proprietress when asked if she had to make a choice: "That's a new one to me. I just want to say I'm as good as any of them." An Ohio skilled worker when faced by the choice problem: "I wouldn't say. (Why?) Well, what is the middle class and working class?" A South Carolina housewife: "I think middle class and working class come under the same heading." A Los Angeles housewife: "I can't say. I just wouldn't know." The wife of a New Mexico miner: "I don't quite understand the difference. I guess we work so we must belong to the working class. I don't quite see it." An Idaho lady: "I'm retired but used to be working class." A Pennsylvania steelworker: "When you're in a mill you're workin'." A North Carolina retail grocer had never thought of herself as being of a class: "I think that class talk is just political talk. Here the Republicans are called the rich man's party, and they run a man who came up from just plain people, and the Democrats say they are the little man's party and they run a millionaire." Wirer in California radio factory: "Well I work for a living so I guess I'm in the working class." Retired Ohio worker: (Ever thought of yourself as being in one of these classes?) "Never gave that a thought, missus." The wife of a Kentucky brewery salesman: (Ever thought of self in class?) "I never thought of that." An interviewer noted: "I've had more trouble with R's in regard to this class thing. Where the distinction is, no one seems to know."

The schedule also contained a question whether the respondent's family when he was growing up was working class or middle class. A Connecticut respondent: "Middle class after '29. Upper class before '29." An Iowa farmer: "I've always been just average—no upper class stuff for me or my family." A Texas widow reported that her family had been upper middle: "We didn't have a college education but we tried to keep ourselves with good characters and things like that." The wife of an Ohio skilled worker: "No just average people; don't know if we came in any class." A retired hospital orderly said his father had been middle class: "Upper part. My father owned a saloon." A Texas lady: "We always had plenty but what class I don't know."

ety of names.[6] From extended observation of a small Connecticut community Lenski concluded that the "status system was not structured in the form of a series of discrete social classes whose limits and membership were common knowledge shared by the members of the community." He thought that it might be more accurate to regard variations in status as ranged along a continuum of minor gradations with no sharp lines of division recognized by the community.[7]

What conclusions can be drawn from all these analyses? For perhaps a third of the adult population the sense of class identification must be slight indeed. They at least say they never think of themselves as belonging to a class. A larger number of persons spontaneously identify with the middle class than with other classes.[8] Without the cue of the term "working class" in the question, workers either don't know the name of their class or scatter themselves among many differently named classes and groups. Nevertheless, when asked to choose among class names, a third or more of a national sample identifies with the middle class, and about 60 per cent with the working class. The groupings, as we have seen, depend somewhat on the form of the question and the time of its administration. Though these nebulous sorts of class consciousness do not make a solid foundation for class war, they are not without political significance.[9]

[6] "Social Class Identification in the Urban Community," *American Sociological Review*, XVIII (1953), 398–404.
[7] Gerhard E. Lenski: "American Social Classes: Statistical Strata or Social Groups," *American Journal of Sociology*, LVIII (1952), 139–44. The odds are that the last word has not been said on the nature of class identification in the United States. Survey research encounters serious obstacles in coping with the problem. The disinclination to acknowledge class identification is especially marked among professional persons. The etiquette of class role may require a rejection of upper status. A high proportion of farmers also say they have never thought of themselves as belonging to a class, a response perhaps not unrelated to the realities of rural life and one influential in the national figures, given the farm origins of so many persons. Unskilled workers least frequently reject the notion of class identification. Party identification may for some persons serve as the functional equivalent of class identification. Other persons may have an acute sense of status which is organized in relation to social categories either narrower than broad classes or with other names.
[8] In response to a 1940 *Fortune* survey question: "What word would you use to name the class in America you belong to?" the percentages were: middle, 38.6; working or laboring, 10.6; and the remainder of the responses scattered among a long list of class names—H. Cantril and M. Strunk: *Public Opinion 1935–1946* (Princeton: Princeton University Press; 1951), p. 116.
[9] Another dimension of class outlook was tapped by a UNESCO survey which asked: "Do you feel that you have anything in common with (own nationality, American, for example) people who are not (your own, e.g., middle) class?" The percentages saying they had something in common with their countrymen not of their own class were: Australia, 78; U.S., 77; Britain, 67; Norway, 64; Germany, 64; France, 63; Mexico, 56; Netherlands, 50; Italy, 50—Buchanan and Cantril: op. cit., p. 18.

Class Identification and Opinion. While differences of opinion exist among occupational groups, considerable overlapping of opinion also prevails among them. Why should some blue-collar workers resemble in their opinion clerical workers and some clerical workers adopt the attitudinal hues of businessmen? In part such deviations from the occupational norm are accounted for by class identifications discrepant with objective occupational status. Manual workers who regard themselves as members of the middle class, on the average, differ in their opinions from those manual workers who place themselves in the working class. Richard Centers first demonstrated the existence of these relationships in the population at large. On the basis of measures

---

TABLE 6.10

OCCUPATION AND CLASS IDENTIFICATION IN RELATION TO POSITION ON DOMESTIC
LIBERALISM SCALE [a]

HEAD'S OCCUPATION	RESPONDENT'S CLASS IDENTIFICATION	
	Working	Middle
White-collar	40%	22%
Blue-collar	50	35
Farm operator	41	32

[a] Entries are percentages of each cell ranking high on domestic liberalism scale. The percentage base excludes those in each cell with too few opinions on the component issues to permit placement on the scale. For construction of the scale, see Appendix II.
DATA SOURCE: *Survey Research Center, University of Michigan, 1956.*

---

of conservatism and radicalism built from responses to questions on domestic economic policy, he found that manual workers identifying with the middle class tended to be more conservative than manual workers identifying with the working class. Yet, by his measures, conservatives from among manual workers with a middle-class identification at the time of the study in 1945 were offset to some extent by radicals from business, professional, and other white-collar strata with a working-class identification.[1] Centers' general findings are confirmed by 1956 data presented in Table 6.10. Among both blue-collar and white-collar workers those who identified with the working class ranked, on the average, higher on a scale of domestic liberalism than those who regarded themselves as middle-class. The scale was con-

[1] Richard Centers: *The Psychology of Social Classes* (Princeton: Princeton University Press; 1949), p. 126. See also Heinz Eulau: "Identification with Class and Political Perspective," *Journal of Politics*, XVIII (1956), 232–53; Oscar Glanz: "Class Consciousness and Political Solidarity," *American Sociological Review*, XXIII (1958), 375–83.

structed from responses about propositions relating to the government's responsibility for the maintenance of employment and in the fields of medical care, education, power and housing, and employment and housing for Negroes. The differences shown in the table are probably less than they would have been had the questions been put at a time of economic stress. Probably the misplaced sense of class identification on balance weakens the lower socio-economic levels in the political process. Their adoption of middle-class standards tends to make their

---

TABLE 6.11

CLASS IDENTIFICATION WITH OCCUPATIONAL GROUPS IN RELATION TO DISTRIBUTION ON SCALE MEASURING INTERNATIONALIST ATTITUDES [a]

INTERNATIONALISM
SCALE

	OCCUPATION AND CLASS IDENTIFICATION					
	White-collar		Blue-collar		Farmer	
	Middle	Working	Middle	Working	Middle	Working
High	64%	56%	55%	54%	54%	50%
Medium	29	24	30	27	20	19
Low	7	20	15	19	26	31
	100%	100%	100%	100%	100%	100%
N	307	184	105	418	39	87

[a] For the construction of the scale, see Appendix II. The percentage base in each instance excludes those respondents with too few opinions to permit their placement on the scale.
DATA SOURCE: *Survey Research Center, University of Michigan, 1956.*

---

political mobilization less complete than that of higher occupational levels.

Class identification also has a slight relationship to attitudes toward American involvement in affairs abroad. Within broad occupational groups those with a middle-class identification are less likely to locate themselves on the isolationist end of an internationalism scale than are persons who identify with the working class. The differences, which appear in Table 6.11, are small. They may be attributable to some factor other than class identification. The broad occupational categories in this table are themselves heterogeneous; those white-collar workers who identify with the working class may not be exactly comparable occupationally with white-collar workers who regard themselves as middle class. The white-collar group in the tabulation includes professional, business, and clerical occupations.

Mobility: Upward and Downward. Upward and downward mobility are often accorded considerable importance as determinants of political attitudes. Upward mobility, the supposition is, prevents the development of radical political opinions. Downward mobility, on the other hand, produces attitudes of discontent. The happy consequences of upward mobility receive more sustained attention. Supposedly the prospect of getting ahead, of climbing up the social ladder, powerfully animates Americans. A land of boundless opportunity, the interpretation goes, breeds few frustrated soreheads determined to upset the political system or to improve their lot by political means. Status fluidity in either this generation or the next discourages the development of classes or groups disposed to get theirs in the here-and-now by taking from others.

To determine how mobility affects political attitude, one must first contrive a measure of mobility. The most workable indicator of mobility from generation to generation is comparison of occupations of father and son that takes into account the relative prestige of these occupations.[2] Using such a standard, approximately two thirds of men in nonfarm occupations enjoy about the same status as their fathers did. About one fifth have been upward mobile, while around one-seventh have dropped down the scale.[3] Inability to maintain the position of their fathers is especially marked among the sons of fathers in higher-status occupations.

The supposition is that these upward and downward movements have their correlations with voting behavior, but the evidence is mixed. The most widely propagated view is that the upward mobile, in their newly found prosperity, tend to vote Republican.[4] Other evidence suggests, however, that changes in the sense of party identification occur with about the same frequency in both directions whether mobility is downward or upward.[5] A wisp of evidence points in a direction sug-

[2] This is a crude, but widely used, measure of mobility. On the niceties of the problem of measurement, see Charles F. Westoff, Marvin Bressler, and Philip C. Sagi: "The Concept of Social Mobility: An Empirical Inquiry," *American Sociological Review,* XXV (1960), 375–85. The most comprehensive analysis of mobility is by Seymour M. Lipset and Reinhard Bendix: *Social Mobility in Industrial Society* (Berkeley: University of California Press; 1959).

[3] The exact figures from the 1952 Survey Research Center sample are: upward mobile, 19 per cent; downward, 13 per cent; stationary, 67 per cent. Other surveys—cited in Lipset and Bendix: op. cit., p. 88—produce slightly differing proportions. For a detailed analysis, see Richard Centers: "Occupational Mobility of Urban Occupational Strata," *American Sociological Review,* XIII (1948), 197–203.

[4] For data on this point together with comparisons with other countries, see Lipset and Bendix: op. cit., pp. 66–67.

[5] Campbell, Converse, Miller, and Stokes: op. cit., pp. 455–60.

gested by neither of these views. White-collar men who have been upward mobile (in comparison with their fathers) tend toward the Republican party, while blue-collar upward-mobile men tend toward the
Democratic party.[6] Yet the numbers whose vote could be regarded as
affected by upward mobility is so small as to be of slight significance
for the political system as a whole.

In their views on domestic policy, the mobile and the nonmobile
manifest differences consistent with these voting contrasts. Among
white-collar males who had been upward mobile a slightly smaller
proportion ranked high in 1956 on a domestic liberalism scale than of

---

TABLE 6.12

INTERGENERATIONAL OCCUPATIONAL MOBILITY, AMONG MALES WITHIN BROAD
OCCUPATIONAL CATEGORIES, IN RELATION TO APPROVAL OF HIGH LEVELS OF
DOMESTIC WELFARE ACTIVITY BY GOVERNMENT [a]

RESPONDENT'S
OCCUPATION

	INTERGENERATIONAL MOBILITY		
	Upward	Stationary	Downward
White-collar	23% (145)	27% (64)	32% (50)
Blue-collar	34 (74)	29 (102)	48 (153)

[a] Entries are percentages of those in each cell ranking high on a scale of
domestic liberalism. For construction of the scale, see Appendix II.
Figures in parentheses are the N's on which the percentages rest.
DATA SOURCE: *Survey Research Center, University of Michigan, 1956.*

---

those who had remained stationary. This difference is consistent with
the higher Republicanism in voting of the upward mobile. On the
other hand, the downward mobile tended to become slightly more
liberal than white-collar persons who had remained stationary. These
differences, which appear in Table 6.12, are not large and should be regarded only as suggestive, for the sample numbers on which they rest
do not suffice to assure statistical significance. Upward-mobile blue-
collar workers tend to be more liberal than the stationary members of
the blue-collar group. Downward-mobile blue-collar workers appear
to be markedly more liberal than blue-collar workers of stationary occupational status. This difference accords with the supposition that

[6] These remarks rest on an analysis of the Survey Research Center data on
the vote by men in the 1956 presidential election. Of upward-mobile white-collar
respondents, 32 per cent reported a Democratic vote, in comparison with 47 per
cent of the stationary respondents. Of upward-mobile blue-collar respondents, 55
per cent reported a Democratic vote in comparison with 47 per cent of the stationary respondents.

deprivation produces political radicalism. The numbers affected may not be great enough to influence the course of events, but if for reason of great social or economic change large numbers of persons were unable to maintain the status of their parents, they would provide fertile soil for the sowers of discontent.

The apparent fact that upward mobility has a different consequence for blue-collar persons than for white-collar persons presents something of a puzzle. The conservatism of upward-mobile white-collar persons is not astonishing, for any reader can call to mind an instance of a self-made man who is as hard as nails. The drift toward liberalism of blue-collar workers raises the explanatory problem. Perhaps the common denominator is the tendency of persons who gain a valued status or position to adopt in special degree the perceived norms of their new status or new group connection. Candid clerics comment with impatience on the meticulous dedication to ritual of the convert. Moreover, the upward-mobile blue-collar worker may have some appreciation of the role of public policy in the maintenance of the prerequisites of status, an interpretation that gains plausibility from the fact that the greater liberalism among upward-mobile blue-collar workers shown in Table 6.12 is accounted for entirely by the union members in this cell of the sample.[7]

Another aspect of the relation between mobility and opinion that has aroused considerable attention is the supposition that downward mobility brings with it a dangerous degree of intolerance. In the main this anxiety has been based on extrapolations from clinical studies to the general population. In one study of 150 veterans in Chicago, for example, Bettelheim and Janowitz found that anti-Semitism and anti-Negro attitudes were most highly concentrated among the downward mobile. Those who had risen in position held far more tolerant attitudes, while the stationary group occupied an intermediate position.[8] Tendencies among those in the custody of psychotherapists do not necessarily also apply in the population at large, but one may well be curious whether they do.

The data permit at least a rough check on the incidence within the general population of the relationship between mobility and attitudes of tolerance and intolerance toward minorities. The findings are con-

[7] Of upward-mobile union respondents, 41 per cent ranked high on the liberalism scale; of the stationary group, 27 per cent. Of the nonunion respondents, the comparable figures were 26 and 32. The base N's, though, were small: in the order of the percentages as presented, 39, 59, 35, and 43.

[8] Bruno Bettelheim and Morris Janowitz: "Ethnic Tolerance: A Function of Social and Personal Control," *American Journal of Sociology*, LV (1949–50), 137–45.

tradictory and confusing. One piece of information consists of expressions of agreement and disagreement in a national sample with the proposition: "If Negroes are not getting fair treatment in jobs and housing, the government in Washington should see to it that they do." Disagreement with this proposition could presumably be regarded as an intolerant opinion. In contradiction to the theory, more of the upward than of the downward mobile, in both white-collar and blue-collar groups, took the intolerant position. The differences among the various groups, as may be seen in Table 6.13, are small; but if the data

---

TABLE 6.13

RELATIONSHIP BETWEEN INTERGENERATIONAL MOBILITY, AMONG MALES WITHIN BROAD OCCUPATIONAL CATEGORIES, AND ATTITUDES ON QUESTIONS RELATED TO TOLERANCE-INTOLERANCE

MOBILITY	NEGRO JOBS AND HOUSING [a] (% DISAGREEING)		FIRE COMMUNIST SUSPECTS (% AGREEING)	
	White-collar	Blue-collar	White-collar	Blue-collar
Upward	25%	31%	14%	21%
Stationary	23	29	14	19
Downward	18	19	20	24

[a] For phrasing of the issue propositions, see Appendix I.
DATA SOURCE: *Survey Research Center, University of Michigan, 1956.*

---

establish anything, it is that downward mobility produces a degree of ethnic tolerance on this question.

On another question the expectations derived from the general theory about the effects of upward and downward mobility are fulfilled. Table 6.13 also relates mobility to opinion about the proposition: "The government ought to fire any government worker who is accused of being a communist even though they don't prove it." Presumably agreement with this outrageous proposition could be regarded as an intolerant position. More of the downward mobile than of the upward mobile agreed. It can scarcely be said, though, that the upward mobile really differed from the stationary, so slight is the margin between them in the sample percentages. What these findings establish about the bearing of mobility on intolerance is difficult to say. They at least suggest that the voluminous comments about the horrendous consequences of downward mobility need to be taken with some reserve.[9]

[9] Doubts about the bearing of mobility on prejudice are expressed by Fred B. Silberstein and Melvin Seeman: "Social Mobility and Prejudice," *American Journal of Sociology*, LXIII (1959), 258–64.

Variability of Relation between Class and Opinion. Discussion of the place of class in political processes has been based mainly on static analysis—that is, an inspection of the relation at a particular point in time between political opinion and subjective class identification. Such analysis, as we have seen, adds an element of explanation to that provided by occupation. Thus, manual workers who regard themselves as members of the working class differ in their political outlook from those manual laborers who place themselves in the middle class. When the role of class is examined through time, however, the significance of class identification in the United States is found to vary widely even over relatively brief periods.

Converse has demonstrated the existence of this change in the period 1945–56 in the United States. During this time a marked decline in the degree of association between attitudes on domestic policy and class identification occurred. Persons classified themselves with the middle and working classes over this period in fairly stable proportions, but the polarization of attitudes along lines of class identification diminished. Similarly, the correlation between the direction of the vote and class identification declined. Obviously a factor of considerable importance in an explanation of the changing relevance of class identification for opinion is variation in economic circumstances. Class identification would be expected to be a more important determinant of policy opinions in times of depression than it would be in periods of prosperity. Converse, though, finds that other variables may also have an effect. Preoccupation with foreign policy may reduce the bearing of class on opinion and on voting. The alternatives presented to the electorate by the parties may also have a relevance. If no class-related alternatives are visible to the elector, his sense of class identification may not be brought to bear on his vote.[1]

3 · Stratification, Opinion, and the Industrial System

This analysis of the distribution of opinion among occupational strata permits an additional step toward an understanding of the place of public opinion in the political order and of the nature of the interactions between political elites and mass attitudes. A major finding from all the analyses is that opinions among those occupational groups from which most political leaders, political activists, and political influentials come differ from those of groups lower in the occupational and class

[1] For Converse's analysis, see "The Shifting Role of Class in Political Attitudes and Behavior," in E. Maccoby, T. Newcomb, and E. Hartley: *Readings in Social Psychology*, 3rd ed. (New York: Holt; 1958), pp. 388–99. It also appears in Campbell, Converse, Miller, and Stokes: *op. cit.*, ch. 13.

hierarchies. These differences vary from issue to issue, and, though one never knows precisely the significance of attitudes tapped by measures of opinion, the contrasts in direction of opinion are plain.

On "bread and butter" issues the upper groups show far less frequent concurrence with measures to improve the lot of the working man than do workers themselves. When the issues of domestic economic policy become more abstruse—the benefits less immediate and less readily perceptible—the laboring classes often cannot see their long-run advantage and concur in lesser degree. On such questions they also register uniformly larger proportions of "no opinion" responses. On matters of foreign policy the direction of difference runs toward an isolationism in skilled and unskilled labor and toward a greater willingness to support American involvement in foreign affairs among the professional and business groups. With respect to civil liberties and related matters of noneconomic liberalism, professional and business persons manifest, on the average, a higher degree of tolerance and of dedication to the values of a democratic order than do workers. The conception of the noble worker devoted to the abstract rights of man misses the mark.

These occupational differences of opinion are differences not of black and white but of degree. That cross-occupational consensus prevails on many issues is of the greatest importance for the politics of an industrial order. All shades of opinion occur in every occupational stratum. Workers are not alone in their support of measures to their economic advantage; they have their allies in the professional and business groups. Not all supporters of internationalism are situated in the upper groups; they find associated with themselves large numbers of skilled and unskilled workers and now and then a farmer. On civil liberties and similar matters, those of the upper groups who take the lead find support as well as dissent and indifference among workers. In short, polarization on political issues does not neatly coincide with occupational and class lines. A fairly high degree of cross-occupational and cross-class agreement prevails. This state of affairs as it bears on the "bread and butter" issues may reflect a fairly general satisfaction with the allocation of the rewards of the industrial system. Doubtless effective operation of an industrial society in its productive function requires at least a minimum acceptance of its economic practices—and that acceptance may be paralleled by a degree of cross-occupational agreement on political issues.

These data on the distribution of opinion among occupational strata suggest further elaboration of the earlier proposition that the democratic governing process involves interactions between leadership circles—the political elite—and mass opinion. The contrasts in opinions among occupations throw into stark relief the significance for the nature of a democratic order of the mores, habits, customs, and values of the thin layer of activists, influentials, and leaders in the political system. Leadership elements work within a context of mass opinion and attitude; in the short run that context fixes opportunities for and limitations upon leadership. The values and internal discipline of leadership elements, in turn, govern the manner in which political activists operate within the context of opportunity and limitation fixed by public opinion.

These observations about the role of leadership in its opinion matrix take on a more perceptible significance when the qualities of opinions are remembered. The shades of opinions within occupations that we have identified should be regarded to an extent as latent. Mass opinion finds expression principally through the mechanisms of political leadership. Responses to survey questions delineate, not necessarily a ghostly entity whose likes and dislikes are automatically transmuted into public policy, but a state of mind susceptible to exploitation by political leadership.

The latent opinions open for exploitation suggest the critical role of self-restraint in leadership circles in the maintenance of a viable balance among the elements of the industrial system. The data on the "bread and butter" questions make patent the possibility, under proper conditions, of arousing the discontent of the lesser occupational groups and of directing it against institutions and practices regarded highly by most upper-status persons. That process could be carried to the point of the alienation of such groups from the values of the democratic order. Restraint in such matters is, within limits, not restraint of a mass public but a consequence of the rules of the game among leadership elements. At the opposite margin of opportunity for discretion in leadership circles, the initiation of measures to alleviate tensions of the lesser occupations in the industrial order is not a reflex of mass opinion but a leadership option. Leadership structures insensitive to the dangers of tension borne of excesses in either direction may be disruptive of the political bases for a democratic industrial order.

In the area of international politics the occupational opinion patterns similarly create both temptations and responsibilities for leadership. Those hell-bent for election at any cost may play upon the isolationist and separatist sentiments of great numbers of workers. In the area of civil liberties the animosities of lesser peoples, often against other lesser peoples, can be inflamed. Obviously the workings of the democratic order, and perhaps its survival, depend in some measure upon those customs of the political game that place limits both of degree and of kind upon the appeals made by its leaders. Though the fate of a democratic order may not depend solely upon the behavior of the "better" people, a heavy responsibility rests upon them. Hence, one may understand the basic significance for a political order of the practices and standards that prevail in the recruitment, advancement, rejection, and indoctrination of leadership.

7

INTERRELATIONS

OF OPINION

When the distribution of opinion within the political system is viewed an issue at a time, an important aspect of public opinion is obscured. Opinions on different issues are distributed through the population in relation to each other; important dimensions of the opinion system may be identified by the simultaneous examination of opinion distributions on several issues. In speculation about political systems reflections recur about interrelations among political attitudes. Although political theoreticians seldom employ that phrase, they deal with the question in one guise or another. One line of thought centers on the interrelation of attitudes within an individual. Gilbert and Sullivan were talking about interrelations of attitude when they wrote of little Conservatives and little Liberals. Persons so named supposedly have within themselves an outlook or orientation that organizes their opinions in a characteristic manner toward specific issues as they arise. Though students of ideology become recondite as they conceive bodies of general doctrine to be mechanisms that control individual opinion and behavior, implicit in their analysis is the theme that opinions are organized in accord with some basic attitude pattern that characterizes the whole personality.

Other speculation concerns the consequences for a political order of opinion interrelationships within the society as a whole. Though the simple division of people into "conservatives" and "liberals" describes an aspect of the system as a whole as well as characteristics of individuals, other and more complex problems are associated with the patterning of opinions within society. For example, when the lines of cleavage on many issues coincide, intensity of conflict within the social system will be relatively high. (The division of society into "liberals" and "conservatives," in effect, assumes this type of coincidence of conflict.) The contrary type of situation—one in which lines of cleavage do not coincide—may muffle political conflict. Enemies on the burning issue of today may be allies on the foremost question of tomorrow. Antagonists will, in short, have common interests, and the mixture of antagonism and alliance may induce restraint in conflict.

Apart from such questions that may go to the roots of the nature of a political order, interrelations of opinions within the electorate may bear significantly on the party system. The workings of a dual party system may be profoundly affected by the degree to which cleavages on the many issues of politics do or do not coincide. And when cleavages coincide, the nature of the party battle may be influenced by the intensity with which opinions are held by opposing groups within the public. On the other hand, when popular cleavages do not coincide, party groups within the electorate may encounter the most serious difficulty in the maintenance of sufficient unity for effective action. Within the representative body party groups may be converted into a congeries of factions, no one of which possesses the power to govern. Under such circumstances, the skills of leadership will be taxed to construct new majorities as each new question arises.

All these observations, while plausible, present obdurate problems of empirical verification. The measurement of mass attitudes, the determination of the distribution of particular opinions within a society, and the delineation of their interrelations are tasks formidable enough in themselves. The next step, the estimation of their bearing upon the behavior of governing structures, presents special hazards of inference. Once the data are examined, it may well be concluded either that the stream of theoretical speculation raises the wrong questions or that the empirical reality is far more complex than the questions assume.

1 · Foreign and Domestic Policy: Congruence and Noncongruence of Opinion of Opinion Groups

When major issues divide the people in different ways, it might be expected that the cohesion of party groups within Congress would be weakened. Moreover, unity of the parties within the electorate would be strained, and the maintenance of popular support for an Administration would be complicated. The interrelations of attitudes on foreign and domestic policy are such that the issues in these fields split the population along different lines. Examination of opinions in these areas will permit us to draw some inferences about the significance of patterns of interrelationships among opinions.

Interrelations of Opinions on Foreign Issues and Domestic Welfare Policies. Opinions on domestic welfare policy are commonly regarded as arrayed along a scale from extreme conservatism to extreme liberalism, whereas foreign-policy opinions are usually pictured as distributed along an isolationism-internationalism continuum. Clearly, among legislators conservatism on domestic policy is not invariably associated with isolationism, nor are internationalists always liberal on domestic questions. Congressional cleavages in the two policy realms cross rather than coincide—a fact that has given rise to the observation that we have in reality a four-party system, which divides in the following way:

Internationalist- conservative	Isolationist- conservative
Internationalist- liberal	Isolationist- liberal

A description of congressional groupings as quadripartite does some violence to the realities, for it ignores gradations of attitude among legislators on both foreign-policy and domestic-welfare issues. Yet to the extent that a four-way division is approximated among legislators, a curiosity develops whether similar clusters of opinion combinations in the public underlie the groupings within Congress. Is there within the public a similar four-way split? The descriptive problem is to portray in some comprehensible way the manner in which the distributions of opinion on foreign and domestic policy are related within the population.

An attack on that problem may begin with an examination of the distribution of opinion on these two dimensions at the time of the 1952 presidential campaign. The distributions on the two dimensions took different forms. On external policy the modal opinion was isolationist, at least as measured by responses to the question on how people felt about whether "this country has gone too far in concerning itself with problems in other parts of the world." The largest bloc of persons thought that we had gone foo far; a substantial number thought that we had not gone too far; and only a few answered in a pro-con manner —as may be seen from the left panel of Figure 7.1. It may be doubted that the answers to the question meant that the country was isolationist in any absolute sense. Probably a majority responded favorably to the Republican exploitation in their campaign of the Korean issue; as they saw the situation of the moment, they thought the country had "gone too far." In contrast, on domestic policy a majority supported the prevailing degree of governmental activity in social welfare or fa-

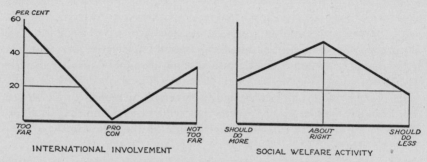

FIGURE 7.1. Opinions on International Involvement and Social Welfare Activity, 1952. DATA SOURCE: Survey Research Center, University of Michigan, 1952. For text of the questions, see Table 7.1. Percentage base includes those with no opinion.

vored even further action. The modal opinion was liberal as measured by responses to the question about whether the government had "done about right, too much, or not enough" in "trying to deal with such problems as unemployment, education, housing, and so on." About half the respondents thought the government had done "about right," as the right panel of Figure 7.1 indicates, while the remainder were about equally divided between those who thought it "should do more" or that it should "do less." [1]

We need only to cross-tabulate the distributions of the responses on these two questions to identify the combinations of opinion within the electorate and to determine their size. The combinations of opinion

[1] The form of the curves in Figure 7.1, it should be explicitly noted, results from the form of the question. The questions do not produce distributions of attitudes along scales. The foreign-policy question yields essentially a yes-no division while the domestic question gives views on what could be called, by generosity, a three-point scale: do less, about right, do more. Other data, however, produce similar results. Analyses of the policy content of open-ended questions put in 1952 show that the modal position within the electorate on foreign policy was pro-Republican and the modal position on domestic policy, pro-Democratic.

supposed to make up the "four-party" system constituted th
ing percentages of the 1952 national sample:

Isolationist-liberal	14%
Internationalist-liberal	9
Isolationist-conservative	12
Internationalist-conservative	5

If those who regarded government policy in the social welfare field as
being "about right" were to be classified as "liberal," a characterization not without basis, the sizes of the blocs of opinion would be:

Isolationist-liberal	41%
Internationalist-liberal	25
Isolationist-conservative	12
Internationalist-conservative	5

These figures should be interpreted strictly in the light of the form of
the questions and of the circumstances of the time. They represent
combinations of opinions expressed at the time of the 1952 campaign
and with respect to the postures of the parties and candidates on the international issues as they then existed. The detailed data from which

TABLE 7.1

RELATIONS BETWEEN OPINION ON INTERNATIONAL INVOLVEMENT AND OPINION
ON GOVERNMENTAL SOCIAL WELFARE ACTIVITY, 1952

SOCIAL WELFARE ACTIVITY [a]	INTERNATIONAL INVOLVEMENT [b]				
	Too far	Pro-con	Not too far	DK	Total
Should do more	14% [c]	* [d]	9%	2%	25%
About right	27	1	16	5	49
Should do less	12	*	5	1	18
DK	3	*	2	3	8
Total	56%	1%	32%	11%	100%

[a] "Some people think the national government should do more in trying
to deal with such problems as unemployment, education, housing, and
so on. Others think the government is already doing too much. On the
whole, would you say that what the government has done has been
about right, too much, or not enough?"
[b] "Some people think that since the end of the last world war this country has gone too far in concerning itself with problems in other parts
of the world. How do you feel about this?"
[c] The entries are percentages of the total sample. N, 1614.
[d] Asterisk denotes less than ½ of 1 per cent.
DATA SOURCE: *Survey Research Center, University of Michigan, 1952.*

ιe above figures were drawn appear in Table 7.1, the arrangement of
vhich requires attentive study for comprehension.[2]

Although data for 1956 precisely comparable to those for 1952 are
not available, by 1956 a change had occurred in the distribution of attitudes toward foreign involvement. The liquidation of the Korean incident altered the situation which people were appraising, and the
Eisenhower Administration brought many Republicans to the support of a higher degree of participation in international affairs.[3]
Nevertheless, other measures made it clear that foreign-policy issues
and domestic issues in 1956 still divided the people along different lines.

TABLE 7.2

RELATION OF POSITION ON DOMESTIC LIBERALISM SCALE TO POSITION ON INTER-
NATIONALISM SCALE, 1956 [a]

INTERNATIONALISM	LIBERALISM		
	Low	Medium	High
High	50%	59%	58%
Medium	32	28	21
Low	18	13	21
	100%	100%	100%
N	226	598	491

[a] For the construction and content of the scales, see Appendix II.
DATA SOURCE: *Survey Research Center, University of Michigan, 1956.*

In 1956 a national sample was rated along a scale of internationalism—
or willingness to tolerate foreign involvement—and a scale of domestic liberalism. Those who ranked high on the liberalism scale were almost as likely to be high on the internationalism scale as were those
who placed at the conservative end of the liberalism scale (see Table 7.2). The lines of cleavage in the two policy areas did not coincide.

Foreign Policy and Fiscal Policy. Interrelations of opinion on foreign
and domestic policies create problems in the contrivance of a program
to command majority support. A domestic action may repel those

[2] Table 7.1 and many of the other tables in this chapter do not show the relationship between variables as do most of the tables in this book, but rather the
proportions of the total sample holding specified combinations of opinions.

[3] In 1954 the proportion of persons taking the position that the United States
had gone "too far" in concerning itself with problems in other parts of the world
was considerably smaller than in 1952, 41 per cent against 55 per cent. See Angus
Campbell and Homer C. Cooper: *Group Differences in Attitudes and Votes* (Ann
Arbor: Survey Research Center; 1956), p. 141.

whose support is needed in the foreign field, and action abroad may outrage those whose disposition might be to support policy at home. Another dimension of this conflict and congruence occurs in the relation between opinions on foreign issues and levels of taxation. Opinion in support of involvement abroad may be worthless unless it is accompanied by a willingness to pay the price.

Odd kinds of noncongruence exist between opinions on taxation and on foreign policy. Judgments of a national sample on taxation were obtained in 1956 by the ascertainment of agreement and disagreement with the proposition: "The government ought to cut taxes even if it means putting off some important things that need to be done." Reaction to the proposition was by no means a simple-minded reflex complaint against taxation: 45 per cent of the sample disagreed with the proposition; only 24 per cent agreed; the remainder either thought it would depend or expressed no opinion. No doubt the question had different meanings for different people, but it also probably isolated a bloc of people with a special kind of concern about taxation.

When responses to the tax question are tabulated against foreign-aid questions, some notion of the nature and size of blocs of opinion supportive of foreign involvement emerges. About one fifth of the total sample supported aid to "poorer countries" even though "they can't pay for it" and simultaneously vowed that taxes ought not to be cut at the expense of "important things that need to be done." Another technically consistent bloc, about one twelfth of the sample, opposed for-

---

TABLE 7.3

COMBINATIONS OF OPINION ON FOREIGN ECONOMIC AID AND ON CUTTING TAXES

CUTTING TAXES [a]		FOREIGN AID [b]			
	Pro	Depends	Con	DK	Total
Pro	11%	4%	8%	3%	26%
Depends	4	3	3	1	11
Con	22	8	11	4	45
DK	5	1	4	8	18
Total	42%	16%	26%	16%	100%

[a] "The government ought to cut taxes even if it means putting off some important things that need to be done."
[b] "The United States should give economic help to the poorer countries of the world even if they can't pay for it."
[c] Entries are percentages of the total sample holding the indicated combinations of opinion. N, 1764.
DATA SOURCE: *Survey Research Center, University of Michigan, 1956.*

eign aid and favored tax cuts. The odds are that the one tenth favoring both foreign aid and tax cuts were not steadfast supporters of foreign aid. The details of these relations appear in Table 7.3.

The relationships may be put in another form. Consider the proportions of persons supporting certain types of foreign involvement who also support tax cuts "even if it means putting off some important things that need to be done." From one fourth to one third of the supporters of foreign involvement as measured by a series of questions also subscribed to the view that taxes ought to be cut "even if it means putting off some important things." For the details, see Table 7.4.

TABLE 7.4

RELATION OF SUPPORT FOR FOREIGN INVOLVEMENT TO OPINIONS ON CUTTING TAXES [a]

CUTTING TAXES	PRO FOREIGN AID	PRO ACT TOUGH	CON STAY HOME
Pro	26%	30%	21%
Depends	10	11	12
Con	52	46	59
No opinion; DK	12	13	8
	100%	100%	100%
N	756	1,095	998

[a] For the wording of the issue propositions, see Appendix I.
DATA SOURCE: *Survey Research Center, University of Michigan, 1956.*

One aspect of the relations between opinions on domestic and foreign policies that these tabulations reveal deserves emphasis. A sizeable bloc of opinion consists of persons who are chary of international involvement, strongly supportive of domestic welfare policies, and hopeful of tax cuts. While this bloc was exceeded in size in 1956 by the cluster of supporters of foreign involvement who recognized that the bill would have to be paid, the relations between the opinions suggest that abrupt changes in domestic economic conditions might quickly increase the strength of the isolationist sector as demands for domestic welfare legislation and tax relief assumed primacy. Warren Miller has analyzed this problem by the use of indicators of attitude different from those employed in the preceding pages. He found that "economic confidence is associated with such general policy directives as: 'The United States should go more than half way in being friendly with other nations,' as well as with issues of economic and military aid." [4] He

[4] Warren E. Miller: "Socio-Economic Analysis of Political Behavior," *Midwest Journal of Political Science*, II (1958), pp. 239-55.

measured economic confidence by responses to inquiries about the prospect for "good times financially, or bad times" during the next twelve months. Those pessimistic about the outlook tended to adopt foreign-policy attitudes of withdrawal. Miller opines that "the base of popular sentiment on which our national foreign policy rests depends" to some degree on the health of the national economy. A sharp downswing in business conditions perhaps "would not only set limits on what the nation's leaders felt could be expended on foreign policy, it would also set limits—and perhaps less well rationalized limits—on what the electorate would condone in the way of internationalist foreign policy activity." [5]

These lines of speculation find illustration, if not proof, in past episodes of American politics. The most obvious connections between domestic conditions and foreign-policy actions occur in the tariff area. Attitude patterns most congenial to the development of autarchy may be associated with domestic economic distress. The triumph of the doctrine of protectionism in the election of 1896 may have rested in a measure on the depression of 1893. The Smoot-Hawley tariff, enacted at the outset of the Great Depression, encountered no mass opposition, only the criticism of the experts. The early part of the Roosevelt Administration was marked more by economic nationalism than by internationalism. Even in the 1950's the sensitivity of people of scattered localities to foreign competition made itself felt in policy actions. Similarly, criticisms of foreign-aid programs by the "average man" often rest on a belief that we should first take care of our own.[6]

It does not follow that domestic economic stress generates a disciplined bloc of opinion that directs its anxieties against the foreigner. Rather, the germination of the type of opinion we have described cre-

---

[5] Ibid., p. 253.

[6] Side comments recorded by interviewers on the questions about economic aid in the 1956 SRC survey indicate the connection of domestic policy and foreign aid in the minds of many people. A Detroit construction worker: "We have a lot of people in Detroit living out of garbage pails and down South its a disgrace the way people have to live. Why do we have to keep sending money over there?" A New York maid: "We have plenty of poor in the United States." An Iowa garage mechanic: "More at home to be helped." A Boston housewife: "Should see that people here are taken care of first." A Mississippi farmer: "Think we need to take care of our own country first." A Detroit housewife: "We should take care of our own here first; there's an awful lot that need it. There are a lot of people not working who need help." Some respondents did not connect domestic and foreign policy but simply opposed generosity. A North Carolina carpenter: "I don't think that we should give them nothing."

ates either opportunity or obstacles for political leadership. A political leadership dedicated to an isolationist position can exploit an undercurrent of anxiety about domestic conditions and thereby gain support for its policies. On the other hand, a political leadership dedicated to foreign trade and foreign involvement faces exceptionally difficult problems of political management when opinions develop that combine domestic anxiety with suspicion of the alien world. Those problems were surmounted by the Roosevelt Administration when it inaugurated the reciprocal-trade program. That success, which was only limited and tentative, was accomplished against a background of positive activity in the field of domestic welfare and by adroit political management.[7]

Consequences of Patterns in Interrelation of Foreign and Domestic Policy. These prosaic tables, indicative of the fact that foreign and domestic issues cut the population in different ways, point to characteristics of the structure of opinion important to the American political system. A basic consequence of the crisscrossing of the electorate by the two kinds of issues concerns the nature of the party system. Given the variety of noncongruent groups produced by these issue cleavages, two parties each consisting of persons like-minded on all issues cannot be constructed. To the extent that these combinations of opinion are projected into the representative system, deference to public opinion can prevail only if legislative groups are fluid.[8] The ruling coalition in Congress must vary in its composition from issue to issue. The maneuvers persisting over two decades to maintain support of foreign policy by the construction of a wavering bipartisan coalition amply illustrate the proposition.

Another major consequence attendant upon the crisscrossing of lines of division upon foreign and domestic policy is the serious problem of tying together the management of the domestic economy and the conduct of foreign policy. The data suggest that the generation of support for an adequate American foreign policy may depend upon the maintenance of a relatively high level of domestic prosperity. As the number of persons pinched economically increases, so also does the

[7] The change in policy was probably facilitated by emphasis on the term "reciprocal trade program" rather than on the tariff. Large numbers of Roosevelt supporters, if the contemporary polls are to be believed, never heard of the reciprocal trade program.

[8] Doubtless considerable variation prevails in the extent to which particular opinion patterns are projected into the representative apparatus. For example, the chances are that in the South political participation among those of isolationist sentiment is extremely low.

number disposed toward withdrawal into our national shell. This is not to say that the poor and distressed rise up in isolationist anger, but only that when such people feel threatened, political leaders, with their own axes to grind, can stir them against involvement abroad. It may be that the modern welfare state has modified, if not repealed, the ancient adage of politics that foreign adventures may be used to blot up domestic discontent. As the state gains both credit and responsibility for the maintenance of economic well-being, discontent with affairs at home may create opinions hostile toward foreign involvement at the cost of domestic welfare.

2 · Interrelations of Opinions on Domestic Policies

Noncongruence between distributions of opinion on foreign and domestic policy creates vexing problems in the management of the political system. Within the domestic policy realm, too, people do not invariably divide along the same line on all issues. Hence a multiplicity of noncongruent cleavages in domestic affairs contributes toward results similar to those produced by the crisscrossing of lines of disagreement on foreign and domestic policy. The foundation of opinion patterns on domestic matters affects more significantly the character of the political system, for the basic structure of American politics rests on domestic issues. Foreign-policy cleavages are only superimposed on that structure.

The Liberal-Conservative Continuum. Division of people into liberal and conservative categories is a great convenience in the description of political opinions. It is also misleading, for people do not divide into two camps, with members of one group in agreement on one side of all domestic economic issues and united to oppose the other group united within itself in opposition on the same issues. If such were the reality, our politics would probably be far different, as well as much more easily described. Instead, the liberal-conservative cleavage divides the population along different lines, depending on the matter at issue. The difference between liberal and conservative is one not of black and white but of degree. At the conservative end of the scale are those who may be agreed in support of all or most measures with a "conservative" tendency, while at the opposite end are those united in support of all or most liberal causes. Between the extremes are those with mixed opinions; they take, in varying combinations, the conservative view on some measures and the liberal on others. In a symmetrical distribution persons at the center of the scale would be half-liberal and half-conservative in their outlooks on a set of issues. In short, the division of the population is peculiar for each liberal-conservative issue.

These observations can be better understood by reference to the scheme set out in Table 7.5. At the liberal end of the scale in the table persons A and B record "yeas" on all issues. At the conservative end, H and I uniformly register "nays." The persons between have varying degrees of agreement and disagreement with those at the two ex-

---

TABLE 7.5

MODEL TO ILLUSTRATE DISTRIBUTION OF PERSONS ALONG LIBERAL-CONSERVATIVE SCALE

PERSONS	ISSUES AND POSITIONS OF PERSONS ON THEM (Y = YEA; N = NAY)	
	1 2 3 4 5 6	
A	Y Y Y Y Y Y	Most Liberal
B	Y Y Y Y Y Y	
C	Y Y Y Y Y N	
D	Y Y Y Y N N	
E	Y Y Y N N N	
F	Y Y N N N N	
G	Y N N N N N	
H	N N N N N N	
I	N N N N N N	Most Conservative

---

tremes. At the center person E is conservative on half the issues and liberal on the other half. The distribution in the table has a property that ought to be especially noted. A program advocating Issues 1, 2, and 3 would command the support of all persons from A through E. A program of opposition to issues 4, 5, and 6 would enlist the support of persons E through I. When responses to a series of questions or about a series of propositions fall in the pattern of the table, they are said to form a Guttman scale, or to be scalable.

On some sets of issues, opinions in the public as a whole approximate the pattern of Table 7.5. Of the questions in the 1956 SRC election survey, those on aid to education, fairness to Negroes in housing and jobs, job guarantee, medical care, and power and housing yielded such a scale. The distributions of those with opinions on these issues are shown in Figure 7.2. Aid to education drew the heaviest support, while government intervention in electric power and housing attracted the least support. Those who favored public activity in housing and electric power usually also supported the liberal position on the other issues. On the other hand, aid to education drew many supporters who were indisposed to adopt the liberal position on the other issues. If finer measures were available, we could identify at one end of the scale the red-hot New Dealer who subscribes to all the tenets of the liberal faith, and at the other end would be isolated the crusty conservative who applies a sturdy individualistic doctrine to all questions. Somewhere in between would be located the "yes, but" liberals and the weak-kneed conservatives. The data of Figure 7.2 supplement the ear-

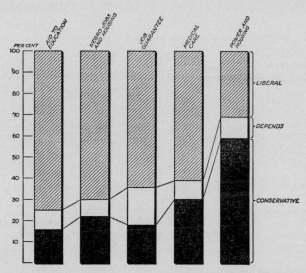

FIGURE 7.2. Distribution of Opinion on Scalable Welfare Questions. DATA SOURCE: Survey Research Center, University of Michigan, 1956. For wording of questions, see Appendix I.

lier observations about the nature of the opinion substructure of the American party system. In the light of these data, the kaleidoscopic character of the groupings that make up congressional majorities becomes comprehensible; that is, if one assumes that representatives to some degree mirror public opinion in their voting.

Domestic Welfare Policy and Fiscal Policy. Although each of the scaled issues just described cuts the population at a separate point, a pattern of order in cleavage prevailed. Other issues, nonscalable, crisscross the population and divide it perhaps with reason but with no rhyme. One such issue that does not fit into the scale is that of taxation. As in the realm of international policy, in domestic policy a balance has to be struck between the demand for public services and the propensity to resist payment of taxes. Those who advocate the enlargement of public services do not invariably support a correlative tax policy.

The odd combinations of opinion that develop about fiscal policy and welfare legislation find illustration in the relations between attitudes on the question of the government's role in assuring that those who want to work can find a job and on the proposition that taxes should be cut at the cost of "things that ought to be done." The various combinations of opinion on these two questions are shown as proportions of a 1956 sample in Table 7.6. Almost one fifth of the total sample (18

TABLE 7.6

COMBINATIONS OF OPINION ON JOB GUARANTEE AND ON CUTTING TAXES [a]

CUTTING TAXES   JOB GUARANTEE

	Pro	Depends	Con	DK	Total
Pro	18%	2%	5%	1%	26%
Depends	6	1	3	1	11
Con	21	4	17	3	45
DK	10	1	2	5	18
	55%	8%	27%	10%	100%

[a] For wording of the issue questions, see Appendix I.
[b] Entries are percentages of the total sample. N, 1764.
DATA SOURCE: *Survey Research Center, University of Michigan, 1956.*

per cent) supported the idea that the government ought to see that those willing to work "can find a job" and adhered also to the notion that taxes ought to be cut. By contrast, another fifth of the sample (21 per cent) maintained a consistent position on both issues, a proportion of approximately the same size as that of the comparably consistent supporters of foreign aid. It may be that only about one fifth of the population can be relied upon to give a consistently sensible and firm support to interrelated policies of the kinds described.

Another tack on the interrelations of opinions on taxes and welfare policy may be taken by an examination of the views on the tax question of two groups: those who support and those who oppose welfare policy. The data appear for a series of policy propositions in Table 7.7. Obviously larger proportions of the pro-welfare than of the anti-welfare individuals concur in the proposition to cut taxes at the cost of important services. Doubtless at the two ends of the tax scale different views prevail on what public services are important. Nevertheless, when a third or so of those who support, for example, federal aid for school construction also feel that taxes ought to be cut at the cost of

TABLE 7.7

RELATION OF OPINION ON WELFARE MEASURES TO OPINION ON CUTTING TAXES [a]

TAX CUTTING   OPINION ON WELFARE MEASURES

	Job Guarantee		School Aid		Medical Care	
	Pro	Con	Pro	Con	Pro	Con
Pro	32%	20%	29%	21%	32%	20%
Depends	11	11	11	12	11	10
Con	38	62	43	59	38	65
No opinion; DK	19	7	17	8	19	5
	100%	100%	100%	100%	100%	100%
N	996	471	1185	259	949	458

[a] For wording of the issue questions, see Appendix I.
DATA SOURCE: *Survey Research Center, University of Michigan, 1956.*

important services, doubt may be entertained about the solidity of the support for aid to education.

If the data are arranged in still another way, it appears that the tax-cut question must isolate a necessitous group of people as well as an odd opinion combination. Let us focus attention on those persons who support the tax-cut proposition and ascertain their views on welfare issues. The persons supporting the tax-cut proposition consist in large measure, as may be seen from Table 7.8, of persons favorably disposed toward welfare measures. Almost one fifth of the electorate falls within this category of persons who commit themselves to self-defeat.[9]

TABLE 7.8

OPINIONS ON WELFARE POLICIES OF PERSONS WHO SUPPORT A TAX CUT EVEN IF IT MEANS PUTTING OFF SOME IMPORTANT THINGS THAT NEED TO BE DONE

OPINION ON

WELFARE PROPOSITION	SCHOOL AID	JOB GUARANTEE	MEDICAL CARE
Pro	76%	70%	67%
Depends	7	5	6
Con	12	21	20
DK; no opinion	5	4	7
	100%	100%	100%
N	453	453	453

DATA SOURCE: *Survey Research Center, University of Michigan, 1956.*

[9] In a study of Detroit, Janowitz finds that "the lower social strata and the lesser status groups demand an extension of the scope of government welfare services and yet simultaneously feel that the burdens imposed by government are not

Yet from their standpoint their position is comprehensible. A simple calculus of self-interest makes simultaneous support of tax reduction and expansion of welfare activities entirely consistent for them. For the system as a whole, however, this type of opinion combination is irrational and creates problems in program-making. The freedom of action for government created by a permissive consensus on a welfare measure may be constricted by opinion on taxation. The existence of a cluster of persons holding this combination of opinions makes it possible for political leadership to befuddle a considerable bloc of people.

The substantial bloc of persons consisting of opponents of social welfare measures who also take the firm position that taxes should not be reduced at the cost of "important things that need to be done" attracts attention. Those persons may be attached to a restricted view of the proper scope of governmental functions, but they place a higher value on public services of which they approve than they do upon a tax cut. These views, of course, may be consistent for the individuals who hold them; they also make sense in terms of the requirements of the political system as a whole. If the weights of blocs of opinion could be nicely reckoned, it probably would turn out that those composed of opinions consistent with the needs of the political system as a whole carry a weight in the political process disproportionate to their numbers.

These interrelations of opinion suggest melancholy thoughts about the practical politics of the interaction of tax policy and substantive policy. Taxation to finance welfare programs meets opposition among those who favor welfare programs even more frequently than among those who oppose them. Progressive taxation is offered as the solution, but it meets opposition from persons who oppose both welfare programs and higher taxation of themselves, a combination of motives that increases intensity of feeling and probably exertions in the political process as well. The balance of forces drives policymakers back toward concealed and indirect taxation, which may be regressive in its incidence. Such an approach may have strategic advantage in that it may be safely assumed that most of those persons who both take the simple-minded position on taxes and support expansion of welfare activities have no impressive comprehension of the theory of the incidence of taxation.

---

worth the services rendered." Further, "negative and hostile feelings" about the worth of government "were concentrated at the bottom of the social pyramid, where simultaneously the demands for more government administration predominate."—Morris Janowitz *et al.: Public Administration and the Public,* pp. 40, 105.

Other Examples of Noncongruent Opinion Groupings. The criss-crossings of opinion cleavages that involve questions of taxation and of expenditure make a comparatively simple pattern; the same people simultaneously want increased expenditures and reduced taxes. If it were feasible to sample opinions on all issues and to construct some representation of their combinations within clusters of individuals in the society as a whole, we should have an incredibly complex picture of many kinds of opinion combinations that occur as different cleavages cut through the society in different planes. That task certainly cannot be essayed with the data at hand, but a few more examples may be set out to give some inkling of the nature of what is a complex reality.

In the field of general economic policy we have data on opinions on two related propositions: the proposition that government ought to see to it that big business corporations do not have much influence on the way government is run and the proposition that the government ought to see to it that everybody who wants to work can find a job. A priori, given the background of American political debate, we might expect that these questions would cut through the population in about the same way. One of the bugaboos of American politics has long been the big business corporation. It might be supposed that those who believe that the government ought to see to it that everybody who "wants to work can find a job" would join in the cry to restrain the influence of big business. In fact, those who opposed government action

TABLE 7.9

COMBINATIONS OF OPINION ON RESTRAINING POLITICAL INFLUENCE OF BIG BUSINESS
AND OF OPINION ON JOB GUARANTEE

JOB GUARANTEE [a]	RESTRAIN BIG BUSINESS INFLUENCE [b]				
	Pro	Depends	Con	DK	Total
Pro	31%	3%	8%	14%	56%
Depends	4	*	1	2	7
Con	14	2	7	4	27
DK	2	*	1	7	10
Total	51%	5%	17%	27%	100%

[a] "The government in Washington ought to see to it that everybody who wants to work can find a job."
[b] "The government ought to see to it that big business corporations don't have much say about how the government is run."
DATA SOURCE: *Survey Research Center, University of Michigan, 1956.*

to assure jobs favored restraint on big business influence in about the same degree as did the pro-job-guarantee group (52 per cent against 56 per cent). Views on restraint of business were, as Table 7.9 shows, quite independent of views on the government job-guarantee question.

The medical-care and school-integration questions create another pair of noncongruent opinion cleavages within the population. Orthodox liberals advocate both medical care and school integration, but these combinations of opinion do not uniformly occur in the general population. The manner in which the cleavages fall on these issues illustrates the capacity of politics to make strange bedfellows. In the South well over half the supporters of government action in the field of medical care oppose federal intervention in school segregation. In the North the relationship was reversed; half of the supporters of medical care favored federal interposition in the problem of school segregation. Many southerners and northerners who are allied on the medical-care question are at odds on the integration question. Similarly, many

TABLE 7.10

COMBINATIONS OF OPINION ON MEDICAL CARE AND SCHOOL INTEGRATION, NORTH AND SOUTH

SCHOOL INTEGRATION	MEDICAL CARE [a]				
	Pro	Depends	Con	DK	Total
			North		
Pro [b]	25% [c]	4%	11%	4%	44%
Depends	3	1	1	1	6
Con	18	3	13	3	37
DK	5	1	2	5	13
	51%	9%	27%	13%	100%
			South		
Pro	17	2	6	2	27
Depends	4	1	1	1	7
Con	35	5	14	4	58
DK	5	*	*	3	8
	61%	8%	21%	10%	100%

[a] "The government ought to help people get doctors and hospital care at low cost."

[b] That is, those who disagreed with the proposition: "The government in Washington should stay out of the question of whether white and colored children go to the same school."

[c] Entries are percentages of the sample holding the specified combinations of opinion.

DATA SOURCE: *Survey Research Center, University of Michigan, 1956.*

persons allied on the integration issue are at odds on the medical-care question. The relative sizes of the various opinion combinations on the two questions in the North and in the South are shown in Table 7.10.

A further illustration of the difficulties of drawing the line between conservatives and liberals comes from an examination of the relationship between position on a scale of domestic liberalism and views on the proposition that the government "ought to fire any government worker who is accused of being a communist even though they don't prove it." The striking relationship, shown in Table 7.11, is that the

---

TABLE 7.11

RELATION OF POSITION ON DOMESTIC ISSUE SCALE TO OPINIONS ON FIRING COMMUNIST SUSPECTS

FIRE COMMUNIST SUSPECTS [a]	LIBERALISM			
	Low	Medium	High	Unscaled [b]
Agree	18%	20%	25%	15%
Depends	8	8	6	7
Disagree	70	64	56	32
No opinion	4	8	13	46
	100%	100%	100%	100%
N	241	660	578	282

[a] "The government ought to fire any government worker who is accused of being a communist even though they don't prove it."
[b] Respondents with too few opinions to permit placement on scale. For the construction of the scale, see Appendix II.
DATA SOURCE: *Survey Research Center, University of Michigan, 1956.*

---

most conservative group, as measured by the liberalism scale, consists largely (70 per cent) of persons who disagreed with the proposition to fire communist suspects. Although well over a majority of those most liberal on welfare measures took the same position, they were far less solid in their position than were the economic conservatives.

Inferentially, these combinations of opinion and crisscrossing of cleavages throw some light on the old supposition that a man's political opinions are but an expression of some broad attitude or of some personality pattern. Studies of limited and highly indoctrinated populations, such as college undergraduates, once led to the conclusion that, since opinions on one specific issue permitted the prediction of opinions on other specific issues, a general or basic attitude governed these responses on individual issues. When the general population is sampled, that inference becomes less tenable. Or if the view is tenable, it is so only on the supposition that within the population there is an enormous variety of individual basic attitudes to produce the various combinations of opinions that exist on specific issues. Rather than to seek the explanation of issue opinions in some basic attitude pattern, it is as sensible to regard individual opinions on specific issues as the product of rationality, immediate self-interest, or other such factors.[1] Such generality or consistency of attitude as prevails may come more from indoctrination by a political party or by other groups with programs than from any characteristic response by individuals to a range of questions.

3 · Escapes from Conflict

Our data convey a dim and overly simple conception of the variety of clusters of opinion that exist within the population, but they suffice to identify several types of opinion combinations. An opinion combination may be technically consistent—that is, made up of opinions supportive of mutually dependent policy; for example, those persons who believe that the "government in Washington" should see to it that everybody has a job and who also take a negative position on tax cuts hold technically consistent opinions. On the other hand, opinion combinations may be technically inconsistent in that contradictory positions are held on operationally related questions. From another viewpoint, an opinion combination may be consistent in partisan terms in that on two or more issues a person holds positions that appear to parallel the leadership line of one party. Or an opinion combination may be inconsistent in partisan terms; for example, those persons who thought in 1952 that the government had "gone too far" in involvement in world affairs but not "far enough" in social-welfare legislation were certain, if they voted, to vote against some of their beliefs, but persons with opinions consistently organized in partisan terms would not have faced the same dilemma.

Escapes, both for the individual and for the system as a whole, mitigate the consequences of conflicts created by noncongruence of opinion groupings. For the individual in the voting situation the rela-

[1] See G. W. Allport: "The Composition of Political Attitudes," *American Journal of Sociology*, XXXV (1929), 220-38; Ross Stagner: "Correlational Analysis of Nationalistic Opinions," *Journal of Social Psychology*, XII (1940), 197-212. The skeptical remarks about the controlling effects of basic attitudes should not be regarded as conflicting with the psychological finding that individuals tend to organize their opinions in a way to promote psychological comfort or to avoid internal conflict. The argument, rather, is that people often accommodate themselves handily to opinion combinations with which the politically sophisticated observer might find it difficult to live.

tive salience of issues may provide an escape from conflict or may, in fact, make what appears to be a conflict no conflict at all. To appreciate this possibility the nature of the data on which the preceding analyses rest must be kept in mind. Interviewers ask for judgments on questions about which the respondent may or may not have thought much one way or another. A person may have said that he strongly believed that the government ought to do more in the field of welfare, housing, etc., but foremost in his mind may have been an anxiety about when the Korean War would be brought to an end.[2] Issues of foreign policy may have been more salient to him than domestic issues, and for that individual the conflict would have been nonexistent. Perhaps he proceeded, insensible of internal conflict, to vote against himself on domestic matters, as doubtless several million persons did in 1952. Or salience may not be between issues but between issues and judgments of candidates or concern about the quality and tenor of government management.

An indication of how the relative salience of issues works in the determination of the vote is provided by analyses of responses in 1956 to open-ended questions on the parties and on the presidential candidates. In the course of their ruminations about the merits and demerits of the political parties and about the candidates, persons made references to foreign and domestic issues. From the number of references in these two policy areas, persons could be classified roughly according to whether foreign or domestic matters were salient for them. As the categorization proceeded, it became necessary to create pigeonholes for those with apparently equal attention on the two areas, as well as for those whose observations were devoid of policy content. The national sample divided in the following way: [3]

Foreign salience	16%
Domestic salience	47
Equal attention	8
No issue content	29

[2] A notion of the way issues change in salience comes from the question occasionally asked by the AIPO: "What do you think is the most important problem facing this country today?" Responses just before and after the Little Rock episode were as follows:

	Sept., 1957	Nov., 1957
Keeping the peace	34%	26%
High cost of living	22	12
Racial problems	10	29

[3] The breakdown by type of issue salience in 1952 was almost precisely the same as in 1956: foreign, 17 per cent; domestic, 54 per cent; equal, 10 per cent; no issue content, 19.

How persons in these several categories voted clearly indicated the bearing of salience on the individual voting decision. Over three fourths of those persons for whom foreign issues were salient voted Republican. Those for whom domestic concerns were more central gave Eisenhower a bare majority. Those who gave equal attention to the two fields also returned a heavy Republican majority. Given the fact that domestic issues were salient for most of the electorate, those who gave equal attention to domestic and foreign affairs had a relatively heavy focus of attention on external matters.[4]

Other investigators have identified the same phenomenon in other ways. Apart from relative salience, voters may have quite deliberate and conscious judgments about the relative importance of policy areas in which they are in attitudinal conflict in partisan terms. Berelson found, for example, that in Elmira those voters who were domestic liberals but inclined toward isolationism in foreign affairs tended to vote in the direction indicated by the relative importance they attached to domestic and foreign issues.[5] In other situations voters seem quite unaware that they are cross-pressured.[6] Some individuals work themselves out of the conflict situation by what the psychologists denominate a "distortion of perception"; that is, they see their candidate or their party as being in agreement with themselves even though informed observers may have contrary perceptions of the relationship.

To be differentiated from those actions that permit the individual to escape from conflict are those adjustments by which the political system as a whole adapts itself to the circumstances created by great groupings holding noncongruent attitudes. For example, governmental action may satisfy a majority on one issue and on a second issue go against the majority, which may be composed in part of some of those who make up the majority on the first issue. The broad record of the Eisenhower Administration provides a classic case of the simultaneous triumph and defeat of noncongruent majorities. Its foreign-policy performance brought majority approval in 1956, while its record

[4] The Republican percentages of the 1956 presidential vote according to the types of issue salience listed in the text were: foreign, 78; domestic, 52; equal attention, 74; no issue content, 57. From these percentages, it is clear that factors other than issue salience accounted for most of the variance in the vote. It should also be said that the measure of salience, contrived *ad hoc* from data collected for other purposes, may have a character of circularity. Salience, as measured, may reflect in part a tendency of people to talk about those policy matters that best support their voting decisions.

[5] Bernard Berelson *et al.: Voting* (Chicago: University of Chicago Press; 1954), p. 200. For a related finding, see Philip K. Hastings: "The Independent Voter in 1952: A Study of Pittsfield, Massachusetts," *American Political Science Review*, XLVII (1953), 805–10.

[6] See Martin Kriesberg: "Cross-Pressures and Attitudes," *Public Opinion Quarterly*, XIII (1949), pp. 5–16.

on domestic policy as a whole evidently earned disapproval. Our governmental structure conveniently permitted the simultaneous expression of both phases of this electoral schizophrenia when in 1956 Eisenhower won re-election as the Democrats carried Congress. But public opinion is not self-executing, and in the determination of which of two noncongruent majorities is to prevail American constitutional arrangements permit the Executive to exercise wide discretion. Even the most friendly observer would not claim that the Eisenhower Administration was characterized by imaginative, venturesome, and energetic initiation of domestic policy. It made its bows to opinion majorities on domestic questions by mild proposals, most of which failed through the weakness of White House legislative leadership.[7] When Congress developed within itself sufficient cohesion to initiate controversial domestic measures, it met presidential veto.

In another fashion, the political system as a whole handles the divergencies of objective manifest in inconsistent opinion groupings by taking some account of the relative weight of opinion clusters. It seems plain that some types of opinion are accorded less deference than others, even though the numbers of their holders in the population may be the same. That this is true there can be no doubt. Whether its truth can be satisfactorily established is another matter. Some of the combinations of opinion we have isolated invite speculation about their strength in the political process. One may suspect, for example, that in many jurisdictions, and perhaps in the nation as a whole, a relatively strong position may be occupied by those hardheaded individuals who oppose extension of the scope of welfare activities yet take a firm stand against tax cuts at the expense of important governmental functions. On the contrary, those clusters of persons who favor more extended welfare activity but can be seduced by promises of tax cuts probably do not weigh heavily in the balance of political forces. Technically inconsistent opinion clusters may not enjoy a strength proportionate to their numbers.

4 · Elites, Programs, Equilibrium

This excursion through the jungle of data on the interrelations of opinion doubtless has created some bewilderment, for the meaning of the facts is by no means self-evident. Nor can their meaning be stated with either simplicity or great assurance. Although the characteristics of opinion described probably have a profound bearing on the nature of

---

[7] The tricks of the art of governing include that of verbal deference to public opinion unaccompanied by correlative concrete action.

the political order, the specification of that bearing requires leaps from the crude facts over dark and obscure terrain toward plausible conclusions whose connection with their point of origin is not readily demonstrable.

Noncongruent Cleavages and Cohesion in the Political Order. Some observers see in the circumstance of multifarious but noncongruent cleavage a source of cohesion within the political system. Obviously, the argument goes, if the state divides itself into two or more groups, each consisting of persons completely in agreement against outsiders on all issues, the potentialities for strident discord and disruptive friction may be great.[8] In the abstract, the hypothesis seems plausible if we assume that the issues involved are not all low-temperature questions. Less obvious, though, is the reasoning underlying the proposition that a multiplicity of cleavages may lend cohesion to the state.

In part, the cohesion hypothesis rests on the fact that crisscrossing cleavages make the same persons allies on some questions and opponents on others, a circumstance that supposedly serves either to mute the intensity of conflict or at least to require that it be conducted in accord with some limiting etiquette. The way this could come about may readily be seen by attentive inspection of the scheme of Table 7.5 on page 164. In that arrangement persons A and B are allied with C on Issues 1 through 5 but opposed to him on Issue 6; C is allied with D on issues 1 through 4 and 6 but opposed on 5; D joins with E on 1 through 3 and 5 through 6, but they are enemies on 4. Or A and B join with G on Issue 1 but oppose him on 2 through 6. Only A and B and H and I are in opposition on all issues. Thus, throughout the social system enmities are paradoxically ameliorated by friendships and disruptive conflicts are offset by cohesive commonalities. An actual opinion situation, to be sure, would deviate from the model in many ways. Simultaneous consensus on a large proportion of issues, for example, would keep narrow the area of conflict.[9] Or the component of conflict

[8] Bartlett observes that "where potentialities of division are very numerous, the possibility of serious splitting may be at a minimum, but where possible lines of division are few, the group may be in serious danger of radical deterioration." —*Political Propaganda* (Cambridge: Cambridge University Press; 1940), p. 8.

[9] For example, Sappenfield finds in a study of university students that those of different religions may be in disagreement on a narrow range of religious questions but united on a range of beliefs about democratic institutions.—"Ideological Agreement and Disagreement Among Religious Groups," *Journal of Abnormal and Social Psychology,* XXXVIII (1943), 532–9. In the same vein, religious "differences may be minimized by the sharing of a large fund of non-religious values." —R. M. Williams, Jr.: "Religion, Value-Orientation, and Intergroup Conflict," *Journal of Social Issues,* XII (1956), 12–20.

might be enlarged by the bipolarization of attitudes on several issues. Yet, with noncongruent opinion groupings, connective links would in varying degrees span the gap between opponents.

These comments in terms of congruent- and noncongruent-opinion categories verge toward theories about the consequences for the nature of the political order of overlapping group membership. A southern worker may be a member of a union (that advocates civil rights for Negroes) and of a white citizens' council (that urges the contrary viewpoint). Persons who maintain a position of conflicting loyalties may, in some instances, try to make the peace (or they may withdraw from one group or take other evasive action). Yet it may be seriously doubted whether the kinds of overlapping or noncongruent opinion groupings described in this chapter have a substantial effect on behavior through the population generally. The southerner who allies himself with the northerner on medical care and opposes him on integration is no less an ardent supporter of white supremacy for that fact. Or the internationalist who finds himself on the same side of foreign issues with a welfare stater whose views on domestic policy he detests is probably in the mass no less an opponent of the welfare state because of that alliance.

The effects upon the political order of multifarious opinion cleavages probably must be sought in their bearing on the behavior of leadership elements. Those who are most sensible of, and most sensitive to the inconsistencies and conflicts of opinion groupings, the contradictory disciplines of cross pressures, are probably the influentials in both public and politically relevant private spheres of leadership. A senator may have in his following both conservative-internationalists and liberal-internationalists, and other combinations as well. A representative may have to worry about constituents who are enthusiastic advocates of public power and medical care and others who desire medical care legislation but cannot stomach public power. Local union officials, urged to promote the international's policy on foreign affairs, may speak only softly to their unskilled brethren with a provincial outlook. A Democratic precinct captain in a suburban neighborhood may push aid to education and sound fiscal policy; another in a working-class precinct may soft-pedal foreign policy and talk up social welfare.

It is probably in the effects of these variegated opinion clusters on the levels of political leadership—using the term to cover a fairly large category of political activists—that one must seek the bearing of a multiplicity of political cleavages on the nature of the political order. Individuals can hold inconsistent opinions with no great personal discomfort. The political leader, though, must contrive some way to enact social welfare legislation to benefit his constituents without at the same time outraging them by the necessary levy of taxes. He must also, if he is a legislator, so conduct himself that he may tomorrow approach for support his enemy of today. If this stab in the dark is correct, to give credence to the hypothesis that multiplicity of cleavages conduces to cohesion, one must include in the explanatory model some account of the complex interactions between mass opinion and the political elite through whose actions the nature of the political order becomes manifest.

And, as we reflect in this vein, another consequence of a multiplicity of cleavage, not often noted, becomes apparent. The strange bedfellows attendant upon noncongruence of cleavage may over the long run muffle political conflict and induce cohesion within the political order. Yet in the short run, in which we spend most of our lives, a multiplicity of cleavage may promote stasis if not paralysis within the state. By multiplication of the uncertainties and the risks for leadership, by subjection of elites to conflicting pressures and directives of dubious clarity, by creation of blocs of opinion susceptible to diversionary exploitation, a set of circumstances conducive to blockage of action comes into being. No majority nicely united on outstanding issues can be readily mobilized; a potential majority on one issue is often shattered by the inclination of some of its members to prefer to kill action on some other issue. Without determined and venturesome leadership, the great leviathan may stall on dead center. All this is not to deny that the Republic may, under some circumstances, flourish even though the government is stalled on dead center. The analysis points, rather, to the nature of checks and balances within the social structure that have to be neutralized when major action becomes necessary.

Elites and Coherent Political Action. The quilted pattern of opinion differentiation is projected upward to condition the behavior of political elites. By the same token these types of opinion patterns place obligations upon the political elite in a democracy. To govern, it must influence opinions as well as be influenced thereby. No aspect of public opinion demonstrates more persuasively the duty of leadership to educate, as well as to follow, than the characteristics of opinion examined in this chapter.

A modicum of consistency or coherence in the program of government as a whole must, of necessity, prevail. In one of its phases that consistency is a technical necessity, for one policy may depend upon another. That technical necessity permeates the detailed actions of government, most of which never come to wide public attention. But, even with the scant data examined, we have identified instances of policies of high visibility which technically demand coherent treatment. The most simple case is that of taxation and welfare policy. The pattern of opinion, whatever lack of faith we may have in the precision of our measurements, is not congruent on the two issues. Substantial numbers of proponents of welfare policies simultaneously rank tax reduction as an action to be taken at the expense of "important things that ought to be done." Obviously the advancement of the public weal requires sufficient skill and courage on the part of political elites to manage interrelated policies in a coherent manner and to win public consent for that action.

Another aspect of consistency in program is a matter not of administrative but of political necessity. A party requires for its existence an inner core of activists fairly well united on a wide range of issues. A degree of difference can be tolerated even within the party elite, but a party leadership cannot survive the centrifugal forces if the party activists are divided along as many lines as is the public generally. If the data were available on the top layers of political influentials—two or three million people—they would probably show, within each party, a much higher degree of consistency of opinion, along party lines, than either their supporters or the public generally. Such evidence as is available indicates that as political activity and political involvement increase, consistency of opinion—in partisan terms—tends to increase.[1] Moreover, between the leadership echelons of the parties fairly consistent and sharp differences exist in broad outlook.[2]

However consistently the party elite may subscribe to the party program, it must win the support of an electorate whose views are not so consistently organized in partisan terms. The task of winning popular consent is complicated by the existence of the kinds of noncongruent opinion clusters that we have identified; whatever combination of positions a party advocates, it will both repel and attract many of the same people. Hence we have considerable appeal to ambiguity, and, in

[1] Angus Campbell, Gerald Gurin, and Warren E. Miller: *The Voter Decides* (Evanston: Row Peterson; 1954), ch. 8. The size of national samples does not permit the isolation from them of sufficient numbers of the thin layer of highly active partisans to demonstrate the degree of contrast in policy consistency between them and the rank and file of partisans. Yet perceptible differences in partisan consistency exist between even the broad strata of party identifiers that can be differentiated by crude measures of political involvement and of participation.

[2] See Herbert McCloskey: "Conservatism and Personality," *American Political Science Review*, LII (1958), 27–45; Angus Campbell, Philip E. Converse, Warren E. Miller, and Donald E. Stokes, *The American Voter* (New York: Wiley; 1960), ch. 9. The early work of S. P. Hayes, Jr., points in the same direction. His professional respondents showed a far higher degree of consistency of views among various policies—in partisan terms—than did factory workers. See "The Inter-Relation of Political Attitudes: II. Consistency in Voters' Attitudes," *Journal of Social Psychology*, X (1939), 359–78.

truth, noncongruent opinion clusters create both the opportunity and the temptation to resort to humbuggery.

The technical tasks placed upon governing elites by the total pattern of noncongruent opinion distributions make patent the excessive simplicity of the customary conceptions of majority rule. Discussion of majority rule tends to assume the existence of a single great issue. Once opinion is ascertained, it remains only to take action in accord therewith. In fact, many questions exist simultaneously. If all issues fell into the same policy dimension, the problems of governments would be far simpler than they are. That is, if all broad policy issues generated responses among people that were scalable in the fashion of the hypothetical issues in Table 7.5 on page 164 a multiplicity of cleavages would create no insuperable problem in governance. Faced by the situation in that table a government would need only to advocate Issues 1, 2, and 3 to be assured of majority support for its entire program.

In reality, all issues do not fall in this manner. The cleavages crisscross, or, in other terms, opinions on some issues are not scalable. And, more important for the argument, it may be assumed that the distributions of opinion on different questions interact as action occurs. Those interactions condition the problem of organization of opinion to maintain support for a government. A policy on a domestic-welfare question may antagonize those sensitive to taxation. An action on segregation may drive away those who have been catered to by a welfare policy. A policy of foreign aid may gain the support of some persons antagonistic to the government's welfare actions and perhaps destroy the support of other persons favorable to the welfare actions.

These remarks touch on the problem of taking simultaneous action in many policy areas in a manner to tap the opinion distribution in each area at a point that will maximize support for government as a whole. Since action in one area may offset gains (or losses) from actions in another area, the problem of majority rule becomes in principle one of higher mathematics. The problem is complicated by the probability that, at least in the long run, attitude toward government policy in one area may be modified by actions taken in another. At the simplest level, an increase in taxation may weaken the supportive end of distributions on welfare and foreign-policy measures. Or an opponent of public power, horrified by the sight of rising dams, may grow lukewarm in his support of milder types of state action. Similarly, an isolationist, his imagination stirred by the accomplishments of TVA, may be moved toward foreign involvement by the prospect of TVAs around the world, or a provincial who dislikes feeding foreigners rather than our own may become more favorably disposed toward the rest of the world as domestic policies maintain steady employment including his own. The uncertainties induced by these and other such factors may help explain why experienced democratic politicians seem to await the development of overwhelming popular support before they act.

Knowledge about such interrelated movements in opinion distributions is practically nil. The odds are that the repercussions from government action in one opinion area on the shape of the distribution in another opinion area are not quickly felt. The process of interaction is doubtless slowed by the time required for perceptions of the new reality to percolate through the population, by the inattention of many persons, by nonpolicy attitudes such as party identification, and by other frictions. It may be, too, that the distributions of some types of opinions that are lightly held, as in some foreign-policy areas, may fairly quickly be altered by the effects of action or inaction in other realms. In any event, the entire discussion points to the complexity of the problem of maintaining the equilibrium of the political system— even if we interpret equilibrium to mean only the maintenance of 51 per cent of the vote on our side.

8

POLITICAL
STRATIFICATION
AND OPINION

THE FINDINGS of recent electoral studies have been disturbing to believers in the copybook maxims of democracy. They have marred the image of the voter as a person possessed of information and judgment on the major issues of the day. They have compelled a modification of the conception of the voter as a person imbued with a sense of civic duty. In their demonstration that few voters possess information on many topics of daily political discourse, these studies provide ammunition for critics of democracy. Thus in 1945 84 per cent of a national sample (AIPO) had no understanding of the meaning of "feather-bedding." That lack of information makes a hilarious bit for critical essays, although it may be doubted that such ignorance carries serious dangers for the Republic. Even so, one is taken aback by the frequency with which common political terms are not understood by the citizenry. Oratory about a balanced budget, for example, must have a relatively limited audience; in 1946 51 per cent of the populace

(AIPO) either confessed that they did not know the meaning of "balancing the budget" or gave incorrect definitions. In 1943 Dr. Gallup concluded that only slightly more than one fourth of Americans had a relatively correct idea of the meaning of "free enterprise." "It means," one respondent said, "ability of industry to exploit labor without government interference," an interpretation not without an element of accuracy but certainly not one in the minds of those who were spending millions of dollars extolling the virtues of free enterprise. Even the terms long current in the castigation of business are without meaning to millions of people. In October, 1950, 46 per cent of a national sample understood none of the following terms: "monopoly," "antitrust suit," "interlocking directorate," and "Sherman Act"; 40 per cent of the sample could identify more than one of the terms, while only 10 per cent knew what the Sherman Act was about.[1]

Though he lacks information on details, a voter may be capable of sensible judgments about the general course of public policy; nevertheless, the large number of persons with extremely limited information piques the curiosity of the political analyst. In what directions do such persons throw their influence, such as it is, in the governing process? Do they lend to the political process an element of unpredictability? Are they especially susceptible to the wiles of the demagogue?

These questions may be approached by an analysis that rests on the assumption that society is stratified politically. The idea of political stratification may not be readily grasped, for discussions of stratification are so often in economic or occupational terms. Let us assume, though, that the political system consists of strata of people differentiated by political characteristics. A few measures of such characteristics are available. Persons vary in the degree to which they participate in campaigns and in other political activity. They differ, too, not only in the intensity of their psychological involvement in politics, but also in their feeling that they may be effective politically. By these and other criteria people may be divided into political strata. To what extent do political strata, so defined, differ in their familiarity with the issues of politics? What differences, if any, prevail in the directions of the opinions held by those who occupy each stratum of the political spectrum? Analysis of these and other similar relationships permits educated guesses about the weights that various shades of opinion carry in the circuitous processes that connect the views and opinions of the citizen with the decisions of those in authority. The same analysis should enable us better to place those who lack opinions in the system of political activity.

[1] Burton R. Fisher and Stephen B. Withey: *Big Business as the People See It* (Ann Arbor: Survey Research Center; 1951), p. 54.

1 · Participation Levels and Opinions

Though politicians must estimate the weights of blocs of opinion, rigorous analysts usually avoid the hazards of such imponderable questions. Yet estimates of influence may be made, in terms of more or less, that have the virtue of plausibility if not of ready verifiability. Those persons who vote regularly surely affect the course of events more than do those who rarely vote. Among those who vote, those who also contribute money or who convey the party gospel to other persons must be assigned more weight than those who limit their endeavors to a quiet expedition to the polls. Those who exert themselves beyond the mere act of voting are also the kinds of persons who write to their congressmen, send letters to editors, sign petitions, and belong to pressure groups. Among large groups we should expect the weight of opinion to vary roughly with degree of participation as well as with numbers. An assumption to the contrary could rest only on the hypothesis that mass political activity affects the course of events not at all.

If sufficient data were available, one could divide the population into strata differentiated by extent of activity in the political process. A thin top stratum would contain the genuine political activists, the professional politicians, the semiprofessionals, and the highly placed individuals in corporate, associational, and community life who have political sidelines and connections. The lowest stratum would include the habitual nonvoters and the persons with little awareness and no concern about political issues—the apoliticals, those who neither talk nor act in a political role. Between these two layers would be others defined by appropriate measures of the extent of their political activity.

Undoubtedly the population divides in some such way; yet the available data permit only crude demarcations of broad participation strata. A top stratum consists of those who not only vote but also engage in some other activity, such as talking up the cause with their friends and acquaintances, wearing a campaign button, contributing money, attending rallies, belonging to a political club, or working in one way or another for the party or the candidate. Some 29 per cent of the 1956 Survey Research Center sample voted and engaged in one or more of these worthy endeavors.[2] A second layer of persons, 44 per cent, limited their participation to voting. Another small category, 5 per cent, consisted of those who did not vote but wore a campaign button or participated in one or another of the additional ways indi-

---

[2] For the incidence of these types of activity in the population in 1952 and 1956, see Angus Campbell, Philip E. Converse, Warren E. Miller, and Donald E. Stokes: *The American Voter* (New York: Wiley; 1960), p. 91.

cated above. This small, and worrisome, category may be largely ignored in the analysis that follows. Another large group consisted of those who neither voted nor participated in any of the other ways specified above.

How is opinion related, if it is, to these variations in participation? Differences in participation acquire significance only if they are associated with differences in kind and direction of opinion. A major contrast consists in the fact that far fewer "don't knows" appear among the high participators than in the bottom stratum. In analysis after analysis of opinions on specific issues, sizeable proportions of persons have been shown to lack an opinion. An "index of issue familiarity" can be used to summarize these responses on a large number of questions.[3] The low participators, the nonvoters, have, on the average, a low level of issue familiarity; in effect, many people who have limited familiarity with broad policy questions disenfranchise themselves. Between the high participators and the medium participators differences in issue familiarity also exist. Those who restrict their political activity to voting have preferences on fewer policy questions and are willing to appraise governmental performance in fewer policy areas than are those persons who vote and engage in other types of political endeavor as well. These contrasts are presented in Table 8.1.

For its interest as an item of political curiosa, Table 8.2 is included to contrast the relations between issue familiarity and political participation among men and women. Women, on the average, have a far

---

TABLE 8.1

RELATION OF POLITICAL PARTICIPATION TO LEVEL OF ISSUE FAMILIARITY

ISSUE FAMILIARITY [a]	LEVEL OF PARTICIPATION [b]		
	Low	Medium	High
High 4	16%	30%	45%
3	17	27	27
2	18	19	16
Low 1	49	24	12
	100%	100%	100%
N	394	770	515

[a] For construction of the index of issue familiarity, see Appendix IV.
[b] Levels of participation: high, voted and engaged in one at least of the other types of participation indicated in the text; medium, voted only; low, neither voted nor participated in any other way. For construction of the participation index, see Appendix IV.
DATA SOURCE: *Survey Research Center, University of Michigan, 1956.*

---

[3] For the construction of the index of issue familiarity, see Appendix IV.

TABLE 8.2

LEVEL OF PARTICIPATION IN RELATION TO ISSUE FAMILIARITY, BY SEX

ISSUE FAMILIARITY   LEVEL OF PARTICIPATION

	Men			Women		
	Low	Medium	High	Low	Medium	High
High 4	25%	44%	58%	12%	20%	28%
3	20	30	22	16	25	34
2	22	15	14	16	23	20
Low 1	33	11	6	56	32	18
	100%	100%	100%	190%	100%	100%
N	126	328	297	267	442	218

DATA SOURCE: *Survey Research Center, University of Michigan, 1956.*

lower level of issue familiarity than men. Even among women who rank high on the scale of political activity, issue familiarity is far lower than among men with the same level of political participation. Women are not alone in developing an incandescent enthusiasm about politics despite a marked lack of information on what it is all about; they do so only relatively more frequently than do men.

While the linkage between the vote and the actions of government is both circuitous and tenuous, these gross differentiations among participation strata probably have real significance for public policy. Whatever opinions nonvoters have must be of slight weight in the political process. Or, perhaps more correctly, those opinions that are heavily represented among nonvoters do not gain whatever strength might come from voting by this sector of the population. Between the strata of medium and high participators, it is plausible to suppose that those who are active in talking up their candidates and parties would as a class exert relatively more weight than would those who merely vote. Moreover, the high participators have opinions and preferences on a wider range of issues than do the mere voters. Even though their store of information may not be impressive, their political activity can, on the average, be more purposive than that of the less-informed medium participators.

The question remains whether the direction of the preferences of high participators differs from that of low participators. If opinions were identical at different participation levels, variation in participation might affect the distribution of influence within the population but not the direction of public policy. Our measures of participation enable us to distinguish only the broadest participation strata; it would be astonishing if sharp differences in the direction of opinion appeared between

TABLE 8.3

RELATION OF POLITICAL PARTICIPATION TO POSITION ON FOREIGN ISSUE SCALE

INTERNATIONALISM [a]	PARTICIPATION LEVEL		
	Low	Medium	High
High	35%	45%	55%
Medium	14	21	23
Low	16	16	12
Not scaled [b]	35	18	10
	100%	100%	100%
N	394	770	515

[a] For construction of the scale, see Appendix II.
[b] Respondents with too few opinions to permit placement on scale.
DATA SOURCE: *Survey Research Center, University of Michigan, 1956.*

strata as heterogeneous as these groupings. Yet some differences in direction of opinion are associated with differences in participation. The high participators are markedly more willing than the nonvoters to support policies of involvement abroad, or at least they were in 1956. They also ranked, on the average, higher on the scale of internationalism than those who simply voted. These differences, as may be seen from Table 8.3, rest in part on the scarcity of opinions of any kind among the low participators.

On domestic issues the high participators, in contrast with the nonvoters, consist in larger proportions of persons who prefer low levels of governmental welfare activity. About one fifth of the top participation stratum ranked low on a domestic-liberalism scale. If we had a

TABLE 8.4

RELATION OF POLITICAL PARTICIPATION TO POSITION ON DOMESTIC ISSUE SCALE

LIBERALISM [a]	LEVEL OF PARTICIPATION		
	Low	Medium	High
High	35%	33%	31%
Medium	31	39	40
Low	9	13	19
Not scaled [b]	27	15	10
	100%	100%	100%
N	394	770	515

[a] For construction of the scale, see Appendix II.
[b] Respondents with too few opinions to permit placement on a scale.
DATA SOURCE: *Survey Research Center, University of Michigan, 1956.*

finer sieve which would subdivide this stratum, wider differences would probably be found to exist between the extremely high and low participators. At any rate, the capacity of those favoring low levels of government activity to obstruct action is greater than might be expected from their proportions in the total population. (See Table 8.4.)

For those who are suspicious of scales—and one can always be unsure about what the mixture in a scale means—the data on direction of opinions in relation to participation are presented for selected specific questions in Table 8.5. The relative conservatism of the high participators finds exemplification in their position on the medical-care question. The high participators are also less inclined to approve the firing without proof of government employees accused of communism and far more disposed to disagree with the proposition that taxes ought to be

TABLE 8.5

Relation of Level of Participation to Direction of Opinion on Selected Issues [a]

ISSUE	LEVEL OF PARTICIPATION		
	Low [b]	Medium	High
Medical Care			
Agree	61%	52%	50%
Disagree	15	26	34
Fire Communist Suspects			
Agree	28	23	19
Disagree	45	56	66
Tax Cut			
Agree	30	26	20
Disagree	27	45	57
Stay Home			
Agree	32	26	19
Disagree	38	56	71
Power and Housing			
Agree	32	42	48
Disagree	17	24	23
School Segregation			
Agree	42	40	49
Disagree	34	41	39

[a] For the wording of the issue propositions, see Appendix I. The wording of the propositions is important in the interpretation of this table for some of them are phrased in a negative fashion; others, positively.
[b] The entries should be read: of the low participators, 61 per cent agreed with the medical care proposition; 15 per cent disagreed; and so forth. The percentages are computed from a base including those with no opinion.
DATA SOURCE: *Survey Research Center, University of Michigan, 1956.*

cut at any cost. They also exhibit notable differences on the proposition that we would be better off if we stayed home and did not concern ourselves with other parts of the world. Probably, by the standards of the day, the high participators tend to take a more sensible position than do the nonvoters. Even if their position is not the more sensible, it is likely to prevail.

2 · Political Involvement and Opinion

Another crude yet serviceable indicator of political stratification is degree of political involvement. Some persons are psychologically more involved, or more concerned, about campaigns and elections than are others. Since political involvement is subjective, it must be measured by self-appraisal, a procedure that gives no assurance that a specified level of involvement is equal from individual to individual.[4] Nevertheless, these ratings are so correlated with other aspects of political behavior that they may be taken to differentiate political strata. Political involvement is correlated with political participation; yet some highly involved persons do not vote, and some with low involvement vote and participate in other ways, as indicated in Table 8.6.

While political stratification as defined by degrees of political involvement does not coincide exactly with stratification as measured by participation, the differences and similarities between levels of involve-

---

[4] For the construction of the index of political involvement, see Appendix IV. Persons with political concern sufficient to bring them to read books such as this one often have no comprehension of the weakness of political involvement among some people. A few quotations from interviews may be revealing. The wife of a worker in a Pittsburgh mattress factory: (Personally care which party wins?) "It doesn't make any difference to me. I'm not interested in stuff like that. I don't listen to nothing; I don't even read about politics in the paper." A Minnesota fisherman: (Care?) "Not a bit." (Anything like about Democratic party?) "No, there ain't; don't believe in politics." A North Carolina housewife: (Care?) "I don't care, I don't guess." California lady who worked 11 hours a day in a cannery: (Care?) "It doesn't make any difference to me." Wife, white, of Georgia laborer: (Care?) "I guess you'd call me not caring since I've never voted, wouldn't you?" Another Georgia housewife: (Care?) "I suppose you'd say I don't care too much about which one gets in. I always say they're all gentlemen when they go in as President but rascals when they come out. Sure enough, you look back and they're all rascals when they come out. I don't vote myself. I leave that for menfolks." Wife of an Iowa telephone lineman, ninth-grade education and married at sixteen: (Care?) "I would say I don't know which one could do the most. I've never paid any attention to parties and have no interest in politics." Retired California minister: (Care?) "I have never registered or voted because I believe that prayers will do more than votes in keeping this country on the right path." On the other hand, some people do care. A Missouri farmer: (Care?) "I do care. I'm politics crazy." The wife of a New Mexico miner: "I do care. I want the Democratic President to win. Things are bad with us, honey."

TABLE 8.6

RELATION BETWEEN LEVEL OF POLITICAL INVOLVEMENT AND VOTING, 1956

VOTE	LEVEL OF INVOLVEMENT			
	Low			High
	1	2	3	4
Voted				
Democratic	21%	28%	28%	40%
Republican	37	42	49	48
Did not vote, preferred				
Democratic	10	7	8	5
Republican	32	23	15	7
Voted	58	70	77	88
Did not vote	42	30	23	12
	100%	100%	100%	100%
N	294	444	487	468

DATA SOURCE: *Survey Research Center, University of Michigan, 1956.*

ment closely resemble those between participation levels. Persons highly involved have on the average a far wider familiarity with the issues, or at least more frequently a willingness to express an opinion about issues and a judgment of governmental performance on the issues, than do persons who have a low interest in campaigns and not much concern about the outcome of elections. Half of those who rank high on the involvement scale also rank high in issue familiarity; half of those low in involvement are also low in issue familiarity. These relationships are shown in Table 8.7.

With respect to direction of opinion, those highly involved rank high in internationalism, just as did those at the top level of political

TABLE 8.7

RELATION OF POLITICAL INVOLVEMENT TO ISSUE FAMILIARITY

ISSUE FAMILIARITY	LEVEL OF INVOLVEMENT			
	Low			High
	1	2	3	4
High 4	13%	26%	35%	47%
3	19	24	27	26
2	16	21	20	16
Low 1	52	29	18	11
	100%	100%	100%	100%
N	333	460	494	475

DATA SOURCE: *Survey Research Center, University of Michigan, 1956.*

TABLE 8.8

RELATION OF POLITICAL INVOLVEMENT TO POSITION ON FOREIGN ISSUE SCALE

INTERNATIONALISM	LEVEL OF INVOLVEMENT			
	Low			High
	1	2	3	4
High	27%	44%	50%	54%
Medium	14	20	22	25
Low	18	17	13	11
Not scaled [a]	41	19	15	10
	100%	100%	100%	100%
N	333	460	494	475

[a] Respondents with too few opinions to permit placement on scale.
DATA SOURCE: *Survey Research Center, University of Michigan, 1956.*

participation. Those who were not much interested or cared little about the campaign consisted in relatively larger proportions of persons disposed toward insularity, as Table 8.8 indicates. These relations should not be taken to mean that the highly involved are always more internationalist in their outlook, but that they were at the time of this sounding in 1956. The better generalization probably is that while persons with high involvement would be expected to have at all times high concern about foreign policy, the direction of their opinion would not necessarily be weighted toward internationalism.

Differences in direction of opinion on domestic issues are also associated with variations in degree of political involvement. Those differences are not wide, as may be seen from Table 8.9. Relatively twice as

TABLE 8.9

RELATION OF POLITICAL INVOLVEMENT TO POSITION ON DOMESTIC ISSUE SCALE

LIBERALISM	POLITICAL INVOLVEMENT			
	Low			High
	1	2	3	4
High	34%	31%	30%	35%
Medium	27	38	43	39
Low	9	13	14	18
Not scaled [a]	30	18	13	8
	100%	100%	100%	100%
N	333	460	494	475

[a] Respondents with too few opinions to permit placement on scale.
DATA SOURCE: *Survey Research Center, University of Michigan, 1956.*

many of highly involved persons as of those least involved concentrate at the conservative end of the scale on domestic issues. Yet for neither group is this conservative proportion large, at least as "conservatism" has been measured here. The policy items included in the scale receive approval from large proportions of those at all levels of the index of involvement. As in other issue areas, a considerable part of the difference between high and low involvement levels is attributable to the fact that the low involvement stratum includes large numbers of persons with so few opinions that they cannot be placed on the scale.

3 · Political Efficacy and Opinion

Some people feel alienated from the political process in that they do not believe that their participation affects the course of events. Others firmly believe that they may cast the deciding vote; hence they may act politically with a sense of mission and of efficacy. This outlook differs in degree among persons. Some know so little about politics that they believe that voting is the only way that they may exert influence. Others have a greater awareness of alternative routes for action and may have experienced the inflation of the political ego that comes from having their views heard with deference by a congressman, a Senator, or an alderman.

In its 1952 and 1956 election surveys the Survey Research Center attempted a measurement of this sense of political efficacy among the members of its national samples. As measured by responses to a series of test items, the sense of political efficacy turned out to be a quality distinguishable from the sense of citizen duty. A person may have a sense of duty that drives him to the polls even though he firmly believes that the entire ritual is pointless and without effect. Moreover, the sense of efficacy appeared to be a motivational drive not entirely dependent upon demographic characteristics. Persons of low education may, on the average, place low in citizen efficacy; yet those of this group who have a high sense of efficacy participate in politics in much higher degree than do their fellows of like educational achievement but of low sense of efficacy.[5]

From the behavior of those persons who rank high in sense of political efficacy it appears that the measure of efficacy taps an important political motivation. Among those with the highest sense of efficacy almost 50 per cent also rated high on the index of political participation; that is, they both voted and engaged in some other campaign activity,

[5] See Angus Campbell, Gerald Gurin, and Warren E. Miller: *The Voter Decides* (Evanston: Row Peterson; 1954), pp. 187-94.

such as talking up their candidate. At the lowest level of efficacy only 13 per cent of the respondents claimed to belong to the high participation group, as may be seen from Table 8.10. Nearly half of those with the lowest sense of efficacy failed to vote, while about 90 per cent of those with a high sense of efficacy said that they had voted in the presidential election of 1956.

The sense of political efficacy, like the sense of political involvement, is correlated with political participation. Hence, as might be expected, relationships between the sense of efficacy and issue familiarity and the direction of opinion are somewhat like those between political

---

TABLE 8.10

SENSE OF POLITICAL EFFICACY IN RELATION TO PARTICIPATION LEVEL

PARTICIPATION LEVEL	SENSE OF POLITICAL EFFICACY				
	Low				High
	1	2	3	4	5
High 4	13%	20%	26%	39%	49%
3	39	40	49	45	42
2	6	5	5	4	4
Low 1	42	35	20	12	5
	100%	100%	100%	100%	100%
N	262	343	461	501	196

DATA SOURCE: *Survey Research Center, University of Michigan, 1956.*

---

involvement and these factors. Persons with a high sense of political efficacy tend also to be persons with a relatively high degree of familiarity with the broad issues of politics; that is, they tend to have views on the sixteen test issues and are willing to express a judgment on what the government is doing about them far more frequently than are those persons low in political efficacy. Only 6 per cent of the persons with a high sense of efficacy (see Table 8.11) were unfamiliar with more than half of the sixteen issues, while over half of those with a low sense of efficacy had so little acquaintance with the issues. These relationships do not establish that persons gain a sense of efficacy by some acquaintance with the broad issues of politics. Probably knowledge stimulates efficacy; on the other hand, a sense of efficacy may also lead a person to search out information. The point of the relationship in this connection is that there exists within the political system a stratum of persons with both a high sense of efficacy and a relatively high acquaintance with the issues.

The sense of political efficacy is positively related to internationalism, at least as it is measured by the scale that we have employed. Those

TABLE 8.11

SENSE OF POLITICAL EFFICACY IN RELATION TO ISSUE FAMILIARITY

ISSUE FAMILIARITY	POLITICAL EFFICACY				
	Low				High
	1	2	3	4	5
High 4	15%	19%	28%	44%	51%
3	16	22	25	29	29
2	15	20	24	16	14
Low 1	54	39	23	11	6
	100%	100%	100%	100%	100%

DATA SOURCE: *Survey Research Center, University of Michigan, 1956.*

with a high sense of political efficacy ranked high on this scale about twice as frequently as did those at the bottom of the efficacy index. The extremely large proportion of persons of low efficacy who had no views one way or another (see Table 8.12) on the items of the internationalism scale suggests that persons of low efficacy may be frequently uninformed as well as lacking in sufficient confidence in themselves to give vent to opinions on cosmic questions of foreign politics.

When the direction of opinion on domestic issues is examined, persons of low efficacy are found in fairly high concentration on the liberal end of the issue scale; that is, they more frequently agree that the government in Washington "ought to see to it that everybody who wants to work can find a job" or that the "government ought to help people get doctors and hospital care at low cost." Or they more frequently take liberal positions on other items constituting the domestic

TABLE 8.12

RELATION OF SENSE OF POLITICAL EFFICACY TO POSITION ON FOREIGN ISSUE SCALE

INTERNATIONALISM	SENSE OF POLITICAL EFFICACY				
	Low				High
	1	2	3	4	5
High	31%	33%	43%	56%	64%
Medium	10	18	25	25	18
Low	18	21	14	10	8
Not scaled [a]	41	28	18	9	10
	100%	100%	100%	100%	100%

[a] Too few opinions to scale.
DATA SOURCE: *Survey Research Center, University of Michigan, 1956.*

issue scale. This relationship, shown in detail in Table 8.13, should not be taken to mean that low efficacy is caused by liberalism on such issues or vice versa. Yet it is not without significance that those social strata possessed of a low sense of efficacy in the political process include relatively large numbers of persons disposed to espouse the liberal position. Given the total pattern of political power, persons with such views who

---

TABLE 8.13

RELATION OF SENSE OF POLITICAL EFFICACY TO POSITION ON DOMESTIC ISSUE SCALE

LIBERALISM	SENSE OF POLITICAL EFFICACY				
	Low				High
	1	2	3	4	5
High	43%	37%	34%	28%	21%
Medium	22	31	38	45	49
Low	4	8	14	21	19
Not scaled	31	24	14	6	11
	100%	100%	100%	100%	100%

DATA SOURCE: *Survey Research Center, University of Michigan, 1956.*

---

give a low rating to their own political efficacy may be appraising their situation with some reality as well as rating their own psychological characteristics.

4 · Other Characteristics of Political Strata

Our measures of participation and of political involvement have an expository frailty in that persons who fall in the various political strata cannot be identified by highly visible insignia of differentiation. Most studies of political participation lean on more readily recognized personal characteristics. They do not deal in ghostly psychological categories, such as levels of involvement and of efficacy, but rather in occupational or other demographic types. Most scholarly effort has been devoted to the determination of variations in voting among such groups. A quick look at the findings of these studies gives some indication of how the political strata we have posited fit into systems of demographic categories.

Participation and Demographic Characteristics. Repeated analyses indicate that within national populations (the situation may differ in lo-

calities under exceptional circumstances) the proportions that vote
increase with each step up the economic ladder. A typical set of participation rates is that reported by Connelly and Field for the presidential
election of 1940: [6]

The upper fourth economically	85%
The middle half economically	69
The lower fourth economically	54

Within these income brackets voting varied with education: 82
per cent of the persons who had gone to college voted, in contrast with
63 per cent of those who had not gone beyond grade school. Other
studies uniformly demonstrate a relation between level of education
and frequency of voting. Thus the Survey Research Center inquiries
found the following percentages voting in the presidential elections of
1948, 1952, and 1956: [7]

	1948	1952	1956
College	79%	90%	90%
High school	67	80	74
Grade school	55	62	60

Occupation, in addition to economic level and education, is related to voting participation in the United States. The turnout rate
regularly increases step by step up the occupational hierarchy. Typical
are the following estimates by the Survey Research Center of percentages of occupational categories voting in 1952:

Professional and managerial	88%
Other white-collar	81
Skilled and semiskilled	74
Unskilled	60
Farm operators	67

Similar differentiations among broad occupational categories regularly
appear, although these heterogeneous groups doubtless conceal smaller
occupational clusters whose rates of participation diverge markedly
from the group norm.

[6] Gordon M. Connelly and Harry H. Field: "The Non-Voter—Who He Is,
What He Thinks," *Public Opinion Quarterly*, VIII (1944), 175–87.

[7] These figures overstate the actual rates of voting participation for two
principal reasons. The sample includes only persons living in households whose
turnout rate is higher than the nonhousehold population, such as persons in the
military service or in institutions. A second source of overestimate is the fact that
more people report to interviewers that they have voted than actually have.

Correlations between voting and demographic characteristics make it clear that occupation, education, income, and other such factors do not necessarily "cause" variations in electoral participation. That other factors are of prime significance in the decision on whether to vote is made apparent by the fact that the great fluctuations in total turnout over time occur in all demographic categories. Persons of all levels of income, degrees of education, and occupation evidently respond to the same influences. The limitations of demographic explanations of voting and nonvoting have led to inquiries to ascertain the psychological characteristics of the nonvoter and the field of social influence in which he exists. A low degree of social integration as manifested, for example, by a low frequency of group membership and a low exposure to political communications characterizes the nonvoter.[8]

Certain psychological characteristics seem also to be common among nonvoters. In summarizing the data on the point, Knupfer opines "that the economic and educational limitations accompanying low status produce a lack of interest in and a lack of self-confidence in dealing with certain important areas of our culture; as a result, there is reduced participation—a withdrawal from participation in these areas." [9] Campbell, Gurin, and Miller find participation to vary with the sense of political efficacy and of citizen duty.[1] Related is Kornhauser's finding that relatively large numbers of industrial workers in Detroit rate high on a scale of feeling of political futility.[2]

Independence of Political Strata. This brief mention of studies of political participation as related to education, income, occupation, and other demographic characteristics serves principally to give a warning about the limitations of their findings. Everyday analysts of politics are accustomed to speaking in terms of businessmen, workers, grade-schoolers, southerners, metropolitanites, and other categories that can be readily comprehended on all sides. The hunch in this argument, though, is that analysis solely in terms of occupational categories is misleading. The assumption has been that the political system is constructed of strata

[8] See, for example, Philip K. Hastings: "The Non-Voter in 1952; A Study of Pittsfield, Massachusetts," *Journal of Psychology*, XXXVIII (1954), 301–12; and John M. Foskett: "Social Structure and Social Participation," *American Sociological Review*, XX (1955), 431–8.

[9] Genevieve Knupfer: "Portrait of the Underdog," *Public Opinion Quarterly*, XI (1947), pp. 103–14.

[1] Campbell, Gurin, and Miller: op. cit., pp. 187–99.

[2] Arthur Kornhauser *et al.: When Labor Votes* (New York: University Books; 1956), p. 156. For an able codification of the extensive literature on participation, see Robert E. Lane: *Political Life* (Glencoe: Free Press; 1959). See also *International Social Science Journal*, XII (1960), 1, a number devoted to "Citizen Participation in Political Life," edited by Stein Rokkan.

definable in terms of political activity and influence and independent of occupational strata, income levels, and other such readily perceptible indicators beloved of the sociologist and the daily commentator. Though relatively more persons of high education than grade-schoolers may be in the higher political strata, education is not the dividing line. A higher proportion of professional men than of unskilled laborers may be in the higher political strata; yet the professional group has a share of the noninfluentials, and the unskilled laborers include a quota of activists.[3]

One of the difficulties about the conception of the political system as consisting of population strata independent of the familiar demographic categories is that we lack satisfactory data on the characteristics of the assumed political strata. In the preceding pages we have employed political participation, the sense of political involvement, and the sense of political efficacy as crude indices of differentiations among political strata. An item of evidence may be added to suggest how the political strata, so defined, cut across occupational categories. The index of issue familiarity, used earlier, has been shown to be closely related to variations in participation, involvement, and efficacy. Within occupational levels participation (as measured by voting alone) varies with issue familiarity, as may be seen from Table 8.14. While issue fa-

---

TABLE 8.14

RELATION OF OCCUPATION AND ISSUE FAMILIARITY TO 1956 VOTING PARTICIPATION [a]

HEAD'S OCCUPATION	ISSUE FAMILIARITY			
	Low			High
	1	2	3	4
Professional	(53%)	(87%)	87%	91%
Business	65	78	87	90
Clerical	(54)	(93)	82	85
Skilled	63	70	81	81
Unskilled	47	50	63	72
Farmer	61	82	73	95

[a] Entries are percentages of those in each cell who said they had voted. Entries in parentheses rest on less than 30 cases.

DATA SOURCE: *Survey Research Center, University of Michigan, 1956.*

---

[3] The limitations of demographic characteristics in the analysis of voting behavior are suggested by the analysis by Morris Janowitz and Warren E. Miller: "The Index of Political Predisposition in the 1948 Election," *Journal of Politics,* XIV (1952), 271–7. See also V. O. Key and Frank Munger: "Social Determinism and Electoral Decision: The Case of Indiana," in Eugene Burdick and A. J. Brodbeck, eds.: *American Voting Behavior* (Glencoe: Free Press; 1959), pp. 281–99.

miliarity itself varies up and down the occupational ladder, among unskilled workers one finds men with high issue familiarity and relatively high rates of voting participation. The same variations prevail among clerical and skilled manual workers. Or, stating the point in another way, one could picture the social strata fixed by occupational prestige as crossed by strata of political participation and involvement. The stratum with preferences on few issues and little disposition to participate in politics includes persons in the professional and business classes as well as skilled and unskilled workers. Similarly, the political stratum with opinions on many issues and high levels of political activity includes persons at all levels of the occupational hierarchy. Higher occupational strata, to be sure, include larger proportions of persons of above-average political activity and involvement than do the lower occupational strata. Yet it is the noncongruence of political and occupational strata that is instructive for political analysis. If a political order is to be democratic, political activists must be sprinkled in some such manner through all levels of the economic-occupational hierarchy. That proposition acquires persuasiveness if one contemplates the situation that would probably prevail if all "activists" were of, say, the business and professional classes.

5 · Political Stratification and the Weight of Opinion

The basic assumption that the electorate is stratified politically can scarcely be questioned, so evident are variations in political influence, status, and activity. Less apparent is it that the weight of opinions in the determination of the affairs of state increases step by step up the posited system of political strata. Yet that hypothesis has an inherent plausibility not often negated in the experience of mankind. It must be stressed, though, that our indicators of political strata are unsatisfactory; they mark only gross differentiations. Even so, they permit instructive inferences.

Opinions and Political Strata. Plausible inferences about relative influence may be drawn from our data. A few broad conclusions seem to be defensible. The lower political strata, whether measured by participation, involvement, or sense of efficacy, include large proportions of persons with opinions on few issues. The "don't knows" appear, to be sure, at all levels of the hierarchy of political activity, but they are especially numerous at the bottom level. Nonparticipators, it should be fair to assume, have little role in shaping the dikes of opinion within which the day-to-day policy of government flows. To the extent that persons at this level have opinions, those opinions probably carry relatively little weight. On the other hand, it conforms with common impression and belief to attribute greater weight to the highly involved and the high participators, who not only have opinions on issues but also talk up their candidates and their parties.

These relative weights take on most importance when the direction of opinion differs among political strata. Insofar as the available data show, the more influential strata are more disposed to support American involvement in world affairs than are those at the bottom of the political system. They may not approve the manner in which a particular administration handles those affairs, but they tend toward a more realistic perception of the international necessities than do those in the lower political strata. In the realm of domestic policy a fairly high degree of "liberalism" characterizes all political strata, but the most involved and most active stratum includes larger proportions of persons of conservative hue.

A way to think about the relative weights of the actives and the inactives in the conditioning of public policy is to consider the incidence of high participators and low participators at points on a distribution of opinion in the entire population. If the small end of a J-curve included relatively large numbers of highly active persons while the tall end of the curve contained relatively few such persons, the failure of government policy to coincide with the permissive consensus indicated by the J-curve would become more comprehensible. Thus, when 41 per cent of those ranking low on the domestic liberalism scale were high participators, while only 27 per cent of those ranking high on the scale were high participators, it might plausibly be supposed that the conservative end of the scale carried more weight than its numbers alone might indicate and the liberal end, less. To some extent a minority can offset its numerical weakness by heightened political exertion. The relative weights of the actives and inactives may depend, too, on the orientation and skills of leadership. One set of party leaders at one time may have special skills in communicating its views to the relatively inactive sector of the population. At another time neither party may bring to the practice of leadership notable artistry in arousing the attention and in mobilizing the support of the less active.

As one examines the similarities and dissimilarities of opinion among opinion strata, questions occur about the dissemination of opinions through the population. Over time do the more active and more involved tend to pull the opinions of the lower political strata into conformity with their own? Or do the opinions of the lesser strata change in the same direction, with some time lag, as do those of the upper political strata? We lack the data to deal adequately with this question. If the latter pattern of relationships exists, it would most readily be seen on questions on which the political elite moved, after some conflict, toward a consensus among themselves, a consensus which in turn was transmitted to those less active, less involved, less concerned, and less informed. Some such sequence of movements in the same direction has probably occurred in foreign policy in recent decades. On those questions on which there is a continuing conflict within the top political strata, transmission of views from the actives to the inactives becomes more a competition to shape the opinions of the lesser political strata than a simple flow of opinion. In the long run the advantage may go to that sector of the actives whose program is more appealing to the inactives or perhaps to those actives who best sense the latent opinions of the inactives.[4]

The Lower Political Strata—the Opinionless—and Political Stability. It seems plausible to suppose that those citizens who have policy preferences and an awareness of the course of government action will, in the aggregate, play a different role in the political system than will those citizens with few or no policy preferences and little awareness of the course of public policy. Many persons of the latter type abdicate by their failure to vote; some of them, though, do vote. How do these persons with few opinions affect the nature of the political system? It is reasonable to suppose that their vote, insofar as they vote, must be governed by considerations other than policy preferences, such as party loyalties, candidate preferences, the admonitions of their friends, or their impressions of the prevailing fashions of the day.

While no trustworthy data are available on the behavior over time of this participant but uninformed political stratum in the nation as a whole, the findings of Campbell, Miller, Converse, and Stokes are suggestive. According to their data, over the period 1948–58 nonvoters shifted in their partisan preferences far more sharply than did voters. Their movement from a Democratic to a Republican candidate preference was far more marked than that of the electorate as a whole.[5] To extrapolate from these findings about nonvoters to the next more active layer—that is, the least-participating, least-informed, and least-

[4] For a consideration of these flows of opinion across political strata, see Elmo Roper: *You and Your Leaders* (New York: Morrow; 1957), ch. 1.

[5] Campbell, Converse, Miller, and Stokes: op. cit., pp. 110–15. National samples usually report a higher percentage for the winner than do the election authorities; the tendency to move to the majority may be especially marked among nonvoters or among those with low involvement.

involved sector of the voting population—requires no farfetched inference.[6] Probably those without anchorage in policy outlook or opinion preferences are blown far more by the winds of the moment than are those of higher political strata.[7] They are probably far more susceptible to manipulation and influence irrelevant to policy.

The consequences for the political system of the manipulability of these low-participant and low-opinion levels of the electorate depend both upon their number and upon the direction in which they are managed. The best guess would be that in recent decades they have swung with the higher political strata, only farther; that is, in 1936 the odds are that they were in high proportion Democratic, but in 1956 they went for Eisenhower. If the free-swinging lower political strata function only to enlarge majorities that would occur anyway, they do no damage. That supposition may build a false sense of comfort about the dangers of ignorance for a democratic order. Circumstances could well develop in which the uninformed strata would move in directions, and in sufficient numbers, to be injurious to, if not destructive of, the order.[8] Clearly, too, the lower political strata move into and out of the active electorate. The direction in which these large occasional accretions to the electorate exert their strength may be of import for the workings, if not the fate, of the political order.[9]

[6] Consistent with the inference are the findings of Saenger about the characteristics of party changers and party consistents in New York from 1940 to 1944. Far more of the changers than of the consistents were unable to perceive differences in the domestic programs of the parties. Fewer changers believed the outcome of the election "was at all important"; fewer changers thought the outcome of the election would affect them "personally."—See G. H. Saenger: "Social Status and Political Behavior," *American Journal of Sociology*, LI (1945–6), 103–13.

[7] Bernard Berelson concludes: "The less informed people are on an issue, the more susceptible they are to opinion conversion through the influence of the communication media."—"Communications and Public Opinion," in W. Schramm: *Mass Communications* (Urbana: University of Illinois Press; 1949), p. 502.

[8] If we had detailed data on the geographical distribution of what we have called the lower political strata—which includes a good many white-collar political illiterates as well as other types—we might better explain the spectacular behavior of the electorate in some states and cities. If a jurisdiction has extremely high proportions of persons without rudders in information, policy attitudes, and preferences, it may be especially susceptible to manipulation by picturesque, or picaresque, political leadership.

[9] Reinhard Bendix opines that "it was the radicalization of people who had not participated actively in party politics and who had been too young to vote which gave a major impetus to the rise of fascism" in Germany.—"Social Stratification and Political Power," *American Political Science Review*, XLVI (1952), 357–75. For a consideration of the problems raised in these pages, see William Kornhauser: *The Politics of Mass Society* (Glencoe: Free Press; 1959).

Part III

PROPERTIES

THE PRECEDING

chapters centered principally on the direction of opinion and on its incidence among persons differently situated in the social structure. Opinions, we say, may be "yes" or "no," pro or con, but they may also arrange themselves along a scale that measures steps in direction smaller than "yes" or "no" in response to a single proposition. Opinions, too, may be differentially distributed among types of persons. In the practical ordering of the political system who has what opinion may be of significant, if not controlling, importance. In any case, an understanding of the structural distribution of opinion illuminates some aspects of the political process.

The analysis moves now to another broad aspect of opinion, a consideration of the properties or qualities of opinion. When we know that a person takes a pro or anti position or locates himself at a specified point on a psychological scale, obviously we do not know all the politically relevant characteristics of his opinion. Opinions possess qualities or properties distinct from their directional character. One of these properties is intensity. A person may, for example, favor compulsory medical insurance but not care deeply about the matter one way or another; his opinion is of low intensity. Opinion may, too, have qualities of stability or instability. A person may oppose compulsory medical insurance and be prepared to stand by his position against all contentions to the contrary. Or his opinions may waver from day to day with *the course of the debate. Opinion may also have a quality of latency in that attitudes may be present only awaiting activation by the appropriate stimulus.*

The discussion of properties of opinion, it should be admitted, must proceed in a tentative and exploratory spirit. The basic theoretical work has not been done to identify the politically relevant properties of opinion or to define well the nature of those properties. In the absence of some plausible basic conceptions of the properties of opinion, survey technicians naturally have not collected extensive data on the qualities of opinions of national populations. Despite these handicaps, the chapters that follow will treat several properties of opinion: intensity, stability, and latency.

9

INTENSITY

SPECULATION about the significance of public opinion must take into account the quality of opinion as well as the number of people who share it. Opinion may range from a preference barely above the level of indifference to a position deeply felt and tenaciously held. A person may agree that the United States should aid underdeveloped countries but not really care whether such a policy is pursued. Or an individual may believe that the United States has gone too far in social legislation and be boiling mad about what he regards as the movement of the Republic toward socialism. Another may subscribe to the abstract proposition that taxes ought to be reduced and yet calculate that there is no point in becoming exercised about the matter, since nothing can be done about taxes anyway. Still another may feel that the government should not interfere with segregation in the public schools and be in a mood to join in the clamor of opposition. If we merely count such persons, each of them carries equal weight in the reckoning of the balance of opinion. Yet it is plausible to suppose that as influences work themselves out through political processes, the qualities of an opinion, as well as the numbers who hold it, enter into the equation of contending political forces. Unfortunately, the qualitative characteristics of opinion are not readily amenable to measurement; nevertheless, some crude appraisals can be made.

1 · Measurement of Intensity of Opinion

Differences in the strength or depth of feeling are usually regarded as variations in the intensity of opinion. The problem of their measurement and analysis raises questions for the student of politics unlike those that concern the psychologist. For the student of psychology intensity of opinion may be an aspect of the problem of the nature of attitude. Or he may be curious whether intensity differs among personality types. From the political viewpoint intensity of opinion assumes importance for other reasons. The distribution of intensities within the population may be related to political action. The presumption, subject to verification, is that persons with opinions of high intensity are more disposed to act, to throw their weight around, than are persons whose opinions approach zero intensity. A further plausible supposition is that the location of intensities within the general patterns of distribution of opinion that fix the context for governmental action may be important. A bimodal conflict distribution, for example, with low intensities of opinion in opposition to an intensely supported course of action, would create a different problem for government than would a conflict distribution that consisted largely of opinions of extremely high intensity both pro and con. Or an opinion distribution reflective of overwhelming consensus may have one consequence if the dominant opinion is of high intensity, another if it is only lukewarm.

To cope with these questions, we need a measure of the intensity of opinion. To understand the conventional measures of intensity, it is essential to distinguish between the direction and the intensity of an opinion. That distinction may be illustrated from an analysis by Hadley Cantril. In 1945 he administered to a national sample of the white population a scale of attitude toward government regulation of business. The respondents were asked which of the following statements best expressed what they thought should be the relationship between business and government after World War II:

1. The government should own and control all big industries, banks, and natural resources.

2. There should be more regulation of business than there was before the war.

3. The government should continue to regulate business about the way it did before we got into war.

4. Some government regulation of business is necessary but there should be less regulation than we had under the New Deal before the war.

5. There should be as little government regulation of business as possible.

This scale was designed to ascertain the *direction* of opinion of the respondent. From the midpoint, approval of regulation about as it had existed before the war, a person might deviate in the direction of more control even unto advocacy of government ownership. Or he might tend in the opposite direction to "as little government regulation of business as possible."

After the respondent had located himself on the opinion scale, he was asked: "How strongly do you hold this opinion—very strongly, fairly strongly, or don't you care much one way or another?" Re-

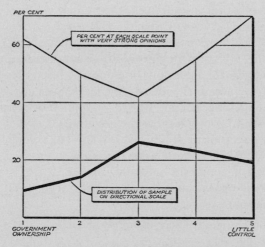

FIGURE 9.1. Distribution of National Sample on Scale of Attitudes on Government Policy Toward Business with Percentage at each Scale Point Holding "Very Strong" Opinions. SOURCE: Hadley Cantril: "The Intensity of an Attitude," *Journal of Abnormal and Social Psychology,* XLI (1946), 129-35.

sponses to this inquiry were presumed to provide a measure, or at least a self-estimate, of intensity of opinion. A person might hold an opinion extreme in one direction—for example, favor public ownership—but the intensity of his opinion could be high, medium, or low. This kind of measurement, of course, creates its doubts. One must assume that self-ratings of individuals are comparable in value at all points on the directional scale.

The distribution of the national sample on Cantril's scale of attitude toward government-business relations appears in Figure 9.1. The same figure shows the proportions of those at the different points on the scale who said they held their views "very strongly." From the figure, intensity of opinion appears to be related to its direction. The more extreme in direction an opinion, the more intense it is, on the average: 62 per cent of those who favored government ownership held their opinions "very strongly," against only 42 per cent of those disposed to continue regulation about as it had been before the war. At the extreme of "as little regulation as possible" 70 per cent appraised their views as "very strongly" held.[1] To some extent, then, a measurement of intensity is also a measurement of direction, which, in turn, is a measurement of intensity.[2]

The discussion of the place of intensity of opinion in the politics of the nation as a whole is greatly handicapped by at least two factors. First, techniques for the measurement of intensity are crude. Second, the data from national surveys of opinion that touch on intensity are limited. The principal materials available for analysis are the responses to questions on the series of policy propositions repeatedly used in the preceding chapters. In the interview situation the respondent was assured that "We don't expect everyone to have an opinion about all of these" questions. If the respondent said he had an opinion on a particular question, he was asked: "Do you think the government *should* do this or do you think the government should *not* do it?" The respondent had been given a card and was asked to choose the phrase on the card which indicated how he felt about the question, such as: "The government in Washington ought to see to it that everybody who wants to work can find a job." The phrases were:

Agree strongly; government definitely should.
Agree but not very strongly.
Not sure, it depends.
Disagree but not very strongly.
Disagree strongly; government definitely should not.
Don't know.

When we use responses to a single question to estimate intensity of opinion, we are operating somewhat differently than was Cantril in the instance cited to illustrate the concept of intensity. He compared average intensities at different points along a Thurstone-type scale composed of several questions. Our data concern intensity of opinion on

[1] Hadley Cantril: "The Intensity of An Attitude," *Journal of Abnormal and Social Psychology*, XLI (1946), 129–35. See also Daniel Katz: "The Measurement of Intensity," in H. Cantril: *Gauging Public Opinion* (Princeton: Princeton University Press; 1944), ch. 3; Reuben Mehling: "A Simple Test for Measuring Intensity of Attitudes," *Public Opinion Quarterly*, XXIII (1959–60), 576–78; and Robert A. Dahl: *A Preface to Democratic Theory* (Chicago: University of Chicago Press; 1956), ch. 4.

[2] On Guttman scales average intensity increases among respondents who place themselves toward the ends of the scale. See E. A. Suchman: "The Intensity Component in Attitude and Opinion Research," in *Measurement and Prediction* (Studies in Social Psychology in World War II), IV, 213–76.

particular questions. This fact requires not only that we contrive arithmetical tricks to use the data, but also that we proceed with caution in
drawing inferences. Our basic assumption has to be that the "Agree
strongly" responses, on the average, differ in intensity from the responses of "Agree but not very strongly." To some extent the soundness of that assumption may be tested. We know, for example, that
southern opinion about federal action on school segregation becomes
very strong. It is also a fair guess that northern opinion, although in a
direction opposite to that of the South, is not of the same intensity. Are
these common-sense impressions reflected in the measures of intensity?
Table 9.1 presents the responses in North and South about the proposi-

---

TABLE 9.1

OPINIONS ON WHETHER FEDERAL GOVERNMENT SHOULD STAY OUT OF SCHOOL
SEGREGATION QUESTION, NORTH AND SOUTH

	U.S.	North	South
Agree strongly; government definitely should (stay out)	35%	27%	53%
Agree but not very strongly	8	10	5
Not sure; it depends	6	6	6
Disagree but not very strongly	10	11	6
Disagree; government definitely should not	29	33	20
No opinion; DK; NA	12	13	10
	100%	100%	100%
N	1763	1250	513

DATA SOURCE: *Survey Research Center, University of Michigan, 1956.*

---

tion: "The government in Washington should stay out of the question
of whether white and colored children go to the same school." In the
South those who "agree strongly" outnumber by over 10:1 those who
"agree but not very strongly." In the North those who disagree
strongly exceed by only about 3:1 those who merely disagree. These
differences in intensity reported by respondents fit our impressions
about the relative sharpness of opinion on this question in the two regions.

Still another step is necessary to establish that intensity of opinion
has import for the political system. These verbal self-appraisals of opinion may have no relation to the way people behave. To check whether
they do, we may relate data on political participation to opinion intensity. Earlier we identified a stratum of high participators: those who not
only vote but also participate in some other way, such as talking up
their candidate, contributing money, or working for the party. On the

segregation issue, those who felt strongly pro or con turned out to include larger proportions of high participators than were among those who merely agreed or disagreed, the percentages in 1956 being:

	Agree strongly	Agree	Disagree	Disagree strongly
North	38%	33%	26%	31%
South	28	24	23	27

We cannot say from these figures that persons with intense opinions became slightly more active in politics because of the intensity of their opinions. Perhaps persons with high levels of participation tend to develop strong opinions. Or some other factor may account for the contrasts. The contrasts are not wide; yet if the mild-opinion group had the same proportion of persons with high levels of participation as the more intense group, several million more persons would have been in the category of high participators.

2 · Opinion Intensity and the Context of Political Action

Government acts within a context of public opinion that may limit either the range or the timing of public action. In turn, the actions of government and of other leadership centers may affect the form of this context. These interactions may to a degree be described or understood from information about the mere numbers of people who are for or against a given policy proposition. Is our understanding of, or our capacity to describe, these interactions enlarged by the addition of knowledge about intensity of opinion?

Before attempting to cope with this question, let us digress for an explanation of a simple ratio by which we may describe intensity numerically. Assume that twenty persons have a "very strong" opinion for a given measure and another ten favor it but not very strongly. A ratio of 2.00 may describe the intensity of support for the measure. If thirty persons strongly oppose and ten oppose not very strongly, the opposition opinion may be tagged with an intensity ratio of 3.00. The application of this ratio is illustrated in Table 9.2, in which the ratios are computed for the concurring and dissenting opinion on a series of propositions about policy and posture of this country toward the rest of the world.

Opinion Intensities on Foreign Policy Questions. The data in Table 9.2 provide us with measures of intensity of opinions about a variety

TABLE 9.2

RATIOS OF OPINION INTENSITY ON FOREIGN POLICY ISSUES

PROPOSITION	INTENSITY RATIO OF OPINION [a]		PER CENT AGREEMENT WITH PROPOSITION		PER CENT OF SAMPLE
	In agreement	In disagreement	Of strong opinion holders	Of total sample [b]	WITH STRONG OPINIONS
Act tough	4.52	1.40	86%	62%	59%
Stay home	1.49	3.17	25	25	58
Be friendly	2.33	0.61	86	63	51
Soldiers abroad	2.06	1.52	83	58	47
Economic aid	0.99	1.67	57	43	37
Aid to neutrals	0.73	2.01	37	29	33

[a] The intensity ratio is the ratio of those who "agree strongly" to those who "agree but not very strongly"; or of those who "disagree strongly" to those who "disagree but not very strongly." For the text of the policy propositions, see Appendix I.

[b] These percentages are affected by the proportions with no opinion as well as by the proportions disagreeing.

DATA SOURCE: *Survey Research Center, University of Michigan, 1956.*

of propositions relating to foreign policy. In some instances the data relate to attitudes of the most general nature. Thus, probably some primeval outlook with a relevance to specific foreign-policy actions is measured by responses to the proposition: "The best way for this country to deal with Russia and Communist China is to act just as tough as they do." Other items, though, bear more directly upon concrete issues, such as: "The United States should give help to foreign countries even if they are not as much against communism as we are." How does the availability of the intensity ratios improve our understanding of the interaction between government and opinion on specific actions related to these questions? It requires a modicum of imagination to divine the significance of intensity; yet it seems apparent that intensity bears on the tenor of popular response to governmental action and that, in the balance of forces, high intensity may to some degree augment the strength of numbers and low intensity may detract from that strength.

Some of the characteristics of the American outlook on foreign policy that perplex both us and the rest of the world may be reflected in, and even partially explained by, the data on intensity. The intensity ratios parallel, for example, the puzzling mixture of bellicosity and friendliness in our responses to the alien world. Opinion of extremely high intensity concurs with the proposition that the way to deal with Russia and China is to act "just as tough" as they do. In contrast, an opinion of quite high intensity also agreed with the statement: "The United States should be willing to go more than half-way in being friendly with the other countries of the world." The few who disagreed with the "be friendly" proposition could not often bring themselves to hearty dissent. Consistent with these mixed attitudes of toughness and friendliness are our alternating postures of spirited acclaim of acts of verbal toughness in our national leadership and of the trustfulness of a delighted puppy when treated in a friendly manner.[3]

Mixtures of our realism and of our romantic longing for withdrawal from the affairs of the external world may also be reflected in the intensity ratios. Probably a recognition of the simple facts of the modern world, rather than emotional preference, forms the basis for the intense disagreement with the proposition: "The country would be better off if we just stayed home and did not concern ourselves with problems in other parts of the world." A similar yielding to the contemporary realities may also characterize the relatively intense agreement with the statement: "The United States should keep soldiers overseas where they can help countries that are against communism." Nevertheless, on each of these propositions a small but fairly intense body of opinion gives vent to a deep-seated yearning, which would probably become larger under proper circumstances, that we might wash our hands of the affairs of the world and tend to our own knitting.

The ratios of intensity of opinion on the propositions about foreign economic aid bear special attention. If our intensity ratios are comparable from question to question—and we have no assurance that they are—the intensity of opinion in support of foreign economic aid is especially low. Americans have opinions of the highest intensity in support of a policy of "acting tough" but of extremely low intensity in support of "economic help to the poorer countries of the world even if they can't pay for it." An even lower level of intensity supports the view: "The United States should give help to foreign countries even if they are not as much against communism as we are." On each of these questions, as Table 9.2 indicates, the opposition sentiment is of higher intensity than the supportive opinion. These relative intensities seem to be mirrored in the periodic consideration by Congress of foreign-aid legislation; aid to neutralist countries seems to encounter more friction in the legislative machinery than do other types of foreign-aid legislation. In any case, the foundation in public opinion for an aggressive American policy of leadership in the economic development of the free world ap-

[3] As people were responding in support of "acting tough," they were also often acclaiming General Eisenhower for winding up the Korean incident. American opinion may be especially disposed toward approval of verbal bellicosity in the conduct of foreign affairs yet not conditioned to support hostilities short of a full-scale war.

pears, from these measures, to be thin—a thinness that may result in part from an inept job of political education by the national leadership, as well as from a deep-seated reluctance to part with a dollar.

Another aspect of the problem of intensity is illuminated by the data of Table 9.2. Persons with opinions of high intensity usually divide in different proportions than does the entire sample. It is not implausible to suppose that persons with opinions of high intensity provide a disproportionate share of the support for policies related to most of the propositions listed in the table. If we had better measures of intensity and of political participation, the import of the zealous believers in a cause could probably be better established.

One may suspect that the low intensities of opinion in support of foreign economic involvement are associated with uncertainties induced by lack of information and lack of understanding of long-run objectives. In fact, over a considerable range of foreign policy there may be a widespread popular disengagement along with a disposition to leave things to the government—so long as nobody is inconvenienced. Suggestive are the responses to the following question put to a sample in the Albany metropolitan region in 1949: "Do you think the government ought to pay attention to the public on these things (foreign affairs) or should it do what it thinks best for the country? Why do you feel that way?" The responses were: [4]

Government ought to pay attention to the public	43%
Government should do what it thinks best	41
Government must do what it thinks best	6
DK and NA	10

Of those who thought that the government ought to pay attention to the public, almost a third could dredge up no reason for their position. About half gave reasons that could be coded under the heading: "That's the democratic procedure." On domestic questions probably not nearly so large a proportion would be disposed to the view that the government should do what it thinks best.

Intensity and Domestic Questions. Variations in intensity in opinion on propositions about foreign policy are such that, at least by *ex post facto* reasoning, they make some sense in relation to our general impressions of the American outlook toward the external world. Variations in opinion intensity on questions of domestic policy do not suggest so

[4] Survey Research Center: *Interest, Information, and Attitudes in the Field of World Affairs* (Ann Arbor: Survey Research Center; 1949), p. 82.

ready a set of interpretations. Yet the data relating to several broad propositions on basic political values (in Table 9.3) are instructive. Observe the high intensity, as well as the magnitude, of opinion in disagreement with the proposition: "The government ought to fire any government worker who is accused of being a communist even though

TABLE 9.3

OPINION INTENSITY ON PROPOSITIONS RELATED TO BROAD POLITICAL VALUES

PROPOSITION	INDEX OF OPINION INTENSITY [a]		PER CENT AGREEMENT WITH PROPOSITION		PER CENT OF TOTAL SAMPLE WITH STRONG OPINIONS
	In agreement	In disagreement	Of strong opinion	Of total sample [b]	
Fire communist suspects	2.18	3.20	25%	21%	57%
Antidiscrimination	2.31	1.95	77	61	56
Union influence	3.10	1.21	78	51	48
Big business influence	3.00	1.08	82	51	46

[a] The index of intensity is the ratio of those who "agree strongly" to those who "agree but not very strongly" or of those who "disagree strongly" to those who "disagree but not very strongly." For the phrasing of the policy propositions, see Appendix I.
[b] These percentages are affected by the proportions without opinions as well as by the proportions in disagreement.
DATA SOURCE: *Survey Research Center, University of Michigan, 1956.*

they don't prove it." This opinion pattern may indicate both a widespread and an intense attachment to the idea of fair play,[5] although those concerned about constitutional values may be perturbed by the relatively high intensity of the opinions of those who agree with the proposition. A basic attachment to equity and fair play may also be evident in the relatively high intensity of opinion in agreement with: "If Negroes *are not* getting fair treatment in jobs and housing, the government in Washington should see to it that they do."

[5] It may be doubted whether opinions on the proposition invariably reflect appreciation of abstract constitutionalism. One respondent explained agreement by the aphorism "where there's smoke, there's fire;" another buttressed disagreement with, "give the devil his due." Far more frequently, though, the volunteered comment was the equivalent of "a person is innocent until proved guilty."

The intensity ratios of opinion holding that the influence of big business and labor unions should be restrained probably give us another dimension of this significant basic political opinion. Note the extremely high intensity ratios of opinion in agreement with the proposition that the government ought to see that big business corporations "don't have much say about how the government is run." With a fine impartiality, about the same intensity exists on the similar proposition about labor unions. It was earlier suggested that concurrence with these propositions probably indicated the existence of a basic view that nobody should have "too much power" in the American system. The intensity ratios suggest that these views are held with a special strength and assurance. The relatively few persons who took the negative position on these questions had, on the average, convictions of no great strength.[6]

On the several additional policy propositions the intensity data (presented in Table 9.4) indicate variations in quality of opinion on individual issues. These variations suggest no generalization; about all one can say is that some questions generate intense opinions among far larger proportions of the public than do others. These differences in proportions of holders of strong opinions, though, make it plain that intensity of opinion, as measured, is not simply the consequence of a disposition among certain types of people to agree or disagree strongly whatever the question may be. The level of intensity depends on the issue. Thus, about two thirds of the sample felt strongly pro or con regarding the proposition: "The government in Washington should stay out of the question of whether white and colored children should go to the same schools." In contrast, only 44 per cent had strong sentiments about the proposition: "The government ought to cut taxes even if it means putting off some important things that need to be done." On school integration opinions in both agreement and disagreement were, on the average, of high intensity, but on the tax-cut question neither supporters nor opponents could develop opinions of high intensity.

On the other questions in Table 9.4 the intensity ratios make some sense in the light of our common-sense judgments about feelings on the issues. The high intensity of opinion against government aid in medical care coincides with our impressions of the determination of those who are opposed. The high intensity of opinion, both pro and con, on public power and housing parallels the spirited leadership for these oppos-

---

[6] Majority opinion of high intensity may either weaken minority convictions or even make converts and thereby affect the division of the population between the yeas and nays on a question. Experimental findings support the point that a zealous majority may cow the minority, but it would require extensive research to trace out the process in the general population. See H. H. Kelley and Thomas W. Lamb: "Uncertainty of Judgment and Resistance to Social Influence," *Journal of Abnormal and Social Psychology*, XXXV (1957), 137–9.

TABLE 9.4

OPINION INTENSITY ON SELECTED DOMESTIC POLICY PROPOSITIONS

PROPOSITION	INDEX OF OPINION INTENSITY [a]		PER CENT AGREEMENT WITH PROPOSITION		PER CENT OF TOTAL SAMPLE WITH STRONG OPINIONS
	In agreement	In disagreement	Of strong opinion holders	Of total sample [b]	
Integration	4.23	3.14	53%	43%	64%
Job guarantee	3.26	1.58	73	56	60
School aid	2.43	1.81	82	68	57
Medical care	2.49	2.29	67	54	56
Power and housing	2.72	2.03	68	41	45
Tax cut	1.47	1.84	35	26	44

[a] The index of intensity is the ratio of those who "agree strongly" to those who "agree but not very strongly" or of those who "disagree strongly" to those who "disagree but not very strongly." For the phrasing of the propositions, see Appendix I.
[b] These percentages are affected by the proportions without opinions as well as by the proportions in disagreement.
DATA SOURCE: *Survey Research Center, University of Michigan, 1956.*

ing viewpoints. The extremely high intensity of opinion supporting the job-guarantee proposition may occasion some astonishment; yet it may be indicative of the existence of a latent opinion or of an expectation of high intensity. An administration that viewed lightly its responsibilities in this field at a moment of economic crisis would probably be in for serious trouble.

3 · Roots of Opinion Intensity

It would be helpful to know why some persons have intense feelings or opinions and why others do not. One explanation is that variations in intensity may be ascribed to the degree to which the ego is affected or disturbed by a stimulus. Sherif and Cantril define the ego as "many attitudes which from infancy on are related to the delimited, differentiated and accumulating 'I,' 'me,' 'mine' experiences." [7] These "me" at-

[7] M. Sherif and H. Cantril: *The Psychology of Ego-Involvements* (New York: Wiley; 1947), p. 4.

titudes may include values, standards, goals, interests, and norms of many kinds. Thus, a person may have so intimate an identification with the Republican party that when it is assaulted he cringes as if he had been attacked personally. Or a miser may feel that a tax to educate other people's children represents the triumph of a conspiracy to rob him of his own, his very own, money. Or a person who has become by interest and indoctrination a "one worlder" may consider his own fortunes to be involved in measures to promote the welfare of his fellow man across the seas. The more an issue involves the ego, so the argument goes, the more intense opinion is likely to be.

A not inconsistent view of opinion intensity has been stated by Miller, who has formulated the following operational propositions:

> Persons for whom a value is more important will be more likely to express intense opinions than will persons for whom the same value is less important.
>
> Persons who perceive issues to be more relevant for their values will be more likely to express intense opinions.[8]

What these theoretical formulations amount to is the contention that the more concerned a person is about an issue, the greater is the probability that his opinion will be intense. Obviously an issue may become of concern to a person in many ways, and that concern may take different forms. A proposed law that would put a man out of business may arouse an intense opinion. A proposed law that clashes with a man's ethical notions, although it would affect him personally not at all, may also arouse an intense opinion, but on a different sort of foundation. It may well be that most issues have such slight effect or potential effect on most individuals that it requires a considerable acculturation to democratic processes—or development of a sense of identification with the community—for a person to feel intensely about many issues. At any rate, the range of opinion intensity must be quite wide within the population generally, and our measures of intensity capture only the most meager suggestion of its variety.

How may we go about the task of locating the factors that seem to bring about intensity of opinion? A method of attack may be illustrated by a case readily comprehensible to college students. In 1948 the Washington Public Opinion Laboratory conducted a survey on the question: "Courses about religion should be required of all students in state institutions of higher learning. Do you strongly agree, agree, disagree, strongly disagree, or are you undecided?" The distributions of the responses for the sample of adults of the state and for university students follow:

[8] Angus Campbell, Philip E. Converse, Warner E. Miller, and Donald E. Stokes: *The American Voter* (New York: Wiley; 1960), pp. 176–9.

	Adults of State	University Students
Strongly agree	5%	3%
Agree	21	8
Undecided	11	4
Disagree	50	32
Strongly disagree	12	53
NA	1	*

University students, as any freshman could have predicted, had no taste for required courses in religion—a manifestation of undergraduate attitudes toward required courses and not necessarily of undergraduate godlessness. Eighty-five per cent of them disagreed, against only 62 per cent of the general population. The intensity factor, though, is of chief relevance here. If we apply our intensity ratio to the data, the intensity of student opinion in disagreement was 1.65, in contrast with the low intensity ratio of 0.24 in the dissenting opinion of the general population. Thus, the more immediate the impact upon a class of persons of policies they oppose, the more intense their opinion may be expected to be. The general population, while not enamored of the idea of compulsory religious instruction, could work up no impressive enthusiasm in its opposition. On the other hand, the lads who contemplated the thought of sitting through a course both compulsory and perhaps dull expressed an opinion of far higher intensity. In the argot of psychology, they were more ego-involved.

Group Identification and Opinion Intensity. Doubtless the foundations of opinion intensity—that is, the ways in which the ego may become involved—are almost as numerous as are the motives that move men, and inquiries into intensity have not been pursued far enough to identify many of these foundations. Within the population there may be excitable persons highly involved politically who possess intense opinions on issues with no immediate impact on their own rights or privileges. The most promising supposition, though, is that persons who are, or would be, affected in some readily apparent manner would be most likely to hold intense opinions. One way in which people are aroused is by threats to the groups with which they have a sense of identification. In view of the importance of group identification in the molding of political attitudes, it might plausibly be expected that persons with a sharp sense of group identification would have more intense opinions on group-related issues than would persons whose sense of identification is slight or who are nonmembers.

Some support for these propositions comes from variations in the intensity of opinion among union members with a high sense of group identification, members with a weak sense of identification, and non-members on the proposition: "The government ought to see to it that labor unions don't have much say about how the government is run." Agreement with this proposition, as we have seen, is both general within the population and of high intensity, perhaps reflective of the acceptance of one of the basic rules of the political game. Among those who "feel pretty close to union members in general," though, the intensity of concurrence is less than among those union members who do not "feel close" as well as far less than among nonmembers. Intensity of opinion also varies similarly at the opposite end of the opinion distribution. Union members disagree with the proposition far more frequently than do nonmembers. Those who "feel close" to the union have a dissenting opinion of far higher intensity than that of either members who do not "feel close" or nonmembers. These relationships appear in detail in Table 9.5, the details of which suggest that many factors

TABLE 9.5

RELATION OF OPINION INTENSITY ON UNION INFLUENCE PROPOSITION TO UNION
MEMBERSHIP AND SENSE OF IDENTIFICATION WITH UNION [a]

AFFILIATION	OPINION ON UNION INFLUENCE ISSUE			
	In agreement		In disagreement	
	Per cent	Intensity ratio	Per cent	Intensity ratio
Union members				
Feel close	35%	2.12	41%	2.86
Feel not close	47%	2.75	29%	1.40
Nonmembers	52%	3.34	15%	0.89

[a] The policy proposition was: "The government ought to see to it that labor unions don't have much say about how the government is run." Where the head of the household or the respondent was a union member, he was asked: "Would you say you feel pretty close to labor union members in general or that you don't feel much closer to them than you do to other kinds of people?"
DATA SOURCE: *Survey Research Center, University of Michigan, 1956.*

other than sense of group identification enter into the determination of opinion direction and intensity. Many persons strong in their sense of union identification still subscribe to the view that unions should not have "too much influence" in government.[9] Some nonmembers,

[9] Data such as those of Table 9.5 need to be put into the perspective of the political system lest erroneous inferences be drawn about the magnitude of blocs of opinion. Union members who felt strongly that union influence should not be restrained amounted to only about 5 per cent of the total national sample. All union members who disagreed with the proposition, either strongly or not very strongly, amounted to only about 8 per cent.

too, take the negative view on the question, but the average intensity of their opinion is low.

Another example of the bearing of group affiliation on intensity is provided by attitudes toward the proposition: "The United States should give help to foreign countries even if they are not as much against communism as we are." The hostility of the Roman Catholic hierarchy toward communist regimes might be expected to produce an opinion of high intensity on this issue among those persons with a sense of close identification with Catholicism. From Table 9.6 it appears that

---

TABLE 9.6

RELATION OF OPINION INTENSITY ON AID TO NEUTRALS TO CATHOLICISM AND SENSE OF IDENTIFICATION WITH CATHOLICS [a]

AFFILIATION	OPINION ON AID TO NEUTRALS			
	In agreement		In disagreement	
	Per cent	Intensity ratio	Per cent	Intensity ratio
Catholic				
Feel close	31%	0.81	34%	2.60
Feel not close	26%	0.69	34%	1.83
Non-Catholics	29%	0.72	30%	1.95

[a] The policy proposition was: "The United States should give help to foreign countries even if they are not as much against communism as we are." The division according to group identification rests on responses to the question: "Would you say you feel pretty close to Catholics in general or that you don't feel much closer to them than you do to other people?"

DATA SOURCE: *Survey Research Center, University of Michigan, 1956.*

---

those Catholics with a sense of closeness to fellow Catholics who oppose aid to neutralist countries do so with an exceptional intensity. Perhaps the significant feature of the table from the standpoint of group influence is the narrow differences between Catholics and non-Catholics in direction of opinion. If the influences of the Church have an effect on the parishioners, it is almost matched, on this issue, by other like influences upon non-Catholics.[1]

[1] Again, the intensity figures need to be put into perspective. Those who felt close to fellow Catholics and also strongly opposed aid to neutrals amounted to only 2 per cent of the total national sample. All Catholics who opposed aid to neutrals, either strongly or not very strongly, amounted to only 7 per cent of the sample. The question drew a large percentage of "don't knows." If one could hold other factors constant, the influence of the Church might appear to be stronger, but the magnitude of this influence in the electorate as a whole is small.

Other Bases of Intensity. The further one proceeds in attempting to identify the correlates of intensity, the more evident it becomes that a wide variety of circumstances can generate intense psychological concern about an issue. On any given issue the analytical problem is one of ascertaining why some people become deeply concerned and others do not. On some questions intensity may rest on the peculiar necessities of a class of persons; raw self-interest may be at the root of some intense opinions. Whether to call this "ego involvement" illuminates the matter may be doubtful.

An illustration of a relation between imputed self-interest and intensity is contained in Table 9.7. One might suppose that those persons

---

TABLE 9.7

INTENSITY OF OPINION ON MEDICAL CARE ISSUE IN RELATION TO SATISFACTION
WITH CURRENT FINANCIAL SITUATION

FINANCIAL
SITUATION [a]

	OPINION ON MEDICAL CARE ISSUE			
	In agreement		In disagreement	
	Per cent	*Intensity ratio*	*Per cent*	*Intensity ratio*
Satisfied	48%	2.28	31%	2.34
More-or-less	56%	2.10	26%	2.15
Dissatisfied	64%	6.35	17%	3.30

[a] "We are also interested in how people are getting along financially these days. So far as you and your family are concerned, would you say that you are pretty well satisfied with your present financial situation, more-or-less satisfied, or not satisfied at all?" The question on medical care read: "The government ought to help people get doctors and hospital care at low cost."
DATA SOURCE: *Survey Research Center, University of Michigan, 1956.*

---

who feel satisfied with their financial situation would be less disposed to favor governmental action to make medical and hospital care available at low cost than would those persons who are "not satisfied at all" with their present financial situation, and that is in fact the case. The financially dissatisfied favor some sort of action with respect to medical care, as the table shows, with an opinion far more intense than that held by those supporters of medical care who are "pretty well satisfied" with their current financial situation. The puzzling aspect of the situation is that the financially dissatisfied who oppose government action on medical care also oppose it with a warmer intensity than do those opponents who are "pretty well satisfied." Since the number of cases in the sample

does not suffice to permit confident identification of the peculiarities of
these dissatisfied opponents of medical care, about all that can be concluded is that intensity of opinion may rest on factors other than personal need and concern as measured by the questions analyzed in the
table.[2]

Some political values may be so widely and so thoroughly implanted in the population that fairly intense opinions prevail even
against immediate self-interest. Thus, on the proposition of federal aid
to education one might suppose that those persons with children of
school age would be most deeply concerned and show the most intense
as well as the most frequent opinions in support of aid to education.

TABLE 9.8

Stage of Life in Relation to Opinion in Support of Aid to Education

LIFE STAGE	PER CENT FAVORING AID	INTENSITY RATIO
Under 45, single	65	3.60
Under 45, married, no children	67	2.80
Married, youngest child under 4½ years	69	2.60
Married, youngest child 4½–14½ years	65	2.65
Married, youngest child over 14½ years	69	2.80
Over 45, married, no children	66	2.14
Over 45, single	61	1.67

DATA SOURCE: *Survey Research Center, University of Michigan, 1956.*

Evidently, however, the doctrine of universal public education is so
much an article of general political faith that it is shared by the child-
less. Table 9.8 shows the degree of support for this proposition among
persons with and without children and with children of different ages.
Among all these sectors of the population support for aid to education is substantial, and the intensity ratio does not vary notably among
the different groups. Only among spinsters and bachelors over 45 years
of age (and presumably without children) does the degree and intensity of support decline. And that decline may have nothing to do with
the childlessness of the respondents concerned.

Intensity in some circumstances may be a function of the community situation. A suggestion of that possibility comes from an analysis
of opinion on the proposition: "If Negroes are not getting fair treat-

[2] White-collar persons contribute disproportionately to the group of financially dissatisfied who are intensely opposed to government action on medical
care.

ment in jobs and housing, the government in Washington should see to it that they do." Among northern whites there is substantial agreement with this proposition. The frequency of concurrence does not differ markedly among whites who live in counties with few Negroes (under 5 per cent) and those who reside in counties with larger proportions (10 per cent or over) of Negroes. Among residents of these types of counties, though, intensity of agreement with the proposition differs remarkably. In counties with few Negroes in the population the tendency is to favor with a high average intensity fair play for Negroes. In counties with larger proportions of Negroes the agreement is expressed with a considerably lower intensity.[3] Persons in communities with larger numbers of Negroes seem to lose some of their zeal for "fair treatment" for Negroes in jobs and housing.[4] This interpretation loses some of its persuasiveness when it is observed that white opinion in disagreement with the fair treatment proposition also becomes of lower intensity in the counties with the higher proportions of nonwhite population (see Table 9.9). For that oddity no ready explanation occurs.[5]

It seems probable that on some questions intensity, as we measure it, reflects no deep emotional concern but indicates a sense of assurance or certainty that rests on information or education. Thus, the intensity ratios differed markedly with level of education on the proposition: "The government ought to cut taxes even if it means putting off some important things that need to be done." The intensity ratio of opinion in disagreement among the college-trained was 2.62; among high school graduates, 1.85; and among grade-schoolers, 1.28. Not only may the foundation for intense opinion be different from question to question; the psychological reality of intensity, as measured, may be different.

[3] Similar, though not so marked, downward gradations of intensity with increasing percentage of nonwhite county population exist in opinion in disagreement with the proposition: "The government in Washington should stay out of the question of whether white and colored children go to the same school."

[4] A Detroit housewife disagreed with the proposition but not strongly: "I've been drove out of three homes by colored people. They swarmed all about me." The wife of a Massachusetts lawyer agreed but not strongly: "But they should also use a little judgment on that." A Michigan salesman disagreed strongly: "They can shift for themselves pretty well. The government doesn't support any other race. Why should they support them?" A millwright disagreed but not strongly: "Here in St. Louis Negroes are getting more than fair treatment." The wife of an Idaho truck driver disagreed strongly: "I think they ought to be shipped back where they came from." The wife of a Missouri auto mechanic disagreed strongly: "Sometimes they make more money than white people. White people need jobs first."

[5] If appropriate data were available, a more suitable correlation than that in Table 9.9 would be possible. One would like to know the opinions of persons with and without community experience or contact with Negroes, a matter only roughly approximated by the grouping of counties in the table.

TABLE 9.9

PERCENTAGE NONWHITE OF COUNTY POPULATION IN RELATION TO OPINIONS OF NORTHERN WHITES ON FAIR TREATMENT FOR NEGROES IN JOBS AND HOUSING [a]

	Nonwhite per cent of county population		
	0–4	5–9	10 and over
Per cent for fair treatment [b]	61	60	54
Intensity ratio of:			
Pro opinion	2.55	1.74	1.33
Con opinion	1.55	1.60	1.10

[a] The question was: "If Negroes are not getting fair treatment in jobs and housing, the government in Washington should see to it that they do."
[b] Percentage base includes those with no opinion on the question.
DATA SOURCE: *Survey Research Center, University of Michigan, 1956.*

An opinion of high intensity on the tax-cut question probably has a psychological reality for the individual and a meaning for the political system unlike an opinion of high intensity on a question such as the issue of school segregation. Another question on which elementary information rather than emotional involvement probably fixes the intensity ratio is the proposition: "This country would be better off if we just stayed home and did not concern ourselves with problems in other parts of the world." The intensity ratio of opinion in dissent among college persons was 6.50, and that among grade-schoolers, 2.12.

Intensity of opinion may be in part a function of a generalized interest and concern in politics; that is, some persons because of their general concern may tend to have opinions of high intensity on most questions on which they have opinions. The data indicate that this may be true for a limited number of persons. Political involvement may roughly be measured by the degree to which a person "personally cares" which party wins and by the degree of his expressed interest in following the campaign. With a fairly high degree of uniformity from question to question, persons with high political involvement more frequently express "strong" agreement or "strong" disagreement than do persons with low political involvement. Thus, 60 per cent of the highly involved had strong opinions on the question of leaving power and housing to private business, while only 31 per cent of those with low involvement had strong opinions. Like details on other issues appear in Table 9.10. It could be supposed that persons who "care" a great deal about election outcomes and are "very much interested" in following campaigns might automatically respond that they "agree strongly" or

TABLE 9.10

POLITICAL INVOLVEMENT IN RELATION TO VERY STRONG AGREEMENT AND VERY
STRONG DISAGREEMENT ON SELECTED POLICY ISSUES [a]

POLICY PROPOSITION	LEVEL OF POLITICAL INVOLVEMENT			
	Low			High
	1	2	3	4
School integration	58%	62%	65%	71%
Job guarantee	54	57	60	68
Fire communist suspects	44	54	59	68
Power and housing	31	41	47	60
Aid to neutrals	24	29	36	42
Foreign aid	36	38	34	37

[a] Entries are percentages of respondents at each level of involvement
who agreed strongly or disagreed strongly with the policy proposition.
The percentage base includes those with no opinion. For a description
of the index of political involvement, see Appendix IV, and for the
phrasing of the policy questions, Appendix I.
DATA SOURCE: *Survey Research Center, University of Michigan, 1956.*

"disagree strongly" with policy propositions. To some extent that appears to be the case, but level of involvement can account for only a
small part of the variation in opinion intensity. Substantial numbers of
persons with weak political involvement have intense opinions. Moreover, the variation within levels of involvement of the proportions with
intense opinions on the series of issues indicates that intensity is a factor
largely independent of involvement.

Reflection on these attempts to identify factors that might be productive of intensity of opinion suggests that intensity or depth of concern rests on the most varied foundations. It may make sense to convert
all these roots of intensity to the common denominator of ego involvement; yet one suspects that intensity, at least as it has been measured,
covers a variety of kinds of concerns. Intensity may rest on a sense of
group identification. It may flow from naked and immediate self-
interest. It may emerge from an attachment to community values. It
may be simply an assurance founded on knowledge. It may come from
an anxiety about threats to an ordered course of existence. Intensity of
opinion seems by and large to develop when persons are confronted by
issues or circumstances that might be expected on a common-sense basis
to arouse their concern most deeply. Yet it may be doubted that intensity, as we have crudely measured it, necessarily has the same meaning
from person to person, situation to situation, or issue to issue.

4 · Intensity of Opinion, Participation, Action

These exercises in the analysis of intensity of opinion remain only exercises unless they can be connected in some way with the workings of the political system. That connection could probably best be made if we had comparable data from different societies, some characterized by opinions of high intensity, others by low levels of opinion intensity. Offhand observation makes it clear that a regime that must deal with opinion blocs of high intensity may be beset by periodic revolutions, driven to dictatorial methods if its decisions are to prevail, or perhaps paralyzed by the intractability of conflicting views of high intensity. On the other hand, a government whose people harbor less intense opinions confronts different kinds of problems in the management of affairs.

Traces of Intensity within a System of Consensus. Since we lack reliable opinion data on sharply contrasting societies, our speculations on the relevance of opinion intensity for governance are restricted to the American situation. The mode of analysis can be a comparison within the American system of problems of governance concerning different issues on which opinion intensity varies. Even that type of analysis is limited, because for the issues on which we have data the range of variation of opinion intensity is relatively narrow. We lack issues distinguished sharply by the intensity of opinion they arouse and, hence, lack sharply different circumstances to contrast as we seek to spot the significance of the variable of intensity for the governing process. In a society characterized in large degree by consensus, intensity of opinion on most issues must be relatively low. This is true by definition; at least it is true under the measures of intensity employed here. Intensity, as we have seen, becomes higher at the extremes of opinion distributions. Most of the distributions of opinion that we have examined approach the consensual form of narrow dispersion, which means that intensities are low. The chances are, too, that the conditions of the times—1956 —when most of the data were collected were conducive to a blandness of outlook.

Even within the American system, though, sufficient variation in intensity prevails among opinions on certain issues to permit a glimpse of the significance of opinion intensity. Among the issues on which the data are available, the most marked intensity of opinion exists on the question of the role of the federal government in school integration. That issue generates a bipolarization of opinion of high intensity, especially high in the South. The consequences of the existence of that type of opinion for government action are evident. Intensity of opinion accentuates conflict and makes the solution of an issue extremely difficult. Contrast the workings of government as it grapples with an issue on which intensity of opinion is extremely low, such as foreign aid. Although that question produces some bipolarization of opinion, feelings about it are of a relatively low intensity. Correspondingly, the maneuvers within the governing process for the attainment of decisions are accompanied by less public anxiety and involvement and are conducted without the limitations that large blocs of intense opinion produce.

Intensity and Political Participation. In another respect our data on opinion intensity handicap us as we seek to estimate the influence of that property of opinion for the political system. We lack adequate data on the characteristics and behavior of that thin layer of persons highly active in politics. From our daily impressions of politics we feel that persons who have opinions of high intensity are likely to seek energetically to achieve the ends in which they believe. These blocs of intense opinion combined with frenetic activity slip through the tines of a national sampling procedure. Yet the endeavors of these small blocs of opinion-holders often energize—or brake—the machinery of state. Little bands of dedicated souls leave their clear imprint on public policy. The duck hunters, the lovers of the national parks, the forestry zealots, the disciples of Izaak Walton, and many other small groups have left their tracks in the statute books. In countless other instances, small blocs of intense opinion are accompanied by exertions of influence that suffice to obstruct action. Yet these patterns of opinion and action can be identified only by far more intensive sampling of attitudes than has occurred.

The broad question is whether this association of opinion intensity with high levels of implementing activity characteristic of the upper stratum of political activists also prevails within the general population. With respect to voting, attributes which are the equivalent of intensity of opinion seem to produce higher levels of political activity. Persons with a high sense of political involvement—that is, persons who care more intensely about who wins—are more likely to vote than are those with a low level of involvement. Persons with a strong sense of party identification, which may be equivalent to a high intensity of opinion, are more likely to vote than are independents or persons with a weak sense of party identification. Persons with a marked enthusiasm about a candidate are more likely to turn up at the polls than are those who retain an indifferent equanimity.

We wish, though, to take the analysis a step further in order to determine whether intense opinion on a series of substantive questions produces a high level of political participation in the population generally. The relationship, while regular, is not large; this should not be astonishing, considering the crudeness of our measures of both intensity of opinion and participation. On most of the issues that we have examined, those persons with high levels of participation—that is, persons who participated in some kind of activity in addition to the mere act of voting—held opinions of a somewhat higher average intensity than did those persons of low levels of participation. The data on this point appear in Table 9.11. On most of the issues there shown, the low

TABLE 9.11

Opinion Intensity Ratios by Participation Levels

POLICY PROPOSITION	PARTICIPATION LEVEL [a]		
	Low	Medium	High
Medical care	2.25	2.40	2.49
Fire communist suspects	2.36	2.59	4.88
Tax cut	1.67	1.62	1.74
Stay home	1.92	2.20	3.18
Be friendly	1.31	1.47	2.38
Power and housing	1.85	2.90	3.22
School integration			
South	8.80	4.70	8.00
North	2.79	2.82	3.42

[a] The ratios in this table are constructed in a different way from those in preceding tables. The ratio here is that of the combined "agree strongly" and "disagree strongly" to the combined "agree" and "disagree" on each question. The entries are the ratios for those falling in each participation level. For the phrasing of the policy propositions, see Appendix I.

DATA SOURCE: *Survey Research Center, University of Michigan, 1956.*

participators—that is, the nonvoters—had opinions of lower intensity than did the high participators. In no instance would it be safe to attribute much increase in participation to intensity of opinion alone; intensity of opinion on the foreign issues in the table, for example, goes along with education and information which have their bearing on participation. Moreover, on some of the questions variations in intensity among participation levels is slight indeed. And the data make it apparent that under some circumstances persons have intense opinions that do not lead to heightened participation, although across the electorate there seems to be a slight tendency for participation to increase with intensity of opinion.

Unchanneled Opinion of High Intensity. The reality seems to be that many persons with opinions of high intensity are not high participators; they may not even vote. Our quest for the significance of opinion intensity must go beyond the hypothesis that intensity produces higher participation among the mass of voters. Perhaps it is worthwhile to look at the circumstances in which high intensity of opinion is accompanied by extremely low levels of political participation. This combination of warm attitude and resignation in behavior may provide us with a clue to the health of political systems. A first step in this examination is taken in Table 9.12, which indicates the proportions of

TABLE 9.12

POLITICAL PARTICIPATION IN RELATION TO OPINION INTENSITY ON SELECTED QUESTIONS [a]

QUESTION	AGREE STRONGLY	AGREE	DISAGREE STRONGLY	DISAGREE	NO OPINION
Tax cut	21%	26%	38%	35%	19%
Medical care	27	27	40	37	17
Fire communist suspects	27	25	36	29	13
Stay home	24	21	38	31	14
Integration					
North	38	33	31	26	18
South	28	24	34	25	19
Power and housing	36	28	34	25	19
Be friendly	39	23	21	25	18

[a] Entries are percentages of those in each cell who ranked high on the index of participation.
DATA SOURCE: *Survey Research Center, University of Michigan, 1956.*

high participators among those who "agree strongly," "disagree strongly," or simply "agree" or "disagree" with various policy propositions. On most of the questions the holders of a strong opinion include larger, but only slightly larger, proportions of high participators than the groups with less intense opinions.

On two of the questions, though, those who held a strong opinion included fewer high participators than the groups with an opinion of less intensity. On the tax-cut question this reversal of expectation prevails on the "agree" side. The tax-cut question, as we saw earlier, evidently isolates a category of persons with peculiar attitudes toward government. The existence of blocs of electors with intense opinions and low levels of participation excites curiosity. These concentrations of discouraged strong believers tend to be more numerous at the end of the opinion scale occupied by the socially disadvantaged.

Concentrations of intense but nonparticipant opinion may represent maladjustments in the political system. Pockets of people with intense opinions are evidently dominated by such feelings of futility and ineffectiveness that they do not exert themselves politically and often fail even to vote. Among those who felt strongly that the government should "help people get doctors and hospital care at low cost," there were in 1956 nonvoters to the number of about 10 per cent of the electorate. This kind of nonparticipation seems to be associated with a low sense of political efficacy.[6] The combination of intense opinion and low sense of efficacy with alienation from participation in the political system may not be the most healthy condition for a democratic order. Such population blocs may be of serious consequence only when they are of considerable magnitude. Such blocs may, if sufficiently agitated, seek to work out their concerns through mob action or by other more direct routes to their ends than the tortuous processes of popular politics; nonparticipators may yearn for short-cuts. As intense opinion is channeled into meaningful political participation, the persons involved may learn to live with the fabianism of public action. The import of this phenomenon could probably be better understood if we had for comparative analysis data on regimes that included large blocs of intense opinion associated with a lack of faith in the efficacy of the normal political processes. Probably if participation is to serve a safety-valve function, it must occur under conditions that give some faith in its ultimate efficacy.

Intensity and Action. The discussion of opinion intensity puts us on the trail of a significant aspect of the place of opinion in the governing process, but the techniques for measuring intensity and the sparseness of the data limit our exploration of that trail. Intensity, one knows from offhand observation, varies over more steps than are suggested by the simple division of opinions into "very strong" and "not very strong." Political concern runs from the most abject indifference through many gradations to an incandescence of interest shared by extremely few people. Moreover, we are handicapped by our measures of political participation. If we could identify more gradations in mass participation, people would arrange themselves from those with absolutely no attention toward political objects and no disposition even to vote to those with command of resources with which to influence

---

[6] Of those who "strongly" favored tax cuts, 49 per cent rated low on the scale of political efficacy; of those "strongly" opposed, 18 per cent ranked low. Among those "strongly" favoring tax cuts, the low-efficacy group included 50 per cent nonvoters; the high-efficacy group, 14 per cent.

many other people. With better measures of both intensity and participation, the chances are that a far more persuasive estimate could be
made of the significance of variations of intensity of opinion in the mass
political process.[7] Yet even as the state of knowledge stands, it is clear
that differences in intensity of opinion are associated with heightened
political activity of several million people. It requires no monstrous
stretch of the imagination to suppose that this fact seeps through the
mechanisms of communication and in one way or another affects the
course of political action. At the other extreme we glimpse traces of
the pathology of democracies in the existence of patches of intense
opinion held by persons who despair of making themselves felt through
the normal channels of democratic action.

[7] These remarks touch on the broad problem of the bearing of attitude on
behavior, a question on which the basic knowledge is in a most unsatisfactory
state. Attitudes of intensity may be dissipated in verbalization or they may lead to
other types of political activism. The factors associated with variation in behavioral consequences of attitude remain inadequately understood.

I 0

STABILITY

COMMENTATORS on democratic processes often speak
of the volatility of public opinion, its whimsicality, its sluggishness, its
stability, its erraticism, and its unpredictability. Yet verified information about the stability or instability of public opinion is scarce. In
comment on the subject it is seldom clear precisely what opinion or
whose opinion is in question. On occasion the appearance rather than
the reality of public opinion is clearly the topic of discourse. "Anyone
who has ever taken part in a political movement," Namier observes,
knows how "a seemingly powerful campaign in the Press can be started
by a few able and zealous writers, how a stage army can be marched
out by one door and brought back by another, and how the appearance
of an 'opinion' can be created (and also how quickly and easily they
peter out once the management is withdrawn)." [1] Such episodes, which
may be cyclonic in their transience, are seldom the reality of public
opinion; most people may be completely unaware of such verbal dis-
turbances, which capture the eye and ear of only a narrow public. At
times the source of lugubrious comment about the instability of public
opinion is the disappointed candidate who, thrown unceremoniously
from office, speaks sadly of the ingratitude of republics.

Psychologists have analyzed with greater precision than publicists
the factors associated with stability of opinion. Their work, often in
the laboratory, is suggestive of the circumstances conducive to dura-

[1] L. B. Namier: "Public Opinion and Representative Government," in *Sky-
scrapers and Other Essays* (London: Macmillan; 1931), p. 40.

bility and instability of opinion. Such findings, however, remain of little import without demonstration that in the real political world sufficient numbers of citizens are so circumstanced that the resultant stability or instability of their opinions affects the course of public action. Persons confronted by ambiguous situations may be highly unstable in their views, but if they are few in number and not strategically located in the political system, their erraticism may be without political effect.

The significance of opinion stability for the political system raises questions impossible to cope with satisfactorily given the present state of knowledge. Even the understanding of just what stability of opinion is leaves something to be desired. In any case, if one hits upon a plausible concept of that property and a satisfactory means for measuring it, he is still left with the omnipresent problem of the opinion analyst: how any opinion, stable or unstable, bears on the governing process.

1 · Bases of Stability; the Idea of Viscosity

As one seeks to clarify the meaning of "stability," it becomes doubtful even whether this term adequately covers the property of opinion that the commentators have in mind. Public opinion might better be described as possessing varying degrees of viscosity. That is, it may change only slowly, if at all, in response to the flow of new ideas and events of the political world. Or it may change rapidly and unpredictably in response to the changing political scene. By translation, then, stability becomes high viscosity; instability, low viscosity. On the American scene mass opinion about most matters of political importance possesses a high viscosity.

Stability of opinion both in idea and in fact can be understood only in relation to the stimuli that affect opinion. Public opinion must be in a substantial degree a product of the stimuli to which the public is subjected: that is, the events, the issues, the problems, the cues from leadership, and the objective circumstances that affect individual well-being. If all the public phenomena to which people react remained constant through time, presumably attitudes and opinions would remain unchanged. Obviously the stimuli do not remain the same.

Patterns of Stability. If the essence of the notion of stability consists in the manner in which people respond to public stimuli, several patterns of relationship between stimulus and response might be expected to occur. In one sense, these patterns would arrange themselves along a continuum depending on the extent to which the stimuli of politics could not be accommodated by pre-existing standards of judgment.

As failure of the old to accommodate to the new becomes more patent, pressures increase toward the alteration of old opinions or the development of entirely new opinions on entirely new topics.

A pure condition of stability would prevail when no new stimuli presented themselves to the public. Opinion would never change for lack of provocation. Certainly politics has its dull and uneventful periods when the picture of the world transmitted to the public remains static. Some people may live through their lives with unchanged perceptions of the world (regardless of how much it actually changes) and, hence, with stable opinions. Yet for the modern polity as a whole change is the rule; therefore, we may dismiss the condition of pure stability as having no relevance for our analysis.

In a sense, all political stimuli are new. Yet many of them are old as well in that they may be brought comfortably into the patterns of past experience and of past practice. They place no strain on pre-existing opinions and are conducive to a stability of opinion, or at least to the continuation of prevailing opinion. Other political stimuli may be really new. A sluggishness of response to these new stimuli may characterize opinion that is viscous. Such sluggishness may result in part from the nature of the attitudes that people bring to the appraisal of the new stimulus. Firmly held beliefs, deeply ingrained attitudes, or thorough indoctrination may underlie opinions that resist alteration by new stimuli: ideas, events, or conditions. Or, when viewed from outside the individual, sluggishness in adaptation may be attributed in part to the nature of the skills of leadership or to the manner in which new ideas or other new stimuli are presented to the public. The resultant sluggishness may or may not be for the good of the Republic. In some circumstances the effect may be only one of a commendable sales resistance to crackpot notions whose adoption would endanger the order. In other circumstances viscosity of opinion could endanger survival of the Republic by an obdurate adherence to outlooks not suitable to the new problems of a new day.

To be contrasted with sluggishness in response and adaptation is an erraticism that may produce wide fluctuations in opinion at least over the short run. Again this type of behavior is a function of the interaction between what is inside the individual's head and the stimuli of the external world. The stimulus (the event, the issue, the public problem) may be novel and may take form suddenly. The individual may be unequipped to appraise, interpret, or respond to the new type of stimulus. The response may be erratic and unstable; opinions of approbation today may be replaced by condemnation tomorrow. The response may be one of bewilderment and panic; or it may be that of an ostrich. Obviously the capacity of individuals to cope with new situations varies enormously. Erraticism in response may be serious for the political order only when the number of excitable and erratic individuals is sufficiently large and influential to cause erraticism in public policy.

Relevant Psychological Notions. All these speculations about the nature of response to political stimuli have some basis in the lore of psychology. The ideas of frame of reference and of structured and unstructured situations have a relevance, but their recondite nature (and perhaps their fuzziness) creates perplexities for the expositor. Perceptual structuring, say Sherif and Sherif, "is jointly determined by the totality of functionally related external factors and internal factors coming into the structuring process at a given time. These interrelated factors—external and internal—constitute the *frame of reference* of the ensuing reaction."

They emphasize that, in their view, frame of reference "does not denote a specific psychological item. It does not refer to a judgment, an attitude, a social norm." A social norm—an attitude, a stereotype, or a prejudice—or a reference symbol may be an element within a frame of reference. But the frame of reference itself is a "system of relations operative at a given time which determine perceptual structuring and hence behavior." The system of relations connects or involves what the authors call internal and external factors. "The external factors are stimulating situations outside of the individual (objects, persons, events, etc.). The internal factors are motives (needs), attitudes, emotions, general state of the organism, effects of past experience, etc." [2]

If we employ terms other than those standard in psychological usage, we may more readily comprehend the relevance of these doctrines of psychology for politics. We may speak of the "opinion-forming" situation rather than of "frame of reference as a system of relations." In the opinion-forming situation we have essentially two variables: the perceptual equipment of the individual and the stimulus. What the individual has in his head before he receives a stimulus will govern to some degree the direction and properties of the opinion he forms in response.[3] The stimuli to which individuals respond vary

[2] M. Sherif and C. Sherif: *Groups in Harmony and Tension* (New York: Harper; 1953), p. 138.

[3] The importance of the conditioning of the individual in how he perceives stimuli becomes strikingly apparent in studies of perception in primitive societies. See A. I. Hallowell: "Cultural Factors in the Structuralization of Perception," in J. H. Rohrer and M. Sherif: *Social Psychology at the Crossroads* (New York: Harper; 1951), pp. 164–95.

along many dimensions; for each individual person, their variance depends to a degree on his perceptual equipment.

Variation among individuals as elements of opinion-forming situations is probably far greater than we might suppose from simplistic ideas about the behavior of public opinion. If we were to seek systematically to ascertain the range of that variation, we would want to identify variation along dimensions politically relevant. One type of variation would be in what has been called "orientation," which is defined as "a readiness to behave with respect to certain events in preference to others." [4] That is, an individual may have a greater or lesser disposition to attend to or pay heed to the stimuli of politics, and within the realm of politics he may be more oriented to some of its phases than to others. For example, he may be oriented toward issues or toward candidates. Variation may occur along the dimension of party and group loyalties; a person may be more or less disposed to appraise, interpret, or give meaning to political stimuli in terms of their bearing on group fortunes or group standards. Variation may occur in the content of the norms by which the individual evaluates actions, events, persons, or proposals. One may be dedicated to the view that men should get what they can and the devil take the hindmost; another may be dominated by a sense of compassion for the weak and the unfortunate. Variation may also exist in the analytical equipment the stimulus strikes. One person may view an event in foreign politics against a background of extensive knowledge and experience; another may judge the same complex situation by the application of folk maxims. Others may bring learning, spurious or real, to the interpretation of a stimulus, while still others are compelled to fall back on their common sense.[5] And lest it be supposed that all persons could be located at some point along these or other politically relevant dimensions, it ought to be added that many persons find themselves with precious little in the way of intellectual equipment or mental predisposition to judge, give meaning to, or place in their world any sort of political stimulus. Not infrequently persons make sense of political stimuli in such peculiar terms that they confound the

[4] W. A. Scott and S. B. Withey: *The United States and the United Nations* (New York: Manhattan; 1958), p. 228.

[5] An aged St. Louis lady agreed very strongly with the statement: "The United States should be willing to go more than half-way in being friendly with the other countries of the world"; she also observed: "You catch more flies with sugar than vinegar." A minor corporate bureaucrat of Indiana agreed with the proposition that taxes ought to be cut even if it meant putting off some important things, and added: "It has been theorized that undue taxation was the cause of the fall of Rome; the very same thing could happen to our nation." A California jewelry salesman responded: "It depends"; he then added: "Would depend on what you meant by some important things. If you mean defense or things like that, then I would disagree."

expectations of those who perceive the political world in terms of general policy.[6]

The second factor in the opinion-forming situation, the stimulus, is also subject to wide variation. Definition of that variable presents a tricky problem; it almost has to be defined in terms of the first variable. Political stimuli include events, communications, ideas, parties, programs, objective conditions, and doubtless many other matters. In opinion-forming situations the same stimulus will be perceived, appraised, and responded to in ways that vary with the characteristics of the individual. The political significance of a particular stimulus, then, depends in part on the distribution within the population of different kinds of mechanisms for its appraisal.[7]

The trickiness in talking about variation in the stimulus in the opinion-forming situation that comes from this subjective variation among individuals may be avoided if we speak of "objective" variation in the stimuli of politics. Objective variation can mean variation among different stimuli for the same individual. Political stimuli for our hypothetical individual may differ along many dimensions. They may be ambiguous or unambiguous. They may be familiar or unfamiliar. They may or may not command attention. They may be immediate or remote in relation to the experience of the individual or in their impact upon the individual. They may or may not be amenable to appraisal by

[6] Consider the comments on the proposition: "The United States should keep soldiers overseas where they can help countries that are against communism." A Nebraska farmer disagreed strongly: "Maybe I wouldn't feel that way if I hadn't been over there myself. I sure didn't like it over there." A Kansas housewife disagreed strongly: "That should be on a volunteer basis; some of the fellows like it over there and would like to go; so let them volunteer." The wife of a Pennsylvania factory foreman agreed: "Of course, when my husband was over there I didn't think so." She added that she thought the government was doing about right on this matter: "They are rotating them." A California skilled worker agreed strongly and added: "But don't let the soldiers marry colored girls over there like Koreans and Japanese."

[7] A vivid illustration of the way persons with contrasting norms appraise an identical event is provided by a survey of French opinion. Respondents were asked to choose from a list of reasons for the Hungarian uprising of 1956. Communist sympathizers and the noncommunist public saw the episode through quite different perceptual filters, as the following partial listing of the reasons they chose to explain the uprising indicates:

Reasons for Uprising	Noncommunist public	Communist sympathizers
Lack of freedom	41%	4%
Hunger and poverty	35	7
Fascist conspiracy	6	60
Instigation by Catholics	6	26
Work of foreign agents	13	60

See Hadley Cantril: *Faith, Hope, and Heresy: The Psychology of the Protest Voter* (Princeton: Institute for International Social Research; 1957), p. X-153.

the individual's value system. They may be accompanied by group pressures to accept or not. They may originate from prestigious or nonprestigious sources.

The import of this distinction between the two variables may become clearer if we consider variation in each of them with the other held constant. Within the population at a particular time there prevails a given distribution of persons classified according to the nature of their perceptual and evaluative apparatus. That is, X per cent have a highly developed capacity to cope with a wide variety of political stimuli, Y per cent have more limited capacities, and Z per cent cannot make much of any object of political relevance. Or individuals could be arrayed along other kinds of dimensions. One might plausibly suppose that these distributions within the population change slowly. Over decades an increasing average level of education would presumably alter these distributions within the body politic. Or a change in the way of life—from, for example, agrarian to industrial—would gradually alter the distribution of types of perceptual and evaluative apparatus. On some questions within a comparatively short period, perhaps months, a large proportion of the population might gain information and standards that it earlier lacked to judge a particular question. Yet on the whole, on the receiving end of the opinion-forming situation we should expect a fairly high degree of stability within the population.

Variation on the stimulus side, which one would expect to be high, consists in changes in the stimuli of political concern. A new object—issue, event, personality, condition—appears in the political field and carries meaning to varying numbers of persons. Only a few may be able to appraise and make sensible evaluations of it, while to many its ambiguity may create only bewilderment. Or the new political stimulus may settle comfortably into well-established grooves in the minds of many persons. The relations between the first and the second variable, of course, never stand still. A new stimulus may be bewildering when it first appears; yet, sometimes sooner and sometimes much later, many persons develop standards for appraisal that give it meaning.

The stimuli of politics often turn out to be ambiguous or to be susceptible to perception in many ways by different individuals. Most people may be compelled, so uniform is our relevant perceptual equipment and cultural conditioning, to concur in seeing grass as green. Their perceptions of the Hon. Richard Nixon or of the Hon. Estes Kefauver are not monitored by such universal norms; evaluations may be both varied and variable. Or many persons may have been so conditioned that they perceive Presidents such as Coolidge and Eisenhower as giants trodding the land, while many others see them as pygmies catapulted to the White House by the unfortunate vagaries of the electorate. The frequent impossibility of ready check on perceptions of matters political against any physical "reality" makes such perceptions especially susceptible to social influence. "The 'reality,' " says Festinger, "which settles the question in the case of social attitudes and opinions is the degree to which others with whom one is in communication are believed to share these same attitudes and opinions." [8] Or, as Sherif and Sherif put it, the "more unstructured, the more uncertain the stimulus situation, the greater are the effects of social influences (personal suggestion, information, group demands, etc.) in perceptual structuring." [9]

The nature of these differentials in opinion-forming situations is illustrated by the analysis of popular response to a broadcast of Orson Welles' radio drama *The Invasion from Mars* in 1938. The drama, amply introduced as drama rather than news, reported a landing of Martians in New Jersey, an expendable piece of real estate, and the strenuous efforts of the civil and military authorities to contain the little visitors and to limit the damage they did. As the broadcast proceeded, panic developed among many listeners. They called for information; they, or a few of them, prayed; they assembled their families for the end of the world; and some of them climbed into their automobiles and took off for the hills, endangering life and limb in the process. And, later, they doubtless felt a little foolish when they realized what they had done. Other listeners, often even if they had not heard the explicit announcement that all this was in fun, saw the performance for what it was, rather than as a news report, and enjoyed it.

An analysis of the response to the broadcast concluded that the anxious people must have possessed an insufficient store of information and an inadequate critical capacity to enable them to appraise what they had heard. Those who refused to become excited must have had a different sort of mental apparatus. Education turned out to be a fair index of these differing capacities to distinguish fact and fiction: 46 per cent of the grammar-school listeners thought the fantasy was a news report; only 28 per cent of the college persons. Cantril opined that the essential difference between those fooled and those not fooled was that the latter had a "critical ability," which may have been obtained through formal education or otherwise. Formal education had not invariably produced that critical ability. For example, one high-school graduate taken in by the show "was a young man in whom no signs of

[8] Leon Festinger: *Social Pressures in Informal Groups* (New York: Harper; 1950), p. 168.
[9] Sherif and Sherif: op. cit., p. 140.

intellectual interest could be detected. He read no books, magazines, or newspapers and listened only to swing music on the radio. It took him seven years to finish high school." [1]

The relation of such findings, as well as those of extensive laboratory experimentation,[2] to the formation of opinion by the kinds of stimuli that are commonly projected from the political stage upon the kinds of people who make up the political world is not a simple task. Yet a few notions of political relevance emerge from the discussion. If the psychological lore has validity, we should expect the formation of fairly stable and predictable opinions about situations, events, persons, and other stimuli that can readily be assimilated by the existing judgmental apparatus of most people. Such opinions would be stable in that they would be continuations or projections of pre-existing attitudes, and in the sense, too, that, given a firm foundation in perception and evaluation, they would not quickly change. When the mass of the people cannot place a political stimulus into a mental pigeonhole, when many have no means of appraising, the consequent perceptions and opinions may be volatile or readily susceptible to change. The capacity of leaders—both demagogues and statesmen—to manipulate may be enlarged. Even newspaper headlines may be believed. Klapper says the media "are quite effective in forming opinions and attitudes in regard to new issues, particularly as these issues are the more unrelated to existing attitude clusters." [3] Perhaps the overarching differentiation among political stimuli is that between the novel and the familiar.

2 · Areas of Stability and Instability

How does psychological theory about the factors conditioning response help us with our problem of stability and instability of opinion, which has been transmuted into a problem of the kinds of response in differing types of opinion-forming situations? Perhaps not at all, for no one has undertaken the task of inventorying the population with respect to its kinds of perceptual equipment in relation to the kinds of political stimuli it receives. One may say, as some of the less-discriminating followers of Lippmann do, that all is explained by the fact that we tend to see with the pictures in our heads. It would be a

[1] Hadley Cantril: *The Invasion from Mars* (Princeton: Princeton University Press; 1947), p. 122.
[2] See Muzafer Sherif: *The Psychology of Social Norms* (New York: Harper; 1936); and Hadley Cantril: *The Psychology of Social Movements* (New York: Wiley; 1941).
[3] Joseph T. Klapper: "What We Know About the Effects of Mass Communication: The Brink of Hope," *Public Opinion Quarterly*, XXI (1957–8), 455–74.

far more appalling task to ascertain which and how many people have what kinds of pictures in their heads and which pictures which people rely on in responding to differing kinds of stimuli. And we should also need to know the political status—influential or noninfluential—of the various categories of persons that might be identified by any such survey of the population.

Though educated guesses can be made about some of these matters, they touch only small segments of the total problem. It requires the most prolonged analysis of even one individual to form judgments about how he responds to political objects.[4] Nevertheless, certain ideas, norms, outlooks, and psychological frames may be so widely distributed within the population that they are employed by many persons in their appraisal and response to a variety of types of political stimuli. To the extent that these are strongly embedded in the minds of individuals, they provide stable reference points in opinion-forming situations. As new stimuli—new objects of political attention—are perceived, they fall into the pigeonholes in the minds of many people and produce outlooks and opinions of a fair degree of stability. The stimuli may be the great source of instability and unpredictability of outlook. Even if men are not unstable, the world is.[5] Yet objects of political attention may vary in the degree to which they are assimilable into our pre-existing mental pictures of the natural order of the political world. Opinions about some objects of political attention might be expected to be more volatile and less predictable than opinions about others.

Party as Standard of Reference. Political parties occupy a prominent place in what we have chosen to call "opinion-forming situations." The vague entity "political party" seems to be both an object to which persons respond and at the same time one of the pictures in our heads, a tool used to see and to evaluate political objects. A person may have attitudes toward parties themselves; these attitudes, in turn, may condition opinions or attitudes about other objects.

Evidently the sense of identification with political parties has, for most people, a durability that lends stability and predictability not only to individual behavior but to the political system as a whole. Party

[4] See the case studies by M. Brewster Smith, Jerome S. Bruner, and Robert W. White: *Opinions and Personality* (New York: Wiley; 1956).

[5] Graham Wallas long ago commented upon the importance of the effect of man's "environment upon his character and actions. It is the extreme instability and uncertainty of this element which constitutes the special difficulty of politics. The human type and the quantitative distribution of its variations are for the politician, who deals with a few generations only, practically permanent."—*Human Nature in Politics*, 3rd ed. (London: Constable; 1920), p. 134.

PART III: PROPERTIES

identification tends to be formed, like religious identification, relatively early in life and by more or less nonrational processes, which produce an enduring sense of party attachment. Over the period 1952–8 the proportions of persons regarding themselves as strong Democrats or as strong Republicans or as partisans in some other degree remained remarkably constant. Some persons, to be sure, from time to time change their party identifications, but for the population as a whole an astonishing persistence of party identification prevails.

Once party identification is established, it is often relied upon to help appraise new objects of attention on the political landscape. Consider the consequences in popular response to the party's nomination of a candidate. Not every Democrat votes for only Democratic candidates; nor does every Republican support only Republican nominees. Yet once a person gains nomination, he is viewed through Democratic or Republican eyes, and the individual appraisal depends, on the average, on the sense of party identification. Persons who consider themselves Democrats will tend to give their party's candidate a high appraisal; they often discover virtues and strengths far beyond those actually possessed by the candidate.[6] They will also tend to take a negative view of the Republican candidate; he may be seen as a scoundrel considerably beyond his deserts. The Republican will perceive the same objects far differently. To him the Democratic candidate may be a person beneath contempt, while the Republican candidate acquires stature, wisdom, and moral qualities rarely combined in one person on this earth. These are commonplace consequences of the interactions in opinion-forming situations. They extend, moreover, beyond the candidate to domestic policies, to foreign policies, and to judgments of the manner in which the government is conducted. The sense of party attachment pervades the population and profoundly conditions our response to the political world.

Unfortunately for the simplicity of the analysis, people have differing combinations of pictures in their heads. Even the same individual

[6] They may also adopt their party's candidate more or less mechanically and without attribution to him of special qualities. Consider the responses to the 1956 inquiry: "Is there anything in particular about Stevenson that might make you want to vote for him?" An Iowa housewife: No. I'll vote for him just because he's a Democrat." The foreman in a Georgia poultry processing plant: "He's a Democrat; that's all that's good about him." A Boston plasterer: "No, just that he's a Democrat, that's all." A Missouri farmer: "Yes, a Democrat makes him a good man. He is honest, efficient, business man." The wife of a Louisville truck driver: "No, not anything particularly—just because he is a Democrat, I guess." A Texas oilfield worker: "He's a Democrat; that's enough." The wife of a retired Texas farmer: "Well, because he's a Democrat. I don't keep up with things like that but I'll vote for the Democrat every time."

may use any one of several pictures to appraise a particular matter. Party may provide the interpretative matrix for events for some persons for some of the time, but the infinite variety among people permits a wide range of responses to the same event. How party may be mixed with other standards in the appraisal of events finds illustration in the American response to our entry into the fighting in Korea. That action claimed wide attention in the 1952 campaign, and the orators let no opportunity pass to comment on the wickedness of the action (or on the wisdom of our speedy response to the challenge to the Free World). The sense of party identification presumably had some bearing on the formation of judgments on this question. Since the decision to enter was indubitably that of a Democratic Administration, those who looked at the world as Democrats would be expected to see a different action than would those equipped with Republican blinders. On the other hand, persons also differed in their information and in their preparation for appraising the place of the action in world politics. Education serves as a crude index of variation among individuals in this capacity. The less educated he was—or the less disposed to view the Korean enterprise in the context of world politics—the more disposed a person might be to fall for campaign arguments such as that Harry Truman had instigated the war to avoid a depression, that the communists controlling the State Department were conspiring to stab General MacArthur in the back, and other such edifying interpretations.

Whatever the explanation, some such differential response occurred. Among strong Republicans 49 per cent of the college-trained but only 10 per cent of the grade-schoolers thought that entry into the Korean affair had been the "right thing" to do. Among Democrats

TABLE 10.1

APPROVAL OF ENTRY INTO KOREAN WAR, BY PARTY IDENTIFICATION AND EDUCATION [a]

EDUCATION	PARTY IDENTIFICATION						
	SD	WD	ID	I	IR	WR	SR
College	58%	50%	60%	(50%)	(68%)	46%	49%
High school	62	46	52	43	46	34	21
Grade school	46	31	38	21	23	16	10

[a] Entries are percentages saying we did "the right thing" in responses to the question, "Do you think we did the right thing in getting into the fighting in Korea two years ago, or should we have stayed out?" Percentages in parentheses rest on less than 30 cases.

DATA SOURCE: *Survey Research Center, University of Michigan, 1952.*

grade-schoolers were pulled away from their natural posture of agreement with the Administration far more than were the college-trained. Yet Democrats, at all levels of education, approved the action in higher degree than did those of comparable education among Republicans, a fact suggesting the bearing of party identification upon the interpretation of a political event. The data appear in Table 10.1.

In opinion surveys findings recur illustrative of the tendency of people to rely upon their sense of party attachment in the appraisal of issues and events. In 1936 the AIPO asked: "Do you believe the acts and policies of the Roosevelt Administration may lead to dictatorship?" An affirmative answer to this proposition had been widely propagated by some leading editors, pundits, and other commentators of the time. Few men had sufficient grasp of the dynamics of history to expatiate learnedly upon the problem, but they had answers—answers probably especially dependent upon party loyalties on such a question. They were:

	Yes	No
National total	45%	55%
Democrats	9	91
Republicans	83	17

The degree of dependence upon the party component of the perceptive apparatus as a means of shaping judgments doubtless varies under different circumstances, and with different kinds of questions, as well as among persons. Certainly the stimulus must be connected with party before party can enter into the response. The possibility of prominent political objects being not so connected is illustrated by the AIPO question of December, 1950, at about the time the Republican congressional leadership was conducting a drive to dump the Democratic Secretary of State: "What do you, yourself think—should Dean Acheson stay on in his present position, or should he be replaced?" The responses were as follows:

	Republicans	Democrats	Independents
Stay on	13%	26%	23%
Be replaced	43	19	31
No opinion	14	14	19
Could not identify	30	41	27
	100%	100%	100%

An impressive proportion of the respondents, especially among the Democrats, had not heard of Dean Acheson. Had the question identified him as the Democratic Secretary of State, doubtless substantial numbers of the uninformed would have responded in party terms. Without the party connection they had no cue for appraisal. One of the weaknesses of American parties is that for large numbers of people many actions, events, and policies cannot be placed clearly in relation to party, so ambiguous are both the perception and the reality of the party system.

Opinions clearly related to group norms, group values, or group loyalties may have a special group-induced quality of stability. This would be expected to be true in highest degree of those secondary groups whose values are reinforced by primary-group pressures. An unambiguous position by party leaders may have special effect on those persons who associate chiefly in their primary groups with fellow partisans. Those with more varied personal contacts probably more often deviate from the party line.

If we revert to the concept of viscosity of opinion, the sense of party identification must be regarded as introducing a quality of viscosity into an important area of political attitude. The balance of party loyalties within the population powerfully conditions the processes of choice of political leaders as well as their behavior once they achieve. office. The balance, to be sure, shifts from time to time to permit alternations in power; yet the population does not consist of a mass of unanchored individuals susceptible to volatile movement by men who appeal to them under strange and changing banners. Moreover, to the extent that parties become encrusted with bodies of doctrine, they become conservative (or viscous) elements in the state, be they radical or conservative parties. Party identification of the policy-sensitive individual provides him with a symbol for his loyalties and also with norms for the appraisal of policy and events.

Personalities. Political personalities make up an important class of political objects—stimuli to which the public reacts, about which it forms opinions. The odds are that opinions about personalities and about other matters dependent upon their relation to personalities possess properties markedly different from opinions about political parties. For one individual the content of the reference symbol "Democratic party" or "Republican party" may remain relatively constant for long periods; party constitutes a stable guidepost by which opinions on candidates and issues may be formed. Political personalities, however, occupy a different type of position in the constellation of political perceptions. To the extent that they are judged independently of party, they present objects for which people have within their perceptual apparatus no common or standardized norms or guides for judgment. Surely from individual to individual response to voice, ap-

pearance, smile, stance, bearing, and manner must be extremely varied
and unpredictable. Further, within the political system as a whole,
opinions about and dependent upon personalities gain an instability because of the rapidity with which new personalities come upon the scene
and require the establishment of new appraisals which, once they become stabilized, must be discarded and replaced by new opinions
about new personalities.

How people make up their minds about presidential candidates (or
about other remote persons generally) must remain a mystery.[7] As they
observe presidential and vice-presidential candidates over TV and radio and through the press, men and women arrive at contrasting and
inexplicable judgments. The inscrutability of man's appraisal of man is
suggested by a few responses to inquiries about whether there was
"anything in particular" that might make "you want to vote for" Eisenhower, Stevenson, and the 1956 vice-presidential candidates. A Connecticut housewife said of Eisenhower: "Yes. He's an honest man."
The same lady on Nixon. "Yes. Nixon is a wonderful man." A retired
Colorado steelworker opined of the vice-presidential candidates: "That
Nixon is no good, he's a big fat liar—that other man, Kefauver, he not
so bad. I think he will try to be a good vice-president." An Ohio
housewife placed Eisenhower in an extra-mundane setting: "Well, I
just like everything about him. He is a religious man and always has
been as far as I know. I think after all God is the only one who can settle things now; we are in too much chaos now."[8] A Detroit housewife
admired Stevenson: "I think he talks beautifully. I think the man has
the most wonderful diction. Of course, that has nothing to do with
running the country." A retired Texas farmer remained skeptical of
Nixon: "I can't put my finger on anything but I've never liked Nixon
from the first campaign. (How's that?) Don't know." In this he was
joined by a Michigan lady: "I don't like Vice-President Nixon and
there isn't any legitimate reason for it. I just plain don't like him. That's

[7] A favorite exercise of psychologists is to confront subjects with sets of
photographs of personages and ask that they be related to a scrambled list of identifications. The gangster has about as much of a chance to be mistaken for the
ambassador or the bishop as he does to be correctly tagged. For a summary of
research on how people perceive and judge other people, see Jerome S. Bruner
and Renato Tagiuri: "The Perception of People," *Handbook of Social Psychology* (Cambridge: Addison-Wesley; 1954), II, 634–54. See also Elmo Roper: *You
and Your Leaders* (New York: Morrow; 1957).

[8] The General's reputation for piety would probably astonish him. Thus, the
wife of an Illinois postal worker: "Oh, yes. I think he is a loyal man, he tries to
do his very best, he is also a churchman. I admire his constant prayer. You can't
ignore God altogether." A North Carolina grocer (Most important reason why
vote for Eisenhower?): "Because I believe he is a godly man; I believe he's a
statesman rather than a politician." A Pennsylvania lady: "Well, he seems like such
a nice man and he is so religious."

all." [9] An upstate New York toll collector saw the Vice-President differently: "Yes I think Nixon is a younger carbon copy of Eisenhower —in time to come he'll be the same type of man. He answered a note I sent him during the 1952 campaign."

The extent to which people are candidate-oriented (rather than issue-oriented or party-oriented) may be of basic import in the determination of the character of the political order. By "candidate orientation" is meant a disposition to pay heed to the candidate rather than to party or issues. Within the American population as a whole the tendency toward a candidate orientation is, or at least was in 1952, to a degree, independent of party orientation. That is, every person who thought the General was a great man did not hold that opinion simply because he was of the Republican party as was the General. Candidate orientation existed more frequently among women than among men.[1] If large proportions of a population are candidate-oriented, we should expect a different kind of political order than if the candidate-oriented were far outnumbered by the issue-oriented and party-oriented. A candidate-oriented polity (or a personality-oriented one) may make it easier to humbug the people, though such a result does not necessarily follow. It depends on the kind of man who happens to capture the fancy of a candidate-oriented electorate. Such an electorate should be easy prey for heroes as well as for free-wheelers and high-binders. Then, too, the extent of candidate orientation may differ with circumstances. At some times people may be more disposed to pay heed to

[9] Other respondents also had difficulty in explaining their views on the candidates. A South Dakota salesman, determined to vote for Stevenson, in response to the question whether there was anything about Stevenson that might make him vote against him: "Yes, there possibly is. (What?) Maybe his personality or the way he smirks, don't know how to explain that, but it's not favorable. Maybe the word is sarcastic. Don't know if it's his nature or if he really is that way. Not like Kefauver who is so friendly—better personality." An Ohio housewife on Stevenson: "Well, I don't like him. (Any other reason?) I think that's reason enough." The wife of a Kansas banker on Stevenson: "I just don't like him. (Can you put your finger on anything in particular?) No." The wife of a Los Angeles machinist: "I don't like Nixon. I don't know why but I just don't." A Pittsburgh sales clerk: "As for Nixon I don't care for him. (How is that?) Well I can't tell you why, I just don't like the man—no special reason." A Georgia farmer on Stevenson: "I ain't so crazy about Stevenson; they could run some better than him if they had tried. (What don't you like about him?) I don't know. I just don't like him." A Kentucky housewife: (Like about Eisenhower?) "Just like him. (What is there you like about him?) He is a better man for it. (Why?) Just is." Others had reasons of sorts. A Brooklyn widow, owner of an apartment house, on Stevenson: "His arrogant manner; holier than thou attitude sends me the wrong way. I don't like his wisecracking attitude. Eisenhower is a really good man. He's a swell man. He's a truly, fine good hearted man." A Georgia truck driver had, he said, "A lot of strong opinions about Nixon. He's not even qualified to be vice-president."

[1] Angus Campbell, Gerald Gurin, and Warren E. Miller: *The Voter Decides* (Evanston: Row, Peterson; 1954), ch. 10.

issues and parties than at others.[2] Given the limitations of the information upon which they must act, those who proudly say, "I vote for the man and not for the party," in the great modern state usually know far less about what they are doing than does the person who has some glimmering sense of the policy inclinations of the parties and unblushingly confesses that he votes the straight party ticket.

The institutional arrangements of a regime may affect its nature by compelling a greater or lesser attention to personalities. In the one-party states of the South, for example, political competition must be conducted in terms of personality rather than of party. Customs and constitutional directives that limit the number of consecutive terms of the governor compel the electorate to respond to new stimuli—that is, new candidates—at frequent intervals without the aid of the guiding symbols of party.[3] This circumstance may contribute an element of unpredictability, as well as picturesqueness, to the politics of the region. To some extent in these states individuals may, however, become "institutionalized" either in themselves or through the rise of factions identified with them and thereby build a psychological situation approaching, at least for short periods, the reality of that created by competition in party terms; that is, impressions of a personality or of a leader may become so fixed in the minds of many individuals that they serve as a reference point for the appraisal of new issues, new circumstances, and new personalities.[4] At another level, some of the differences between British and American politics may be attributable to the customs that assure a more continuing, a more stable, party leadership in Britain than is the American practice. American voters must form judgments more often about new sets of leading personalities.

Opinions about issues or substantive events may be dependent upon the political personality with whom they are associated. Appraisals of the personality may become an internal element of the opinion-forming situation and are extended, negatively or positively, to policies the personality advocates or opposes. This effect becomes of importance chiefly with respect to the President; few other individuals make enough of an imprint on the public mind of the nation for this transference to occur on a large scale. "When public opinion about policies is simply a reflection of opinion or attitude toward their pre-

[2] Yet as one speculates upon the combinations of factors that throw particular leaders into power at particular moments he can only be impressed by the role of chance in the governance of democratic orders.

[3] Probably response to personality in small communities where firsthand acquaintance is wide scarcely resembles that in electorates so large that most people gain their impressions of candidates through the media.

[4] Presidents, too, become for relatively brief periods stable elements of the political landscape and generate within the population fairly stable patterns of response.

sumed authors or supporters," says Goldhamer, "the public opinion is likely to be labile and unprincipled." [5] Whether such opinion is labile in the short run, it must certainly be in the intermediate and long run, for personalities come and go.

The precise determination in specific circumstances of the interdependence of attitudes toward a personality and toward other related matters of political relevance requires refined and intensive inquiry. Though no thoroughgoing analyses of the matter have been made, simple data suggest that opinions are often related to, if not dependent upon, attitudes toward personalities. Several surveys that bear upon the relation of issue opinions and attitudes toward Franklin D. Roosevelt, a person with the capacity to generate both adulation and enmity, are illustrative. In October, 1936, during Roosevelt's campaign for a second term, when dire consequences were predicted for the nation if he were re-elected, the *Fortune* survey put the question: "Do you think the country will be facing any kind of crisis if the Democrats are elected?" The responses, by attitude toward Roosevelt, were:

	Yes	No	Don't know
National total	24.1	58.7	17.2
Attitude toward Roosevelt			
Roosevelt re-election essential	4.6	79.2	16.2
Best man despite mistakes	9.8	73.6	16.6
His usefulness now over	36.4	45.3	18.3
His re-election the worst thing	64.7	23.9	11.4
Uncertain about Roosevelt	12.0	38.3	49.7

In 1940, when Roosevelt was running for a third term and war threatened, *Fortune* put the following question: "If it comes to a question of the United States declaring war, in whose judgment would you have the greater confidence, that of the President and the Department of State—whoever they are at the time—or that represented by a vote of Congress after debate?" The responses were doubtless colored by factors in addition to attachment to personalities; nevertheless, the differences between the outlooks of Roosevelt supporters and of Willkie partisans suggest that the image of Roosevelt strongly affected the responses, which divided as follows:

	Presi-dent	Depends on who is President	Con-gress	Both	Neither	Don't know
National	25.7%	6.2%	50.8%	6.8%	1.4%	9.1%
For Roosevelt	39.3	7.0	37.8	7.1	0.9	7.9
For Willkie	12.1	4.1	70.2	5.9	1.5	6.2

[5] Herbert Goldhamer: "Public Opinion and Personality," *American Journal of Sociology*, LV (1949–50), 353.

On a plane of less-grave policy Roosevelt's name was associated with a shift in the date of Thanksgiving, an action taken at the behest of businessmen who wanted a better arrangement of the shopping season before Christmas. An opinion survey that employed the question: "Do you like President Roosevelt's idea of having Thanksgiving a week earlier this year?" drew an additional 5 per cent approval over the question: "Do you like the idea of having Thanksgiving a week earlier this year?" [6]

Questions of personality and of party may become mixed in the minds of men as they use them as standards for the appraisal of events. An illustration comes from an inquiry about whether an endorsement of a candidate by the late Senator McCarthy would make a vote for the candidate more or less likely. The response to the question depended fundamentally on one's opinion of the Senator, but it was also connected with party identification. Democrats far more often than Republicans said that the Senator's endorsement would make it less likely that they would vote for the anointed candidate. Relatively twice as many Republicans as Democrats said that the endorsement would make it more likely that the candidate would receive their vote. On balance, though, the responses indicated that McCarthy's endorsement would hurt a candidate more than it would help him. The data appear in Table 10.2. The outcomes of senatorial elections in 1954 and 1956 that

---

TABLE 10.2

RELATION OF PARTY IDENTIFICATION TO LIKELIHOOD OF VOTING FOR OR AGAINST
CANDIDATE ENDORSED BY SENATOR McCARTHY [a]

EFFECT ON VOTE	PARTY IDENTIFICATION		
	Democratic	Independent	Republican
More likely to vote for	8%	9%	16%
No difference	46	53	50
Less likely to vote for	41	32	29
No opinion	5	6	5
	100%	100%	100%
N	525	243	300

[a] The question was: "If you knew that Senator McCarthy was supporting a candidate for Congress, would you be more likely to vote for the candidate, or less likely, or wouldn't it make any difference to you?"
DATA SOURCE: *Survey Research Center, University of Michigan, 1954.*

---

[6] A. B. Blankenship: "The Influence of the Question Form Upon the Response in a Public Opinion Poll," *Psychological Record*, III (1939–40), 355.

reduced the ranks of the McCarthyites make it plausible to suppose that the responses shown in the table had some relationship with preferences actually expressed at the polls.

It remains to speculate on the significance for the political system of the peculiar processes by which people form opinions of personalities. The apparent lack of standardized norms for the appraisal of personalities may introduce an element of caprice into political systems. The modal popular response to parties and perhaps to many issues and values may be fairly standardized, with the consequence that fixed attitudes form a brake on political change. However, when issues and actions are transmuted into terms of personalities, attitudinal blockages may be by-passed. Or it may be that imposing personalities can capture the loyalties of sectors of the population that are unencumbered by abstract concerns about policies, values, or institutions. In any case, personalities, whether they be heroic or demoniac, may serve as especially effective instruments for political change. The strain of approbation of government by law and of fear of government by men that runs through American political theory may have a sound psychological base.[7] Where the strain of thought errs is in its supposition that men with a genius for popular leadership are invariably dangerous to men of substance.

Events. Stability and predictability of opinion have been interpreted here as the consequence of characteristics of the opinion-forming situation—the interaction between the pictures in individuals' heads and the stimuli of the political world. To the extent that events of the political drama are seen in terms of political parties, a relatively high degree of predictability and of stability of opinion prevails among large sectors of the population. For party-oriented individuals party is a continuing reference symbol of stable effect although of varying content. The perception of personalities presents a less-predictable matter, for we lack similar and widely distributed internalized standards for judging personalities. Opinions about and opinions dependent upon personalities may be erratic not only because personalities come and go but because of the lack of common standards for their appraisal. The events of the political world constitute another type of stimulus. A constant flow of new events parades before the citizen; the properties of opinion about them may be dependent upon whether his perceptual

[7] For examples of the possibilities of exploitation of types of popular responses to men, see F. H. Jonas: "The Art of Political Dynamiting," *Western Political Quarterly,* X (1957), 374–491.

apparatus enables him quickly to pigeonhole them and treat them as items he has seen before or whether they are perceived as invasions from Mars.

If we regard opinions as the result of the interaction between attitudes and the stimuli of the political world, we may be able to say something sensible, although unsupported by detailed data, about the stability of public opinion as it responds to events. It seems clear enough that those opinions bearing upon our basic governmental arrangements, practices, and policies have been remarkably stable or have had a high viscosity. Consider the impact of one kind of "event"—the gradual changes over a century involved in the industrialization and urbanization of the nation—a slow process of change, with consequences for the status, the security, the conditions of life of most people. How was it perceived? While nobody really knows, the supposition is plausible that the events were filtered through a set of pictures in heads well adapted to the older agrarian world. Proposals for ameliorative public policy competed with the ingrained philosophy of individual initiative, of individual responsibility, of the virtues and rewards of hard work. Only extremely slowly, and then with the aid of events of widespread impact, did a general opinion develop supportive of public action in the management of the economy to protect those made vulnerable by the new division of labor. True, over the period 1870–1930, unrest welled up from time to time, with unhappy results for individual candidates and parties; yet these outbursts soon subsided, and only at a glacial rate did new opinions develop. As late as the early 1930's even the American Federation of Labor opposed unemployment insurance. Thus, the response to some types of new events may be a lack of response, a maintenance of the ancient values despite the impact of inconsiderately inconsistent events.

Although we cannot know what the distribution of attitudes in the public was or how it changed over the seventy-five years preceding, say, the adoption of the Employment Act of 1946, the movement of governmental action is consistent with the supposition of the existence of a public opinion resistant to change. "In things that matter," says Schramm, "the individual and his social organization are generally inclined to resist change. On any subject where his attitudes are long and firmly established, where they have an emotional content, where they relate to things he deeply values, the individual is highly resistant to change, whether it is suggested by mass communication or any other source." [8] It may be supposed that there exist in any well-established political order viscous opinions about fundamental

---

[8] Wilbur Schramm: *Responsibility in Mass Communication* (New York: Harper; 1957), p. 55.

political practices, which, though not necessarily well articulated in all sectors of the population, are especially resistant to alteration. These are not pictures but engravings in citizens' heads.

Once the pattern of basic opinion is altered, a new framework comes into existence for the appraisal of transient events and conditions. In effect, expectations of government are broadened and opinions about a wider scope of objects become politically relevant. It may have taken decades for a basic opinion to develop that the government should exert itself to keep the economy operating. Now that it has developed, however, the response to slight fluctuations in economic activity may be both immediate and pronounced. Traces of this broad shift in outlook may remain in the contrasting outlooks of the genera-

---

TABLE 10.3

AGE IN RELATION TO OPINIONS ON PROPER SCOPE OF GOVERNMENT WELFARE ACTIVITY AMONG WHITE-COLLAR RESPONDENTS [a]

Opinion	Under 35	35–55	Over 55
Should do more	28%	28%	23%
Doing about right	51	43	34
Should do less	15	25	39
Don't know	6	4	4
	100%	100%	100%
N	148	226	106

[a] For text of the welfare question, see Appendix III.
DATA SOURCE: *Survey Research Center, University of Michigan, 1952.*

---

tions. Though the data on the point are thin, some suggestion of the possibility is contained in Table 10.3, which relates age to responses to a 1952 question about the desirable scope of national activity in dealing with "such problems as unemployment, education, housing, and so on" by white-collar persons. Those over 55 in considerably larger proportions than those under 35 thought that the government should be doing less in these welfare fields. The numbers of the sample do not suffice to permit analysis to tie these differences definitely to age, but if they are so connected, the more conservative views of those of the earlier generation may reflect a stronger attachment among them to the values of an earlier era.[9]

[9] It is to be doubted, though, that the newer outlooks are accompanied by any widespread understanding in the population of the niceties of governmental intervention in the economy. Consider the side comments of respondents in 1956 on the proposition that the government in Washington ought to see to it that everybody who wants to work can find a job. All the persons quoted disagreed with the proposition. An Idaho farmer: "I think that would be an awful big or-

By no means do all events of domestic politics present stimuli that meet resistance and incomprehension as they interact with the pictures in our heads. The more easily an event may be brought within the terms of the experience and basic values of a person, probably the more assured and the more rapid the opinion formation. People may not, for example, readily grasp the meaning of the industrial revolution or the latest developments in Viet Nam but they can understand divorces, mink coats, deep freezes, and golf-playing on workdays.[1]

Although the realm of international affairs is supposedly one in which public opinion is most volatile, evidently certain types of basic opinions possess over the long run a high degree of stability. They may fix the limits within which opinions on transient matters develop, as well as give direction to these opinions. Basic opinions on international policy rest, first, on an attitude of loyalty to the nation. The obverse of loyalty is an attitude of hostility to those who threaten the nation. Attitudes toward other nations differ from nation to nation, and these gradations in outlooks have a relatively high stability.

Still another area of relatively stable attitude concerns the broad stance the nation should take with respect to the external world. Although we have no series of soundings of opinion over a long enough period to capture the change, it seems unquestionable that public opinion from 1925 to 1950, say, shifted from a predominantly isolationist tinge to an opinion more favorably disposed to participation in international affairs. To be sure, this shift occurred only gradually and against the resistance of older ideas. The quality of the new opinion is not one of aggressiveness, nor does it contain much "one-worldness." It is more in the spirit of a reluctant admission that the nature of the world has changed and we must change with it—so long as we don't have to fight

---

der." A Mississippi farmer: "I think that would be impossible for the government to do." A Pennsylvania TV repairman: "There's enough work for those that look." A New Jersey accountant: "That is not the government's job. It is the businessman's job. Government should leave the businessman alone and let him work out his problems. It could create jobs." A North Carolina farm widow: "People that wants to work can find it." But a Missouri farm housewife agreed strongly: "Everyone should have work to be busy to stay out of crime."

[1] A maxim of American politics is that if you are to be crooked, be crooked in a manner not comprehensible to the average man. For example, the award of a license for a television station may be a bit of graft in the millions, but to grasp its import one must understand the possibility of capitalizing the value of an intangible privilege and the probability of being able to realize these gains despite the formally revocable nature of the license. Such information is not widely distributed in the population. Apart from such incomprehension, events are often perceived in ways astounding to persons who are equipped with a good deal of political lore themselves. Relevant is the finding that many persons saw the televised Army-McCarthy hearings more as a neighborhood squabble than as a conflict over great issues. See G. D. Wiebe: "A New Dimension in Journalism," *Journalism Quarterly*, XXXI (1954), 411–20.

in Korea or some outlandish place of which nobody ever heard. And it may be doubted that the new outlook toward the outside world has the same solidity and durability as did the one it replaced.

The set of outlooks toward the outside world includes fairly stable attitudes toward individual countries, attitudes that have been built up over long periods of time and are resistant to alteration. These sets of attitudes may set up systems of dikes within which the normal actions of policy may occur without arousing popular dissent or question. Thus, the fairly durable opinion toward Great Britain sharply contrasts with that toward Russia. Even in the period of our alliance with Russia during World War II popular expectations about Russian friendship did not become great. From 1942 to 1946 a series of surveys was conducted on the question, "Do you think Russia can be trusted to cooperate with us after the war is over?" The "yes" percentage never rose above 55. Fluctuations occurred in these responses, but on the whole the long-standing distrust of the Russians demonstrated an imposing stability against the pressures of wartime sentiment.[2]

It would be instructive to have a census of the norms, standards, and criteria that people use in appraising questions of foreign policy. Such information would give us a better understanding of the attitudinal foundations of public opinion about foreign-policy issues. A few remarks culled from volunteered comments in 1956 interviews suggest types of pictures in people's heads, but these illustrations give us no indication of the frequency of their occurrence. Doubtless an important underlying attitude is that of nationalism in the broad sense of "we" against "them." A Nebraska housewife, who disagreed with the proposition that we should "give economic help to the poorer countries of the world even if they can't pay for it," said: "I think they should help the people at home first. There's a lot of little children going hungry in the United States that need help." A South Dakota cafeteria worker in the same vein said: "We have a lot of people here and older people who need help here first." The wife of a Detroit machinist also disagreed: "I think they should help but first clean up these slums in the United States and make better living for these people right here."

Folk maxims may be brought to the service of the interpretation of international affairs. A Louisville house painter who disagreed strongly with the statement that we should give help to "foreign countries even if they are not as much against communism as we are" said: "Let them paddle their own canoes and let us paddle ours." On the issue of economic aid generally a Missouri farmer opined: "Charity should begin at home." A New Jersey postal clerk took the view: "The

[2] For the results of the surveys, see H. Cantril and M. Strunk: *Public Opinion, 1935–1946*, pp. 370–371.

more you give the more they want." A Missouri farm housewife thought: "We should stay home and mind our own business."

Some people use their biblical learning or their ideas of humanitarianism to prop up their opinions on foreign questions. On the proposition that the way to deal with Russia and China "is to act just as tough as they do," a New Jersey postal clerk observed: "That is not the golden rule. No, I wouldn't want us to get as tough as they are." On economic aid to poorer countries an upstate New York housewife remarked: "They are human beings; they need help." A North Carolina farm widow: "It's the Christian thing to do, and our government has always done more of that than anybody else."

Other individuals apply their views of the proprieties in interpersonal relations to international relations. On the proposition that we ought to "act tough" toward Russia and China a Philadelphia skilled worker concurred strongly: "No one ever took a punch at Joe Louis." The wife of an Idaho construction foreman drew an analogy from another realm: "They can be bluffed the same as they try to bluff us." But a New Jersey nurse thought: "It would be a nice mess if we did." A Missouri farm housewife opposed economic aid on grounds of etiquette: "Never. They don't appreciate our help." A North Carolina carpenter had a similar view: "We spend more money in Europe than we do here and nobody don't give us nothing." A Missouri housewife, drawing on the obligations of friendship when she doubted that we should "go more than half-way in being friendly with the other countries of the world," said: "We don't want to get too friendly; they might start a war and we would have to help out." A Kansas housewife thought the United States ought to be friendly, "If they can. Some folks you can't be friendly with."

Occasionally persons call on their personal experience or their philosophical lore to underpin their opinions. A Missouri truck driver favored economic aid to poorer countries: "I have been and seen where help could be important." A minor corporate supervisor reflected: "A hungry mouth breeds discontentment in the world." A lady worker in a South Dakota sausage factory had had experience: "Help people in the United States first. My husband was out of a job for three months. They gave DP's jobs instead of him. A lot of poor families around here need the pay."

Though not typical, these examples of the perceptual filters through which people view issues of foreign policy suffice to indicate some of the hazards of the practice of foreign politics in a democracy. The gap between the way a diplomat and the average man view foreign policy almost has to be measured in light years. Translation of practice and policy into comprehensible terms that will win the necessary internal support for external policy requires political adroitness of a high order—that is to say, a sense of the way the average man sees the world of foreign politics. The hazards of failure to accomplish this are dual. Government may take the easy course of adapting its foreign policy to the lines most easily sold domestically: "act tough," paddle our own canoe, down with the outsider, be he friend or foe. If government does not choose this easy course and fails to obtain popular understanding, its policies may languish for lack of popular support or it may find itself voted from office.

3 · Political Elites and Opinion Stability

As one puzzles about the nature and function of mass opinion, it seems that, no matter what aspect of the problem he struggles with, he must sooner or later return to the question of the relation between political leadership and mass opinion. The properties of opinion, as well as its distribution, have no great political significance unless they bear upon the processes of government; and governments, if they are worth their salt, have their effects upon the properties of mass opinion. One way to speculate upon the significance of the property of stability or instability in opinion is to assume that interactions occur between political elite and mass opinion. The unfortunate connotations of the term "elite" make it necessary to state explicitly that it is used in a broad sense to include political leaders, governmental functionaries, party activists, opinion makers, and others of that vaguely defined stratum of society who talk and act in political roles. We may assume that mass opinion both conditions elite behavior and is itself affected by elite performance.

Consider the circumstances in which the political elite must act when the dominant public opinion is stable. As this situation has been defined, it is one in which the issues and events of politics fit nicely into the norms and standards of the people. If opinion in the system as a whole is stable,[3] most people share similar standards of value or judgment. Probably most actions of government are taken against a background of stable opinion. The response of the public is predictable, and its opinion is not likely quickly to change. Thus, long, long ago the supremacy of the federal government over the states was established; no great debate has to be initiated when new instances of federal-state conflict occur, although there may be warm discussion about the propriety of action in particular situations. The issue over whether government shall provide free public education has long since been set-

[3] As contrasted with stability of opinion of an individual.

tled. The question of whether a degree of social security shall be assured by public action is water over the dam; it does not have to be reconsidered when the issue of the number of weeks coverage for unemployment insurance arises. A good many decades ago a warm conflict was fought out over the question of federal participation in internal improvements. And some time ago it was decided that it did not destroy an employee's liberty if his employer were compelled to maintain safe working conditions in the plant.

On many questions, thus, government and those immediately concerned with action and proposed action act as if they knew precisely what public opinion is and as if they judged it to be quite stable. The proponents and opponents of measures restrict themselves to argument about what the "facts" are; they know what opinion is. Not even cranberry growers deny the propriety of prohibition of the sale of cranberries coated with cancer-producing weed-killer; they merely contend that it would take a lot of weed-killer to do the trick.

In situations of stable opinion (in the system as a whole), then, mass opinion tends to support action taken in line with it. Many actions are taken without much conscious thought about public opinion. Whether there is really an opinion supportive of the action may be immaterial. If all concerned believe the questions of principle to be settled and to be stable in the public mind, for all practical purposes they are.[4] Under these circumstances the role of the political elite becomes in part technical, in part managerial, in the sense of reconciling actions with what they judge to be the dominant and stable opinion. One can only be impressed by the recurring efforts of drafters of policy proposals, and of the interpreters of actions and events, to express, interpret, or rationalize them in terms of what they judge to be both relevant and enduring values of the Republic.

Let us contrast the position of the leadership elite in situations of unstable opinion. Those situations are characterized by novel events, proposals, and problems—that is, stimuli that cannot be brought within the range of any generally distributed picture in our heads. Many kinds of norms may be applied to the judgment of the novel stimulus. It may conflict with old norms, or it may simply be viewed with apprehension or alarm. In short, the public does not know what to make of the new situation; or at least many little publics, to the extent that they are attentive, may each make something different of the new stimulus.[5]

[4] One suspects that elite judgments of mass opinion are not invariably correct. It may be that political activists have a better memory of the accords reached in the battles of the past than does the mass of the citizenry.

[5] A significant question, though impossible to answer satisfactorily, is how the outlooks of voters relate to their partisan regularity in voting which is a stability of sorts. A strong sense of party identification is the most notable corre-

In this kind of circumstance, without a stable opinion pattern, leadership levels face a trying problem. One type of disposition is to let things ride "until opinion crystallizes." Yet governments cannot always await such a crystallization. The political elite—the talkers, the persuaders, the speculators, the philosophers, the advocates, the opponents—mediate between the world of remote and complex events and the mass of the public. A great function of political leadership is the clarification of public problems and the presentation of courses of action. To the extent that governments depend upon public favor, the success or failure of leadership in fulfillment of its function of clarification may be, if not always a matter of life and death for the nation, often a matter of the gravest importance.[6]

The leadership of public opinion in these circumstances of fluid or unstable opinion depends in considerable measure on the systems of public ethics that guide the elite. Irresponsible centers of leadership enjoy their greatest opportunities under circumstances of fluid opinion. A policy most urgent in the national interest, unless it rests on stable opinion, may be scuttled because those who seek individual or group advantage can manipulate a fluid opinion or an opinion not grounded in firmly fixed beliefs or standards. The ancient claim of politicians that they put country before party may rest on a dim recognition that under some circumstances they are tempted to do just the reverse. The norms that govern the elite, as well as the threat of retribution at the polls, constitute an element of the democratic governing process.

If these broad interpretations are correct—that is, if opinion tends to remain fairly stable under conditions of relative well-being with a disciplined elite—they may point to one of the great miscalculations of those who fought the rise of democracy in the western world. They pictured the people as a beast ready to rise against its masters, eager to

---

late of voting regularity. In the 1956 SRC survey those who had voted in presidential elections were asked: "Have you always voted for the same party or have you voted for different parties for president?" Seventy-eight per cent of the strong Democrats and 74 per cent of the strong Republicans said they had always voted for the candidates of their parties; the comparable percentages for weak Democrats and weak Republicans were 55 and 52. Of those with a high sense of political involvement, 51 per cent had always voted for the same party; of those with a low sense of involvement, 38 per cent. Of those with high issue familiarity, 66 per cent had voted for the same party; of those with a low issue familiarity, 44 per cent.

[6] For example, the failure of the Truman Administration to make plain the reasons for American involvement in the Korean episode—a novel sort of enterprise for the United States—may have made it impossible to drum up public support for American participation in brush wars and thereby restricted us to atomic wars. At any rate, the successful Republican exploitation of the issue in 1952 will give statesmen cause for the greatest reluctance to engage in comparable enterprises, no matter what the need or provocation.

use the apparatus of power to right all wrongs. In truth, at least under American conditions, the people do not often flex their muscles. Even then they do so under the ministrations of the most skilled and artful leaders—and such leaders need as allies conditions that make life intolerable, either materially or psychologically, for many people. A critical element in the maintenance of stable orders consists in the recruitment into the leadership ranks of those with leadership skills and in their indoctrination in the etiquette of the order. At choke-points in the system for the advancement of leadership, those elements of society desirous of maintaining the ancient ways can apply their strength and resources with considerable leverage on the entire system.[7]

[7] And they often do. The means best calculated to assure a young lawyer legislator offers of retainers is for him to display some talent—and integrity—in leading popular causes.

11

LATENCY

I F PUBLIC OPINION has a quality of latency, discussion of such opinion would appear to present a singularly slippery problem. Until the opinion moves by activation from its state of hibernation, one can know neither its form nor its direction. So long as it remains latent, it cannot well be inspected. By the time it reaches a state of activation, it has ceased to be latent. Yet in the practice of politics and government latent opinion is really about the only type of opinion that generates much anxiety. What opinion will develop about this prospective candidate? What opinions will be stirred by this legislative proposal? What opinions, anxieties, and moods will be generated by this event or by that action?

Certain prominent lines of political speculation are related to this concern about what the public will think if government acts this way or that. Friedrich has propounded his "rule of anticipated reactions" to describe the tendency by those responsible for decision to estimate response to a contemplated course of action. One of the basic elements of David Truman's group theory is a concept that resembles that of latent opinion. He speaks of the "potential interest group." By "interest" he means a shared attitude. A group exists when interactions, or relationships, occur beyond some minimum frequency among individuals. By "interest group" he means a group that "on the basis of one or more shared attitudes, makes certain claims upon other groups in the so-

ciety." [1] Any set of shared attitudes may become the basis of an interest group. At one point in time no pattern of interactions may exist
among persons (that is, they may not constitute a group) although
they may share a particular set of attitudes. Some disturbance, though,
may set off interactions among persons with those common attitudes.
A potential group becomes a group in actuality. Truman assigns great
importance to these "potential groups" in the workings of the political
systems, for they are often based on interests or expectations widely
held in the society—the general and basic political values, the "rules of
the game." [2] It may not do violence to the argument to translate it into
the observation that certain attitudes or opinions may exist in the minds
of men without their being activated politically. Given relevant or appropriate stimulus, the opinion will be triggered into expression or action. In a quiet suburban neighborhood there may be a pervasive attitude of hostility toward burglary (a latent opinion or a potential
group). The opinion remains latent until, say, a wave of burglaries sets
off a movement to oust the chief of police.

1 · Ramifications of the Concept of Latency

The concept of latency of opinion, when expressed with grace and assurance, may seem to be a sovereign explanation of fundamental aspects
of the democratic governing process. If one encounters analytical obstacles as he seeks to tie governmental action to public opinion, he can
blandly assert that actions are based on estimates of latent opinion. Underlying the idea of latency, in one of its versions, are the psychological
notions employed in Chapter 10 in the discussion of stability of opinion. The citizen is equipped with ingrained sets of values, criteria for
judgment, attitudes, preferences, dislikes—pictures in his head—that
come into play when a relevant action, event, or proposal arises. To
know how the public will respond to a contemplated course of action,
those in positions of leadership and authority need only to relate that
action to their estimate of the pictures in people's heads—and adjust
their strategy accordingly. The actual situations in which governments operate are far more complex than the simple model of the impact of action upon a pre-existing attitude. An exploration of the ramifications of the idea of latency makes clear that in actual governing
situations the estimation of latent opinion presents perplexing questions.
Moreover, the conclusion may be that the genuinely critical problems
of government and public opinion rest, not in the anticipation of latent

[1] *The Governmental Process* (New York: Knopf; 1951), p. 33.

opinion, but in the calculation of response to actions and events the analogues of which have not occurred before—about which there is really no latent opinion; or if relevant latent attitudes exist, they may be obstructive of action that the national interest requires because they are not constructively relevant to the new event.

Whose Latent Opinion? When one speaks of latent opinion, an obvious first question is, whose opinion? The public consists of an attentive public, or a series of attentive publics, and the great inattentive public. Ordinarily the latent opinions of the attentive publics may be estimated in advance. These publics have their party line, their established positions, their ideologies, and in many instances, their professional spokesmen. Over the short run the latent opinions of the American Medical Association, the American Farm Bureau Federation, the National Association of Manufacturers, or the AFL–CIO can be well known. And many other smaller and less prominent groups have reaction patterns so well established that one can know in what manner they will kick when they are needled. How well their spokesmen reflect the views of the group members may be another question, but the views of the spokesmen are usually well known in advance of action.

These attentive publics have their patterns of reaction that serve as bases for predictable response. The relatively inattentive mass public presents a more vexing problem for those who would sense the nature of latent opinion. The problem may be not so much the estimation of the direction of that latent opinion as the prediction of the extent to which an action, a proposal, or an event will even attract the attention of the mass public or of a significant fraction of it. So few public questions cross the threshold of attention of most people that for purposes of practical governance the problem of latency is not so much a matter of general public opinion as of the opinions of special and attentive publics.

The risks of governance come in part from uncertainties about whether mass attention will be mobilized or whether it will remain indifferent and uninformed. "Those who hold public office or work in the mass media know that while it is often difficult to stimulate public response on important issues, it is also difficult to foresee when some apparently trivial point will release widespread public protest." [3] Further, it is difficult to foresee when that public response will be a tempest, which flares up and dies away within a few weeks, and when it will be

[3] G. D. Wiebe: "The Army-McCarthy Hearings and the Public Conscience," *Public Opinion Quarterly*, XXII (1958-9), 490–502.

firm enough to endure. These uncertainties help account for the supposed "power of public opinion." Even though few questions attract
wide attention, those who decide may consciously adhere to the doctrine that they should proceed as if their every act were certain to be
emblazoned on the front pages (or at least on the pages of the *Congressional Record*) and to command universal attention.

In any case, estimation of latent opinion is not simply estimation of
the direction of majority sentiment. The problem extends to the estimation of what sectors of society, influential or noninfluential, will
have opinions. It involves the question whether an issue will command
the attention of a large public. On such estimates from time to time
may turn decisions that could scarcely withstand the uproar that
would be created if they came to universal attention.

Kinds of Questions. Latent opinion may be regarded from the standpoint of whose opinion or from that of the kind of issue, question,
or event that may arouse latent opinion. The two matters are interrelated; one may be simply the obverse of the other. Issues vary in their
capacity to capture public attention. Obviously if a matter does not attract attention, it activates no latent opinion. Some issues and events
carry so universal a threat or impact that they command wide attention. Others are seen, or felt, by only small numbers of people. Furthermore, in the competition for the public eye and ear an issue that attracts attention at one time may go unnoticed at another because of the
diversion of attention by other and more compelling events.

Issues may also vary in the extent and manner to which they are
related to relevant norms and standards held by the public. Some actions may attract wide attention but touch no value or concern among
most people, who, uninvolved, remain spectators. Other issues may
touch sentiments or beliefs widely held within the population. Still
others may affect values held within restricted sectors of the population. An action that clearly conflicts with a widely held attitude may be
expected to stir up controversy if it comes to public attention; an action patently within the limits of the firmly held norms may pass unnoticed or arouse only mild approbation. Many governmental actions
attract little attention because they raise questions within the permissive
limits fixed by latent opinion. The excoriation of cancer, the idealiza-
tion of the American mother, and the condemnation of sin never get a
politician into trouble. Still another range of questions commands only
limited attention because their technical character makes it impossible or difficult to present them in terms comprehensible to a wide public.

Latency and Rationality. The idea of latency rests on an assumption that does not always fit the real world of politics. That assumption tends toward the belief that there is a fairly automatic interaction between the stereotypes in our heads and political stimuli. Undoubtedly many people respond in this way to many of the stimuli of politics, but we pass beyond the bounds of this simple concept of latency when we consider the circumstances in which the public copes with new and great events and questions without the comforting guidance of grooves in the mind. In such situations the process is not so much one of the activation of a latent opinion as it is one of more or less rational efforts of a public to make up its mind about new and great questions that thrust themselves forward for decision. True, the public may rely upon its notions of fairness, of national interest, of individual self-interest, but essentially it is wrestling with a question new to it. And in these interactions governments confront great uncertainties, for the ultimate crystallization of dominant opinion may be governed by an appraisal of events over which government has no control and the response to which is utterly unpredictable. This may be one of the reasons why governments so often temporize and mouth ambiguities as they await the appearance of a crystallization of opinion before they act.

Latency and Electoral Reprisal. The concept of latency itself requires more elaboration the further one examines it. When may latent opinion be regarded as activated, and what is the evidence of its activation? The manner in which public questions develop permits governments to avoid the problem of estimation of latent opinion in many instances. Consideration of an entirely new question may be accompanied by anxiety about what the public response will be. Yet few entirely new questions are so quickly decided that opinion develops entirely after action. Ordinarily debate proceeds over sufficient time to permit the ventilation of viewpoints before decisions are made. The expressions heard during this period may be regarded as the activation of opinion. Those who must decide may take into account the opinions they hear and the opinions they intuitively sense before they take decision.

From another viewpoint, latent opinion may not be truly activated until it is converted into a vote in appraisal of those who make public decisions. Estimation of latent opinion in this sense becomes the tricky job of forecasting the relation of particular actions and events to future popular votes. An action may activate a latent opinion. It may generate a public response of approval, of anger, or of frustration. These sentiments may be dissipated in time, or they may persist and be converted into a vote of reward, or of penalty, on election day. Yet we know that the factors that determine how people vote are so varied and the actions of government so numerous that the estimation of the electoral consequences of most specific actions is beyond the wit or skill of man. Governments are, to be sure, mindful of the probability that their actions will have electoral consequences, but their capacity to forecast those consequences is quite limited. And on many great matters they have no capacity to control events in a manner to discount those electoral consequences. Anxieties about electoral reprisal doubtless condition the operations of democratic governments. Their gauge of that possibility, though, is apt to be rather the momentary complaints that actions arouse than any trustworthy forecast of the translation of latent opinion into popular votes.

Nor do the responses to survey questions designed to ascertain the division of opinion give a clue to the convertibility of opinion into votes. The opinion discovered by survey questions is often a latent opinion in the sense that the question has not been salient in the minds of the respondents until the query was put to them by the interviewer. They express an opinion on a matter about which they have never thought one way or another. The opinion may also be latent in the sense that it is improbable that it will bear on the vote when the next election rolls around. The laws of probability give us some confidence that if the questions asked of samples were asked of the entire population, the division of opinion would be about the same as it was in the sample. Yet the responses give us no indication of what the opinion would be on a question after full debate and discussion.

One aspect of this problem of the estimation of the electoral bite in an opinion that is doubtless partially latent is indicated by the relation between opinion on medical care and the appraisal of governmental performance in that realm. A large majority of the respondents in the 1956 sample agreed with the proposition: "The government ought to help people get doctors and hospital care at low cost." Those persons with an opinion on this question were asked later in the interview whether on this problem the government was going too far, doing less than it should, or what. Appraisals of government performance provide some indication of the quality of latency in the opinions on the issue itself. Of those who favored governmental aid in medical care, almost a third hadn't heard what the government was doing in this field or had no opinion about its performance. A slightly larger proportion of those opposed to governmental participation had not heard what was happening or had no judgment of governmental performance. These blocs of persons obviously had opinions that would probably have no bearing on the vote without activation by further information or argumentation. Nor would it be probable that those who thought the government was doing "about right" would give much attention to medical care in their vote. The bloc of votes with a potential electoral bite consisted of those who both favored governmental participation and thought that the government was doing less than it should in this field.[4] The figures appear in Table 11.1.

TABLE 11.1

RELATION OF OPINION ON MEDICAL CARE TO APPRAISAL OF GOVERNMENTAL PERFORMANCE IN FIELD OF MEDICAL CARE [a]

APPRAISAL OF
GOVERNMENTAL
PERFORMANCE

	OPINION ON GOVERNMENT HELP IN MEDICAL CARE				
	Strongly favor	Favor	Pro-con	Oppose	Strongly oppose
Government going too far	*	*	3%	5%	9%
About right	12	22	27	49	51
Doing less than it should	61	44	23	10	5
Haven't heard what government doing; DK	27	34	47	36	35
	100	100	100	100	100
N	676	272	148	139	320

[a] Those respondents with an opinion on the proposition, "The government ought to help people get doctors and hospital care at low cost," were asked: "On the question of the government helping people get doctors and hospital care at low cost, is the government going too far, doing less than it should, or what?" Respondents were given a card with the following alternatives: Haven't heard what the government is doing: definitely too far; a little too far; about right; a little less than it should; a lot less than it should; don't know.

DATA SOURCE: *Survey Research Center, University of Michigan, 1956.*

---

2 · Activation of Latent Opinion

The idea of latency as a simple reflex response to stimulus explains only in part the opinion that develops with the movement of events. Some people certainly form opinions almost automatically by the application of the norms or conceptions in their heads as they are confronted by political stimuli. On other questions and in other types of situations mass opinion may be formed predominantly by more or less rational responses to proposals and events. Such an assertion may appear improbable, so widely disseminated are the psychological propositions about

[4] This bloc made up about 30 per cent of the sample.

opinions as automatic responses to stimuli. To be sure, the great issues
that involve this reflective process and attract the attention of large
proportions of the population are few indeed. The issues of any kind
that attract the attention of large proportions of the people are few.
Yet from time to time questions arise that command general attention
and set off wide discussion, which eventually crystallizes an opinion not
readily explicable as an unthinking reaction guided by the pictures in
our heads.

The kinds of stimuli that bring latent opinion to life also have a significance for one's conception of the place of the anticipation of latent
opinion in the governing process. Composers of horror essays about
politics occasionally portray politicians as devilish characters guided by
their psychological advisers as they estimate the probable public response to this or that proposal or position or verbal theme. This kind of
conception assumes a high degree of involvement in and attention to
political acts by the general public. It is quite a feat to induce the public
to listen, much less to manipulate it. The probabilities are that the kinds
of stimuli that arouse latent opinions widely within the public are not
the simple verbal stimuli of politicians. They are, if one may guess, more
usually objective conditions that affect or capture the attention of the
masses of people. As they develop, these objective conditions—economic deprivation, external threat, grave injustice—produce responses
whose nature may be affected by the values and expectations held by
people. And the triggering effect of circumstance may certainly be
reinforced by the oratory of those politicians who come forward with
diagnoses and prescriptions. Yet the impression that develops is not one
of cunning governments that manipulate opinion on these subjects. It
is rather the hunch that governments cannot control the circumstances
that activate hostile opinions. Opinion takes shape as the public responds to events and appraises governmental efforts to cope with them.
We may gain a better understanding of these processes by the examination of several types of situations in which latent opinion becomes
activated.

The Rebound Effect. In essence the idea of latent opinion assumes
that a rebound effect exists.[5] A stimulus strikes an attitude, and a latent

[5] It scarcely needs to be said that an overly simple psychology underlies this
entire discussion of latent opinion. More sophisticated theories of the nature of attitudes and of the conditions for their arousal and change have been developed.
Once the necessary empirical observations have been made, these theories may
provide the basis for more persuasive explanations of the processes and consequences of the activation of latent opinion. See Daniel Katz: "The Functional
Approach to the Study of Attitudes," *Public Opinion Quarterly*, XXV (1960),
163–204.

opinion bounces into being. Obviously the conception of activation of latent opinion as a simple stimulus-response process must be modified to take into account imperfections in communications, in information, and in perceptions.[6] These modifications are of importance in speculation about the place of the process of activation of latent opinion for the workings of the political system. If one pictures the system as consisting of individuals with latent opinion that can be triggered by the manipulation of the appropriate symbols, he emerges with a system readily manageable by those skilled in the choice of magic words. Certainly some survey findings strongly indicate that on some questions a more or less Pavlovian response in opinion and action occurs as a stimulus triggers a latent opinion. That stimulus, though, often affects few people. Few may be reached by it; or many persons who respond to it may be subject to counteracting influences that pull them in the opposite direction.

A case indicative of both the simple rebound effect and of its relatively small magnitude (in the particular instance) is provided by the effect of Franklin D. Roosevelt's allusion in the campaign of 1940 to Mussolini's "stab in the back." The common supposition is that Roosevelt's disrespectful comment about Mussolini drove voters of Italian origin into the Republican ranks. If we are to place credence in the Crossley poll, the shift occurred but it was not of great magnitude. The findings of a survey shortly before the election were as follows:

1936 Voters	*1940 Vote Intention*		
			Undecided;
	Roosevelt	*Willkie*	*nonvoters*
Men for:			
Landon	3.4%	95.0%	1.6%
Roosevelt	70.2	24.2	5.6
Italian origin for:			
Landon	2.8	91.6	5.6
Roosevelt	64.4	23.9	11.7

Only a slightly larger proportion of voters of Italian origin than of men generally shifted their support from Roosevelt in 1936 to Willkie in 1940. One may well suspect that this survey underestimated the mag-

[6] The complexity of the process of activation of opinion on issues is suggested by Lazarsfeld's analyses of the voting decision. Basic attitudes, group identifications, and other factors interact with the perception of events in a complex process to crystallize decision, to activate latent partisanship, and to bring individuals to a voting decision. Presumably some such process of similar complexity may occur as the public, or parts of it, arrive at a position on policy issues. Of that process, though, we have no studies on the order of *The People's Choice*.

nitude of this difference. Even with some allowance for error, though, the data point to the limited magnitude in this instance of the rebound effect and suggest the importance of many other influences for voting behavior that outweighed concern about the homeland. Latent opinion even on this kind of emotional question may be offset by frictions, imperfections in communication, and conflicting standards of action.

Yet the case of the sensitive voters of Italian origin suggests that on some kinds of questions a latent opinion in the minds of some persons is expressed almost as a one-to-one reaction to a triggering event. One such type of situation may be that in which a fairly small attentive public has highly developed sensitivities and unambiguous standards about particular types of questions. Another type may be that in which an action receives wide attention and happens to bear on a widely distributed attitude—for example, the disposition to condemn petty thievery in high public office.

Estimation of the nature of the opinion that may be activated by a particular proposal or action (as well as the consequences of its activation) is complicated by the fact that the stimulus may touch off a response that is guided by different and even conflicting standards of value among different people. The possibilities are illustrated by two questions put by the AIPO in 1957. The first question was as follows: "People in favor of 'Right to work' or open shop laws say that no American should be required to join any private organization like a labor union against his will. Do you agree or disagree with this?" To this question the responses were distributed as follows:

	General Public	Union Members
Agree	73%	52%
Disagree	18	41
No opinion	9	7

Probably in its responses the general public drew upon its dislike for compulsion in any form while union members had in some degree other standards for judgment on the question. When the issue was put in different terms, another norm of fairness produced a contrasting distribution of opinion. The second formulation was: "Those opposed to 'Right to work' or open shop laws say that when all workers share the gains won by the labor union all workers should have to join and pay dues to give the union financial support. Do you agree or disagree with this?" This phrasing produced the following division of opinion:

	General Public	Union Members
Agree	45%	74%
Disagree	41	23
No opinion	14	3

The contrasting responses to the two formulations suggest why it is of importance how issues are presented to the public. If they appear in one light, they may evoke approval; in another, they may arouse opposition.[7] The contrasting responses also indicate the limits of the insights provided by the idea of latency. When men have different standards of judgment that can be applied to the same question and when the barrage of political stimuli includes appeals to all those standards, the collective response can as readily be pictured as the result of a process of rational calculation as one of simple rebound.

TABLE 11.2

SATISFACTION WITH CURRENT FINANCIAL SITUATION IN RELATION TO OPINION ON JOB GUARANTEE, WITHIN OCCUPATIONAL CATEGORIES [a]

FINANCIAL SATISFACTION	OCCUPATION AND POSITION ON JOB ISSUE					
	White-collar		Blue-collar		Farmers	
	Pro	Con	Pro	Con	Pro	Con
Satisfied	43%	39%	60%	25%	51%	27%
More-or-less satisfied	44	38	63	22	51	28
Dissatisfied	51	38	77	12	63	12

[a] The question on financial satisfaction was as follows: "We are also interested in how people are getting along financially these days. So far as you and your family are concerned, would you say that you are pretty well satisfied with your present financial situation, more-or-less satisfied, or not satisfied at all?" The entries may be read as follows: Of white-collar respondents satisfied with their current financial situation, 43 per cent agreed that the government ought to see to it that everybody who wants to work can find a job; 39 per cent disagreed. And so on. The differences between the two figures and 100 are accounted for by the responses of "it depends" and by those with no opinion.

DATA SOURCE: *Survey Research Center, University of Michigan, 1956.*

---

[7] Sample surveys make possible an informed guess about what the public response will be to specified campaign themes or, in the terminology of this chapter, to estimate the nature of the latent opinion that will be stirred by campaign themes. Thus, in a survey early in a campaign on a "right to work" law it was discovered that Negroes regarded "right to work" laws as measures calculated to assure to Negroes equality in job opportunity. Intensive educational efforts corrected this impression.

Another aspect of latent opinion that both facilitates its prediction and circumscribes its importance in the political process is its association with objective circumstance. Given the values of the American political culture, some kinds of objective threats or deprivations may, when properly exploited, produce opinion in demand of governmental action. Whether much is gained by calling this response to reality the activation of latent opinion may be doubtful, but this is a type of reaction that governments must be concerned about as they weigh the possible effect of events on public opinion. As an illustration consider the data of Table 11.2, which show the relationship between varying degrees of satisfaction with personal financial situation and opinion on the proposition that the government should see that those who want to work can find a job. Support is considerably more frequent among those "not satisfied at all" with their financial situation. It may plausibly be expected that if economic conditions changed sufficiently to increase substantially the number of persons "not satisfied at all," the number of persons approving the job guarantee proposition would increase. Proposals would be heard in the land—and cheered—to create another WPA.[8] Yet to grasp the place of this kind of "latent opinion" in the governing process the particular case must be placed in a setting of the political values of the culture. The response approbative of governmental assurance of employment can occur only after a society has developed the notion that political action is an appropriate way to deal with unemployment. (In some cultures the hat might be passed, or the medicine men might be called upon.) Moreover, the norm needs to be widely accepted within the society; that is, more must be involved than the anxiety of the unemployed if opinion is to be of much effect on public policy. Consider, for example, the opinions of those "pretty well satisfied." As the table indicates, large proportions of such persons also agreed with the idea of governmental responsibility for the assurance of employment. The response to agitation or circumstances (or a combination thereof) depends on the broad kinds of values and expectations held by the people.

An additional illustration of the relationship between the sense of satisfaction with personal financial situation and policy outlook is provided by the data of Table 11.3. Satisfaction and dissatisfaction are there related to opinion on the proposition: "The government ought to help people get doctors and hospital care at low cost." Among blue-collar workers the variation in opinion with degree of satisfaction is most marked. About three fourths of those "not satisfied at all" took the position that the government should help on medical care, while

[8] See the discussion by Bernard Berelson: "Events as an Influence upon Public Opinion," *Journalism Quarterly*, XXVI (1949), 145-8.

only a bare majority of those "satisfied" concurred with the proposition. Here, again, it is probably safe to predict that the movement of more people into the ranks of those "not satisfied at all" would increase the percentage of approval of the medical care proposition in the society as a whole.[9]

The effects of events on opinions take place against the background of beliefs and attitudes within the population. For example, a

TABLE 11.3

SATISFACTION WITH CURRENT FINANCIAL SITUATION IN RELATION TO OPINION ON GOVERNMENT AID IN MEDICAL CARE, WITHIN OCCUPATIONAL CATEGORIES [a]

FINANCIAL SATISFACTION	OCCUPATION AND POSITION ON MEDICAL-CARE ISSUE			
	White-collar		Blue-collar	
	Pro	Con	Pro	Con
Satisfied	38%	40%	53%	24%
More-or-less satisfied	52	32	57	22
Dissatisfied	49	31	72	10

[a] Entries to be read as in Table 11.2.
DATA SOURCE: *Survey Research Center, University of Michigan, 1956.*

widespread humanitarianism that assumes some sort of community responsibility to care for the sick probably underlies attitudes on medical care. Often actions and propaganda to generate opinion are in considerable measure efforts to make the facts known about the adequacy of medical care available to people differently circumstanced. Information thus may activate a latent opinion. In a society with another set of values information might have no effect if the prevailing doctrine were "let the weak perish." Existence of wide agreement on broad objectives probably accounts for the fact that American political disputation at times has the character of a debate over what the facts are. Resistance to the establishment of the facts may be fierce because of the assumption that once the facts are known the decision is made.

Perhaps in a technical sense the objective realities do not activate latent opinion; politicians mediate between the facts and the public by

[9] To establish the consequences in opinion of such changes in conditions requires soundings of opinion at intervals through time. While such time series are scarce, an example comes from periodic surveys by the *Wisconsin Agriculturalist* of the opinions of Wisconsin farmers on the question whether Secretary of Agriculture Ezra Taft Benson was doing a good job. In July, 1953, 13 per cent thought the Secretary was doing a poor job. That proportion rose to 55 per cent by January, 1956. Between these two points in time the lot of the Wisconsin dairy farmer in particular had deteriorated, a fact not neglected in political oratory addressed to these farmers.

calling the facts to public attention and by putting forth proposals for action. Modern techniques of social observation make it possible for political leaders to observe fairly closely those trends in objective conditions that may activate opinion. Politicians, especially minority politicians, are prone to watch the statistical indicators and to come forward with their remedies and critiques of government even before the persons immediately affected begin to squawk. The availability of these statistical indicators probably has had important consequences for governments that profess a deference to public opinion. Before the availability of the newer techniques of social accounting, much more drastic shifts in objective circumstance were probably required for the development of a widespread awareness of changes. As recently as the 1930's, for example, the scarcity of data made the debate over unemployment sound as if some people doubted that unusual unemployment existed.

Rebound versus Reorientation of Opinion. In some situations the expectation may be that latent opinion will be activated in a one-to-one relationship between stimulus and response in a more or less mechanical fashion. It may be doubted that this outlook often has much relevance in the anticipation of public reactions on those great questions that stir the people deeply and activate a mass opinion that may be really decisive of governmental action. Such instances of widespread and intense focus of attention on great public issues, infrequent though they are, seem rather to be occasions for the consideration of new problems, for the revision of old pictures in our heads, than moments at which the public automatically applies old standards to new situations. An impression emerges of a public moved under these circumstances by more or less rational considerations in appraisal of great issues toward a majority sentiment. And in the generation of opinion about great events and issues the impression also develops that attempts to manage and manipulate opinion do not necessarily control; the implacable movement of events attracts attention, and old stereotypes are discarded as new opinion is formed. Advocacy gains an apparent strength, but chiefly as it reinforces and verbalizes common-sense appraisals by the mass public of conditions, problems, and events.

Episodes that fit this general description are infrequent and those about which opinion data are available are even rarer. Perhaps the most striking example consists in the sharp shifts in American attitudes as the public responded to the events leading to our entry into World War II. The impact of these events brought a reversal of well-established opinions on a series of public issues. Opposition to compulsory military service, which had long been a cardinal tenet of American opinion, declined as events in Europe made the threat of war more apparent. At intervals the AIPO put the question: "Do you think that every able-bodied young man 20 years old should be made to serve in the army, navy, or air forces for one year?" The changing responses as events unfolded were as follows:

	Favoring	*Opposing*
December, 1938 (after Munich)	37%	63%
October, 1939 (after war began)	39	61
June 2, 1940 (after battle of Flanders)	50	50
June 23, 1940 (after French surrender)	64	36
July, 1940	67	33
August, 1940	66	34

As sentiment about military conscription was changing, substantial numbers of persons were also modifying the long-standing opinion that Presidents should serve only two terms. Events abroad had their repercussions on opinions about governmental practices at home that might be related to our capacity to cope with external affairs. To the question: "If President Roosevelt runs for a third term, will you vote for him?" (and variations on that question), the "yes" proportion of responses shifted as follows: November, 1938, 40 per cent; June, 1939, 38 per cent; August, 1939, 40 per cent; December, 1939, 46 per cent; May, 1940, 57 per cent.

Along with these changes in outlook the public was also revising its interpretation of history. The efflorescence of isolationism after World War I had evidently produced a widespread belief that the United States should never have entered that conflict. Yet as disorder welled up in Europe again, people began to revise their opinions. A series of responses to the AIPO question: "Do you think it was a mistake for the United States to enter the last war?" follows:

	Yes	*No*	*No opinion*
January, 1937	70%	30% = 100%	8%
February, 1939	48	37	15 = 100%
October, 1939	59	28	13
November, 1939	39	42	19
January, 1941	40	44	16
March, 1941	39	43	18
April, 1941	35	47	18
December, 1941	21	61	18

In a parallel movement of opinion, popular attitudes toward international organization shifted as events developed. More people began to believe that it had been a mistake for the United States not to join the League of Nations. Responses to a series of surveys on the question: "Do you think the United States should have joined the League of Nations after the last war?" were as follows:

	Yes	No	No opinion
AIPO, July, 1941	37%	37%	26%
NORC, July, 1942	46	23	31
NORC, August, 1942	47	28	25
NORC, January, 1943	51	23	26
AIPO, June, 1944	53	20	27

While it could be contended that all these movements of opinion amounted only to a mechanical interaction between unchanging latent opinions and the stimuli of politics, the argument would not carry much conviction. The process could quite as well, and more plausibly, be described as the more or less rational development of opinion under the impact of events and of the competing programs advanced by political leaders. The second interpretation assigns a radically different role to public opinion at turning points in national policy than the first.

Mixtures of Reorientation and Rebound. Doubtless as issues and problems arise, the nature of the popular response differs. In some instances an almost universal stereotype may govern the opinions of most people. In other instances the question is so new that a virtually complete reorientation of opinion occurs, erected upon at least partially new considerations. In still other instances the circumstances may be mixed. The opinions of some people may be only a reflex of well-established attitudes. Other persons may form opinions that rest on modifications of or departures from attitudinal predispositions by a more-or-less rational process. The movement of opinion during the 1937 controversy over President Roosevelt's proposal to reorganize the Supreme Court probably represented one of these mixed situations.

Though we have no systematic data on the point, the odds are that the traditional adulation of the Supreme Court had created in the minds of most people a disposition to respect its position, its authority, and its decisions. The sanctity of the Court became somewhat tarnished as it struck down statute after statute designed to cope with problems brought to a head by the Great Depression. The place of the Court became a warm issue with Roosevelt's proposal to rejuvenate it by the enactment of legislation permitting appointment of additional justices. This scheme set off a spirited debate. Opponents of the reorganization plan challenged it as a threat to the foundations of the Republic, an act of dictatorship, a threat to the rule of law, and a scheme subversive of the Constitution. The plan's defenders were hard put to cope with these arguments but contended that some reconsideration of the place of the Court in the political system was essential if the popular will was to prevail and if the urgent problems of the time were to be dealt with. To win public support for the proposals, the advocates, with the aid of events and circumstances, had to produce a reorientation of opinion; to arouse latent opposition, the opponents merely had to activate and to strengthen ancient shibboleths.

As the debate on the plan proceeded, the Court itself acted to change the terms of the conflict. After Roosevelt's proposal in February, the Court late in March, 1937, reversed itself on the question of the constitutionality of state minimum wage legislation and followed up this coup with decisions upholding the National Labor Relations Act and the Social Security Act. As the debate proceeded, the AIPO took weekly samplings of opinions on the reorganization proposal, the data from which permit inferences about the interplay of events and opinion. At the beginning of the discussion in February those with opinions on the issue divided 50:50 for and against court reorganization. The Court's decision on the minimum wage question, however, seemed to break the back of the support for reorganization. Approval in the general public declined; and as the debate proceeded, a majority seemed to conclude that if the Court had decided to reform its behavior, nothing was to be gained by bloodying its collective nose. The state of opinion at several points in the debate is indicated by these figures:[1]

	Feb. 15	May 17	June 17
Favor reorganization	45%	31%	35%
Oppose reorganization	45	44	50
No opinion	10	25	15

Commonly the impact of events may be to compel a reorientation of old attitudes and norms, but in this instance as events unfolded during the debate—as the Court trimmed its own sails—events reinforced the established attitudes of deference toward the Court.

[1] Frank V. Cantwell: "Public Opinion and the Legislative Process," *American Political Science Review*, XL (1946), 924-35.

Attitudinal Foundations of Latency. The foregoing observations have enabled us to pull the simple conception of latency as stimulus-response down into the realities of politics sufficiently to place vague boundaries around the phenomenon of activation of latent opinion in political practice. The phenomenon is limited by the processes that limit the numbers of persons who become aware of a political stimulus. It is limited by the clarity of relevant norms in the minds of those who perceive the stimulus. It is limited by the fact that policy proposals often need to be associated with objective circumstances if latent opinion is to be stirred. It is limited, or at least given character, by the fact that opinion may be rationally developed on some great issues.

Still another conditioning factor, as has been suggested, is the extent to which there may be present in people's minds latent opinions which can be activated by the appropriate stimulus. The map of the topography of the public mind is most sketchy, but information is available about some types of terrain that are not to be found in the public mind or that occur most infrequently. All readers are familiar with sweeping interpretations of the public mind that assume the existence within the general public of some systematic ideological outlook. We are told that the electorate by its vote of yesterday took a decisive turn to the right. Or that the country is in a radical mood. Or that the middle-of-the-road philosophy is now triumphant. If any such sets of outlooks existed generally within the public, the process for the activation of latent opinion could easily be explained. The right-winger would be expected automatically to take a right-wing stance on individual issues as they arose; the left-winger would respond in a manner compatible with his ideology. The fact seems to be that the assumption of the existence of such ideological schemes in the public mind misses the mark by far. Extremely few persons in the total population view political events in any such manner.

The evidence leading to such conclusions consists of data assembled and analyzed by Campbell, Converse, Miller, and Stokes in their study of the 1956 election. By the analysis of responses to open-ended questions on what respondents liked and disliked about the Republican and Democratic parties and the presidential candidates, it was possible to group persons according to the conceptions they had of politics (at least as those conceptions were evoked by these questions). In their categorization they identified a class of individuals who perceived a liberal-conservative scale along which issues and persons might be placed. These individuals, who might be expected to respond to issues in terms of their own system or scale of values, constituted only 2.5 per cent of the sample. By a fairly generous policy in classification, another

9 per cent could be called near-ideologues. Another 42 per cent of the sample had no conception of a systematic left-right differentiation but saw the political process as one concerned largely with group benefits.[2] These persons were differentiated in the manner in which they perceived groups and politics. Some saw a fairly elaborate process of group rivalry, while others had a much more primitive conception of the place of groups in politics. Another 24 per cent of the sample saw politics in terms of the goodness or badness of the times, which some of them associated with the Administration or with a political party. Another 22.5 per cent of the sample consisted of persons in whose responses not a trace of issue content could be found; the conception of left and right, liberal and conservative, would probably be meaningless to most of this group. In some instances they were candidate-oriented or party-oriented, but in no instance did they display even the most rudimentary conception of politics as involving questions along a liberal-conservative continuum.[3]

The relevancies of these findings for the broad problem of this chapter are several. The terms of political discourse common among scholars and even among many politicians have no referent in the attitudinal baggage of most voters; there is, for most people, no latent ideological outlook along a liberal-conservative scale to be activated by the manipulation of the appropriate symbol. The great mass of voters form their opinions according to other types of standards, which may often involve group interests or simple estimates of the conditions of the times along with an assignment of party responsibility therefor. Other kinds of inquiries would probably identify vague standards widely distributed within the population, but the evidence yields more a picture of the public as one that would form its opinions (on domestic economic issues) in a pragmatic manner than by the application of even a simple ideological scheme for the appraisal of events and actions. Most people may believe that a man who wants to work ought to be able to find a job, but they do not view governmental interposition to insure this possibility as an episode in the grand struggle between individualism and collectivism. The relative absence of systematic ideological outlooks in the public mind suggests that American opinion has

[2] In July, 1960, the AIPO asked a national sample: "Do you happen to know what is meant when someone is called a 'liberal' in politics?" Then a second question was put about the meaning of a "conservative." Forty-four per cent demonstrated that they had some understanding of the meaning of both terms.

[3] For the discussion of these matters with the full definitions of the categories and illustrative excerpts from interviews, see Angus Campbell, Philip E. Converse, Warren E. Miller, and Donald E. Stokes: *The American Voter* (New York: Wiley; 1960), ch. 10.

a considerable plasticity and is susceptible to being shaped by the conditions and requirements of the times.[4]

3 · Governance and Opinion Latency

Government has been pictured as operating within a matrix of opinion, a matrix that establishes vague limits of permissiveness within which governmental action may occur without arousing a commotion. The concept of latency of opinion enables us to elaborate this model of the relation between government and opinion. As government moves through time, the form and firmness of the matrix of opinion change as new events and new actions activate latent opinion in greater or lesser degree or induce the development of entirely new opinion. A crisis may so mobilize opinions that government permits its anxieties to freeze it into inaction, or the direction of public demand may be regarded as so obvious that government acts impulsively and even unwisely. Or the opinion activated may be regarded as so unstable and impermanent that it evokes from government pacificatory speeches and pronouncements with no perceptible effect on reality as the subsidence of public concern is awaited. As time moves, the crisis may be dissipated; the activated opinion again becomes latent. As new events and circumstances develop, the focus of public attention shifts; the matrix of opinion assumes new forms and new policy content.

Interplay of the Attentive and Inattentive Public. In one respect the problem of opinion latency and of the changing content and form of activated opinion is one of public attention. Unless the public becomes aware of actions or events, whatever latent attitudes exist will not be converted into conscious opinion with a potential bearing on behavior through voting or otherwise. The determination of what latent opinions will be activated rests upon the shifts through time of the foci of public attention and, perhaps more importantly, upon the changing extent to which the public centers its attention upon political objects.

The strangest paradox of so-called government by public opin-

---

[4] This focus on mass opinion should not lead one to underestimate the import for the course of government policy of the ideological grooves in the minds of the relatively few persons in the population who are political activists. An analysis instructive about the significance of ideological commitments could be made of the domestic actions of the Eisenhower Administration. Its laissez-faire ideologies apparently controlled its specific decisions on many matters through a wide range of governmental activities.

ion is the slight degree to which opinions of the mass of the people are aroused by most actions of government. This odd situation comes about in two ways: first, by the assiduous (and on occasion short-sighted) quest by governments for types of actions that will not antagonize opinion; second, from the fact that so few actions by government have so widespread an impact or a quality to command the attention of many persons and thereby to activate whatever relevant latent opinion may exist.[5]

Many actions—those of the first type—fall so clearly within the limits of what is widely regarded as proper that those immediately affected well know that the decision would gain public concurrence if it were made the subject of a campaign of public agitation. The universal norms have apparently governed the decision, or the decision reflects so well the expectations deducible from "national character" that it may be said that public opinion has prevailed without having been either informed or consulted. This state of affairs may come about as a result of prayerful consideration of the probable public reaction; more commonly it comes about without conscious concern about public opinion. Those responsible for decision may be themselves so imbued with the dominant values of the society that no thought of public reaction need cross their minds. And they may have consulted so extensively with those immediately concerned by the decision as to foreclose all possibilities of cries of outrage from them.

The second consideration—the capacity of issues to capture attention—creates uncertainties for government. The extent to which public attention is captured will govern the extent to which latent opinions are activated. A considerable proportion of the decisions of Congress and of the Executive, decisions which may often be regarded by the sophisticated observer as of great significance, attract only limited attention. Those small publics that are attentive to a particular type of question are readily activated. The uncertainty exists in the extent to which the latent opinions of the mass of people not immediately concerned with the question will be activated.

On these questions, whose visibility to the mass public is unpredictable, decision may be a matter of interplay of the opinions (and wishes and preferences) of small attentive publics and of official estimates of the opinions of the inattentive public which may or may not become activated. Those small publics with intense opinions for or against a contemplated course of action make themselves heard; no art

[5] The problem of capturing public attention is not limited to democracies. Graham Wallas in 1908 recorded the views of a Russian terrorist who reported that there was "no use arguing with the peasants." The revolutionary movements attracted attention if a Tzar, a Grand Duke, or a minister could be assassinated.— *Human Nature in Politics*, 3rd ed. (London: Constable; 1920), p. 175.

is required to foresee the direction their opinions will take, nor are they misunderstood when the time for action arises. On the other hand, most of the time governments know that latent opinions of the inattentive public will not be aroused; or that if they are, they will be of low intensity. Moreover, if they are aroused, the probability of their being ultimately converted into reward or penalty at the polls is slight indeed. Thus, on a range of questions, which we admittedly cannot define with precision, governments enjoy, insofar as mass opinion is concerned, a high degree of discretion in the determination of what action they will take and which sector of the attentive public they will heed. On such questions governments need only clothe their action so as to make it appear that equity has prevailed—a hedge against the possibility that an action may capture public attention and energize latent attitudes.

Attention, Inattention, Latency, and Governmental Initiative. Limitation of public attention to small, interested publics on so many questions and the concomitant failure to activate the latent opinions of the mass public may help explain why so much of American government appears to be (and on occasion is) a matter of distributing the spoils of policy to the interests. Yet at infrequent intervals mass attention appears to be aroused and latent opinion seems to be activated in support of measures expressive of democratic ideals which at other times would scarcely be seriously considered. It is at these times that mass opinion may seem to have the bit in its teeth, and government exerts its authority to batter down the resistance and opposition of narrow, and ordinarily controlling, publics.

We may wonder what features characterize these times of action when an aroused mass public seems to prevail. Perhaps one characteristic is the manner in which the President interprets his role. To arouse latent opinion, attention must be captured, and on the American national scene only the president can capture the attention of the ordinarily inattentive public. Mass attention must be aroused, but the public also must be given cues; the situation must be clarified for it. Thus, a President who recognizes no role for himself in initiative of policy or leadership of opinion is without effect on mass opinion about policy though he may be personally a popular figure. A President who abdicates the duty of leadership of opinion leaves the country rudderless; the babel of other voices ordinarily goes unheard by most people. The country is without a conspicuous clarifier of the stream of events. It is during such eras that the litterateurs turned political commentators expatiate upon the lack of a sense of national purpose, the decline of moral values, the alienation of mass man, and other such recondite matters.

Talk, even from the most conspicuous sources, is not enough to arouse widespread attention or demand. Propaganda seems to be most effective when reinforced by objective conditions.[6] Presidential leadership seems most effective in the activation of latent opinion when a sense of threat, frustration, or deprivation is widely felt within the population.[7] The public, Lippmann observed, does not "rouse itself normally at the existence of evil. It is aroused at evil made manifest by the interruption of a habitual process of life." [8] "Crisis," says Lasswell, "concentrates attention; non-crisis disperses it." [9] Under circumstances of crisis or deprivation, a President (or perhaps in smaller jurisdictions other leaders) may capture the attention of the ordinarily inattentive public, provide cues of direction and clarification, and amass a support that makes itself felt throughout the policy manufacturing machinery of government.[1]

Yet these episodes are infrequent, a fact that may account for some of the peculiarities of a government that leans on the doctrine of government in accord with public opinion. Public opinion does not emerge like a cyclone and push obstacles before it. Rather, it develops under leadership. Governmental functionaries addicted to the notion that

[6] For example, psychological warfare has many claims made on its behalf, but its effects on the enemy seem to be most notable when the enemy is losing anyway. Thus, in World War I German civilian morale fluctuated with the fortunes of German armies, not with the volume of Allied propaganda. Propaganda to German troops began to have effect after a series of unsuccessful battles and the hunger blockade had prepared the way. See George G. Bruntz: "Allied Propaganda and the Collapse of German Morale in 1918," *Public Opinion Quarterly*, II (1938), 61–76; and George W. Hartmann: "Immediate and Remote Goals as Political Motives," *Journal of Abnormal and Social Psychology*, XXXIII (1938), 86–99.

[7] Thus, Harry Truman, in his policy programs, advocated a more powerful brand of political medicine than did Franklin Roosevelt. Yet the public response was not overwhelming, perhaps because the times were less parlous in 1949 than in 1933.

[8] Walter Lippmann: *The Phantom Public* (New York: Harcourt, Brace; 1925), p. 67.

[9] Harold Lasswell: "Attention Structure and Social Structure" in Lyman Bryson, ed.: *The Communication of Ideas* (New York: Harper; 1948), p. 262.

[1] In his study of the Townsend movement Hadley Cantril interviewed a 73-year-old man, born and raised on a marginal farm, schooled through the sixth grade, who qualified as a political theorist: "The Townsend Plan would be the best god-damned thing that ever happened for this country—if they'd only give it a chance. And I'll tell you why it don't get a chance. People are too damn lazy to take any interest in a good thing like this when they've got a little money and a job, and there's more people like that than there are old ones and unemployed. The only time you can get anything done to help the people is in a depression, when they're all poor and worried. Then the Congress knows its gotta pass things like the Social Security and Employment Insurance, because they know the whole country wants it."—Hadley Cantril: *The Psychology of Social Movements* (New York: Wiley; 1941), p. 195.

they must govern in accord with public wishes thus may be especially susceptible to the error of mistaking wisps of opinion for public opinion. More often, and more seriously, they hesitate to take action predictably necessary because they await the development of popular support. It may well be that the more closely politicians keep their ears to the ground, the less likely they are to govern in accord with the long-run movements of public opinion.

To put the matter in another way, the public cannot innovate; it can only acclaim or reject innovation. And the chances are that as government confronts the unfolding future, most of the highly attentive sectors of the public tend to oppose innovation which, insofar as it depends on public opinion, must draw its support from those sectors of the public least attentive, most difficult to mobilize. Governments that listen most respectfully to the attentive public (whose influence at elections is often overestimated) thus may be driven to paralysis.[2] The odds are that leadership echelons with a compulsive deference to public opinion become cautious, even to the point of failure to take the initiative on issues of the gravest importance. Politicians so habituated are mightily tempted to avoid disturbing sleeping dogs.

Often the process of adapting public opinion as new problems and new circumstances emerge may be more of a problem in the adaptation of elite opinion than in the conversion of the masses. To illustrate, during the 1940's there gradually developed an outlook in the ranks of opinion leadership across party lines, and across other group lines, that something other than an isolationist posture was appropriate for the United States in postwar world affairs. Or among the political elite there gradually arose an assumption that the economy need not be managed entirely on a dog-eat-dog basis. Such shifts in philosophy and outlook among that vaguely defined category we call the "political elite"

[2] Evidence suggests that under some circumstances innovation may precede rather than follow changes in opinion among highly attentive and interested sectors of the public. On the adaptation of the business community to New Deal measures, see Robert E. Lane: "Law and Opinion in the Business Community," *Public Opinion Quarterly*, XVII (1953), 239–57. In a Pittsburgh interracial housing project, three of every four who had expected serious racial conflict found, after living in the project a while, that their fears had been unfounded. Moreover, more of those who had worked with Negroes were willing to live in the same community than of those who had not worked with Negroes.—Paul F. Lazarsfeld: "Some Remarks on the Role of Mass Media in So-called Tolerance Propaganda," *Journal of Social Issues*, III, 3 (1937), pp. 17–25. On a less grave level, a *Fortune* poll in 1935 found that 88 per cent of a national sample preferred to have milk delivered in a glass bottle; 6 per cent, in a paper container; with the remaining responses scattered. Two thirds of those who favored paper came from the few places where paper containers had been in use. To be sure, not all opinion change occurs after action. Yet opinion on certain questions is sometimes not altered until after an innovation has become a reality, a factor of importance in speculation about the place of public opinion in government.

are accompanied by a good deal of technical analysis and by the formulation of elaborate justifications and rationalizations. But for most people shifts of preference do not need to overcome nicely rationalized philosophies or systems of thought. Once the elite cues become relatively clear, mass opinion may move along in harmony.

Part IV

FORMATION

EVERY FACTOR

that makes the individual what he is attitudinally enters into the formation of political opinion. Frequent allusion has been made in the preceding chapters to the bearing on mass opinion of the outlooks and operations of political leadership—political activists of many types and kinds, ranging from presidential candidates to the fellow at the next workbench who seems to know the score and is not unwilling to share his wisdom. The political alternatives and outlooks current among political activists find their reflections in the views and opinions of persons less active politically. The different conditions in contrasting occupational life situations have, as we have also seen, a fundamental bearing on political outlook of the individual. The impact of the "objective" conditions of the times may also be reflected in the direction and intensity of opinion and may contribute to fundamental reorientations of political attitude on broad questions of public policy.

Certain institutions also have an immediate and telling impact upon political opinions and outlooks, and the following chapters examine the role of some of these institutions. Obviously, in the formation of the general outlook of the individual the family must be of prime importance. The social and political views current within the family tend to be acquired by the child. The schools also function as a great engine for the formation of attitudes, outlooks, and abilities of political relevance. The media of communication—press, radio, TV—provide us with a picture of the current political world and convey cues from other sources of influence within the polity as well as propagate the views of of their proprietors. The media link us to remote events, and the manner in which they do so may greatly influence our response to them.

Other institutions also function in the formation of mass opinion. Political parties and that array of organizations known as "pressure groups" mold as well as reflect opinion. Since their opinion-forming functions cannot readily be separated from their functions of representation of opinion, their treatment may be postponed to a later part of the book.

I 2

THE FAMILY

THE FAMILY is obviously a major agency in the formation of basic political attitude.[1] In addition to whatever qualities he inherits, the child acquires in the family circle social outlooks of varying political content and relevance. Some anthropologists ascribe fundamental characteristics of political systems to individual behavior resulting from specified child-rearing practices: swaddling or not, permissive or not, rigid toilet training or not, families child-centered or not, feeding by the clock or demand. Thus if the little monsters are fed whenever they yell, they are said to become, not apathetic nonvoters, but adults with confidence in their control of their environment and with a sense of efficacy in relation to those in authority.[2] Such interpretations lend themselves to statement with plausibility, but their persuasiveness evaporates once the sparseness of their support in systematic observation is perceived. The object here, though, is not to push the analysis back to the impact of family on personality. Rather, it is to ascertain the relations, if any, between a limited number of family political char-

---

[1] See Herbert Hyman's admirable analysis of existing information about the topic: *Political Socialization* (Glencoe: Free Press; 1959).

[2] It might be as plausible to deduce that demand-feeding would produce adults who would complain loudly when even slightly frustrated and, hence, a political system in continuous and senseless turmoil. One of the troubles about Freudian psychology is that once a person begins to believe it, he can believe anything. For some Freudianism, see E. H. Erikson: *Childhood and Society* (New York: Norton; 1950).

acteristics and the political outlooks of offspring within the American political culture.

Estimation of the relation of family experience as a child to the political opinions of the adult meets formidable research obstacles. First, available data about the early family environment of adults are limited. They also depend upon the individual's recall of his family situation, which may be colored by projection of his own attitudes back to his family. Further, there is the problem of disentangling family influences from other factors that mold political outlook. Children come under the influence of other children, of the schools, and often early in life they begin to sense the political stimuli that play upon the community generally. Ordinarily these factors may reinforce the family; its circumstances may determine what kinds of peer influences, what types of school environment, and what sorts of media reach the child. In some instances, though, these external influences may weaken the effect of the family. As a person grows older, his early family experience becomes remote and other considerations enter into his political outlook. They may again either reinforce or weaken the political orientation a person had at, say, age eighteen. Withal, one must take with a large grain of salt correlations between present political outlooks of adults and their memories of the politics of their families. Nevertheless, the data strongly suggest that early family experiences have important consequences in adult political behavior.

1 · Party Identification

Given the significance of party identification in the behavior of the American electorate, any institution that contributes to the shaping of party loyalties is an important political agency. Family evidently plays a major role in the fixing of attachments to political parties. Children acquire early in life a feeling of party identification; they have sensitive antennae and, since they are imitative animals, soon take on the political color of their family.[3] Partisanship is only one of the identifications acquired by children through the family. Religious identification, usually also so acquired, has a remarkable persistence.[4] Negro and

[3] In October, 1952, H. H. Remmers asked his national sample of high school students: "If you were going to take part in this year's election, for which of the following candidates would you vote: Eisenhower-Nixon, Stevenson-Sparkman, Some Other?" The division of the response to this question came within 1 per cent of the actual vote.—H. H. Remmers: "Early Socialization of Attitudes," in Eugene Burdick and A. J. Brodbeck, eds.: *American Voting Behavior* (Glencoe: Free Press; 1959), pp. 55–67.

[4] In 1959 the AIPO asked Catholics: "Have you ever seriously considered becoming a Protestant?" Only 6 per cent replied in the affirmative. The same proportion of Protestants had considered becoming Catholic.

white group identifications, with the associated preferences and prejudices, also develop early in a child's life.[5]

College Students and Parental Partisanship. Early studies of the
inheritance of partisanship centered on that ever-handy subject, the
college student. At the time of the 1928 campaign Allport found that
79 per cent of a group of 375 students in elementary psychology at
Dartmouth had the same candidate preferences as their fathers.[6] In 1932
Fay and Middleton found at De Pauw a similar correspondence between student and paternal party preference, with the direction of
apostasy toward the Democratic party.[7] While both of the studies illustrated the impress of the father upon son's political preferences,
each study also reflected the erosive effect of the temper of the times on
inherited party identification.[8]

Adults and Parental Partisanship. While a correspondence between
the party preference of a teenager or of a college student and that
of his parents may be regarded without much quibble as an indication of parental influence, the same correspondence between a middle-
aged person and his parents may not be equally persuasive evidence of
that relationship. Nevertheless, the evidence on the partisanship of the
offspring of different types of families establishes the long persistence
of party loyalties fixed by the family. Families homogeneous politically—that is, with both parents of the same party—produce fewer offspring that turn out to be independents than do families whose children
remember both parents as shifting or whose children have no memories of parental political inclinations. Homogeneous families also produce more offspring who in later life regard themselves as strong parti-

[5] M. Sherif and C. Sherif: *Groups in Harmony and Tension* (New York:
Harper; 1953), pp. 98–9. For regional contrasts in the views of teenagers on school
integration, see H. H. Remmers and D. H. Radler: *The American Teenager* (Indianapolis: Bobbs-Merrill; 1957), p. 220. Southern children take on the regional
outlook by the time they reach high school, doubtless in considerable measure
through parental tutelage.

[6] Gordon W. Allport: "The Composition of Political Attitudes," *American
Journal of Sociology*, XXXV (1929), 220–38.

[7] Paul J. Fay and Warren C. Middleton: "Certain Factors Related to Liberal
and Conservative Attitudes of College Students: II. Father's Political Preference;
Presidential Candidates Favored in the 1932 and 1936 Elections," *Journal of Social
Psychology*, XI (1940), 107–19.

[8] Also interesting is the question whether youngsters may not be a political
influence within the family. They may function as neutral transmitters of external
influences into the family circle, especially into families that are out of line with
their immediate external world.

sans, either Democratic or Republican, than do mixed families. The child of a Democratic father and a Republican mother may not know what to believe. These differences in the partisanship of children of various types of families are highly indicative of the durability of family influence. Yet, as the data of Table 12.1 show, at least a quarter of

---

TABLE 12.1

Relation of Parents' Party Identification to That of Offspring

PARTY IDENTIFICATION
OF RESPONDENT

PARTY IDENTIFICATION OF PARENTS [a]

	Both D	Both R	One R, one D	One D or R, other un- certain	Both shifted	DK about either	Neither voted
Strong Democrat	36%	7%	12%	14%	11%	15%	15%
Weak Democrat	36	9	32	23	23	21	22
Independent	16	20	10	33	39	30	36
Weak Republican	6	30	22	12	14	9	9
Strong Republican	6	33	22	15	11	3	3
None, minor party, or not ascertained	. . .	1	2	3	2	22	15
	100%	100%	100%	100%	100%	100%	100%
N	657	387	41	102	103	140	59
Per cent of total sample	41%	24%	3%	6%	6%	9%	4%

[a] "Do you remember when you were growing up whether your parents thought of themselves as mostly Democrats, or Republicans, or did they shift around from one party to another?"

SOURCE: *Angus Campbell et al.: The Voter Decides, p. 99. This transcription of the original table consolidates as independents those independents who leaned Democratic, those who leaned Republican, and those who said they leaned in neither direction.*

---

the children covered by the analysis of a national sample had departed from their fathers' party faith. The influence of the family, potent though it is, does not suffice to prevent a good deal of fluidity in party groupings through the generations.[9]

[9] A study of 1952 voting of a sample of the members of the United Auto Workers in Detroit provides another bit of evidence on the persistence of family influence. These persons had had similar employment experiences and had been subjected to a modicum of Democratic indoctrination by their union; yet of those with Republican fathers 51 per cent were for Eisenhower, and of those with Democratic fathers, 16 per cent.—Arthur Kornhauser *et al.: When Labor Votes* (New York: University Books; 1956), p. 43.

Offspring of Democratic families are likely to be Democrats; off-spring of Republican families, Republicans. From these relationships we infer that family has a bearing on partisanship.[1] Evidence for the connection, though, does not consist of the correlation alone. Responses to open-ended questions often include explanations of party attachment in terms of family inheritance. Consider the following comments extracted from answers to the question: "Is there anything in particular that you like about the Republican party?" The wife of a Connecticut pharmacist: "Just being brought up a Republican; Eisenhower is doing a wonderful job; just don't keep up on politics." A California housewife: "Well, I was just raised a Republican." An upstate New York lady who does housework by the day: "My father was a Republican." An unskilled worker in Queens: "My dad is a Republican and we are all hot Republicans." To a question about the most important reason for his decision to vote for Eisenhower a Missouri farmer replied: "I'm from a strong Republican family."

Equally illuminating comments can be culled from responses to the question: "Is there anything in particular that you like about the Democratic party?" A South Dakota dental technician: "No, I'm a Democrat; that's what my folks are. No reason otherwise." A New York housewife: "Well, my father is a Democrat and I am one by inheritance sort of. I know nothing about politics but I like the Democratic party because I know they are more for the poorer people." The wife of a Chicago skilled worker: "My father was a Democrat. I don't know too much about it. I've always been Democratic too." An Arkansas laborer: "No. I couldn't say. I was raised as a Democrat. My father was a Democrat." A North Carolina lady: "I was born a Democrat, but my father was a broad-minded man." The wife of a Massachusetts lawyer: "Our forefathers have been Democrats and we have naturally always stuck with the Democratic party." The wife of a Massachusetts psychiatrist liked the Democrats: "Well, let's put it this way. I was brought up in the Democratic party and I have never found anything so terrific in the Republican party that I would want to change." The wife of a Minnesota salesman could find nothing to like about the Democrats: "No, nothing at all. Mind you, no reason but I don't know much about the

[1] The sharp-eyed reader may wonder whether the Republican offspring of Republican parents have always been Republican. In its 1958 survey the Survey Research Center asked party identifiers whether they had ever thought of themselves as a member of a party other than that of their current identification. Of the Republican offspring of Republican parents 6 per cent had at some time or another thought of themselves as Democrats. Of the Democratic offspring of Democratic parents 4 per cent had at one time or another regarded themselves as Republicans.

Democratic party. I just know my folks and family always voted Republican and so I vote Republican." [2]

Erosion of Family Imprint. The long persistence of family-fixed party identification may come in considerable measure from its reinforcement by events subsequent to maturation. Contrarily, when events after departure from the family fold conflict with inherited party identification, they tend to pull the offspring away from the party of their parents.[3] Inherited identification may thus persist simply because no circumstance arises in conflict with it.

These factors of reinforcement and conflict are illustrated by data from the 1948 Elmira study by Berelson and his associates. In Elmira voters of all age groups whose fathers had been Republican voted Republican in about the same degree. Presumably the community influences in this predominantly Republican locality (and a good many other factors as well) operated to reinforce the inherited Republicanism of these voters no matter how long they had been away from the family group. On the other hand, among the older voters with Democratic fathers considerably higher proportions voted Republican in 1948 than did those young voters of Democratic parentage not far removed from family influences. Possibly the net pull of influences as they operated on Democrats by inheritance weakened rather than reinforced their attachment to the party of their parents.[4] Since the abandonment of parental party by persons born Democratic was more frequent among older voters, duration of exposure to community influences may have been related to strain on inherited loyalties.

Reasons for departures from the parental party are doubtless as numerous as those that move persons to vote in this or that direction. A major factor consists in events, such as the Great Depression, with an impact advantageous to one of the parties.[5] On the American scene up-

[2] All these quotations are from interviews taken by the Survey Research Center during the 1956 campaign.

[3] Evidence on these points, as well as the role of the family generally, is provided by a Minnesota study by Herbert McClosky and Harold E. Dahlgren: "Primary Group Influence on Party Loyalty," *American Political Science Review,* LIII (1959), pp. 757-76.

[4] Bernard Berelson *et al.: Voting* (Chicago: University of Chicago Press; 1954), p. 88.

[5] A Michigan janitor, once a Republican, in 1956 regarded himself as an independent with Republican leanings: (When did you change?) "Roosevelt's election." (Why?) "Depression of '29." A St. Louis steel worker, a Democrat, had shed his Republicanism during the Hoover Administration: (Why?) "I must have been drunk when I voted for him. They offered me a job for 20¢ an hour when Hoover was President." A Pittsburgh saleslady, now a Democrat, once a Republican, changed during Hoover's Administration: (Why?) "My husband was a gov-

ward mobility may cut Democratic moorings and bring a Republican identification. At least that may be the consequence if mobility introduces a person into Republican circles.[6] A common source of partisan change among women is marriage outside the political faith of their fathers.[7] Like or dislike of a political personality or a party policy[8] and many other factors bring shifts in party identification.[9] In some instances such shifts may be a form of rebellion against parental authority.[1]

An estimate of the frequency with which these pulls from family party identification are effective for different types of families under different circumstances may be made from the data of Table 12.2. That table shows the relation between parental politics and party identification of offspring by age groups. Of those under age fifty-five in 1952 relatively more children of Republican parents had forsworn the politics of their parents than had those born into Democratic families.

---

ernment employee and we got three cuts in pay and we lost our home on account of that." The depression, though, cut both ways. A Baltimore school teacher, once a Democrat now a Republican, changed during the Roosevelt Administration: (Why?) "I guess projects like the WPA. The government was encouraging people to be bums."

[6] For evidence on this tendency in Cambridge, Massachusetts, see Eleanor E. Maccoby: "Youth and Political Change," *Public Opinion Quarterly*, XVIII (1954), 23–39.

[7] A Kansas housewife, once a Republican became a Democrat: (When?) "When I got married." (Why?) "Just that my husband was a Democrat." To the question whether there was anything in particular she liked about the Democratic party, the wife of an Ohio bank teller responded: "No. I'm a Democrat by marriage." The wife of a Minnesota farmer: "Nothing. I'm a Democrat because my husband is one." The wife of a Texas insurance salesman: "I'll tell you. I was reared a Democrat and I married a Republican. So I think I am turning into a Republican."

[8] A Michigan Negro housewife once Republican leaned Democratic: (Why?) "Platform stand for colored in 1952." A worker in interior decoration in Manhattan shifted from Democratic to Republican: (When?) "After Roosevelt died." (Why?) "I didn't like Truman." A Louisville grocery cashier had been Democratic but was now an independent: (Why?) "I just like Eisenhower, that's all, and I like John Sherman Cooper—he's my boy."

[9] An Idaho housewife, by vocation a bookkeeper, once thought of herself as a Republican but had become a weak Democrat: (When did you change?) "About the time I was old enough to vote. I had a crazy notion that Democrats were drunkards and no good. I was just a dumb kid." (Why change?) "I got out in the world and saw the conditions and realized I was wrong. Probably happened to like Democratic candidates better." A Kansas housewife had become a Democrat: "I did a lot of reading and felt they [the Democrats] were more for the common people."

[1] Maccoby: loc. cit., presents evidence that "rejection of parental political values" among persons aged twenty-one to twenty-four is associated with "strict discipline in the home." An upstate New York housewife responded to a question about what she disliked about the Democratic party: "I have a hatred for it that is ingrained by a Democratic mother who had a job with the party and made all of us kids vote Democratic until I left home when I was 28."

TABLE 12.2

PARENTAL POLITICS IN RELATION TO PARTY IDENTIFICATION AND
AGE OF RESPONDENT

AGE AND PARTY IDENTIFICATION OF RESPONDENT	PARENTAL POLITICS [a]		
	D-D	R-R	Shifted, Don't know, Neither voted
Under 35			
Democratic	72%	15%	37%
Independent [b]	22	25	40
Republican	6	60	23
	100%	100%	100%
N	231	220	88
35–55			
Democratic	74	18	43
Independent	14	23	37
Republican	12	59	20
	100%	100%	100%
N	276	163	119
55 and over			
Democratic	71	15	44
Independent	10	14	40
Republican	19	71	16
	100%	100%	100%
N	139	118	50

[a] "Do you remember when you were growing up whether your parents thought of themselves mostly as Democrats or Republicans or did they shift around from one party to another?"
[b] Independents include those who, when pressed, confessed that they felt closer to one or the other of the parties.
DATA SOURCE: *Survey Research Center, University of Michigan, 1952.*

During the lifetime of those under fifty-five, the influences of the times operated on balance to wear away inherited Republican loyalties with greater frequency than they did to weaken inherited Democratic loyalties. On the other hand, among persons over fifty-five years of age in 1952 those with Republican parents retained their family party identification more frequently than did younger persons of Republican parentage. The older group may have consisted of persons whose party loyalties had become firmly fixed before the country became Democratic in its orientation in the 1930's.[2]

[2] Another indicator of the erosion of family party identification is provided by the respondent's recall of the party for whose presidential candidate he first voted. The first vote corresponds more closely with family politics than does cur-

The sketchy data on the attenuation of the connection between party identification of parent and offspring suggest that the apparent (and perhaps the real) political significance of the family may depend in part on the nature of the society within which the family exists. The capacity of the family to project party identification into the next generation may depend on factors external to the family as well as on the nature of the family. Families with outlooks parallel to the dominant outlooks of the society appear to be most influential on the party identification of their offspring; the forces of the society reinforce the impress of the family. The impact of the family that is at variance with the societal forces to which the offspring is subjected seems to be offset in greater degree by post-familial influences. Republican sons who had to adjust to a Democratic world seem to have been under more compelling pressure to abandon their family politics than were Democratic sons who lived in a Democratic era. The apparent impact of the family on the politics of its offspring may tend to be greater in stable or tradition-directed societies than in dynamic or rapidly changing societies. In the latter type of society the forces that run counter to the orientations fixed by family may be more numerous and more powerful.[3]

2 · Parents and Political Interest

Familial influence probably extends beyond the transmission of party identification to include the inculcation of an orientation toward politics and of habits of political behavior. It is plausible to expect the offspring of a family in which political questions are a topic of frequent discussion to acquire an interest in politics. It is equally plausible to expect the son of a family with no concern about politics to develop a lesser interest. Few families function as incubators of statesmen;

---

rent sense of party identification. Of those with homogeneous Democratic families, 88 per cent in 1952 remembered their first vote as Democratic; the corresponding figure for the offspring of Republican families was 71.

[3] It would be important to know whether the proportion of families with strong partisan attachments, either Republican or Democratic, is changing through time. Presumably an increase in the proportion of independent or indifferent families would produce an increase in the proportion of persons in the next generation with independent outlooks or weak party attachments. No significant differences were reported by the respondents in the age groups analyzed in Table 12.2 in the proportions who remembered their families as homogeneous politically, either D-D or R-R. The proportion with such recall among those fifty-five and over was 70 per cent; those thirty-five to fifty-five, 71 per cent; those under thirty-five, 69 per cent. Even if these proportions have remained stable over time, the impact of family on the political behavior of offspring may have changed through a decline in the intensity of family partisanship.

many family environments have almost a zero political content. Yet to the extent that differences prevail among families they might be expected to be reflected in their offspring.

Parental Interest in Politics and Political Involvement. Offspring of families with high levels of political interest tend toward a higher degree of psychological involvement in politics than do those who remember their families as not paying much attention to politics. This conclusion rests on the responses of a 1958 national sample to the question: "Do you remember when you were growing up whether your father was very much interested in politics, somewhat interested, or didn't he pay much attention to it?" This question, together with a parallel inquiry about the mother's interest, permits a grouping of families according to level of political interest as remembered by their offspring. For the respondents themselves a measure of political involvement is available. That index, it may be recalled, rests on a classification of persons according to their expressed degree of interest in the campaign and the nature of their response to the question: "Generally speaking, would you say that you personally cared a great deal about which party won the elections to the Congress in Washington this

---

TABLE 12.3

RELATION BETWEEN PARENTAL INTEREST IN POLITICS AND RESPONDENTS' POLITICAL INVOLVEMENT

LEVEL OF INVOLVEMENT	PARENTAL POLITICAL INTEREST [a]		
	High	Medium	Low
High 1	36%	19%	14%
2	25	27	12
3	19	29	19
Low 4	20	25	55
	100%	100%	100%
N	658	422	274

[a] Parental political interest was determined by the question: "Do you remember when you were growing up whether your father was very much interested in politics, somewhat interested, or didn't he pay much attention to it?" A similar question was put about the respondent's mother. Parental interest was classified as high if at least one parent was reported as "very much interested." The medium interest category consists of those instances in which at least one parent was "somewhat interested." In the low-interest group both parents were said not to pay much attention to politics.

DATA SOURCE: *Survey Research Center, University of Michigan, 1958.*

fall or that you didn't care very much which party won?" Respondents whose parents had a high interest in politics had, more than twice as often as the offspring of parents with low political interest, a high sense of involvement in the 1958 campaign, as Table 12.3 indicates. A striking fact from the table is the extremely high proportion of the offspring of low-interest families with a low sense of involvement. While a family with high-level political interest may not so often have children highly involved politically, only infrequently do the children of families with low political interest become highly involved themselves.

Parental Occupation and Sense of Political Efficacy. The known differentiations in political activity and outlook among occupational groups suggest the possibility of checking the political characteristics of the present electorate against parental occupation. If the sons of unskilled workers differ from the sons of professional men, the possibility arises that familial influences may have had something to do with these differences. An index of the sense of political efficacy, as we have seen, measures political attitudes of some significance. Persons with a high sense of political efficacy tend to participate in politics in higher degree than do persons with a low sense of efficacy and to possess distinctive characteristics of other kinds.[4]

Parental occupation has a marked relationship to the sense of political efficacy of the offspring: 63 per cent of those with fathers in the professions rank high in political efficacy; only 28 per cent of those

TABLE 12.4

RELATION BETWEEN FATHER'S OCCUPATION AND RESPONDENT'S SENSE OF POLITICAL EFFICACY

SENSE OF POLITICAL EFFICACY	FATHER'S OCCUPATION					
	Professional	Business	Clerical	Skilled	Unskilled	Farmer
Low	10%	19%	25%	25%	40%	47%
Medium	17	22	25	31	28	25
High	73	59	50	44	32	28
	100%	100%	100%	100%	100%	100%
N	99	217	65	302	233	660

DATA SOURCE: *Survey Research Center, University of Michigan, 1956.*

[4] For a description of the index, see Appendix IV.

with farming fathers place high on the efficacy index (see Table 12.4). Whatever outlooks are fixed in the family circle are compounded by experiences in the later life of offspring; children of different occupational groups tend to have contrasting education and work experiences.

Parental Politics and Ticket Splitting. Another interesting bit of evidence on the impact of family on political behavior comes from an analysis of responses, shown in Table 12.5, to the following inquiry:

TABLE 12.5

PARENTAL POLITICS IN RELATION TO WILLINGNESS OF OFFSPRING TO SUPPORT PARTY TICKET

ATTITUDE TOWARD   PARENTAL POLITICS [b]
UNDESIRED CANDIDATE [a]

	D-R	Shifted	D? R?	R-R	D-D	Don't know, or Neither voted
Would vote for anyway	5%	18%	14%	22%	22%	37%
Would not vote for either candidate	17	15	22	19	26	26
Would vote for other party's candidate	78	67	64	59	52	37
	100%	100%	100%	100%	100%	100%
N	36	61	64	291	531	89

[a] "Suppose there was an election where your party was running a candidate that you didn't like or you didn't agree with, which of the following things comes closest to what you think you would do? 1. I probably would vote for him anyway because a person should be loyal to his party. 2. I probably would not vote for either candidate in that election. 3. I probably would vote for the other party's candidate."
[b] "Do you remember when you were growing up whether your parents thought of themselves mostly as Democrats or Republicans or did they shift around from one party to another?"
DATA SOURCE: *Survey Research Center, University of Michigan, 1952.*

"Suppose there was an election where your party was running a candidate that you didn't like or you didn't agree with, which of the following things comes closest to what you think you would do? 1. I probably would vote for him anyway because a person should be loyal to his party. 2. I probably would not vote for either candidate in that election. 3. I probably would vote for the other party's candidate." This is an "iffy" sort of question; yet the replies to it depended somewhat on the kind of family a person had had. The frequency with which persons said they would vote for the other party's candidate was higher among those from families of split party loyalties or families that shifted around from party to party than it was among persons with politically homogeneous families. Oddly enough, those least disposed to cut the ticket were those with no recollection of their family's politics. Relatively few of such individuals develop a party identification, but when they do, it seems to be especially strong. Since it may rest on experience or ratiocination rather than on the explanation, "I was just raised a Democrat," their allegiance may gain great strength.[5]

3 · Family and the Direction of Opinion

There can be little doubt that family influences contribute to the shaping of basic values and outlooks, which in turn may affect the individual's views on political issues long after he has left the family fold. To establish that proposition, however, places a strain on both the ingenuity and resources of the researcher. What, if any, bearing does early family influence have on the views of a person fifty years of age on a question that may have been unheard of when he was a boy? Whatever the relation might be, it would naturally be expected to differ widely among individuals. Even if by intensive study the relation could be satisfactorily determined for a few individuals, the question would remain whether the phenomenon was of such a character and so generally distributed within the population as to have importance for the political system.

Policy Attitudes of Parents and Young Children. One way to attack the question is to compare the attitudes of parents and young children. The most direct approach is to measure the attitudes of both parents and children and then make the necessary correlations. It is fairly sim-

---

[5] Another check on the general question discussed in the text may be made from responses to a 1958 SRC question: "How about the elections for state and local offices—did you vote a straight ticket or did you vote for candidates from different parties?" The relations between answers to this question and parental politics for those respondents voting for state and local candidates at the time of the 1958 congressional election were:

Parental Politics	Straight Democratic	Straight Republican	Split	Total
D-D	65%	8%	27%	100%
D-R	31	24	45	100
R-R	17	52	31	100

ple to corral school children and to administer an attitude scale to them, but it is more wearing to search out their parents and to induce them to check the boxes on such a scale. Hardy souls, though, have carried out a few small-scale studies of this type. The findings generally indicate a positive correlation between attitudes of parents and children, and hence bolster the inference that the child acquires views on policy issues from his parents. These relations tend, however, to be markedly lower than the correlation between parent and child in party identification. The odds are that conversation around the home makes party identification far more visible than it does parental outlook on policy questions. This contrast leads Newcomb to isolate "institutional allegiances as the crucial influences which are transmitted by families."[6] Nevertheless, children tend to take on their parents' views on current issues, a type of influence that may decline in significance later in the child's life as new issues and new questions develop and as the child becomes subject to more nonparental influences.[7]

Another attack that throws light, more indirectly, upon the relation between attitudes of parent and child is comparison of the distribution of attitudes among groups of children with the distribution of attitudes among the adult population generally on the same question. Comparisons of high-school children and the adult population indicate similar distributions of attitude, a procedure that does not connect directly the attitude of parent and child but permits inferences about the influence of parents. Illustrative is a study by Centers of the attitudes of 1,000 high-school students in a small city near New York City. These students fell along a scale of attitude toward labor in the following manner:

Parental Occupation	Very Pro-labor	Pro-labor	Indeterminate	Anti-labor	Very Anti-labor
Business executive	*	*	11%	17%	72%
Professional	13%	9%	7	19	52
Small business	27	14	18	12	29
White collar	31	18	11	15	25
Skilled manual	40	13	13	15	19
Semiskilled	49	22	10	11	8
Unskilled manual	60	13	8	12	7

[6] Theodore Newcomb: "Determinants of Opinion," *Public Opinion Quarterly*, October, 1937, 71–6.

[7] For a critical review of the studies of family-child relationships in attitude, see Sarah Carolyn Fisher: *Relationships in Attitudes, Opinions, and Values Among Family Members* (Berkeley: University of California Press; 1948). A more recent and less technical summary-analysis is that by Herbert Hyman: op. cit., pp. 69–72.

These differentiations among high-school children paralleled the pattern known to exist for adults, though the extent to which they reflected family influences is debatable. Other factors doubtless also affect the figures, but the data strongly suggest the existence of a marked family influence on political outlook at the high school ages.[8]

Parental Class and Adult Policy Orientation. Studies of high-school students and of groups of collegians turn up interesting kinds of relations between the attitudes of the younger generation and the known or assumed attitudes of their parents. It is a different, and far more difficult, question whether in the population generally the family plays a role in the fixation of basic outlooks of sufficient magnitude to be of much significance in the political system. It would require a prolonged interview to obtain an individual's recollections of the nature of the political content of his early family environment. And it would require many such cases to be able to separate the impact of family from the influences of later life on political attitude. The data conveniently available touch only the surface of the problem and are suggestive rather than conclusive.

Although in the United States the sense of class identification is tenuous, it has a relation to attitudes on scales of liberalism-conservatism about domestic issues. The question arises whether parental class might project itself into the attitudes of the offspring. In 1956 the respondents in the SRC national sample were asked, in addition to a question about their own class identification, the following question: "What would you say your family was when you were growing up, middle class or working class?" Whatever such recall of family status may be taken to mean, it is worth inquiring whether people regarding themselves as working class and reporting their parents as working class differ in attitude from those who ascribe a middle-class status to their parents. On the average, working-class offspring of middle-class parents, as Table 12.6 indicates, rank considerably lower on the scale of domestic liberalism than do working-class offspring of working-class parents. The figures could be taken to mean that middle-class sons and daughters retain to a degree a middle-class outlook even though they come to be working-class themselves. If this interpretation is correct, so minute a fraction of the population acquires through familial influences these deviant outlooks that it can have no great bearing on the political system. On the other hand, middle-class offspring of working-class

[8] Richard Centers: "Children of the New Deal: Social Stratification and Adolescent Attitudes," *International Journal of Opinion and Attitude Research*, IV (1950), 315–35.

parents differ only slightly on the scale from the middle-class offspring of middle-class parents. Yet they differ in the direction that would be expected if we assumed that upward-mobile children retained to a degree the outlooks that their parents might have been expected to hold.

TABLE 12.6

RELATION OF PARENTAL SOCIAL CLASS TO RESPONDENTS' RANKING ON DOMESTIC ISSUE SCALE

R'S CLASS IDENTIFICATION AND REPORT OF PARENTAL CLASS [a]	LOW	MEDIUM	HIGH	NOT SCALED [b]	TOTAL	N
R working class						
Parents working class	9%	32%	40%	19%	100	972
Parents middle class	21	47	19	13	100	82
R middle class						
Parents working class	20	41	28	11	100	185
Parents middle class	19	48	23	10	100	436

[a] The question was: "What would you say your family was when you were growing up, middle class or working class?"
[b] Expressed too few opinions to permit scaling.
DATA SOURCE: *Survey Research Center, University of Michigan, 1956.*

Parental Occupation and Policy Outlooks of Offspring. Another way to inspect the parent-offspring relationship is to relate current attitudes to paternal occupation. While we have again no direct information on the policy outlooks of parents, probably differences in attitude not unlike those of the present have long prevailed among occupational groups. On a scale measuring internationalism the offspring of professional men, as may be seen from Table 12.7, rank considerably higher than do the offspring of farmers: 60 per cent of the offspring of the former place high on the scale, as against only 41 per cent of the latter. These differences doubtless result in part from the influences of post-familial life which either maintain or alter the trajectory into which the child was placed by his family. Nevertheless, isolationism of the farm offspring makes it probable that rural isolationism persists into the next generation even though the boys may not have remained on the farm.[9]

The relationship between parental occupation and position on a

[9] Concealed in the table is a statistic of long-run significance for American politics—the large number of farmers' offspring included in the national sample. If the family does project its influence into the outlook of the next generation, the attitudes characteristic of farm families will in due course become of far less magnitude in the polity as a whole.

TABLE 12.7

RELATION OF FATHER'S OCCUPATION TO RESPONDENTS' POSITION ON
INTERNATIONALISM SCALE

INTERNATIONALISM	FATHER'S OCCUPATION					
	Pro-fessional	Business	Clerical	Skilled	Un-skilled	Farmer
High	60%	55%	48%	48%	41%	41%
Medium	21	23	35	23	22	16
Low	8	11	6	13	13	18
Not scaled	11	11	11	16	24	25
	100%	100%	100%	100%	100%	100%
N	99	217	65	402	233	660

DATA SOURCE: *Survey Research Center, University of Michigan, 1956.*

scale of liberalism-conservatism on domestic issues appears in Table 12.8. While the differences among groups according to parental occupation exhibit some oddities, in the main they are of the kinds that might be expected. Nevertheless, the relations shown to exist in these tables have several shortcomings. On the average, voters whose fathers were unskilled laborers rank higher on a scale of domestic liberalism than do those whose fathers were professional men. Yet that contrast may be in substantial degree attributable to the contrasting life experiences of the two groups rather than to any familial impact. The off-spring of unskilled laborers tend to have life experiences unlike those of the progeny of professional fathers. A second source of reservations about the relationships is that the attitudes are measured by responses

TABLE 12.8

RELATION OF FATHER'S OCCUPATION TO POSITION ON DOMESTIC ISSUE SCALE

LIBERALISM SCALE	FATHER'S OCCUPATION					
	Pro-fessional	Business	Clerical	Skilled	Un-skilled	Farmer
Low	25%	17%	21%	15%	9%	11%
Medium	50	41	54	39	31	35
High	20	30	20	32	40	34
Not scaled	5	12	5	14	20	20
	100%	100%	100%	100%	100%	100%
N	99	217	65	402	233	660

DATA SOURCE: *Survey Research Center, University of Michigan, 1956.*

to a series of set policy propositions, most of which are new. Early
familial influence on such issues could come about only if it were assumed that some broad outlook was implanted that influenced attitude
on specific issues that developed much later.

Parental Partisanship and Attitudes of Adult Offspring. Another approach to the problem of parental formation of political outlook leads
roughly to the same conclusions about family influence but meets some
of the analytical shortcomings of the preceding analyses. The findings
of this alternative approach are essentially that the offspring of Republican families tend to take pro-Republican outlooks in their comments about issues as they respond to open-ended questions; the offspring of Democratic parents tend to take pro-Democratic positions
on the same questions.

The data on these propositions appear in Table 12.9. To appraise
the table, the data underlying it must be clearly understood, for they
differ from the earlier materials. The issue positions as recorded in this
table were determined, not by responses to a series of set questions on

TABLE 12.9

POSITION ON DOMESTIC AND FOREIGN ISSUES IN RELATION TO EDUCATION AND
PARENTAL POLITICS [a]

EDUCATION AND PARENTAL POLITICS	DOMESTIC ISSUES			FOREIGN ISSUES				N
	Pro R	O	Pro D	Pro R	O	Pro D		
College								
D-D	27%	35%	38%	39%	49%	12%	100%	102
R-R	44	28	28	55	38	7	100	74
Others [b]	29	37	34	48	38	14	100	56
High School								
D-D	17	32	51	35	55	10	100	318
R-R	33	42	25	50	46	4	100	172
Other	19	39	42	31	61	8	100	184
Grammar School								
D-D	14	30	56	28	63	9	100	236
R-R	20	38	42	40	52	8	100	141
Other	10	50	40	21	72	7	100	203

[a] For construction of the scales, see the text discussion of this table.
[b] This category includes respondents who remembered their parents as
D-R, D-?, R-?, as shifting around or as not voting and those who had no
recollection of their parents' politics.
DATA SOURCE: *Survey Research Center, University of Michigan, 1956.*

issues about which the respondents' parents had never heard, but by comments on a series of open-ended inquiries in 1952. The respondents were asked: "Is there anything in particular that you like about the Democratic party?" "Is there anything in particular that you don't like about the Democratic party?" The same questions were put about the Republican party and open-ended inquiries were made about the candidates. Included in the responses were policy references that could be regarded as pro-Democratic and anti-Republican or anti-Democratic and pro-Republican. Some respondents expressed no policy views; they were placed at zero on a policy scale. Also ranked at zero were those persons whose pro-Republican policy comments equalled in number their pro-Democratic observations. When pro-Republican policy references outnumbered pro-Democratic references, the respondent was placed at the appropriate point on the pro-Republican end of the scale. When the preponderance of comment was pro-Democratic, he earned a place on the Democratic end of the scale. Essentially the data permit us to group persons into three categories: those who saw the Democratic party as adhering to policy positions they liked, persons who viewed the Republican party in that light, and persons whose comments contained no policy content or who viewed the policy positions of the parties with approximately equal approbation.

The respondent's recall of the partisanship of his parents was available to set against his current policy attitudes. The question whether the offspring of Republican parents differ in their policy outlooks from those of Democratic parents raises the problem of how to take into account post-familial experiences. Education serves as a fair index of a variety of kinds of post-familial experience. Persons who do not go beyond high school may be supposed to have, on the average, similar life experiences, whatever their family political background. The same expectations are plausible for the college-educated. Education, therefore, can be used as a partial control on post-familial experience.

With education held constant, the offspring of Democratic families differ from those of Republican families on both domestic and foreign issues as measured by responses to open-ended questions. The analysis still leaves open the question of how much of this difference is attributable to the impact of family. No data are to be had to show what, if any, policy differences existed between the Democratic families and the Republican families from which this generation of voters sprang. The odds are that, on the average, differences existed between the two types of families. Moreover, the contrasts between the educational levels lend some plausibility to the hypothesis of the persistence of familial influence. Observe from the table that the college-trained offspring of D-D families tended to move toward a Republican policy position; on the other hand, the grammar school offspring of R-R families moved toward the Democratic policy position as held by the grammar school of offspring of D-D parents. Both tendencies are in accord with what might be expected from the differential pulls of the times and circumstances during which the voters of 1952 grew up. Yet at each educational level differences associated with familial politics persist. These differences are probably closely associated with family transmission of the sense of party identification. An inherited tendency to identify with the Democratic party may carry with it a tendency not only to regard oneself as a Democrat but also to see issues as a Democrat.

Parental politics also has another relationship with the manner in which offspring view the political world. In answers to: "Is there anything in particular that you like about the Democratic party?" and other such questions, respondents often spoke favorably or unfavorably of the group interests to which they perceived the parties to be attached. They liked the Democratic party because it was the party of

---

TABLE 12.10

POSITION ON SCALE OF FAVORABLE AND UNFAVORABLE REFERENCES TO GROUP INTERESTS OF PARTIES IN RELATION TO EDUCATION AND PARENTAL POLITICS

EDUCATION AND PARENTAL POLITICS	GROUP REFERENCES			
	Pro R	O	Pro D	
College				
D-D	31%	36%	33%	100%
R-R	42	34	24	100
Others [a]	34	43	23	100
High School				
D-D	20	46	34	100
R-R	41	40	19	100
Others	20	46	34	100
Grade School				
D-D	21	38	41	100
R-R	23	43	34	100
Others	13	56	31	100

[a] This category includes respondents who remembered their parents as D-R, D-?, R-?, as shifting around or as not voting and those who had no recollection of their parents' politics.
DATA SOURCE: *Survey Research Center, University of Michigan, 1952.*

the working man, or, on occasion, they disliked it for the same reason. They disliked the Republican party because they saw it as the party of business; occasionally they liked it for the same reason. All such references could be coded into pro-Democratic or pro-Republican categories. Some respondents made no such group references, or those they made in one partisan direction were balanced by those made in the other direction. These were placed at a neutral or zero position on a scale of group references. When all these group references are related to parental politics, within education levels of the respondents, the offspring of Democratic families more frequently viewed favorably the group affiliates of the Democratic party than did the offspring of Republican families. The differences are not sharp, but some relationship persists between parental partisanship and the view of the political world by the current generation. The figures are shown in Table 12.10.

4 · The Family and the Political System

While the evidence about the bearing of family experience on the subsequent political activities and outlooks of children is scant, it is consistent with the view that the family must be regarded as a conserving factor in the political system. The family is conserving in that it tends to project into the future the prevailing pattern of social and occupational status with the associated political outlooks. It is conserving in that it tends to perpetuate the prevailing system of identifications with political parties and other politically relevant groups. To a degree offspring probably also take on attitudinal orientations in the general direction of those of their parents. Yet to say that the family is a conserving influence is not to say that it is necessarily conservative in the usage of our day. A radical father may also have a radical son, but collectively families tend to project the existent national pattern of party loyalties and to a lesser extent the existent attitudinal pattern on policy into the future where it becomes subject to reinforcement or alteration by new forces.[1] Families may or may not develop in the offspring an interest in and concern about politics. Doubtless the family indoc-

[1] Alex Inkeles, on the basis of a study of Russian defectors, concludes that parents who have themselves undergone the experience of extreme social change may not, in rearing their own children, simply recapitulate their own experience but may attempt to adjust their child rearing practices "the better to prepare their children for the life" they expect "those children to lead."—"Social Change and Social Character: The Role of Parental Mediation," *Journal of Social Issues*, XI, 2 (1955), 12–23.

trinates the child with a variety of social norms and values some of
which in the long run have an importance for the nature of the political
order.[2]

This broad interpretation of the place of the family in the political
order receives recognition, if not verification, in the practices of revolutionary regimes—and reactionary regimes as well. Those orders—be
they communist, fascist, Nazi, or whatnot—that seek to break with
their political past establish special youth organizations to separate the
young, even the very young, from family influences and to impress
the new political orthodoxy upon the youth. And they may go to the
contemptible extreme of converting the child into a political spy to
ferret out parental deviationism.[3]

One of the most significant political functions of the family is almost completely missed as the few cases concerned slip through the
tines of the apparatus for sampling national populations—the function
of producing political leaders, political activists, politicians. Evidence
on the sources from which political activists come, though thin, indicates that families of politicians, of public officials, of bureaucrats, and
of officeholders contribute a disproportionate share of those who run
for office and otherwise provide leadership within the community. It
would be unexpected if full evidence established that this relationship
did not prevail. Conspicuous political families—the Adamses, the Tafts,
the Lodges, the Kennedys, the Roosevelts, the Longs, the Talmadges—
come to mind, but doubtless sprinkled through the population are many
families in which there runs a political activism of a less spectacular
sort.

[2] See the provocative discussion, based on prolonged interviews with 15 New
Haven adults, by Robert E. Lane: "Fathers and Sons: Foundations of Political
Belief," *American Sociological Review*, XXIV (1959), 502–11.

[3] The insistence of the Roman Catholic Church that children of mixed mar-
riages be reared in the faith represents another practical recognition of the role of
the family as the mold of the adult. The church fathers are skilled applied social
scientists.

13

THE EDUCATIONAL
SYSTEM

USUALLY the schools are regarded as apart from politics. They are thought of as agencies to equip young persons with those basic skills of literacy essential for the practice of even the simplest vocations of an industrial society. Or at the upper levels the schools transmit the skills and information necessary to practice the professions or provide a grounding for young men who, properly trained on the job, may become junior executives and, perhaps eventually, useful citizens. While the schools perform these and other similar functions, they also constitute a major element of the apparatus of the modern state.

Elementary and secondary schools mold children into little Americans, little Germans, little Russians. They propagate the historical lore of the people, the myths, the beliefs, and the faiths and thereby aid in the process of political indoctrination. Beyond its inculcation of values and beliefs, the educational system develops intellectual skills and basic attitudes that are reflected in the political behavior and opinion of the adult long after he has left school. Tributes to the potency of the schools in the political system come in the exertions of groups as disparate as the Audubon Society and the National Association of Manufacturers to impress their special brands of policy upon the next generation through the school system.

1 · Education in the Structure of Power

An institution that enjoys the repute for influence held by the schools would scarcely be expected to be permitted by those dominant in the political order to roam freely. Yet the place of the schools in the power system may be perceived with far greater clarity in some systems than in others. In the establishment of revolutionary regimes of this century the place of the schools in the political order has been glaringly visible. One of the first tasks of new rulers has been to rewrite textbooks and to purge the school system of adherents to the old ways in order that memories of the old society might be erased and that the educational machine might be used to imprint the goals of the new order upon the plastic minds of the youth of the land. In the American setting the schools are not so obviously seen as arms of governance; yet in the large they play a significant role in the perpetuation of the values of the culture, including those habits, patterns of action, norms, and outlooks that are fundamental to the political order.

Inculcation of Political Values. All national educational systems indoctrinate the oncoming generation with the basic outlooks and values of the political order. The American public-school system, though, plays an additional role of prime political importance. Or at least the philosophy behind its foundation explicitly expounded the doctrine that free public education should serve as a sieve to separate from the population those of talent, who would be given opportunity to develop that talent regardless of their social origin. This function, to the extent that it is performed, is of profound significance for the political system.

The modern educational system conducts a massive operation in transmission of the traditions, learning, and skills necessary to maintain a society. The rise of compulsory universal education coincided with both the rise of modern nationalism and the industrialization of society. The operation of an industrial system requires wide dissemination of at least rudimentary skills in reading, writing, and mathematics. The maintenance of the national state requires the indoctrination of the society with the values, beliefs, and loyalties of the order. This role has been of special importance in the United States, a society that has had to assimilate wave after wave of immigration and to create new loyalties to the new homeland.

The characteristic national values and outlooks permeate the entire school curriculum from the kinds of problems posed in arithmetic to the formal instruction in civics. School children acquire some knowledge of American literature, a matter by no means lacking in political significance. Instruction in American history acquaints the child with the great episodes in our past, with our traditional national heroes, and with many of the ideals of the society. History tends to be a sensitive subject; instruction is somewhat selective. The great of the past are elevated into paragons who would scarcely be recognized by their contemporaries; those episodes that redound most to our national glory receive emphasis; and the picture of the past is deficient in cracks and crevices.[1] Courses in civics are explicitly designed to acquaint students with the broad character of the constitutional system and are often billed, somewhat hopefully, as courses in applied citizenship. In recent decades the high schools have sought to make the elements of the social sciences intelligible through instruction in social studies. Whatever the content and whatever the approach, the school system functions as a powerful molder of politically relevant attitudes and as a means for induction into citizenship.[2]

School instruction alters attitudes that tend to persist as changed. Yet knowledge of the magnitude and nature of these changes within the total population is limited. Certainly a degree of ritualistic patriotism is inculcated. People are equipped with a common store of national memories in order that they may respond knowledgeably when George Washington is mentioned in political discourse. Beyond such matters of common knowledge about the effects of education, we have the evidence from the extensive compilations of attitude tests of national samples by H. H. Remmers. His detailed data indicate a gradual enlargement of view and a growing political realism as students move through high school. Fewer seniors than ninth-graders concur with the proposition: "Foreign countries have little to contribute to American society." More disagree with the statement: "Certain groups should not be allowed to hold public meetings even though they gather peaceably and only make speeches." More seniors than ninth-graders concur with the view that "modern society is moved chiefly by the desire for profit"; while fewer seniors than ninth-graders take the view that large "estates, on which the land lies idle and unused, should be divided up among the poor for farming."[3]

[1] See Bessie L. Pierce: *Public Opinion and the Teaching of History* (1926); *Civic Attitudes in American School Textbooks* (Chicago: University of Chicago Press; 1930) and *Citizens' Organizations and the Civic Training of Youth* (New York: Scribner's; 1933); and also Albert Alexander: "The Gray Flannel Cover on the American History Textbook," *Social Education*, XXIV (1960), 11–14.

[2] For the classic comparative view, see Charles E. Merriam: *The Making of Citizens* (Chicago: University of Chicago Press; 1931).

[3] See H. H. Remmers and D. H. Radler: *The American Teenager* (Indianapolis: Bobbs-Merrill; 1957), p. 212, for these and other similar data.

Education and Opportunity for Talent. In another respect the American educational system performs a political function of import. The United States pioneered in the establishment of free, public education, and the theoretical justification was explicitly political—that is, in implementation of the egalitarian doctrines of the day. Jefferson envisaged a school system whose function would be to identify talent, whatever its social origin, and to provide education to the limits of its capacity at public expense. The system represented a departure from the practices of older, class-bound societies. The incompleteness of the attainment of the ideal of the educational system as a means for the recruitment and utilization of talent has occasioned expressions of unhappiness. Despite the development of state-supported colleges and universities, the cost of education has always barred many, but by no means all, of the sons of poorer parents from higher education. The social researchers have found that lack of motivation as well as lack of means may bar higher education to young persons of talent. Children of parents of higher social status, often persons with college training, tend to be motivated to attend college even though they may lack the necessary intellectual endowments. On the other hand, sons of parents of low social status, at least in some areas of the country, tend to lack motivation to go to college, even though they may be, in the language of the college admissions officers, college material.[4]

On the whole, social scientists probably underestimate the political significance of the educational system as it facilitates social mobility. They deal in rates of mobility, a habit which seems to lead them to ignore the absolute numbers of persons who are mobile. A typical mobility analysis appears in Table 13.1; it shows the proportions of the

TABLE 13.1

FATHER'S OCCUPATION IN RELATION TO RESPONDENT'S LEVEL OF EDUCATION

R'S EDUCATION	FATHER'S OCCUPATION					
	Professional	Business	Clerical	Skilled	Unskilled	Farmer
Grade School	2%	15%	9%	22%	37%	48%
High School	37	45	57	62	54	43
College	61	40	34	16	9	9
	100%	100%	100%	100%	100%	100%
N	99	215	65	401	233	655

DATA SOURCE: *Survey Research Center, University of Michigan, 1956.*

[4] See S. M. Lipset and R. Bendix: *Social Mobility in Industrial Society* (Berkeley: University of California Press; 1959), p. 230.

offspring of fathers of different occupational groups who reached various educational levels. Of the sons and daughters of farmers only 9 per cent had some college training. The corresponding figure for the offspring of professional persons was 61 per cent. Thus, when these people were growing up, the son of a professional man was about six times as likely to go to college as was the son of a farmer. The odds were about four times as great that the son of a businessman would go to college as would the son of an unskilled laborer.

These rates, significant though they are, conceal facts of great importance. The rate of college attendance for farmers' sons was low, but the absolute number of farmers' sons who went to college was at least equal to the number of sons of professional men who did so. The number of sons of skilled and semiskilled workers who had college training exceeded the number of sons of professional men with the same educational experience. Hence, the college-trained population is not dominated by the offspring of the elite occupations. Almost half of it consists of sons and daughters of blue-collar workers and of farmers. The college-trained sector of society, which manifests an especially high degree of political activity, consists, not of persons with a narrow and homogeneous class background, but of persons with a diversity of experience in their formative years. Exactly what this means for the tone and outlook of the political activists of the system could be discovered only by extensive inquiry; yet the bare fact commands attention in speculation about the bearing of educational opportunity on the political system.[5]

Whether a young man gets to college depends to a considerable degree on the occupation and income of his father. Those who go to college, though, have a better chance than persons with grade-school or high-school training to move into occupations of higher status than those of their fathers. By the same token, persons with college training are less likely to undergo downward movement in the occupational hierarchy, as the data of Table 13.2 indicate. The frequency of intergenerational downward mobility shown by the table may arouse skepticism. Yet the movements shown become plausible as one reviews his own circle of acquaintances and recalls that the offspring of persons of high-status occupations are not invariably equipped to maintain the parental level in the occupational world.

As the educational system advances and rejects persons in the generational flow, one of its incidental functions is the training of a

---

[5] The social origins of the college-educated population will be altered as the contribution of farm families to the total population declines. Yet, given the higher rates of college attendance by the children of blue-collar families than by those of farm families, it is unlikely that the college-trained population will come to be dominated by offspring of the elite occupations.

TABLE 13.2

LEVEL OF EDUCATION IN RELATION TO INTERGENERATIONAL MOBILITY AS MEASURED BY DISCREPANCY BETWEEN STATUS OF FATHER'S OCCUPATION AND STATUS OF OCCUPATION OF HEAD OF HOUSEHOLD [a]

INTERGENERATIONAL MOBILITY	EDUCATION		
	Grade school	High school	College
Lower	43%	33%	26%
Same	28	28	27
Higher	29	39	47
	100%	100%	100%
N	506	800	301

[a] The analysis assigns housewives to the occupations of their husbands. That procedure would affect the relations shown only if women generally married "up" or "down" in relation to their fathers' occupations. DATA SOURCE: *Survey Research Center, University of Michigan, 1956.*

corps of political leadership. While Americans often picture politicians as low persons of questionable literacy, college-trained persons manage to capture a large share of the posts of formal political leadership; and they predominate, too, in leadership in private groups and institutions of all kinds. In these private capacities they constitute an element of the political elite. By and large, the influentials are college-trained. What college training does to and for them is another question. Though it does not form them in a common mold, it may impart verbal and intellectual skills to persons of all kinds of political orientation.[6]
Strains in Crisis and Change. So long as the nation seems to be moving on an even keel and no great problems agitate the people, the political role of the schools tends to be fulfilled without much deliberate thought and with little or no controversy about its broad objectives. In such times the modal values are so dominant that the educational system, like other institutions of society, dedicates itself to the assiduous affirmation of the status quo. When the major tenets of the broad political consensus appear to be inadequate for the problems of the time, voices are likely to be raised in question of the suitability of the pro-

[6] On occasion concern is expressed about the consequences that might flow from more complete success in the effort to locate talent and, by means of education, funnel it into the occupations typically filled by college-trained. Men of political skill and acumen would become far more highly concentrated in the elite occupations. Further, from the standpoint of the productive system, the process might drain from the shop and the farm men with enough brains to figure out how to get things done.

gram of education to equip the oncoming generation to cope with emerging problems. And the voices of the old order, too, will be heard in defense of the virtues of our fathers and against new-fangled notions in education. An occasional eccentric will utter a plea for a return to McGuffey's readers, and he will be hailed by his fellow crackpots as a veritable embodiment of the ancient wisdom.

The most recent thoroughgoing reconsideration of the political role of the schools occurred at the time of the Great Depression. Serious misgivings about our general political arrangements were abroad in the land, and the suitability of the prevailing political philosophy itself came to be questioned. Concurrently the issue was raised whether the schools were adequately fulfilling their duty. Were they simply functioning as an agency to perpetuate beliefs suitable only for a status quo already discredited? Even in the 1920's social critics, small voices in a babel of peace and prosperity, had expressed their doubts about the schools. In 1922 John Dewey stated that the school system fostered an eagerness "to be duped" by its "systematic, almost deliberate, avoidance of the spirit of criticism in dealing with history, politics and economics." [7] In the 1930's these concerns became far more general as private commissions, professional groups, scholars, and educational leaders conducted surveys and issued pronunciamentos all to the general effect that the schools should strive toward instruction calculated to equip young people to cope with a world certain to be different, certain to be dynamic rather than static.[8] How the public schools were to accomplish so great a mission remained imprecise; yet no one doubted that the school system played a significant role in the political order. Faith in its efficacy came to be expressed also from sources to the right, from which came demands that the schools should stand fast for the principles of our forefathers.

Integration of Schools with the Political Apparatus. In many regimes the educational system is far more intimately articulated administratively with the governing apparatus than is the American practice. No central ministry of education in Washington controls the content of instruction. Even within the states a considerable degree of decentralization to local authorities characterizes the elementary and

[7] "Education as Politics," *New Republic*, XXXII (1922), 139–41.

[8] The most imposing of these inquiries was conducted under the auspices of the American Historical Association. Its Commission on the Social Studies summarized its position in its *Conclusions and Recommendations* (New York: Scribner's; 1934). Among the sixteen volumes prepared for the Commission, especially relevant is C. E. Merriam: *Civic Education in the United States* (New York: Scribner's; 1934).

secondary schools, while institutions of higher education, both public
and private, enjoy a high degree of independence from the general governmental structure. Nevertheless, ways and means are found to assure
that the school system does not deviate markedly from the modal political values of the culture. The administrative position of the educational system is essentially a mixture of autonomy and of intermittent
and piecemeal control at the margins of that area of autonomy.

As the school authorities manage schools, they tend to guide
themselves by the basic but unwritten norms of the society. In a society
whose political outlook is colored by wide consensus, no extensive
monitoring of the school system is required to assure the maintenance
of orthodox political instruction. "A well-established ideology," Lasswell remarks, "perpetuates itself with little planned propaganda by
those whom it benefits most. When thought is taken about ways and
means of sowing conviction, conviction has already languished, the
basic outlook of society has decayed, or a new, triumphant outlook has
not yet gripped the automatic loyalties of the young and the old." [9]

Naturally all is not left to the discipline of the prescriptions of the
culture. Boards of education and other such lay administrative bodies
tend to be dominated by the more influential elements of society; that
is, they ordinarily do not reflect even the mild sorts of dissent from the
traditional mores prevalent in American society.[1] On the whole the
interpositions of these authorities in the instructional process restrain
deviation from past practice and from the hallowed mores of the society. In a sense, the professional leadership of the school system may
be regarded as a more or less autonomous entity in a pluralistic social
system, which strives, with some success, to maintain its autonomy
yet yields here and there as it comes into contact with other elements
of the system. And the professional leadership of the public-school
system, insofar as it has a political orientation, may seek to be future-
oriented; from time to time, therefore, it collides with other elements
of the social system.

Control at the margins of the operation of the educational system
may be by either formal or informal means. Groups with specialized
concerns often obtain legislation to require types of instruction thought
to be desirable: instruction in the Constitution, in American history, in
the evils of tobacco, in the perils of liquor, and in the social rewards
of conservation. Control may also be directed toward the school personnel. For example, statutes may be enacted to require special oaths of

[9] Harold D. Lasswell: *Politics* (New York: Whittlesey House; 1936), pp.
29–30.
[1] See George S. Counts: *The Social Composition of Boards of Education.*

teachers and college instructors—oaths not required of newspaper reporters, editors, TV commentators, ministers, politicians, publishers, or other disseminators of information.

Such formal controls are supplemented by informal pressures at the margin to assure the political orthodoxy of the educational system. American Legion posts and other organizations occasionally set up committees of semiliterate characters to review textbooks and raise a commotion if the authors have taken note of the fact that the era of McKinley came to an end some time ago. On occasion such groups succeed in having teachers fired who displease them. Even in some colleges and universities the unfortunate instructor who happens to utter an idea unacceptable to a member of the governing board may find himself without a job. These episodic acts of intervention doubtless have an exemplary influence on those who are not directly affected by them. Interests outside the school system also attempt to enlist its positive support by less brutal methods. Many groups propagandize school teachers and make available teaching materials setting forth the virtues of privately owned utilities, the contributions of labor unions to the American way of life, the blessings of the free-enterprise system, the romance of the steel industry, and the wonders of petroleum. If the educational systems yielded to all the stronger pressures upon them—and could accomplish through the schools what the lobbyists wish—the American mental state would soon be one of ossification.

2 · Education and Political Outlook

Education forms the individual's productive skills and equips him to thread his way through a world in which a modicum of literacy and other capacities are helpful. It also affects his attitudes about his place in the social system and his outlook toward participation in politics. The educational system is but one of many influences that shape the citizen. In Chapter 12 the conclusion seemed inescapable that family influences on the partisan direction of political experience persisted to some extent against subsequent influences in the life of the individual. Occupational interests and status often either maintain or alter the outlooks a person derives from his family and from his schooling.

An analytical difficulty in the estimation of the effects of education on the individual in his political role is that education and other factors are closely intertwined. College education and high occupational status tend to go together; both college-trained persons and persons of high occupational status tend to possess political characteristics that differentiate them from persons of lesser educational attainments and lower occupational status. Yet repeated inquiries have established that level of education bears on political characteristics when other factors are held constant. Attention may be directed first to certain characteristics of political attitude and behavior that have no relation to the direction of opinion. The evidence indicates that level of education has a relationship to the "sense of citizen duty," the "sense of political efficacy," to psychological involvement in politics, and to political participation. The more extended the educational experience, the more likely is the individual to feel that he should play a role as a citizen and that it makes a difference when he does.

Education and the Sense of Citizen Duty. In the American system the individual is subjected to an indoctrination from the time he begins to be aware of politics that it is his duty to vote and to fulfill his political role in other ways. The schools, the newspapers, and other sources of information and admonition convey the recurring message. These influences, it might be supposed, would implant in most persons the sense that they had a duty or responsibility to vote whether an election would make any difference to them or whether their vote would make any difference in its outcome. It might be supposed, too, that the degree of the feeling of citizen duty would vary among individuals.

A rough measure of this sense of citizen duty is possible by the use of a scale consisting of four items with which a person may agree or disagree. These items are as follows:

1. It isn't so important to vote when you know your party doesn't have a chance to win.
2. A good many local elections aren't important enough to bother with.
3. So many other people vote in the national elections that it doesn't matter much to me whether I vote or not.
4. If a person doesn't care how an election comes out he shouldn't vote in it.

The Survey Research Center checked agreement and disagreement with these items in its 1952 and 1956 elections surveys. As might be expected, given the high social approval of positive citizen action, most of the population clustered toward the high end of a scale constructed from agreement and disagreement with these propositions. Nevertheless, the sense of citizen duty, so measured, evidently reflected a psychological motivation of some import. Political participation was related to the sense of citizen duty even when other obvious factors bearing on participation were held constant.[2]

Education probably accounts in part for the development of this sense of political obligation. The schools themselves implant the sense of duty to some extent. Further, the more highly educated a person is, the more likely he is to be thrown into the path of other influences—through the media and otherwise—that preach the doctrine that a citizen should vote. He is also likely to occupy a socio-economic status that develops in him a lively awareness of the relevance of political

---

TABLE 13.3

RELATION OF LEVEL OF EDUCATION TO SENSE OF CITIZEN DUTY

SENSE OF CITIZEN DUTY	EDUCATIONAL LEVEL		
	Grade school	High school	College
High 4	29%	50%	60%
3	39	40	37
2	12	6	2
1	8	2	1
Low 0	12	2	*
	100%	100%	100%
N	894	1371	486

DATA SOURCE: *Survey Research Center, University of Michigan, a combination of 1952 and 1956 samples.*

---

activity for the maintenance of that status. At any rate, quite marked differences exist in the distribution along the scale of citizen duty of college-trained persons and of those persons whose schooling was limited to the elementary grades. Relatively twice as many college persons as grade-schoolers, as Table 13.3 shows, ranked high on the scale of citizen duty.

The contrasts among educational levels in the sense of citizen duty that appear in Table 13.3 conceal other factors that bear upon that sense of obligation. It is known, for example, that members of the professions, the occupational category most given to verbalizations of ethical imperatives, tend to concur in expressions of propriety regardless of what their own behavior may be. Farmers and unskilled workers, less given to hypocrisy and perhaps more earthy in their outlook,

[2] For the data on these points, see Angus Campbell, Gerald Gurin, and Warren E. Miller: *The Voter Decides* (Evanston: Row, Peterson; 1954), pp. 194-9.

have contrasting tendencies. Yet, as Table 13.4 suggests, the sense of citizen duty seems to be related to extent of education when occupational status is controlled. Among college-educated farmers almost as large a proportion ranks high in citizen duty as of the professional group. Within every occupational group the sense of citizen duty increases with level of education.[3]

TABLE 13.4

SENSE OF CITIZEN DUTY IN RELATION TO EDUCATION AND OCCUPATION [a]

HEAD'S OCCUPATION	LEVEL OF EDUCATION					
	Grade school		High school		College	
Professional	[b]	(10)	56%	(88)	63%	(170)
Business	41%	(84)	53	(260)	62	(127)
Clerical	35	(49)	55	(186)	60	(84)
Skilled	31	(347)	49	(541)	57	(67)
Unskilled	24	(230)	40	(162)	[b]	(8)
Farmers	25	(174)	46	(134)	53	(30)
Total	29	(894)	50	(1,371)	60	(486)

[a] Entries are percentages of those in each cell ranking high on scale of sense of citizen duty as defined in Table 13.3. Figures in parentheses are the base N's for each percentage.
[b] Too few cases to percentage.
DATA SOURCE: *Survey Research Center, University of Michigan, 1952 and 1956.*

Education and the Sense of Political Efficacy. The sense of citizen duty may be dismissed as a reflection of more or less universal lip service to trite expressions of the obligation to vote. A more significant psychological set, however, may be tapped by a scale designed to measure the sense of political efficacy. An individual may see himself obliged to vote, but he may also feel that the performance of his civic duties makes no difference. On the other hand, a citizen may have a sense that he throws some weight around in the political process both by voting and in other ways.

[3] In speculating about the meaning of Table 13.4, one should keep in mind that the occupational categories themselves include a wide range of status levels. The clerical category, for example, includes persons as far apart as the clerk with the simplest skills to the high-powered salesman. Some of the variation associated with education may, in fact, be accounted for by variation within broad occupational category. On the other hand, the educational groupings themselves are fairly diverse. The college group may include both the person with a law degree and the individual who went to college but was advised at the end of the first semester that his talents pointed to opportunities for him in other fields.

Characterization of the population according to its sense of political efficacy was attempted by the Survey Research Center in 1952 and in 1956. A rough measure of the sense of efficacy was made by obtaining views from the respondents in a national sample on a series of test items (reproduced in Appendix IV). It developed that the sense of efficacy, as measured, had a positive relationship with variations in political participation, even with factors such as occupation, education, income, age, and race held constant. The sense of efficacy is even more closely associated with level of education than is the sense of citizen duty. Many more college-educated persons than grade-schoolers thought that government had some regard for them, that citizens

---

TABLE 13.5

RELATION OF LEVEL OF EDUCATION TO SENSE OF POLITICAL EFFICACY

SENSE OF POLITICAL EFFICACY	EDUCATIONAL LEVEL		
	Grade school	High school	College
High 4	3%	8%	27%
3	14	28	37
2	29	38	26
1	23	15	6
Low 0	31	11	4
	100%	100%	100%
N	897	1370	485

DATA SOURCE: *Survey Research Center, University of Michigan, 1952 and 1956 combined.*

---

could reach their government by means other than the ballot box, and that the decisions of government are not necessarily the consequences of maneuvers of the interests but may reflect the way people vote. And more of the college-trained than grade-schoolers could, or at least thought they could, make sense of the political world. All these differences, as summarized by the efficacy index, appear in Table 13.5.

The question remains of whether the sense of political efficacy is correlated with education when other factors are held constant. That exercise is accomplished for occupation in Table 13.6, which indicates that within occupational categories the proportions possessed of a high sense of political efficacy generally increase, and usually quite sharply, with level of education. Among farm operators, for example, relatively nearly six times as many of the college-trained as of the grade-schoolers rank high in political efficacy. Similarly, among skilled workers about

TABLE 13.6

SENSE OF POLITICAL EFFICACY IN RELATION TO EDUCATION AND OCCUPATION [a]

HEAD'S OCCUPATION	LEVEL OF EDUCATION		
	Grade school	High school	College
Professional	[b]	47%	72%
Business	35%	42	59
Clerical	20	41	64
Skilled	19	36	54
Unskilled	11	26	[b]
Farmers	10	21	57

[a] Entries are sums of the two high categories in political efficacy as shown in Table 13.3. The N's are approximately the same as in Table 13.4.
[b] Too few cases in cell to percentage.
DATA SOURCE: *Survey Research Center, University of Michigan, 1952 and 1956 combined.*

three times as large a proportion of the college-trained place high on the scale as of the grade-schoolers. Yet when these differences are projected to the citizenry as a whole, it must be remembered that only a few farmers and skilled workers are college-trained.

Education and Political Involvement. Earlier in the discussion the index of political involvement was found to be an important correlate of opinion and action. The question occurs here whether level of education is related to the sense of political involvement. The index of involvement, it may be recalled, purports to measure involvement in a specific campaign. Its construction is explained in Appendix IV.

Fairly sharp contrasts existed in extent of involvement in the 1952 and 1956 presidential campaigns among persons of different educational levels. Relatively over twice as many college persons as grade-schoolers ranked high on the scale of political involvement; extremely few college persons—only 3 per cent—placed at the bottom of the scale, in contrast to 29 per cent of the grade-schoolers. Again, the question may be raised whether differences in education do not simply mask other differences that might plausibly be expected to account for contrasts in involvement. To check this matter, occupation is held constant in Table 13.7. The differences in the table, while suggesting that education has an independent influence, also point to the possibility that interests associated with occupational status are strong generators of a sense of political involvement. Business persons with only a grade-school education had a high sense of involvement almost as frequently as the college-trained businessmen.

In the appraisal of all these tables one important point needs to be kept in mind: college training does not invariably produce persons with a high sense of citizen duty, a high sense of efficacy, and a high level of political involvement. College-trained persons have these attributes more frequently than do persons of high school education. On the other hand, limitation of education to grade school does not invariably result in a person who has no sense of obligation to vote, who has a sense of political futility, and who does not care who wins. Factors

TABLE 13.7

RELATION OF POLITICAL INVOLVEMENT TO LEVEL OF EDUCATION AND OCCUPATION [a]

HEAD'S OCCUPATION	LEVEL OF EDUCATION		
	Grade school	High school	College
Professional	[b]	36%	53%
Business	40%	37	48
Clerical	26	36	53
Skilled	22	30	40
Unskilled	17	19	[b]
Farmers	18	23	37

[a] Entries are percentages of those in each cell ranking high on the index of political involvement.
[b] Too few cases in cell to percentage.
DATA SOURCE: *Survey Research Center, University of Michigan, 1952 and 1956 combined.*

other than education give many grade-schoolers a sense of sharing in political affairs. Only on the average are grade-schoolers less involved, less impelled by a sense of citizen duty, and less animated by a sense of political efficacy than the college crowd.

Education and Political Participation. Education not only tends to imbue persons with a sense of citizen duty and a sense of political efficacy; it also propels them into political activity. By the available measures, persons with college education show themselves to be markedly more active in politics than are persons whose education has been restricted to grade schools. These differences prevail at different educational levels within broad occupational categories.

By the simplest measure of political participation, voting or not voting, persons of varying educational achievement demonstrate sharp

contrasts. This difference in participation may not be so important
for the political process as are other differences about which no really
satisfactory data are available. Yet the special political coloration of the
college group is suggested by its rank on our index of political participation. In every occupational group the proportion of high participators increases with education. If satisfactory information were available on the incidence of more specialized types of political participation
—skilled propagandizing, public leadership, running for office, per-
suading officials—doubtless an even wider difference would be found
to prevail among educational levels than those that appear in Table 13.8.
Those differences would be attributable only in part to education. Occupational status goes along with certain types of political roles. On the

TABLE 13.8

EDUCATION IN RELATION TO LEVELS OF POLITICAL PARTICIPATION WITHIN OCCU-
PATIONAL GROUPS

HEAD'S OCCUPATION AND R'S PARTICIPATION LEVEL	LEVEL OF EDUCATION		
	Grade school	High school	College
Professional			
High [a]	*	36%	48%
Low	*	16	5
Business			
High	37%	36	50
Low	20	15	6
Clerical			
High	16	26	53
Low	32	18	4
Skilled			
High	18	32	42
Low	28	18	9
Unskilled			
High	9	20	*
Low	48	27	*
Farmers			
High	18	24	36
Low	36	19	7

[a] The entries are percentages of those in each cell high and low on the
index of political participation. High participators include those who
voted and reported having engaged in at least one other type of campaign participation. Low participators neither voted nor participated
otherwise. See Appendix IV.
DATA SOURCE: *Survey Research Center, University of Michigan, a combination of 1952 and 1956 samples.*

other hand, education provides the skills and information essential for the performance of those roles.

A factor that contributes to the contrasts in Table 13.8, and doubtless also to the differences shown in the immediately preceding tables, consists in the contrasting political roles of men and of women (see Table 13.9). The grant of the franchise to women equipped them with the legal right to vote but not necessarily with the motivation, interest, or information to do so. To a large extent, though, education erases the contrasts between men and women in the gross types of political par-

TABLE 13.9

RELATION OF EDUCATION TO LEVEL OF POLITICAL PARTICIPATION, BY SEX

PARTICIPATION
LEVEL [a]   LEVEL OF EDUCATION

	Grade school		High school		College	
	M	F	M	F	M	F
High 4	30%	11%	37%	23%	50%	41%
3	40	41	43	48	41	47
2	4	4	5	5	5	6
Low 1	26	44	15	24	4	6
	100%	100%	100%	100%	100%	100%
N	253	289	353	531	177	153

[a] For construction of the index of participation, see Appendix IV.
DATA SOURCE: *Survey Research Center, University of Michigan, 1956.*

ticipation. Women with a grade-school education contribute disproportionately to the nonvoting group among persons of this educational level. On the average these women are older than college-trained women and spent their formative years in an era when political activity by women was not regarded as the best of form. On the other hand, as far as voting alone is concerned, college-trained women have about as high a participation rate as do college-trained men. The incidence of other types of political activism among college women is slightly lower than among college men, but there can be no denying that a junior-league type with the political fever is a truly awesome spectacle.

3 · Education, Opinion, and Opinion Direction

While education certainly contributes to the formation of attitudes, motivations, and understandings that lead to heightened political activity, the question remains whether education affects direction of opinion on issues of public policy. One proposition is incontrovertible: namely, extent of education has a good deal to do with the probability that a person has an opinion. Its bearing on the direction of opinion is far less clear. The best guess is that education makes a difference for the direction of opinion on some topics, but on other issues direction of opinion may be more nearly independent of level of education.

Opinion or No Opinion. Survey results abound with findings that show a sharp relationship between level of education and level of information on political questions. Those of lesser education frequently have no information about concepts and terms that are the building blocks of everyday discourse among those with even the most elementary political sophistication. In 1946, for example, Dr. Gallup asked his national sample the question: "Can you tell me what is meant by balancing the federal budget?" The responses, by level of education, were:

Education	Correct	Incorrect or don't know
College	77%	23%
High School	55	45
Grammar school or none	37	63

The college group, with about one fourth unable to answer the question, made no impressive showing (doubtless because of the depressing influence of the ignorance of English majors and other such college products), but they were at least more often informed on this elementary question than were those whose education was limited to grammar school.

Differentials among educational groups go beyond simple variations in quantity of information. Ordinarily on questions that relate not to information but to broad policy preferences, relatively far more persons of little education profess to have no opinion than do those with college training. The policy propositions that have been repeatedly used in the preceding chapters were in large degree not questions on which a person had to have a store of specific information to express an opinion. As these questions were put by the interviewers, they were preceded by the comment: "Of course, different things are important to different people, so we don't expect everyone to have an opinion about all of these. If you don't have an opinion, just tell me that; if you do have an opinion, choose one of the other answers." After each policy proposition was read to the respondent, he was asked: "Now, would you say you have an opinion on this or not?"

While there may be some quibble about the meaning of a refusal to express an opinion in this kind of situation, differences in frequency of declination vary sharply with education. Moreover, the frequency of lack of opinion varies among questions of different kinds, a fact that may give a clue to the bearing of education on opinion. On questions of foreign policy the disinclination to express an opinion is especially marked among persons with only grade-school education. The details are presented for a series of such questions in Table 13.10. In the preparation of that table it was assumed that post-educational experience

---

TABLE 13.10

RELATION OF LACK OF OPINION ON INTERNATIONAL ISSUES TO LEVEL OF EDUCATION AND OCCUPATION

ISSUE PROPOSITION AND EDUCATION	PER CENT WITH NO OPINION BY OCCUPATION		
	White-collar [a]	Blue-collar	Farmer
Stay home [b]			
College	6%	4%	* [c]
High school	8	11	13%
Grammar school	14	23	18
Foreign Aid			
College	6	13	*
High school	10	20	17
Grammar school	26	24	14
Be Tough			
College	8	10	*
High school	13	19	21
Grammar school	19	27	26
Forces Overseas			
College	12	10	*
High school	15	21	29
Grammar school	23	28	32
Be Friendly			
College	2	1	*
High school	9	11	7
Grammar school	21	17	15
Aid to Neutrals			
College	12	8	*
High school	18	30	27
Grammar school	34	40	40

[a] Includes clerical, sales, business, professions.
[b] For text of the issue propositions, see Appendix I.
[c] Too few cases to percentage.
DATA SOURCE: *Survey Research Center, University of Michigan, 1956.*

might also have some bearing on willingness to grapple with issues of foreign policy. A high-school graduate who enters a white-collar occupation may be expected, on the average, to have more contact with the media and more opportunity to pick up a fleeting acquaintance with foreign-policy issues than a high-school graduate who becomes an industrial worker. To provide a rough control on these variations, each level of education is grouped in the table into white-collar workers, blue-collar workers, and farm operators. Within the occupational groups the proportion with no opinion almost invariably declines with increase in education.

Evidently exposure to the educational process has an effect on people's willingness to express opinions on broad propositions such as those used in this survey. Probably information acquired by formal education on international politics is not the significant factor, for a person might well have an attitude on these propositions without a heavy encumbrance of information. Thus a response to a proposition such as the following may be an expression of a fairly generalized attitude rather than an opinion resting on information: "This country would be better off if we just stayed home and did not concern ourselves with problems in other parts of the world." [4] Education, along with its secondary effects of assuring some exposure to the media, probably generates at least a verbal confidence to cope with such questions.

Then, too, whether a person has an opinion may be related to his capacity to bring the problem within the range of his understanding; that capacity may depend on the nature of the question as well as on an individual's educational experience. The validity of this interpretation is suggested by an examination of opinion and lack of opinion on a series of questions of domestic policy, shown in Table 13.11. On those questions that could be brought immediately into relation with a person's understanding of his self-interest, few persons declined to express a view. On the proposition: "The government in Washington ought to see to it that everybody who wants to work can find a job," most persons, whatever their level of education, had an opinion. Most respondents also agreed or disagreed with the proposition: "The government ought to help people get doctors and hospital care at low cost." While persons with grade-school education declined more frequently than others to express an opinion on such questions, the differences among educational levels were small.

Contrast, though, the proportions with no opinion on other questions in the table that presuppose at least some faint knowledge of rela-

---

[4] Yet it must be agreed that a trace of information might be conducive to an opinion. A retired Iowa farmer: "Airplanes, TV and radio unite us in the world." A St. Louis policeman: "I don't believe we can hardly do that anymore."

tively abstract questions of politics. Note the large proportion of grade-schoolers with no views on: "The government ought to see to it that big business corporations don't have much say about how the government is run." Similarly, large proportions declined to cope with the

TABLE 13.11

RELATION OF LACK OF OPINION ON SELECTED DOMESTIC ISSUES TO OCCUPATION WITHIN EDUCATIONAL LEVELS

ISSUE PROPOSITION
AND EDUCATION

	PER CENT WITH NO OPINION		
	White-collar	Blue-collar	Farmer
Job Guarantee			
College	7%	2%	*
High school	10	8	12%
Grammar school	8	10	13
Medical Care			
College	5	12	*
High school	10	11	9
Grammar school	15	15	9
Aid to Education			
College	4	6	*
High school	8	9	12
Grammar school	10	12	21
Restrain Business			
College	14	13	*
High school	20	24	23
Grammar school	41	45	36
Power and Housing			
College	15	15	*
High school	23	28	28
Grammar school	43	41	39
Restrain Unions			
College	13	2	*
High school	18	24	33
Grammar school	31	36	42

DATA SOURCE: *Survey Research Center, University of Michigan, 1956.*

philosophical problem: "The government should leave things like electric power and housing for private businessmen to handle." On such questions the contrasts in frequency of lack of opinion among educational levels are sharp. Education probably equips people with sufficient familiarity with general ideas and probably also with a sufficient supply of value preferences to enable them to respond to issues put in rather general terms. The less the education, the more directly must an issue bear upon a person's immediate interest or experience to evoke an opinion.[5]

Direction of Opinion: International Issues. The bearing of level of education on direction of opinion presents a difficult problem in both analysis and interpretation. The kind of education a person possesses is so closely related to occupation, to income, and to other such factors that it is difficult to disentangle the contribution of education to his opinions. The statistical relations between education and direction of opinion are also most varied, and it is not easy to divine the general meaning of education for direction of opinion. These uncertain and hedging comments are to be contrasted with earlier discussions of the question. Early studies of college sophomores indicated that A-students were more radical than gentlemen C's and far more radical than grade-school students.[6] The moral was that the dangers of education perhaps outweighed its advantages. Later it turned out that college-trained persons voted Republican and held Republican views in higher proportions than did persons blessed with only an eighth-grade education. Hence, we were spectators at a race between educational expansion and the disaster of Democratic rule. In fact, the opinion data from surveys of national samples do not neatly fit any single interpretative scheme.

On questions of foreign policy evidence seems to indicate that education has a relationship with direction of opinion. Probably these relationships exist, not because the issues involve foreign policy, but because they are of a wider category of issues whose qualities are such that persons with better education are better able to see their larger implications and, hence, more likely, under the circumstances in which the nation finds itself, to move toward preordained conclusions.[7] A summarization of the position of a national sample on several foreign policy

[5] Philip K. Hastings concludes, from a Pittsfield survey: "Level of information is related to the fact of having an opinion of some kind, no matter what the nature of and basis for the opinion may be."—"Level of Information and Opinion Content," *Political Science Quarterly*, LXIX (1954), 234-40.

[6] For a summary of the literature, see W. A. M. Kerr: "Correlates of Politico-Economic Liberalism-Conservatism," *Journal of Social Psychology*, XX (1944), pp. 61-7.

[7] These remarks are consistent with the finding of George H. Smith from a 1946 survey: "Very low information is associated with low internationalism no matter whether people are radicals, indeterminates, or conservatives. Thus, though differing sharply on domestic issues, uninformed radicals and uninformed conservatives think much alike when they look beyond our shores."—George H. Smith, "Information, Radicalism, and Internationalism," *Public Opinion Quarterly*, XII (1948), 125-7. Level of information would be expected to bear on direction of opinion only when an increase in information activates some pre-

questions is provided by Table 13.12. On a scale which roughly measured acceptance or tolerance of involvement abroad 60 per cent of
those with college training ranked high, in contrast with 37 per cent of
the grade-schoolers. Of equal interest is the fact that almost four times
as large a proportion of grade-schoolers as of college persons had so few
opinions on the issues comprising the scale that they could not be
ranked on it.[8] These differences in distribution on the internationalism
scale are not a product of the hidden effect of occupation. Within edu-

---

TABLE 13.12

EDUCATION IN RELATION TO POSITION ON INTERNATIONALISM SCALE

INTERNATIONALISM	LEVEL OF EDUCATION		
	Grammar school	High school	College
High	37%	44%	60%
Medium	14	24	25
Low	19	14	7
Not scaled [a]	30	18	8
	100%	100%	100%
N	542	883	330

[a] Too few responses to permit scaling.
DATA SOURCE: *Survey Research Center, University of Michigan, 1956.*

---

cational levels distributions of occupational groups along the scale are
similar.

The relation between internationalism and education in the 1950's
should not be taken to mean that education generally predisposes people to an internationalist position. Rather, the probabilities are that
when a dominant view develops on international policy it will be most
notably present among persons concerned and informed about foreign
policy, and these individuals are especially numerous in the upper educational strata. If, for example, data were available on attitudes on foreign policy between, say, 1890 and 1910, a nationalist (if not an imperi-
alist) position would probably have been held with a high frequency
among the better-educated. Interest in and a capacity to see the impli-

---

existing basic outlook. If that outlook is widely distributed in the population, to
raise the general level of information is to alter the directional distribution of
opinion. Without some such prerequisite, information alone could not be expected to alter opinion direction.

[8] A factor to be kept in mind in the comparison of persons with grade-
school and college education is that the grade-school group is of considerably
higher average age. In the 1956 sample 42 per cent of the grade school group was
over fifty-five, against only 16 per cent of the college group; 13 per cent of the
grade-school group was under thirty-five, but 36 per cent of the college group.

cations of questions of external policy, while by no means a monopoly of the better-educated, occur more frequently among this group. These observations are consistent with findings about the relation of opinion and education and economic status in the period before World War II. Education was "found to be more important" as a determinant of opinion "where factual knowledge gives an insight into implications, for example, in determining opinion toward a negotiated peace or toward post-war problems." [9] Just after the fall of France an interventionist position was "more likely to be held by well-educated than by high-income people. The former group continued to see the implications of a German victory and wanted to help make it impossible, while the latter group tended more to retreat into the temporary safety of the status quo." [1] These differences between economic status and education as determinants disappeared after Pearl Harbor.

Direction of Opinion: Domestic Issues. While the books are filled with clear-cut assertions about the bearing of education on the direction of opinion on domestic issues, the data do not enable us to speak with great assurance. The hesitancy comes in part from the fact that education is so closely correlated with occupation that when one isolates a special viewpoint of the college-educated, for example, it is almost impossible to know whether that opinion reflects the consequences of education or of the peculiar interest of the business and professional group. One may reasonably suspect that on some kinds of questions the differences in outlook among occupations are attributable in reality to education. Yet so diverse are the contrasts among educational levels that a variety of explanations has to be called into service to account for them.

If a cue is taken from the discussion of education and opinion on international affairs, one might search for a test of the question of whether an increase in education brings with it a greater capacity to judge some of the more remote consequences of particular domestic questions. Persons with high-school or college education would be expected to see those consequences more readily than those with only a grade-school education, and their opinion would be affected accordingly. Relevant to this problem may be the responses of agreement and disagreement to the policy statement: "The government ought to cut taxes even if it means putting off some important things that need to be done." Now this proposition presents to the person with even the

[9] Hadley Cantril: *Gauging Public Opinion* (Princeton: Princeton University Press; 1944), p. 107.
[1] Ibid.

slightest political sophistication no remote implication, but its consequences escape some persons. In fact, about a quarter of the sample
wanted taxes cut and failed to see that they might be cutting off their
noses to spite their faces.

These differences in outlook on taxes were fairly closely associated
with level of education, as inspection of Table 13.13 will indicate. A
partial explanation of these contrasts may be that the grade-school
group includes low-income individuals who may be especially attracted
by the prospect for improvement of their lot, whether by tax reduction

---

TABLE 13.13

RELATION OF LEVEL OF EDUCATION TO VIEWS ON TAX-CUT ISSUE [a]

POSITION	LEVEL OF EDUCATION		
	Grade school	High school	College
Disagree strongly	17%	30%	47%
Disagree	13	16	18
Depends	8	12	13
Agree	10	12	7
Agree strongly	24	14	7
No opinion	28	16	8
	100%	100%	100%
N	542	883	330

[a] The policy statement was: "The government ought to cut taxes even
if it means putting off some important things that need to be done."
DATA SOURCE: *Survey Research Center, University of Michigan, 1956.*

---

or otherwise. Nevertheless, on this question education seems to account
in the main for the differences among the groups. Within educational
levels the responses to the question were approximately the same among
broad occupational groups. The not implausible inference is that education tends to increase the capacity to cope with relationships among political issues.

When we go beyond such simple-minded questions as the tax-cut
proposition, the estimation of the bearing of education on direction of
opinion encounters serious obstacles. Assertions can be made with more
assurance about what education does not do than they can about what
it does. The belief, held with some belligerence in certain circles, that
college education produces economic radicals, for example, is demon-
strably false. College experience in some institutions may impart a liberal cast of mind; in others the effect may be the opposite; and still other
colleges may succeed magnificently in affecting the attitudes of their
students not at all. Yet college-trained persons generally manifest more

conservative attitudes on economic issues than do persons of lesser education. The distributions of opinion on several such issues are shown, by level of education, in Table 13.14. On these issues "conservative" opinion increases step by step up the educational ladder. The size of the sample permits no completely satisfactory check on the extent to which

---

TABLE 13.14

RELATION OF EDUCATION TO OPINIONS ON SELECTED PROPOSITIONS OF ECONOMIC POLICY

ISSUE AND EDUCATION [a]	PRO	DEPENDS	CON	NO OPINION
Medical care				
College	14%	13%	65%	8%
High school	26	12	46	16
Grade school	34	8	30	28
Job guarantee				
College	39	7	47	7
High school	54	9	28	9
Grade school	71	4	13	12
Aid to education				
College	57	13	25	5
High school	68	8	16	8
Grade school	73	7	6	14
Housing and power, keep private				
College	52	10	24	14
High school	42	6	26	26
Grade school	35	6	16	43

[a] For issue phrasing, see Appendix I.
DATA SOURCE: *Survey Research Center, University of Michigan, 1956.*

---

educational differences mask occupational differences, but the data suggest that even with other things equal the better educated tend to be more conservative.

Another hypothesis is that formal education may serve to indoctrinate people with the more-or-less official political values of the culture. To the extent that it does so, opinion will be brought into line with those values. The evidence on this matter is neither voluminous nor persuasive; yet some studies have yielded findings generally consistent with the proposition. Samuel Stouffer's study of attitudes towards communism included a scale to measure "tolerance," which included items on free speech for nonconformists and other such rights. The number

of cases sufficed to establish that within occupational categories the proportions ranking "high" on this scale increased with education.[2] Parallel are findings that larger proportions of the college-educated in both
the South and the North approve of school integration.[3]

Probably a major consequence of education for opinion consists in
the bearing of education on the kinds of influences to which a person is
subjected throughout his life. The more extended the educational experience, the more probable is it that a person will be exposed to the discussions of issues as they arise. When, as so often occurs, the current
discussion is heavily loaded on one side, it might be expected that this
educationally conditioned exposure would have some bearing on the direction of opinion.[4] Thus, the increase in opposition to governmental
participation in medical care with level of education doubtless depends
in part on income and occupational characteristics associated with education. Probably it also depends in part on the greater exposure of upper educational levels to doctrines critical of government activity of
this sort.[5] Subjection to the stream of propaganda on this and other issues might be expected to offset whatever reaction of immediate self-
interest one might have.

4 · Education and the Opinion Structure

While it is plain that education significantly shapes politically relevant
attitudes, it must be conceded that isolation of the effects of the
school system from other influences forming political man is not
readily accomplished. Intensive studies of life histories of individuals

[2] Seymour Lipset presents a special tabulation of Stouffer's data on this point
in "Democracy and Working-Class Authoritarianism," *American Sociological Review*, XXIV (1959), 482–501.

[3] Herbert Hyman and Paul B. Sheatsley, "Attitudes Towards Desegrega-
tion," *Scientific American*, December, 1956. Similarly, in Texas in 1950 (the Texas
Poll) far fewer college persons than grade-schoolers favored separate schools for
Latin-American children: 28 per cent, against 47 per cent.

[4] In a national survey George H. Smith found that disapproval of the Taft-
Hartley Act increased with level of information which in turn is correlated with
educational level.—"Information and Opinions About the Taft-Hartley Act," *International Journal of Opinion and Attitude Research*, II (1948), 169–82.

[5] As any student might surmise the bearing of college education on the direction of political attitude depends in a measure on what subjects are studied in
college. Hard information on these varying effects is limited, but a study by the
Opinion Research Corporation in 1959 demonstrated marked differences in attitude between college seniors with an economics major and other groups of
students. For example, on the average, economics majors took positions on a series
of ideological questions far more closely resembling those of a sample of business
executives than did college freshmen, education majors, or college seniors generally. See also Seymour Lipset: *Political Man* (New York: Doubleday; 1960),
ch. 10.

would permit more confident assignment of weights to the factors of family, education, occupational interest, social status, and other such influences. The sketchy data on persons constituting samples of the national electorate permit us to draw only crude inferences about the bearing of education on the political outlook of the national population.

Whether education is the cause of it all, important types of political outlook vary with extent of education. High levels of political participation, a high sense of citizen efficacy, and a high sense of citizen duty occur far more frequently among persons with college training than among those whose formal education ended at the elementary state. Similarly, the range of information on, or at least of acquaintance with, questions of public policy tends to increase with education. The political significance of these differences is blunted by the sizes of the absolute numbers involved. Though high political interest occurs more frequently among college graduates than among high-school graduates, there are more high-school graduates in the population.

Although differences in the direction of opinion often exist among groups of varying educational achievement, similarities among these groups may be politically more significant than their contrasts. Zones of substantial agreement cut across all educational levels. Probably the differences that exist could be grouped roughly into two broad kinds. First are those contrasts that may have little to do with education. College-trained persons drift largely into business and the professions and to some extent acquire political outlooks with foundations in occupational interest. Persons with less educational experience more commonly become blue-collar or clerical workers. Occupationally oriented outlooks, although correlated with education, do not rest fundamentally on education.

A second series of contrasts in opinion direction occurs largely around issues not immediately connected with occupational concern. Rather, they are questions on which there may be an overriding national interest or which are closely connected with values and norms of basic importance to the political culture but not necessarily economically based. On this type of question level of education may have a significant directional effect. For example, on questions of American policy abroad the information and outlook that come with extension of education may enable people to see the ramifications of issues and may make policies of international involvement (at least under certain circumstances) more congenial to persons with greater education than to grade-schoolers. Here again these outlooks are by no means confined to particular educational levels. They are simply more frequent at higher educational levels. On issues that involve basic national values, persons with more extended education evidently have been more thoroughly indoctrinated in the norms of the political culture and respond accordingly. On the average, persons with less education probably react to these matters more by raw and relatively unconditioned human impulse, if they react at all; they often confess to the possession of no opinion.

Beyond these and other such contrasts among educational levels made discernible in the mass of people by sample surveys, it is important to remember that the educational system in its upper reaches produces persons with extremely varied political outlooks. That is to say, the ranks of the highly educated—from which we draw, disproportionately, persons with leadership skills, with evangelistic inclinations, with capacities for social invention—are not homogeneous in political attitude. Colleges and universities willy-nilly provide the leadership for right and left, for isolationism and internationalism, for innovation and inertia. In the largest sense the educational system is a great mechanism for conserving the values, the institutions, the practices of the political order, as it inculcates from the primary school even through college the memories, the unities, and the norms of the system. Yet the educational process does not completely embalm the political system. From it there come the political innovators as well as the conservers.[6]

[6] Occasionally the assertion is made that persons of little education tend to be conservative. Such observations often rest on responses to questions such as the AIPO inquiry of April, 1945: "After the war, would you like to see many changes or reforms made in the United States, or would you rather have the country remain pretty much the way it was before the war?" While 57 per cent of the grade school level wanted things as they were, only 37 per cent of the college-trained shared that view. The contrast is doubtless explained in part by the fact that the college-trained know of possibilities for reform or have sufficient imagination to conjure up ideas for change. The grade-schoolers have not so often had their minds stretched to an awareness of the possibilities which they can recall when a question such as this one is put to them. They have to be sold on reforms, and it seems probable that in the domestic sphere, at least when the alternatives have been clearly put to them, they have not acted generally in a conservative manner.

14

MEDIA: SPECTER AND
REALITY

THOSE WEARY with the modern world seem especially disposed to attribute an overwhelming influence over public opinion to the media of mass communication: television, radio, newspapers, magazines, and movies. Their indictment runs to the effect that modern politics—through the interdependence of all parts of the world and through the transfer of decision from local to national authorities—becomes remote from the average man. His information about events and personalities must be acquired through the media, with no possibility of independent check against his own observation or experience. This dependence, the argument goes, makes the public a plastic to be molded by the masters of the media into almost any form they desire. The free and independent citizen beloved of democratic theorists becomes an automaton actuated by impulses transmitted by anonymous rulers through the system of communication. While the capacity of the media collectively to affect public attitudes and behavior cannot be doubted, the luxuriant verbiage on the subject contains a generous component of buncombe. The problem is to separate the fairly well-established propositions from the buncombe.

The fairly well-established propositions, it should be emphasized at the outset, are few. There are especially few on the topics of concern in this discussion. We should like to be able to sum up in some comprehensible way what the media do to make people what they are politically. What are the effects of the media on the policy outlooks, preferences, and expectations of the citizenry as a whole? Even with a plenitude of research resources, such questions would present almost insurmountable problems of observation and analysis. Given the limits of knowledge of the political role and effects of mass communications, about all that can be done is to make educated guesses around the edges of the problem. Those guesses, though, should enable us to define some of the boundaries of the role of mass communications as molders of opinion.

1 · Audiences and the Objects of their Attention

The literary model of the world of modern mass communications is one in which the messages of the media fall upon the just and the unjust alike, as does the rain; from the relentless clamor of the media modern man has no escape. Moreover, that model in its political versions assumes that the flow of communications includes a large component of political content. In the appraisal of the place of mass media in the political order, a first step is to deflate these assumptions. Modern man fortunately retains a degree of freedom of choice. He may or may not, as he wishes, attend to the mass media. If he listens to the radio or watches television, he may, within the limits of what is available, be selective in his attention. To some extent, each medium of communication has its characteristic audience, and within those audiences the extent of attention to differing types of messages varies enormously.

Choices Among Media. Perhaps the principal incontestable moral of the data about politics and mass communications is that many of the political messages carried by the communications network do not reach many people. The limits of the audience fix the area of direct influence of the mass media; a message unheard is a message unheeded. The audience for mass communications defines itself as people choose that to which they will attend. Some people have a wider range of choice than others, but all people have some control over their intake from the mass media. A major factor in the determination of the information to which one will expose himself is the choice among media, for the range and even the kind of political content differs among the media.

Media audiences are not, of course, sharply divided; they overlap. Some clues to the nature of that overlap and to the relative sizes of the audiences come from studies of campaigns. At such times the level of political attention is doubtless much higher than between campaigns, but the relative importance of media as continuing sources of general political information may resemble that which prevails during campaigns. A rough notion of the relative magnitude of the audiences for the principal media comes from the responses of samples interviewed after the 1952 and 1956 presidential campaigns. Of the total sample: [1]

	1952	1956
Read about the campaign in newspapers	79%	69%
Listened to radio speeches or discussions	69	45
Watched campaign programs on television	49	74
Read about the campaign in magazines	40	31

The contrasts between the two years reflect principally the extension of television facilities and the growth of the TV audience at the expense of other media.

Even minimal exposure placed a person in these grossly defined media audiences. A "Yes" reply to the question: "Did you read about the campaign in any newspapers?" qualified a person for inclusion in the 69 per cent of the sample in the 1956 newspaper audience. More of a differentiation of the media audiences came from responses to the question: "Of all these ways of following the campaign which one would you say you got the most information from—newspapers, radio, television, or magazines?" The distributions on this question perhaps define better the relative importance of sources of information. The percentages who said that they "got the most information" from the various media were:

	1952	1956
Newspapers	22%	24%
Radio	28	10
Television	31	49
Magazines	5	5
Combinations of media	5	3
Didn't follow campaign	6	8
DK and NA	3	1

Thus, in 1956 by far the largest bloc of people rated television as their most important source of campaign information.[2] About half as many

[1] Data source: Survey Research Center, University of Michigan, 1952 and 1956.

[2] The import of television for voting behavior remains to be established. One 1952 analysis, based on studies of areas with and without television, failed to isolate any special effect of television.—Herbert A. Simon and Frederick Stern: "The Effect of Television upon Voting Behavior in Iowa in the 1952 Presidential Election," *American Political Science Review*, XLIX (1955), 470–7. One study offers

gave that rating to the newspapers; radio fell far behind. Magazines were ranked as the most important source by 5 per cent, and, as we shall see, this audience has special characteristics.

Striking contrasts in political attitude and behavior exist among those chiefly dependent on each of the media. The small group that relies mainly on magazines ranks markedly higher than other media audiences in willingness to express opinions on issues and in disposition to appraise governmental performance on the issues. Twice as high a proportion of this group as of radio listeners—54 per cent against 24 per cent—placed high on a scale of issue familiarity in 1956. Magazine readers, though, are persons who tend also to follow campaigns through several media. Newspaper readers also ranked on the average considerably higher than radio listeners. Those who reported that they followed the campaign not at all were least informed; yet they included, relatively, almost half as many persons high in issue familiarity as did the radio-listening group. The data appear in Table 14.1.[3]

TABLE 14.1

Most Important Source of Campaign Information in Relation to Issue Familiarity [a]

ISSUE FAMILIARITY	MOST IMPORTANT SOURCE					
	Magazines	Combinations of media	Newspapers	TV	Radio	Didn't follow campaign
High 4	54%	42%	35%	32%	24%	11%
3	25	32	28	25	23	12
2	14	11	21	20	15	14
Low 1	7	15	16	23	38	63
	100%	100%	100%	100%	100%	100%
N	80	47	423	862	185	147

[a] The question was: "Of all these ways of following the campaign, which one would you say you got the most information from—newspapers, radio, television or magazines?" For construction of the index of issue familiarity, see Appendix IV.

DATA SOURCE: *Survey Research Center, University of Michigan, 1956.*

the subversive suggestion that it is what a campaigner says, not the medium of transmission that determines whether people remember the message.—Charles E. Swanson, James Jenkins, and Robert L. Jones: "President Truman Speaks: A Study of Ideas vs. Media," *Journalism Quarterly,* XXVII (1950), 251–62.

[3] Many studies establish the high information level of the magazine audience. On a test of familiarity with names in the news, 82 per cent of readers of three or more magazines in Minnesota villages ranked high, but only 39 per cent of those who read no magazines.—R. O. Nafziger *et al.:* "The Mass Media and an Informed Public," *Public Opinion Quarterly,* XV (1951), 105–14.

Media audiences also vary in political participation. The magazine audience includes a large proportion of high participators—that is, persons who both vote and participate in some other way, such as by contributing money or talking up their candidate—while those who rely chiefly on radio include relatively only one fourth as many high participators. As might be expected, those who do not follow political campaigns through any of the media are in high proportion nonvoters. In 1956 61 per cent of this group failed to vote. In appraising these differences in proportions of high participators one must, of course, re-

---

TABLE 14.2

RELATION OF MOST IMPORTANT SOURCE OF CAMPAIGN INFORMATION TO LEVEL OF POLITICAL PARTICIPATION [a]

PARTICIPATION
LEVEL   MOST IMPORTANT SOURCE

	Magazines	Combina-tions of media	News-papers	TV	Radio	Didn't follow
High 4	56%	56%	34%	32%	13%	5%
3	34	36	46	44	44	34
2	4	4	5	5	5	5
Low 1	6	4	15	19	38	56
	100%	100%	100%	100%	100%	100%
N	80	47	423	862	185	147

[a] For construction of the index of political participation, see Appendix IV.
DATA SOURCE: *Survey Research Center, University of Michigan, 1956.*

---

member that the television audience accounts for a far larger part of the electorate than does the magazine audience. The magazine audience includes only a high concentration of activists. High participators among the magazine readers are far outnumbered by comparable persons in the television audience. Participation figures for the several media audiences are shown in Table 14.2.

An important difference in media audiences is education. The better-educated rely in far higher degree on printed sources for their campaign information than do those with the least formal education; the latter depend more upon radio and television.[4] Formal education does not drive persons away from the radio and TV but leads them, or at least many of them, to be attentive to several media. An index of

[4] Angus Campbell, Gerald Gurin, and Warren E. Miller, "Television and the Election," *Scientific American*, CLXXXVIII, 5 (1953), 46–8.

media exposure during the 1956 campaign provides data on the point. Those who had paid attention to the campaign through all the media were ranked high in media exposure; those who had followed the campaign through none of the media earned a low ranking in media exposure; others placed at intermediate points depending upon the number of media to which they had exposed themselves. As may be seen from Table 14.3, 40 per cent of those who reported exposure to all the principal media had at least some college education. Only 3 per cent of the low-

TABLE 14.3

Media Exposure in Relation to Level of Education

EDUCATION	MEDIA EXPOSURE [a]				
	Low				High
	0	1	2	3	4
College	3%	4%	15%	28%	40%
High school	39	48	57	48	51
Grade school	58	48	28	24	9
	100%	100%	100%	100%	100%
N	147	355	559	494	228

[a] Ranks are fixed by the number of media the respondent reported exposure to during the campaign. Thus, those in the high category had read about the campaign in newspapers, listened to radio speeches or discussions, watched political programs on television, and read about the campaign in magazines. The low category consists of those who followed the campaign in none of these ways.

DATA SOURCE: *Survey Research Center, University of Michigan, 1956.*

exposure group were college persons. Grammar-schoolers made up almost 60 per cent of the low-exposure category.[5]

The choice among media is also probably related to the degree and kind of interest in political matters. Persons who seek information about their political interests soon reach a ceiling on the possibilities if they rely chiefly on radio. Thus, persons with more than a superficial interest in international affairs find radio and television singularly unsatisfying as the sole source of their information. Consider the data of Table 14.4, which relates the principal source of campaign information to position on a scale of favorableness toward involvement in international

[5] Geographical contrasts also prevail among media audiences, according to a Minnesota study of five media: newspapers, magazines, books, movies, radio. "The proportion of people attending all five media decreased consistently from metropolis through small city and village to the farms."—Malcolm S. MacLean, Jr.; "Mass Media Audiences: City, Small City, Village and Farm," *Journalism Quarterly*, XXIX (1952), 271–82.

affairs. Of those persons who rely on radio, over one fourth had so few opinions on the issues constituting the scale that they could not be ranked on it. On the other hand, 68 per cent of the magazine readers placed at the top of the scale of internationalism. It is not to be supposed that such persons have these opinions solely because they read magazines; the odds are that they read magazines in part because they have these opinions.[6]

TABLE 14.4

RELATION OF MOST IMPORTANT SOURCE OF CAMPAIGN INFORMATION TO POSITION
ON FOREIGN ISSUE SCALE

INTERNATION-
ALISM   MOST IMPORTANT SOURCE

	Magazines	Combinations of media	Newspapers	TV	Radio	Didn't follow
High	68%	57%	50%	45%	35%	29%
Medium	15	17	25	22	17	10
Low	10	15	12	15	20	12
Not scaled [a]	7	11	13	18	28	49
	100%	100%	100%	100%	100%	100%
N	80	47	423	861	185	147

[a] Respondents with too few opinions to permit placement on scale.
DATA SOURCE: *Survey Research Center, University of Michigan, 1956.*

All these data on audiences of the media at times of campaigns do not provide any solid information on who relies on what media for their day-to-day political intelligence during the intervals between elections. Yet those who rely principally on radio and television for their campaign information probably are not voracious readers during the periods between elections. If half or more of the population depends heavily on radio and television for its regular supply of political information, a substantial sector of the citizenry places a limit on its own political enlightenment. The technical characteristics of these media, as well as the economic conditions of their operation, affect the kinds and quantities of information they can convey. Despite an occasional

[6] On the domestic-issue scale a large proportion of the radio listeners, 42 per cent, ranked high in "liberalism" or favorableness toward governmental intervention. Only 28 per cent of the magazine readers occupied that position. The moral may be that a sector of the population with most liberal leanings has least facilities for learning what the score is politically. For an instructive analysis of the mass media and the audience for discussion of world affairs, see Alfred O. Hero: *Mass Media and World Affairs* (Boston: World Peace Foundation; 1959).

production of extraordinary power, television must limit itself to the tidbits of the events of the day. Radio and television can convey a tone toward political events and an impression of the personalities and the human interest, but ordinarily they can carry little analysis in depth. Moreover, the message of the electronic media is as evanescent as the trill of the songbird. Newspaper and magazine readers, or at least the readers of some newspapers and some magazines, have the opportunity to pursue their interests at length and in some depth, an option not open to those who restrict themselves to television and radio.

Selectivity in Attention. A person may, through choice or by force of circumstance, rely principally on one or another of the great mass media for his political information. Other types of self-selection also contribute to the definition of the audience of the media. A person may be a newspaper reader, but he may choose to read one paper rather than another. If he relies on magazines, he may read one, another, or several.[7] If he is a radio listener, commonly he may choose among stations. If he is a TV watcher, he is likely to have his favorite channel. Still further choices fix the boundaries of the media audiences. The newspaper reader may only skim the headlines, or he may peruse the cerebrations of the editors and of Mr. Walter Lippmann with a grim determination. Some radio listeners hang onto the loaded phrases of Mr. Fulton Lewis, Jr. while others hear only scattered sentences from the newscasts interspersed between the rock 'n' roll. The magazine reader may subject himself to the indignant editorials of the *Saturday Evening Post*, he may reflectively linger over its political articles, or he may read only the fiction. Perhaps he reads the lugubrious political analyses with their strange middle-class Hearstian tinge in the *Reader's Digest* or perhaps he concentrates on its joke sections.

When the opportunity exists for readers to choose, newspapers attract somewhat differentiated audiences. A New Yorker, for example, can read the *Daily News* or the *Times* and, on the whole, different interests actuate the readers of such distinctive journals. Newspaper audiences tend to be differentiated by education, by economic status, and probably also by degree and kind of political interests. A clue to the difference comes from an analysis of the reading habits of women in New York in the early 1940's. Of those women who spent on the average $30 or more for a dress, 42.5 per cent read the *Times* and 7.2 per cent, the *Daily News*. Of those women who in those days spent less than $5

[7] For an analysis of the types of audiences of a series of magazines, see Paul F. Lazarsfeld and Rowena Wyant: "Magazines in 90 Cities—Who Reads What?" *Public Opinion Quarterly*, October, 1937, 29–41.

on the average for a dress, 8.6 per cent read the *Times* and 46 per cent, the *Daily News*.[8] Thus, in multipaper towns individual newspapers tend to develop their characteristic audiences. The Hearst press has a special attraction for those of lower education and low political interest. In Detroit, for example, Kornhauser found that one half of the nonvoters among UAW members who read any paper read the Hearst *Times*. This paper was read to a much greater extent by nonvoters than either of the other two papers.[9]

TABLE 14.5

"WOULD YOU SAY YOU READ NATIONAL AND INTERNATIONAL NEWS RATHER
CAREFULLY OR DO YOU USUALLY READ JUST THE HEADLINES?":
METROPOLITAN ALBANY, 1949

CARE IN READING NEWS	ALL ALBANY ADULTS
Do not read news	4%
Just headlines, skim	47
More than headlines, not much	4
Sometimes carefully, sometimes not	14
Carefully, skip some things	19
Very carefully	6
National carefully, international not	3
International carefully, national not	1
Not ascertained	2
	100%

SOURCE: *Survey Research Center*, Interest, Information, and Attitudes in the Field of World Affairs (*November, 1949*), *being a report of a sample survey in metropolitan Albany in April, 1949.*

Readers of newspapers are highly selective in what they pay heed to in the varied fare laid before them. The vagaries of its readers clip the power of the press.[1] Even when editors bring out their boldest display type, faithful readers may not intercept the message. In the summer of 1940 the Cleveland *Plain Dealer*, the paper with the largest circulation in Erie County, Ohio, splashed on the front page an announcement in support of Willkie; it followed up during the campaign with

[8] Paul F. Lazarsfeld: "The Daily Newspaper and Its Competitors," *Annals of the American Academy of Political and Social Science*, CCXIX (1942), 32–43.
[9] Kornhauser *et al.*: *When Labor Votes*, 82–3.
[1] Of this fact publishers are well aware. They attempt on occasion to offset the obscurity of the editorial page by transferring their political message to the comics. Consider, for example, the political morals of the adventures of "Little Orphan Annie."

daily front-page editorials. In September, 59 per cent of a sample of Erie County did not know which candidate the *Plain Dealer* was supporting. Only about one in seven of those persons with a Democratic predisposition—those who would have to be converted if the paper was to have influence—knew of the paper's editorial position.[2]

Although the evidence is scant, it suggests that an extremely small proportion of the population follows political news in the press with care. Doubtless attention to this type of news increases during the excitement of a presidential campaign. Day in and day out the odds are that less than 10 per cent of the adult population could be regarded as careful readers of the political news. Some evidence on this point appears in Table 14.5, which shows responses to a survey inquiry in the Albany metropolitan area in April, 1949: 47 per cent of the sample said they read "just the headlines" of the national and international news,[3] while only 6 per cent claimed to read both types of news "very carefully." While Albany is not the United States, similar inquiries of a national sample probably would not turn up larger proportions of persons closely attentive to the political news in the press.[4]

While radio once was and television now is the medium that attracts an audience most dispersed through all social and economic levels, sharp differences apparently exist in the audiences for programs with various types of content. Major speeches by the candidates in presidential campaigns may be heard and watched by an audience spread across the socio-economic spectrum, but serious programs in the lulls between campaigns attract relatively far more persons in the upper socio-economic reaches. In 1937, for example, a controversy developed over the appointment of Senator Hugo Black to the Supreme Court. He was traveling in Europe when it was revealed that in his earlier years he had been a member of the Ku Klux Klan and, so the reports went, the country awaited breathlessly the explanatory radio speech to be delivered on his return. The surveys showed that the proportions of various socio-economic classes listening to his speech were: [5]

[2] Elmo C. Wilson: "The Press and Public Opinion in Erie County, Ohio," *Journalism Quarterly*, XVIII (1941), 14–17.

[3] The headlines of a paper are an important means for affecting the outlook of readers. For experimental evidence, see Percy H. Tannenbaum, "The Effect of Headlines on the Interpretation of News Stories," *Journalism Quarterly*, XXX (1953), 189–97. A laboratory experiment demonstrated differences in impressions among readers of the same story captioned with different heads. The headline effect was especially marked among scanners.

[4] The comics seem to command wider attention than any other category of newspaper content. See Charles E. Swanson: "What They Read in 130 Daily Newspapers," *Journalism Quarterly*, XXXII (1955), 411–21.

[5] Paul F. Lazarsfeld: *Radio and the Printed Page* (New York: Duell, Sloan, and Pearce; 1940), p. 26.

Socio-economic Class	Listening	N
High	62%	366
Upper-middle	49	934
Lower-middle	42	427
Low	35	452

Similar evidence comes from a survey to identify the listeners to two speeches in the same year by President Roosevelt on his proposal to reform the Supreme Court. These are the proportions of urban listeners to these speeches within socio-economic classes: [6]

Socio-economic Class	Listening	N
High	43%	187
Upper-middle	38	433
Lower-middle	35	210
Low	28	255

In short, when learned (or even exciting) political discourses begin to move over the electronic waves, a great many listeners and viewers turn off the power or tune in another station.[7]

Still another process in individual selection of items in the mass media for attention may be of the greatest significance for the political role of the mass media. People seem to pay attention to those items with which they agree, not those that seek to convert them.[8] Insofar as campaign propaganda is concerned, it has repeatedly been found that people tend to pay heed to those communications supportive of their own predispositions.[9] A good Republican tends to listen to sound Republican oratory; Democrats listen to their own brand of propaganda. Campaigns are not, of course, entirely a matter of Republicans talking to Republicans and Democrats talking to Democrats. The tidings of the day manage to seep across party lines and to make some converts. The

[6] Ibid., pp. 27–8.

[7] In 1956 the average audience for nighttime political programs on CBS was about 60 per cent below the usual audience for entertainment programs. The size of the audience for individual political broadcasts varied with the size of the audiences for the entertainment regularly scheduled for the time period.— Richard S. Salant: "Political Campaigns and the Broadcaster," *Public Policy*, VIII (1958), 336–67.

[8] Katz and Lazarsfeld put the matter wryly: "Perhaps the most important generalization in this area—at least as far as an understanding of the process of effective persuasion is concerned—is that those groups which are most hopefully regarded as the target of a communication are often least likely to be in the audience."—*Personal Influence* (Glencoe: Free Press; 1955), pp. 21–2.

[9] Paul Lazarsfeld, Bernard Berelson, and Hazel Gaudet: *The People's Choice* (New York: Duell, Sloan and Pearce; 1944), 129–33; and Wilbur Schramm and R. F. Carter: "Effectiveness of a Political Telethon," *Public Opinion Quarterly*, XXIII (1959), 121–7.

information on whether this same selective process operates as people winnow the day-to-day flow of political communications in non-campaign periods is limited. It is perhaps not practicable for even the most alert and agile person to avoid communications content divergent from his own notions; yet the best guess is that the audiences of the mass media tend toward a selectivity that supports rather than weakens their pre-existing outlooks. A bit of evidence comes from a study of an intensive campaign of education in Cincinnati about the United Nations. Those most exposed to the campaign turned out, regrettably, to be those already most favorably disposed toward the United Nations. The same study found that interest in international affairs tended to be a function of a sense of personal concern. Of those, for example, who felt that "they would be better off personally" if foreign trade increased, 57 per cent had an interest in international affairs. Of those who did not see this personal advantage, only 37 per cent had an interest in international affairs by the tests used in this study.[1] From what is known of the generally low levels of interest in political matters, we should expect that factor to be of continuing influence on the nature and extent of popular attention to the flow of political communications.

Even though a person pays attention to a medium of communication, he may regard it with a defensive skepticism. In many localities it has long been a maxim of practical politics that press opposition is a positive asset. Perhaps among some people, who may at times be numerous, newspaper communications have an inverted effect: such people either do not believe what they read in the papers, or they believe that the opposite is true. The extent of this mistrust in the national population is not known,[2] but small-scale inquiries throw some light on the matter. In his study of a random sample of United Auto Workers in Detroit, Kornhauser found that 50 per cent ranked television as the most-trusted source of political information; only 23 per cent placed newspapers in the first rank. When asked which source they trusted least, 42 per cent ranked newspapers first. Distrust of the press was especially high among Stevenson voters in 1952; Eisenhower voters among UAW members on the average regarded newspapers more favorably.

[1] S. A. Starr and H. M. Hughes: "Report on an Educational Campaign: The Cincinnati Plan for the United Nations," *American Journal of Sociology*, LV (1949–50), 389–400. For a thoughtful discussion of individual selection of communications for attention, see W. Phillips Davidson: "On the Effects of Communication," *Public Opinion Quarterly*, XXIII (1959), 343–60.

[2] Quite apart from the defense of conscious skepticism, some people under some circumstances unconsciously misinterpret propaganda messages and thereby sidetrack them. For experimental evidence, see Eunice Cooper and Marie Jahoda: "The Evasion of Propaganda: How Prejudiced People Respond to Anti-Prejudice Propaganda," *Journal of Psychology*, XXIII (1947), 12–25.

While these levels of trust and distrust of the media reflect the peculiarities of the sample and of the Detroit press, they suggest that many people build for themselves a defensive shell against the mass media, especially the press.[3]

The sources of information to which an individual attends fix the range of content to which he may choose to subject himself. An extremely small proportion of the flow through the channels of mass communication has an overtly political content. To expose himself extensively to political content, a person must search for it and, having found it, exert himself at least to the extent of reading beyond the newspaper headlines or the captions of magazine articles. Even the passive radio listener or televiewer with political concerns has to go to the trouble of remembering to tune in at the right time if he wishes to sift political items out of the flow of information. In the heyday of radio, in 1946, only 13 per cent of the total air time of a sample of members of the National Association of Broadcasters was dedicated to news and comment; another 3 per cent went for "talks."[4] Although newspapers give political news prominent position, it constitutes only a small proportion of the items in the paper; other kinds of items compete for space (more successfully in some papers than others) and for the attention of the reader. Sports contribute the largest proportion of newspaper items, 11.6 per cent in a sample of 130 daily newspapers. Items about national government accounted for 2.8 per cent of the items; politics, 2.5 per cent; social and economic international relations, 1.2 per cent; and political international relations, 1.9 per cent.[5] In many communities the political content of the local daily is so thin that the most persevering quest for political information of any depth is certain to be futile.

Stratification of the Audience of the Mass Media. Though these data on who attends to what in the mass media are sketchy, they suffice to support some observations about the politically significant characteristics of the media audience. They modify the conception of mass man as one upon whom the impulses of the media strike without pity and with-

[3] Kornhauser: *When Labor Votes,* pp. 89–90. These findings suggest also that the mass of people have yet to learn that television reports of events can be doctored. The public-relations men have developed the practice of generously providing TV stations with films on newsworthy events, including political events; such films rarely show the clients to disadvantage. See Maurice Schonfeld: "Seeing Is Not Believing," *The Reporter,* June 25, 1959.

[4] Kenneth Baker: "An Analysis of Radio's Programming," in Paul Lazarsfeld and Frank Stanton: *Communications Research 1948–1949* (New York: Harper; 1949).

[5] Swanson; op. cit.

out defense. The flow of the messages of the mass media is rather like dropping a handful of confetti from the rim of the Grand Canyon with the object of striking a man astride a burro on the canyon floor. In some measure chance determines which messages reach what targets.

Although information is scant on who pays how much attention regularly to what political content of the media, a fruitful way to visualize the audience for political communications is to regard it as stratified. It is stratified according to interest and involvement in politics. The greater the sense of political involvement, the greater the exposure to political communications tends to be. Strata also differ in the types of communications to which they attend. The highly and continuously attentive stratum includes relatively large numbers of magazine readers, book readers, and readers of the quality newspapers. The same group listens in higher proportion to radio and TV programs with a high assay of political content than do other strata. This upper stratum doubtless includes most of the political activists, probably no more than 10 per cent of the population at the most.

At the opposite extreme of the communications audience are those who pay little or no attention to the political content of the flow of communications. The size of this group depends on where one locates the cutting point as he defines the bottom stratum. Almost 10 per cent of a national sample confessed that it had followed the 1956 campaign in none of the major media. For at least a quarter of the population the day-to-day attention to politics must be slight indeed. To the extent that this group is attentive at all, it includes large proportions of persons who rely in high degree upon the radio or the tabloid and tabloid-like press for their information. It includes many persons whose interest in politics is insufficient to bring them to the polls. Their average level of education is low. Obviously the kinds of political communications, as well as the quantities, to which these people expose themselves also differ from those to which the upper 10 per cent devote their attention.

Between these two strata are intermediate strata whose characteristics cannot well be defined for lack of data. They certainly include large proportions of persons who rely on the newspapers as their principal source of political information. They are made up of persons more likely to vote than are those of the bottom stratum and less likely to be active in other ways politically than are members of the top stratum. All of these observations find some support in the relationship between media exposure and political involvement. Those who are highly exposed to the media tend to rank high on the scale of political involvement that has been used at several preceding points; those who rank low in exposure also have on the average a low level of political involvement. Doubtless the relationship works in both ways. Exposure may produce involvement and, in turn, highly involved persons may expose themselves more to the media. (See Table 14.6.)

Doubtless the audience for political communications also varies in size through time. The great regular pulsation in size occurs with the quadrennial presidential campaigns. Other events and episodes may bring huge but temporary enlargements of the political audience; the telecasts of the Kefauver crime investigations and of the Army-McCarthy hearings held the attention of large audiences. The marginal

TABLE 14.6

EXPOSURE TO MEDIA IN RELATION TO LEVELS OF POLITICAL INVOLVEMENT

LEVEL OF
POLITICAL
INVOLVEMENT   MEDIA EXPOSURE

	Low				High
	0	1	2	3	4
High 4	5%	10%	23%	41%	46%
3	13	24	32	30	31
2	33	35	27	21	17
Low 1	49	31	18	8	6
	100%	100%	100%	100%	100%
N	147	335	559	494	228

DATA SOURCE: *Survey Research Center, University of Michigan, 1956.*

or in-and-out audience probably makes up a larger proportion of each subsequent lower stratum of the audience for political communications. Probably the upper 5 or 10 per cent, the most politically attentive, are also the most nearly continuously attentive. Those least intimately connected with the communication system tend to be intermittent in their attention.

When we speak of the stratification of the media audience, one warning must be kept in mind. This stratification is not identical with stratification by occupation, by income, or by social status. While some correlation between exposure to the media and occupational status prevails, the two types of strata are by no means congruent.[6] The independence of the strata of the media from other types of stratification is of such importance for the political order that the point deserves elaboration.

[6] Stratification of the media audience probably more closely parallels what has been treated as political stratification in Chapter 8.

2 · The Flow of Communications

The direct impact of the communications media is fixed by the limits of their audiences and by the selectivity in attention of the members of those audiences. In another way the impact of the media is both enlarged and restricted by the system by which communications flow within the population. People who become best informed through exposure to the media are most frequently found among the politically influential—that is, those who talk with and advise others. By this means the audience of the media may be enlarged; their messages reach indirectly many people who pay no direct attention to the media. By the same token, their impact may be reduced, for the influentials are not neutral relayers of the messages of the media but tend to give their own interpretation to the events of the world as they pass the word along.

The Two-Step Flow. The principal inquiries into the nature of this two-step or multistep flow of communications have been by Paul F. Lazarsfeld, Bernard Berelson, and their associates. In their study of the 1940 presidential election in Erie County, Ohio, they were impressed by the importance of "personal influence" in the determination of the vote in contrast with the supposed influence of the mass media. Those who changed their voting intentions during the campaign mentioned friends or members of their family more frequently as sources of influence than did those who remained steadfast in their voting decision during the campaign. Those who made up their minds late in the campaign reported personal influence as a factor in their decision. People least interested in the campaign relied more on conversation than on the media for their information.[7]

The question naturally arose, who are the influentials, that is, those who seek to convince or advise their friends and acquaintances how to vote? They were persons with relatively high exposure to the media. Those who did not essay the role of the influential ranked friends and relatives with high frequency as their chief sources of information, whereas the influentials relied on the media. Differentiation between

[7] Lazarsfeld, Berelson, and Gaudet: op. cit., ch. 16. Findings impressively demonstrative of the role of personal influence in a state gubernatorial campaign are reported by C. E. Parker: "Polling Problems in State Primary Elections," *Public Opinion Quarterly*, XII (1948–9), 728–31. Indicative of the nature of the personal influence situation is the response of the wife of a Michigan factory worker to the inquiry as to whether there was "anything in particular" about Stevenson that might make her want to vote for him: "Not that I know of. I'm more or less swayed by opinions of other people because I don't know enough about them myself."

the influentials and others were based on two questions: "Have you tried
to convince anyone of your political opinions recently?" and "Has anyone asked your advice about a political question recently?" Persons who
answered "yes" to both questions were labeled "convincers and advisers"; those who answered "yes" to only the first question were called
"convincers"; those who answered "yes" to only the second question
were categorized as "advisers." Presumably those who answered "no"
to both questions included the influenced. These groups of persons
named their chief sources of political information as follows:

	Convincers and Advisers	Convincers	Advisers	Neither
Radio	63.6%	59.6%	54.3%	41.3%
Newspapers	63.6	54.8	42.8	37.5
Magazines	27.2	4.8	8.5	5.6
Friends or relatives	9.1	12.8	22.8	28.8
N	11	84	47	465

Some respondents inconsiderately named more than one "chief source"
of political information; hence the percentages add to more than 100.
Yet the differentials in attention to the media and to personal acquaintances among the groups support the hunch that persons most exposed to
the media may act as transmission belts to carry, perhaps in contami-
nated form, the messages of the media to the inattentive.[8]

Further work in other localities either by Lazarsfeld or under his
inspiration verified and further refined the findings of the Erie County
study. One of the research questions of special interest for politics was
the location in the social structure of the influentials, that is, those who
served as communication relays. In Decatur, Illinois, it was found that
in the realm of public affairs there tended to be more of a downward
flow of communications than in other realms—than, for example, in the
field of fashions, where women sought information from their equals.
Persons who sought advice on public affairs often went to persons of
somewhat higher status.[9] Yet the person who seeks advice or listens
does not depart far from his own status. In Elmira Berelson and his associates found that persons seeking political information tended to talk
with people of their own broad occupational status, but that the opinion leaders tended to come from the better-educated members of their

[8] Elmo C. Wilson: "The Press and Public Opinion in Erie County, Ohio,"
Journalism Quarterly, XVIII (1941), 14–17.

[9] Elihu Katz and Paul F. Lazarsfeld: *Personal Influence* (Glencoe: Free
Press; 1955), p. 330. This volume contains an admirable synthesis of the available
information on the flow of mass communications. See also Elihu Katz: "Communication Research and the Image of Society: Convergence of Two Traditions,"
American Journal of Sociology, LXIV (1960), 435–40.

respective groups. Flow of information and influence tended to be downward through the occupational structure but by small steps.[1]

Consistent with these local studies are data from a 1956 national sample. The respondents were asked whether during the campaign they had talked to people to "try to show them why they should vote for one of the parties or candidates." These "talkers" were fairly widely distributed through the population, but they were especially numerous among those persons most exposed to the media. Almost half of the persons who reported that they had paid some heed to each of the four principal media also said that they had talked to people to persuade them how to vote. Only 9 per cent, as Table 14.7 indicates, of those per-

TABLE 14.7

MEDIA EXPOSURE IN RELATION TO TALKING TO PEOPLE TO PERSUADE THEM TO VOTE FOR ONE OF THE PARTIES OR CANDIDATES [a]

TALKED TO PEOPLE	MEDIA EXPOSURE [b]				
	Low				High
	0	1	2	3	4
Yes	9%	18%	26%	35%	46%
No	91	82	74	65	54
	100%	100%	100%	100%	100%
N	147	335	559	494	228

[a] The question was: "Did you talk to any people and try to show them why they should vote for one of the parties or candidates?"
[b] Media exposure is measured by the number of media to which the respondent reported exposure during the campaign.
DATA SOURCE: *Survey Research Center, University of Michigan, 1956.*

sons who had not followed the campaign in any of the media claimed to have been "talkers." This information tells us nothing, of course, about what kinds of people were the objects of these persuasive conversations. Readers may have talked to readers. Yet the data are also consistent with the supposition that media content to some degree flows through the "constant" readers to other persons, among whom may be included persons who pay less attention to the media.[2]

[1] Berelson *et al.: Voting* (Chicago: University of Chicago Press; 1954), pp. 93–115.
[2] The two-step flow is not limited to one of media to reader to nonreader. Within the communications industry some centers of origination of news receive close attention from other media enterprises. In his study of the Washington correspondent, Leo Rosten found that most correspondents read with diligence the *New York Times* and several other eastern papers and often used their stories as the basis for the reports they wired to their own papers.—*The Washington Correspondents* (New York: Harcourt, Brace; 1937), p. 94.

Another suggestive piece of evidence on the flow of communications comes from Stouffer's study of the opinions on communism of community leaders and of a national cross section. In the summer of 1954 his interviewers asked: "Now, take a different topic which is on some people's minds: the question of whether we're heading toward more unemployment or harder times. On this subject, would you say you get your information mostly from what you read or hear on the air, or mostly from what you hear in conversation with other people?" The contrasts in response between his community leaders and the cross section of the general population were quite marked: [3]

	Community leaders	Cross section
Read or heard on air	64%	48%
Conversations with people	28	45
Don't know	8	7
N	1,500	4,933

This evidence suggests that the differentials in exposure to media that prevail during presidential campaigns also exist at other times and on other aspects of public affairs and, too, that they are associated with the system of flow of intelligence in noncampaign periods as well as during campaigns.

The theory of the multistep flow of communications compels a modification of the conception of the world of mass communications as one in which the communications barons place their imprint directly on helpless mass man. This hypothesis brings the recognition that the flow of mass communications to people is to some degree not direct but occurs in part through the network of personal relationships within society. It might be called a "trickle down" theory of communications flow.[4] From studies of communications generally it is known, as might be suspected, that the network of personal communications does not act as a neutral transmitter but that people "color, amplify, distort, limit, or otherwise change the information as it is passed along."[5] Instead of a pure system of influence by media, the system includes a large element of personal influence. Between the media and at least part of

---

[3] Samuel A. Stouffer: *Communism, Conformity, and Civil Liberties* (New York: Doubleday; 1955), p. 227.

[4] The theory, of course, existed long before modern sociologists discovered it. The late Ellery Sedgwick, editor of the *Atlantic Monthly*, declared: "To inoculate the few who influence the many is the *Atlantic's* perpetual formula." —Quoted by James Playstead Wood: *Magazines in the United States*, 2nd ed. (New York: Ronald; 1956), p. 84.

[5] Melvin L. De Fleur and Otto N. Larsen: *The Flow of Information* (New York: Harper; 1958), p. 264.

their audiences is a human screen that filters and modifies the messages of the media as they are passed on. We lack comprehensive information on the content of this personal flow of information.[6] Nor can we make well-supported appraisals of the place of this flow in the political system, save perhaps that it compels a revision of the romantic estimates of the place of the mass media in the molding of attitudes.[7]

Social Distribution of the Influentials. Once the existence of the multistep flow of communications is established, it becomes important to know the distribution in the social structure of those persons who serve as relay points in that flow. The map of this network of relations in the nation as a whole is sketchy. The essence of the findings of intensive studies in a few localities is that the persons through whom communications flow are not restricted to any occupational stratum or economic level. They are scattered through the occupational hierarchy; collectively, the influentials, the communicators, constitute a category of persons who might be labeled as political activists.

Clues to the nature of the communications network come from studies of the characteristics of persons politically active—at least their findings may be regarded as clues if we make the not implausible assumption that those persons who are politically active tend to be the persons who constitute the communications network for political information. In a 1950 study the late Julian Woodward categorized a national sample according to level of political activity which he measured by frequency of voting, frequency of conversation about public issues, number of memberships in organizations taking stands on public issues, frequency of writing or talking to congressmen or other officials to convey opinions, working for candidates, and contribution of money to political causes. On an index constructed of these items, about 10 per cent of the population placed in the "very active" category. This 10 per cent came from all economic strata. The upper economic levels

[6] Inquiry into the nature and structure of the person-to-person flow of communication has been so limited that it may be worth emphasizing that this system of personal communication may possess an importance and a complexity now scarcely suspected. For example, in small communities and in metropolitan neighborhoods impressionistic observation suggests that a heavy flow of local information often only partly drawn from the media may move through these channels. Even in national campaigns one is astonished by the rapidity of the spread of slanderous yarns by word-of-mouth from coast to coast.

[7] The nature of the two-step flow in an extreme type of situation is suggested by the 1956 comment of a semiskilled California worker with a grade school education: "They (politics) do get complicated, but I try to understand and ask someone if necessary. It's no good trying to read the papers, they use such big words a person can't understand. You have to ask somebody who knows stuff."

contributed a disproportionate share of the "very active," but 54 per cent of them came from the "C" economic level and 10 per cent from the "D" level. The details appear in Table 14.8. These findings, although based on a study with a different object, are consistent with the findings of the local studies by Professor Lazarsfeld and his associates.[8]

The simple test of whether persons talked to others to try to show them why they should vote for a party or a candidate provides a less-

TABLE 14.8

DISTRIBUTION OF POLITICAL-ACTIVITY STRATA AMONG ECONOMIC LEVELS

ECONOMIC LEVEL
OF RESPONDENTS

	Very active	Fairly active	Fairly inactive	Very inactive	Total
A	13%	7%	3%	1%	4%
B	23	15	10	4	10
C	54	59	58	44	52
D	10	19	29	50	33
Not ascertained	*	*	*	1	1
	100%	100%	100%	100%	100%
N	830	1,341	2,772	3,063	8,006

SOURCE: *Special tabulation provided by the late J. L. Woodward. The same data appear in another form in J. L. Woodward and Elmo Roper: "Political Activity of American Citizens,"* American Political Science Review, LXIV *(1950), 872–85. For a description of the differentiations according to level of political activity, see the textual discussion of this table.*

refined index of political activity than Woodward's scale; nevertheless, it also suggests that the persons through whom the messages of the media flow are themselves located throughout the social structure. At each level of education, which serves as an indicator of occupational and economic status, a goodly proportion of "talkers" exists. And within each level of education those more highly exposed to the media tend more frequently to try to show other people the proper political path, as may be seen from Table 14.9. These relations are, of course,

[8] For a discussion of the data, see the article by Woodward cited in Table 14.8, and also Elmo Roper and Louis Harris: "Crime, Reform and the Voter," *Saturday Review of Literature*, April 7, 1951. For related findings, see Ralph H. Smuckler and George M. Belknap: *Leadership and Participation In Urban Political Affairs* (East Lansing: Michigan State University, Government Research Bureau; 1956), ch. 3.

those of campaign time, but they give reason to suppose that the persons participant in the two-step flow of political communication are scattered throughout the social structure.[9]

These findings, based on national samples, convey only a gross impression of the distribution of the politically influential through the social system. They give no vivid picture of the details, which are merely suggested by scattered studies of minute situations. Wilensky, in a study of a UAW local in the 1948 presidential campaign, describes persons

---

TABLE 14.9

EDUCATION AND MEDIA EXPOSURE IN RELATION TO TALKING TO PEOPLE TO PERSUADE THEM TO VOTE FOR ONE OF THE PARTIES OR CANDIDATES [a]

MEDIA EXPOSURE [b]	EDUCATION		
	Grade school	High school	College
High	30%	37%	47%
Medium	25	26	29
Low	11	18	[c]

[a] Entries are percentages of those in each cell who said that they had talked to people to "try to show them why they should vote for one of the parties or candidates."
[b] The exposure levels shown in the earlier tables are here consolidated as follows: 0 and 1 into low; 2, medium; 3 and 4, high.
[c] Too few cases to percentage.
DATA SOURCE: *Survey Research Center, University of Michigan, 1956.*

---

at the lower end of the scale: "Or," he says, "knowing that respondents 10 and 61 are both Negro 'lower-lows' living in the Black belt is not enough, for one memorizes CIO-PAC voting charts in his spare time, the other never heard of their existence and is not quite sure what union he belongs to, anyway." [1] Adler and Bobrow describe the foreign-policy influentials at the other end of the scale in a Chicago suburb. These influentials read the *New York Times* and the *London Economist*. When they want to influence public opinion, they find a "ready

---

[9] The percentages of those who said in 1956 that they had talked to others about candidate or party who came from the indicated occupational categories were: professional, 13; business, 16; clerical, 10; skilled, 39; unskilled, 9; farmers, 8; and others, including retired, unemployed, and housewives who were heads of households, 15. Of those who talked to people, 43 per cent had a Democratic party identification; 32 per cent, Republican; and 25 per cent, independent. Probably a goodly number of the Democrats were talking for Eisenhower.

[1] Harold I. Wilensky: "The Labor Vote: A Local Union's Impact on the Political Conduct of Its Members," *Social Forces*, XXXV (1956), 111–20.

rostrum before any number of civic, professional, educational, or political organizations" in their own area or elsewhere.[2]

3 · Group Absorbents of Media Radiation

Still another element in the system of mass communications may either weaken or strengthen the impact of the media. The literary model of the pattern of mass communications erects the lonely individual on the receiving end, a person who seems to be without predispositions of his own and without any support in whatever inclination he might have to resist what he reads or hears. The mass so conceived, as Friedson pointed out, is a myth. Group influences often have a hand in the individual's selection of the messages to which he chooses to attend. Moreover, as Friedson puts it, the "individual participates in an interpersonal grid of spectators who discuss the meaning of past experience with mass communications and the anticipated significance of future experience."[3] A mass audience exists, to be sure, but it consists of many small audiences; and the tone, norms, and influences of these groups affect both the choice of media messages and the manner of their reception. Consider, for example, the treatment accorded by the men around the mine head to one of their number who indicates anything other than the most profound distrust of the morning newspaper's diatribe against Mr. John L. Lewis. It is almost a law of American politics that group leaders strengthen the loyalties of their followers to the degree that the vigor with which they advocate the common cause makes them objects of attack by or through the mass media.

The idea distills down to the proposition that the mass audience consists of individuals living within and subject to a variety of group influences. The individual's own standards, beliefs, and outlooks are in part a product of his interaction in these groups, both informal and formal. As he is subjected to the play of the messages of the media, he continues to exist within a group context that operates to resist or reinforce the cues culled from the communications flow. These group influences may affect the choice of media, or they may affect the interpretations placed on the content of the media. The messages of the media do not strike the isolated and atomistic individual; they strike, if they reach

[2] Kenneth P. Adler and Davis Bobrow: "Interest and Influence in Foreign Affairs," *Public Opinion Quarterly*, XX (1956), 89–101. In another community, "Revere," Robert K. Merton finds a differentiation between the "locals" and the "cosmopolitans." Locals read the local press and focus their attention on "Revere." The cosmopolitans read the magazines and center their interest on national and international affairs.—"Patterns of Influence," in Lazarsfeld and Stanton: op. cit.

[3] Eliot Friedson: "Communications Research and the Concept of the Mass," *American Sociological Review*, XVIII (1953), 313–17.

their target at all, an individual living in a network of personal relationships that affect his outlook toward the objects of the external world, including the mass media.

Small Scale Studies of Groups and Communications. The most casual observation makes it plain that in large measure mass communications reach individuals who are not isolated but are ensconced in protective group cocoons. Yet to estimate the significance of this phenomenon in the total system of mass communications is hazardous. We can scarcely know what proportions of what kinds of political content reach what proportions of the population with what kinds of beliefs reinforced by what sorts of group influences. The kinds, if not the magnitudes, of the effects of communications reception under group conditions can be specified. For some people and for some communications, group influence reinforces the effects of the propaganda, which may lend legitimacy to the group norms. A sense of the fundamental soundness of their views percolates through the consciousness of the gentlemen around the bridge table in the bankers' club as they remark on the keen insights in the most recent editorial by David Lawrence. In other types of situations group phenomena operate to discount, to rebut, or even to screen out the messages of the mass media. The best guess may be that in the total social system, given the dominant tone and content of the American mass media, group forces on balance provide a net resistance to those messages of the media calculated to alter attitudes and a net reinforcement of messages calculated to maintain the status quo.

Such estimates of the magnitudes of group absorption and reinforcement of the impact of the media are conjectural; nevertheless, studies of small situations support observations about the kinds of effects of the interposition of groups in the communication process. For example, it could scarcely be doubted that the characteristic content of the American press, both in editorial and news columns, has long conveyed a mood or tone of hostility toward the political activities of labor unions. Yet study after study has demonstrated that those persons most active in and most attached to the unions are those most disposed to follow the unions' political line as they perceive it. Those least attached to unions and presumably less under the group influence are less consistent in their adherence to the union line (and more disposed to follow the media). Group loyalties and group norms thus provide defenses against the hostility of the mass media.[4]

[4] See Angus Campbell, Philip E. Converse, Warren E. Miller, and Donald E. Stokes: *The American Voter* (New York: Wiley; 1960), ch. 12.

Related laboratory evidence suggests that salience of group membership probably has a bearing on the capacity of group-anchored attitudes to resist change. For example, a Roman Catholic markedly conscious of his Catholicism would show more resistance to the advocacy of a policy promotive of birth control than would a person scarcely aware that he was a Catholic.[5] Other experimental work concludes that persons exposed to propaganda contrary to their beliefs who have been given opportunity to discuss the matter after exposure tend to listen to those persons who agree with them. The hypothesis is "that participation in free group discussion tends to counteract the influence of the communication."[6]

Easy acceptance of all these findings could convince one that political attitudes are frozen beyond alteration by their encasement in the protective cloak of the group. But the group may reinforce as well as counteract the exhortations of the media. Lazarsfeld and Merton comment on the spectacular propagandistic success of Father Coughlin, a radio spellbinder of the 1930's. They attribute the effects of his radio talks to supplementation by a system of local groups whose members gathered to listen to Coughlin and then discussed among themselves his message of "social justice." The same network of local organizations served as a channel for the distribution of the newspapers and pamphlets of the Coughlin movement.[7] Another study, in another realm, provides parallel and consistent findings. In the flow of personal communications, Menzel and Katz suggest, a factor in the effect of communications is an individual's integration in a group. "An individual is ordinarily reluctant to depart from the norms of his particular group, unless the departure itself receives some form of group support, and a communication aimed at influencing his thoughts or actions may therefore fail. When changes occur, it is usually only when the individual perceives that his group approves, or that support comes from a dissident sub-group, or from an outside group toward which the individual sees himself moving or whose presumed standards he accepts."[8]

Such findings lead to the question of just what mechanism sets changes in motion. One small study is not a sufficient foundation for a general theory, but Lipset's analysis of the rise of the Canadian Co-

[5] Harold H. Kelley: "Salience of Membership and Resistance to Change of Group-Anchored Attitudes," *Human Relations*, VIII (1955), 275–89.

[6] May Brodbeck: "The Role of Small Groups in Mediating the Effects of Propaganda," *Journal of Abnormal and Social Psychology*, LII (1956), 166–70.

[7] P. F. Lazarsfeld and R. K. Merton, "Mass Communication, Popular Taste and Organized Social Action," in Lyman Bryson, ed.: *The Communication of Ideas* (New York: Harper; 1948), p. 115.

[8] H. Menzel and E. Katz: "Social Relations and Innovation in the Medical Profession: The Epidemiology of a New Drug," *Public Opinion Quarterly*, XIX (1955–6), 339–52.

operative Commonwealth Federation is suggestive. He traces the motive power for this movement to individuals who were most group-integrated—that is, the local leaders of farm organizations and of trade unions in Saskatchewan. These persons, as they saw that the traditional methods no longer sufficed, changed their attitudes first; others followed along. "Their position made it incumbent on them to make decisions and set new patterns for the rest of the class." [9]

Estimates and Caveats. This attempt to place mass media in the context of the political system provides us with estimates, if not of their influence, of limitations on their impact. Those limitations are fixed broadly by the choices made by those who constitute the potential total audience of the mass media. People may choose to attend or not to attend to the media. They may choose among the media. And they may choose among the messages of any particular medium. In all these choices they may avoid to a considerable extent messages contradictory of their current beliefs and attitudes. Perhaps the most striking general finding is the extent to which people exclude themselves from the media audience or belong to it only in a marginal way.

Mass communications strike another buffer in the system of personal flow of communications. Inquiries, by no means as comprehensive as we should like, establish that a considerable volume of communications flows, not directly from the media to the ultimate consumer, but through chains of personal relationships. Those persons who function as relays in such chains may transmit or not transmit to others the tidings they gather from their own more extensive exposure to the media. If and when they do so, they may color the news of events and actions with their personal predilections.

An additional absorber of the impact of the media consists in the group anchorage of opinions. Group influences within which the individual lives may counteract or reinforce the messages of the media. Insofar as they are advocates of innovation and change of attitude, the media probably on balance encounter more friction than they do support in the vast miscellany of groups, formal and informal, that crisscross the population. Yet, as advocates of the status quo, the media may find reinforcement for their messages as they come to rest in congenial group settings. The status-quo attitude may, of course, differ in meaning from person to person as the orientation of the group environment differs.[1]

[9] S. M. Lipset: "Leadership and Social Movements," in A. W. Gouldner, ed.: *Studies in Leadership* (New York: Harper; 1950), 342–62.

[1] A thoughtful and comprehensive synthesis of studies of communications is Joseph T. Klapper: *The Effects of Mass Communications* (Glencoe: Free Press; 1960).

15

MEDIA: STRUCTURE
AND IMPACT

ESPITE the stratagems by which people screen themselves from the flow of communications, it must not be deduced that
the media lack influence. On the contrary, the system of mass communications certainly has import for the political system, both in its role
as a neutral transmitter of intelligence of political relevance and as an
independent source of outlook toward politics. In the appraisal of this
influence two broad problems confront us: to identify types of effects
of mass communications on opinions and to estimate the function of
those effects in the political system as a whole. The preceding chapter
centered on limitations on the power of the media, a matter not often
given as prominent recognition as it deserves. The object here is to
move toward an estimate of the kinds of positive influence that may
be attributed to the mass media.

1 · Economic Organization and Position

In the estimation of the place of the media in the political system, the
most important single fact may be that the units of the communications

industries are relatively small enterprises whose economic posture during the past half-century has largely been defensive. That fact has its consequences in several directions for the performance of the media. The struggle for survival within those industries results in forms of organization—for example, local press monopolies and chain newspapers —that fundamentally condition communications enterprises in the performance of their political function. Competition among types of media, as well as the small size of individual enterprises, weakens the communication industries as a whole in their position vis-a-vis other, often more powerful, centers in society. There are exceptions to these broad propositions; some publishing concerns, for example, have been built into minor empires—often over the wreckage of other publishing enterprises. Yet by and large communications firms have lived a precarious economic existence, often threatened by bankruptcy from competition of their own kind or from newer media of communication.

Trends in Newspaper Organization. Approximately 1,750 daily, English-language newspapers are published in the United States. They reach about four of every five adult Americans and constitute a major means for the communication of political intelligence to the electorate, as well as a means for the amusement and enlightenment of the people. The manner in which the newspapers perform their function of political communication is conditioned by their economic circumstances. While newspaper publishing has always been economically hazardous,[1] during the past half-century the industry has been beset by new and pervasive economic risks. Publishing has become a mature, if not a stagnant, industry. Aggregate circulation now grows, not by the discovery and development of new markets, but only gradually with the increase in adult population.[2] Instead of being animated by the optimism of an expanding industry, newspaper publishers have for decades been preoccupied with the problem of survival. The intensity of competition for both readers and advertisers and the vagaries of the costs of newspaper production have driven hundreds of newspapers to the wall.

For politics, a major consequence of the vicissitudes of newspaper publishing has been the growth in the number of cities dominated by newspaper monopolies. As bankruptcies, mergers, and liquidations have taken their toll, more and more people have become dependent on a

[1] A vivid impression of the rapidity and frequency of the rise and decline of newspapers through the history of American journalism may be gleaned from Frank Luther Mott: *American Journalism: A History of Newspapers in the United States through 260 Years,* rev. ed. (New York: Macmillan; 1950).

[2] Wilbur Peterson: "Is Daily Circulation Keeping Pace with the Nation's Growth?" *Journalism Quarterly,* XXXVI (1959), 12–22.

single publisher for their picture of the political world. The number of daily newspapers in the United States reached a peak in 1909, when 2,600 dailies were published.[3] By 1955 this number had declined by more than one fourth, to 1,785.[4] And the end is not in sight as additional papers fold, merge, or seek the infusion of new capital from men of means who wish to engage in the expensive hobby of publishing marginal newspapers. One-ownership towns—that is, towns with either a single newspaper or newspapers under common ownership—have become the rule. In 1920 42 per cent of the cities with daily newspapers had competing dailies; in 1950, less than 10 per cent.[5] Monopoly occurs far more frequently in smaller cities. In 1955 only two of the 25 cities of over 400,000 were monopoly cities.[6] Thus, though 90 per cent of the cities may be ministered to by only a single newspaper publisher, more than 10 per cent of all newspaper readers may choose between competing local dailies.

Some newspaper publishers contend that the security of local monopoly frees them of economic anxiety and permits them to devote their efforts to the fulfillment of the glorious traditions of the press. An analysis of thirteen pairs of newspapers in competitive and noncompetitive cities by friendly critics concludes that the evidence does not "support the contention of single-ownership advocates that these papers *as a class* have been taking advantage of their more favorable economic position to improve their news, editorial, and feature content." [7] Whether monopolistic publishers strive for a protective colorlessness or seek to maximize their power, the disappearance of competition fundamentally alters the influences bearing upon publishers.

As the number of newspapers declined, the proportion of papers included in chains increased. The Hearst and Scripps-Howard chains achieved the greatest size though many smaller chains were put together. This process of consolidation occurred with rapidity following World War I. If a chain is defined as two or more papers under com-

---

[3] Raymond B. Nixon: "Concentration and Absenteeism in Daily Newspaper Ownership," *Journalism Quarterly*, XXII (1945), 97–114.

[4] Raymond B. Nixon: "Trends in Daily Newspaper Ownership Since 1945," *Journalism Quarterly*, XXXI (1945), 3–14.

[5] Alfred McClung Lee: "Freedom of the Press: Services of a Catch Phrase," in G. P. Murdock, ed.: *Studies in the Science of Society* (New Haven: Yale University Press; 1937) and *The Daily Newspaper in America* (New York: Macmillan; 1937).

[6] Raymond B. Nixon and Robert L. Jones: "The Content of Non-Competitive vs. Competitive Newspapers," *Journalism Quarterly*, XXXIII (1956), 299–314.

[7] *Ibid.*, p. 312. The local news monopoly is not a complete blackout; political intelligence flows into the community through magazines, radio, TV, and out-of-town papers. Even so, a considerable range of purely local information may be screened from the local population.

mon financial control, 8 per cent of the dailies were chain papers in 1923 and 17 per cent in 1935. Chain dailies accounted for 31 per cent of the circulation in 1923 and for 42 per cent in 1935.[8] Perhaps the urge for economic survival has had some bearing on the growth of newspaper chains, but it is doubtful that chain newspapers enjoy great economic advantage. They can pool some editorial costs, but the major costs, manufacture and distribution, remain unaffected by consolidation.[9] Whatever the economic effects of chain organization, it fundamentally conditions the performance of the publishing function. A locally owned newspaper may be, if not the authentic voice of Smithville, the voice of a man of consequence in Smithville. Convert it into a chain paper, and it becomes an outlet for a viewpoint piped into town from corporate headquarters. Observers of the American newspaper scene can point to few, if any, examples of great newspapers built by the salaried viceroys of absentee corporations.

A feature of the newspaper industry with a major influence on the character of the press is the organization for the collection and distribution of news. The collection of any major portion of the news it publishes is beyond the resources of any save the largest newspaper. To spread the cost some type of joint service is essential. The Associated Press, a nonprofit, cooperative, membership association, serves that function for its members through its own staff and by the exchange of news originating with member papers. Though the AP took its present organizational form in 1900, it was the product of a long experience in local and regional cooperative news gathering.[1] The magnitude of the AP operation is suggested by the size of its budget—around $36,000,-000 in 1960. Early restrictions on admission to AP membership encouraged the development of competing news services. The chief surviving commercial service is the United Press International, a 1958 consolidation of the United Press, founded by E. W. Scripps, and International News Service, once a unit of the Hearst organization.

The news services have to their credit impressive technical achievements in the rapid dissemination of their dispatches to newspapers and broadcasters. Within minutes the news of an event can be spread to every corner of the land; it may not be worth knowing, but it

[8] W. Weinfeld: "The Growth of Daily Newspaper Chains in the United States: 1923, 1926–1935," *Journalism Quarterly*, XII (1936), 357–80.

[9] Both the Scripps-Howard and Hearst chains have had their financial troubles. Even in so prosperous a year as 1959 Hearst Consolidated Publications, Inc. lost $2,400,000 on an operating revenue of $188,000,000. On the other hand, the Newhouse newspapers are said to be highly profitable.

[1] For a brief treatment of the AP background, see Edwin Emery and Henry Ladd Smith: *The Press and America* (New York: Prentice-Hall; 1954), ch. 23.

can quickly be made known.[2] On the other hand, the necessity of serving many masters forces upon the news services the cultivation of a style of reporting that will antagonize no man. "The thriving existence of the Associated Press," its board of directors declares, "guarantees that the public will have access to honest news, free of bias, free of domination by political or economic groups, and free of taint from selfish interests." By the same token the public has access to vast quantities of news that is essentially meaningless.[3]

Radio and TV. The new electronic media, radio and television, supplement and in some respects supplant the press. About 3,400 AM broadcast stations, 750 FM broadcast stations, and 650 television stations together make up a formidable mechanism for the dissemination of entertainment and political intelligence. Yet the major moral to be drawn from their performance is that neither radio nor television has been able to grow into an independent source of political information or interpretation. In the main these new instruments have been brought into the orbit and into the pattern of the older news media; they are, by and large, transmitters rather than originators of political intelligence. As such, radio and television have not become institutions of political influence in their own right. They have now and then a Murrow but they are more likely to have men of mellifluous voice who read the abbreviated news report from the AP or the UPI.

During the 1920's and the 1930's the press jockeyed for position with radio. The principal complaint by the newspapers was that radio station proprietors were thieves; that is, they broadcast news the press had collected at some cost to itself and in which it claimed a property right. Annoyance turned into downright antagonism when the broadcasters began to compete for advertising revenue.[4] In 1933 the newspapers combined to limit radio to two five-minute, unsponsored news broadcasts daily, the material to be furnished by the press. Under the pressure of their newspaper customers, the United Press and Interna-

[2] Among the 1959 news beats claimed by the UPI were the first reports of the birth of Prince Andrew and of the engagement of Princess Margaret. The quick availability over the nation of such information is mightily promotive of the welfare of the Republic.

[3] An incidental consequence of the news services is that the small-town daily, with only a little ingenuity and effort, can be as good a newspaper as many metropolitan newspapers. And some of them are. Thus, by almost any standard the *Ann Arbor News* (circulation 30,000) is as good a newspaper as the *Detroit Free Press* (circulation 460,000).

[4] See Russell J. Hammargren: "The Origin of Press-Radio Conflict," *Journalism Quarterly*, XIII (1936), 91–3. See also Emery and Smith, op. cit., ch. 26.

tional News, which had been selling news reports to radio stations, joined in this program of rationing. This attempt to reduce to a rivulet the flow of news to radio stations invited radio to set up its own news-gathering facilities. Moves in that direction soon forced the press to retreat. Commercial news services made their dispatches available to radio for a price, as did the AP, which later, in 1946, opened its membership to broadcasting stations. The movement of events thus left radio, and later television, largely dependent on the news services for political intelligence, although the radio and TV chains, notably the Columbia Broadcasting System and a few of the larger stations, have developed small news staffs of their own.

The newspapers also accommodated themselves to the new competition by going into radio and television on their own. Newspaper ownership of radio stations had obvious consequences for the communications system. The maintenance of radio as an independent and competing medium would have maximized the opportunity for variety in the presentation of political intelligence. Federal licensing authorities eventually became aware of the error into which they had crept by granting radio licenses to newspapers, but the damage had been done. In 1954 about 18 per cent of the AM radio stations were affiliated with newspapers, as were 32 per cent of the FM stations and about one third of all television stations.[5] In some cities, over 100 in 1941, the only newspaper publisher was associated with the only radio station.

Important for the manner of performance of the political function of the electronic media is the existence of radio and TV networks. Radio networks developed in order to serve the dual purpose of selling national advertising and of providing noteworthy programs for local stations. Affiliation of a station with a network destroyed whatever pretentions it had to existence as an autonomous institution; it merely relayed materials that came in over the wire.[6] While the rise of television did not destroy network radio, the radio networks became far less profitable enterprises.[7] Television, though, made individual stations even more subject to network control than radio stations had been. The cost of producing live television severely limited what individual stations could do in programing. The individual station had to depend on the networks both for programs and for access to national advertising

[5] Harvey J. Levin: "Economies in Cross Channel Affiliation of Media," *Journalism Quarterly*, XXXI (1954), 167–74.

[6] The numbers of stations affiliated with the radio networks in 1959 were: American Broadcasting Company, 298; Columbia Broadcasting System, 198; Mutual Broadcasting System, 445; National Broadcasting Company, 210.

[7] NBC announced in June, 1960, that its radio network was operating in the black for the first time in almost eight years.

revenues. The value of a TV station came to depend in large measure on whether it had a network affiliation.[8]

At several points in the development of the electronic media opportunity arose to create a communication system independent of the press, but these opportunities were muffed. In the early days of AM radio, foresight did not suffice to comprehend the possibility of radio as a communication system in its own right. A substantial number of AM licenses fell into the hands of newspapers. The invention of FM radio provided another chance, but the existing AM stations and the press captured most FM licenses and treated the public to a rebroadcast on FM of the same elevating fare available on AM radio.[9] When television came along, it fell prey in considerable measure to the existing broadcasting licensees.

Magazines. Magazines can, and sometimes do, play a role in political education markedly different from that of the newspaper or the TV. Not pressed to meet the daily deadline and not limited by the newspapers' narrow conception of what is news, they can present political analyses of some depth. Their varied sources of advertising support and their base in national circulation permit them to explore in detail messy political situations that local newspapers prefer to sweep under the rug. Magazines, too, on the whole reach a better-educated audience than do other mass media, a circumstance that permits a higher level of analysis than prevails in newspapers which, through the custom of the trade, dedicate themselves in the main to the "hard news"—that is, the transitory surface phenomena of politics.

The extent to which magazines take advantage of these opportunities varies. The impression is probably correct that during this century politics has been a topic of declining prominence in magazines of general circulation. In the decade or two before World War I popular magazines—such as *McClure's, Everybody's,* and the *American Magazine*—exerted great influence through their political analyses. The *Ladies' Home Journal* conducted a crusade against the abuses of the patent-medicine companies, an endeavor in which *Collier's Weekly* eventually joined. In that era the popular magazines advocated what seemed to be great causes, assaulted the citadels of power, and in general made a useful nuisance of themselves.[1]

[8] See Robert Horton: "The Economic Squeeze on Mass TV," *The Reporter,* April 28, 1960.

[9] See Charles A. Siepmann: *Radio, Television, and Society* (New York: Oxford University Press; 1950), p. 58.

[1] They probably, too, left a constricting heritage for the newsman who, unequipped to cope with the more complex social and political problems of a later

The great crusading magazines have long since died out and new kinds of magazines have come to dominate the mass-circulation field.[2] Of the 7,500 or so periodicals published in the United States, only a few attain a mass circulation, and not all of these few pay much heed to politics.[3] *Reader's Digest*, with its circulation of over 13,000,000 in the United States, leads the pack. The *Digest* will never live in the hearts of men for its advocacy of noble causes, but its great circulation gives wide currency to its political outlook, which is a mixture of low-order muckraking and propaganda leaning usually to the right.

Another relatively new development in the magazine field is the picture magazine. *Life*, established in 1936, had in 1959 a circulation of over 6 million. Dedicated principally to pictorial essays, it has to put most of its political message into its picture captions. *Look*, an imitator of *Life* but with a somewhat higher assay of political content, was established in 1937 and maintains, as a biweekly, a circulation of nearly 6 million. These new magazines vie for position with the older *Saturday Evening Post*, one of the few general magazines of mass circulation that antedate 1920; it has altered its format and fought to maintain its position in the fierce competition for circulation and advertising. While its editorial policy is unabashedly conservative, it deserves more credit than it receives for the quality of its articles on domestic and foreign politics.

The weekly news magazines are another new development in American periodical journalism. Of the mass magazines they are perhaps most significant as sources of political information and outlook. *Time*, founded in 1923 as the first of the weekly news magazines, formed the basis for the Luce publishing empire—*Time, Life, Fortune, Sports Illustrated*, and other miscellaneous enterprises. With a circulation of over 2 million, it conveys a picture of the political world, its critics say, as Henry Luce sees it or as Henry Luce would like it to be. However that may be, *Time* is not bound by notions of objective reporting. Its condensation of the news of the week involves a selectivity dictated by editorial policy, an evaluative tone fixed by the same standard, and often a warped picture of the political world. The world of

---

day, could dream of becoming another Lincoln Steffens. Thereby, he concentrates on cases of petit larceny and largely fails to interpret for his readers the great administrative and political problems of our era.

[2] On American magazines generally, see James Playstead Wood: *Magazines in the United States*, 2nd ed. (New York: Ronald; 1956); Frank Luther Mott: *A History of American Magazines* (Cambridge: Harvard University Press; 1957); and Theodore Peterson: *Magazines in the Twentieth Century* (Urbana: University of Illinois Press; 1956).

[3] *True Story*, with its circulation of about 2,500,000, is a mass magazine but not a major source of political information.

Time is one of black and white; that may be one of the reasons for its great success. *Newsweek*, founded in 1933, has a circulation of over 1 million and is less opinionated than *Time*. *U.S. News and World Report*, published weekly since 1933 but as a continuation of an earlier periodical, devotes considerable space to documents and complete texts.[4]

Doubtless mass periodicals have their importance in the dissemination of political intelligence. If the truth could be known, though, they may be outweighed in that respect by the aggregate performance of the hundreds of magazines of relatively small circulation that cater to specialized audiences. *The New Yorker*, *Harper's*, the *Atlantic*, the *Reporter*, the *New Republic*, the *Nation*, *Foreign Affairs*, and other such journals reach small audiences, but their political content is of a relatively high order and their readers include many of the influentials. Journals that serve professional or occupational groups usually carry the political word on matters of immediate concern to their readers. The *Journal of the American Medical Association*, *Nation's Business*, union periodicals, and hundreds of other such magazines cope with those aspects of government and politics of interest to their readers.

Even a cursory look at the history of the magazines of great general circulation suggests that magazine publishing may be a way to make a fortune but not necessarily the way to establish an immortal institution. Most general magazines of great circulation cannot trace their history back beyond 1920, and few of the giants of the years before 1920 survive. In recent years the mass magazines have been caught up in competitive wars among themselves. Their costs have risen and their share of the advertising dollar has declined as television has grown. Even the greatest magazines have had to apply themselves earnestly to the struggle for maintenance of position.

Economic Circumstances and Political Expectations. This account of the organization and economic circumstances of the communications industries may convey an exaggerated notion of their problems of survival. Yet it cannot be denied that entrepreneurs in these lines have faced appalling uncertainties. Moreover, attention to the economic aspects of the communications industries serves to emphasize the fact that they consist of commercial enterprises, not public service institutions. Their operation is conditioned by their commercial nature. They sell advertising in one form or another, and they bait it principally with

[4] Of interest is a series of three articles on the news magazines by Ben H. Bagdikian, of the *Providence Journal-Bulletin*, in the *New Republic*, February 2, 16, 23, 1959.

entertainment. Only incidentally do they collect and disseminate political intelligence.

Unhappiness about the performance of the media as instruments of political education or as tribunes of the people arises from expectations that are quite unrealistic. It is their accomplishments for the public weal, not their shortcomings, that are astonishing. The press encourages the highest expectations about its performance. Publishers and editors are prone to dwell on the glorious past of the press, the duties and responsibilities associated with freedom of speech, and the great deeds of the heroes of their calling. They embalm noble sentiments in codes of ethics and resolutions commendatory of high purpose. Yet newspaper publishers are essentially people who sell white space on newsprint to advertisers. Many of them are beset by the continuing problem of how much to spend for what to fill the space around the ads to maintain enough paid circulation to make it unnecessary to convert the sheet into a shopping-news throwaway.[5] Other problems, too, vex them: How may they meet the competition for the advertising dollar from local radio and television stations? How may they retain a share of national advertising against the competition of magazines? What can be done to keep the price of newsprint down? And how can they keep both their employees and their stockholders happy? In moments of leisure they can give thought to the emulation of Horace Greeley or of Henry Watterson.[6]

Radio and TV broadcasters have built up expectations of the blessings to flow from electronic communications. Yet they operate under economic conditions that sharply limit their performance, whatever their aspirations may be. The fact that newspapers are sold gives the reader some claim on the publisher. Radio and television programs are electronic throwaways. Whatever function radio and TV stations undertake in the collection and dissemination of political intelligence beyond the transmission of abbreviated reports from the news services is likely to be at their own cost and, moreover, to bring them only grief. Lineal descendants of operators of music halls and peep shows as they are, only moderate expectations should be entertained about the performance of operators of TV and radio stations in the dissemination of

[5] The odds are that a newspaper with pretensions to greatness must accept a relatively low rate of return on its capital. At least some newspapers with a claim to excellence have been operated by men who plowed most of the earnings back into the business to improve facilities and news coverage.

[6] No major technological break-through in the manufacture of newspapers has occurred for about three quarters of a century. Refinements there have been, but no innovation of basic importance has been introduced since the rotary press and linotype. One explanation might be that the limits have been reached; another, more plausible, is that an industry of relatively small units cannot afford the research necessary to discover cost-cutting innovations.

political intelligence. Further, limitations on television, economic and otherwise, are such that no individual television station is likely to flower into the equivalent of, say, a *St. Louis Post-Dispatch*. Television networks might develop for themselves roles of significance as agencies of political interpretation, but the obstacles are formidable.

In addition to all these constrictions, individual communications enterprises—newspapers, radio stations, TV stations—are caught up in a system in which their own role in the origination of media content has been severely limited. They approach the condition of the movie-house proprietor under the old system of block-booking, a practice of full-line forcing by which the producers could compel him to take all or none of a series of films. Proprietors of newspapers and radio-TV stations are, in varying degrees, only processors and disseminators of raw materials that they buy from others. In most newspapers a substantial part of the content comes from the press services, the syndicates, and the press agents. Radio and TV stations rely on the networks, the news services, and the producers of film, tapes, and records.

2 · Discipline of the Media by Marginal Control

Interpreters of the place of the communications system in the structure of political power and of mass attitudes are tempted to paint pictures of shadowy executive committees of the communications industries, each dedicated to making certain that only orthodox and undisturbing political content will flow through the industry channels. A less naive theory of the integration of mass communications with the power system commends itself. This theory recognizes the existence of a looseness in the organization of communications and of a range of autonomy within the elements of the system. The limits of this autonomy are fixed by scattered acts of discipline of individual newspapers, radio or TV stations, or agencies of other media as they go beyond the limits tolerable to those with the capacity to discipline.

The media, operating under such intermittent restraints, must further be placed within the general structure of opinion formation. Public opinion, it has been argued, results to a considerable extent from the interaction of elite and mass. The media may be regarded both as elements of the political elite and as means by which other sectors of the elite propagate their views. In the power struggles within the elite (in part for access to the public) the media are subjected to restraints or controls at the margin. That control does not need to be exercised often, for few newspaper publishers or magnates of the electronic media have burning urges toward political unorthodoxy. Though they may operate with the illusion of freedom and autonomy, when they exceed the limits of what is permissible they are brought to heel. Over the long run, the innate conservatism of the proprietors of the communications industries is reenforced by scattered acts of discipline of individual deviates, which episodes have a wider exemplary impact.[7] Oscar Handlin makes about the same point when he says that the "only accurate way of describing the situation of the mass media is to say they operate within a series of largely negative restraints. There are many things they cannot do. But within the boundaries of what they may do, there is an aimless quality, with no one in a position to establish a positive direction." [8]

Press. Consideration of the political role of the press is often in terms of its treatment of political campaigns in which its bias is usually evident and to some extent discounted by its readers. More significant in relation to the general pattern of political attitude is its orthodoxy on most matters of public policy. Extraordinarily few journals, either daily newspapers or magazines, act as agencies of political criticism. They may dig to find the facts about individual acts of corruption,[9] but the grand problems of the political system by and large escape their critical attention. Perhaps the characteristic outlook of the press was put by Ben Hibbs when he became editor of the *Saturday Evening Post* in 1942: "I believe firmly in the American system—freedom of living—freedom of enterprise. Above all, I believe it is the patriotic duty of the *Post* to help keep alive in the minds of the people that free enterprise literally has made America—that it is the only system under which we can prosper and enjoy the fruits of democracy." [1] Publishers, in short, tend by and large to be bead counters, a respectable endeavor but not one calculated to cope with the practical problems of the here and now.

The bland tone of the press is not the consequence of a powerful and continuing restraint of a fourth estate eager to exercise its prerogatives under the constitutional guarantee of the press. Newspaper and magazine publishers are generally of the conservative classes themselves. Moreover, most of them operate on a thin resource base and cannot afford to assume risks—or to generate anxieties in the minds of their bankers. Pressure does not need to be brought upon them to keep them

---

[7] The broad hypothesis about the nature of the position of the communications industries in the power system resembles that suggested in Chapter 13 with respect to the schools.

[8] "Mass Culture and Mass Media," *Daedalus*, LXXXIX (1960), 325–32.

[9] See Silas Bent: *Newspaper Crusaders* (New York: Whittlesey House, 1939).

[1] Quoted in Wood: op. cit., p. 160.

safe and sane; they are not often bribed or coerced, for they do not have to be. Yet the principle of control of the deviant at the margin applies from time to time as individual papers get out of line. The sources of control include advertisers, those who appear to be able to carry out threats to boycott circulation, and, on occasion, politicians.

To estimate the significance of advertisers in press policy would present a neat problem in the measurement of influence even if all the facts could be known. The reason for the difficulty is simply that advertisers do not need to exercise their power to be influential. Newspapers that depart markedly from the norms of the business community, save in the most exceptional instances, seem to have a way of languishing and dying. Whether their mortality rate is attributable to a reluctance among businessmen to buy advertising space in such papers or simply to poor management, it seems to prevail and serves as a standing warning to all. Advertisers do not have much occasion or motive to concern themselves with the general policies of the press; they tend to be concerned more, when they are concerned at all, about specific editorial policies or about the handling of specific items of news. The electrical utilities have long sought to influence newspaper editorial outlook toward power policy. This leads to such occurrences as an identical editorial in 59 newspapers, the source being a clipsheet circulated by a public relations firm working in the interest of private power companies.[2] The Commission on the Freedom of the Press reported an instance in which the American Press Association placed policy advertising of the United States Steel Corporation in 1,400 small-town newspapers in connection with a strike. The APA wrote to the publishers: ". . . we are counting on you to give them all the support that your good judgment dictates. This is your chance to show the steel people what the rural press can do for them. Go to it, and pave the way for more national advertising." [3]

Circulation boycott or the threat of boycott may influence newspapers on occasion. Probably the most potent threat is in the hands of the ecclesiastics; their quiet words more often result in acceptance of censorship than in boycott. Pressure from politicians may be calculated to affect both circulation and advertising income. In 1951 *Time* ran a

[2] Wilbur Schramm: *Responsibility in Mass Communications* (New York: Harper; 1957), p. 147. The power companies were probably far more active in efforts to suborn the press in the 1920's than they have been more recently. See Federal Trade Commission: *Summary Report . . . on Efforts by Associations and Agencies of Electric and Gas Utilities to Influence Public Opinion* (Sen. Doc. No. 92, pt. 71A, 70th Cong., 1st sess. (1934).

[3] Commission on Freedom of the Press: *A Free and Responsible Press* (Chicago: University of Chicago Press; 1947), pp. 62-3.

story about the late Senator Joseph McCarthy displeasing to him. He wrote to several national advertisers saying: "Time's advertisers make it possible for the Luce chain to send into millions of American homes . . . dishonest, twisted news. . . . Many of those advertisers are militantly anti-Communist and intensely American. When I know they are not aware of the facts and because of that are unknowingly helping to pollute and poison the waterholes of information, I have a duty to bring that to their attention."[4] Pressures from political sources may take the form of the threat of discriminatory taxation—and some publishers regard any taxation as discriminatory.[5] Or politicians with access to the public payroll may reward smaller publishers with sinecures. Thus, in the 1940's in Illinois some $300,000 went to editors and publishers of weekly and semiweekly papers, supporters of the state's Republican regime. Some of these distinguished journalists turned up on the payroll under titles such as "highway department messenger clerk," though others, it should be said, gave the major part of their time to state work.[6]

An imposing catalogue of instances of pressure upon the press and of its response to those pressures could be constructed. It would, however, convey an erroneous impression of the frequency with which pressure has to be brought. The press does not often have to be nudged to mind its political manners. In the long run when the chips are down on the basic issues, the press has to be on the side of its advertisers as a class. It may be able to afford to antagonize this or that individual advertiser, and some papers have greater economic independence than others. Yet in the large the press must maintain the good will of the industrial and mercantile elements of the country.

The Movies. While it is unlikely that many people would pay to see movies dedicated to outright partisan causes, the motion picture has powerful potentialities in the molding of attitudes of political relevance. Dramatization may be far more effective in the shaping of opinions, even in the kindling of political passions, than the learned disquisitions of the editorial pages or the strident speeches of the soapboxers. Moreover, the movie, through the inclination of people to believe what they see, could be a frightening instrument of political humbug-

[4] Schramm: op. cit., p. 152.

[5] Thus, the Supreme Court invalidated a Louisiana law to levy a tax of 2 per cent on the gross receipts of newspapers having a circulation of more than 20,000 a week, alleged to be a law designed to annoy newspapers hostile to Huey Long. —*Grosjean v. American Press Co.*, 297 U.S. 233 (1936).

[6] *New York Times*, April 26, 1949.

gery.[7] That the movies have remained largely sterile politically and have restricted themselves mainly to chronicling the pursuit of girls by boys (or vice versa) is a tribute to the sensitivity of the industry to the exertion of controls at the margin. Only infrequently do moviemakers feel disposed to cinematic essays of social criticism. When they do, they may find themselves charged with communism, pressured by boycotts, haled before congressional investigating committees, and subjected to other indignities. Life, they discover, is far more comfortable if they restrict themselves to safe topics. Pressures on Hollywood at times come from private organizations with the capacity to organize mass boycotts; on other occasions, from within the industry itself; and at times, from government. Boycotts cut movie attendance and income, and congressional committees can subject movie makers to the expense and inconvenience of defending themselves as well as to the annoyance of public harassment.

To police itself (and to protect itself from boycotts) the movie industry has long maintained an organization for the review of movies. This organization has functioned to reinforce the anxieties of men already made nervous by the economic risks of movie production. The following comment by the Production Code Administration in 1937 on the script of *Dead End*, though unusual—perhaps because that type of picture is unusual—suggests the delicacy with which topics with political potential are regarded: [8]

We would like to recommend, in passing, that you be less emphatic throughout, in the photographing of this script, in showing the contrast between conditions of the poor in tenements and those of the rich in apartment houses. Specifically, we recommend you do not show at any time, or at least that you do not emphasize, the presence of filth, or smelly garbage cans, or garbage floating in the river, into which the boys jump for a swim. This recommendation is made under the general heading of good and welfare, because our reaction is that such scenes are likely to give offense.

[7] The episode of the movie industry and the 1934 race of Upton Sinclair for the governorship of California illustrates the potential of the movies. Sinclair, the Democratic nominee, proposed to "End Poverty in California," and the movie industry, disturbed by the implications of the end of poverty, distributed gratis to theaters a series of fabricated newsreels. Hordes of vagrants were pictured entering the state in the hope that they might end their poverty if Sinclair won. These threatening characters, extras on the studio payrolls, were actually photographed on the streets of Los Angeles.—See Leo C. Rosten: *Hollywood* (New York: Harcourt, Brace; 1941), p. 136.

[8] Quoted in Ruth A. Inglis: *Freedom of the Movies* (Chicago: University of Chicago Press; 1947). p. 182.

The congressional investigation has served as an effective instrument for influencing, if not coercing, the movie industry. Moviemakers, like other people, do not enjoy being pilloried before their fellow man, but congressional concern about the content of their product also reminds them that Congress could enact regulatory legislation. Better to knuckle under at the moment than to have to deal with regulatory agencies in perpetuity. In the long series of investigations of communism by congressional committees the movie industry received intermittent attention; a few communists were unearthed, but no convincing evidence turned up that the movies had been converted into a transmission belt for communist doctrines. Shortly before Pearl Harbor the leaders of the movie industry who were haled before a Senate committee dominated by isolationists were accused of making anti-Nazi films. Such episodes led Darryl Zanuck to conclude: "The fear of political reprisal and persecution has been a millstone about the neck of the industry for many years." [9]

A full account of the pressures brought against the movie industry would be voluminous. It would give considerable attention to the Legion of Decency, an organization under Roman Catholic sponsorship formed to advise the faithful what movies are permissible, whose operation is not without its effect on which movies are made. The professional patriots of the American Legion exert themselves to intimidate the industry. All such pressures help keep the movies politically inert. Moreover, the rise of television placed the movie industry in so precarious an economic position that it had no resources to venture on dramas of social significance.

Electronic Media. Dedication by the electronic media of most of their time to light entertainment, as well as their operation under special statutory policies, has placed them in a different position from the

[9] Quoted in Schramm: op. cit., p. 113. The punitive powers of Congress are greater than its power to reward, but the spirit of right-wing congressional attitude toward movies is suggested by the remarks of the Hon. Karl Mundt, of South Dakota, in June, 1959, to his senatorial colleagues. He recommended to them the motion picture, "It Happened to Jane." The Senator had, he said, often criticized left-wing propaganda of the movies, but here was a movie that merited approbation. "It portrays the American free enterprise story. It is the kind of picture which I think, with a little revision, would help sell the American concept of freedom in various areas throughout the world. The motion picture . . . depicts the story of a young widow, played by Doris Day, who is intent on going into the lobster business in a small town in Maine. This delightful story is replete with instances of American ingenuity, stick-to-itiveness, and the portrayal of the American free enterprise process as a great way of life, which all of us should, in every way, seek to perpetuate."—*Congressional Record* (daily ed.), June 12, 1959, p. 9580.

press. Newspapers have behind them a traditional political role, the nonfulfillment of which leaves their proprietors with some sense of guilt. Radio and TV are not moved by any such understanding of an inherited public responsibility. Consequently, control at the margin of an area of autonomy has not often been exerted over radio or TV for lack of provocation.

Though the entertainment content of radio and TV could have a political import, the stranglehold of advertisers over program content has insured that programs with the widest appeal would arouse no controversy, irritate no sensitivity, disturb no gray cell. The fact that advertisers are associated in the public mind with the program as well as with the commercials gives them reason to have anxiety lest the program annoy potential customers. The advertising agencies have functioned as the principal monitors of program content. In the heyday of network radio a small number of agencies handled the radio accounts of the major advertisers and produced the programs.[1] As TV developed, production of programs moved into the hands of the networks and of specialized producers, but the advertising agencies and sponsors maintained close supervision of program content. Radio was said to be unique in that it was "the only medium in which the advertisers prepare the 'reading matter.' "[2] Advertisers may not prepare the TV epics, but fundamentally they control television content, although a degree of independence is maintained by the journalistic wing of television and radio. The broad nature of the position of the advertiser was made clear by the general astonishment that greeted the decision of Standard Oil of New Jersey in 1960 to sponsor "The Play of the Week" and to leave the choice of plays, their content, casting, and production to the professionals.[3]

At its peak radio was heavily dependent upon a comparatively few large advertisers, as television now is. This circumstance can only make media managers extraordinarily sensitive to the wishes, either expressed or deduced, of these advertisers. A pair of episodes in the 1940's suggest the hesitancy of the networks to annoy their principal revenue sources. The Co-operative League of the United States arranged to put on the air "Let's Get Together, Neighbor," a series of programs on co-operative merchandising. On second thought the networks cancelled

[1] Commission on Freedom of the Press: *A Free and Responsible Press* (Chicago: University of Chicago Press; 1947), p. 63.

[2] Llewellyn White: *The American Radio* (Chicago: University of Chicago Press; 1947), p. 4. See also Clifford J. Durr, "Freedom of Speech for Whom?" *Public Opinion Quarterly*, 8 (1944), pp. 391–406.

[3] For a spirited defense of television by Frank Stanton, President of CBS, see "Television in Our Society," *Printers' Ink*, August 14, 1959. Mr. Stanton, it should be said, has earned the reputation as the most responsible leader of the television industry.

the arrangement. They explained to the Federal Communications Commission that the programs should not be aired because they were controversial, proposed a new system of marketing, and would involve solicitations of membership in the league. After the commotion subsided, the networks backed down to some extent but would not permit the league to solicit members. Again, in 1943 the United Auto Workers had considerable difficulty in buying time to advocate a program of postwar reconversion and stabilization. The National Association of Broadcasters had advised its members not to sell time to the UAW.[4] The networks are in an unenviable economic position. They are not completely free to sell their product—air time. If they make their facilities available to those who advocate causes slightly off color politically, they may antagonize their major customers.

Radio and television are also limited by a statutory provision that requires them to give equal time to opposing candidates. The practical effect has been that no candidate is given time because the station would then be under an obligation to extend the same privilege to the candidates of splinter parties. In 1959 quite a stir developed when the Federal Communications Commission interpreted this legislation to require that equal time be given to opposing candidates even in news broadcasts. A mayor who was a candidate for re-election could not be televised in a ribbon-cutting ceremony without creating for other candidates a right to demand equal time. Or splinter-party candidates could demand equal time when the activities of major-party candidates were covered in the newscasts. Congress in 1959 revised the statute to exempt from the equal-time requirement any appearance by a legally qualified candidate on any "bona fide newscast, bona fide news interview, bona fide news documentary, or on-the-spot coverage of bona fide events including political conventions." It did, however, declare that its action did not relieve the broadcaster from the obligation "to afford reasonable opportunity for the discussion of conflicting views on issues of public importance," a statement not completely unequivocal in its import.

As the presidential campaign of 1960 approached, Congress suspended for the campaign of 1960 the equal-time requirement as it applied to Presidential and Vice-Presidential candidates. This action permitted the TV networks to offer to the major parties their facilities for the so-called great debates between Kennedy and Nixon without incurring a responsibility to give equal time to the candidates of minor parties. The networks, with their fear of an opening wedge for general regulation, had opposed proposals that they be required by law to give a specified number of hours of time to each major-party candidate.

[4] White; op. cit., pp. 75–80.

Statutory and administrative pressures on networks and broadcasters are supplemented by informal pressures. The President can, for example, demand and obtain coverage of his speeches by all networks, at least for major speeches when he is not patently engaged in campaigning for re-election. Broadcasters, as holders of licenses subject to periodic renewal, are sensitive to the wishes of those who control the federal government. They further are susceptible to coercion by individual politicians. Senate investigations and threats of investigation are said to have been motivated by senatorial ire about network documentaries and news comment. Life is much more serene for a station operator or a network executive if he pursues an innocuous policy calculated to antagonize no Senator of importance. Broadcasters, too, stand in fear if not in awe of the Federal Communications Commission, a body that has often been controlled by a fairly contemptible set of men. Even so, it can cause anxiety when licenses are up for renewal.

The fact that radio and television stations exploit under public grant a limited resource—the broadcast channels—has created a worrisome problem of public policy. Should stations enjoy the freedom of advocacy that goes with freedom of the press, or should they be obliged to see that all points of view are represented in their programing? In its Mayflower decision of 1941, the Federal Communications Commission, in passing upon the renewal of the license of WAAB in Boston, laid down a rule against editorializing by radio stations. In 1949 the FCC modified the Mayflower decision to permit broadcasters to editorialize, provided that they gave ample opportunity for the presentation of conflicting viewpoints. Few stations took advantage of the new ruling to establish "editorial columns." [5] In 1958 the chairman of the FCC, John C. Doerfer, observed that the broadcasters had "not yet approached their potential in developing the art of commenting on the news or local problems." Mr. Doerfer had a capacity for understatement, but TV and radio station owners also may be hesitant to editorialize lest their editorials not please the licensing authorities. Moreover, only a few stations have been willing to make the outlays necessary to support an editorial staff. Enterprises manned by disc jockeys and variety show impressarios are not likely to become opinion leaders.

Media in the Power System. The long development that has defined the place of the media in relation to other centers of influence in the political system has restricted their role. Communication agencies have the potential of great power in a governing system. As newspapers

_____
[5] Roy E. Carter, Jr.: "Radio Editorializing Aboard the 'New Mayflower,'" *Journalism Quarterly*, XXVIII (1951), 469–73.

developed in England, the governing orders recognized that potentiality and sought to annex the power of the press to themselves. Punitive measures were supplemented by subsidies, at times from parties and patrons and at times from the public treasury. The growth of circulation and advertising enabled the press to win independence from the governing circles and to become in effect the avowed voice of "public opinion"—or at least the voice of the upper middle class and an autonomous power in its own right, one to be reckoned with. These tendencies found their most striking expression in the *Times* of London in the first half of the nineteenth century.[6]

Not many editors had to go to jail in the early development of the American press, but they were often assimilated into the governing system through subsidies from party leaders and through the patronage of public printing. As they acquired an economic independence from political subsidy, many of them became great party organs through the beliefs and inclinations of their owners and editors. Gradually even these connections became shadowy, and the press became a Fourth Estate that asserted the dignity of a position of power but found itself, in fact, in a position in which that power remained only a potential or a power that could be exercised only in one direction. In short, one set of masters had been replaced by another. As the press became a commercial interest in its own right and dependent on the greater commercial interests in society, it acquired a freedom from party and government but a freedom that could be exercised chiefly, if at all, in only one direction. The press could serve, in the large, the commercial interests, or it could remain neutral. The liberal interests could not afford to buy the press; the conservative interests did not need to.

The electronic media have never cultivated the illusions of grandeur that the press cherishes as a heritage from its boisterous past. The owners of radio and television stations cannot foregather and revel in oratory acclaiming the glorious battles of their predecessors against the iniquities of tyrants. From the outset, radio and TV proprietors were hucksters and little more.

The position of the media in the power system must be explained, not by some devil theory, but in terms of the consequences of their place in relation to the other elements of the system and the nature of the system itself. The etiquette and understandings of the American political order prescribe a relatively narrow range of freedom for debate and criticism. The position of the media in relation to other elements of the system limits them to only a part of that permissible spectrum of debate. The range of alternatives, for example, offered by the

---

[6] For a lively account of the British press, see Francis Williams: *Dangerous Estate, The Anatomy of Newspapers* (London: Arrow Books; 1959).

political parties and by individual politicians may not be broad, but it is broader than the range of advocacy by the media, which are bound mainly either to a bland neutrality or to an alliance with the commercial sector of society. As innovation in public policy has developed, the media have tended to be cast in defensive roles rather than as innovators or advocates at the evolving edge of public policy.

3 · Impact and Import

Most of the discussion of the media to this point has been in definition of the limits of their place in the political system and in deflation of the more extravagant estimates of their influence. It should not be concluded, though, that the communications media are powerless. When a newspaper editor or a radio commentator wishes, he can ruin almost any man's reputation and make life uncomfortable for him indeed. In some communities the chap who owns both the local daily and the radio station can, at least for a time, determine in large degree what the public may and may not learn about local public affairs. While a lurid catalogue of the crimes of the media against common decency could readily be assembled, these exertions of raw and arbitrary power are exceptional.

Appraisal of the place of the media in the national political system should perhaps be in terms of role rather than of power. The press, for example, claims to hold up a mirror by which its readers can see the world. The problem of the role of the media in the political process resolves itself in part to the estimation of the distortions and biases introduced by the media into their picture of the world and to the estimation of the consequences for political behavior and attitudes. What phases of the political world are reflected in the mirror? Which phases are suppressed or ignored? How are the realities warped? Beyond the function of the management of the mirrors through which the world is seen, the press at least also views itself in the role of advocate and counselor. In the expression of editorial judgment the press plays a different role than it does as it holds a mirror to the world. When we examine the broad role of communications in the political system, we raise questions difficult to handle. A leading student of the topic suggests that "the chief discovery of field studies of the effects of mass communications is that it is exceedingly difficult to identify such effects." [7] Nevertheless, some propositions about the role of the media in the political system have a degree of plausibility.

[7] Raymond A. Bauer: "Comments," *Public Opinion Quarterly*, XXIII (1959), 15.

From Cue-Giver to Common Carrier. Probably the trends of the past half-century or so have altered radically the political role of the press. Those changes are epitomized, and exaggerated, by the suggestion that the press has moved from the role of cue-giver toward that of common carrier. The old-fashioned partisan press served as political philosopher and guide for its devoted readers; the modern newspaper purports to report objectively the news about the political world. To the extent that this has been the trend, it alters the character of the content of the press and probably also its political role.

Skepticism may greet the suggestion that the press has moved toward the role of a common carrier. Content studies have established that newspapers tend to favor in the news columns the candidates they support editorially. Their candidate receives more space, and stories about him are often given more prominent display. In presidential campaigns the advantage has gone to Republican presidential candidates, since most of the press, despite claims to independence, leans toward the Republicans.[8] At times the bias, to be sure, is scandalous in its disingenuity, and the activities of some local candidates may be even completely blacked out. Thus, in a 1956 Michigan congressional race, the daily in the home town of a Democratic candidate "printed not a single news story about that candidate."[9] Yet, save for the few remaining avowed partisan journals, the ascertainment of bias in the treatment of presidential campaigns has come to be a matter to be determined by content analysts who measure column-inches, count frequencies of appearance of news stories in positions of prominence on the front page and back in among the classified ads, assign weights to all these factors, and produce an index of bias. The genuine partisan press could be identified without a ruler, a calculator, and a Ph.D. In the campaign of 1896, Batlin finds, the *San Francisco Call* printed 1,075 column-inches of pictures in coverage of the McKinley-Hobart campaign and only 11 inches about the Bryan-Sewall campaign.[1]

Responses of publishers to charges of bias indicate that their own conceptions of their roles have changed. In the day of the honest partisan press, neither publishers nor readers expected impartiality.[2] Nowa-

[8] See, for example, Nathan B. Blumberg: *One-Party Press?* (Lincoln: University of Nebraska Press; 1954); Charles E. Higbie: "Wisconsin Dailies in the 1952 Campaign: Space vs. Display," *Journalism Quarterly*, XXXI (1954), 56–60; Sidney Kobre: "How Florida Dailies Handled the 1952 Presidential Campaign," *Journalism Quarterly*, XXX (1953), 163–9; Ralph M. Goldman: "How Republican Is the Press?" *New Republic*, September 15, 1952.

[9] Douglas Kelley: "Press Coverage of Two Michigan Congressional Elections," *Journalism Quarterly*, XXXV (1958), 447–9.

[1] Robert Batlin: "San Francisco Newspapers' Campaign Coverage: 1895, 1952," *Journalism Quarterly*, XXXI (1954), 297–303.

[2] See William Preston Beazell: "The Party Flag Comes Down," *Atlantic Monthly*, March, 1931.

days when charges of bias are made, publishers challenge them in expressions of pained innocence but withal recognize an obligation to fairness of news treatment in campaigns. They measure column-inches themselves to prove that they are meeting the obligations of a common carrier, and on occasion they bring their practices more nearly into accord with the canon of impartiality in the news.

The manner of the press in reporting presidential campaigns is only an aspect, though an important one, of the relation of the press to public opinion. One gains the impression, too, that in the day-to-day reporting of political events the tendency toward the role of common carrier has altered the function of the press. In the outright partisan press the devoted reader was usually told what the news meant; he could read the correspondence from Washington and the state capital and provide himself with an interpretation of the world that made sense in the light of his partisan predispositions. The assumption on which modern reporting rests is that the reader should be given the "facts" so that he can then decide for himself what they mean. "The facts" usually mean what the public figure interviewed tells a reporter or what he hands the reporter in a mimeographed press release. Objective reporting denies to the correspondent the privileges of the old-time partisan reporter, who would have interpolated comments on the interviewee's reputation for veracity, his underhanded motives in making this statement, and how it all related to the party battle. The "news" tended to be permeated with partisan interpretation. Even in its most biased reporting of public affairs the modern newspaper makes a show of objectivity and often seeks to achieve its policy ends, not by editorializing directly in the news, but by manipulating the emphasis given to news themes in accord with its policy.[3]

The developments in the economic organization of the press earlier described are conducive to the gradual modification of the press into a common carrier of neutral, and often meaningless, political intelligence. The monopolization of local circulation areas makes it prudent to turn out a product whose content antagonizes few readers. Some monopolistic owners develop common-carrier conceptions of their role, justified in terms both of fairness and of the strategy of maintenance of monopoly. On occasion the conception extends to editorial policy which consists of a mixture of "Afghanistanism" and abdication.

[3] Kimball Young analyzed the attention given themes pro and con on the Marshall Plan in the *New York Times* and the *Chicago Tribune*. The *Tribune* gave far less emphasis to pro themes, such as "Stop Communism," than did the *Times*. The *Times* gave far less attention to anti-themes, such as "Plan is Inflationary," than did the *Tribune*.—"Content Analysis of the Treatment of the Marshall Plan in Certain Representative American Newspapers," *Journal of Social Psychology*, XXXIII (1951), 163–85.

"Afghanistanism" is the practice of speaking with great forthrightness on matters very remote.[4] Abdication may take the form of delegating the job of hardhitting editorial interpretation and even the rough reporting to the columnists.

The effects of monopolization on the tone of the press are reinforced by the dependence of most papers upon the press services for a large proportion of their news. The news services must produce dispatches that will be acceptable to all kinds of publishers. "Objective reporting" serves the purpose admirably. Consequently, newspapers published on the same day from coast to coast convey an almost identical bland and meaningless picture of the political world.

The effects of all these circumstances are compounded by the movement from individual ownership to corporate and chain control of newspapers. Bureaucratized organization for the production of news has in large degree replaced personal journalism.[5] The hired manager, rather than an owner both able and disposed to call his soul his own, comes to occupy the publisher's chair. Now and then a paper acquires a character of its own, but, with time, control comes to be vested in the cautious hands of the trustees of estates or of boards of directors beholden to shareholders. Certainly, not all major newspapers fall under these strictures, but knowledgeable newspapermen do not need more than their ten fingers to count the notable exceptions.

Large research resources would have to be employed to determine even roughly the extent and precise nature of the trends that have been identified only impressionistically. Yet the direction of movement has probably been stated with a crude accuracy. The significant question is what are the consequences for the role of the press in the political system. In the large, the long-term changes in the treatment of political events have converted the press from a giver of cues into a common carrier. When editorial policy, often of a partisan tone, permeated the entire content of the press, the loyal reader had cues of considerable clarity. The partisan press put a degree of order into the confusing world of politics. The modern press tends to convey all its disorder; only the best informed reader who also happens to read one of the best papers can place events into a meaningful scheme. In a sense, the press has moved from the role of actor to that of narrator. As actor it had its beliefs, its likes, and its hates. As narrator it behaves as a specta-

[4] Charles A. Sprague: "The Editor's Job Today," *Journalism Quarterly*, XXIX (1952), 265–70.

[5] Few are the newspapers whose publishers could be described as was the late Robert R. McCormick, of the *Chicago Tribune:* "He not only knows what will sell and how to manage his big business shrewdly; he also knows what he believes and is willing to go to hell for it."—John Bartlow Martin, "Colonel McCormick of the *Tribune*," *Harper's Magazine*, October, 1944.

tor and probably induces in the reader a sense of being a spectator
rather than a participant in events that matter. If events are not fraught
with significance for reporters, readers are likely to be equally unmoved. As objective reporter of events, the press fails the one great
task of interpretation most likely to arm the people with information
on which they could act; that is, the readers never know for certain
which crowd is trying to do what to whom. The identity, motives, and
objectives of the antagonists in politics add up to the basic information
on which popular rule can rest.

Furthermore, the conception of a duty to report the news "objectively" places the press at the mercy of the humbug and the charlatan.
Once the press commits itself to the proposition that its duty is to
transmit a dead-pan account of the sayings of statesmen, it commits itself not to let its readers in on the secret shared by every reporter in
Washington: that the perpetrator of these sayings may be a fraud of
the first magnitude. Such would be "interpretative" reporting or
"editorializing" in the news columns.[6] Long before the late Senator
McCarthy brilliantly demonstrated the proposition, Leo Rosten put
the matter this way: "The American press has few effective techniques
for preventing skillful propagandists from bending the newspapers
to the bow of their own strategy."[7]

This exposition is not to be regarded as a plea for the resuscitation
of the old-time partisan press, which probably never existed in unde-
filed form anyway. Its purpose is, rather, to emphasize that the circumstances, economic and otherwise, as well as the technical customs of
the newspaper trade, profoundly condition the role of the press in the
political system.[8] The picture of the press collectively as the wielder
of great power on its own initiative does not fit the facts. Actually the

[6] For a distinguished editor's comments on the consequences of the prevailing definition of news, see Herbert Brucker: "What's News," *Nieman Reports,*
January, 1960, 5–9.

[7] Leo C. Rosten: "Political Leadership and the Press," in L. D. White, ed.:
The Future of Government in the United States (Chicago: University of Chicago
Press; 1942), p. 98.

[8] These circumstances are reinforced by the standards of qualification for
newspaper personnel. Even yet a substantial strain of belief remains in the newspaper world that ignorance of the lore of economics, of political science, and of
history constitutes a positive advantage for an entrant into the reporting trade.
Critics of newspapers often forget that to turn out daily stories that go even
slightly above the level of, "Senator So-and-so said today . . . ," requires broad
learning to provide a context to give meaning to the events of the day and an
unusual command of the art of English composition. Newspapers, like most comparatively small enterprises, cannot afford—as can, say, General Electric—to do
effective training on the job. And it can scarcely be said that the schools of
journalism equip their graduates for anything more than the most routine tasks.
The marvel is not that the level of political reporting is so low; it is that so many
men of skill in political interpretation develop.

press tends to be buffeted about by other elements in society and hamstrung by the limitations of its own conception of its role, as well as by its obligations to other elements in society.

To regard the media as approaching the status of common carriers may be to identify some important aspects of their function in the American political system. To specify the characteristics of that function is not simple, and to demonstrate the correctness of such specifications would be far from simple. Yet the peculiar American role of the mass media may be reflected in the uniformity of their content, in the relative ease of access to the public through the media for those who operate within the rules of the game, and in the generality of the audiences of the media. Over the long run, the communication of a fairly uniform picture of the political world to all classes and kinds of people—in contrast with a specialization of mass media by religion, by party, by section, or by some other fractionalization of the population —may contribute to the political homogenization of the American people. Or perhaps the process provides many people with a common conception of the political world. The so-called American consensus may have its foundations partially in the characteristics of the American media. In turn, ready access to the public through the general media may facilitate feedback of sentiments to government as well as communication among diverse elements of the political elite. The significance of the common-carrier function becomes most clear in the electronic media. The availability of their channels for a price enables some of those interests in society that do not enjoy the favor of the press to obtain direct access to the public. In the hands of a Franklin D. Roosevelt, for example, the radio became a counterpoise to the press.[9]

Reinforcement of the Status Quo. If the broad thesis of the preceding paragraphs contains a strain of validity, the question of the power of the managers of the media becomes in a sense the wrong question. To the extent that the media have become common carriers, their managers should no more be held accountable for the materials that flow through their channels than should managers of transportation concerns be blamed for the quality of the printed matter they transport from place to place. The tone and quality of the content of the media tend to be mightily influenced, if not fixed, by those who manufacture news and by those who fix the nature of other politically relevant content available for the media. And in the choice of what they shall

[9] For reflective observations on the function of communications, see Gabriel Almond in G. Almond and J. Coleman: *The Politics of the Developing Areas* (Princeton: Princeton University Press; 1960), ch. 1.

"transport," the managers of the media operate within the field of those influences that condition their commercial survival.

Without the benefit of the findings of any large-scale analysis of the content of the media, it is safe to conclude that the major influence of the media upon political attitudes is by and large a reinforcement of the status quo. A comprehensive measurement of the content of the press or of TV and radio broadcasts would doubtless confirm the casual impression that the media contain only the slightest trace of content in advocacy of alteration of the political order. The content rather tends to reaffirm existing values, to buttress prevailing institutions, and to support ancient ways of doing things. Advocacy, to be sure, creeps even into the news columns, but it is fair to say that, on the whole, that advocacy has either a tone of nostalgia for the good old days or a tinge of bitterness toward innovations that have occurred over the objections of a wise and enlightened Fourth Estate.

The reinforcement effect of the media in the social system is magnified by the fact that for practical purposes they function as instruments in a situation of monopoly propaganda. Propaganda has its greatest effect when it is unchallenged, when only a single theme is disseminated. To a remarkable degree the American mass media propagate the same broad political line, a result perhaps to be expected in a political system of the American type. Whatever the explanation, the unity of policy themes in the media doubtless enlarges their reinforcing effects. Evidence from the psychological laboratories supports the proposition that unchallenged presentation, even when false, gains greater acceptance under monopoly conditions than when persons are subjected to competing interpretations. That finding may be projected, to be sure without any supporting data, to the larger society.

Even that substantial proportion of the content of the mass media that is not directly political—entertainment—tends also to reinforce the values of the system and to maintain an indifference to questions that might touch upon controversial matters. The commercial sponsorship of the entertainment content of radio and TV assures that the entertainment will reaffirm the sanctioned values. A soap salesman does not want to annoy any potential soap customers. As Klapper concludes, "the entertainment content of mass media in this democracy continually reaffirms sanctioned attitudes." [1] Or, as he puts it elsewhere, the need for "holding a massive audience leads the media, particularly in their entertainment fare, to hew to the accepted, and thus to tend to resanctify the sanctified." [2]

[1] Joseph T. Klapper: "Mass Media and the Engineering of Consent," *American Scholar*, XVII (1948), 419–29.

[2] Joseph T. Klapper: "What We Know About the Effects of Mass Communication: The Brink of Hope," *Public Opinion Quarterly*, XXI (1957–8), 453–74.

The media may tend to reinforce the orthodox values; yet a considerable sector of the population has its reservations about some of those values. That sector of the population may have a capacity to resist the messages of the media, and estimates of the strength of that resistance should give us at least a negative appraisal of the significance of the media. Probably a defensible estimate is that parts of the population maintain, at least on some broad political outlooks, an imposing resistance to conversion by the media. The plausibility of that proposition may be suggested by a few illustrations which, if they do not measure the influence of the media, at least suggest that in some areas of attitude not much change occurs despite the rain of messages from the media. Consider the stability of party identification within the total population. If a content analysis of the total flow of mass communications from 1948 to 1958 were available, it would almost certainly show on balance a tone and emphasis anti-Democratic and pro-Republican. From 1952 to 1958 the proportions within the population calling themselves Democrats and Republicans changed scarcely at all. Perhaps the media caused conversions, but they were offset by conversions in the opposite direction.

No convincing measurement of the effects of the media through time on policy attitudes has been attempted. Such data as we can muster are consistent with the supposition that the media affect opinions, but they are also consistent with the supposition that the effects are comparatively small in the total population. A wisp of evidence comes from an analysis of opinion on the question of public policy toward medical and hospital care. Perhaps it would be conceded that the content of the media for the period 1948–56 was on balance hostile toward "socialized medicine," a condition attributable not entirely to the editorial stands of the media but in part to the skill of the opponents in bringing the media to the service of their propaganda. In 1956, though, there remained a substantial sentiment supportive of some type of governmental action in this field. Of the national sample, 44 per cent of those with opinions agreed "strongly" with the proposition: "The government ought to help people get doctors and hospital care at low cost." Another 17 per cent agreed "but not very strongly."

If the media have an effect, it should appear most markedly among those persons most exposed to the media. When opinions are compared with media exposure, it turns out that those persons most exposed include the largest proportions who disagree with the medical-care proposition. These comparisons, shown in Table 15.1, are made within educational levels to eliminate at least some of the other factors that might be expected to bear on opinion. The maximum effects that might be attributed to the media, though, are comparatively small. Thus, of

TABLE 15.1

Media Exposure, within Educational Levels, in Relation to Opinions on Medical Care Issue

OPINION [a]	EDUCATION AND MEDIA EXPOSURE [b]								
	Grade school			High school			College		
	1	*2*	*3*	*1*	*2*	*3*	*1*	*2*	*3*
Agree	65%	67%	76%	51%	52%	53%		40%	32%
Pro-con	4	5	4	10	9	9		8	13
Disagree	9	17	15	21	27	31		40	48
No opinion	22	11	5	18	12	7		12	7
	100%	100%	100%	100%	100%	100%	100%	100%	100%
N	246	158	138	216	314	353	18 [e]	85	227

[a] The question was: "The government ought to help people get doctors and hospital care at low cost."
[b] The three levels of media exposure consisted of persons who said that they had followed the 1956 campaign in the specified number of media: 1, 0–1; 2, 2; 3, 3–4.
[e] Too few cases to percentage.
DATA SOURCE: *Survey Research Center, University of Michigan, 1956.*

the high-school group with high exposure to the media, 31 per cent opposed government action in medical care; of the high-school group with low exposure, 21 per cent opposed. While we should not delude ourselves that we have here a measure of media influence on opinion, we have a trace of evidence that whatever that influence may be it is not great on this issue at least in the short run. The high proportions with no opinion among those with low media exposure may be more convincing evidence of the effects of media on opinion.

A similar analysis of opinion on another question produces similar results but perhaps more persuasive evidence of media influence. On the question of public power there can be no doubt that the media content from 1935 to 1960 consisted predominantly of materials hostile toward public ownership.[3] And the materials specifically on public power were supplemented by a steady drum beating for "free enterprise." The flow of the media for several decades, though, did not suffice to wear away a hard core of support for public power. A 1956 question that mixed power with housing—"The government should leave things like electric power and housing for private businessmen to handle."—drew "strong" disagreement from 21 per cent of the sample with

[3] Part of this content consisted of mendacious advertising by the electric power industry which was but a minute proportion of the media content on the topic and doubtless of insignificant effect. This advertising must be regarded more as a reward for editorial support than as a serious attempt to affect public opinion.

opinions and "not very strong" disagreement from 10 per cent.[4] When these opinions are related to media exposure, those persons more exposed turn out to be more inclined to leave "things like power and housing" to private business, a relationship consistent with the supposition that the media may have influence. The differences associated with media exposure are more marked than on the medical-care question, as inspection of Table 15.2 will make plain. It may be that the media are more effective on a rather abstract proposition of principle such

---

TABLE 15.2

MEDIA EXPOSURE, WITHIN EDUCATIONAL LEVELS, IN RELATION TO OPINIONS ON LEAVING "THINGS LIKE ELECTRIC POWER AND HOUSING" TO PRIVATE BUSINESS [a]

OPINION	EDUCATION AND MEDIA EXPOSURE [b]								
	Grade school			High school			College		
	1	*2*	*3*	*1*	*2*	*3*	*1*	*2*	*3*
Agree	28%	38%	44%	31%	46%	46%		49%	54%
Pro-con	3	10	7	5	8	5		8	10
Disagree	12	19	23	27	25	26		25	24
No opinion	57	33	26	37	21	23		18	12
	100%	100%	100%	100%	100%	100%	100%	100%	100%

[a] The question was: "The government should leave things like electric power and housing for private business men to handle."
[b] The three levels of media exposure consisted of persons who said they had followed the 1956 campaign in the specified number of media: 1, 0–1; 2, 2; 3, 3–4.
[c] Too few cases to percentage.
DATA SOURCE: *Survey Research Center, University of Michigan, 1956.*

---

as the power and housing question than they are on a question such as medical care to which an individual can readily relate his own concerns.[5]

[4] Included in the sample were a few persons associated with REA cooperatives as employees or customers; they were forthright in their views. The soundness of the strategy of private power companies in their hostility to the REA rests probably not on economic grounds, for the REA business is minuscule and often not in profitable territories, but on a psychological basis. The REA creates pockets of adamantine sentiment supportive of public power.

[5] Such data as there are indicate that since the 1930's sentiment supportive of public ownership of power facilities has declined in strength. In 1937, when memories of scandals in the management of utilities and of the battles over the Public Utility Holding Company Act were fresh, slightly over half of the persons polled favored government ownership of electric power companies. With the subsidence of attention to utility questions, public power sentiment declined to 28 per cent in 1946. For reports on a series of surveys on the question, see Hadley Cantril and Mildred Strunk: *Public Opinion, 1935–1946* (Princeton: Princeton University Press; 1951), p. 694. Such trends in sentiment may indicate nothing about the influence of the media; the moral may be that the utilities are in trouble when they deserve to be in trouble.

Short-Term and Long-Term Effects. Determination of the impact of mass communications on attitudes meets almost insurmountable obstacles. Under laboratory conditions, findings of precision regularly emerge about what kinds of communications have what effects on what sorts of people.[6] But information about what happens to real people in the real world of mass communications is thin. This shortage of verified knowledge gives us room for riskless speculation about the effects of the media. The question could be dismissed with the apparently well-founded conclusion that a major effect of the media on the American scene is the reinforcement of the status quo on basic matters. Yet guesses not completely untutored may be made about other effects in the political system. For convenience such guesses may be grouped into those about short-term effects and those about long-term effects.

In the short run the effects of the media probably are greatest on topics for which readers and viewers have only the vaguest internalized norms or standards for independent judgment. On the contrary, over the short run the media might be expected to have relatively less effect on opinions and attitudes about topics on which most people have their own standards of judgment, perhaps buttressed by group norms and pressures. Earlier it was suggested that opinions about personalities probably in special degree lack foundations in norms and standards. Such opinions may be especially dependent on the images conveyed by the media.[7] Thus, the predominantly adulatory and protective role of the media in relation to Eisenhower surely must have contributed to the maintenance of a favorable public image despite mistakes that in the hands of an unsympathetic press could have been used to convert the image of the General into one of ineptitude. The capacity of the media to distort reality is not unlimited, but as they mold the public images of personalities they touch a critical point in the democratic process.[8]

[6] See Carl I. Hovland: "Reconciling Conflicting Results Derived from Experimental and Survey Studies of Attitude Change," *The American Psychologist,* XIV (1959), 8–17, and also "Effects of the Mass Media of Communication," in *Handbook of Social Psychology* (Cambridge: Addison-Wesley, 1945); II, 1062–1103.

[7] For example, in primary elections when voters lack the cue of party identification that is available in general elections, the press may be influential especially on candidates for more obscure offices. See the supportive findings in Harold F. Gosnell and Margaret J. Schmidt: "Relation of the Press to Voting in Chicago," *Journalism Quarterly,* June, 1936, 129–47.

[8] The TV enthusiasts seem to believe that the electronic camera enables voters better to judge persons. Sig Mickelson, of CBS News, thus observes: "Looks, charm, and personality have always been political assets—but, curiously enough, less so today than in the days of the torchlight parade and the monster rally. Why? Because the television camera is merciless and uncanny in the way it can pierce through sham and insincerity. The political pitchman of the past cannot survive the probing camera."—"TV and the Candidate," *Saturday Review,* April 16, 1960. A man must take pride in his trade, but prose so rich in non-

The media may be especially influential in the formation of opinion, at least in the short run, about substantive issues and events which are remote from the experience of people and to the appraisal of which they can bring no applicable general convictions. As Klapper summarizes the knowledge on the point, the media "are quite effective in forming opinions and attitudes in regard to new issues, particularly as these issues are the more unrelated to existing attitude clusters." [9] The never-never world of foreign affairs, a mixture of secrecy and of remote events with meaning only to the relatively well-informed, may be such an area of special media influence.[1] Even in foreign affairs the media may become powerless when events and policies become so clear in their implications that most people are able to bring them within their judgmental capacities. Some of the effects of the media in the field of

---

TABLE 15.3

MEDIA EXPOSURE WITHIN EDUCATIONAL LEVELS, IN RELATION TO POSITION ON INTERNATIONALISM SCALE [a]

INTERNATIONALISM	EDUCATION AND MEDIA EXPOSURE [b]								
	Grade school			High school			College		
	1	*2*	*3*	*1*	*2*	*3*	*1*	*2*	*3*
High	30%	40%	48%	35%	44%	50%		52%	63%
Medium	7	18	21	18	24	27		27	25
Low	18	18	22	16	16	12		14	5
Not scaled [c]	45	24	9	31	16	11		7	7
	100%	100%	100%	100%	100%	100%	100%	100%	100%
N	246	158	138	216	314	227	18	85	227

[a] For construction of the scale, see Appendix II.
[b] The exposure groupings are according to the number of media through which the respondent followed the 1956 campaign: 1, 0–1; 2, 2; 3, 3–4.
[c] Respondents with too few opinions to scale.
DATA SOURCE: *Survey Research Center, University of Michigan, 1956.*

---

sense is scarcely in order after the quiz-show operators demonstrated that even amateur actors could delude tens of millions of TV viewers. The effect of TV is simply to give certain types of frauds access to a larger audience than they could reach in the good old days.

[9] "What We Know About the Effects of Mass Communication: The Brink of Hope," *Public Opinion Quarterly*, XXI (1957–8), p. 462.

[1] Some empirical support for the proposition may be read into the findings of a New York City survey in 1944. Readers of the reactionary-isolationist press of the city tended to follow their newspapers on abstract questions about foreign affairs and domestic policy. However, on specific questions within the range of their experience—unemployment insurance, for example—they remained unmoved by the admonitions of their newspapers.—Gerhart Saenger: "The Press and Public Opinion," *New Republic*, July 31 and August 7, 1944.

foreign policy may be reflected in the data of Table 15.3. With education held constant, as the table indicates, those persons most exposed to
the mass media are most disposed to take an internationalist position.
The scale used to measure this attitude did not necessarily separate people into true-blue isolationists and bleeding "one-worlders." It probably
really measured awareness of the elementary facts of the modern
world; that awareness, given the circumstances, would lead people to
agree with the kinds of propositions included in the scale. And that
awareness apparently increases with exposure to the media.

Speculation about long-run effects of the media raises the question
of whether the suggestions of the media, day after day, year after year,
may not substantially affect people's opinions even on basic issues. The
Hearst press thus enjoys a circulation concentrated among the less-edu-
cated. What can be said of the impact over the long run on the attitudes of its readers of its disposition to see a red under every bed? Or
over the decades, what sort of consequences in outlook toward community problems could be expected among the readers of the *St. Louis
Post-Dispatch* and the *Los Angeles Times* or of the *Louisville Courier-
Journal* and the *Dallas Morning News*, to mention only two pairs of
contrasting journals? Or is the latter day *Denver Post* gradually re-
shaping the basic attitudes of Denverites from whatever form the *Post*
gave them in its gaudier days?

Such a question of long-term effects cannot be analyzed systematically in any satisfactory way. Probably on some matters of basic and
perceptible immediate self-interest the impact of the media may not
be impressively large even over the long run. Thus, there would be no
doubt that since the heyday of the New Deal the content of the media
has been hostile to the idea of government responsibility for assuring
employment. This is not to say that this has been a topic of unremit-
ting attention by the media, but the themes of the merits of individual
self-reliance and of the wickedness of governmental intervention in the
economy recur with frequency. Moreover, insofar as opposing themes
receive attention, they receive principally unfavorable attention. Yet in
1956 about two thirds of a national sample agreed with the proposition:
"The government in Washington ought to see to it that everybody
who wants to work can find a job." That proportion remained about
the same in 1958.

Over the long run the media may have their effects on attitudes
less immediately self-related than are those about the question of job
assurance and perhaps even on questions of that type. Repetition day
after day may have its effects. Small-scale experiments suggest also that
changes of opinion may be greater weeks after exposure to communication than they are immediately after exposure. This delayed change, or

"sleeper effect," seems to be more frequent among the less-well-educated.[2] Experiments also give support to the hypothesis that messages rejected because of their untrustworthy source may be eventually accepted. People tend to forget that information came from a distrusted source; they remember the message and are influenced by it.[3] The unknown is whether some such process operates in the world outside the laboratory on a sufficient scale to affect the direction of mass opinion perceptibly.[4]

The steady flow of the propaganda of the media between elections also probably strikes people at a time when their defenses are less effectively mobilized than they are during presidential campaigns. Probably at campaign time group identifications are most highly activated, the pressures of group norms most effective, and the connection of particular policy outlooks most clearly tied to group interest. In the periods of political relaxation between campaigns these defenses are probably down, confusion and ambiguity meet less challenge, and individuals become more receptive to the messages of the media. At these times people are more likely to be blown about by the winds of the media than when political interest is more completely activitated. Some people, too, may be more susceptible to these influences than others. "The less informed people are on an issue," says Berelson, "the more susceptible they are to opinion conversion through the influence of the communication media." [5]

Relentless repetition of the themes of the media may, even if it does not convert, weaken or modify opinions. That consequence may affect the intensity of opinion; it may also affect the direction of opinion. Again the findings of small-scale studies have a suggestive relevance. When the attitudes of those subjected to experimental propaganda are measured by psychological scales, it may be found that, though the subjects have not been converted to the view of the propagandizer, their attitudes have shifted along the scale toward those views advocated by the experimental communications.[6] Conceivably, such changes of degree may result from the impact of the media over the long run. Of the

[2] Carl I. Hovland *et al.: Experiments in Mass Communication* (Princeton: Princeton University Press; 1949), 273–4.

[3] Carl I. Hovland and Walter Weiss: "The Influence of Source Credibility on Communication Effectiveness," *Public Opinion Quarterly*, XV (1951), 635–50.

[4] Consider the 1956 reply of a Los Angeles registered nurse to the question whether there was anything she liked about the Democratic party: "No. I don't know. It *seems* the Democrats remind me of communists. I know this isn't *true* but it just reminds me of this."

[5] Bernard Berelson: "Communications and Public Opinion," in Wilbur Schram: *Mass Communications* (Urbana: University of Illinois Press; 1949), p. 500.

[6] V. M. Sims: "Factors Influencing Attitude Toward the TVA," *Journal of Abnormal and Social Psychology*, XXXIII (1938), 34–56.

magnitude of such change in the political system as a whole, nothing well-founded can be said.[7]

Diversionary Effects of the Media. In the last half-century the growth in the volume of nonpolitical content carried to people by the new system of mass communications may have diverted people's attention from politics. Television, radio, cinema, magazines, paperback books, and syndication to newspapers of nonpolitical materials have brought new and cheap or even free amusement to the masses. "The political elements in the constitution of the human being," John Dewey noted as early as 1927, "those having to do with citizenship, are crowded to one side." [8] This phenomenon may be what Lazarsfeld and Merton had in mind when they spoke of the "narcotizing dysfunction" of the media, but they added the thought that the sheer volume of information now available might "serve to narcotize rather than to energize the average reader or listener." [9] A vast flow of information may certainly add to the befuddlement of man, especially when the media have themselves in large measure abdicated the function of trying to make sense of the stream of events for their audiences. The long-term decline in voting is consistent with the theory that the diversions of the new mass media have encroached upon politics as a topic of attention and, possibly, as a source of entertainment.[1] Whether mass media are really responsible for this decline in the focus of attention upon politics, it is safe enough to say that politics occupied a relatively larger place in the media in the 1880's than in the 1950's.[2]

[7] Some extreme types of propaganda are doubtless self-defeating. Extravagant right-wing propaganda serves in the American context probably chiefly to satisfy those already saved rather than to convert lost souls. As the distance, measured along a psychological scale, between the position of the propagandist and the objects of propaganda increases, the less likely is the attitude of the objects of the message to be changed, or so some studies indicate.—Carl I. Hovland, O. J. Harvey, and Muzafer Sherif: "Assimilation and Contrast Effects in Reactions to Communication and Attitude Change," *Journal of Abnormal and Social Psychology*, LV (1957), 244–52.

[8] *The Public and Its Problems* (New York: Holt; 1927), p. 139.

[9] P. F. Lazarsfeld and R. K. Merton: "Mass Communication, Popular Taste and Organized Social Action," in Lyman Bryson, ed.: *The Communication of Ideas* (New York: Harper; 1948), p. 105.

[1] Doubtless qualitative changes have also occurred in the nature of the attention given to politics, a topic that has been imaginatively explored in David Riesman: *The Lonely Crowd* (New Haven: Yale University Press, 1950).

[2] Hard data on trends in media content are scarce, but in a study of biographies in popular magazines, Lowenthal found that after 1922 (in contrast with 1901–14) attention to figures from political life had been cut by 40 per cent, while entertainers as subjects of popular biography had gained by 50 per cent. Over the same period business and professional men had also declined in im-

Special Role of the Quality Media. Some sectors of the press, a few magazines and a few daily newspapers, play a special role in the political process, a role of a type not encompassed by our discussions of the media and mass opinion. They dedicate themselves to the provision of large quantities of political information, often in documentary form, and to relatively high level political interpretation. *The New York Times*, the New York *Herald Tribune*, the Washington *Post*, the Baltimore *Sun*, and a few other newspapers command the attention of a highly politicized and very influential audience. The principal actors in national politics can read these papers on the day of publication; all those persons of importance in bureaucratic and political circles are apt to read at least the *Times*. Another layer of activists and influentials scattered over the country are included within the audience of some of the "quality" papers.

These newspapers serve a special function in communication among the major political actors and the lesser activists. These people talk to each other through these papers; thus they provide, in a sense, an arena for the continuing discussion of politics among those principally concerned. The *Times* and the Washington *Post*, in particular, serve as a means for supplementing the internal lines of communication of the sprawling federal establishment. Men in political circles have to read these papers if they are to know what is going on and what is being said in the wider political world of which they are a part. The events the papers choose to report and the manner in which they report them influence a critical and knowledgeable audience composed in part of political actors, who do not remain unaffected by the image of themselves that they see mirrored in the press. The editorial appraisals of the quality press, founded as they often are on far more extensive information than are the ruminations of most of the press with less adequate independent sources of Washington information, are likely to gain a special attention in governmental and near-governmental circles. In these and other related ways the quality press plays a role among the influentials quite unlike that commonly attributed to the media in their relation to the mass of the people. This role has led Cater to dub the press "the fourth branch of government," a characterization that involves a degree of exaggeration but which gives recognition to the differentiated role of at least a small part of the press.[3]

---

portance as the subject of popular magazine biography. See Leo Lowenthal: "Biographies in Popular Magazines," in Lazarsfeld and Stanton, *Radio Research, 1942–1943* (New York: Duell, Sloan and Pearce; 1944).

[3] Douglass Cater: *The Fourth Branch of Government* (Boston: Houghton Mifflin; 1959).

Part V

LINKAGE

THE PRECEDING

analyses make it evident that in dealing with public opinion we are attempting to cope with a set of elusive problems. Yet in some ways the questions that have been dealt with are comparatively easy to manage. The shapes of opinion distributions can be described with some assurance. The distribution of opinions within the social structure emerges from simple analytical procedures. Analysis of opinion properties encounters obstacles, but some sense can be made of even these nebulous factors. As we labored with the processes of opinion formation we were on firmer ground, although many of their aspects remained unilluminated.

The problems in dealing with all these questions, though obdurate, seem relatively simple alongside the riddles encountered in the attempt to identify the linkages between public opinion and governmental action. At points through the preceding chapters advantage has been taken of opportunities to suggest plausible consequences for governmental behavior of particular aspects of public opinion. Yet when one approaches systematically the broad question of the interaction between government and opinion, he soon recognizes that the phenomenon cannot be broken into neat pieces and nicely tabulated to produce persuasive two-way tables indicative of the interconnections between mass opinion and public decision.

At the outset one must discard simplistic conceptions, such as the notion that in some way public opinion exudes from the mass of men and produces guide lines for governmental action. A complex interaction occurs, with government (and other centers of influence as well) affecting the form and content of opinion; and, in turn, public opinion may condition the manner, content, and timing of public action. Again, opinion may be of no effect, for many public actions seem to be beyond popular concern or influence. Systematic analysis of these relations is complicated by the fact that they are restricted to no clear and rigid channels or patterns. Yet some of the relations between opinion and government are institutionalized. The chief burden of the chapters that follow will be an examination of these formalized means for give and take between government and opinion: elections, political parties, pressure groups, and representative procedures.

16

LINKAGE: GENERAL CONSIDERATIONS

DISCUSSION of public opinion often loses persuasiveness as it deals with the crucial question of how public opinion and governmental action are linked. The democratic theorist founds his doctrines on the assumption that an interplay occurs between mass opinion and government. When he seeks to delineate that interaction and to demonstrate the precise bearing of the opinions of private citizens on official decision, he encounters almost insurmountable obstacles. In despair he may conclude that the supposition that public opinion enjoys weight in public decision is myth and nothing more, albeit a myth that strengthens a regime so long as people believe it.

That governments pay heed to public opinion is, of course, more than a myth. Even a dictatorial regime cannot remain oblivious to mass opinion. In the analysis of the interaction between government and opinion, though, we have an odd reversal of the problem of the forest and the trees. The forest is more visible than the trees. The broad concern of a popular government for mass opinion appears in stark relief, especially when governments are viewed comparatively. The trees are not so readily seen. In the determination of the relation of opinion to specific governmental actions, the analytical problem becomes sticky. Doubtless the difficulty comes in part from the tacit assumption that in a popular government there exists, or should exist, mechanistic articulation between opinion and action. At times the problem is further compounded by the disposition to personify public opinion as an initiating entity that pulls strings to actuate governments.

Comprehension of the interaction of government and public opinion depends on the contrivance of an appropriate broad conception of the process. All governments, we may set out axiomatically, must concern themselves with public opinion. They do not maintain their authority by brute force alone; they must seek willing acceptance and conformity from most of their citizens. Popular government may be considered as a special case of governments in general. Popular government has its peculiarities, one of which is the basis for the exercise of its authority: that governors shall seek out popular opinion, that they shall give it weight if not the determinative voice in decision, and that persons outside the government have a right to be heard. This legitimization of the view that the preferences of the governed shall be accorded weight by governors constitutes the moral basis of popular government, an ethical imperative that in mature democracies is converted into consistent habits and patterns of action among those in places of authority and leadership.

Linkage of opinion and government occurs as governors and governed behave in ways consistent with these ethical assumptions of popular government. Thus, the essence of government by public opinion may rest, not in any precise mirroring of opinion by government, but in concern in good faith by governments for public preferences and in dedication to mass interests. As government and public interact from day to day, the process is not one of translating a single popular will into public policy. On those questions on which people generally have opinions, the process may be an intricate one of estimating what kinds of people have what opinions and of a search for a decision that will give appropriate weights to conflicting equities and interests. Moreover, the interaction works in the opposite direction as government and other centers of political influence attempt to form opinion.

In popular governments this formation of opinion tends less to be a calculating manipulation of opinion for the advantage of narrow interests. When it is guided by the ethical imperatives of popular government, it often attempts to form support for measures advocated in good faith but whose relevance for the wider interest may not be immediately perceived by the public. In any case, in popular government the day-to-day work of government is conducted with an eye to the mechanisms of linkage between government and opinion peculiar to popular governments, the chief of which is the electoral process. At elections public opinion is clearly controlling; that is, it determines who shall govern. The vexing analytical problem comes in the comprehension of the extent to which, and the processes whereby, public opinion is linked to the actions of government in the periods between elections.

1 · Communication and Feedback

The conception of popular government as interaction between public opinion and government assumes a two-way flow of communications between citizen and government. From government itself communications may move to the citizen to maintain or to obtain consent by persuasion or by conveying information. From sources independent of government, information about governmental actions may be transmitted to the citizen. All these streams of intelligence affect or activate public opinion. In turn, a feedback of opinion to centers of authority occurs. Responses of approval to past or projected courses of action may be evoked. Or responses of violent disapproval may clog the channels for the transmission of opinions to Washington. As critical communications come to outweigh commendatory communications, the course of governmental action may be brought into more real or apparent harmony with public opinion.[1] A wavering equilibrium is maintained between opinion and policy as each side of the interaction adapts itself to the other.

This model of government as a two-way system of communications has its analytical uses, although it must be modified to take into account major departures from it in the workaday world. A chief deviation from the model is the extent of participation by the public in the communications interaction. At any particular time attentiveness and responsiveness to political communications vary widely among political strata of the population; some people are listening and responding, perhaps vociferously, while others are inattentive and unresponsive. The size of the attentive public may vary from time to time as new issues and new problems arise. A second departure from the model flows from the conduct of government in a manner to anticipate negative or resistive response. Many governmental actions generate not a ripple of reaction; to some degree that consequence occurs because decision-makers have correctly estimated the temper of those to be affected by

[1] For a study of interaction between diplomatic policy and public opinion in pre-World War I Germany, see Richard R. Fagen: "Some Assessments and Uses of Public Opinion in Diplomacy," *Public Opinion Quarterly*, XXIV (1960), 439–57.

action. Government, thus, may be most nearly attuned to public opinion when its actions raise no clamor—when, in fact, the communications feedback does not occur.

A third deviation from the model involves the rapidity of public response. At times the attentive public may be large and quickly responsive to events and actions. At other times and on other questions public discontent may be generated only slowly; it may require years or decades for a public sentiment to develop. Finally, the model must allow for imperfection in the flow of information. Incompleteness in information flow may come from deliberate misrepresentation by those who seek to mold public attitudes; it may come from inattentiveness of all or certain sectors of the public; it may come from distortions and obstructions in the channels of communication. In these and other ways the simple model of governance as a communications interaction does not encompass the reality like a glove; yet the central idea of communication and feedback between public and government has validity. To take into account the deviations from the model is only to recognize variety in the reality.

President and Public Opinion. In the maneuvers of government to shape public opinion the President plays a primary role.[2] Because of the prominence of his position he can command the attention of all the media. Radio and television networks are at his call when he wishes to make a major statement directly to the people. His formal pronouncements command space in the press. Through his press conferences he can greatly influence the manner in which the major news is treated and can, moreover, manufacture a great deal of that news himself.

The presidential press conference is a unique American institution, which enables the President to feed information into the communications system and gives reporters an opportunity to quiz him on matters of public concern. The head of no other great state permits himself to be subjected to the rough questioning by reporters that is routine in the American presidential press conference. The rise of the press conference has occurred during this century. The germ of the conference took form in Theodore Roosevelt's time. Roosevelt—a man of vitality, color, and histrionic talent—invited friendly correspondents to chat

[2] The relative prominence of the President in the media has been increasing. Elmer E. Cornwell finds that attention to the President, as measured by column inches, has risen with special rapidity since World War I. The change does not seem to be the result of the impact of strong Presidents; even weak Presidents command greater press space. Over the same period there has been no such increase in congressional news.—"Presidential News: The Expanding Public Image," *Journalism Quarterly*, XXXVI (1959), 275-85.

with him as he was shaved by a Negro barber, a journeyman of genius who managed, as he performed his rites, to avoid daubing the soap brush into the mouth of the vocal and gesticulating President. Woodrow Wilson placed the press conference on a more regularized and less informal basis. Harding, Coolidge, and Hoover continued it with variations.[3]

The press conference came into its glory during the era of Franklin D. Roosevelt. Unlike some of his predecessors who had required that questions be submitted in advance, Roosevelt permitted inquiries without notice. He often provided background information off the record that might be useful to reporters in shaping their stories and developed a relationship with the working press that offset to some degree the hostility of their publishers toward him and his Administration. He made, says Pollard, the press conference "such an integral part of his working program that comparisons with any previous administration are largely pointless." [4] A major change in practice came in Eisenhower's Administration when television and radio reporters were permitted to tape the proceedings, a step that newspaper reporters thought reduced the utility of the conference. Only those things could be said that could be allowed to go out over the airwaves. In the hands of a lesser man than Eisenhower this step could have had disastrous consequences. The quality of the President's extemporaneous prose assured that whatever misstep he made in the give-and-take of the conference could not prove embarrassing; it was almost certain to be concealed by his highly individual syntax.

The function of the President as he seeks to inform and to shape public opinion depends not only upon the personality of the President, but upon the character of his Administration as well. If his policy is an aggressive one, the President may attempt to explain, to lead, to shape opinion in support of legislation. He may use his position to direct pressure upon Congress. In times of crisis, domestic or international, the President may inform and reassure the people and thereby gain support for his policies or for himself.[5]

Perhaps the basic function of the President in relation to public opinion is not readily defined, and its effects are even less readily measured. By the general image he creates the President may generate a

---

[3] On the history of the press conference, see Leo C. Rosten: *The Washington Correspondents* (New York: Harcourt, Brace; 1937), ch. 2. See also Elmer E. Cornwell, Jr.: "The Presidential Press Conference: A Study in Institutionalization," *Midwest Journal of Political Science*, IV (1960), 370–89.

[4] James E. Pollard: "Franklin D. Roosevelt and the Press," *Journalism Quarterly*, XXII (1945), 197–206.

[5] See Elmer E. Cornwell, Jr.: "Wilson, Creel, and the Presidency," *Public Opinion Quarterly*, XXIII (1959), 189–202.

broad public approval of himself and of his Administration. His failure
to do so may make his Administration vulnerable. Aspects of his program and particular leaders within the Administration do not enjoy the
protection from sniping that a general sentiment broadly favorable to
the Administration would give them. Eisenhower's good fortune in his
relation to public opinion seemed to rest in a capacity to make himself
liked and trusted. Critics and opponents of particular policies and actions of his Administration encountered difficulties when they attempted to break through the protective shield of popular confidence
enjoyed by the President to attack elements of his Administration.[6]

Subpresidential Public Relations. No other official can match the President in his capacity to utilize the media of communication, but every
federal agency equips itself with a public-relations staff and conducts
an information program of some sort. The endeavors of these agencies
range widely in both content and objectives. The great bulk of publicity material released by governmental agencies consists of simple factual material which is distributed for the information of the public. The
stream of publicity releases includes large numbers of announcements
of decisions in individual cases and of rules and orders. These materials
inform the interested sectors of the public, and their dissemination
may induce better compliance. Many other items are released to fulfill
a function; census findings, farmers bulletins, or the results of scientific
research constitute a part of the materials disseminated to the public.[7]

Most of these kinds of publicity are not designed to influence public opinion, though their circulation through the channels of information may incidentally create a favorable impression of the work of the
agencies concerned. The public-relations endeavors of some officials
and agencies are definitely calculated to form public opinion. The
speeches and statements of the Secretary of State may be an attempt to
explain and attract support for a foreign policy. Ezra Taft Benson,
Eisenhower's Secretary of Agriculture, spent a good deal of time and
effort trying to drum up support for his farm policy. All such opinion-
molding efforts have in recent decades been far overshadowed by large-
scale programs of the various branches of the military to sell to the public their own particular brand of strategic policy. Each service—using a
variety of activities, ranging from the pronouncements of its high brass
to the propaganda worked into movies produced with the aid of back-

[6] On Eisenhower and the press, see Walter Johnson: *The American President and the Art of Communication* (Oxford: Clarendon; 1958).
[7] J. L. McCamy: *Government Publicity* (Chicago: University of Chicago
Press; 1939).

drops, such as battlewagons and bombers, provided at public expense —has sought to build a favorable public attitude toward its objectives.[8]

To public-relations activities the services assign officers in numbers that in the early history of the Republic would have constituted a formidable military force. The Air Force has pursued public favor with an especial zeal. It regards words as weapons. "Facts must be convincing, demonstrated, living salesmen of practical benefits," the Air Force tells its information officers. "These are the only kind of facts that mold opinion and channel the vibrant tensions of public thinking; always deciding issues in the end, altering military policy as surely as defeat in war—they make public opinion the most powerful tool of all, more powerful even than war itself." [9] This beautiful prose manifests the characteristic illusion of the public-relations man that he is in contact with reality. Yet the services have enough faith in this sort of doctrine to provide extensive facilities to reporters and writers.[1]

Feedback from Public Opinion. To some extent the linkage of government and public opinion consists in the response of the public both to the government's endeavors to shape opinion and to its actions as they affect the citizenry. Specialized organs and procedures carry perhaps the major part of the feedback. The representative body is in a sense an assemblage of persons at the seat of government, with the role of articulating the sentiments of their constituents. In varying degrees they maintain touch with their constituents and make themselves heard in the executive departments and agencies in no uncertain terms; the *Congressional Record* is read with the utmost care in the bureaucracy.

[8] See, for example, Walter Schneir: "The Campaign to Make Chemical Warfare Respectable," *The Reporter*, October 1, 1959, 24–8.

[9] Quoted in Douglass Cater: *The Fourth Branch of Government* (Boston: Houghton Mifflin; 1959), p. 166.

[1] Government public-relations men, like their colleagues in the private publicity mills, sometimes let zeal for their cause offset their dedication to truth. Hanson W. Baldwin records that in the late 1940's the Air Force, in an attempt to influence policy, fed to newspapermen the tidings that Russia had 14,000 operational combat planes and was producing from 40,000 to 50,000 planes annually. It turned out that only 8,200 of Russia's 14,000 operating planes were combat types and that the production figure was the maximum wartime production. The current production was in the range of from 6,000 to 12,000.—Hanson W. Baldwin: "When the Big Guns Speak," in Lester Markel, ed.: *Public Opinion and Foreign Policy* (New York: Harper; 1949), p. 112. In the early years of the Eisenhower Administration the government announced that large numbers of "security risks" had been discharged and attempted to build up a picture of heroic and dedicated souls cleansing the bureaucracy of subversives. Eventually it turned out that the sorry performance consisted principally of a transformation into subversives of the routine departures from the public service of drunkards, incompetents, and the like, a large proportion of whom had been employed by the Eisenhower Administration itself.

The political parties constitute another of the institutions that channel public opinions and attitudes into government as do pressure groups. Elections are basic means for the expression of public sentiment.

These more-or-less formalized mechanisms for the transmission of public opinion to government, to be treated in more detail in later chapters, are supplemented by other modes of communication from the citizenry to government, communication that flows informally and day to day as the actions of government occur. A heavy volume of communications, usually in the form of letters, flows from the citizenry to public officials. During the past half-century, according to studies by Leila Sussman, the volume of mail to the White House has increased at a sharp rate. In Lincoln's time the number of letters annually sent to the President per 10,000 literate adults was 44. During Wilson's tenure in World War I the rate was 47. In Franklin Roosevelt's day the rate reached 160. These increases are said to be attributable in part to the increasing level of education of the population; the rates of letter writing in relation to the total numbers of high-school graduates have increased only slightly. Though data are not available on the volume of mail to members of Congress, doubtless parallel increases have occurred in the numbers of citizens who feel moved to take pen in hand and give their Senator or Representative the benefit of their judgment on the issues confronting the Republic.[2]

Those who write letters to the White House tend to write in support or approbation rather than in criticism. Consequently, when the proportion of critical letters in the flow of White House mail about a particular problem begins to climb toward 50 per cent, experienced appraisers of the stream of communications know that the President is in serious trouble. At the time of Roosevelt's fight to reorganize the Supreme Court, for example, opposition letters amounted to about half of the stream of mail for three days. The tendency to write letters of approval doubtless gives presidents, Senators, congressmen, and other officials a distorted notion of the nature of the public response to their actions and positions.

The notion of the letter or the telegram to Congressmen as a way of influencing governmental action has found fairly wide acceptance within the American population. Far more people, though, have the idea that they might exert influence by writing their Congressmen than actually write. In a survey in Albany, New York, in 1949, 32 per cent of the respondents said that writing to their Congressman was a way that "ordinary citizens" could influence the government's actions

---

[2] Leila Sussman: "Mass Political Letter Writing in America: The Growth of an Institution," *Public Opinion Quarterly*, XXIII (1959), 203–12.

in foreign affairs. Yet only 11 per cent of the sample said that they had written to a Congressman.[3] In an AIPO survey made in 1946, 14 per cent of a national sample said that they had at some time or another written or wired to their Congressman or Senator. The proportions claiming to have engaged in this type of activity varied from 35 per cent of those with college education to 9 per cent of the grammar-school group.

Newspaper comment and reports may be regarded by public officials as a feedback from public opinion. In an earlier day, when the structure and role of the press were different, this interpretation had some warrant; even now press comment represents the response of an influential group—the publishers. And if the press pays no attention to an action or pronouncement, the public functionary may be justified in the conclusion that he is beating a dead horse. On the other hand, widespread press attention, either condemnatory or approbative, does not necessarily mean that many persons in the general public are concerned.

The most deliberate capitalization on the feedback phenomenon is the "trial balloon"—a proposal or statement, often issued anonymously by "high authority," for the purpose of testing public opinion. Ordinarily few people ever notice a trial balloon, but responses may be expected from members of the attentive public, and, more importantly, from members of Congress, from other political leaders, from the press, and from group spokesmen. If the response indicates that the proposed action will fall on sensitive toes, the scheme may be dropped or altered, or measures may be initiated to convert particular opinion leadership centers. Most major measures have the benefit of a trial-balloon procedure, though not necessarily deliberately, for Washington officialdom is as leaky as a sieve and rumors of contemplated action often find their way into the news columns before formal announcements have been made or even before firm decisions have been taken.

A favorable response to a public action may have the effect of reinforcing and encouraging the position taken. An instance frequently cited, of considerable importance in American foreign policy, was the response in 1945 to a speech by the late Senator Arthur Vandenberg. In this speech he took a line at variance with the traditional Republican isolationist position and struck out for wider American participation in international affairs. The great play given the story by the newspapers astonished the Senator, and the flow of messages of approbation persuaded him that he had taken a position attractive to public opinion.

[3] Survey Research Center: *Interest, Information, and Attitudes in the Field of World Affairs* (Ann Arbor: Survey Research Center; 1949), p. 84.

Thus fortified he went on to become a major figure in the development of a foreign policy that won bipartisan support.[4]

In other instances the reception given an evolving policy may induce its modification, the better to take into account the temper of public opinion as made manifest by the feedback. Cater, for example, concludes that the ultimate form of the Marshall Plan was affected by the public response in the early stages. In its earlier versions the program was directed against "hunger and want," but estimates of the pressures of opinion converted it more completely into a program aimed against communism.[5]

Perhaps the most direct feedback of public attitudes and the most immediate response to those attitudes occur as candidates adjust their speeches to the temper of their audiences. As they travel from place to place, they experiment with appeals and with phrasings, discarding those appeals that evoke disapproval and repeating those that bring cheers. Some politicians are equipped with an empathy so sensitive that they can adapt their discourse to the necessities as they speak. Candidates with adequate resources may use sample surveys to extend their knowledge of popular response beyond the limits of the audiences they actually see and hear. While the adaptation of electoral appeal to campaign audiences is not the adjustment of policy to public opinion, the process probably in the long run has its effects on public policy.

We can cite examples of opinion feedback, but the data permit no estimate of the total role of the process in the political system. What kinds of proposals and actions induce response? Which elements of the public respond? What sources of response are most influential, and which actions stimulate little or no public response? On all such matters there simply is no comprehensive information. About all that it is safe to say is that on issues that attract attention and involve the interests of large numbers of people many persons write to the White House and to Capitol Hill, with varying consequences. These issues are not always those of the greatest significance for the Republic. A plan to exterminate the squirrels on the White House lawn may arouse wider and more intense response than a proposal to spend several billion dollars on foreign aid.

Intuition and System in Feedback. In their appraisal of public response to actions and proposals, officials proceed by impressionistic or systematic means, although hunch, intuition, impression are by far the

[4] See Arthur H. Vandenberg, Jr., ed.: *The Private Papers of Senator Vandenberg* (Boston: Houghton Mifflin; 1952), ch. 8.
[5] Cater: op. cit., pp. 15–17.

more widely used. Legislators live in a tradition in which one of their functions is to estimate and to represent opinion. In an earlier day instructions from appropriate bodies of their constituents were not uncommon. The disappearance of these binding directives did not convert legislators into Burkes dedicated to the right without regard to the opinions of their constituents. Most of them are but extensions of their constituents; they have grown up with them and share their interests and aspirations. On many matters they need not consult the will of their supporters, for they embody it. Yet they do not rely solely on their impression of sentiment at home. They read the local papers; they give weight to their mail; they listen attentively to visitors; they make pilgrimages around their constituencies and invite one and all to give them their views on the state of the union; they request the considered opinions of especially influential backers; they ponder the results of past elections and estimate the results of future elections. By these and other means they arrive at crude estimates of the opinions of those elements in their constituency to whom they are beholden.

These unsystematic procedures for the gauging of opinions have always been a part of the kit of tools of the public official. They have been supplemented to a limited extent by opinion polls, which provide an estimate of dimensions of opinion not often identified by impressionistic judgment. Individual Representatives and Senators from time to time conduct polls of their constituents. Only a few of these operations are carried on with any technical competence. The questions are usually on the order of: "Would you like to see taxes reduced?" More extensive surveys of opinion are conducted by the administrative agencies, and, given the interests of their sponsors, the concern of these surveys is not so much with major policy questions as with information useful in the administration of going programs. Are the objects of the program understood? Do the administrators have an adequate comprehension of how the program is understood by the persons whom it affects? Do the administrators have adequate information about the circumstances at the point of impact of the program that bear on its success? If the program is an educational or promotional effort, is the message reaching in an intelligible form those for whom it is intended? Surveys calculated to obtain the answers to such questions are examples of systematic efforts to measure directly the response or feedback from public policies and may provide the information necessary for appropriate modifications in modes of administration.[6]

[6] See Henry A. Wallace and James L. McCamy: "Straw Polls and Public Administration," *Public Opinion Quarterly*, IV (1940), 221–3; Angus Campbell: "The Uses of Interview Surveys in Federal Administration," *Journal of Social Issues*, II, (1946), 14–22; Hans E. Skott: "Attitude Research in the Department of Agriculture," *Public Opinion Quarterly*, VII (1943), 280–92; Harold F. Gosnell

In some agencies of government specialized units monitor public opinion and furnish their findings to the operating officials of the agency. The Public Studies Division of the Department of State follows radio and television comment, excerpts from which find their way to the desks of the officers concerned and into the Division's "Daily Opinion Summary." The Division clips a selected group of papers. It follows the activities of the interest groups and keeps an eye on the published polls. Occasionally it arranges for the conduct of special polls of opinion by private polling agencies. Summaries and analyses of information from all these and other sources are circulated to those officials of the department who should know about the state of public response to the department's actions.[7]

The techniques employed by government for the appraisal of the response in public opinion to governmental actions and to changing circumstances are relatively crude. Perhaps the most serious consequence of inadequate opinion appraisal is that officials often fear to act on matters of conceded urgency lest the public response be hostile. Thus, in the summer of 1940 when the world situation was, to say the least, ominous a majority of those writing to congressmen opposed compulsory military service. The traditional opposition to conscription in peacetime was both felt and heard by congressmen. On the other hand, an AIPO survey of August, 1940, found the public as a whole to be about two to one in favor of conscription.[8] Moreover, a majority in every state favored compulsory military service. The highest support occurred in Mississippi (87 per cent), and the lowest in Indiana (55 per cent).

2 · Conditioning Effects of the Opinion Context

Government, as we have seen, attempts to mold public opinion toward support of the programs and policies it espouses. Given that en-

---

and Moyca C. David: "Public Opinion Research in Government," *American Political Science Review*, XLIII (1949), 564–72; Martin Kriesberg: "Opinion Research and Public Policy," *International Journal of Opinion and Attitude Research*, III (1949), 373–84; and Harry Alpert: "Opinion and Attitude Surveys in the U.S. Government," *Public Opinion Quarterly*, XVI (1952), 33–41.

[7] See Robert E. Elder: "The Public Studies Division of the Department of State: Public Opinion Analysts in the Formulation and Conduct of American Foreign Policy," *Western Political Quarterly*, X (1957), 783–92; W. Phillips Davison: "More than Diplomacy," in Markel: op. cit., pp. 121–40; H. Schuyler Foster: "American Public Opinion and U.S. Foreign Policy," *Department of State Bulletin*, November 30, 1959.

[8] The question was "Do you think that every able-bodied young man 20 years old should be made to serve in the army, navy or air forces for one year?"

deavor, a perfect congruence between public policy and public opinion could be government of public opinion rather than government by public opinion. One can never be certain of the extent to which the parallelism of governmental action and public preference results from governmental influence on opinion and to what extent it results from the adjustment of public policy to bring it into accord with public opinion.[9] Yet it is plain that on the American scene congruence between action and public preference results from the flow of influence to as well as from government.

As it seeks to shape opinion toward acceptance of its policies, the American government enjoys no monopoly of propaganda. Competing policies are urged upon the public by the opposition party and by private centers of power and influence. These alternative lines of action may prove, when the votes are counted, to be closer to public taste than those of the government of the moment. Moreover, government tends to be affected as a molder of opinion by the ethical imperatives that influence the actions of mature popular governments—namely, that public decision should promote the public interest and should, given time and opportunity for discussion and the dissemination of information, command public support. With an acceptance of this fundamental rule of the game, governors tend to estimate and to discount opinion in advance, as well as to seek to form it.

Government may be regarded as operating within a context of public opinion that conditions its actions. That context is not a rigid matrix that fixes a precise form for government action. Nor is it unchangeable. It consists of opinions irregularly distributed among the people and of varying intensity, of attitudes of differing convertibility into votes, and of sentiments not always readily capable of appraisal. Yet that context, as it is perceived by those responsible for action, conditions many of the acts of those who must make what we may call "opinion-related decisions." The opinion context may affect the substance of action, the form of action, or the manner of action.

[9] Herbert Simon concludes that the determination of the direction of the flow of influence depends on miscalculations by decisionmakers of the state of opinion. He says: "If the President is elected, his decisions may be affected not only by what the citizens did in the last election, but also by his expectations of what they will do in the next. I think it can be seen that the possibility of measuring the separate links in the chain of influence depend, in this instance, on the presence of some ignorance in the system. So long as the President is able to form exact expectations of the citizens' reactions, and they of what a candidate will do if elected, his influence on them cannot be distinguished from their influence on him, but let his or their forecasts be in error and the possibilities of disentangling the relations are re-established."—"Notes on the Observation and Measurement of Political Power," *Journal of Politics*, XV (1953), 505.

Opinion and the Substance of Action. Obviously opinion in the sense of mass opinion has no immediate bearing on many actions of government. They are taken administratively or even legislatively with no conscious concern about general public opinion, for there is no general public opinion about them. They may be of so routine a nature that there need be no concern about opinion, though at times a question becomes routine because opinion on the general principle has long since become crystallized. Or they may concern only limited publics whose will, in the absence of challenge, may govern decision.

Mass opinion becomes relevant on those issues, great or small, that attract widespread attention, that involve the emotions and interests of many people, and that in fact generate a mass opinion. The bearing of the opinion context on these decisions is probably felt more in a negative than in a positive way. On such questions governments hesitate to act until the weight of mass opinion becomes fairly well defined. Even when opinion assumes the form of what we have called a "permissive consensus," [1] government is not necessarily impelled to action. Yet until a permissive consensus develops governments are hesitant to adopt new policies on major opinion-related issues. The practical doctrine is one not of majority rule but of the rule of considerably more than a majority. So unpredictable are the reactions of people to governmental action that politicians prefer to be sure that if they act they will not find themselves far out on a limb. Even when a substantial majority sentiment prevails, governments may conclude that the permissive consensus does not deserve enactment. The costs, both psychic and monetary, to those who will be adversely affected by the proposed line of action may dictate inaction, restraint, or delay.

The opinion context, therefore, may be regarded as a negative factor; it fixes the limitations within which action may be taken but does not assure that action will be taken. To be sure, negative interpretation of the role of the opinion context does not prevail universally. On occasion a storm of public opinion, or at least the appearance of a storm of opinion, may be aroused and seem to sweep officials before it. More often, governments employ delaying tactics to permit the storm to subside—or better to permit the determination whether it is really a storm. On occasion, too, Presidents may gain enough of a following to be able to push through legislation whose support in popular opinion is limited. Yet over the long run it appears that the enactment of major attention-commanding measures tends to await the development of a predominant permissive opinion.

[1] See Chapter 2.

Opinion and the Form of Action. The context of opinion does not consist of clearly etched guidelines. Moreover, the values of the political culture contain contradictory streams. Whether a line of action accords with dominant opinion may depend upon the strain of that opinion to which it is related. Consequently, the dominant opinions and values often affect the form an action takes. Those who advocate a new policy exert their ingenuity to phrase it in terms that will make it consistent with values widely accepted. Those who are in opposition attempt to picture the action as one that diverges markedly from all that is regarded as good and holy by the populace. Security payments to the aged, for example, may be portrayed as a ruthless assault on American individualism or as a noble implementation of our humanitarian belief that the aged should not lack food or shelter.[2]

A recurring illustration of these propositions consists in the attempts of opponents of reform measures to pin a socialist label on such measures. The American people, in an inconsistency incomprehensible to doctrinaires, oppose socialism yet manifest a tendency to support specific measures that may be in principle socialistic. In a 1934 study of a Pennsylvania county George W. Hartmann concluded that most of the voters of his sample wanted specific measures for which socialism stood but did not "want to have them labelled that way." In the locality of the study, he opined, the people "would prefer to have the Republican Party be the vehicle for introducing socialism to America."[3] National samples have shown a similar pattern of opposition to "socialism" and support of measures regarded by the analyst as socialistic. The Psychological Corporation, shortly after World War II, found that 75 per cent of their national sample opposed socialism "in this country." Goodly numbers of their respondents, though, supported specific measures, such as the TVA, which they even conceded might be steps toward socialism.

Such findings doubtless underlay the determined attempt of the Republican party in the campaign of 1950 to emphasize its slogan "Liberty Against Socialism" without intensive endeavor to specify the content of that phrase. Advocates of measures, on the contrary, do not urge socialism; they urge specific acts which they attempt to tie into

[2] The public, like the Supreme Court, can draw on contradictory precedents to justify its current temper.

[3] "The Contradiction between the Feeling-Tone of Political Party Names and Public Response to Their Platforms," *Journal of Social Psychology*, VII (1936), 336–55. For related findings, see Selden C. Menefee: "The Effect of Stereotyped Words on Political Judgments," *American Sociological Review*, I (1936), 614–21; Daniel Katz and Hadley Cantril: "An Analysis of Attitudes Toward Fascism and Communism," *Journal of Abnormal and Social Psychology*, XXXV (1940), 356–66.

congenial elements of American tradition and opinion. The Townsend Plan, a scheme for old-age pensions that won wide popular support in the 1930's, was presented, for example, in this way: "It is a simple American plan dedicated to the cause of prosperity and the abolition of poverty." [4] "The Townsend Plan is religion in action." It requires a hardy soul to oppose prosperity, the abolition of poverty, and religion.

Opinion and the Manner of Action. In a regime that attaches high value to notice of contemplated action, to the opportunity to be heard in protest, to due process of law, to the avoidance of arbitrary action, and to other such procedures, public opinion may normally be supposed to impose conditions on the manner in which government acts. In addition to such formalized practices of deference to public opinion, governments are often influenced in other ways in the manner of their action by the context of opinion. While no exhaustive categorization of these effects on manner of action has been made, several types of effects may be indicated.

Often to generate support for a policy the incantations of a prestigious authority may be invoked. A commission of distinguished and presumably disinterested citizens may lend their names. The ritual may involve a study and report on a problem whose solution requires general public acceptance. Thus, in the early stages of World War II gasoline rationing was instituted as a means of conserving tires because of the shortage of rubber. No little grumbling accompanied the institution of rationing. Bernard Baruch, a gentleman who had for years cultivated a reputation as a disinterested statesman of uncommon sagacity, was called upon to conduct a study of the entire question. In due course his report reached its preordained conclusion and received extensive attention in the mass media. The report and other concurrent agitation brought a marked change in public opinion toward gasoline rationing. Before and after the Baruch report the AIPO asked national samples, "Are you in favor of nation-wide gasoline rationing to conserve tires?" The before and after divisions of opinion were:

	Favor	Oppose	Undecided
Before Baruch report	49%	44%	7%
After Baruch report	73	22	5

At times the context of opinion compels far greater attention to the explanation of the underlying reasons for an action than those respon-

[4] Hadley Cantril: *The Psychology of Social Movements* (New York: Wiley; 1941), pp. 202–7.

sible for decision at first regard as necessary. Information and under-standing do not always bring acceptance and cooperation, but often they do. Action in accord with general opinion may be resisted or sabotaged simply because it is not understood. Thus, during World War II a so-called job freeze was introduced incident to the rationing of manpower among industries. The freeze, though, included several escapes for the individual worker. Men might shift into more skilled employment; they could change jobs if they were in low-pay work; they could change jobs if they lived far from their places of work. Apart from administrative headaches in the plan, it stimulated only re-strained enthusiasm among workers. Opinion surveys indicated that disapproval of the scheme by workers was associated with their under-standing of it. Of those aware of all three loopholes, 78 per cent ap-proved the action; of those who thought all job changes were for-bidden, only 25 per cent approved. Clearly an informational campaign was in order. In an administrative system with a pervasive legalistic tradition—ignorance of the law is no defense—administrators some-times miss the obvious.

On occasion administrative practices are modified to improve com-munications to achieve compliance with public objectives. In World War II surveys of war-bond purchasers revealed that purchases were far more frequent among persons who had been personally solicited than among those persons who were reached by the media alone. That finding was not astonishing, but the obvious needs to be frequently re-established in this workaday world. The moral was to introduce a more extensive program of personal solicitation into the next war bond cam-paign, a step that produced higher sales.[5]

Even as they deviate from the cultural norms prescriptive of proper modes of action, governments may pay tribute to those stand-ards of opinion. They may take action secretly in a manner as if to concede that had they acted in the light of day the pressure of opinion would have compelled them to make a different decision. The annals of state legislatures contain endless examples of maneuvers at the end of the session to put through legislation hurriedly so that opponents are taken unawares and have no opportunity to raise a hue and cry. Such actions are not unknown in federal administrative agencies. Thus, after Eisenhower came to power, the Department of the Interior re-scinded a rule adopted during the Truman Administration requiring, as a condition to the grant of easements for power transmission lines across public lands, agreement by private utilities to rent excess trans-mission capacity to the government for the wheeling of public power.

[5] See Rensis Likert: "Opinion Studies and Government Policy," *Proceed-ings of the American Philosophical Society*, XCII (1948), 341–50.

At the behest of western utilities, the regulation was rescinded without notice to or consultation with either private or governmental agencies interested in the matter. The decision thus became a fait accompli before those concerned could raise a public commotion.

3 · Opinion: Immediate and Remote

In the interactions between government and its opinion context another characteristic of the context takes on considerable practical importance. The cocoon of opinion that envelops government may be regarded as a cloudy sort of structure consisting of layers of opinion near to government and others remote from government. These characteristics of immediacy and remoteness have themselves several dimensions, each important for the nature of the bearing of public opinion upon public action.

At any particular time with respect to a given issue, immediate opinion consists of that of the alert, attentive, interested, and informed public. These are the people who talk to officials, write letters to their congressmen, comment in print or on public occasions, nudge other people to action, or who manifest a low boiling point in other ways. More remote from government is the opinion of persons with lower levels of participation in public affairs, with less attention, less information, and a less immediate concern. By a variety of analyses in the preceding chapters these differentiations among strata in the opinion system have been shown to exist. The persons in the strata remote from government often, insofar as they have opinions, have opinions that do not parallel those of persons more deeply involved in public affairs. In the operations of government those who make themselves heard, those who argue their case, and those who take a hand enjoy an advantage. Perhaps over the long pull theirs is the opinion that enters most frequently into the calculations of those who make most of the decisions that must be related to opinion.

These immediate and remote strata of the opinion context have another property significant for the place of opinion in action—a property that creates special perplexities for government. Opinion that is remote at the moment of decision may also express itself at a point remote in time. The positions of the lobbyists, of the special interests, and of the highly active sectors of the public are made known with vigor and persuasiveness day by day as government grapples with the problems of the moment. They may, in fact, make themselves heard before the government comes to grips with a problem, often to the effect that government should do nothing. The outer layers of less involved opinion, though, may be slow to be aroused, and expression may be delayed until the next election or even the next election after that. The direction this opinion will take when it is stirred to action may be unpredictable. What its memory of past actions will be and whether its perceptions will be converted into electoral approbation or animosity are equally imponderable.

To some degree the difference between immediate and remote opinion is that between organized and unorganized opinion. The alert and sensitive opinion is likely to be organized into formal groups whose spokesmen are on hand when Congress and state legislatures are considering action. They make their views known in the executive and administrative offices and to the public through the media. Remote opinion is less likely to be so organized. It has no lobbyists, although politicians may give prayerful consideration to the nature of that opinion and to the probability that it will find expression at the next election.

In a sense a government that takes public opinion into account tends to be cross-pressured by both immediate and remote opinion. Government is beset by spokesmen for immediate opinion; the politically active sectors of society make their preferences clearly known. However, it is also pressed by its own estimates of the state of more remote opinion and by its anxieties about the possibility of the activation and translation of that opinion into votes at some time in the future. Insofar as considerations of opinion enter into decision, governmental decisionmakers must calculate how much they should discount the clamor of immediate opinion and what weight they should give to latent preferences that are remote, both in communication and in time, from the point of action.

All these broad points may be given practical meaning by mention of the warm debate in the spring of 1959 over the level of public expenditures. President Eisenhower dedicated himself to the advocacy of the proposition that the fate of the Republic depended on the expenditure of a sum no larger than he recommended. In Congress the liberal Democrats dedicated themselves to the advocacy of more adequate appropriations for education and for national defense. The hubbub of the debate made headlines for weeks and generated a good deal of interest in Washington. But the general public was not greatly excited; in fact, most of it had not heard about the policy commotion in Washington. In its release of May 1, 1959, the AIPO reported the following responses to the question: "Do you think there is anything for which the government should be spending MORE money than it is at present?"

Schools, education   11%
Defense   9
Unemployment benefits   3
All other items   15
Nothing   62

Simultaneously the AIPO asked: "Do you think there is anything for which the government should be spending LESS money than it is at present?" To this question the responses were:

Foreign aid   17%
Government expenses, salaries   13
Defense   9
Farm subsidies   4
All other items   9
Nothing   48

Perhaps the opinion measured by the AIPO survey represented immediate opinion. In the sentiments reported no clear directive of action was perceptible. Yet the issues involved in the debate were of a kind that might well be sufficiently agitated to be of some import in the subsequent election. Insofar as public opinion could enter into the decision, it had to be not the opinion of the moment but estimates of future opinion. The nature of that future opinion would depend on the course of events and on the effectiveness with which the contending points of view were put to the public.

An illustration of this tension between immediate and remote opinion is provided by the maneuvers of the Republican Administration in the spring of 1960 after Richard Nixon was apparently assured of the presidential nomination. Eisenhower, committed by both inclination and political debt to the American Medical Association and to activist elements of his party holding parallel views, stood firm against measures sponsored by Democrats in Congress to provide medical care for the aged through the social security system. Similarly, Eisenhower, committed to the views of the American Farm Bureau Federation, steadfastly supported the agricultural policies of Secretary Benson. In all these positions the President doubtless found a happy congeniality between his own views and those of the streams of immediate opinion that had access to the White House. Mr. Nixon found himself most unhappily situated in the crossfire between the opinion of the day and estimates of the possible opinion in November. On medical care for the aged, the intelligence began to filter out, with no denial from Mr. Nixon, that the Vice-President was waging a fight within the Administration for the aged. The impression seemed to be conveyed that the Vice-President stood four-square for the old folks but that the delicacy of his position as a member of the Administration made it improper for him to make an issue against the beloved but wrongheaded President. On farm policy, there began to appear news stories based on "high authority" suggesting that the Vice-President would, at the proper time, reveal his true sympathy for the hard-pressed farmer.

The interaction between government and public opinion in the day-to-day work of government presents, it must be conceded, a phenomenon about which our systematic data are limited; to describe it, a certain amount of surmise must substitute for hard knowledge. Nevertheless, there can be no doubt of the significance of official concern for public sentiment as question after question is dealt with. The informal give and take between government and public opinion may be difficult to perceive and appraise. The more formal channels through which the public is linked with government—elections, political parties, pressure groups, and representative processes—are more readily portrayed. It is to those topics that the discussion now turns.

17

POLITICAL PARTIES

POLITICAL PARTIES are basic institutions for the translation of mass preferences into public policy. At the simplest conceptual level the political party is regarded as a leadership clique that formulates policy proposals, advocates them before the electorate in campaigns, and—if it wins the mandate—proceeds to conduct the government in accord with the majority will as it is inferred from the election results. So austere a conception of party role, as even the most casual observer knows, does not fit the facts of party life in its rich and varied detail.

Deviations from this model of perfect articulation of mass opinion and governmental action through the party mechanism are numerous. There are departures from the presumed clarity of the intentions of party leadership and of the preferences of its supporters. Party programs are ambiguous on many matters on which mass opinion, too, may be uncertain or nonexistent. On many issues the party leadership may even have no announced position, or it may be noisily divided. Moreover, the model tacitly assumes that no friction exists within the political system. In fact, congruence between mass opinion and the programs of leadership may develop gradually, and conversion of programs into public policy may be accomplished only after long delay. Nevertheless, after allowance for slippages and imperfections, a solid basis remains for the theory of the party as a link between public opinion and public policy. Over time parties acquire a general policy tendency that in some primeval way parallels the modal preferences of their followers. From time to time they espouse great causes, and, at widely separated moments, they close ranks and enact against the fiercest opposition programs that come to be regarded by common consent as promotive of the welfare of mankind.

1 · Popular Images of the Parties

Though the conception of the political party as an instrument by which the citizen relates himself to the governing process has a validity, the citizen does not necessarily make party instrumental of his ends by a simple rational choice. Citizen John Doe does not often study the issues, decide in what direction his preferences lie, ascertain which party more nearly espouses his preferences, and then affiliate with that party. Many citizens take actions that are equivalent in effect to this sequence of steps but which involve a choice far less conscious and deliberate. People tend to have a broad image of parties. They see a party as generally dedicated to the interests of a particular set of groups within society, or as committed to a broad range of policy objectives. Their shorthand image of party may encompass a bundle of particular policies about which information and opinions may be sparse; yet their commitment to party may give them leverage on that range of issues to the extent that the party machinery is animated by both good faith and competence as it translates into detailed actions its mandate to govern.[1]

Groups and the Popular Portrait of Parties. People often link themselves to the governing process through their images and impressions of the group sympathies and alliances of political parties. They carry crude diagrams in their heads that identify the group affiliates and allies of the major political parties. They regard this party as the friend of the workingman and that party as the advocate of the cause of business. These impressions of group interests of parties are probably formed fairly early in life, along with party identifications, and have a stability that is not unconnected with the persistent class and group antagonisms within the polity. These images reflect some of the elemental rivalries

[1] Graham Wallas long ago observed that party "is primarily a name, which, like other names, calls up when it is heard or seen an 'image' that shades imperceptibly into the voluntary realization of its meaning. As in other cases, emotional reactions can be set up by the name and its automatic mental associations. It is the business of the party managers to secure that these automatic associations shall be as clear as possible, shall be shared by as large a number as possible, and shall call up as many and as strong emotions as possible."—*Human Nature in Politics,* 3d ed. (London: Constable; 1920), pp. 83–4.

and conflicts that persist in the political order. In this context their importance is that they may serve as a handy shortcut to more or less rational action by the citizen. While his information about the questions that plague those with responsibility for decision may be limited and his grasp of the nuances of the discussion of public policy may be slight, he may have an image of one or the other of the parties as dedicated generally to the interests of his kind of people. To the extent that his perceptions correspond with the realities, he can, as he acts in terms of the broad image, act simultaneously on a series of specific issues.

The most common image of parties relates them to the causes of occupational and economic interests. Business and professional people have tended by large majorities to picture the Republican party as the party that best serves their interests. At the opposite end of the occupational hierarchy, unskilled workers picture the Democratic party as the agent of their interests. The occupational distribution of these perceptions of parties, as indicated by one of Dr. Gallup's surveys in 1959, appears in Table 17.1. That table indicates, too, that in all occupational categories sizable numbers of people saw no difference between the parties with respect to the question or dared not venture an opinion. Yet well over half the people probably have images of political parties as advocates of group interest. Furthermore, these images, though they may change over time, are fairly durable. At least since the invention of polling techniques the differential images of the Republican and of

TABLE 17.1

GROUP OPINIONS ABOUT WHICH PARTY BEST SERVES GROUP INTERESTS [a]

PARTY THAT
BEST SERVES
GROUP   RESPONDENT GROUP

	Business and professional	White-collar	Skilled workers	Unskilled workers	Farmers
Republican	58%	34%	16%	15%	20%
Democratic	15	32	50	54	54
No difference	14	23	16	14	17
No opinion	13	11	18	17	9
	100%	100%	100%	100%	100%

[a] The question was: "As you feel today, which political party—the Democratic or the Republican—do you think serves the interests of the following groups best:" with the appropriate group phrase put to those in each occupational category.
DATA SOURCE: *American Institute of Public Opinion, release of November, 10, 1959.*

the Democratic party have prevailed. Perhaps if we had comparable data for, say, 1900, the Republican party would have appeared then in a more prominent role as the ally of the industrial worker. However these images change through time, they serve as a means for the expression of an omnibus decision on a range of issues when group concerns happen to be foremost in the mind of the voter.

The dead figures in Table 17.1 give us little of the flavor of people's conceptions of parties and their group affiliates. They may even give us an erroneous notion of the differentials in the popular images of the two parties. People may respond to a set question even though the position they state is not one they would offer if they were not cued by the question. As the people who make up a randomly chosen national sample ruminate in response to open-ended questions on what they like and dislike about the major parties, they make five or six times as many references to group affiliations favorable to the Democratic party as to the Republican party.[2] The Democratic party is described favorably as the party of the farmer, of the workingman, of the poorer class, of the average man. Persons who make such comments often couple with them unfavorable references to the Republican party as the party of business, of the rich, of the corporations.

Excerpts from interviews during the 1956 presidential campaign indicate the tone of these group references. People were asked: "Is there anything in particular that you like about the Democratic party?" and "Is there anything in particular that you don't like about the Democratic party?" Like questions were put about the Republican party. The questions, thus, did not compel a group answer. Group references of party approbation and disapprobation came off the top of the respondents' heads. Though not chosen at random the following quotations do not misrepresent the spirit of the pro-Democratic and anti-Republican group references.

> A St. Louis electrician: (Like about the Democratic party?) "Yes, there is—the Democratic party is for the working people. I like what they do for the working man. I am a Democrat."

> A semiskilled California worker: (Like about the Democratic party?) "So far, the Democrats always interested in farmers. I was a farmer, my folks still are. The Republicans promise they will help farmers and then never do. We have no trouble with the sale of farm products and poor people have a better chance with the Democrats and the workingman does have, too, with Democrats."

[2] See Angus Campbell, Philip E. Converse, Warren E. Miller, and Donald E. Stokes: *The American Voter* (New York: Wiley; 1960), ch. 3.

The wife of a Connecticut salesman: (Like about the Democratic party?) "I like what they do for the laboring class. They try to improve working conditions—work for shorter hours—a higher wage rate—and are more interested in benefits for the workingman."

A Texas janitor: (Like about the Democratic party?) "I think Democrats are more for the workingman; give more help to the laboring class." (Dislike about the Republican party?) "That party has always been for moneyed men. I don't like them. They are for the big man; people with money."

A Bronx postal clerk: (Like about the Democratic party?) "They are for the small working man, who is me. The Republicans always stand for big business."

Waiter in San Francisco: (Like about the Democratic party?) "I like the Democrats because they fulfill what they promise. With the Democrats I always had a job and with the Republicans I was in the breadlines. (What else?) I feel the Democrats are for the small businessman and the poor people."

A Kentucky minister: (Like about the Democratic party?) "More a people's party. I think the Republican party has a different philosophy from the Democrats. They say prosperity trickles down rather than up from the people. It is a big business party."

A St. Louis policeman: (Like about the Democratic party?) "They are strictly for small individuals instead of for big corporations like the Republican party is. Republican leaders are controlled by monied men—that's what I don't like about the Republican party—it is run by large corporations."

A New York hotel maid: (Dislike about the Republican party?) "They are all right for the big shots in Wall Street."

South Dakota lady worker in a meat packing plant: (Like about the Republican party?) "Like I say they have their faults. Some say they're more for big business instead of the little people. (What do you think?) Oh, gee, I don't know. Maybe so."

Farm laborer in North Carolina: (Dislike about Republican party?) "I just don't like it at all. (Why is that?) Because they is for the rich people."

Georgia Negro maid of all work: (Like about the Democratic party?) "Yes, they don't be no depressions, when them Democrats is in. They just lets that money roll on and that's what I likes."

Little Rock housewife: (Like about the Democratic party?) "To me the Democratic party has always stood for the farmer and the workingman more than the Republican party."

Approving references to the group affiliates of the Republican party occur far less frequently. Occasionally a disarmingly straightforward observation turns up in interviews, but when people are asked what they like about the Republican party, they respond more often in nongroup terms. They may like its foreign policy, its candidate, or its skills in management, but not often do they volunteer a good word for its group associates. The popular image of the group affiliates of the Republican party is, on balance, negative. On the whole, people have other types of good things to say about the party. A few, doubtless unrepresentative, quotations suggest the types of responses people make.

A retired butler: (Like about Republicans?) "They're better learned and scholared than the Democrat's men. The millionaires are all Republicans. I've worked for ——, ——, ——, and others."

Retired Boston wholesaler: (Like about Republicans?) "The Democrats is all right but it's not a money party. I like to string along with big business and big money. Well, I'll also tell you under the Republicans the country has prospered."

North Carolina farm widow: (Like about Republican party?) "Sure, I like the high prices we get for our products and it's always been their policy to do that. The Democrats have always been a low cost of living party. We always felt that they don't cheat over votes like the Democrats." (Electoral practices in the vicinity of the lady's farm indicate that her perceptions are not entirely at war with reality.)

Registered nurse of South Dakota: (Like about Republican party?) "Oh gee, that's a hard question, I'm not too versed on politics that's for sure. I couldn't argue about this with anybody." (Anything at all?) "They haven't fought any battles in the last four years." (Anything else?) "No."

A Michigan janitor: (Like about the Republican party?) "My dad and his dad were strong Republicans and I guess it is in my blood too. Republican party is more of a party that promotes business and believes more in business principles."

Los Angeles saleslady: (Like about the Republican party?) "Well, I think they try not to dictate too much. They try hard to keep the promises they make. They are better qualified to run our government."

California doctor: (Like about the Republican party?) "A more stable and dignified party, a party able to handle all affairs at home and abroad. The party has clear vision. Serious minded people in office."

Indiana bank nightwatchman: (Like about the Republican party?) "They stand up for a good clean Constitution. In this age it is hard to keep clean politics but they do pretty good. They don't throw mud at the others."

Missouri farm housewife: (Dislike about the Democratic party?) "I just don't like them. Too much war minded." (Like about the Republican party?) "Sure, with Republicans they stand more for peace than Democrats do."

Wife of a Michigan minister: (Like about the Republican party?) "Their principles and ethics are of a higher caliber and are better founded in their religious views."

Pennsylvania farmer: (Like about the Republican party?) "Yes, They do more for the country and clean up Washington— never any drinking down there when the Republicans are in."

Detroit electrical construction worker: (Like about the Republican party?) "Right off hand I couldn't tell you. I'd have to read up on that."

The Reality of Party. When he reflects upon the nature of his favorite political party, the observant citizen must surely be puzzled about what it is in which he puts his faith. What kind of instrument is the party which theorists tell him serves his purpose? Its organizational apparatus consists of scattered pieces—the national committee, congressional party organizations, state committees, party clubs, and perhaps the precinct captain down the street—but these pieces seem to be tied together in common purpose only at the time of presidential campaigns, if then. The programs of the parties, if they come to the attention of the harried citizen, may seem to speak firmly only about such topics as support of peace and prosperity and opposition to socialism. Connection between the broad drives that seem to animate parties and the eventual output of the governmental machine is so tenuous that it may escape all save the most assiduous students of politics. Yet in one way or another the ponderous apparatus of party manages at times to mobilize the people in a way to affect the broad course of public policy.

One way in which the party manages to embody the aspirations of those who perceive it to be devoted to the concerns of specified groups is that it tends to be of those groups, or its most active components are of those groups. Our information about the composition of the party activists is inadequate. If we had a sample large enough, with sufficient information on the nature of the political activities of persons variously involved in politics, meaningful contrasts between party leadership echelons could be made. Even with the crude measures available, some revealing comparisons are possible. From time to time in the preceding chapters we have used an index of political participation in which those who both voted and participated in campaigns in one of a variety of other ways were classified as high participators. High participators in the Democratic and Republican parties doubtless set the general tone and orientation of the parties. The contrasting com-

TABLE 17.2

OCCUPATIONAL COMPOSITION OF PARTICIPATION STRATA WITHIN PARTY IDENTIFI-
CATION GROUPS

HEAD'S OCCUPATION   PARTICIPATION LEVEL AND PARTY IDENTIFICATION

	Low						High	
	1		2		3		4	
	D	R	D	R	D	R	D	R
White-collar	19%	19%	24%	24%	30%	34%	34%	48%
Blue-collar	46	48	55	41	43	31	43	27
Farmer	15	11	5	16	11	13	9	5
Other	20	22	16	19	16	22	14	20
	100%	100%	100%	100%	100%	100%	100%	100%
N	337	134	75	37	675	416	426	363

DATA SOURCE: *Survey Research Center, University of Michigan, a combination of 1952 and 1956 samples.*

position of the high-participation category in the two parties is consistent with the notion that the parties are of their group interests, not simply representative of them. Of Democratic high participators (Table 17.2), only 34 per cent fall into white-collar occupations; of the Republican group comparable in political activity, 48 per cent are from white-collar occupations. Substantially more Democratic than Republican high participators are blue-collar workers. Occupational differences between the party identifiers become more marked as level of political participation increases. Occupational contrasts hardly exist between nonvoting party identifiers. It is from among the high participators that the leadership echelons emerge, and, giving the contrasting occupational composition of the active partisans, the expectation would be that divergent policy emphases would be impressed upon the parties by their leadership cores.

Too few cases of genuinely high-level activists turn up in a national sample to permit their identification and a comparison of their policy outlook with that of the mass of the party. Yet some suggestion of the existence of an inner core of persons especially dedicated to the party's policy line may be obtained from an analysis of party identifiers according to their degree of political involvement. Involvement, it may

---

TABLE 17.3

RELATION BETWEEN LEVEL OF POLITICAL INVOLVEMENT OF REPUBLICAN PARTY
IDENTIFIERS AND THEIR POSITION ON SELECTED DOMESTIC ISSUES

ISSUE AND ISSUE POSITION	LEVEL OF INVOLVEMENT			
	Low			High
	1	2	3	4
Medical Care				
Disagree	21%	24%	36%	49%
Pro-con	9	7	14	10
Agree	49	54	41	33
No opinion	21	15	9	8
	100%	100%	100%	100%
Job Guarantee				
Disagree	11	30	34	45
Pro-con	9	5	4	9
Agree	59	55	52	40
No opinion	21	10	10	6
	100%	100%	100%	100%
Power and Housing				
Agree	24	44	56	68
Pro-con	8	7	7	4
Disagree	21	18	15	9
No opinion	47	31	22	19
	100%	100%	100%	100%
N	66	125	161	158

DATA SOURCE: *Survey Research Center, University of Michigan, 1956.*

---

be recalled, is measured by the degree of interest in the presidential campaign and the intensity of "care" about its outcome. The Republican party, it will surely be conceded, presents itself through its more prominent spokesmen as the party of laissez-faire, of "free enterprise," and of limited governmental activity. The more highly involved identifiers with the Republican party, as Table 17.3 indicates, subscribe to the orthodox tenets of this party doctrine far more frequently than do those Republicans with a low degree of political involvement. Of those with high involvement, for example, 68 per cent agreed with the proposition that such matters as power and housing ought to be left to private businessmen; of those with low involvement, only 24 per cent. Similarly, on the propositions about government help in medical care and in the assurance of job opportunities, far larger proportions of highly involved Republicans took the orthodox party position. The more highly involved 30 per cent or so of Republican identifiers manifest, thus, a higher degree of ideological purity than do the party strata of lesser political involvement.[3]

Similar differences in outlook among persons at different levels of involvement appear in Table 17.4, which relates level of involvement to views on the question whether the national government should do more, less, or about the same in trying to deal with "such problems as

TABLE 17.4

LEVEL OF POLITICAL INVOLVEMENT, WITHIN PARTY IDENTIFICATION GROUPS, IN RELATION TO OUTLOOK ON SOCIAL WELFARE ISSUE [a]

PARTY IDENTIFICATION AND POLICY OUTLOOK	LEVEL OF INVOLVEMENT			
	Low			High
	1	2	3	4
Democratic Identifiers				
Democratic outlook [b]	21%	20%	26%	35%
Republican outlook [c]	9	11	7	12
Republican Identifiers				
Republican outlook	8	21	29	41
Democratic outlook	18	27	23	17

[a] Responses to a question on whether the national government should do more or less in trying "to deal with such problems as unemployment, education, housing and so on." For text, see Appendix III.
[b] Classified as Democratic in outlook were those respondents who said that the national government should "definitely do more," "should do more," or "should do more on some." Entries are percentages of those at each participation level who made such responses.
[c] Classified as Republican in outlook were those responses coded "should do less," "definitely should do less," "less on some."
DATA SOURCE: *Survey Research Center, University of Michigan, 1952.*

[3] The differences in policy position among Democrats by levels of involvement on the questions dealt with in Table 17.3 differ from the Republican in the expected directions, but the contrasts between Democrats with high and low involvement are not so wide. Thus, on the medical-care issue 67 per cent of highly involved Democrats agree, in comparison with 57 per cent of those with low involvement. The wider intra-Republican than intra-Democratic contrasts probably come from the fact that the Democratic leadership position has a more powerful appeal to the relatively uninvolved, whatever their party identification, than does the Republican position.

unemployment, education, housing, and so on." It is fair to regard the yearning to do more in these fields as an orthodox Democratic position. The proportion of Democratic identifiers who take the orthodox Democratic position increases up the scale of political involvement. Similarly, among Republican identifiers the orthodox Republican becomes more frequent at the higher levels of involvement: 41 per cent of the highly involved Republican identifiers preferred that the national government do less in these fields of social welfare, while only 8 per cent of Republicans of least involvement took that position.

These data suggest that if information were available on the policy outlooks, say, of the upper 5 per cent of the party as determined by some measure of involvement or participation, this stratum would show an even more marked conformity with party doctrine than does the upper group as defined by the measures of involvement we have used. Moreover, we should expect the contrasts between the outlooks of these small leadership groups to be far sharper than the contrasts between our highly involved groups. Information consistent with these hunches has been accumulated by Herbert McClosky, who induced most of the delegates to the 1956 Democratic and Republican national conventions to check schedules that could be used to compute attitude scores on a liberalism-conservatism scale. These leaders showed far sharper attitudinal differences than did national samples of party voters. Moreover, the leadership groups in each party tended to develop far more homogeneity of attitude than did the party groups within the electorate.[4] Had it been possible to repeat the test in 1960, the delegates to the Republican national convention would probably have turned out to be on the average closer in outlook to Senator Goldwater than to Governor Rockefeller, and the delegates to the Democratic convention closer to Senator Humphrey than to Senator Byrd.[5]

2 · Party Identification and Policy Orientation

Many persons bring parties to their service by a mental shortcut. They see parties as committed to the interests of their kind of people or of kinds of people with whom they sympathize, but they may have no

[4] See Herbert McClosky, Paul J. Hoffman, and Rosemary O'Hara: "Issue Conflict and Consensus Among Party Leaders and Followers," *American Political Science Review*, LIV (1960), 406–27.

[5] The differences in attitudes between leadership levels and the mass of party identifiers should not be regarded as necessarily a reflection of intraparty conflict. In some instances, to be sure, such conflict may exist. Probably more often, though, highly active and involved partisans have more opportunity to learn the party rituals and slogans. The less-active group includes many loyal party followers not so well indoctrinated in the party outlook as the activists.

clear understanding of the substantive policies that will advance such causes. For many others a more direct connection between policy preference and party identification prevails; they have views on policy issues and see their party as dedicated to the advocacy of those views. This connection may develop in either of two ways. Persons may first have policy preferences and then ally themselves with the party they regard as more disposed to promote those preferences. Or they may have a sense of identification with a party and adopt those policy views that they perceive to be the party line. To be sure, the reality of the process of relation of policy preferences to party identification is more complex than this dichotomy suggests. Nevertheless, in one way or another correlations develop between issue opinions and party attachments, and the party becomes an instrument for the transformation of opinions into governmental action.[6]

Relation of Party Identification and Issue Position. Our information on the relation between party identification and issue position is neither comprehensive nor satisfactory. National sample surveys of attitudes have sought far more to explain the vote than to observe and understand the issue opinions of people. Surveys, though, have turned up a good deal of incidental information on the relation between party identification and issue position. The evidence suggests that party affiliation is more closely correlated with issue opinions on some questions than on others. On some contentious issues of domestic economic policy the center of gravity of "liberalism" has tended to be on the Democratic side and that of "conservatism," on the Republican side. Yet on other domestic economic issues resemblances between followers of the two parties far outweigh their dissimilarities. Issue cleavages probably more closely parallel party lines at some times than at others, although changes in the partisanship of issues over time have not been adequately recorded.

Illustrative of the broad contrast in outlooks of party identifiers is the fact that Democratic identifiers, on the average, support a wider scope of public-welfare activity than Republicans find congenial. An omnibus question that captures this broad contrast in domestic policy

[6] The conception of party as an instrument for popular action is a relatively sophisticated political idea, and it rests on a long sequence of invention of political institutions and practices as well as on a long process of mass adaptation to those institutions and practices. In the era of the American and the French revolutions, we are told, "the first manifestations of mass rather than class democracy took the form of mob action. . . . Mob action provided the first concrete indication of the common man's claim to participate in the decision-making process which is government, of his demand for a share of political power."—Lloyd I. Rudolph: "The Eighteenth Century Mob in America and Europe," *American Quarterly*, XI (1959), 447-69, quote 447.

outlook is the following: "Some people think the national government should do more in trying to deal with such problems as unemployment, education, housing and so on. Others think that the government is already doing too much. On the whole would you say that what the government is doing is about right, too much, or not enough?" While such a question may not tap opinion on the specific issues that enliven the front pages, it ought to check the general outlook of people toward the scope of governmental welfare activity. When put to a national sample in 1954, this question brought the responses that appear in Table 17.5.

TABLE 17.5

RELATION OF PARTY IDENTIFICATION TO OPINIONS ON SCOPE OF SOCIAL LEGISLATION [a]

OPINION	SD	WD	ID	I	IR	WR	SR
Should do more	41%	20%	23%	35%	38%	22%	11%
Doing about right	38	55	55	34	35	45	50
Should do less	4	8	4	7	12	15	22
Other responses	17	17	18	24	15	18	17
	100%	100%	100%	100%	100%	100%	100%
N	248	288	97	82	68	159	146

[a] The question was: "Some people think the national government should do more in trying to deal with such problems as unemployment, education, housing, and so on. Others think that the government is already doing too much. On the whole would you say that what the government is doing is about right, too much, or not enough?"
SOURCE: *A telescoping of table from Angus Campbell and Homer C. Cooper,* Group Differences in Attitudes and Votes (*Ann Arbor: Survey Research Center, 1956*), *p. 91.*

Among strong Democrats, those who thought the government should do more outnumbered by about ten to one those who thought it should do less. Among strong Republicans the ratio was about two to one in the opposite direction. While these differences in policy outlook at the extremes of party identification are sharp, goodly proportions of all party identification groups thought that what the government was doing was about right.

When attention is turned to more specific questions, Democratic and Republican identifiers are in sharp disagreement on some issues; on others majorities of Republicans and of Democrats are in agreement. The situation on a series of issues appears in the data of Table 17.6. Note there that on the question of leaving "things like electric power and housing" to private business Democratic identifiers are about evenly divided, while an overwhelming majority of Republican identifiers take

TABLE 17.6

RELATION BETWEEN PARTY IDENTIFICATION AND POSITION ON DOMESTIC ISSUES [a]

ISSUE POSITION	JOB GUARANTEE		MEDICAL CARE	
	D	R	D	R
Agree	68%	53%	69%	46%
Pro-con	6	8	8	12
Disagree	26	39	23	42
	100%	100%	100%	100%
N	507	365	497	359
	School Aid		Power and Housing	
Agree	79%	66%	45%	73%
Pro-con	6	11	9	9
Disagree	15	23	46	18
	100%	100%	100%	100%
N	516	373	411	307

[a] The party groups include only the strong and weak identifiers.
DATA SOURCE: *Survey Research Center, University of Michigan, 1956.*

the laissez-faire position. On the issue of government and medical care Republicans divide about evenly, while a substantial majority of Democrats take the stand that the government ought to do something to make medical and hospital care more readily available. On the other hand, on federal aid for school construction substantial majorities of the followers of both parties are in agreement.

The fact that all Republicans do not line up on one side of an issue and all Democrats on the other causes unhappiness among some commentators on the American party system. Yet overlapping distributions of opinion, such as those in Table 17.6, are precisely what we should expect, given the nature of the American system. Those opinion patterns show varying degrees of approach toward concurrent consensus between the parties. On all the issues a shadow of conflict remains, and the shades of difference between the parties are sharper on some issues than on others. In a regime that proceeds in considerable degree by the attempt to achieve common consent, we should expect agreement gradually to develop across party lines on major issues. Differences in the opinions of party identification groups may be most marked in the developmental or agitational stage in the life of issues. Issues arise, are settled, and die, or at least some of them die. At the point of most heated conflict the attitudinal differences between party identifiers may be clearest. If we had attitude data on issues running over a long enough period, we could picture the evolution of opinion from conflict to consensus and thus better understand the role of the party system in that process.[7]

Prevalence of policy agreement across party lines has led some observers to the conclusion that under such circumstances party cannot serve as an instrument for its identifiers and supporters. The fact seems to be that under conditions of consensus party may be instrumental in a nonpolicy sense. The question may become one of which party is better equipped to carry out policies about which there is precious little disagreement. The area of foreign policy is one in which in recent years the parties have come to be perceived largely in terms of nonpolicy differentiations.

Determination of what popular attitudes have a relevance for foreign policy is not a simple undertaking, but by some measures the distributions of the opinions of the mass of Republican and of Democratic partisans are almost exactly alike. Consider the remarkable similarity of the distribution of the opinions of Republican and Democratic identifiers along the Survey Research Center's 1956 scale of attitude toward international involvement as it appears in Table 17.7. That scale, it may be recalled, provides a rough indication of willingness to tolerate involvement abroad as indicated by opinions on propositions, such as those about aid to poorer countries, aid to foreign countries even

---

TABLE 17.7

RELATION OF PARTY IDENTIFICATION TO POSITION ON FOREIGN ISSUE SCALE

INTERNATIONALISM	DEMOCRAT	INDEPENDENT [a]	REPUBLICAN
High 5	24%	28%	27%
4	21	20	20
3	20	21	24
2	9	9	6
Low 1	6	7	6
Not scaled [b]	20	15	17
	100%	100%	100%
N	769	415	515

[a] Independents include those who leaned Democratic or Republican.
[b] Too few opinions to permit scaling.
DATA SOURCE: *Survey Research Center, University of Michigan, 1956.*

---

[7] Any theory of the American party system must take into account those issues that cannot be accommodated by the system. Those matters, such as school segregation, may be settled, if they ever are, to a large degree through channels other than the party system. Public opinion does not invariably work through the party system. Relations between citizen and government may be direct rather than mediated by the party.

though they are not so much against communism as we are, and the maintenance of soldiers overseas to help countries against communism. That few Democrats or Republicans rank low on such a scale should not be taken to mean that one-worlders predominate in both parties. Rather, most identifiers of both parties more or less reluctantly concede that the United States must maintain a high degree of economic and military involvement abroad to save our own neck.

Perhaps what the cross-party consensus on foreign policy amounts to is a willingness to support measures calculated to maintain the peace, although that willingness may not extend to "brush" wars. Cross-party consensus on policy, though, does not mean that the choice between parties becomes a matter of indifference. There may be no agreement on the question of which party is the better equipped or more disposed to move toward the achievement of an end generally accepted as good. On this question people may have bitter differences.

In the 1952 and 1956 campaigns the popular image was predominantly one of the Republican party as the party more likely to maintain peace. Past events reinforced the attempts of the Republican party to hang the tag of "war party" on the Democrats. Shortly before the 1956 election the AIPO reported that among those who had opinions on the topic those who thought the Republican party was more likely to keep the United States out of World War III outnumbered by more than two to one those who saw the Democratic party in that light.[8] The Republican party enjoyed at the same time a far greater advantage among those sufficiently concerned about war and peace to volunteer comments on this matter in response to open-ended questions about what they liked and disliked about the parties.[9] A few quotations from comments people made in 1956 in response to these open-ended questions will convey the tenor of sentiments about the Republican and Democratic parties in the field of foreign affairs.

A Connecticut tinsmith: (Like about Eisenhower?) "I think he's a great leader and a great President. If anyone can keep the country out of war, he can."

Wife of upstate New York building contractor: (Like about the Republican party?) "We have stayed away from war." (How

[8] The question was: "Which political party do you think would be more likely to keep the United States out of World War III—the Republican party or the Democratic party?" The responses: Republican party, 42 per cent; Democratic party, 17 per cent; no difference, 20 per cent; no opinion, 21 per cent. AIPO release of October 2, 1956.

[9] For the details, see Campbell, Converse, Miller, and Stokes: op. cit., ch. 3.

vote?) "I like Ike. I feel that he has kept us out of war—with two boys in the family that's outstanding in my mind."

Wife of Maryland salesman: (Vote for Ike, why?) "Because the war has been so close to us and Eisenhower knows what he is doing."

Wife of Boston streetcar operator: (Like about the Republican party?) "Well Eisenhower kept us out of war. We have had two wars under Democratic Presidents—World War II and the Korean War. The Republicans—or I should say Eisenhower has kept us out of war."

Wife of Bronx taxi driver: (Like about the Republican party?) "They kept us out of war and we were in a war when they took over."

Retired Missouri maid: (Dislike about Democrats?) "Yes, Roosevelt was head of the party that sent us to war. Boys trained to kill has provided present crime wave to kill at home. Sold our boys for prosperity, we did. They have provided too much education for youth these days."

When all such responses were classified into pro-Republican and pro-Democratic comments, the Republican party enjoyed an advantage

TABLE 17.8

PARTY IDENTIFICATION IN RELATION TO POSITION ON INDEX OF ATTITUDE ON FOREIGN ISSUES [a]

PARTISAN DIRECTION OF ATTITUDE	PARTY IDENTIFICATION				
	SD	WD	I	WR	SR
Pro R	12%	23%	37%	44%	51%
Neutral	78	72	59	52	46
Pro D	10	5	4	4	3
	100%	100%	100%	100%	100%
N	356	386	404	246	261

[a] This scale is based, not on responses to specific policy questions, but on the numbers of pro-Republican and pro-Democratic references on foreign issues in response to open-ended questions. Those respondents classified as pro-Republican made more references on foreign issues favorable to the Republicans. The neutral category consists of persons who made no references to foreign issues or who made an equal number of pro-Democratic and pro-Republican references.
DATA SOURCE: *Survey Research Center, University of Michigan, 1956.*

in all party identification groups. Strong Democrats were less disposed than strong Republicans to perceive the Republican party favorably; Democratic identifiers tended to take refuge in a neutral position. Even so, many Democratic identifiers shared the image of the Republican party as a party of peace. Republican intimations that the Democratic party was a war party, perhaps not even above the initiation of a war to maintain prosperity, had taken some root within the electorate. These differences among groups of party identifiers are shown in Table 17.8. In 1956 people tended to view the Republican party as the one more likely to keep the peace, although that opinion probably focused more on Eisenhower than on the Republican party.

Party As Opinion Maker. While the preceding discussion showed the relation between party identification and policy opinion, it touched scarcely on how that connection comes about. A political party, as we have seen, may be regarded either as an instrument for persons who are attracted to it by its policy posture or as a molder of the opinions of those who are already identified with it. The distinction between the two roles, however, becomes blurred when we place them in the time context in which party attachments are formed. For many persons party identification and the congruent policy outlooks are probably simultaneously formed, though over a lengthy period of time. A boy born into a business family, for example, may early acquire a Republican party identification and an image of that party as dedicated to the interests of his kind of people. He also gradually develops opinions on issues that are congenial to his party and group identifications. In a poetic sense, he is "attracted" to the party because the party's issue positions parallel his own. Yet other individuals, probably relatively few in the entire electorate, more or less deliberately adopt a party identification congruent with their beliefs on public policy. Evidence on changes in party identification shows that conservative individuals tend to move from a Democratic to a Republican identification and liberals to shift their party attachments from Republican to Democratic.[1] For these persons the instrumental function of party appears in its clearest form.

A party may mold, as well as reflect, opinions. Party followers may adopt the policy postures of the party leadership. To some extent this process of shaping opinions doubtless occurs slowly during the political maturation of the party identifier. One source of the opinions of our hypothetical son of a business family may be the pronouncements of the party leadership that fall within his range of perception. The

[1] Ibid., p. 214.

party also shapes opinions on new and transient issues over shorter periods of time. Such short-term influence may even alter the direction of
party-associated opinions of fairly long standing. Usually, though, to
affect the balance of opinion within the party group by such changes
requires time. Not all partisans read the party line in the newspaper at
breakfast and proceed to talk it up during the day. The party line itself
changes gradually, and as it becomes clearer and clearer, more party
identifiers reconcile themselves to the new directions of party policy.

Probably the limitations on the party as an opinion molder are severe. Its influence is restricted to those persons who have both an awareness of an issue and a clear perception of the party position on it. It is
also restricted to those issues about which the party leadership holds a
position of some clarity. The party's influence doubtless also encounters
varying degrees of resistance and acceptance among those who perceive
the party position. One would expect the effect to be most marked on
those who value their party attachments most highly and have the least
personal interest or concern in conflict with the perceived party position.

Though the extent of party influence on the views of its identifiers
is not easily established, the evidence clearly indicates that it exists. Survey questions that give the respondent a cue to party position are likely,
at least in some instances, to produce a sharp cleavage in response
among partisans. Thus, the following question was put by Dr. Gallup in
1935 in the infancy of opinion polling: "Are you in favor of the present
administration's agricultural policy as embraced in the AAA?" The response by Democrats and Republicans was:

	Democrats	Republicans
Yes	70%	8%
No	30	92

The question gave a cue to those who may have never heard of the policy and really had no opinion one way or another. Many Democrats
supported and many Republicans opposed the agricultural policy because of its association in the question with the Democratic Administration.

The most persuasive evidence on the influence of party as a molder
of opinion comes from studies of the relation of party identification to
attitudes on foreign-policy questions. This policy area, in which few
people have guides in their own immediate experience or interest (in
contrast with, for example, the job-guarantee issue), is one in which
people might be expected to be especially prone to look to trusted cen-

ters of leadership for guidance.[2] Evidence suggests that as the position of party leaders on foreign-policy issues is altered, the opinions of party identifiers also change to come into line with the new position of party leadership. Belknap and Campbell in 1951 analyzed the correlates of opinion on a series of foreign-policy questions and found that party identification was more closely related to opinion than were such variables as type of residence (rural or metropolitan), religion, and income. With such factors held constant, foreign-policy opinions differed with party identification. The hypothesis was put forward that "for many people Democratic or Republican attitudes regarding foreign policy result from conscious or unconscious adherence to a perceived party line, rather than from influences independent of party identification." [3]

Evidence in support of the hypothesis that party cues shaped the foreign-policy opinions of party identifiers gained strength from a subsequent showing that attitudes had changed, apparently in response to altered leadership cues. Campbell and Cooper found that in the country as a whole from 1952 to 1954 a marked shift in position had occurred on the general question whether the country had gone too far in involvement with problems in other parts of the world.[4] After General Eisenhower's investiture as President, most Republican leaders of prominence began to take a far more internationalist position than had been generally associated with the party. The change in the related public opinion between 1952 and 1954 consisted in large part of a change among Republican party identifiers and was especially marked among those who called themselves strong Republicans. Some Republicans may have altered their opinions to accomodate themselves to the new party line, though it must be remembered that both party leaders and identifiers had been subjected to the new realities of the place of the United States in the world.

The best guess is that the party's actual impact in the short run as a molder of opinion is ordinarily limited to a small proportion of the entire electorate. Those limitations fall within the numbers of persons

[2] Recall here the laboratory evidence on group influence. From one of his experiments Asch concluded: "When confronted with a fictitious standard of a congenial group and a sharply divergent authentic ego-standard, there was a tendency to take the standpoint indicated by the group-standard." These conclusions apply only to judgments about matters which "are objectively unclear," which may describe many foreign-policy questions.—S. E. Asch: "Studies in the Principles of Judgments and Attitudes: II. Determination of Judgments by Group and by Ego Standards," *Journal of Social Psychology*, XII (1940), 433–65.

[3] George Belknap and Angus Campbell: "Political Party Identification and Attitudes Toward Foreign Policy," *Public Opinion Quarterly*, XV (1951–2), 601–23.

[4] Angus Campbell and Homer C. Cooper: *Group Differences in Attitudes and Votes* (Ann Arbor: Survey Research Center; 1956), pp. 88–90.

with sufficient attention to public affairs to perceive the positions of the party leaders. These persons may make up no more than from a fourth to a third of the electorate; those who adapt their opinions to conform to the party norm constitute some unknown fraction of these proportions.[5] Quite another phenomenon exists when persons support or go along with their party even though they may be either uninformed or indifferent about its policy positions. This type of behavior may be extremely important in the political process, but it constitutes party mobilization of support, not party formation of issue opinion.

American parties are poorly equipped to inform and shape the opinions of their followers. Formation of party policy is itself haphazard. Platforms customarily make fairly clear the contrasting policy positions on the few issues on which the parties differ, but these critical elements of the platforms are usually veiled by a good deal of verbiage and are not brought effectively to the attention of the party identifiers. Presidential candidates may or may not make the party position clear. In the periods between campaigns machinery for the formation of the minority party position is either nonexistent, or many party spokesmen enunciate various policies both conflicting and consistent but invariably confusing.

Accommodation to Party Situation by Distortion of Perception. The materials we have examined on the relation between party identification and policy position incidentally show considerable divergence between the more or less objective policy positions of party leaderships and the policy positions of party identifiers. Many Republicans agreed that the "government in Washington ought to see to it that everybody who wants to work can find a job." They also thought that the "government ought to help people get doctors and hospital care at low cost." While the Republican and Democratic positions on these ques-

---

[5] The basis for these comments is as follows. In its 1956 survey the Survey Research Center obtained opinions on a series of broad policy questions which have been repeatedly cited in these chapters. A set of screening questions permitted an estimate, probably an underestimate, of the numbers of persons with an awareness of party position. Those who had no opinion on each issue were screened out. Those with an opinion were asked: "On the question of the government (helping people get medical care or what not) is the government going too far, doing less than it should or what?" When those who had not heard what the government was doing or had no opinion about its performance were screened out, those who remained were asked: "Would the Democrats or the Republicans be closer to what you want on this issue, or wouldn't there be any difference?" Those who saw either the Democrats or the Republicans as closer to their own position constituted from a minimum of 22 per cent to a maximum of 37 per cent of the national sample on the 16 questions. Probably chiefly within these groups would be found those whose views had been formed by party cues.

tions in 1956 were not as different as night and day, there is little question that the Democratic party was more disposed to exert federal authority in these fields.

How do people reconcile their party faith with their conflicting policy beliefs? They do so in many ways. They may not be aware of party differences. They may not be greatly concerned about the issue on which they see conflict. To some extent they warp the party position to fit their own views. Berelson found that in Elmira some people simply twisted their perceptions of the stand of their favored candidate into accord with their own views. Those Republicans who favored price control, an issue of prominence in 1948, tended to see Governor Dewey as also favoring price control, a view that involved a misperception of the Governor's forthright stand.[6]

Party as Coupler of Opinion and Government: Summary Comments. All these data permit us to make a few summary observations on the role of political party as an instrument of public opinion. The discussion began with the conception of the political party as a means for the aggregation of the opinions of like-minded people and for the conduct of government in accord with those opinions. That simple view, though it has a kernel of validity, must be supplemented if it is better to approximate the reality.

The party group, the evidence makes plain, is not the product of a mercurial combination of individuals with like opinions to promote or resist policy proposals of the moment. It is, rather, a fairly stable group whose broad policy orientations roughly parallel the group interests

[6] Not much can be said with confidence about what proportions of the national electorate distort the position of their party to fit their own predilections, save that the proportions probably vary from issue to issue and from time to time. Some data about perception of party position on the 1956 job-guarantee question are of relevance. If support of the position that "the government in Washington ought to see to it that everybody who wants to work can find a job" is regarded as the Democratic position, 3 per cent of the national sample consisted of Democratic identifiers who took the Republican position but saw the Democratic party as closer to their own position. Another 5 per cent consisted of Republicans who took the Democratic position but saw the Republican party as closer to their own position. Another 1 per cent consisted of reverse distorters, Democrats who took the Democratic position but saw the Republican party as closer to their own position. Republicans with a Republican view who saw the Democratic party as closer to their own opinion made up less than half of 1 per cent of the sample. These figures probably understate distortion of perception, since the question about party position came after those unable or unwilling to express an appraisal of government performance with respect to the question had been screened out. Further, some of those who professed to see no difference between the parties may have been accommodating themselves to conflict by a distortion of perception.

and general policy expectations of a substantial proportion of its identifiers. The images people hold make parties instruments available for use
when the broad standing differences between the parties become salient
in public attention.

Given the nature of the party as an instrument and the kinds of
broad issues with which it is associated in the minds of its followers, one
should not necessarily expect an immediate articulation in time or a precise congruence in fit between the opinions of party identifiers and
party leadership. Yet of the capacity of mass opinion to bring party to
its service in the long run there can be little doubt. Nor does the recognition of the function of party as an instrument of opinion require acceptance of the notion that party leadership must "mirror" the opinion
of partisans. Opinions within party groups are not of a uniform shade
on any issue. Techniques of opinion measurement make it plain that in
large groups of persons opinions on almost any issue are dispersed along
some sort of scale. To reflect those gradations as by a mirror would
make governance difficult. Respect at leadership levels for mass opinion
must to a degree involve a misrepresentation of mass opinion.

Further, interaction between party leadership and party identifiers
may form as well as reflect opinion. By their evangelism party advocates create opinion. They may also create opinion after as well as before governmental action. Some great governmental innovations occur
in advance of public acceptance rather than after. Bold and imaginative
action may be followed by the generation of a supportive opinion—or
the party leadership may find itself discredited.

In another way, linkage of opinion and action becomes loose, perhaps especially in areas of policy consensus, because the issues may not
be about broad ends but about means. At stages in the development of
policy, parties may be effective instruments for decision about larger
ends of public policy. Once consensus develops, it is often senseless to
talk in terms of public opinion, for the issue may be a highly technical
question of means. Most people may, for example, agree that government should maintain employment, but they are unlikely to have views
about whether a boost in the interest rate or an adjustment of the tax
rate at a given time will achieve the desired end. And even if an opinion
could be whipped up on such matters, it would probably be worthless.
(Even the experts may not know the answers.)

These remarks require reference again to the special ethical imperatives under which governing levels of democratic orders must operate.
The steps from the broad aspirations of a people to their effectuation in
public policy are numerous and tortuous. Opportunities for humbug-
ging the people are also numerous. Achievement of popular government consists, not in a simple leadership reflex in response to popular

mandate, but in fidelity in the attempt to give definition to vague popular aspirations and in the search for technical means for their effectuation. The governance of a popular regime requires a powerful indoctrination of leadership elements with its special norms of governance. If exploitation is the object of governance, different rules of the game prevail.

3 · Minority Party in the Opinion System

The political party in a crude fashion bundles up the preferences and aspirations of individuals—in the process contributing to the formation of those preferences and aspirations—and seeks over the long run to move public policies in the appropriate direction. The conceptions of opinion formation that have emerged as the analysis has proceeded enable us to specify another role of the minority party in a system that professes to pay heed to public opinion. The idea has become apparent that opinion cannot be treated in isolation from its institutional setting. In considerable measure it must be a product of mass interaction with points of leadership—both formal political leadership and the many nonofficial centers for the dissemination of intelligence and the advocacy of points of view.

In the light of this conception the minority party acquires a role of special significance in democratic systems. It falls heir to that position in part because of the behavioral tendencies of those who control governments. Universal truths about human behavior are suspect, but one behavior that is predictable is the tendency of governments to present their actions in the most favorable light possible. They try to conceal their errors and derelictions. They seek to control the flow of information about their activities. They attempt to bring public opinion to the service of their allies and supporters in the political system. At bottom, they tend toward a monopolization of the flow of information and of the function of molding opinion. The extent to which governments carry these tendencies varies enormously; governments are restrained in one way or another. Yet even in mature democracies these tendencies manifest themselves to some degree.

These broad circumstances invest the minority party with its special role vis-a-vis public opinion. Its leaders, especially those in representative bodies, are in a position to crack the government's monopoly of information and to bring to public attention the blunders and misdeeds of the party in power. This function of informing the public is exercised against the background of latent opinions and attitudes not only among the minority partisans in the electorate but among people generally. The function of prying out information and of exposure of misdeeds becomes effective principally when some general consensus prevails on values or on policy objectives—that is, when the moral of the facts is obvious. When majority opinion condones thievery or special privilege, castigation of the government arouses no latent opinion of disapprobation. The minority purveys intelligence to the public, or at least to the attentive parts of it. The minority thereby forms opinion on both the substantive policies of government and the conduct of government. In the performance of its role the minority must, of course, have access to the public through the media.

In a sense, then, the minority becomes not only an instrument for the formation of opinion but the weapon that gives majority opinion its ultimate sanction. Without some such instrument at hand the public may complain, it may mutter, it may convene in groups and pass resolutions, and it may gather in mobs. Yet its ultimate sanction against those who control government is the availability of a minority leadership capable of governing. Governments may pay heed to public wishes and preferences in part because of the norms of value and behavior internalized by the impact of the political culture on the political activists. They may also pay heed because of the fear that if they do not do so, another crowd of politicians will.

In another respect, the minority may occupy a special position vis-à-vis public opinion in the advocacy of policy innovation. Opinion supportive of policy innovation does not bubble from the public as steam from a kettle. Opinion is generated as a response to leadership proposals that are propitiously timed and appropriately framed. Leadership of the minority party functions as one of the centers for the origination and advocacy of innovative policy ideas. A common supposition of American politics is that parties only pick up proposals for policy innovation after they have gained some momentum from their advocacy by other centers of leadership. Be that as it may, new policy proposals on matters of wide significance are not likely to make much headway unless they are adopted by a political party.

The performance of these functions of the minority party is conditional on the possession by the political system of certain special characteristics. The range of objectives of the minority must exclude revolution. The existence of agreement on a range of broad issues defines in part the area within which the minority may exercise its functions. In a sense the operation of a responsible minority also depends on the nature of the latent opinions and attitudes within the population. A population that includes large numbers of persons receptive to destructive leadership encourages the development of such leadership. The performance of the minority role thus depends on a restraint and a recognition of the rules of the game in the leadership echelons and on a compatible set of expectations and norms within the population.

Whether the American institutional arrangements are properly designed for the best execution of the minority role may be doubted. The aggrandizement of the President, especially by the electronic media, has made the dispersed minority leadership one of low public visibility. Even more serious is the limitation induced by the occasional control of the presidency by one party and of Congress by another. The mixture of majority and minority roles in Congress under these circumstances greatly limits the party that does not control the Executive. Its fulfillment of the minority role is embarrassed by the necessity that it must to some extent behave as a majority if government is to be maintained. One must add to these problems of long standing the special obstacles to the performance of the minority role in opinion leadership in what has become to no small degree a garrison state. When it digs out the facts on the conditions of the defense system and the performance of the Administration, the opposition may risk disclosure of data that would give aid and comfort to the enemy. Without public disclosure public opinion in appraisal of governmental performance can only be uninformed. Moreover, in some other aspects of foreign policy the maintenance of an impression of firmness of purpose abroad requires to some degree the maintenance of conflict at home at a subdued level.

Of another order and perhaps of profound significance is the role of the minor party in the development of accretions to the body of consensus on broad issues. Party leaders focus their attention on the attainment of office and are not much disposed to fight for lost causes. They tend to abandon positions that have clearly been rejected by majority opinion. As they do so, they also tend to bring their followers around to acceptance of that which has prevailed. In this manner the minority leadership plays a part in the reconciliation of its followers to the new order of things.

18

ELECTIONS

ELECTIONS are basic means by which the people of a democracy bend government to their wishes. In both their symbolism and their reality free elections distinguish democratic regimes. They occupy a prominent place in the political faith of democratic orders. The morale of a democracy depends in part on the maintenance of the belief that elections really serve as instruments of popular government, that they are not rituals calculated only to generate the illusion of deference to mass opinion. Since American parties attract the loyalties of persons with considerable similarity of policy views, it might be supposed that elections would merely record the numbers who identify with the major parties. Although the sense of party identification introduces a degree of stability into voting behavior, the looseness of party attachments also assures that at each polling a sector of the electorate considers the alternatives anew. Elections are not occasions at which solid partisan phalanxes march to the polls; they are opportunities for decision, and politicians are not without anxiety as they await their outcome.

The travails of democracies in the past half-century have tarnished the image of elections as an instrument of popular decision. Abortive installations of democratic practices in nations scattered over the world have contributed to this disenchantment, though the moral may be that democratic procedures are workable only under some circumstances and then only by people habituated to their requirements. Yet even

American publicists seem to share the global disillusionment with electoral decision. The ancient distrust of democracy gains reinforcement from the indiscriminate projection to mass electoral behavior of the findings of psychology that men's behavior contains an element of irrationality. Dissemination of these views makes it easy for many people to believe that the highbinders of Madison Avenue can humbug the American people in an election.[1] Among some intellectuals doubts about the vitality of the electoral process may flow from sociological interpretations of electoral behavior as but the conditioned by-product of social status, occupational position, or some other deterministic relation. Of the relevance of these factors for electoral behavior there can be no doubt, but of their controlling influence in the political system there must be serious reservation. The American electorate sooner or later belies all predictions built on deterministic assumptions.

Obviously one cannot maintain that public opinion is projected through elections with a crystalline clarity to animate governments to actions in accord with patterns it prescribes in precise detail. If such were the reality, governments would be hamstrung. Nevertheless, by elections the people make great decisions, which may have a heavy substantive policy content. Elections probably serve better as instruments for popular decision on broad and great issues; the details and the trivia may be beyond popular control, a fact that at times may lead to a defeat of the majority preferences in the minutiae of administration. The popular decision has components in addition to those of substantive policy. Elections cannot be regarded solely as a conduit for the transmission of policy preferences to government. They also express other judgments and preferences—such as those about candidates and about past performance of government—as well as policy desires. In short, elections matter, and they serve in the political system as a basic connection between public opinion and government. The problem is to indicate how this linkage occurs and on what kinds of questions it seems most clearly controlling.

1 · Voting and Substantive Issues

The despair that leads some analysts to dismiss elections as of no avail in the expression of public opinion comes in part from the simpleminded model against which they test actual elections. That model as-

[1] It may be doubted that Madison Avenue foisted General Eisenhower off on the American electorate. Probably about all the advertising agencies did was to embellish the image of a presold product. At earlier epochs in American history party managers have found prominent generals both available and capable of election.

sumes that elections ought in some way to separate people into two groups: a majority consisting of persons in agreement on a series of propositions to the execution of which their candidate was committed and the minority made up of persons on the other side of the same issues to which position their candidate had committed himself. So stark a model is so remote from reality that its uses are limited in speculation about the place of elections in the political process. Its assumption that the world of opinion is one of blacks and whites does not accord with the existence of gradations of opinion. Nor does the model take into account variations in intensity of opinion from question to question. In it the relative salience of issues for people finds no recognition. Nor does it make allowance for the fact that on many specific questions mass opinion may be uninformed, though most people may have broad sentiments or preferences that may be regarded as logically, if not always practically, controlling of subsidiary issues. Moreover, the model assumes that public opinion is to be regarded as acting prospectively when, in fact, its most forceful expressions may be retrospective judgments about policy and performance.

As has been demonstrated, the citizen's identification with party tends to produce a tie consistent with his policy preferences. To some extent this results from the matching of conscious policy preferences with policy positions taken with some clarity by the parties. To some extent it consists in policy through agency as the citizen perceives his party to be dedicated to the interests of persons like himself. When election day rolls around, though, the citizen may not vote in accord with his party identification. His party attachment is somewhat like his church membership; he regards it as no binding commitment to attend Sunday services. The looseness of their party attachments permits many Americans to bring their voting closer into line with the concerns salient to them at the moment of the election than it would be if undeviating partisan loyalty prevailed. As the voters respond to the changing realities, a fairly impressive correlation prevails between the vote and policy preferences on the salient issues. Moreover, voting decisions inconsistent with party identification often result from policy preferences. The act of voting is by no means devoid of policy content and intent.

Relation between Vote and Policy Preference. The more conscious the American voter is of policy issues and the more aware he is of party policy, the more likely he is to cast a ballot consistent with his policy preferences. This interpretation runs counter to easy generalizations to the effect that the voter is a boob at the mercy of slick operators. Certainly some voters magnificently fulfill that specification, but the motivations that bring many people to a decision about their presidential vote include a policy component. For some voters substantive policy is far more central than for others; yet few who take the trouble to vote are entirely lacking in policy preferences.

The relationship between policy preference and vote is neatly demonstrated by Table 18.1, which merits close examination. That table relates the individual's vote to his perception of the positions of the parties on issues on which he had opinions. Those who had opinions

---

TABLE 18.1

PRESIDENTIAL VOTE IN RELATION TO VOTER'S PERCEPTION OF CLOSENESS OF THE PARTIES TO HIS POSITION ON SIXTEEN POLICY ISSUES [a]

NUMBER OF PRO-DEMOCRATIC PERCEPTIONS	NUMBER OF PRO-REPUBLICAN ISSUE PERCEPTIONS			
	0	1–2	3–5	6–16
0	36%	14%	3%	2%
1–2	72	41	16	3
3–5	81	60	33	14
6–16	89	78	b	c

[a] Entries are percentages of those in each cell reporting a Democratic presidential vote in 1956. See text for discussion of construction of table.
[b] Only 12 cases fell in this cell; 8 reported a Democratic vote.
[c] No cases in this cell.
DATA SOURCE: *Survey Research Center, University of Michigan, 1956.*

---

on the issue propositions included in the 1956 Survey Research Center inquiry were asked whether they thought the government was going too far, about right, or not far enough in each policy field.[2] Some people had no notion of what the government had been doing or no opinion about whether its action was too much or too little; these persons were screened out. Those who survived this test were asked whether the Democrats or Republicans were closer to their preferences on the issue. Response to this inquiry separated out people who saw a distinction between the parties on the issue. A person thus might have a pro-Democratic perception or a pro-Republican perception on from one to sixteen issues. Or he might see the Democrats as closer to him on one issue and the Republicans as closer to his preferences on a dozen issues. Or the predominance of perception and preference might be in the other direction.

[2] For the text of the issue propositions, see Appendix I.

The relationships to the reported vote of these perceptions of party positions on issues, shown in Table 18.1, are startling in their clarity. Of those persons who saw the Republicans as "closer" to what they wanted on from six to sixteen issues and simultaneously gave the Democrats the nod on not a single issue, 98 per cent voted Republican. At the other extreme, of those who saw the Democrats in a comparably favorable issue light, 89 per cent voted Democratic. Between these extremes the division of the vote varied roughly with correspondence between the perceptions of issue positions of the parties and the voters' preferences. Those most concerned with issues, as measured by the numbers of issues on which they had perceptions of party positions, most frequently brought their vote into line with their policy perceptions. The table also clearly indicates that factors in addition to substantive issues enter into the vote decision. Of those who had no impression of party position on any of the sixteen issues, only 36 per cent voted Democratic.[3] If factors other than policy issues had been equal between the parties, a 50:50 split would have been expected in this cell. The other intermediate cells of the table also reflect the net balance of Republican advantage in the nonpolicy influences in this election.[4]

Determination of the political attitudes of a national sample of people and estimation of which attitudes are most relevant to the vote are not operations readily accomplished with imposing precision. One reason, though, why some confidence can be placed in what we have discovered is that alternative procedures yield essentially the same results. In addition to the data on responses to inquiries about specific issues, data are available on issue attitudes expressed in response to open-ended questions. Respondents could indicate what happened to be on their minds as they commented on such questions as: "Is there anything in particular that you like about the Democratic party?" "Is there anything in particular that you don't like about the Democratic party?" In their replies respondents often remarked that they liked a party because of its social security policy, its farm policy, its military policy, or for

[3] The form of the interview schedule probably excluded the possibility of identifying some issue concern within this group; that is, some of those persons screened out because they could make no estimate of government performance may have, nevertheless, perceived one of the parties as dedicated to their own opinion.

[4] The technician may be concerned about the numbers in each cell of the table. The 0–0 cell, those with no perceptions of party positions on policy as measured by the schedule, made up 16 per cent of the sample of voters. (Had nonvoters been included in this tabulation the proportion in the 0–0 cell probably would have been higher.) The extreme Republican cell, no pro-Democratic perceptions and from six to sixteen pro-Republican perceptions, constituted 18 per cent of the sample of voters. The comparable extreme pro-Democratic cell made up 14 per cent of the sample.

other reasons with some policy content. From the form of the questions these observations were in approbation or disapproval of a party. When coded, the responses might indicate that a person took a pro-Democratic position in that the number of his pro-Democratic policy comments exceeded the number of pro-Republican comments; a neutral position might be indicated by no policy comments or an equal number of comments in opposite partisan directions; or a person might have a net pro-Republican policy position. When the partisan direction of policy position is determined in this way, a fairly high degree of correspondence prevails between policy outlook and the reported presidential vote. These relationships, in domestic and foreign policy, appear in Table 18.2.

TABLE 18.2

RELATIONSHIP OF ISSUE POSITION AS DETERMINED BY RESPONSES TO OPEN-ENDED QUESTIONS AND PRESIDENTIAL VOTE

VOTE		DOMESTIC-ISSUE POSITION		
		Pro R	Neutral	Pro D
R		86%	62%	32%
D		14	38	68
		100%	100%	100%
	N	338	557	377
		FOREIGN-ISSUE POSITION		
R		82%	51%	32%
D		18	49	68
		100%	100%	100%
	N	423	774	75

DATA SOURCE: *Survey Research Center, University of Michigan, 1956.*

The relationships between the direction of vote and policy position do not necessarily mean that people voted Democratic or Republican because of their policy inclinations. Some of them adopted these policy positions because they voted Democratic or Republican. Moreover, probably relatively few persons change their votes at each election to bring them into conformity with their policy preferences. The correlations picture in large part a standing relationship rather than one developed anew at each polling. The relationships also doubtless reflect some misinformation and wishful thinking as people warped their perception of their candidate's position into agreement with their own views. Nevertheless, the parallelism among issue-oriented people between their vote and their perceptions is impressive, however it comes about.[5]

Movement toward Harmony between Vote and Policy Preference. The conformity of policy preference with vote does not result from a happenstance association between party choice and policy preference. As people shift their voting position, they tend to bring it into harmony with their policy preferences. The resulting parallelism never achieves completeness, for people have diverse interests and combinations of preferences in politics. Conformity of vote and policy preference is closer on some issues than on others and closer at some times than at other times.

These movements toward conformity are shown to exist by two types of data. They take place through time when a person shifts from a Democratic vote in 1948, say, to a Republican vote in 1952 and by this step brings his vote into line with his policy preferences and his perceptions of the policy orientations of the parties. In another way a person may at a particular election move away from his party identification to vote in a manner that he feels better fits his policy preferences. Thus, a farmer who professes to be a strong Republican may vote for a Democratic candidate because he dislikes Republican farm policy.

Illustrative of the first type of data are findings on shifts of voters from 1928 to 1932. The movements, Republican to Democratic and Democratic to Republican, between these two elections formed a pattern that recurs. From 1928 to 1932 the "more conservative voters tended to move toward the Republican party and the more progressive toward the Democratic." The result of the movement was to increase the attitudinal differences between the party groups. Conservatives who had voted for Al Smith in 1928 tended to become Hoover supporters in 1932; liberals who had voted for Hoover tended to vote for Roosevelt in 1932.[6]

The movement from the candidate of one party to that of another

[5] On the relation between issue position and presidential vote in 1952, see Angus Campbell, Gerald Gurin, and Warren E. Miller: "Political Issues and the Vote: November, 1952," *American Political Science Review*, XLVII (1953), 359–85.

[6] Samuel P. Hayes, Jr.: "The Inter-Relations of Political Attitudes: IV. Political Attitudes and Party Regularity," *Journal of Social Psychology*, X (1939), 503–52. This study was based on 8,000 schedules collected by members of the League of Women Voters before the election of 1932. The mode of selecting the respondents would not meet the standards of modern sampling practice, but there cannot be much doubt about the validity of the finding cited above.

through time does not consist solely of persons motivated by policy considerations. Even in the same individual policy motivations may be mixed with other concerns. From 1948 to 1952 large numbers of Truman voters moved to the support of Eisenhower. These D-R voters were on the average less dedicated to pro-Democratic positions on a series of policy issues than were the faithful who adhered to the Democrats in both 1948 and 1952, a contrast especially marked among the D-R switchers in the South. Yet the D-R group as a whole did not take a pro-Republican policy position in the same degree as did the hard core that voted Republican in both 1948 and 1952. Policy motivations among the D-R shifters were supplemented by their favorable impressions of the Republican candidate.[7] While voters may shift their support from the candidate of one party to that of another for policy reasons, they may also shift for other causes. There is some support for the belief that the group most susceptible to shift through time with the popular tide consists of those individuals completely devoid of policy interests or concerns.

Another illustration of the urge toward congruence of policy and voting preference rests on the tendency of voters to bolt the party with which they are identified when its policies displease them; they consider themselves strong Democrats or strong Republicans but decide to

TABLE 18.3

PRESIDENTIAL VOTE IN RELATION TO PARTY IDENTIFICATION AND OPINION ON SCOPE OF SOCIAL WELFARE ACTIVITIES OF GOVERNMENT [a]

PARTY IDENTIFICATION	OPINION ON WELFARE ACTIVITIES		
	Should do less	Is about right	Should do more
Strong Democratic	35%	85%	90%
Weak Democratic	35	66	68
Independent	10	36	56
Weak Republican	0	6	15
Strong Republican	0	1	2

[a] Entries are percentages of those in each cell reporting a Democratic vote in 1952. The question was: "Some people think the national government should do more in trying to deal with such problems as unemployment, education, housing, and so on. Others think that the government is already doing too much. On the whole, would you say that what the government has done has been about right, too much, or not enough?"

DATA SOURCE: *Survey Research Center, University of Michigan, 1952.*

[7] See Angus Campbell, Gerald Gurin, and Warren E. Miller: *The Voter Decides* (Evanston: Row, Peterson; 1954), 168–72.

vote for the opposition candidate at a particular election. This process finds illustration in the tendency in 1952 for those Democrats to vote Republican who thought their party had gone too far in the social-welfare field. Of those Democratic identifiers who took a conservative position on welfare policy, 65 per cent voted Republican. Only 10 per cent of those strong Democrats who thought the national government should do more in the welfare field were drawn to Eisenhower by the siren calls of the 1952 campaign. In the other direction, 15 per cent of that small band of weak Republicans favoring broader welfare activity resisted the pressures of the campaign and voted for Stevenson. The details appear in Table 18.3.

The relation between policy preference and vote appears also in a negative way; that is, the less interest and information a person has about policy, the less likely he is to vote. The greater the policy content of an individual's political concern, the more powerful is this interest in both bringing him to the polls and in fixing the direction of his vote. There are other dimensions to autonomous disfranchisement. Some people are so little involved politically that they care not at all how the election comes out.[8] Measures of degree of "care" about election outcomes are crude, but the less a person cares, the less likely he is to vote. The rates of voting in 1952 in relation to response to the question: "Generally speaking, would you say that you personally care a good deal which party wins the presidential election this fall, or that you don't care very much which party wins?" were as follows:

	Per Cent Voting
Care very much	83%
Care somewhat	79
Don't care very much	70
Don't care at all	57

These estimates overstate the actual voting rates, but they doubtless indicate accurately the positive relationship between "care" about outcome and participation.

2 · Nonissue Content of the Vote

The discussion of elections as means for the expression of opinion on substantive issues is embarrassed by the fact that American elections al-

[8] The extreme of indifference is exemplified by the response of the wife of a Minnesota farm laborer to the question whether she personally cared "which party wins the presidential election" in the fall of 1956. "No difference; didn't know there was an election coming." The interviewer persisted through the lengthy schedule, and about the only political perception gleaned was the thought that the Democrats "are supposed to help the farmers. My husband says so."

most invariably have other types of decisional content as well. Surely everyone has heard a wise old politician or newspaper reporter sagely opine, "It's all a matter of the candidate's personality." Or, at a time when another interpretation seems more suitable, the same philosophers will deliver themselves of the dictum, "They just vote the straight party ticket." Or the heavy thinkers who compose for the editorial page will conclude, "The voters, in their wrath, threw the rascals out." The fact is that the American electorate, if it is to perform its role in the political system, must concern itself with problems in addition to those of substantive policy. It must, so fortuitous are the processes by which parties designate candidates, make some appraisal of the qualities of aspirants for office. Yet so numerous are the decisions they make that voters must also be guided in a measure by party cues as a matter of economy of effort. Almost invariably, an election involves appraisal often directed not to policy but to the manner of execution of policies about which there is no dispute.

The analytical problem of making sense of elections comes in part from the technical difficulties in the separation of the elements of the electoral decision and in the assignment of weights to each. Within a single election considerations of policy, of party, of candidate, and of other questions may be, and usually are, mixed. The proportions in which these elements occur vary from election to election. In one election the personality and competence of the candidates may occupy a predominant position in the minds of the voters as they reach decision. In American campaigns the question of which candidate is "the best man" probably plays an especially important part. When a consensus on policy prevails, voters are free to direct their attention to other aspects of electoral choice. Yet the candidate or personality component of electoral choice differs from election to election. Though a man may personify a general policy position, often campaign debate has only the slightest taint of policy content as it concentrates on the question of the "best" man. When a serene rural county chooses a sheriff, its electors may have to determine which of two equally agreeable candidates will probably create the least disturbance as he maintains order in an already peaceful community. Questions of "honesty," competence, and the like pervade the discussion. In state and national elections these questions are more often mixed with policy considerations; yet even in presidential elections they are sometimes of high salience.

In some elections the mixture of questions at issue may be dominated by the matter of the competence in the management of public affairs, either of the candidate or of his entourage. The issue may be one of past performance entirely uncolored by policy considerations. The frequency of elections in state and local governments and the custom of

re-election convert many of these pollings into a simple referendum
on the record of past management. In other instances the questions are:
Shall the rascals be thrown out because they have demonstrated themselves to be crooked and incompetent in the execution of policies about
which there may be no deep disagreement? What of the alternative
crowd? Would it turn out to be any better?

Kinds of Questions and Kinds of Voters. The technical task of estimating the decisional content of elections involves essentially two elements. First, one must establish some system of categories of the elements of electoral decision, such as the choice between parties, the
element of substantive policy decision, and so forth. Second, one must
estimate in some manner the weights given these factors by individual
voters and sum the weights of each factor in the entire electorate in
order to arrive at the relative significance of the several elements in a
particular election.

These operations involve obdurate problems in the obtaining of
information from a sample of the electorate and in its analysis and interpretation. Only two systematic attempts have been made to analyze
presidential elections in these terms. In their study of the 1952 election
Campbell, Gurin, and Miller worked on the assumption that voters
might be motivated by a concern about issues, about parties, or about
candidates. Once this trichotomy was established, the analytical problem was to determine the relationship of the focus of attention of voters
on these subjects to their vote. The examination of responses to questions about parties, candidates, and issues revealed that some voters paid
attention almost solely to parties. An example of a person who could be
regarded as party-oriented comes from the protocol of a 1956 interview
with the wife of a Navy enlisted man. Her statements did not soar
above the laconic, but the direction of her orientation was clear. The
relevant comments follow:

> (Is there anything in particular that you like about the
> Democratic party?) "No, nothing in particular. I just like them
> because they are Democrats."
>
> (Is there anything in particular that you don't like about the
> Democratic party?) "No."
>
> (Is there anything in particular that you like about the Re-
> publican party?) "No, I don't like Republicans."
>
> (Is there anything in particular that you don't like about the
> Republican party?) "No, not that I know of."

(Is there anything in particular about Stevenson that might make you want to vote *for* him?) "I think he would make a good President because he is a Democrat." (Any other reason?) "No."

(Is there anything in particular about Stevenson that might make you want to vote *against* him?) "No."

(Is there anything in particular about Eisenhower that might make you want to vote *for* him?) "No, he is a Republican and I wouldn't vote for him." (Any other reason?) "No."

(Is there anything in particular about Eisenhower that might make you want to vote *against* him?) "I don't have any reason to vote against him, except he is a Republican."

This respondent's store of political lore did not suffice to nourish loquacity, but her political attention centered on party to the exclusion of the candidates' qualities. A pure type of contrasting orientation toward the candidates comes from the sparse comments of a self-styled Texas accountant, probably really a bookkeeper, on the same questions.

(Like about the Democratic party?) "I'm not very strong on parties. I go more on the man than the party. I don't know the basic beliefs and differences between the two parties. I'm not informed."

(Dislike about the Democratic party?) "No."

(Like about the Republican party?) "No."

(Dislike about the Republican party?) "No."

(Reasons why vote for Stevenson?) "No. There is nothing that I can think of."

(Reasons to vote against Stevenson?) "I don't like our President to be divorced and I don't go along with his religion."

(Reasons why vote for Eisenhower?) "Yes, I've admired him through the years. He does what he thinks is the correct thing to do regardless of politics. Isn't easily swayed. He has sterling character and people can't push him around. He stands up for his convictions."

(Reasons to vote against Eisenhower?) "No. I can't think of anything." [9]

Persons whose attention is so monopolized by a single aspect of a campaign are relatively few. Better-informed persons usually have a

[9] Perusal of the thinner interview protocols from a national sample of voters will remove any doubt that one may entertain about the utility of even the dullest course in high school civics.

mixture of issue, party, and candidate concerns and motivations. Yet in their 1952 study, Campbell, Gurin, and Miller established that to some extent motivations toward party, candidate, and issues were independent each of the other; that is, when one inspected the dimension of candidate orientation within the electorate he was not simply examining a mask for party orientation. Their analysis, though, did not lead to an estimate of the relative weights of the three factors in the total electoral decision, but, rather, to the finding that presidential preference was associated with the direction of preference on each of the three factors. Those persons with Democratic orientations on party, candidate, and issues voted Democratic in extremely high degree. Likewise those with an R-R-R motivational pattern almost to a man voted Republican. Among those persons with mixed orientation and motivation—for example, among persons with a Republican candidate orientation and Democratic inclinations on party and issues—the solidarity of the vote was reduced by the conflict in concerns.[1]

An Estimate of Weights of Components of Electoral Decision. Another step in the analysis of the factors entering into the electoral decision was taken by Campbell, Converse, Miller, and Stokes in their study of the 1956 election, which involved, incidentally, a re-examination of the data accumulated in the 1952 Survey Research Center study. In the 1956 study the categories of voter motivation were increased in number to permit a more complete representation of the considerations that entered the minds of the voters as they cast their ballots. Some of the variety in the decisional content of the vote had been obscured when all motivations were compressed into the 1952 tripartite division: party, candidate, issues. The classification of attitudes of voters in the 1956 analysis consisted of the following pigeonholes:

> Attitude toward Stevenson
> Attitude toward Eisenhower
> Group-related Attitudes
> Attitude toward Parties as Managers of Government
> Attitude on Domestic Issues
> Attitude on Foreign Issues

In the main these categories subdivided the categories of the earlier analysis and are mostly self-explanatory. Attitudes toward the candidates, Stevenson and Eisenhower, might be negative or positive. In its

[1] For the discussion of the independence of the three types of motivation, see Campbell, Gurin, and Miller: *op. cit.*, ch. 10; for treatment of the relation between patterns of motivation and the vote, see ch. 12.

purest form the attitude toward candidates is completely devoid of policy content: "I just don't like Stevenson," or "Ike is a wonderful man." Group-related attitudes may be pro-Democratic or pro-Republican. A person may like the Democratic party because he regards it as the party of the workingman. "Attitudes toward Parties as Managers of Government" includes estimates of the Democrats and Republicans in their performance, past and prospective, as operators of the governmental apparatus. As might be expected, the assignment of weight to these attitudes by the coding of responses to open-ended questions presents difficulties; yet it can be done. When one knows whether a person's opinions are pro-Democratic or pro-Republican on the matters so classified and has some idea of their intensity, he knows with a fair degree of accuracy how the individual will vote. The vote becomes an expression of these attitudes about the various kinds of questions at issue in an election.

Once one has determined the relationship between the attitudes of individuals and the direction of their presidential vote, the problem still remains of the estimation of the relative weight of each of these factors in the total electorate. Was the electorate as a whole moved more by issues than by candidates? Or by what? One of the principal innovations by Campbell and his associates in their analysis of the 1956 election was the attempt to ascertain the relative weights of these types of concerns in the entire electorate. Using mathematical procedures too complex to be explained here, it was estimated that the direction of net partisan advantage in each of the areas of concern in 1952 and 1956 was as follows:

	Direction of Partisan Advantage	
	1952	1956
Attitude toward candidates	R	R
Group-related attitudes	D	D
Attitude toward parties as managers of government	R	R
Attitude on domestic issues	D	D
Attitude on foreign issues	R	R

The areas in which the net balance of attitude favored the Democrats were, of course, outweighed by the Republican advantage in other areas. Among the attitudinal areas favoring the Republicans in 1952 the weight of those voter responses classified as "Attitude toward Parties as Managers of Government" ranked first, followed by "Attitude toward Eisenhower." In the 1956 polling "Attitude toward Eisenhower" had become by far the top ranking factor in pro-Republican weight.[2]

These attempts to estimate the character and relative strengths of the attitudes that go into the decision of the electorate as a whole are necessarily crude. They serve, though, to indicate the variety of considerations that enter into the electoral decision. The policy component always enters into the equation, but it is supplemented by other considerations that the voter must weigh and at times may be subordinated to them. Yet all these analyses, despite the new light they throw on the electoral process, leave other aspects of the broad electoral decision undescribed. Some of those aspects concern the broad effect of the electoral decision in the general stream of governmental action. Perhaps by building on these analyses of the relation of attitudes and the vote, some informed guesses may be made about this question.

3 · Elections as Collective Decisions

If elections express a public opinion, it should be possible to assign meaning to them as they are examined in the context of the circumstances of the moment at which they occur. Scholars habitually shy away from the task of translating the indistinct mutterings of the people's voice as it projects itself through the ballot boxes and the voting machines, but politicians must as a matter of course attribute a decisional content to elections. While their readings of the verdict of the people may on occasion be erroneous, they have a quality of authority. Scholars, too, should by the findings of electoral research be able to make appraisals of the meaning of the grand decisions by the electorate. In a minor referendum—as, for example, a vote on a proposal for the issuance of building bonds by a school district—the expression of public opinion is direct and unmistakable in its meaning, but interpretation of the meaning of great national electoral contests presents a problem of far greater complexity. Granted that these grand electoral decisions have a meaning whose clarity differs from election to election, the problem remains of appraising particular elections or types of elections in their total context to divine the nature of the collective purpose expressed in the balloting. Such an attempt assumes that, despite the variety of motives and preferences that guide individual voters, their individual actions can be summed into a broad decision of one or more major components of some clarity, at least in some elections.

[2] For the detailed analysis, see Angus Campbell, Philip E. Converse, Warren E. Miller, and Donald E. Stokes: *The American Voter* (New York: Wiley; 1960), ch. 19.

Disapprobation. Perhaps the public can express itself with greatest clarity when it speaks in disapprobation of the past policy or performance of an administration, though the collective decision may not specify with minuteness the elements of policy or performance of which it disapproves and cannot indicate with precision the lines of policy that should be pursued, save that changes should be made. The presidential election of 1932 could be regarded as one in which the collective decision was one of disapproval of past performance. Although from the vantage point of hindsight, many elements of the New Deal may be read into Roosevelt's campaign speeches and into his earlier record as Governor of New York, the dominant element of the collective decision consisted in a rejection of the broad policies of the Hoover Administration rather than a mandate for future action. About the only clear prospective instruction contained in the electoral verdict was a mandate for the repeal of the Prohibition Amendment, and that action itself constituted to a degree a judgment of past experience.

Another election in which a major component of the decision consisted in the disapproval of past performance was that of 1952. From data presented earlier, the conclusion is inescapable that the election marked no majority rejection of the major trends of domestic policy under the New Deal and the Fair Deal, although Eisenhower had the support of those bitterly opposed to intervention in the economy. The major content of the decision related rather to the performance of the Truman Administration in the field of foreign policy. That interpretation is supported by the relationships between party identification and

---

TABLE 18.4

PRESIDENTIAL VOTE IN RELATION TO PARTY IDENTIFICATION AND TO OPINION ON UNITED STATES RESPONSIBILITY FOR COMMUNIST CAPTURE OF CONTROL OF CHINA [a]

PARTY IDENTIFICATION — OPINION ON CHINA POLICY

	Our fault	Don't know	Nothing U.S. could do
Strong D	69%	84%	89%
Weak D	40	66	67
Independent	28	20	45
Weak R	3	6	8
Strong R	1	0	1

[a] Entries are Democratic percentages of reported presidential vote for the groups in each cell in 1952. The question was: "Some people feel that it was our government's fault that China went Communist, others say there was nothing that we could do to stop it. How do you feel about this?"

DATA SOURCE: *Survey Research Center, University of Michigan, 1952.*

vote that appear in Table 18.4. The question of whether "it was our government's fault that China went Communist" or whether there was "nothing that we could do to stop it" separated out with some clarity those who deserted the Democratic party to vote for Eisenhower. Of those strong Democrats who thought that it was our government's fault that China went communist, only 69 per cent voted Democratic. Of those who thought that there was nothing "we could do to stop it," 89 per cent voted Democratic. Similar contrasts appear at other levels of party identification. This is not to say that the election turned on the China issue alone. Rather, the probabilities are that this question tapped a broad dimension of dissatisfaction with the conduct of foreign affairs that found expression in the vote. And that dissatisfaction was compounded by an unhappiness about the conduct of domestic affairs as well.[3]

Confirmation and Ratification. If public opinion expresses itself with relative clarity in retrospective disapproval of performance or policy, it may also express itself in the same manner in confirmation or ratification of past policy or performance. Only infrequently is a new program or a new course of action advocated with such force and the attention it receives so widespread that the polling may be regarded as advance approval of a proposed course of action. Those governments that regard elections as clear mandates for new policy actions probably often mirror the beliefs of the political elite rather than reflect an understanding of the vote widely shared in the population.

The congressional election of 1934 and the presidential election of 1936 are probably the elections in recent American history that could most certainly be regarded as mass approvals of newly instituted public policies. The actions taken from 1933 to the election of 1936 constituted a program of unusual range and novelty in American domestic policy. Subjected to frontal challenge by the minority, that program undoubtedly won broad popular ratification in the increased Democratic congressional majorities of 1934 and in the overwhelming vote by which Roosevelt was re-elected in 1936.

At a different level the election of 1956 could be regarded as a mass

[3] Expression of electoral disapprobation, it is relevant to note, depends on the existence of political parties with some continuity and some sense of corporate accountability. When a President seeks re-election, he cannot avoid that accountability; his record is approved or it is not approved. When the President's party puts forward a nominee as a successor to the incumbent, the candidate must, if the electorate is to be effective, be accountable for the record of his party. When such a presidential candidate seeks to work out of such responsibility, he attempts to subvert a basic tenet of the constitutional customs.

confirmation or approval of the performance of the Eisenhower Administration perhaps principally in the field of foreign affairs. The motivation of the vote contained a generous component of a political admiration for Eisenhower as a person; it contained practically no motivation of approbation for his innovations in domestic policy—which were, of course, negligible. Probably the approval of past performance in the foreign field, as well as expectations about the future, were captured by the responses to the question: "Now looking ahead, do you think the problem of keeping out of war would be handled better in the next four years by the Republicans, or by the Democrats, or about the same by both?" Comments in the replies to this inquiry were heavily loaded with professions of confidence in Eisenhower based on his military and diplomatic experience and with expressions of approbation for his success in "keeping us out of war." And the position on this question, as may be seen from Table 18.5, was closely associated

TABLE 18.5

PRESIDENTIAL VOTE IN RELATION TO PARTY IDENTIFICATION AND TO OPINION ABOUT PARTY CAPABILITIES IN HANDLING "PROBLEM OF KEEPING OUT OF WAR" [a]

PARTY IDENTIFICATION	BETTER BY DEMOCRATS	SAME BY BOTH	BETTER BY REPUBLICANS
Strong D	87%	90%	47%
Weak D	96[b]	71	24
Independent	[c]	42	11
Weak R	[c]	14	2
Strong R	[d]	0	[e]

[a] Entries are percentages of those in each cell reporting a Democratic presidential vote. The question was: "Now looking ahead, do you think the problem of keeping out of war would be handled better in the next four years by the Republicans, or by the Democrats, or about the same by both?"
[b] This percentage rests on only 24 cases.
[c] Too few cases to percentage.
[d] No case fell in this cell.
[e] Less than one-half of 1 per cent.
DATA SOURCE: *Survey Research Center, University of Michigan, 1956.*

with the vote. Those Democrats who thought the problem of "keeping out of war" would be better handled by the Republicans deserted their candidate with far greater frequency than did those Democrats who had confidence with the peace-maintaining capacity of their own party.[4]

[4] It should not be presumed that these Democrats voted Republican necessarily because they had greater confidence in Eisenhower on the peace question. In some instances they may have had this confidence because they had decided to vote for Eisenhower. However it came about, the parallelism of expectation and vote had an importance.

The consideration was not an issue of policy; the Democrats had not advocated war. Although expressed as an expectation about the future, it reflected fundamentally a broad approval of past performance.

Rejection. As has been said, one source of difficulty in discerning the import of the popular decision in an election has been the supposition that elections do, or ought to, involve a choice between new and alternative policies for the future. American public policy rarely develops in this manner. Its evolution is more commonly by gradual stages. Policy breaks with the past, when they occur, more generally come about without precise prospective mandate; popular action takes place mainly in retrospect rather than in prospect.

Something can be said, however, for the existence of a type of election in which the electorate rejects a proposed panacea. By so doing, it may or may not give positive approval to the alternative. A clear-cut instance of an election of this type is that of 1896. William Jennings Bryan took control of the Democratic party from the conservative Cleveland forces and crusaded in advocacy of the free coinage of silver as a cure for the ills that beset the country. Here was a positive proposal, certainly widely known if not always understood in its details, to depart from the prevailing monetary policy. If we had for 1896 data of the kind that have been available for recent elections, we could speak with more confidence about what was in the minds of people as they rejected Bryan for McKinley. But the electors clearly rejected the radical alternative offered by Bryan, and it is not implausible to suppose that doubt and anxiety about free silver had more to do with their actions than did a powerful attraction to the gold standard.

Frustration of Policy-Motivated Decision. The structure of the American electoral system is such that certain types of policy-motivated decisions are frustrated or cannot be made by election. Or the more correct interpretation may be that certain types of combinations of opinions encounter obstruction as they percolate through almost any electoral system. When two or more issues divide an electorate along different planes, if a majority on one of the issues prevails, the majority on the other may be defeated. These problems were touched upon in the earlier discussion of the interrelationship of opinions.[5] In recent decades those who cherished both isolationist and liberal views have suffered some inconvenience in adapting themselves to the alternatives offered by the American party system. Similarly, those who embraced both

[5] See Chapter 7.

internationalist and conservative opinions had some uncertainty about how their opinions might best be translated into electoral preference. On lesser issues such conflict is commonplace.

In the American system several routes are open for the avoidance of the political dead-ends created by the existence of noncongruent majorities on a series of issues. Some of these ways around the problem are individual; others are institutional. The individual often places a higher value on his position on this issue than on another; or one issue may be more salient than the other. This permits him as he votes to bring his candidate preference into line with his dominant policy preference. Berelson, Lazarsfeld, and McPhee suggest that the unity of the supporters of a candidate may consist, not in their agreement on a series of issues, but in their opposition to one or another of the policy positions of the candidate they reject. "One Republican," they conclude from their Elmira study, "may be most concerned with foreign policy, and on that subject he is against the Democrats. Another Republican may be most concerned with domestic economics, and on that subject he is against the Democrats." [6] Unity may thus exist along a common denominator of disagreement with the opposition on a series of issues, but this is unity for election day only. Someone is bound to find himself in the majority on election day and in a minority on policies of interest to him the next day. Nevertheless, individuals may accommodate themselves to the situation to some extent by emphasizing in their actions those considerations most important to them.

Institutional structures also enable, or even require, governments to take into account the circumstance of the simultaneous existence of noncongruent majorities. The looseness of the party system, especially in its nominating practices, permits the election of Senators and Representatives with unorthodox combinations of policy outlook. Thus, the isolationist-liberal combination of opinion can find its spokesmen through the representative system. Witness the career of the late Senator William Langer, of North Dakota. A New Dealer with most pronounced convictions on domestic matters and a man markedly lacking in zeal for one-worldism, he probably reflected relatively well the mixed policy pattern of his constituency. Such adjustments through the representative system are commonplace.

In a more notable fashion, the system of separated powers on occasion, perhaps accidentally, permits governmental adaptation to the requirements of noncongruent majorities. The most striking case, or at least the one on which the data are most complete, is that of the election of 1952 and its consequences. A foreign policy majority supported

---

[6] Berelson, *et al.: Voting* (Chicago: University of Chicago Press; 1954), p. 206.

Eisenhower in his promise to do something other than that which
Truman had been doing. That majority, though, was not also, as some
dedicated Republicans believed, committed to a rollback in domestic-
welfare policy. The two noncongruent majorities, as a result of the
congressional elections of 1954, found their voice through different
organs of government. The President spoke for one majority; Congress, with its Democratic complexion, was beholden to the other majority.

When noncongruent majorities exist, the meaning of the outcome
of an election may be obscure; the election may, in fact, settle only one
of the great issues. There are also other types of questions that are not
apt to be settled in any clear fashion by elections. Those are questions
on which the popular opinion distribution is of the type we earlier denominated as "concentrated"—that is, questions about which comparatively few persons have an opinion one way or another.[7] In the excitement of the presidential campaign these matters are overshadowed by
more important questions, and few persons would regard their vote as
an expression of opinion on them. Such questions are not likely to be
settled by elections unless they are definitely related to some major
ideological position of the winner or governed by the group interests
associated with the winner.

Acceptability of Election Results. It is plain that elections involve
broad decisions on policy questions, although estimation of precisely
what those determinations are requires a degree of artistry. A more important feature of elections, whatever else they decide, is their production of acceptable decisions on the succession to power in the state. At
the leadership levels that quality of elections manifests itself when the
losers surrender the seals of authority to the winners of the popular
majority. The development of norms, expectations, and restraints that
enable those with authority to surrender it in response to popular decision is a rare phenomenon among the rulers of men; they usually fear
that they may suffer personal discomfort if they transfer the apparatus
of state power to their enemies. Nevertheless, in a few regimes those
who occupy office have learned how to accomplish the peaceable transfer of authority. Or perhaps they have learned how to conduct themselves in office so that they will not be shot by the outs who win an
election.

Within the mass of the people, too, some sort of reconciliation to
the defeat of one's candidate evidently occurs. Though the opposition
winner may not be embraced with enthusiasm, many people accom-

[7] Chapter 4.

plish a psychological adjustment to the loss of an election. That adjustment may take the form of concluding that the stakes of the election were not after all so important as they were thought to be in the heat of the campaign. That process is illustrated by the data of Table 18.6. Before the election in 1952 a national sample was asked whether it thought that it would "make a good deal of difference to the country whether the Democrats or the Republicans win the election." About three

TABLE 18.6

APPRAISALS OF IMPORTANCE OF OUTCOME OF 1952 ELECTION BEFORE AND AFTER
THE ELECTION BY STRONG PARTY IDENTIFIERS [a]

OPINIONS ON ELECTION IMPORTANCE	STRONG DEMOCRATS		STRONG REPUBLICANS	
	Pre	Post	Pre	Post
Very important differences; big difference; important differences; some difference	72%	46%	78%	80%
Minor differences; no difference; about the same; depends	24	45	20	18
Don't know	4	8	1	2
NA	–	1	1	–
	100%	100%	100%	100%
N	392	402	241	217

[a] The pre-election question was: "Do you think it will make a good deal of difference to the country whether the Democrats or the Republicans win the elections this November or that it won't make much difference which side wins?" The post-election question was: "Do you think it will make a good deal of difference to the country that Eisenhower won instead of Stevenson, or don't you think it will make much difference?"

DATA SOURCE: *Survey Research Center, University of Michigan, 1952.*

fourths of the strong Democrats and strong Republicans opined that important differences, big differences, or at least some difference was at stake. After the election a substantial proportion of the strong Democrats made their peace with the situation by adopting the view that the Eisenhower victory would make no difference, only minor differences, or perhaps no difference at all.

This phenomenon of reconciliation to defeat has been noted in many surveys.[8] It also manifests itself in other ways. In postelection surveys that inquire about the vote, an overreport of the vote for the

[8] See, for example, Arthur Kornhauser *et al.*: *When Labor Votes* (New York: University Books; 1956), pp. 135, 161.

winner ordinarily occurs. Some people do not wish to admit that they
were on the losing side and, ex post facto, change their vote, so to
speak. The odds are that some of the acceptance of election outcomes
may be attributable to a sportsmanship whose efficacy may be most
marked among people with the least knowledge and awareness of the
stakes of the political game. Then, too, after an election other persons
may come around to the view that, though their man lost, the result
was the "best thing" for the country.[9]

[9] *Fortune*, February, 1941, has a relevant post-mortem on the 1940 presidential election; a goodly number of Willkie voters concluded that it was the "best thing" for the country that Roosevelt had won.

19

REPRESENTATION

In their genesis, representative bodies were institutions more or less deliberately designed to link public opinion and government. Their members were assembled from the four corners of the realm to advise the king and to give consent to his measures or to those of his ministers. Even yet some representative bodies act as if they were apart from the governing process. They criticize, ratify, or withhold ratification of executive actions. Other representative bodies, such as the American Congress, assert for themselves a wider function in governance. They criticize, ratify, or withhold ratification; they also initiate legislation, reshape administration measures, and sometimes act as if the executive in his role of legislative leadership had usurped functions rightly belonging to the representatives. Yet, whatever broad place the representative body holds in a constitutional system, its members are inclined to assert a special role as the voice of the people.

In the long stream of rationalization and debate on the role of the representative, a continuous concern has been manifest about the proper relation between the representative and his constituency. The bald issue appears in the contrast between the representative bound by instructions from his constituents and the representative bound by conscience to exercise his best judgment in the interest of the nation. Burke, in his famed exposition of the second viewpoint, contended: "Parliament is not a congress of ambassadors from different and hostile interests, which interests each must maintain, as an agent and ad-

vocate, against other agents and advocates; but Parliament is a deliberative assembly of one nation, with one interest, that of the whole—
where not local purposes, not local prejudices, ought to guide, but the
general good, resulting from the general reason of the whole."

The practice of constituency instructions to representatives has
long since ceased, in part because the broadening of the suffrage and
the direct election of representatives left no organ competent, either
legally or practically, to issue instructions. Nevertheless, the discussion of representation has continued in large measure in the terms set in
Burke's time. Excessive devotion by the representative to his constituency has been thought to insure a sacrifice of national interest to local
and parochial concerns. Burke's position has also been embraced by
those with broader fears of public opinion. On the American scene,
representatives who appear to be supporters of the corporate interests
against the wishes of their constituents find themselves adorned with
Burkean virtue by the kept commentators.

A concern about how representatives ought to respond to the
opinion of their constituents is a worthy preoccupation, but it is likely
to be futile unless illuminated by some knowledge about how representatives respond. That legislators have an abiding interest in the nature
of opinion in their constituencies there can be no doubt. How their estimates of that opinion bear on their work in the assembly is not nearly
so clear. At times they bow down before constituency opinion, and at
times they ignore it. On many questions there may be no discernible
constituency opinion, but on a few issues constituency opinion may be
imperious in its demands. On all these matters, however, our information is limited. The objective in this chapter is to assemble information
that is available.

1 · Roll-Call Votes and Constituency Opinion

Most of the time the elegant prose spilled over the question of whether
a legislator should be a man and vote his mature convictions in the national interest or be a mouse and bow abjectly to the parochial demands
of his constituents is irrelevant to the realities. Few of his constituents
have even the slightest awareness of most of the questions on which the
legislator must stand up and be counted. On those few issues about
which awareness is widespread among his constituents, he usually has
no trustworthy estimate of the distribution of opinions of his constituents. In some districts on some issues the legislator may know well
enough what opinion is. A southern congressman from a predominantly Negro district may have no doubt that his supporters—that is,

the whites—oppose federal intervention in race relations. Such instances of clarity of opinion, however, are relatively few among all the questions a legislator must consider. On the same issue, the congressman from a northern, white constituency may vote in the opposite way from his southern colleague, though usually he has no reliable information on the attitudes of his constituency. Generally, a legislator may hear from a few people on a few issues. He must always, as he votes, assume the risk of antagonizing some constituents, but he is rarely faced by the difficult choice of rejecting or accepting the mandate of his constituency, for he does not know what it is. And, indeed, there may be none.

Legislative Votes and Imputed Constituency Attitudes. The sketchiness of knowledge about constituency opinion creates its embarrassments for any discussion of the relation between the voting of legislators and the attitudes of the people of their districts. Sampling the opinions of a congressional district—so strange are the properties of survey methods—amounts to almost as great a task as sampling the people of the nation. Hence, given the data now available, any treatment of how any representative links opinion in his constituency to the governing process must be less than exact. Political analysts approach the problem chiefly by indirection. They ascertain demographic characteristics of legislative districts. They reason that people of specified characteristics —industrial workers, for example—ought to have a specified outlook toward a given legislative issue. Therefore, it is concluded, a representative reflects the opinion of his district if he takes a position in harmony with the opinion imputed to a majority of his constituents. The frailty of the analysis rests in the fact that people's opinions often are not the same as those imputed to them. Nevertheless, on some kinds of issues this type of analysis yields plausible results and is, in reality, about the only sort of information that is available on the relation between representative and constituency.[1]

One method to check the relations between constituents and representatives without the necessity of imputing opinions to constituents is to make global comparisons of party groups in the electorate and in the representative body. That method has its obvious shortcomings because we cannot connect representative A with constituency A'. Yet it has its uses. Opinion surveys show that, on the average, Democrats and Republicans in the country as a whole differ on questions of

[1] Warren E. Miller, of the Survey Research Center of the University of Michigan, has under way an analysis of the relation between legislators' roll-call votes and attitudes of their constituents as measured by a 1958 national survey.

domestic economic policy.[2] If the voting records of members of the
House of Representatives resemble the outlook of the people who
elected them, we should expect Republican legislators to differ from
Democratic legislators in their voting records on issues of domestic
economic policy. In fact, given the tendency for leadership echelons to
espouse group doctrines in an especially pure form, we should expect

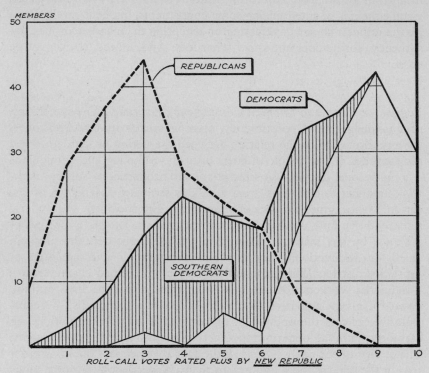

FIGURE 19.1. Distribution of House Members, by Party,
on Roll-Call Index Constructed from 1956 Votes Rated
by *New Republic*

wider differences to prevail between the two groups of legislators than
between their supporters in the electorate.

Such comparisons of the voting records of Republicans and of
Democrats in the House of Representatives are commonplace; they
show the expected concentration of Republicans toward the conservative end of the scale and of Democrats toward the opposite end. A
specimen of this type of distribution appears in Figure 19.1, which ar-
rays Democratic and Republican members of the House on an index
built of their votes on ten roll calls in 1955 and 1956. The *New Repub-*

[2] Chapter 17.

lic characterized the votes on each of these roll calls by a plus or a minus, depending on whether it coincided with that journal's position. While the resulting index is not a work of psychometric art, it is a serviceable separator of persons of contrasting political outlooks.[3] The distribution of House members on the scale in Figure 19.1 conforms to expectations built on the assumption that legislators will differ as their constituencies differ. In another respect, though, the relations diverge from such expectations. In the figure, southern Democrats are shown separate from Democrats generally, and they manifest a less-liberal average record than do nonsouthern Democrats, which results in part from the inclusion in the index of a roll call on civil rights. Southerners, as was shown earlier, do not have a markedly more conservative outlook than people elsewhere. The divergence of southern Democratic members may have a partial explanation in the low levels of political participation of persons disposed to be liberal in outlook; these legislators may lean toward their politically active constituents rather than toward their constituents generally.

Such a contrast between groups of voters and groups of legislators does not tell us much about the relation between representative A and his own constituents in district A'. A second stage in the analysis, which involves the imputation of opinions to types of constituents, will take us a step nearer to the demonstration of communion between representative and constituent. In Figure 19.1 Republican Representatives are spread rather widely along the index of liberalism. What kinds of districts do the more liberal Republicans come from? The *Congressional Quarterly Almanac* has obligingly fitted the census data to congressional districts and classified them into these four groups:

I, primarily rural districts with no city of over 25,000;
II, small-town districts, with no city over 50,000;
III, mid-urban districts, "substantially influenced" by a city of from 50,000 to 200,000; and
IV, metropolitan districts, with cities of 200,000 or over or within such cities.

These categories cannot be related to our opinion data, but earlier tabulations of survey data indicated that a cutting point of 50,000 tended to mark fairly sharp differences in opinion between places of different population size.[4] If Republican Representatives resemble their constituents, we should expect the Republicans from metropolitan districts to

---

[3] For its use in this context the index is also marred by the fact that it includes three roll calls on foreign policy and one on civil rights. For the items included in the index, see the compilation in *New Republic*, October 15, 1956.

[4] Chapter 5.

rank higher, on the average, on the index in Figure 19.1 than Republicans from rural districts, and that is in fact the case. The percentages of those Republicans from each type of district with index scores of four or more are as follows:

District Type	Per Cent of Representatives with Score of 4 or More
I	22%
II	24
III	43
IV	57

Expectations about the relations of the voting records of Democratic Representatives and the character of the constituency would be the same—namely, that Representatives from metropolitan districts would rank higher on the index more frequently than would Democrats from rural districts. Though this is true, the contrast is more marked among nonsouthern Democrats than among all Democrats. The percentages of nonsouthern Democrats from each of the types of district with scores of eight or more on the index are as follows:

District Type	Per Cent of Representatives with Score of 8 or More
I	59%
II	59
III	81
IV	90

These tabulations make the relationship between the constituency and the vote of its Representative in Congress far more simple than it is. The limitations of constituency characteristics in the explanation of the vote are apparent in the figures themselves. If we had a measure of determinative constituency opinion, we should expect, for example, all our rural Democrats to rank at 0 on the scale and all the metropolitan Democrats to place at 10. From the data we have, however, about all that can be concluded is that constituency opinion—as inferred from the particular demographic characteristics—is only one of a complex of factors that bear on a legislator's vote.

Varieties and Directions of Constituency Opinion. Our illustrative case incidentally explains the techniques by which analysts attempt to deduce the relationships that prevail between constituency opinion and the position of the legislator. Application of these techniques suggests that constituency influences upon a legislator are numerous and often mutually contradictory. The diversity of demands upon him, as well as the varying probability that these demands will affect the outcome on election day, leaves a range of freedom of choice for most legislators on many questions. That discretion is exercised in a manner to suggest a relationship between legislative voting and constituency characteristic, but at times the relationship is slight. Nevertheless, such correlations contribute to the description of the role of the legislator in the linkage of opinion to government. A summary of the chief findings on the matter may be useful.

Apparently party affiliation must be ranked as the factor most influential in the determination of a legislator's vote. Whether this phenomenon should be classified as an influence of constituency is not always clear. Party influence—that is, the influence of the party leadership—is usually reinforced by constituency; thus, the two types of influence may be indistinguishable. One type of constituency tends toward the Democratic party, and another toward the Republican.[5] At the extremes these are working-class districts and silk-stocking constituencies. On those issues relevant to these constituency differentials, a legislator's perception of constituency opinion strengthens his inclination to vote with his party. On this type of issue the party effect also may strengthen the inclination of a Representative to vote with the sentiment of his constituency.

Yet the chances are that the party factor should be regarded as consisting, at least in part, of elements other than pure constituency influence—that is, something in addition to the legislator's concern about the views of the people who elect him. When he follows the party line, the legislator may be responding to the mandate of a constituency larger than his district. On occasion, this process even brings him to reject the dominant opinions of his own district. More often, party provides guides for position on measures about which the people of his own constituency have no real concern or about which the opinions of his constituency are divided or ambiguous. Although we have no district-by-district opinion data, our earlier occupational analyses of opinion support the assumption that in a considerable number of districts opinion and information on many issues must be low indeed.

So pervasive is the factor of party that analysts of legislative behavior employ the party line as a norm from which to measure deviations that may be associated with a special constituency opinion. Ingen-

[5] For a scatter diagram that relates the Democratic percentages of the vote for Representatives and the occupational composition of House districts, see Duncan MacRae, Jr.: *Dimensions of Congressional Voting* (Berkeley: University of California Press; 1958), p. 259.

ious scholars have expended an appalling amount of energy in efforts to obtain some line on the extent to which constituency opinions bring legislators to diverge from the party position. The late Julius Turner, in a pioneer work, identified several constituency characteristics that seemed to give a peculiar form to the voting records of members of the U.S. House of Representatives. Within party groups Representatives from particular sections, from districts predominantly native-born or foreign-born, or from metropolitan or rural districts tended to establish voting records of a special cast. However, these were but deviations from the party norm, which, Turner emphasized, evidently outweighed these other factors as explanations for the total legislative record.[6]

In the attempt to identify by inference the influences bearing on the votes of legislators, more recent studies apply more refined measurements than Turner used to legislative voting records and constituency characteristics. Duncan MacRae worked through the task of arranging members of the House of Representatives along Guttman scales constructed from votes on roll calls. These scales provided, of course, a ranking of members on the dimension embodied in the scale far superior to that yielded by the crude indices employed in the earlier studies and in the illustrative case in the opening pages of this chapter. He also compiled, to match against the scale rankings of Representatives, demographic data on their districts—namely, the percentages of farmers and farm laborers and of professionals and managers among employed males.

When MacRae correlated the positions of Representatives on Guttman scales with the district occupational percentages, some familiar relations appeared as well as some not so familiar. On a "Fair Deal" scale regional differences existed among Democratic Representatives, with Representatives from the Far West ranking as most liberal and those from the South as most conservative. Within each region Representatives from farming districts tended to locate themselves toward the conservative end of the scale and urban Representatives toward the liberal end of the scale.

Another relationship that suggests the nature of the role of party appeared among Democratic House members from urban districts. These districts, as might be expected, varied considerably in the occupational status of their population, a factor that might be expected to be reflected in the voting records of their Representatives as measured

[6] Julius Turner: *Party and Constituency: Pressures on Congress* (Baltimore: Johns Hopkins Press; 1951). For a similar and related analysis, see George L. Grassmuck: *Sectional Biases in Congress on Foreign Policy* (Baltimore: Johns Hopkins Press; 1951).

by the "Fair Deal" scale, even though all the districts were predominantly urban. On the contrary, Democrats from relatively high-status urban districts placed about as high on the scale as did Democrats from low-status urban districts. Presumably party pressures kept Representatives from high-status districts in line; or, alternatively, the voters of these districts had opinions out of line with what might be expected from their occupational status.

On the basis of scales constructed from votes on agricultural measures, MacRae concludes that it is on these measures that constituency interest appears to be strongest and party weakest in legislative voting. A Representative from a dairying district, be he Republican or Democratic, may not hesitate to abandon his party to vote as the dairy farmers wish. If cotton is grown in his district, he looks out for the cotton farmer; and he cannot fail to be impressed by the plight of the peanut growers, if any of them happen to inhabit his district.

On foreign aid MacRae was unable to discern any correlation between the occupational characteristics of constituencies and scale positions of Democratic Representatives. Steps to maintain party unity in the support of Administration measures probably offset whatever variations in district opinion may have existed. Given the nature of the occupational distribution of opinions as shown by our earlier analysis, some Democratic working-class districts almost certainly had a high proportion of voters with isolationist sentiments; yet these variations in district sentiment were not paralleled by differences in voting records. Among Republican House members, however, those from rural districts tended to rank lower on the foreign-aid scale than did those from urban districts, a relationship that would be expected to prevail if legislators tended to take on the attitudes of their districts.[7]

These extracts from research findings suggest some of the complexities of the relations between constituency characteristics and legislators' voting records. They can be fully appreciated only by working with the data and by trying to make sense of it, but a few other kinds of deviations from the simple model of constituency pressure on legislator may be suggested. For example, the consistency with which Representatives from the same state vote together makes it plain that the Democrats or Republicans from a single state often informally caucus and agree upon a position although their districts may be quite varied in demographic composition.[8] Responsiveness to constituency opinion may be affected mightily by the impact of an issue upon the people of

[7] On these and other relations, see MacRae: op. cit., ch. 3. His work in the comparison of constituency and legislative voting record represents the highest technical proficiency so far achieved in this type of work.

[8] See David B. Truman: *The Congressional Party* (New York: Wiley; 1959), ch. 7.

the district. If only 5 per cent of the population is interested and the remainder unconcerned about an issue, the legislator may zealously advocate the cause of the 5 per cent under some conditions.[9] If the district is split 60:40 or 40:60, he may confront a more trying situation, for the degree of homogeneity of the constituency probably has some bearing on the relation between constituency and legislator's vote. A legislator from a district composed overwhelmingly of industrial workers must on the whole have a clearer perception of the opinions of his district than does one from a mixed white-collar and blue-collar district. The long-run trend has probably been a decline in the number of homogeneous districts.[1]

Obviously a legislator's anxiety about the views of his constituents will depend somewhat on the salience of the issue for them and the intensity of their opinion. A southern legislator may, for example, be far more responsive to his constituency on an issue of school segregation than on one of public power, even though popular opinion might be divided in about the same way on both issues. Or pressure from a constituency may take directions opposite to those that might be imputed to it by the pure reason of the analyst. Thus, from 1954 to 1955 two thirds of the shifts from support for "flexible" to "rigid" price supports for agricultural products occurred among Representatives from industrial districts. All this apparently was the result, not of constituency pressure in the ordinary sense, but of the work of labor leaders in bringing to the support of the Democratic leadership Representatives from urban working-class districts.[2]

A critical look at all the evidence on the relation between legislative voting and constituency characteristic must conclude with the observation that we have persuasive circumstantial evidence that constitu-

[9] Thus, on a 1956 vote in the House on a civil rights measure, 100 per cent of northern Republicans from districts 5 per cent or more Negro in population voted for the measure (if we exclude one Oklahoma vote as not really a "northern" vote). Of northern Republicans with districts of less than 5 per cent Negro population, 84 per cent voted for the measure (11 per cent against, 5 per cent not voting). Perhaps in districts with more than 5 per cent Negro even relatively small numbers of Negroes reinforced the Representatives' disposition to follow the party line. In districts less than 5 per cent Negro a Representative might feel somewhat freer to follow personal predilection, but it is doubtful that many of the Representatives from these districts felt under strong pressure from home to vote for the measure. Incidentally, reflection on these data illustrates some of the difficulties of drawing inferences about the relations between constituency and representative from demographic data about the district.

[1] State legislative districts, because they are smaller, approach homogeneity more often than congressional districts. See Duncan MacRae, Jr.: "The Relation between Roll Call Votes and Constituencies in the Massachusetts House of Representatives," *American Political Science Review*, XLVI (1952), 1046–55.

[2] See J. Roland Pennock: "Party and Constituency in Postwar Agricultural Price-Support Legislation," *Journal of Politics*, XVIII (1956), 167–210.

ency opinion affects a legislator's position. Yet we have no evidence on constituency opinion itself, only the imputation of opinion based on demographic characteristics. Moreover, the relation between vote and constituency characteristic is much more marked on some types of measures than on others, more marked among some types of constituencies than others. Finally, practically no research has been done on many types of issues for which no obvious cue for legislator might be spotted among constituency characteristics. The articulation between legislator and constituency opinion is by no means a rigid relationship.

2 · Communication of Constituency Opinion

Implicit in much of the discussion of the role of representative vis-a-vis constituency is the assumption that the constituency has ways and means of expressing its views to its representative. When electors were few in number, they might foregather and caucus to formulate instructions to their representative. In modern times no small group with determinate opinions speaks for the constituency. Some estimate of the sentiment of the constituency may be made from the flow of communications from constituency to legislator. Obviously the legislator, from all the sources of information that accrue to a successful politician, has an impression of the preferences of his constituents that rests on more than sheer intuition. That impression is supplemented by a variety of information that flows to him in informal ways on preferences about specific measures that are pending in the legislature. Nevertheless, he is without reliable guides to the opinions of his constituency as a whole on most measures. Even if a representative vowed to be a slave to his constituency, he would be hard put to identify, in the information that flows to him, the commands of his constituency.

Constituency Mail. One indicator of constituency opinion is the mail that flows into a legislator's office. The mail probably never represents the views of a cross section of the constituency. It may, in some instances, result from organized letter-writing campaigns led by some interest group. Organizations often provide their members with form letters, which ordinarily carry no weight with a congressman.[3] If such letters urge him to do what he plans to do anyway, a legislator may not be above mentioning the avalanche of mail from his constituents in approbation of his position. If they urge him to do what he does not plan

[3] For samples of such letters, see Estes Kefauver and Jack Levin: *A Twentieth Century Congress* (New York: Duell, Sloan and Pearce; 1947).

to do, he will describe with scorn the spontaneous composition of identical letters by many persons. The volunteer mail—that is, the mail
written by individuals on their own initiative—is likely to be representative of the upper social and educational classes. The AIPO, for
example, in 1949 put the question: "Have you ever written or wired
your Congressman or Senator in Washington?" The affirmative replies
by level of education were: college, 39 per cent; high school, 21 per
cent; grade school, 11 per cent.

On issues on which occupational status or education marks lines of
cleavage a legislator is thus almost certain to get from the mail an erroneous impression of his constituency as a whole. This biased picture of
the constituency is apt to be even more marked on great issues that stir
deep emotions and stimulate a good deal of mail. Thus, the proposal to
repeal the arms embargo in September, 1939, generated a good deal of
congressional mail in opposition. A study of the mail of a sample of
congressmen led to the conclusion that more than half of them "voted
against the expressed opinion of their constituents as judged by their
mailbags." [4] In a later study of senatorial mail at the time of the enactment of the Burke-Wadsworth selective service bill just before World
War II, the conclusion was that the mail ran 90 per cent against conscription. At the same time, the Gallup poll showed the country as a
whole to be 70 per cent for conscription.[5] Dexter found that a large
proportion of congressional mail on the reciprocal trade bill had been
sent at the instigation of interested parties.[6] The inference from the nature of the flow of mail could be that most people are disposed to
leave the running of the country to their congressmen, or at any rate
are willing to wait until the next election to express a judgment on how
the country has been run. In any case, the mail is not a satisfactory index to the opinion of the constituency as a whole.

Congressional Polls. Since the invention of opinion polling a few
members of Congress have been moved to conduct polls of their districts. Polls should permit a better estimate than can be made from mail
of the sentiments of a district, but, since most of these polls are conducted with little technical competence, they yield no trustworthy information on the distribution of attitudes in the constituencies. They
are, in fact, usually conducted, not for the purpose of ascertaining the

[4] L. E. Gleeck: "96 Congressmen Make Up their Minds," *Public Opinion
Quarterly*, IV (1940), 3–24.
[5] Rowena Wyant: "Voting Via the Senate Mailbag," *Public Opinion Quarterly*, V (1941), 359–83, 590–624.
[6] L. A. Dexter: "What Do Congressmen Hear: The Mail," *Public Opinion
Quarterly*, XX (1956), 16–27.

drift of constituency thinking, but rather to promote the cause of the legislator. A constituent, in receipt of a questionnaire from his congressman, is certainly reminded of the Representative and is probably flattered that so august a personage has manifested an interest in his views.

In 1954 slightly over 10 per cent of the members of the House of Representatives had used polls of one sort or another.[7] While a few members have assistants skilled in sampling techniques, most congressional polls are so designed that they are certain to produce results not reflective of opinion in the district. Most are based on mail questionnaires, and those who read, fill out, and return questionnaires are not likely to be a random sample of the population. But it may be surmised that those who respond to mail inquiries have a special interest in politics and that their views are worthy of special consideration by the legislator.

The phrasing of some, but by no means all, of the questions in these congressional polls can provoke no response of much meaning or utility. A 1960 question—"Do you agree with the administration that disarmament must be accompanied by a foolproof inspection system?"—produced an agreement of 89 per cent in a North Carolina district. Only 3 per cent of the 1951 respondents in a Wisconsin district checked the "no" box on the question: "Do you favor a reduction in nonessential civilian expenditures?" Impressions, though, from a casual perusal of poll reports, which Representatives often print in the *Congressional Record*, suggest that they have improved the form of the questions in their polls over the past decade.

Despite technical weaknesses of congressional polls, they may serve a purpose in the stream of intelligence that flows to the House member about opinion in his district. Poll results may restrain what seems to be a tendency for legislators to regard their constituents as fools. Thus, congressmen seem always to approach the question of postal rates gingerly as if the voters were poised to put them out of office if the rates were raised to the level necessary to cover costs. Individual congressional district polls have shown the contrary to be true, as have national polls. Polls also provide a guide in discounting the tone of the mail. As one congressional assistant opined as a result of polling experience, "we don't put too much weight in our ability to guess what the people at home are thinking." [8]

[7] Carl Hawver: "The Congressman and His Public Opinion Poll," *Public Opinion Quarterly*, XVIII (1954), 123–9.

[8] Philip M. DeVany: "The 'Town Meeting' Poll in South Dakota," *Public Opinion Quarterly*, XVIII (1954), 138. See also Winston Allard: "Congressional Attitudes Toward Public Opinion Polls," *Journalism Quarterly*, XVIII (1941), 47–50.

Constituency Perceptions of Legislators. The supposition that the actions of legislators may be thought of as a response to the sentiments of their constituents carries with it the tacit notion that constituents inform themselves about the records of their representatives. Without receiving a copious flow of information, the constituency can exercise no electoral sanction against the errant legislator. Instead of voting for or against a candidate on the basis of his record, the elector has to fall back on the cue of party or permit himself to be moved by the fact that the candidate is a handsome figure of a man, in good standing as a member of the VFW, a communicant of the right church, and reputed to be a kind husband and an indulgent father.

From the data scattered through the preceding chapters on the distribution of political information within the population and on the extent of popular focus of attention on political matters, it would be astonishing if we should discover that many people had anything more than the sketchiest information about the performance of their Representatives or Senators. At intervals during the 1940's the AIPO put questions such as: "Do you happen to know the name of the Congressman from your district?" The percentages of the national sample able to give a correct answer ranged from 41 to 55, varying from time to time and with the wording of the question. An analysis by place of residence of the March, 1942, respondents has its instructive aspects. Among farmers 67 per cent could name their Representative. In towns of under 10,000, 61 per cent could name their Representative; in cities of over 500,000, only 23 per cent. The high familiarity of farmers with the names of their Representatives may have some connection with the sensitivity of Representatives to the interests of their farmer constituents.

Knowledge of the Representative's name is an essential piece of information for a voter if he is to concern himself with the record of his Representative. If in the average constituency only half the electors know the name of the Representative, the proportion with any information about his performance must be far less. While only scattered pieces of data on constituent information about their Representatives are available, they accord with expectation. When in March, 1942, the AIPO asked: "Before America entered the war, was your Congressman in favor of entering the war or staying out?" 65 per cent of the national sample did not know what position their congressman had taken. (In truth, the question was somewhat complicated by the fact many congressmen had cultivated an ambiguity of position on the issue.) In 1946 the AIPO asked those who knew their Representatives' names: "Have you had a chance to follow his work in Congress—for example, do you know what committees he is on and how he has voted on important issues?" A number equal to 19 per cent of the national sample claimed to have followed the work of the congressmen, doubtless an overstatement of the reality but a figure that begins to get down toward the magnitude of the numbers with a relatively high level of interest and concern about politics.

Communication and Role. All these bits of information make it clear that a more complex conception of the relation between legislator and constituency is required than the simple one of a legislator who responds or does not respond to the will of the majority of his constituents. Whatever correspondence develops between the sentiment of the constituency and the outlook of the legislator comes about by more complex means than the mechanical communication to him of the views of the constituency. He is, in fact, most of the time without any systematic guide to constituency opinion, and in most of his work even the most intensive polling would not turn up constituency opinion relevant to the decisions he has to make. Such work might identify broad sentiments comprehending the specific issues confronting the legislator, but there would be no assurance that when election day rolled around the voters would connect the two. The image of a constituency informed about the performance of its representative and ever alert to reward conformity or to punish deviation misses the mark.

The legislator, then, by force of circumstance is thrown in considerable measure into a position in which he has to use his own judgment rather than follow constituency mandate. He may become the equivalent of Burke's admirable soul who follows his conscience in the pursuit of the general interest. Or his conscience may lead him in other directions. Or he may regard himself as bound to speak for identifiable special interests in or out of his constituency. If he regards himself as a spokesman for his constituency, it remains largely for him, in the exercise of his judgment, to determine wherein the interests of the constituency lie. How he will behave depends to a degree on his conception of his role and those conceptions vary among legislators.[9] His conception of his duty may lead him to bow to constituency opinion or to vote against it on occasion.[1]

[9] For an instructive analysis, see Heinz Eulau, John C. Wahlke, William Buchanan, and LeRoy C. Ferguson: "The Role of the Representative: Some Empirical Observations on the Theory of Edmund Burke," *American Political Science Review*, LIII (1959), 742–56.

[1] Hartmann records the case of the New York legislator who received 5,000 personal letters on an issue, not a dozen of which were on the side on which he voted. He wrote, he said, to all his correspondents telling them that "they were each and every one completely wrong in the position which they were taking

Though these observations about the discretion of the legislator are correct, they must in some way be reconciled with the fact that legislators seem to be guided, to some extent at least, by opinions that can plausibly be imputed to their constituencies. This comes about in part because many legislators see themselves dedicated to a role of advocacy of the viewpoint of their constituencies. As they meditate about their decisions on specific issues, they come to conclusions congruent with the dominant interest of their constituency. They arrive at that position often without benefit of guidance from the constituency; often they know better the interests of the constituency as it relates to particular measures than the constituency itself knows them. On issues of great salience to the constituency and about which opinion may be intense, the legislator may, of course, operate under a condition almost equivalent to a mandate binding in its effect.[2] Yet such issues are few. The data also establish that on some types of questions legislators in the exercise of their discretion may be influenced by party policy or other considerations that run counter to the opinions of their constituencies. Withal, the impression develops that the matrix of constituency opinion within which a representative operates allows a good deal of play in which he must exercise his own judgment, whatever his conception of his role.[3]

3 · Sanctions of Opinion

By its array of data and the inferences therefrom, the analysis has nosed its way into a box. The data indicate a widespread lack of information among voters about the policy position of their legislators; they also indicate the existence, insofar as figurative mandates from constituencies

---

and for the reasons set forth in my communication." His plurality was doubled at the next election. See George W. Hartmann: "Judgments of State Legislators Concerning Public Opinion," *Journal of Social Psychology*, XXI (1945), 105–14.

[2] On some issues legislators may accurately estimate constituency sentiments. Crane, in an ingenious study, compared voting by Wisconsin legislators on a daylight-saving bill with the district votes in a subsequent referendum on the issue. About 85 per cent of the legislators voted in the same way as their constituencies. In interviews with legislators it turned out that the most important explanation of a vote divergent from the district sentiment was "uncertainty as to what that opinion was." See Wilder W. Crane, Jr.: "Do Representatives Represent?" *Journal of Politics*, XXII (1960), 295–9. The daylight-saving issue is one about which it is comparatively simple to estimate constituency opinion; it is also one without great import for the Republic and, therefore, one on which a legislator need have no sense of guilt if he humors the preferences of his constituents.

[3] For an analysis of Representatives' perceptions of their role and related matters, see L. A. Dexter: "The Representative and His District," *Human Organization*, XVI, 1 (1957), 2–13.

are concerned, of a considerable range of freedom for the legislator. Yet on his own initiative the legislator may vote as he deems the interest of his constituency requires. Under these circumstances of electoral ignorance and legislative freedom, what happens when a legislator deviates markedly from the norms of the constituency? What is the sanction of public opinion over this type of legislator? How is he brought to heel if he departs sharply from the majority sentiments of his constituency? Or is the dedication of the legislator to public opinion merely a habit of the political culture, not a posture ultimately enforcible by political sanction?

Constituency opinion is not without sanction, though some of the sanctions are so commonplace that we scarcely recognize their existence. In the pre-election stage constituency processes operate prospectively to screen out those candidates who deviate from the locally dominant sentiments. An aspirant's broad policy orientation must not diverge far from the norms of his constituency if he is to be nominated or to have a chance for election. In most northern Democratic constituencies a rip-roaring devotee of the rights of management would fare poorly in the battle for his party's nomination. In northern, suburban Republican constituencies a person sympathetic to labor unions would scarcely expect to contend with success for the Republican nomination. In neither type of district would a Socialist Labor candidate aspire with optimism to election. The customary norms of the constituency which must be met if a person is to be "available" as a candidate limit the field to those candidates with broad views consonant with those of the district.

Another type of sanction comes into play when a legislator seeks renomination or re-election, as most of them do. The constituency by its refusal to re-elect a legislator may express its disapproval of his record; or by returning him for another term it may express its approval. Yet the operation of this sanction involves more institutional apparatus and more indirection than might be suggested by this simple statement of the process. The exercise of electoral judgment about the performance of a legislator requires that a goodly number of voters be informed about his record. That condition is not often fulfilled.

The mechanism of party is interposed between legislator and voter to give an electorate, even though uninformed about the minutiae of a legislator's record, some sanction over his behavior. In elections to the national House of Representatives, the movement of votes from one election to the next does not vary erratically from district to district as would be expected if the dominant consideration in the mind of the electorate was the performance of the individual legislator from the individual district. Rather, the movement tends to result almost entirely in gains or losses for the majority party of the moment. The inference may be that the legislator benefits or suffers from the general appraisal of the performance of his party, although exceptions to that proposition occur. The efficacy of this electoral sanction depends on the existence of a degree of party discipline within the governmental apparatus. In a sense, also, the recognition of the role of party as an intervening link in the connection between voter and legislator suggests that the legislator may in fact be accountable not individually but as a member of a larger corporate entity.[4]

In their choice of candidates for representative far more voters vote the party slate than vote for (or against) an individual candidate.[5] This fact alone confronts the legislator with an insurmountable task if he hopes to establish in the minds of his constituents an image of sufficient strength to have much effect on election day. A few legislators gain sufficient recognition of their peculiar policy position to give them an electoral strength quite independent of their party (and others may establish a position in one-party districts to give them a like advantage over their potential opponents), but only a few. Thus, when Jacob Javits of New York was a Republican member of the House of Representatives, his voting record deviated so far from the Republican norm and became so well known that he was able to win several elections in an overwhelmingly Democratic district. Such instances are few, though a good many legislators gain some independence from electoral tides against their party. That independence probably comes in the main from the contacts between legislator and constituent that promote familiarity with the solon's name rather than from a clearly perceived policy position fitted to the sentiments of the district as a whole.[6]

As one constructs a general model of the sanction of constituency opinion, he must include means for the information of the constituency either on the general record of the representative or on his performance

[4] Probably for individual survival the realities do not require the degree of freedom from party ties within the House of Representatives that is commonly supposed. The assertion is that to survive a Representative must vote his district and abandon his party. On some issues and in some districts that is undoubtedly true. More often, though, abandonment of the party line may be only a concession to interests of minor electoral strength within the district.

[5] In 1956 the SRC schedule included these questions: "How about the vote for Congressman? Did you vote for a candidate for Congress? (If yes.) Who did you vote for? (If R doesn't know candidate's name.) Which party was that?" The response divided in the following way: 11 per cent mentioned correct Democratic candidate; 1 per cent mentioned incorrect Democratic candidate; 23 per cent mentioned Democratic party only; 11 per cent mentioned correct Republican candidate; 20 per cent mentioned Republican party only; 5 per cent had not voted for Congressman or did not know whether they had; the remainder were nonvoters.

[6] On this matter, see V. O. Key, Jr.: *Politics, Parties, and Pressure Groups*, 4th ed. (New York: Crowell; 1958), ch. 20.

on roll calls of special concern to his district. If a legislator is to worry about the attitude of his district, what he needs really to worry about is, not whether his performance pleases the constituency at the moment, but what the response of his constituency will be in the next campaign when persons aggrieved by his position attack his record. The constituency, thus, acquires a sanction largely through those political instruments that assure a challenge of the record. In the large, that function is an activity of the minority party; it may also be an activity of individual candidates who contend against the incumbent for either nomination or election. The long continuance of a legislator in office may reflect his skill in the avoidance of positions that would arouse effective challenge. Success in that endeavor may be conditioned by the characteristics of the political structure and habits of the district as well as by the legislator's skill in avoiding the arousal of latent opposition. However that may be, sanction of majority sentiment within the district depends ultimately on centers of leadership either within or without the district adequately equipped to challenge the legislator who seeks re-election.

2 0

PRESSURE GROUPS

PRESSURE GROUPS occupy a prominent place in analyses of American politics. In a regime characterized by official deference to public opinion and by adherence to the doctrine of freedom of association, private organizations may be regarded as links that connect the citizen and government. They are differentiated in both composition and function from political parties. Ordinarily they concern themselves with only a narrow range of policies, those related to the peculiar interests of the group membership. Their aim is primarily to influence the content of public policy rather than the results of elections. Those groups with a mass membership, though, may oppose or support particular candidates; in that case they are treated as groups with power to affect election results and, thereby, with the capacity to pressure party leaders, legislators, and others in official position to act in accord with their wishes.

Despite the extensive literature on pressure groups, our knowledge of their role and mode of operation in the political system remains inadequate. One source of the unsatisfactory quality of our knowledge may be the muckraking tendency to magnify the import of political practices that occur outside the formal structure of the regime. Pressure groups can readily be pictured as privileged interests whose shadowy operations determine the course of public policy in a manner contrary to the general interest. Another difficulty in the analysis of pressure groups is that they include a variety of types of institutions. Generalizations about pressure groups often produce observations that correctly describe some groups but miss the mark with respect to others. "Pressure group" is by no means a homogeneous category. Such groups differ in purpose and vary widely in size of membership. They may or may not be homogeneous in membership. They differ in the faithfulness with which they mirror the preferences of their members, as well as in many other respects.

A dimension of differentiation extremely significant in the conditioning of the nature and operation of pressure groups is that of membership. The AFL-CIO is an entity unlike the American Bottlers of Carbonated Beverages. The American Farm Bureau Federation can scarcely be classified with the American Greyhound Track Operators Association. Organizations that speak for, or claim to speak for, a mass membership are relevant in a discussion of the linkage of public opinion and government. On the other hand, while the American Beekeeping Federation may have its legitimate claims on government, it speaks for no formidable body of public opinion. To some extent the mode of operation of large and small groups must differ. Yet a small group in one situation may be a large group in another: a neighborhood association with 300 members may be huge to a city councilman but invisible to a United States Senator.

Whether the group be large or small, its organizational apparatus may serve as a link between its membership and government. In this chapter some aspects of this function will be examined, with the principal emphasis on mass-membership organizations; incidental attention will be given to smaller organizations in order to indicate the contrasting problems of the two types of groups.

1 · The Organized and the Unorganized

In the estimation of the place of pressure groups in the interactions between government and citizen a first step is the determination of the incidence of membership in organizations. That problem has at least two important aspects. As one looks at the political system as a whole, the question arises of what kinds of people are most frequently involved in the organizations that bind people together in concerns of political relevance. Second, an examination of individual organizations, especially those with a mass membership, arouses curiosity about the extent to which they enroll their potential membership.

Incidence of Membership. The delineation of the web of group memberships of political relevance is a task that strains the available data. Perhaps almost every circumstance that brings people together in

group interaction has potential import for political opinion and behavior—the family, the work group, the neighborhood, the car pool,
the church, the social gathering of friends, the union, the professional
society, the poker club, as well as more formal organizations. Surveys
of group membership do not provide us with a complete map of politically relevant group relationships. The data regarding informal group
memberships may be especially weak. Surveys, though, consistently
show that frequency of group membership tends to vary with income,
occupation, education, and other such indices of status. Illustrative of
this general tendency are the data of Table 20.1, which indicate the

TABLE 20.1

OCCUPATION OF HEAD OF HOUSEHOLD IN RELATION TO TOTAL NUMBER OF FORMAL
AND INFORMAL GROUP MEMBERSHIPS OF RESPONDENT [a]

NUMBER OF MEMBERSHIPS	PRO-FESSIONAL	BUSINESS	CLERICAL	SKILLED	UNSKILLED	FARMER
None	19%	25%	32%	35%	43%	41%
One	14	33	36	33	36	33
Two	14	18	18	21	16	11
Three or more	53	24	14	11	5	15
	100%	100%	100%	100%	100%	100%
N	43	75	50	147	56	66

[a] The question was designed to obtain information on memberships
ranging from labor unions, through veterans organizations, neighborhood clubs, professional groups, poker clubs, and any others. For the
questions, see Angus Campbell *et al., The Voter Decides,* p. 224, questions 32 and 33.
DATA SOURCE: *Survey Research Center, University of Michigan, 1952.*

proportions of persons at different occupational levels reporting specified numbers of group memberships. Over half the respondents in professional households claimed three or more group memberships, while
only 5 per cent of those in the households of unskilled workers
claimed a frequency of organizational affiliation.

In the accumulation of the data for this table the respondents were
confronted with a list of fourteen types of organizations, ranging from
labor unions to informal groups such as sewing circles and poker
clubs. Church-related organizations were included but not churches.
After they had reviewed the list, respondents were given a chance to
mention "any other" organization to which they belonged. Almost a
third of the sample could not claim a membership in any group.[1] Al-

[1] Wright and Hyman report a 1953 survey in which respondents in 47 per
cent of the households reported no memberships in the family in voluntary organizations. Their question was more restrictive than the SRC inquiry. It was:

though the table shows that sharp differentials exist in frequency of group affiliation up and down the occupational hierarchy, occupation does not necessarily account for these differences. Rather, the data show only the distribution within the occupational hierarchy of those prone to become group members.

Extent of Enlistment of Potential Membership. While the justice of its cause should determine the success of an organization's endeavors, the size and coverage of its membership are not without importance in a regime that gives weight to numbers. Numbers alone may carry weight; the more completely an organization encompasses its potential membership, the greater is its moral authority when it claims to speak for an interest in society. Analyses of all kinds of organizations, both large and small, indicate that usually they fail by far to enroll their potential membership. The mass-membership organizations have, to be sure, large numbers of persons within their ranks and may be politically formidable, but many eligible for membership remain unaffiliated. Probably not much more than one third of farm households, for example, include members of farm organizations.[2] Doubtless the proportion of full-fledged commercial farmers belonging to farm organizations is greater than one third, but substantial numbers even of such farmers abstain from activity in farm groups.[3] Of those who report membership in a farm organization, those affiliated with the American

---

"Does anyone in the family belong to any sort of club, lodge, fraternal order, or union with ten or more members in it?"—Charles R. Wright and Herbert H. Hyman: "Voluntary Association Memberships of American Adults: Evidence from National Sample Surveys," *American Sociological Review*, XXIII (1958), 284–94.

[2] Of the farm households in the 1956 Survey Research Center sample 66 per cent included no member of a farm organization. This proportion rests on 191 cases.

[3] As one puzzles about the political strength of the American farmer, it may be relevant to remember that many city-dwellers were once farm boys and girls. Thus, in 1956 a city lady said of Eisenhower: "I think he's done a good job. Helped the farmers with the soil bank which has been wonderful. My folks live on a farm. I know." Another person who grew up on a farm liked the Democrats: "The farmers aren't getting as much for crops; factories aren't running as well; more strikes since the Republicans got in. I'm for the Democrats for the farmers' sake mostly." A young lady who did not vote but had hoped the Democrats would win: "I just wanted a Democrat in. (Why?) They protect the farmer and I'm a farm girl." At the time she planned to go to vote, her new boy friend turned up: "I didn't know him well enough to tell him to leave." More city-dwellers grew up on farms than might be supposed. In 1956, 15 per cent of metropolitan respondents reported farm origins. This proportion increased, roughly as size of place declined, to 41 per cent in places of from 2,500 to 10,000 and 50 per cent in places of less than 2,500.

Farm Bureau Federation are most numerous; the National Grange and the National Farmers Union rank second and third.

Even the trade unions, in which membership may be in fact compulsory for workers in particular plants or industries, fail by far to achieve their membership potential, although their coverage is wider than that of farm organizations. When arranged according to the occupation of the head of the household, the following proportions in 1956 reported union membership in the household: professional, 9 per cent; business, 9 per cent; clerical, 21 per cent; skilled worker, 57 per cent; unskilled worker, 36 per cent; farm operator, 2 per cent; other, 11 per cent. Of the households with a union member, 77 per cent were in the skilled and unskilled categories.[4]

Joiners and Nonjoiners. Studies of the members of organized groups and of their potential members in different times, places, and circumstances uniformly show that persons who belong to organizations are, on the average, distinguishable from the nonjoiners. The better-off and better-educated in almost any category of potential members are more likely to be members than are those not so well off or those with less education. The prosperous, the alert, the informed, and the educated join together in organizations to promote their concerns. Beyond these differences, the joiners and nonjoiners differ in their political characteristics, in their political participation, in their sense of political efficacy, and in their psychological involvement in the political process.

A major characteristic of joiners is that they have higher levels of political participation than do nonjoiners. Persons who belong to organizations and are active in them are also likely to vote and to be active in politics in other ways. Those who say they are "active" in the groups to which they belong are far less numerous than those who merely belong. Those in a national sample who said that they were "active" in three or more groups included relatively almost twice as many persons of high levels of political participation as did those who said they were "active" in no formal group. On the other hand, the person not "active" in any formal organization was about three times as likely to be a nonvoter as the person "active" in three or more groups, as indicated by Table 20.2. This index of activity in formal groups may

---

[4] The presence of union members in professional, business, and farm households doubtless has some political import. Consider the widow operating a farm who said that she had been unsympathetic toward unions until her son, a union member, acquainted her with the facts of industrial life. The amount of this cross-occupational seepage of attitude is probably slight for the entire country but in some localities, for example, where many farmers work part-time in factories, it may be of sufficient magnitude to matter.

TABLE 20.2

NUMBER OF ACTIVE MEMBERSHIPS IN FORMAL GROUPS IN RELATION TO LEVELS OF
POLITICAL PARTICIPATION [a]

LEVEL OF PARTICIPATION	NUMBER OF ACTIVE MEMBERSHIPS			
	None	One	Two	Three or more
High 4	24%	28%	32%	41%
3	46	55	47	48
2	3	1	5	0
Low 1	27	16	16	11
	100%	100%	100%	100%
N	336	116	57	27

[a] Persons who reported membership in formal organizations in response to the question analyzed in Table 20.1 were asked: "First, let's take the ———— group. Would you say you are an active member of this group or not very active?" For construction of the index of participation, see Appendix IV.

DATA SOURCE: *Survey Research Center, University of Michigan, 1952.*

identify an especially influential sector of the population; only about 5 per cent of the sample claimed to be active in three or more such groups. Those who claimed to be active in two or more groups made up about 10 per cent of the sample.

Other indices of political differentiation also show contrasts between members and nonmembers within classes of persons eligible for affiliation with an organization. Farmers who belong to farm organizations, for example, are on the average higher in their sense of political

TABLE 20.3

SENSE OF POLITICAL EFFICACY AND POLITICAL INVOLVEMENT OF RESPONDENTS
IN FARM HOUSEHOLDS WITH MEMBERS OF FARM ORGANIZATIONS AND IN FARM
HOUSEHOLDS WITHOUT SUCH MEMBERS

	POLITICAL EFFICACY		POLITICAL INVOLVEMENT	
	Members	Nonmembers	Members	Nonmembers
High 4	3%	1%	34%	17%
3	38	17	22	19
2	27	28	28	35
1	20	35	16	29
Low 0	12	19		
	100%	100%	100%	100%
N	64	127	64	127

DATA SOURCE: *Survey Research Center, University of Michigan, 1956.*

efficacy and in their degree of political involvement than are farmers who do not belong. The measure of political involvement is a measure of interest and concern about a particular presidential election, but farmers who do not become involved in presidential campaigns must have little concern about public affairs between elections. The data on political efficacy and political involvement of respondents in farm households with and without farm organization members appear in Table 20.3.

From the relationship of membership in farm organizations to political efficacy and political involvement, group members would be expected to show a higher degree of political activity than nonmembers. This expectation is fulfilled even in unions whose members include many persons with only a nominal attachment to the organization, as may be seen from Table 20.4. The striking fact in the table is the mark-

TABLE 20.4

UNION MEMBERSHIP IN RELATION TO LEVEL OF POLITICAL PARTICIPATION [a]

PARTICIPATION

LEVEL	SKILLED		UNSKILLED	
	Union	Nonunion	Union	Nonunion
High 4	28%	23%	19%	8%
3	49	48	52	44
2	5	7	3	5
Low 1	18	22	26	43
	100%	100%	100%	100%
N	267	195	69	105

[a] Distributions according to level of participation are of respondents in households headed by skilled and unskilled workers with and without a union member in the household. Thus in the union columns the respondent is usually the union member or his wife.
DATA SOURCE: *Survey Research Center, University of Michigan, 1952.*

edly higher level of participation among unskilled workers who belong to unions than among unskilled nonmembers. Organizations may have their greatest potential to affect political activity, and also the direction of the vote, among those persons not otherwise motivated to political action. Highly skilled persons have characteristics apart from union membership that move them to political participation. The least skilled, if left to their own devices, may not even vote. Among this category of persons the nudge of the union may have an especially notable effect.

Degrees of Group Identification. These comparisons of members and nonmembers should not obscure the fact that among those who belong to groups, differences prevail not unlike those that exist between members and nonmembers. Members of farm organizations have a higher sense of political efficacy than nonmembers, and a higher degree of political involvement also. Members of unions participate in higher degree than do nonmembers. Yet among the members of such organizations gradations of political efficacy, political involvement, and political participation exist which belie the popular suppositions of the solidarity of mass-membership groups.

Each mass-membership organization probably includes a hard core of members who are closely identified with the group and who in turn are most active and most involved in political matters. This contrast between the political characteristics of the hard core and the peripheral members prevails within trade unions. Relevant data may be obtained from a rough measure of closeness of identification with the union by its members. Of those with the lowest sense of union identification, as may be seen in Table 20.5, over one fourth rank low on the index of political involvement. Of those with the closest sense of union identification only one eighth rank low in political involvement.[5] Unions evi-

TABLE 20.5

Sense of Union Identification in Relation to Level of Political Involvement

POLITICAL INVOLVEMENT	LEAST IDENTIFIED [a]			MOST IDENTIFIED
	I	2	3	4
High 4	17%	14%	26%	34%
3	19	29	24	23
2	36	33	26	31
Low 1	28	24	24	12
	100%	100%	100%	100%
N	83	126	109	110

[a] The index of union identification was constructed from responses to two questions: "Would you say you feel pretty close to labor union members in general or that you don't feel much closer to them than you do to other kinds of people?" "How much interest would you say you (or head of household) have in how union people as a whole are getting along in this country? Do you have a good deal of interest in it, some interest, or not much interest at all?"
DATA SOURCE: *Survey Research Center, University of Michigan, 1956.*

[5] Of those most identified with unions 10 per cent ranked low on the index of citizen duty; of those least identified, 27 per cent.

dently include an inner core of persons who are deeply concerned about both union affairs and politics.

Mass Organization and Political Stratification. What do these data about membership in mass organizations add to our information on the general system of opinion? Perhaps their major importance is that they provide another bit of information for our conception of the system of political stratification. It was earlier suggested [6] that the citizenry might be pictured as a system of strata differentiated according to political activity, participation, efficacy, and other criteria. Another index of political differentiation is membership in voluntary associations. Each higher political stratum seems to be characterized by a greater frequency of membership in groups, formal and informal. The higher political strata may gain leverage in the political process by their participation in politically relevant private groups.

Data on membership also throw light on the groups themselves and on their place in the political system. Group members tend to have a higher degree of political involvement than do those persons eligible but unaffiliated with the group. Even among group members identification with the group varies, and with that variation there occurs a variation in politically significant characteristics. These differences between members and nonmembers and among members give us some clue to the capacity of the group to muster its potential strength in the political process and to serve as a link between the citizen and government.

2 · Groups and Opinion

In its efforts to mold opinion the leadership of a pressure group has at least two major targets—the public and its own membership. One of the conventional suppositions is that any pressure group dedicates itself to the molding of public opinion toward the group's viewpoint. Once "the public" is educated to the soundness of group policies, then government itself may be more malleable in the hands of the group lobbyists. That groups engage in general propaganda there can be no doubt, but they must also devote no little energy to the indoctrination of their own members. Attitudes of group members are not always a product of their objective circumstances. Group leaders must take a hand in molding the attitudes of the rank and file.[7] While that function is performed

---

[6] Chapter 8.

[7] Oliver Garceau early emphasized the role of group leadership in the manufacture of the group line. See his *The Political Life of the American Medical Association* (Cambridge: Harvard University Press; 1941).

in even the smallest groups, it assumes a special significance in mass-membership organizations. An organization that claims several million members can maximize its strength only as it is successful in the indoctrination of its membership.

Opinion Homogeneity within Groups. Opinion surveys permit rough estimates of the success of mass organizations in impressing their policies upon their members. While the available information does not go deeply into the subtleties of the attitudes of members and of comparable nonmembers, it generally supports the observation that a gap exists between the attitudes of the leadership of mass-membership organizations and those of the rank and file. This is not to say that the membership necessarily dissents from the position of the leadership. Perhaps a more common explanation of the divergence is the imperfection of communications within the group. If the members had occasion to inform themselves and to reflect on issues, they might well bring their views into accord with those of the leadership. Nevertheless, whatever the explanation, the indoctrination of the membership is far from complete.

One gauge of these matters, which comes from a survey at the time of the 1952 presidential campaign, yields a measure of the attitude of union members and nonmembers on the Taft-Hartley Act. That Act had been debated in the 1948 campaign, talked about for several

TABLE 20.6

OPINIONS OF RESPONDENTS IN WHITE-COLLAR AND BLUE-COLLAR HOUSEHOLDS WITH AND WITHOUT UNION MEMBERS ON TAFT-HARTLEY ISSUE [a]

OPINION	WHITE-COLLAR [b]		BLUE-COLLAR	
	Union [c]	Nonunion	Union	Nonunion
Repeal or change prolabor	23%	12%	29%	10%
Leave as is or change promanagement	20	20	12	9
Change, NA how	22	25	18	9
No opinion	35	43	41	72
	100%	100%	100%	100%
N	60	413	333	292

[a] For the wording of the question, see Appendix II.
[b] That is, the head of the household of the respondent was white-collar: professional, business, or clerical.
[c] The respondent falls in the union column if he or some other member of the household belongs to a union.
DATA SOURCE: *Survey Research Center, University of Michigan, 1952.*

years, and raised again as an issue in 1952. The official union line, at least
for most unions, was advocacy of repeal of the Act; one would suppose
that union members had had ample opportunity to hear the union view.
Yet union members were not universally concerned about the question.
The respondents of the national sample in blue-collar households with a
union member were about three times (29 per cent against 10 per cent)
as likely to support repeal of the Act or its amendment in favor of labor
as were respondents in blue-collar households without a union member.
The message reached some union people, but an astonishingly large
proportion of the respondents in both union and nonunion blue-collar
households had no opinion on the question (41 and 72 per cent, respec-
tively). The details appear in Table 20.6.

Probably on an issue such as the Taft-Hartley Act, which went directly to the question of their existence and mode of operation, unions
exerted an unusual effort to bring members into line. On questions relating to social welfare generally, unions may be less motivated to
energetic campaigns of membership indoctrination. Nevertheless, on
such questions union members express views in accord with union policy with greater frequency than do comparable nonmembers. An illustration comes from responses to a 1952 question on social welfare policy: "Some people think the national government should do more in
trying to deal with such problems as unemployment, education, housing, and so on. Others think that the government is already doing too
much. On the whole, would you say that what the government has

TABLE 20.7

OPINIONS ON SCOPE OF GOVERNMENTAL SOCIAL WELFARE ACTIVITY OF RESPOND-
ENTS IN WHITE-COLLAR AND BLUE-COLLAR HOUSEHOLDS WITH AND WITHOUT
UNION MEMBERS [a]

OPINION	WHITE-COLLAR [b]		BLUE-COLLAR	
	Union [c]	Nonunion	Union [c]	Nonunion
Should do more	33%	26%	34%	24%
Is doing about right	46	44	52	57
Should do less	18	27	10	10
Don't know	3	3	4	9
	100%	100%	100%	100%
N	63	419	326	294

[a] For the wording of the question, see Appendix II.
[b] That is, the head of the household of the respondent was white-collar.
[c] A member of the household, usually its head, was a union member.
DATA SOURCE: *Survey Research Center, University of Michigan, 1952.*

done has been about right, too much, or not enough?" The more politicized unions had generally adhered to the position that the government should do more in these fields. Union members and respondents in union households took the position that the government "should do more" with greater frequency than did persons in nonunion households of roughly comparable occupational status. Even so, as Table 20.7 shows, the differences were not marked and were doubtless attributable in part to factors other than union influence. Then, too, the differences may have been greater at an earlier time when the issues involved were topics of sharper controversy.[8]

Group Identification and Opinions. While these data indicate that group members far from uniformly adopt what might be regarded as the group line, they give no explanation of why group policies should be so incompletely assimilated by the members. At various points we have touched on the processes by which groups impose their norms and values upon their members. The effectiveness of these processes varies with many circumstances. The clarity of the norm, the manner of its communication to members, the extent of reinforcement by small groups within the larger entity, the relevance of the particular norm to the perceived scope of legitimate action by the group, the value attached by an individual to his membership, and other factors bear upon the effectiveness of the group as it seeks to imprint its norms upon its members.

Mass organizations may be pictured as consisting of categories of members ranging from those least attached to the organization and least susceptible to its influence to those most attached to it and most disposed to adopt its policy line. This latter category could, if we had the detailed data, be shown to include the leadership echelons and activists. A crude measure of these gradations indicates that the more closely a person identifies with labor unions, the more likely he is to have opinions in the directions that might be expected if he followed the union's policy line.[9]

[8] Unions are not alone in their failure to impose their norms on all their members. A *Fortune* poll in 1936 asked: "Do you believe in the teaching and practice of birth control?" Of the entire national sample 63 per cent said yes, and of Roman Catholics, 43 per cent. Probably even within small groups in which homogeneity of attitude would be expected divisions of opinion also exist. Thus, W. H. Whyte, Jr., found among members of the National Association of Manufacturers violent dissent from its free enterprise campaign of 1950.—*Is Anybody Listening?* (New York: Simon and Schuster; 1952), ch. 1.

[9] Some union members have no sharp consciousness of membership. For example, in Arthur Kornhauser's sample of UAW workers in Detroit, 7 per cent did

Illustrative of this relation between union identification and policy opinions are the data of Table 20.8. Those with the highest union identification agreed far more frequently than those least identified with the proposition: "The government ought to see to it that big business corporations don't have much say about how the government is run." Consistently, those most highly identified disagreed far more often than those least identified with the proposition: "The government

---

TABLE 20.8

SENSE OF UNION IDENTIFICATION OF UNION MEMBERS IN RELATION TO AGREEMENT
WITH SELECTED POLICY PROPOSITIONS [a]

| | LEAST IDENTIFIED [b] | | | MOST IDENTIFIED |
ISSUE	1	2	3	4
Business influence	42 [c]	55	55	64
Union influence	51	43	40	36
Job guarantee	70	58	66	75
Medical care	52	52	56	67

[a] Entries are percentages of those in each level of union identification expressing agreement with the specified policy proposition. The sample numbers underlying the percentages from least to most identified are as follows: 83, 126, 109, 110. For the text of the policy questions, see Appendix I.

[b] For the construction of the index of union identification, see the notes to Table 20.5.

[c] An exceptionally high proportion, 43 per cent, of those in this cell had no opinion on this proposition.

DATA SOURCE: *Survey Research Center, University of Michigan, 1956.*

---

ought to see to it that labor unions don't have much say about how the government is run." Similarly, those most closely identified with unions agreed with higher frequency than those least identified with the proposition that the federal government should see to it that those who want to work can find a job.[1] Those identified most closely with unions

---

not mention their union membership when asked about their organizational affiliations.—*When Labor Votes* (New York: University Books; 1956), p. 28. Or consider the lady who worked in a Michigan carton factory interviewed in the 1956 SRC survey about whom the interviewer noted: "Respondent could not find her union card and neither she nor her husband knew the name of her union." The lady was a "born" Republican without a keen sense of union identification and supported Eisenhower with an impressive zeal.

[1] On the job-guarantee question, as may be noticed in the table, those with lowest union identification also agreed in high degree with the proposition. Probably among those least identified with unions there is an especially large proportion of persons in insecure positions, a factor which produces agreement with this proposition quite independently of union influence.

more often agree that the government ought to help people get doctors and hospital care at low cost, a position of concord with a standard line of union policy. The chances are that in all mass-membership groups in which political activity is regarded as a legitimate group activity those members who are psychologically most closely identified with the group adopt its policy line with greater frequency than do the marginal or nominal members.[2]

While the apparatus of group leadership propagates a policy line that takes firmer root among those members closely identified with the group, factors apart from group machinery may also shape opinion. Persons who occupy similar positions in society and who undergo similar life experiences may develop similar opinions independently of organizational influence. Labor unions, for example, may preach a policy line, but the message may never reach many of their less-attentive members. These persons, because they are industrial workers, often

TABLE 20.9

IDENTIFICATION WITH JEWISH GROUP IN RELATION TO OPINION ON ISSUES OF JOB GUARANTEE AND MEDICAL CARE

OPINION	JOB GUARANTEE			MEDICAL CARE		
	Less identified [a]	More identified	Control group [b]	Less identified	More identified	Control group
Agree	59%	85%	52%	65%	78%	59%
Pro-con	3	0	7	7	0	9
Disagree	35	11	32	21	18	21
No opinion	3	4	9	7	4	11
	100%	100%	100%	100%	100%	100%
N	27	29		27	29	

[a] Identification differentiations based on responses to the questions: "Would you say you feel pretty close to Jews in general or that you don't feel much closer to them than you do to other kinds of people?" "How much interest would you say you have in how Jews as a whole are getting along in this country? Do you have a good deal of interest in it, some interest in it, or not much interest at all?"
[b] A group of non-Jews comparable to Jews in the sample with respect to occupation, education, union membership, and several other factors. The control group was contrived by Philip Converse. For a detailed explanation, see *The American Voter*, ch. 12.
DATA SOURCE: *Survey Research Center, University of Michigan, 1956.*

[2] March finds in a study of a local League of Women Voters that the active members more often supported the group political norms than did the inactive members.—James G. March: "Group Norms and the Active Minority," *American Sociological Review*, XIX (1954), 733-41.

form opinions on job-related or status-related issues that approximate the union line but through no influence of the union.[3]

Apart from response to such objective circumstances and from acceptance of announced group policy lines, subcultures within the population doubtless carry and maintain characteristic outlooks significant for opinion upon public policy. Jews may constitute a case in point. Although the numbers in the sample are too few to produce findings in which much confidence can be placed, it seems probable that the sense of identification among Jews with the Jewish group is associated with opinion differentials. On the questions of governmental action to see that those who want to work can find a job and on governmental aid in medical care, those with the sharpest sense of Jewish identification have markedly more liberal views than those Jews least identified with the group. Those least identified did not differ significantly from a comparable group of non-Jews. The relationship provides some support for Lawrence Fuchs' thesis that the Jewish culture places a high value on humanitarian action.[4] Alternatively, those most identified may have preserved a group attachment to the social democratic policies of the nations of their ancestral origin where many social welfare issues had long since been settled. The details of the data appear in Table 20.9.

Pressure Groups and Nonmember Opinion. By a circuitous route we have arrived at a point at which some plausible but largely unsupported comment may be made about the function of pressure organizations in the formation of general public opinion and its mobilization in support of group aims. The official rationale of group propaganda seems to be that by the expenditure of enough money, general public attitudes may be manipulated to support group policy preferences. Against this background of permissive public attitudes groups have easy sledding as they deal with government which, if not moved to positive action in their favor, will hesitate to take steps detrimental to them.[5] This theory of group action has a special appeal to groups small

[3] Persons who have a sense of identification with a group may form opinions by reference to the group even though the group apparatus has not engaged in extensive group propagandization on a question.

[4] See L. H. Fuchs: *The Political Behavior of American Jews* (Glencoe, Ill.: Free Press; 1956).

[5] For example, in testimony before a Senate committee in 1956 Paul Keyser, President of El Paso Natural Gas Company, spoke of a campaign of propaganda carried on by the Natural Gas and Oil Resources Committee, in connection with the industry's efforts to obtain a modification of regulatory legislation: "If the consumer understood he couldn't get supplies in a free economy unless the producer had an incentive, the problem was two-thirds solved." Then legislation would almost take care of itself, the reasoning went.

in membership, which are most often composed of businessmen. Unlike mass organizations, they command directly the support of only a few people, and they can readily subscribe to the doctrine that they must carry their cause by the generous support of propaganda to shape the opinions of the general public.

The broad conception of pressure groups as activators of general public opinion which in turn softens up government seldom conforms with the reality. This skeptical conclusion does not come from measurements of the effects of group propaganda campaigns, for those effects defy precise measurement. Rather, it flows from inferences from other data. First, scattered through the preceding chapters are illustrations of many issues that have received prolonged and prominent attention in the media. Despite that attention, large proportions of the citizenry remained without opinions on the questions or completely without information. Compare the press and radio time dedicated to the Taft-Hartley Act—which left even many union members without opinions—with the propaganda efforts that even the largest private groups can muster. The impact of the propaganda campaigns of most private groups upon the general public must be almost infinitesimal. The Association of American Railroads, for example, may buy many pages in the *Saturday Evening Post* to propagate the viewpoint that the railroads are getting a raw deal, but the odds are that the impact on public opinion and the feedback to policymakers will be negligible.[6] The scale of operation necessary to have substantial impact on public opinion is beyond the resources of most groups. They may reach selected groups of political activists through one channel or another with considerable effect, but by and large their lone efforts to mold mass opinion must be of small consequence.

Another indirect gauge of the probable effects of group propaganda campaigns on the general public comes from reflection on the efficacy of mass-membership groups in shaping the opinions of their own members, those who would be expected to be most susceptible to their message. Consider the data on the attitudes of union members. Union leadership has no impressive record in propagandizing its own members. Many members remain unaware of issues that the leadership regards as of prime importance to the union itself. Of those members who have opinions many take positions that depart from the official union line. No doubt the efficacy of mobilization of member opinions varies widely among individual unions, and that variation may be as-

[6] It is an interesting practical and theoretical question whether special interest groups of small membership might better promote their cause by the dissemination of competent and trustworthy technical analyses to demonstrate the facts and equities of their position to a relatively few political activists and influentials than by mass propaganda.

sociated with the magnitude of union efforts in member education. Yet if a mass-membership organization meets limited success in managing the attitudes of its own members, how much more ineffective must be campaigns of propaganda designed to settle like a mist over the population generally? In fact, most pressure organizations make no attempt to conduct general campaigns of public education. The lobbying efficacy of most organized groups, which is often impressive, depends on factors other than manipulation of mass attitudes.

An important way in which a pressure group can make an impact on public opinion is by exploiting the multiplier effect of alliance with a political party. If the party makes the group's cause its cause, the group line may be brought to the attention of a comparatively large sector of the public. Even if no substantial number of converts is made, latent opinions congenial to the group cause may be activated. The great campaign conducted in 1950 by the American Medical Association against "socialized medicine" provides an illustration. The AMA bought advertising space costing over $1 million just before the 1950 congressional elections to defend freedom against "the fantastic promises of this un-American excursion into State Socialism." In announcing its propaganda effort, the AMA authorities said: "We want an articulate public opinion, speaking with a voice that the socializers in Washington cannot defy or ignore." The campaign doubtless activated an opinion among many persons predisposed to react negatively to the word "socialism," but the chances are that such effect as the program of the AMA had depended more on its adoption by the Republican party than on its direct influence on public opinion. Republican campaigners in 1950, 1952, and later gave attention to "socialized medicine" and the good doctors reciprocated with strenuous efforts in support of the Republican party.[7] Even so the Eisenhower Administration felt compelled to show some deference to a public opinion that had not been converted to the AMA position, but the Administration proposals for medical care were weak, and its support of them was both inept and halfhearted, postures appropriate for the unheroic discharge of its debt of honor to the AMA. Given the limits of the capacity of pressure groups—even those with the greatest resources and largest memberships—to manage public opinion independently, their causes are prob-

---

[7] Whether the AMA or the Republican orators were responsible for it, the translation of "compulsory medical insurance" into "socialized medicine" was accomplished in the minds of many people. That term was often used in the volunteered comments by respondents on the 1956 SRC question: "The government ought to help people get doctors and hospital care at low cost." An upstate New York auto dealer agreed with the proposition but added, "I don't want socialized medicine." A Detroit housewife turned the tables: "I think they should have socialized medicine, is that what they call it?"

ably better advanced by confederacy with political parties than by independent action.

Open propagandization of the public by pressure organizations may even be damaging to the group cause; at least that is the judgment that from time to time dictates concealment of the source of support of group propaganda. Concealment seems to occur most frequently among business groups, although the general principle probably is that any group that feels itself to be in the doghouse will tend to hide behind false fronts when it propagandizes the public. Thus, in the late 1940's the Small Business Economic Foundation made something of a splash in the ocean of propaganda in a campaign to save free enterprise. The small-business supporters of the Foundation turned out to include such struggling enterprises as The Texas Company, United States Steel Corporation, Goodyear Tire & Rubber Company, Lone Star Cement Corporation, and others of comparable size.[8] Almost every investigation of large-scale pressure propaganda turns up some illustration of the tendency to conceal the origins of educational information by the creation of dummy committees or by the capture and conversion of legitimate organizations.

Whether general campaigns of publicity have much effect one way or another, their sponsors sometimes fear that they may have a negative effect if the source of their support becomes known. Given people's tendency to forget the sources of information, these apprehensions are not invariably well founded—at least for long-term campaigns directed toward the general public. Dissemination of information steadily over a long period of time may have an impact on public opinion despite the fact that the source is identified.[9]

Even though mass propaganda campaigns may have limited effects, groups from time to time are forced into positions that seem to compel them to engage in mass education. Action by government, for example, may appear to discredit an organization, and its leaders come to believe that, if it is to operate at all, its public image must be refurbished. Otherwise, the expectation seems to be, any proposal with which their name is associated is apt to be rejected out of hand. Thus, the AFL-CIO gave serious attention to its public relations after the Senate investiga-

[8] *Congressional Record* (daily ed.), March 2, 1950, p. 2726.

[9] Another negative effect of propaganda campaigns is that they may activate opposition. Thus, campaigns by power companies against the rural electrification program incidentally stir up the partisans of rural electrification. In turn, power propaganda may reduce the freedom of action of those congressmen whose constituencies include supporters of the REA. These solons are placed in a position where, if they support changes in some of the less defensible features of REA policy, they may be made to appear to be supporting the enemies of their constituents by knuckling under to the power interests. Some groups might better achieve their purposes with less ballyhoo.

tion under the chairmanship of Senator McClellan had aired some of
the less rosy aspects of union activity.[1] Over a long period the National Association of Manufacturers has served as a whipping boy for
liberals and has been naturally concerned about its public image. Surveys conducted for the Association have indicated that its reputation
with the public is far better than its own members judge it to be. In a
1954 survey, the "informed" respondents in a national sample—namely,
those who had heard of the NAM and could name one or more ways
in which they had heard of it—were asked: "On the stand it takes in national affairs, would you say NAM is forward looking or behind the
times?" The replies were as follows: forward looking, 67 per cent; behind the times, 9 per cent; depends, 3 per cent; no opinion, 21 per cent.
Moreover, slightly over half of the "informed" public approved of
"most things that NAM does or stands for."

A 1960 survey for the NAM sought to test the bearing of NAM
sponsorship on policy propositions about inflation. Thus 64 per cent
of a national sample of the public generally approved the statement:
"The cost of the present federal government budget works out to
$1,440 per American household. That's too much government spend-
ing." When a repetition of the statement to another sample included an
attribution of the statement to the National Association of Manufacturers, 66 per cent agreed. That is, within the general public on a series
of statements sponsorship by the NAM made only a negligible difference, if any, in their acceptance.[2] The moral of these data probably
is that erroneous judgments about mass opinion are common in the
give and take among those highly active in politics. When a bit of oratory that uses NAM as an epithet reaches the "average man," his response is more likely to be, "What's the NAM?" than one of either
acceptance or rejection of the argument because of its association with
the NAM.

3 · Leverage of the Group Vote

A maxim of early pressure-group theory was that private groups, dis-
pleased with the performance of legislators and other officials, would
respond by punishing their enemies and rewarding their friends at the
polls. That group influences affect the vote there can be no doubt, but

[1] See Gerald Pomper: "The Public Relations of Organized Labor," *Public
Opinion Quarterly*, XXIII (1959-60), 483-94.
[2] The materials for the surveys conducted for the NAM are used by the
courtesy of Mr. Ramon B. Dixon, Public Affairs Director in NAM's Detroit
office.

the nature of that effect and the role of pressure-group leadership in delivering the vote scarcely fit simplistic theories. Severe limitations attend the efforts of group leaders to rally their followers to punish their enemies and reward their friends. Some of these limitations have already been made obvious. A sense of commitment to group goals is weak among large proportions of the members of mass organizations. Communication of information to members about the derelictions of officials with respect to group interest is erratic. Often the reality of official behavior is itself ambiguous. A congressman from a labor district who clearly espouses the NAM line may expect the tidings to be heard by his constituents, but if he preserves an appropriate ambiguity in his record he may survive despite the best efforts of union leaders. The broad kinds of indirect evidence that can be amassed make it fairly clear that group strength in the governmental process, insofar as it rests on the vote, does not depend on the capacity of private-group leaders to manipulate the votes of a large proportion of their members in the short run.

Most pressure organizations as they deal with government, of course, gain not the slightest leverage from the vote of their members. Even if the votes could be delivered, they are too few to have an effect one way or another. And the smaller organizations make no pretense that they deliver the vote of their members. Mass-membership organizations may have within their circles millions of voters; yet data on the way people behave in their voting make it plain that a theory of standing alliance with parties and politicians more nearly explains the electoral basis of group strength than does a theory of intimidation by group threats to move their members one way or another come the next election.

Legitimacy of Group Electoral Activity. Mass-membership groups in their electoral activity labor under the handicap that many of their members do not regard it as legitimate for the organization to attempt to influence their vote. In part, this attitude stems from the fact that for many organizations—trade unions, for example—political activity is regarded as secondary to other group functions. Beyond this, people resent efforts to influence their vote or resent the imputation that they belong to a voting bloc. They may vote for every union-endorsed candidate on the ticket or for every Catholic on the ballot and simultaneously declare with some belligerence that they make up their own minds how to vote.

A crude indicator of the extent to which group electoral activity is regarded as legitimate by members is provided by the 1956 question directed to respondents in farm households: "How do you feel about farm organizations trying to help certain candidates get elected? Do you think it's all right for them to do that or do you think they ought to stay out of that?" Only 58 per cent of the sample thought it was "all right"; 35 per cent thought that farm organizations ought to "stay out"; the remainder had no opinion. For some unknown reason, respondents in households with members approved campaign participation by farm organizations less frequently than did those in nonmember households: 48 per cent against 62 per cent. To a question on legitimacy of union activity in support of candidates, the response in union households was 49 per cent "all right"; 39 per cent thought unions should stay out of campaigns.

These national figures conceal wide variation certainly among unions and probably among farm organizations. Some of the newer unions, especially those organized by the CIO, from the time of their formation placed considerable importance on political activity. Others, usually older, had long centered their efforts almost solely on bargaining and related matters. The attempt to superimpose political action on these activities met with some resistance; members often regarded these new endeavors as no business of the union. An intensive study of a local union suggests, though, that even the older unions are becoming more favorably disposed toward political action. "But ten years ago," one of its leaders remarked, "you'd have been booed down if you tried to talk to members about politics at a local meeting. That isn't so today. When I look at the progress we've made, I'm not worried that members aren't all out for political action at present." [3]

The view that an organization should not take a hand in campaigns may not invariably mean that a member will reject the group's electoral advice, but the sentiment that organizations should stay out of campaigns does not facilitate management of the membership. The task is further compounded by the weakness of identification with the organization by many of its members. Those least identified follow the electoral cues of the organization to a lesser degree, just as they adopt the policy lines of the organization to a lesser degree.[4] Those who "feel close" to their union, for example, far more frequently say that they "trust" the candidate recommendations of labor unions than do

[3] Hjalmer Rosen and R. A. Hudson Rosen: *The Union Member Speaks* (New York: Prentice-Hall; 1955), p. 47.

[4] The relation of vote and strength of group identification is analyzed in detail by Angus Campbell, Philip E. Converse, Warren E. Miller, and Donald E. Stokes: *The American Voter* (New York: Wiley; 1960), ch. 12. Similarly, the greater the clarity of the group position in the campaign, the greater is the probability that its members will follow the group line.

those who do not feel especially close to their union.[5] This "trust" reflects itself in the voting records.

Electoral activity by pressure groups is nearly always a two-edged sword. Group support of a candidate or a party may repel as well as attract voters. In the heyday of the CIO, for example, the evidence suggested that its support might hurt a candidate more than it would help him. Far more persons in the public generally said that CIO endorsement would make it likely that they would vote against the candidate than said such approval would lead them to vote for the candidate.[6] Such expressions are not necessarily controlling when the ballot is cast, but they indicate a hazard often taken into account in practical politics. Devoted supporters of a candidate may regard it as advantageous to work quietly and not to spread the tidings of their endorsement in circles where it might damage the cause.

An estimate of the net effects of these positive and negative influences of group endorsement was made in 1950 in the state of Washington. A sample of persons was asked: "If you were not well informed about the candidates or issues in the forthcoming election, which three of a list of organizations' advice would you most likely take?" And a similar question was used to identify the organizations whose advice the respondent said he was "least likely" to take. The balance between acceptance and rejection of organization advice was invariably positive among the members of the organizations concerned. Some members of certain groups—such as the Grange or the American Legion—had no high regard for the advice of their organizations, but they were outnumbered by the members who said they were likely to take their advice.[7] Within the electorate of the state as a whole, though, some groups drew far more negative than positive appraisals of their candidate advice. For example, those who rated the CIO and the Catholic Church as organizations whose advice they were most likely to

---

[5] In 1956 the SRC asked respondents in union households: "Would you say you feel pretty close to labor union members in general or that you don't feel much closer to them than you do to other kinds of people?" Another question: "Are there any groups on this list that you particularly trust—that is, would you be more likely to vote for candidates they recommend?" Of those who "felt close" to union members 52 per cent indicated a trust in the candidate recommendations of labor unions. Of those who did not feel especially close only 22 per cent did so.

[6] An AIPO question of May, 1944: "If the CIO union supported a candidate, would you be more likely to vote for that candidate or against him?" For, 10 per cent; against, 53 per cent; no difference, 20 per cent; no opinion, 17 per cent.

[7] A 1956 illustration of the rejection of organization advice comes from a reply of a butcher to the question whether unions should help candidates get elected. He thought unions should stay out of campaigns: "Any candidate would be better off if he didn't have the support of the leaders of my union. (Why?) Because they're a bunch of crooks and everybody in the union knows it."

take were far outnumbered by those who placed these groups among those whose advice they were least likely to take.[8] These relationships were, of course, a function of the composition of the population of the locality and of the circumstances of the times.

While the connection between the attitudes revealed by all these data and the vote itself is certainly loose, the information makes it clear that the leaders of mass pressure groups do not head disciplined blocs uniformly disposed to vote group interests at the polls. When pressure-group spokesmen threaten reprisal at the polls, as one unwisely does now and then, they are usually pointing an unloaded gun at the legislator.[9] Such persuasiveness as they gain thereby comes from the fact that one is never certain when a gun is loaded.[1]

Inertia and Tides. The place of pressure groups in the management of the vote is restricted by the salience of nongroup factors in the determination of the vote, factors that usually outweigh the admonitions of group leaders. Of these factors at least two merit mention in any appraisal of the place of group leadership in the electoral process. Many voters maintain the same partisan position election after election. Their party identification, even their inherited party identification, sets them upon a political trajectory from which they are infrequently deflected by pressure-group recommendations. (Those trajectories may, and often do, parallel group recommendations.) In the short run at least, group leaders can move only a few of their followers away from their customary partisan attachment. If the president of the Chamber of Commerce of the United States, unhappy about the effectiveness and fidelity of a Republican Administration in the fulfillment of its commitments to business, were to issue a clarion call to American businessmen to vote Democratic, he would not be followed by an impressive proportion of his members. Even so great a union leader as John L. Lewis discovered that his miners remained in the Democratic fold when he sought to bring them to the support of Wendell Willkie.

A second major limitation on the electoral efforts of group leaders is the fact that the broad movements of the electorate appear to be

[8] Howard E. Freeman and Morris Showel: "Differential Political Influence of Voluntary Associations," *Public Opinion Quarterly*, XV (1951–2), 703–14.

[9] In the practice of lobbying the threat of electoral reprisal is infrequent. See Lester W. Milbrath: "Lobbying as a Communication Process," *Public Opinion Quarterly*, XXIV (1960), 32–53.

[1] Another source of electoral weakness of mass-membership organizations is that their leaders generally do a poor job in mobilizing the vote. In a 1952 survey Elmo Roper found that only 28 per cent of union members said that they had "ever received from the union" any literature about candidates running for public office. The comparable figure for members of farm organizations was 20 per cent.

great tides that carry along to some extent all kinds and classes of people regardless of the admonitions of the leaders of even the most disciplined mass pressure groups. In the series of presidential elections following 1936, for example, the trend among union members was away from the Democrats just as it was in other categories of the population. Dr. Gallup's estimates of the Republican percentages of the presidential vote in union households and in all manual-worker families were as follows: [2]

	Union Families	Manual-Worker Families
1936	20%	26%
1940	28	34
1944	28	38
1948	27	34
1952	39	45
1956	43	50
1960	35	40

Throughout this period union members were Democratic in higher proportions than were unorganized workers, but the trends among the two types of voters were in the same direction. While union activity probably helped maintain the Democratic loyalties of union members, union leadership could not stay the broad shifts in voting motivated by factors other than group concerns.

Risk, Uncertainty, and Power. The tenor of the argument may make it seem that we have proved too much, that we have reduced pressure groups to zero in their influence, a proposition that flies in the face of the facts. Classes of people certainly gain deference from government by their possession and exercise of the vote. Downgrading of the supposed influence of private pressure groups in the acquisition of that deference merely means that influence flows through other channels. The influence of pressure groups upon government may not depend heavily on the short-term manipulability of their members' votes.

Instead of the picture of group leaders with the capacity to sandbag officials by their command of blocs of votes, the more realistic conception is one of a standing alliance between party leaders and pressure-group leaders. Confederates, if not friends, they tend to stand together for the interests of the party and of the group insofar as the two interests are compatible. The leadership of, for example, the Chamber

[2] George Gallup: "How Labor Votes," *Annals of the American Academy of Political and Social Science*, CCLXXIV (1951), 118-24.

of Commerce of the United States or of the National Association of Manufacturers has been, if not avowedly, in reality as closely allied with the Republican party as the leadership of the AFL-CIO has been with the Democratic party. In the long run leaders of pressure groups with mass memberships are apt to be the junior partners in their alliances with politicians, for the membership cannot be delivered even in support of their standing ally. Farmers and workers in the mass are not as faithful allies of their partisan friends as are their leaders. To some extent their inconstancy comes from their concern about factors other than group interests; to some extent, from the skill of politicians in weaning them away from those interests.

In another sense the strength of those groups based on a mass membership comes not through the organization but from the direct connection between constituencies and government. Farmers, workers, Protestants, Catholics, and other large categories of persons are certain to receive a modicum of deference from politicians even when they have no lobbyists. Senators and Representatives are often as closely in touch with farm sentiment as is the American Farm Bureau Federation. They may be even more aggressive than pressure organizations in their advocacy of the cause of persons numerous in their constituencies. A class of persons, such as farmers, may be most effective with their Representative because they dominate his district, but the same group is not ignored in the national arena. A congressional candidate in some districts can afford to be known as an enemy of the farmer or of union labor, but no presidential candidate can indulge in the luxury of identification as an enemy of groups with mass membership. The sincerity of his dedication to group interest may be doubtful, but that should never be apparent. The oddities of politics are such that at times the sliver of votes delivered by a pressure organization may appear to have turned the tide. More often it may seem in prospect that the group can turn the tide. Candidates face uncertainties that lead them to commitments to group interests unwarranted by electoral necessities. But this is a politics of pre-election commitment, not one of post-election fulfillment.

4 · Puzzles of Pressure Politics

At this point the analysis leaves us with a series of puzzles as we seek to describe the role of pressure groups as links between opinion and government. Clearly the model of the lobbyist who speaks for a united following, determined in its aims and prepared to reward its friends and punish its enemies at the polls, does not often fit reality. Nor is it probable that the unassisted effort of pressure organizations to mold public opinion in support of their position has a large effect upon mass opinion. Yet legislators listen respectfully to the representations of the spokesmen of private groups, which in turn spend millions of dollars every year in propagandizing the public. Leaders of private groups articulate the concerns of substantial numbers of persons, even though they may not have succeeded in indoctrinating completely the members of their own groups. All this activity must have some functional significance in the political system. The problem is to identify its functions in a manner that seems to make sense. In this endeavor a distinction of utility is that made earlier in the discussion between mass-membership organizations and nonmass organizations, which far outnumber the former.

Representation of Mass-Membership Groups. Only the spokesmen for mass-membership organizations can give the appearance of representing voters in sufficient numbers to impress (or intimidate) government. The influence of nonmass groups, which often have only a few hundred or a few thousand members, must rest upon something other than the threat of electoral retribution. As has been seen, the reality of the behavior of members of mass organizations is that in the short run they are not manipulable in large numbers by their leaders. Their party identification anchors many of them to a partisan position, and over the longer run they seem to be moved from party to party in presidential elections by the influences that affect all types and classes of people.

The spokesmen of mass-membership groups also labor under the handicap that they may be made to appear to be unrepresentative of the opinions of their members. When the president of an organization announces to a congressional committee that he speaks for several million people, the odds are that a substantial proportion of his members can be shown to have no opinion or even to express views contrary to those voiced by their spokesmen. This divergency is often explained as a wicked betrayal of the membership or as a deliberate departure from the mass mandate. Yet it is not unlikely that another type of explanation more often fits the facts. Opinions, as we have seen in many contexts, do not fall into blacks and whites. It may be the nature of mass groups that attachment to the positions voiced by the peak spokesmen varies with attachment to and involvement in the group. At the leadership level the group position is voiced in its purest and most uncompromising form. A substantial layer of group activists subscribes to the official line, but among those with less involvement the faith wins less general acceptance. At the periphery of the group, though, the departure from the official line may be more a matter of indifference than of dissent. Leadership policy is often pictured as the consequence of interaction between leadership and group membership, which may be only partially true. Leaders may be more accurately regarded as dedicated souls who bid for group support of their position. Almost invariably they receive something less than universal acquiescence.[3] This may be especially true in mass organizations in which political endeavor is to a degree a side issue—as, for example, in trade unions and farm organizations. As one traces attitudes and opinions across the strata of group membership, the clarity of position and the extremeness of position become more marked at the level of high involvement and activism.

If it is more or less the nature of mass organizations to encompass a spectrum of opinion rather than a single hue, much of the discussion of the representativeness of group leadership may be beside the point. However that may be, circumstances surrounding the leadership elements of mass organizations place them, in their work of influencing government, in a position not entirely dissimilar to that of leaders of nonmass groups. They must rely in large measure on means not unlike those that must be employed by groups with only the smallest membership. The world of pressure politics becomes more a politics among the activists than a politics that involves many people. Yet politics among the activists occurs in a context of concern about public opinion, a concern that colors the mode of action if not invariably its substance.

Arenas of Decision and Norms of Action. The maneuvers of pressure-group politics thus come ordinarily to occur among those highly involved and immediately concerned about public policy; the connection of these maneuvers with public opinion and even with the opinions of mass-membership organizations tends to be tenuous. Many questions of policy are fought out within vaguely bounded arenas in which the activists concerned are clustered. A major factor in the determination of the balance of forces within each arena is party control of the relevant governmental apparatus. Included among the participants in each issue-cluster of activists are the spokesmen for the pressure groups concerned, the members of the House and Senate committees with jurisdiction, and the officials of the administrative departments and agencies

[3] We expect the clergy to be more pious than the laity, but we do not often apply the same standard of judgment to the relations between leaders and led in nonecclesiastical groups. In the latter groups, at least in their political role, we expect the leaders to mirror accurately the sentiments of the mass, an expectation that may be based on an erroneous premise about the nature of group behavior.

concerned. In the alliances of pressure politics those between administrative agencies and private groups are often extremely significant in
the determination of courses of action. The cluster of concerned activists may include highly interested persons, firms, and organizations
scattered over the country, though the boundaries delimiting those concerned vary from question to question, from arena to arena.[4] In short,
pressure politics among the activists takes something of the form that
it would take if there were no elections or no concern about the nature
of public opinion; that is, those immediately concerned make themselves heard in the process of decision.

In the give and take among the activists, norms and values with
foundations in public opinion are conditioning factors. The broad
values of the society determine to a degree who will be heard, who can
play the game. Those who claim to speak for groups that advocate
causes outside the range of consensus may be given short shrift. Some
groups advocating perfectly respectable causes may be heard with less
deference than others. Subtle standards define what David Truman
calls "access" to the decisionmakers. To some extent this is a party matter: an AFL-CIO delegation does not expect to be heard with much
sympathy by a committee dominated by right-wing Republicans. The
reality of access, too, may provide an index to the tacit standards in
definition of those interests regarded as having a legitimate concern
about public policy. The spokesmen of groups both large and small
are often heard with respect, not because they wield power, but because they are perceived as the representatives of interests entitled to
be heard and to be accorded consideration as a matter of right.

Within the range of the permissible, the process of politics among
the activists is governed to some extent by the expectation that all entitled to play the game shall get a fair deal (or at least a fair hearing
before their noses are rubbed in the dirt). Doubtless these practices parallel a fairly widespread set of attitudes within the population generally. Probably those attitudes could be characterized as a disposition
to let every group—big business and labor unions as well—have its say,
but that such groups should not be permitted to dominate the government. In the implementation of these attitudes the legalism of American
legislators plays a role. Frequently congressional committeemen regard
themselves as engaged in a judicial role of hearing the evidence and of
arriving at decisions based on some sort of standards of equity.

[4] Floyd Hunter reports that in some areas the largest corporations often
work directly with government rather than through pressure associations: "I
would not go to the associations to get a policy hammered out. I'd go directly to
a friend. a cabinet member, the President, or to top Congressmen and get satisfaction."—*Top Leadership, U.S.A.* (Chapel Hill: University of North Carolina
Press; 1959), p. 149.

Rituals of the Activists. The maneuvers of group spokesmen, be they spokesmen for mass or nonmass organizations, are often accompanied by rituals in obeisance to the doctrine that public opinion governs. The belief often seems to be that congressmen will be impressed by a demonstration that public opinion demands the proposed line of action or inaction. Hence, groups organize publicity campaigns and turn up sheafs of editorials in support of their position. They stimulate people to write or to wire their congressmen; if the labor of stimulation is too arduous, they begin to sign to telegrams names chosen at random from the telephone directory. They solicit the endorsement of other organizations for their position. They lobby the American Legion and the General Federation of Women's Clubs for allies willing to permit their names to be used. On occasion they buy the support of individuals who happen to hold official positions in other organizations. They form fraudulent organizations with impressive letterheads to advance the cause. They attempt to anticipate and to soften the opposition of organizations that might be opposed to their position.[5] Groups of similar ideological orientation tend to "run" together or to form constellations in confederation for mutual advantage.

All these maneuvers we have labelled "rituals"; that is, they are on the order of the dance of the rainmakers. That may be too brutal a characterization, for sometimes these campaigns have their effects— just as rain sometimes follows the rainmakers' dance. Yet the data make it fairly clear that most of these campaigns do not affect the opinion of many people and even clearer that they have small effect by way of punitive or approbative feedback in the vote.[6] Their function in the political process is difficult to divine. The fact that organizations engage in these practices, though, is in itself a tribute to the importance of public opinion. To some extent, too, these opinion campaigns are not so much directed to mass opinion as to other activists who do not speak for many people either but have access to the arena of decision-making and perhaps have a viewpoint entitled to consideration. In another direction widespread publicity, by its creation of the illusion of mass support, may legitimize a position taken by a legislator. If a legislator votes for a measure that seems to arouse diverse support, his vote is not so likely to appear to be a concession to a special interest.

[5] A recent celebrated case that involved many of these tactics was the campaign conducted by Carl Byoir & Associates for the railroads in Pennsylvania against legislation to permit longer trucks to use the highways. See the account in Robert Bendiner: "The 'Engineering of Consent'—A Case Study," *The Reporter*, August 11, 1955.

[6] A congressman whose voting record places him too far out of line with the sentiments of his constituency will probably suffer without the interposition of pressure groups.

Barnums among the Businessmen. An additional explanation that apparently accounts for a good deal of group activity is simply that businessmen (who finance most of the campaigns of public education by pressure groups) are soft touches for publicity men. The advertising and public-relations men have demonstrated that they can sell goods; they proceed on the assumption that the business of obtaining changes in public policy is analagous to selling soap.[7] They succeed in separating businessmen from large sums of money to propagate causes, often in a manner that sooner or later produces a boomerang effect.

Professional bureaucrats of the continuing and well-established organizations practice restraint in their public-relations campaigns. They need to gain the confidence of congressmen and other officials with whom they also need to be able to speak the next time they meet. The fly-by-night organization or the business group that falls into the clutches of an unscrupulous public-relations firm is more likely to indulge in the fantastic public relations and pressure campaign. Thus the National Tax Equality Association raised some $600,000 to finance a campaign against the tax exemptions of cooperatives, the most important of which are farm coops. Contributions came from concerns as scattered as the Central Power & Light Co., of Corpus Christi, Texas; Fairmont Foods Co., of Omaha, Nebraska; Central Hudson Gas and Electric Corporation, of Poughkeepsie, New York; and the Rheem Manufacturing Co., of San Francisco. The late Representative Reed, of New York, who was not one to attack business lightly, declared:

> Mr. Speaker, an unscrupulous racket, known as the National Tax Equality Association, has been in operation for some time, directing its vicious propaganda against the farm co-operatives. To get contributions from businessmen, this racketeering organization has propagandized businessmen with false statements to the effect that if farm co-operatives were taxed and not exempted the revenue to the government would amount annually to over $800,000,000. [The treasury estimate was in the neighborhood of $20,000,000.] This is, of course, absolutely false and nothing more nor less than getting money under false pretenses. . . . This outfit of racketeers known as the Tax Equality Association has led honest businessmen to believe that their contributions were deductible from gross income as ordinary and necessary business expense with reference to their Federal income-tax return.[8]

[7] Why the analogy is false should by now be self-evident. Apart from considerations of morality and equity in public decision, the fundamental difference is that the customers, animated by advertising, cannot go into the store and buy public policy. Implementation through government of whatever motives are aroused by propaganda is a complex process.

[8] *Congressional Record* (daily ed.), March 20, 1951, p. 2793.

The Tax Equality Association provided its subscribers with the following form letter to send to their Congressmen:

> Dear Mr. Congressman: You raised my income taxes. Now I hear you are going to do it again. But you still let billions in business and profits escape. How come you raise my taxes, but let co-ops, mutuals, and other profit-making corporations get off scot free, or nearly so? I want a straight answer—and I want these businesses fully taxed before you increase my or anyone else's income taxes again.

Letters so phrased are not well designed to produce favorable congressional response. The ineptness of this sort of campaign creates no little curiosity about the political judgment of solvent businessmen who put their money or their corporation's money into the support of obviously stupidly managed endeavors.

Autonomous Actors or Links? This review of the activities of pressure groups may raise doubts about the validity of the conception of these groups as links between public opinion and government. The reality seems to be that the conception applies with greater accuracy to some groups than to others. Certainly group spokesmen may represent a shade of opinion to government even though not all their own members share the views they express. Yet to a considerable degree the work of the spokesmen of private groups, both large and small, proceeds without extensive involvement of either the membership or a wider public. Their operations as they seek to influence legislation and administration, though, occur in a milieu of concern about opinion, either actual or latent. That concern also disposes decision-makers to attend to shades of opinion and preference relevant to decision though not necessarily of great electoral strength—a disposition of no mean importance in the promotion of the equitable treatment of people in a democratic order.[9] The chances are that the effects of organized groups

[9] The speculations and the data of this chapter may throw some light on the nature of "pluralism" and the circumstances congenial to the existence of a pluralistic order. Pluralistic explication of the nature of a political order may conjure up notions of a society divided into great groups; interaction between these groups produces a precipitate of public policy. The data suggest the question whether the conditions precedent to the existence of a pluralistic order may not include a relative absence or weakness of attachment among the mass of people to group causes. The pluralistic interactions among leadership echelons may occur, and may be tolerable, precisely because leadership clusters can command only a relatively small following among the mass. That circumstance both predisposes leadership sectors toward a practice of give-and-take and avoids the paralyzing conflict that might come with intense mass attachment to group causes.

on public opinion occur mainly over the long run rather than in short-run maneuvers concerned with particular congressional votes. Moreover, group success may be governed more by the general balance of partisan strength than by the results of group endeavors to win friends in the mass public. An industry reputed to be led by swindlers may not expect the most cordial reception from legislative committees, especially at times when the balance of strength is not friendly to any kind of business. If the industry can modify its public image, a task that requires time, its position as it maneuvers on particulars (about which few of the public can ever know anything) may be less unhappy. That modification may be better attained by performance than by propaganda.

Part VI

CONCLUSIONS

2 1

PUBLIC OPINION
AND DEMOCRATIC
POLITICS

THE EXPLORATION of public attitudes is a pursuit of endless fascination—and frustration. Depiction of the distribution of opinions within the public, identification of the qualities of opinion, isolation of the odd and of the obvious correlates of opinion, and ascertainment of the modes of opinion formation are pursuits that excite human curiosity. Yet these endeavors are bootless unless the findings about the preferences, aspirations, and prejudices of the public can be connected with the workings of the governmental system. The nature of that connection has been suggested by the examination of the channels by which governments become aware of public sentiment and the institutions through which opinion finds more or less formal expression.

When all these linkages are treated, the place of public opinion in government has still not been adequately portrayed. The problem of opinion and government needs to be viewed in an even broader context. Consideration of the role of public opinion drives the observer to the more fundamental question of how it is that democratic governments manage to operate at all. Despite endless speculation on that problem, perplexities still exist about what critical circumstances, beliefs, outlooks, faiths, and conditions are conducive to the maintenance of regimes under which public opinion is controlling, at least in principle, and is, in fact, highly influential.

1 · A Missing Piece of the Puzzle

Though the preceding analyses did not uncover the secret of the conditions precedent to the practice of democratic politics, they pointed to a major piece of the puzzle that was missing as we sought to assemble the elements that go into the construction of a democratic regime. The significance of that missing piece may be made apparent in an indirect manner. In an earlier day public opinion seemed to be pictured as a mysterious vapor that emanated from the undifferentiated citizenry and in some way or another enveloped the apparatus of government to bring it into conformity with the public will. These weird conceptions, some of which were mentioned in our introductory chapter, passed out of style as the technique of the sample survey permitted the determination, with some accuracy, of the distribution of opinions within the population. Vast areas of ignorance remain in our information about people's opinions and aspirations; nevertheless, a far more revealing map of the gross topography of public opinion can now be drawn than could have been a quarter of a century ago.

Despite their power as instruments for the observation of mass opinion, sampling procedures do not bring within their range elements of the political system basic for the understanding of the role of mass opinion within the system. Repeatedly, as we have sought to explain particular distributions, movements, and qualities of mass opinion, we have had to go beyond the survey data and make assumptions and estimates about the role and behavior of that thin stratum of persons referred to variously as the political elite, the political activists, the leadership echelons, or the influentials. In the normal operation of surveys designed to obtain tests of mass sentiment, so few persons from this activist stratum fall into the sample that they cannot well be differentiated, even in a static description, from those persons less involved politically. The data tell us almost nothing about the dynamic relations between the upper layer of activists and mass opinion. The missing piece of our puzzle is this elite element of the opinion system.

That these political influentials both affect mass opinion and are conditioned in their behavior by it is obvious. Yet systematic knowledge of the composition, distribution in the social structure, and patterns of behavior of this sector of the political system remains far from satisfactory.

The longer one frets with the puzzle of how democratic regimes manage to function, the more plausible it appears that a substantial part of the explanation is to be found in the motives that actuate the leadership echelon, the values that it holds, in the rules of the political game to which it adheres, in the expectations which it entertains about its own status in society, and perhaps in some of the objective circumstances, both material and institutional, in which it functions. Focus of attention on this sector of the opinion system contrasts with the more usual quest for the qualities of the people that may be thought to make democratic practices feasible. That focus does not deny the importance of mass attitudes. It rather emphasizes that the pieces of the puzzle are different in form and function, and that for the existence of a democratic opinion-oriented system each piece must possess the characteristics necessary for it to fit together with the others in a working whole. The superimposition over a people habituated to tyranny of a leadership imbued with democratic ideals probably would not create a viable democratic order.

Values and Motives of the Activist Subculture. The traits and characteristics of political activists assume importance in the light of a theory about why the leadership and governing levels in any society behave as they do. That theory amounts to the proposition that these political actors constitute in effect a subculture with its own peculiar set of norms of behavior, motives, and approved standards. Processes of indoctrination internalize such norms among those who are born to or climb to positions of power and leadership; they serve as standards of action, which are reinforced by a social discipline among the political activists. In some regimes the standards of the ruling groups prescribe practices of firmness toward the governed who are regarded as menials with no rights; they deserve no more than the rough and arbitrary treatment they receive. The rules of the game may prescribe that the proper practice for rulers is to maximize their own advantage as well as the correlative deprivations of the ruled. The ignorant, the poor, and the incompetent may be seen as entitled to what they get, which is very little. Or the rules of the game of a regime may mitigate the harshness of these outlooks by a compassionate attitude toward the wretched masses who cannot help themselves. Hence, we may have little fathers of the people. The point is that the politically active classes may develop characteristic norms and practices that tend to guide their behavior. In a loose sense these may be the norms of a sub-culture, that of the specialists in politics and government. Beliefs generally accepted among these persons tend to establish habits and patterns of behavior with considerable power of self-maintenance or persistence through time.

While the ruling classes of a democratic order are in a way invisible because of the vagueness of the lines defining the influentials and the relative ease of entry to their ranks, it is plain that the modal norms and standards of a democratic elite have their peculiarities. Not all persons in leadership echelons have precisely the same basic beliefs; some may even regard the people as a beast. Yet a fairly high concentration prevails around the modal beliefs, even though the definition of those beliefs must be imprecise. Fundamental is a regard for public opinion, a belief that in some way or another it should prevail. Even those who cynically humbug the people make a great show of deference to the populace. The basic doctrine goes further to include a sense of trusteeship for the people generally and an adherence to the basic doctrine that collective efforts should be dedicated to the promotion of mass gains rather than of narrow class advantage; elite elements tethered to narrow group interest have no slack for maneuver to accommodate themselves to mass aspirations. Ultimate expression of these faiths comes in the willingness to abide by the outcome of popular elections. The growth of leadership structures with beliefs including these broad articles of faith is probably accomplished only over a considerable period of time, and then only under auspicious circumstances.

If an elite is not to monopolize power and thereby to bring an end to democratic practices, its rules of the game must include restraints in the exploitation of public opinion. Dimly perceptible are rules of etiquette that limit the kinds of appeals to public opinion that may be properly made. If it is assumed that the public is manipulable at the hands of unscrupulous leadership (as it is under some conditions), the maintenance of a democratic order requires the inculcation in leadership elements of a taboo against appeals that would endanger the existence of democratic practices. Inflammation of the sentiments of a sector of the public disposed to exert the tyranny of an intolerant majority (or minority) would be a means of destruction of a democratic order. Or by the exploitation of latent differences and conflicts within the citizenry it may at times be possible to paralyze a regime as intense hatreds among classes of people come to dominate public affairs. Or by encouraging unrealistic expectations among the people a clique of politicians may rise to power, a position to be kept by repression as dis-illusionment sets in.[1] In an experienced democracy such tactics may be "unfair" competition among members of the politically active class. In short, certain restraints on political competition help keep competition within tolerable limits. The observation of a few American political campaigns might lead one to the conclusion that there are no restraints on politicians as they attempt to humbug the people. Even so, ad-monitions ever recur against arousing class against class, against stirring the animosities of religious groups, and against demagoguery in its more extreme forms. American politicians manifest considerable restraint in this regard when they are tested against the standards of behavior of politicians of most of those regimes that have failed in the attempt to establish or maintain democratic practices.

The norms of the practice of politics in an order that has regard for public opinion include broad rules of etiquette governing relations among the activists, as well as rules governing the relations of activists with the public. Those rules, in their fundamental effect, assure the existence of a minority among the political activists; if those who con-trol government can suppress opposition activists, an instrument es-sential for the formation and expression of public opinion is destroyed. A body of customs that amounts to a policy of "live and let live" must prevail. In constitutional democracies some of these rules are crystal-lized into fundamental law in guarantees such as those of freedom of speech, freedom of press, and the right to appeal to the electorate for power. Relevant also are procedures for the protection of property rights; a political opposition may be destroyed by expropriation as well as by execution.[2] While such rules extend in their application to the en-tire population, one of their major functions is to prevent politicians from putting each other into jail or from destroying each other in the ordinary course of their competitive endeavors. All these elements of the rules of the game gain strength, not from their statement in the statutes and codes, but from their incorporation into the norms that guide the behavior of the political activists.[3]

[1] The politicians of some of the new democracies have installed new re-gimes as they took the unfortunate step of arousing popular expectations beyond hope of early fulfillment.

[2] Rules against the use of public authority for the private advantage of offi-cials also have their political bearing. Officials who build huge fortunes or enter-prises by the abuse of official position can yield power only at enormous cost.

[3] Probably a critical stage in the evolution toward democracy occurs at the moment when those in authority conclude that their acceptance of the un-favorable outcome of an election would not result in grievous harm to them. Genetic analyses of democracies with a focus of attention on this point would be instructive.

Form and Structure. Certain broad structural or organizational characteristics may need to be maintained among the activists of a democratic order if they are to perform their functions in the system.
Fundamental is the absence of sufficient cohesion among the activists
to unite them into a single group dedicated to the management of public affairs and public opinion. Solidification of the elite by definition
forecloses opportunity for public choice among alternative governing groups and also destroys the mechanism for the unfettered expression of public opinion or of the opinions of the many subpublics. Maintenance of division and competition among political activists requires
the kinds of etiquette that have been mentioned to govern their relations among themselves. Those rules, though, do not create the cleavages among the activists. Competitive segments of the leadership echelons normally have their roots in interests or opinion blocs within
society. A degree of social diversity thus may be, if not a prerequisite,
at least helpful in the construction of a leadership appropriate for a
democratic regime. A series of independent social bases provide the
foundations for a political elite difficult to bring to the state of unifica-
tion that either prevents the rise of democratic processes or converts
them into sham rituals.

At a more earthy level, maintenance of a multiplicity of centers of
leadership and political activism requires arrangements by which men
may gain a livelihood despite the fact that they are out of power. Consider the consequences for the structure of opinion leadership of a socio-
economic system in which those skilled in the arts of governance have
open to them no way of obtaining a livelihood save by the exercise of
those skills. In the United States the high incidence of lawyers among
the politically influential provides a base of economic independence; the
defeated politician can always find a few clients. Extensive reliance
on part-time, amateur politicians in representative bodies and in many
governing commissions has assured an economic cushion for many political activists. The custom of making many such offices economically
unattractive has, in effect, required that they be filled by persons with
an economic base independent of the public treasury. Opinion leaders
and managers often find economic independence in posts with business associations and other voluntary societies. Communications enterprises, important in the operation of democracies, gain independence
from government by their commercial position. The structure of government itself, through its many independent units and agencies, assures havens of some security for spokesmen for a variety of viewpoints. All this may boil down to the contention that development and
maintenance of the type of leadership essential for the operation of a
democratic political order is facilitated by the existence of a social

system of some complexity with many centers that have some autonomy and economic independence. Perhaps a safer formulation
would be that societies that do not meet these requisites may encounter
difficult problems in the support of a fractionalized stratum of political activists; they need to construct functional equivalents of the
means we have been describing to assure the maintenance of competing centers of leadership.[4]

When viewed from another angle, these comments about the utility of independent foundations for competing sectors of the political elite relate to the more general proposition that regimes deferential
to public opinion may best flourish when the deprivations contingent
upon the loss of an election are limited. The structure of government
itself may also contribute to that loss limitation. In federal regimes and
in regimes with extensive devolution to elective local governmental
authorities the prospect of loss of a national election may be faced with
some equanimity, for the national minority may retain its position in
many subordinate units of the nation and remain in a measure undis-
turbed by the alternations of control within the nation as a whole. The
same function of loss limitation may be served by constitutional and
customary expectations that limit the permissible range of governmental action.

Another characteristic may be mentioned as one that, if not a prerequisite to government by public opinion, may profoundly affect the
nature of a democratic order. This is the distribution through the social
structure of those persons highly active in politics. By various analyses,
none founded on completely satisfactory data, we have shown that in
the United States the political activists—if we define the term broadly
—are scattered through the socio-economic hierarchy. The upper-in-
come and occupational groups, to be sure, contribute disproportionately; nevertheless, individuals of high political participation are
sprinkled throughout the lesser occupational strata. Contrast the circumstances when the highly active political stratum coincides with the
high socio-economic stratum. Conceivably the winning of consent and
the creation of a sense of political participation and of sharing in public affairs may be far simpler when political activists of some degree are
spread through all social strata. The alternative circumstance may induce an insensitivity to mass opinion, a special reliance on mass communications, and a sharpened sense of cleavage and separatism within
the political order. The contention made here amounts to more than
the axiom that democracies can exist only in societies that possess a
well-developed middle class. In a modern industrial society with uni-

---

[4] Consider the problem of a regime that seeks to carry out economic development in large measure through governmental enterprise.

versal suffrage the chances are that a considerable sprinkling of political activists needs to exist in groups below the "middle class," however that term of vague referent may be defined. The correct general proposition may be that the operation of democratic processes may be facilitated by the distribution of persons participating in the order through all strata of the electorate. When the belief that democracy depended upon the middle class flourished, a comparatively narrow suffrage prevailed.

Allied with these questions is the matter of access to the wider circles of political leadership and of the recruitment and indoctrination of these political activists. Relative ease of access to the arena of active politics may be a preventive of the rise of intransigent blocs of opinion managed by those denied participation in the regularized processes of politics. In a sense, ease of access is a necessary consequence of the existence of a somewhat fragmented stratum of political activists. Systems built on rigid class lines or on the dominance of clusters of families may be especially prone to the exclusion of those not to the proper status born—or married. Yet ease of access does not alone suffice. It must be accompanied by means, either deliberate or informal, for the indoctrination of those admitted in the special mores and customs of the activist elements of the polity. Otherwise, ease of access may only facilitate the depredations of those alienated from the values of the political order. By their nature democratic political systems have large opportunity—if there is the necessary will—to extend widely opportunities for political participation in lesser capacities and thereby to sift out those capable of achieving access to the more restricted circles of influentials. Whether the builders of political orders ever set about deliberately and systematically to tackle such problems of recruitment and indoctrination may be doubtful. Those problems may be solved, when they are solved, by the unconscious and unwilled processes of evolutionary adaptation of social systems.

This discussion in terms of leadership echelons, political activists, or elites falls painfully on the ears of democratic romantics. The mystique of democracy has in it no place for ruling classes. As perhaps with all powerful systems of faith, it is vague on the operating details. Yet by their nature governing systems, be they democratic or not, involve a division of social labor. Once that axiom is accepted, the comprehension of democratic practices requires a search for the peculiar characteristics of the political influentials in such an order, for the special conditions under which they work, and for the means by which the people keep them in check. The vagueness of the mystique of democracy is matched by the intricacy of its operating practices. If it is true that those who rule tend sooner or later to prove themselves enemies of the rights of man—and there is something to be said for the validity of this proposition—then any system that restrains that tendency however slightly can excite only awe.

2 · Mass Opinion: Variations in Nature and Function

The demarcation between the political activists and the "mass" must be regarded as a zone of gray rather than as a sharp line, but we may make a distinction between the two types of people with respect to their roles in a system in which public opinion conditions governmental action. The assumption of the preceding paragraphs has been that political activists must possess certain modal characteristics if a political system is to be a viable democracy. Without an imposing foundation of empirical data, an attempt was made to specify some of these characteristics of the activist stratum. Presumably the mass of the people must also possess attitudes and behavioral tendencies congenial to the necessities of a democratic order. That assumption involves us in a process of some circularity, for it has been repeatedly noted that the political activists may shape the opinions of the rest of the people. If the activists control, there is no need to consider mass opinion. Yet the remolding of popular attitudes is not the work of a day; they have a considerable viscosity. Hence, it is permissible to speak of the mass of the people as independent in their characteristics of the activist stratum and as one of the elements that combine with appropriate types of leadership behavior to create a functioning system. Specification of what modal qualities or attitudes should characterize the mass of the people if a society is to have a working democracy presents its difficulties. Although the survey data tell us a great deal about mass opinion, the available materials still leave wide gaps in the information relevant to the broad question that concerns us at the moment. Nevertheless, from what is known and surmised about mass opinion, we may grope toward an identification of those characteristics that may make it compatible with the practice of democracy.

Differentiations within the Public: Clues to Democratic Capabilities. Students of public opinion quickly learn that it is not illuminating to speak of "the public." In their biological characteristics men are animals of endless diversity; in their political behavior they may be equally varied. To bring that diversity within our comprehension, students of public opinion often attempt broad classifications of the citizenry. Thus, we have differentiations according to kinds of participation in political matters, ranging from the sector of the public with a continuing interest in public affairs and an inclination to write their congressman at the drop of a hat to those persons who pay virtually no attention to politics and rarely bother even to vote. The relevance of such categories at this point lies in the possibility that they may provide clues as we search for those qualities of outlook and behavior of the mass of the people or of large sectors of the public that are congenial to the workings of a democratic order—that help make possible the existence of a regime in which public opinion plays a role.

A recurring classification is that of the attentive public (or publics) and the inattentive public. So crude a statement conceals a variety in the objects as well as in the degrees of attention. Our data have identified, for example, variations in attention to presidential campaigns. Some people—nearly 10 per cent—do not follow even presidential campaigns through any of the media, while at the opposite end of the scale are others who follow the campaigns through all the media and entertain a deep concern about their outcome.

Doubtless those who manifest high interest in campaigns also maintain a continuing interest in the flow of action between campaigns. Their focus of attention on the stream of events certainly has its consequences at the next election, not only in their votes but in their influence on the less attentive to whom they communicate their views. Beyond this audience with its focus of attention on a range of political events generally, there exists a complex population of special publics whose attentions center more or less continuously on specific governmental agencies or fields of policy. We lack surveys to define the dimensions of these publics, the objects of their attention, or the extent to which they overlap. Nevertheless, some types of such publics can be indicated. The most obvious attentive publics consist of those with a direct concern in particular policies or actions. That concern may rest, though not necessarily, on an economic self-interest. In any case, these special publics extend considerably beyond the leaders and spokesmen of formalized organizations. For example, farmers make up an attentive public; to be sure, not all farmers earn a place in that public, but the better-informed and more alert of them center attention on farm policy and its administrators, and have their views both solicited and taken into account by officialdom. Or consider the old folks. With both the leisure and the motivation of interest, many of them have a familiarity with policies and practices with respect to benefits for the aged as well as an eager eye for helpful new proposals. Congressmen are likely to hear from them.

Veterans constitute another attentive public whose attention seems to be especially capable of producing a feedback into the halls of government. Another attentive public keeps a continuing watch over policy toward education: teachers associations and PTA's are the more prominent spokesmen for this public, but many (sometimes, one suspects, too many) people consider themselves to be experts on education and do not hesitate to give confident vent to their assured views. One could identify for almost every governmental function comparable attentive publics varying both in size and in the intensity of their concern. Not all such publics are motivated by a direct self-interest. Consider the public attentive to foreign policy. Sprinkled over the land are societies, associations, circles, and study groups whose members give attention to international affairs, entertain visiting ambassadors, advise both the government and their fellow citizens on recondite issues of foreign policy, and look down generally on those clods among their fellow men who do not pay heed to the really important questions of this world.

Another type of attentive public, probably of special influence, consists of professional groups. Professions develop their own codes of ethics as well as their standards of practice. Members of the professions who deviate from the norms of their group may be cold-shouldered by their brethren and under some circumstances even deprived of the right to earn a livelihood by the practice of their trade. Members of the professions who occupy official positions carry on their functions under the scrutiny of the nongovernmental members of the profession and are thus subjected to the gaze of an attentive public equipped with standards of appraisal of some precision. Consider the relations between the bench and the bar. Judges may have the last word with attorneys who practice before them, but they are not unmindful of the expectations of the bar generally. Their work is open to the criticism of their professional peers. Engineers are equipped with greater technical precision than lawyers but with a less compelling system of professional ethics. Nevertheless, engineers in public posts, when they botch a job, incur the disapproval of the attentive public of engineers. Medical men in public posts are not beyond the pull of their professional norms even as they develop public policy on medical care. Among persons engaged in general administration professional norms seem to be in the process of development, and these group standards emerge from an attentive public which is largely, but not entirely, intragovernmental.[5]

This kind of differentiation between the attentive and nonatten-

[5] An interesting question relevant to the relation of attentive publics and government is the effect of the competition of different areas of public activity for attention. For example, some of the troubles of urban government may come from the fact that the more dramatic activities of the federal government divert to it the attention of those persons who might, under other conditions, constitute the watchful audience for the conductors of municipal affairs.

tive public is a commonplace of speculation about the place of the citizenry in a democracy. It is often accompanied by attempts to estimate the proportions of the public that share varying degrees and kinds of attentiveness, estimates often unsupported by the data of observation. But surely the highly attentive and active public of which we have been speaking constitutes normally no more than 10 to 15 per cent of the adult population, although at times of crisis far higher proportions may focus their attention on particular actions of government.

The reason, though, for the introduction here of the question of political differentiations among people was the hope that it might suggest popular characteristics conducive to, if not essential for, the existence of democratic practices. Obviously the highly attentive publics, as they monitor the actions of government and let their judgments be known, play a critical role in assuring a degree of responsiveness of government to nongovernmental opinion. For these publics to perform that function, though, an understanding and acceptance of their role must prevail among many people. The belief must exist that it is the public's business to engage in such activities of surveillance and criticism of government. Societies have existed and do exist in which there is a radically different role system; it may be improper for private persons to concern themselves with the business of officials. For lack of adequate comparative data, it is difficult to make vivid the significance of behaviors we regard as commonplace.[6] It is sufficient to note that there is nothing in human nature to assure that the attentive publics will act as they do. Development of understandings of roles and of appropriate behaviors among large numbers of people requires considerable time and a good deal of trial and error; this is one reason why democracies are not created by decree but, rather, evolve.[7]

Attentiveness with its correlative behaviors will wane unless it is associated with a belief that watchfulness and articulateness ultimately have some bearing on what government does or does not do. That belief can be engendered only if it has some foundation in reality. In turn, that reality depends upon the outlooks of those persons who constitute the highly activist element—the officials, the occupants of points of nongovernmental power, the persons who may next occupy points of private and public power. That is, each of the elements of the political system must have characteristics that make it possible for them

[6] Probably what all this boils down to is that in a democratic order the indignant private citizen regards it as proper to raise a popular commotion. When he does so, he acts with the expectation that he will not be jailed, but that he will be heard with courtesy and that his views may have some effect.

[7] One way in which the understandings and behaviors appropriate for national democracies may develop is through widespread participation in the relatively simple affairs of local government.

to fit together. Thus, democratic politicians defer to expressions of opinion. They listen with patience to the crackpot and even maintain their composure in the face of unfair and uninformed criticism—especially when it comes from an influential constituent. In all this there is a core of genuine concern about public opinion even though impracticable and intemperate expressions of opinion may be greeted with a ceremonial courtesy devoid of substantive deference. All these observations may amount to is the contention that if a democracy is to exist, the belief must be widespread that public opinion, at least in the long run, affects the course of public action. In a technical sense that belief may be a myth, an article of faith, yet its maintenance requires that it possess a degree of validity. It seems even that those clerics who most successfully perpetuate their myths are those who can turn up a miracle for their communicants now and then.

Political involvement is another type of differentiation among the citizenry that may provide clues to those characteristics of people which are congenial to the workings of a democracy. Variations in the degree of psychological "care" and "interest" in campaigns have served as a crude but useful index for many of our analyses. Almost by definition there must exist a fairly widespread psychological involvement in political affairs if a society is to operate by democratic procedures. Involvement probably carries with it at least a degree of attention to political affairs. Yet as we move from the most highly attentive and most highly involved sector of society, involvement may take on rather special dimensions. A substantial proportion of the citizenry may not belong to the highly attentive sector of the public of which we have spoken but may pay a routine heed to politics, may "care" about how elections come out, and may have an "interest" in campaigns. This involvement tends to carry with it some sense of sharing in the political process, some belief that participation makes a difference, some faith in the reality of the dogmas of democracy. Yet the activities associated with this sense of involvement are of a different order from those of the highly attentive publics whose members may be especially well informed and fairly closely in touch with political processes.

The psychological involvement of a substantial sector of the populace represents, of course, an acquired cultural characteristic. It takes some learning and habituation for a people to acquire a sense of participation, a sense of sharing in a political order.[8] Yet this sense of involvement may be of prime significance. It is basic for any popular

---

[8] Hence, one may express some pessimism about the outcome when a society that is attempting to move almost from the Stone Age to the Atomic Age overnight immediately franchises all its people. None of the more mature democracies acquired the habit patterns of democratic governance at so rapid a rate.

participation in governmental processes. Beyond this, the sense of involvement may be a fundamental means by which discontents and ambitions and desires are steered into constitutional channels. Earlier we identified even in the American system blocs of opinion of high intensity that were associated with low involvement, with a low sense of political efficacy, and with low levels of political participation. Groups of persons not involved in democratic processes but possessed of intense discontents may occur in any order. The practical question is how large such blocs of sentiment need to be and what circumstances need to exist for them to become destructive of the normal democratic processes.[9]

Loyalties, Orientations, Expectations. In the division of labor in a democratic order the highly attentive publics, a comparatively small sector of the whole, need to develop an understanding of their special role in the workings of the system. Other kinds of understandings and outlooks, which may be associated with considerably less in the way of overt participation, must permeate most of the population. To specify those understandings and outlooks requires that we grope beyond data that can be neatly set forth in demonstrative tables.

A basic prerequisite is that the population be pervaded by a national loyalty. Or, perhaps more accurately, that the population not consist of segments each with its own sense of separateness. The condition is best illustrated by synthetic nations consisting of blocs with their own history, language, culture, and memories of, if not aspirations for, a separate national identity. Students of public opinion long ago noted the incompatibility of these circumstances with democratic processes. That incompatibility comes not so much from the psychological characteristics of the mass of the people as from the fact that those characteristics invite exploitation by elements of leadership. Reckless leaders can disrupt the processes of government by diversionary appeals that weaken or destroy the foundations of national unity. Regimes with tight discipline in the ranks of political leadership—dictatorships, semidictatorships, monarchies—can restrain those who would activate the latent or not so latent divisive animosities of the mass of people. Democratic elites ordinarily have less capacity to restrain their irre-

[9] For a sense of political involvement to be widespread within the population, the conditions of life must be such that the struggle for subsistence does not monopolize the efforts of most men. In a random sample of the American population a few respondents are found whose struggle for the bare necessities of life so occupy their time and energy that their political involvement is at a zero level.

sponsible elements. Hence, mass attitudes that yield readily to divisive appeals create special difficulties for democratic orders.[1]

Closely related to this acceptance of the regime is what might be called a sense of the collectivity or of the community. Probably for the existence of an order deferential to public opinion the mass of people must share some sense of the legitimacy of the collectivity, in contrast with a situation in which large sectors of the population have no sense of a community of interest but center their attachments upon group, class, or even upon some smaller subnational entity. Perhaps a shadow of this sentiment of commonality was captured by the survey questions analyzed earlier about the influence on government of big business and trade unions. People of all occupational and income levels tended to think that both these interests should be kept in their place, that each should have its say but neither should have too much power. The view among the articulate seemed to be that some greater common interest should prevail. The same sense of the collectivity may manifest itself when people say that they have "something in common" with their fellow citizens of other social classes. It appears again on policy question after policy question as people of all sorts share attitudes on issues that might be expected, on a simple calculus of self-interest, to draw sharp class cleavages.

The bearing of this sense of community or of commonality upon democratic processes can best be surmised by estimates of what occurs when it is absent. If mass attachments are to subdivisions of the nation and if elements of the leadership both exploit those attachments and become anchored to them, the basis exists for national paralysis, since there is no freedom for a quest for common interest.[2] Sooner or later people, or some of them, may weary of the democratic game and resort to nondemocratic steps to attain their ends.

How people acquire this sense of political community is not clear. Doubtless, as with all basic social outlooks, the development of these attitudes is the product of a prolonged process. While all the apparatus

[1] Federal regimes may, to some extent, overcome the difficulties of cultural diversity but even so a price must be paid. Thus, the Canadian system, as it took form under the protection of the British Crown, developed a political elite with norms appropriate to the mixed culture of the Commonwealth. Yet the cost of unity includes both constitutional and customary restraints on governmental action.

[2] In the preceding chapters demonstrations recur of the incohesiveness of subnational interests on the American scene. Social researchers give great emphasis to manifestations of solidarity of subsectors of the nation, but the fact of greater import for the nature of the political system is the relative weakness of such solidarity. Group cohesiveness, always something less than complete, waxes and wanes as considerations transcending group concerns assume greater or lesser salience.

of civic education plays a part, the sense of community must also be in part a product of public policy; that is, without appropriate practices in leadership echelons to give it a basis in reality the sense of community may languish.

These observations resemble the proposition that a consensus needs to prevail for democracy to exist; yet they should not be taken as the equivalent of that proposition. Perhaps among the upper-activist stratum a consensus does need to prevail on the technical rules of the game by which the system operates. What kind of consensus, if any, extends throughout the population beyond a general acceptance of the regime remains problematic. In the main, the notion of consensus has sprung from the inventive minds of theorists untainted by acquaintance with mass attitudes. Knowledge of the relevant mass attitudes is slight, but such as it is it does not give much comfort to those who suppose that most people carry around in their heads the elements of democratic theory even in the most attenuated form. Nevertheless, the mass may possess outlooks that permit the regime to function as if a consensus prevailed, though precisely what those outlooks are is another question.

Another psychological characteristic of the mass of people that probably bears upon the workability of democratic processes relates to popular expectations. We may differentiate level and focus of expectations. Some optimum level of expectation may render a populace susceptible to the wiles of the high bidder whose unrealistic promises may sweep him to power and bring only disillusionment to the people. Governmental instability may develop as the bids are raised and one set of rulers replaces another. At the other pole, an extremely low level of expectation may be a reflection of mass cynicism and alienation from democratic processes. Doubtless, a good deal of experience and political indoctrination must go into the formation of mass attitudes characterized by the appropriate mixture of realism and optimism, of patience and eagerness. Good faith on the part of the leadership echelons is essential for this state of mind to exist in the mass of people; there also must be sprinkled through the population a substantial number of persons with sufficient understanding of the limitations and possibilities of politically induced social change to generate an optimum level of expectation in the mass.[3]

The question of the focus of mass expectations raises a problem

[3] The reader has doubtless observed that in these characterizations of mass prerequisites for democratic processes we have moved far away from hard data. The kinds of problems of which we speak have not been explored by the use of sample surveys which have centered mostly on more manageable problems such as the explanation of voting behavior. Yet it seems clear that appropriate use of survey procedures could bring far more understanding of mass political attitudes than we have.

different from that of their level. People's expectations may center on political or nonpolitical sources of fulfillment. Since one set of expectations tends to be fulfilled (except in a rapidly expanding economy) at the expense of others, it might plausibly be expected that a sustained high level of expectation associated with a focus upon government for fulfillment would tend to generate high stresses within a society.[4] On the contrary, with the focus of expectations diffused—upon the self, upon the family, upon business corporations, upon trade unions, and upon other nonpolitical institutions—the stakes of the political game might be expected to be more readily kept within those limits that make defeat tolerable. This is, in effect, a translation of the hackneyed question of whether democracy is feasible only under some variant of capitalism. When governmental decree controls almost completely the allocation of the social product as well as the assignment of resources, human and material, to productive tasks, the stakes of politics become enormous indeed. The easy answer to the problem is that mass tensions that could be stirred over such questions by competing factions of the political elite make it impossible for the struggle to be contained within the bounds of the easy give-and-take of democratic processes. The correct answer, though, may be that under the conditions described the development of democratic practices require the creation of rules of the game among the political activists together with expectations among the masses of the people appropriate to the special requirements of a socialist economy. Though such an evolution of behavioral patterns would have to surmount formidable obstacles, the possibility of its occurrence should not be excluded, for political man is a malleable creature.[5]

3 · Interaction and Discretion

Analytically it is useful to conceive of the structure of a democratic order as consisting of the political activists and the mass of people. Yet

[4] Democratic politicians, though, are skilled in the contrivance of formal actions that fulfill expectations at a verbal level but are cushioned in the reality of their application. Thus, though the American progressive income tax in form heavily taxes the rich, in fact the statutes are such that most men of wealth, with the advice of a competent tax lawyer, can greatly mitigate the impact of the high rates in the upper brackets. See Murray Edelman: "Symbols and Political Quiescence," *American Political Science Review*, LIV (1960), 695–704.

[5] The problem mentioned in the text is not hypothetical but a pressing reality in young and underdeveloped countries with democratic aspirations. If our broad analysis of the conditions requisite for the rise of democratic practice has validity, these nations, as they attempt to install such practices, work under the most unfavorable circumstances. Whatever evolves will probably diverge markedly from the patterns of the mature western democracies.

this differentiation becomes deceptive unless it is kept in mind that the democratic activists consist of people arranged along a spectrum of political participation and involvement, ranging from those in the highest posts of official leadership to the amateurs who become sufficiently interested to try to round up a few votes for their favorite in the presidential campaign. In the preceding discussion we sought to isolate some of the characteristics of both activists and mass that appear to be compatible with, if not essential for, the operation of a democratic order, thus setting up a static picture of two broad political strata. It is in the dynamics of the system, the interactions between these strata, that the import of public opinion in democratic orders becomes manifest. Between the activists and the mass there exists a system of communication and interplay so complex as to defy simple description; yet identification of a few major features of that system may aid in our construction of a general conception of democratic processes.

Opinion Dikes. In the interactions between democratic leadership echelons and the mass of people some insight comes from the conception of public opinion as a system of dikes which channel public action or which fix a range of discretion within which government may act or within which debate at official levels may proceed. This conception avoids the error of personifying "public opinion" as an entity that exercises initiative and in some way functions as an operating organism to translate its purposes into governmental action.

In one of their aspects the dikes of opinion have a substantive nature in that they define areas within which day-to-day debate about the course of specific action may occur. Some types of legislative proposals, given the content of general opinion, can scarcely expect to attract serious attention. They depart too far from the general understandings of what is proper. A scheme for public ownership of the automobile industry, for example, would probably be regarded as so far outside the area of legitimate public action that not even the industry would become greatly concerned. On the other hand, other types of questions arise within areas of what we have called permissive consensus. A widespread, if not a unanimous, sentiment prevails that supports action toward some general objective, such as the care of the ill or the mitigation of the economic hazards of the individual. Probably quite commonly mass opinion of a permissive character tends to develop in advance of governmental action in many areas of domestic policy. That opinion grows out of public discussion against the background of the modal aspirations and values of people generally. As it takes shape, the time becomes ripe for action that will be generally acceptable or may even arouse popular acclaim for its authors.

The qualities of this substantive opinion doubtless differ widely from issue to issue and from person to person. On some issues opinion may be oriented favorably toward broadly defined objectives; on others, perhaps extremely few, opinion may become focused on sharply defined proposals. On any issue the more alert and informed persons may have fairly well-formed opinions about sharply defined issues; others may have broad preferences—for example, something ought to be done for the farmers but not too much.

Opinion dikes may bear on the manner as well as on the substance of action. And it may be that in a democratic order those opinions that control or guide the mode of action may be of special importance as substantive action moves into areas where it encounters formidable opposition. Action taken in a seemingly fair and equitable manner may be acceptable, but arbitrary action to the same effect may be regarded as intolerable. The procedural content of American public opinion has been little explored. The division of opinion and the spontaneous comment on the proposition that government employees accused of communism ought to be fired even though the charge is not proved suggest that notions of fair play may be widely held within the population. Doubtless other procedural notions have wide popular acceptance that could be demonstrated by survey methods.

The idea of public opinion as forming a system of dikes which channel action yields a different conception of the place of public opinion than does the notion of a government by public opinion as one in which by some mysterious means a referendum occurs on every major issue. In the former conception the articulation between government and opinion is relatively loose. Parallelism between action and opinion tends not to be precise in matters of detail; it prevails rather with respect to broad purpose. And in the correlation of purpose and action time lags may occur between the crystallization of a sense of mass purpose and its fulfillment in public action. Yet in the long run majority purpose and public action tend to be brought into harmony.

Modifications of the Opinion Context. The content of mass opinion changes through time; it is perhaps in such alterations that the power of mass opinion is made manifest. Though changes in opinion content occur continuously, at some moments combinations of events, imaginative leadership, and action induce relatively rapid and marked changes in popular preferences and expectations. These episodes may bring new opinion orientations, which in turn become rather rigid elements of the pattern of popular attitudes.

The movement of opinions and the expectations that accompanied the fulfillment of the program of the New Deal illustrate well the process of change and its consequences for governmental action. A spirited leadership with programs of action deviating markedly from past practice won approval and generated a new set of popular expectations about governmental action. The "power" of public opinion manifested itself in a negative way. Those candidates and leaders tainted with the suspicion that they wanted to turn the clock back had hard sledding for years. Until they could make a show of acceptance of changes they could not capture control of the government. Thus, through elections opinion ratified past reforms by its rejection of those who appeared to be at odds with the new balance of public sentiment.

Similarly, in the area of foreign policy World War II brought with it a reorientation of the context of public opinion, which became more supportive of involvement in international politics. Probably the body of popular opinion in this area has a less solid base and a less constricting effect upon public action than does opinion on domestic welfare policy. The radically changed position of the United States in world affairs creates new problems not only for a government that rests on public opinion, but also for those who seek to inform and to lead that opinion. The conduct of domestic debates over foreign policy carries hazards for external policy. On the other hand, repression of debate results in a failure to inform the people of incompetence in the conduct of foreign affairs.[6]

Mass opinions, aspirations, and expectations change as the political system moves through time. It is in this moving situation that the power of mass opinion makes itself manifest in its interactions with democratic leadership—chiefly in its rejection of leadership factions whose outlook lags notably behind or strikes out markedly ahead of the moving average of opinion. Those who wish to turn the clock back, to reverse decisions already rooted in popular acceptance, gradually learn their lesson as they meet rebuff after rebuff. Those too far ahead of opinion, though they may contribute to the forces impelling alteration of the opinion context, likewise find themselves rejected. Deviants from

[6] The dilemma which the circumstances of a garrison state creates for democracies leads some American scholars to advocate fundamental reconstruction of the structure of government. The fixed term of the president makes it impossible for a bumbling administration to be thrown out of power until the date for the next presidential election rolls around. The limitations on debate and discussion imposed by the necessities of external unity and by diplomatic secrecy make it difficult adequately to inform the electorate. The remedy urged by some scholars is some variant of the cabinet system by which Congress, a body better informed than the electorate, could cast out an incompetent administration.

dominant opinion, though, play a critical role in the preservation of the vitality of a democratic order as they urge alterations and modifications better to achieve the aspirations of men. Hence the fundamental significance of freedom of speech and agitation. Those activists closest to the core of power may hesitate to assume the risks of political entrepreneurship, but others, with less to lose, may by their efforts gradually make the endeavor that is not "practical politics" today feasible tomorrow.

Opinion Context and Governmental Discretion. This discussion of the anchorage of leadership to public opinion should not be taken to mean that wide ranges of discretion do not exist within which a creative role may be played by popular leadership. Glum political philosophers meditate in their melancholy fashion about how the pursuit of the good of the Republic is frustrated as the mass pulls superior men down to its own mean and grasping material level. The long-run good of the polity, the argument goes, must be neglected as leadership is compelled to cater to the greed and to the ignorance of the masses. Measures that obviously promote the greater public good cannot be undertaken because of mass opposition and misunderstanding.

That at times mass opinion may handicap desirable action cannot be denied. Yet as one puzzles over the nature of interactions between government and mass opinion and ponders such empirical data as can be assembled on the matter, he can arrive only at the conclusion that a wide range of discretion exists for whatever wisdom leadership echelons can muster in the public service. The generality of public preferences, the low intensity of the opinions of many people, the low level of political animosities of substantial sectors of the public, the tortuousness of the process of translation of disapproval of specific policies into electoral reprisal, and many other factors point to the existence of a wide latitude for the exercise of creative leadership. While the winning of consent for innovation may require skill in popular exposition and in political technique, those political leaders who shirk the task of popular education are misfits who do not understand the responsibilities of their jobs. And those leaders who act as if they thought the people to be fools responsive only to the meanest appeals deserve only scorn.

The Basic Weapon of Public Opinion. These concluding observations about the interaction of the activists and the mass take on an ethereal tenor, and they should be tied to their referent in institutional reality, which is the party system. In the give-and-take between the leadership echelons, with their intense policy drives and attachments, and the mass of people, the ultimate weapon of public opinion is the minority party. The effect of opinion on the grand course of public opinion depends on the existence of a crowd of outs who can be elevated to power—and the capacity to boot the ins from office. The mechanism is cumbersome and produces no minute fit of public preference and public policy. At times the remedy to the public becomes effective only over the long run, for the outs may offer no alternative congruent with the dissatisfactions against the ins. Yet the party system introduces the possibility of a fluidity in the political order to offset the policy myopia of governments long secure in their position. Parodoxically the party system may also introduce a saving degree of stability into orders dependent upon public opinion. It creates among many people loyalties that transcend and neutralize the vagaries of the opinion of the moment. It introduces traditional and stable policy outlooks with strength but susceptible of modification as they are abraded by their moving contact with the future. It provides ways and means of recruitment of leadership and for its indoctrination with the basic values and working habits of the political order.

Inevitability of the Decay of Democracies? Our exposition of the interactions between leadership and mass opinion enables us better to understand the argument that democracies, by their inner logic, tend toward decay. That in the long sweep of time all regimes tend toward decay is a proposition at least not negated by the annals of recorded history. Yet the contention, advanced by respectable authorities, is that democracies possess within themselves defects that inevitably lead to their decay in a manner peculiar to democracies.

The fatal weakness of modern mass democracies, so the argument goes, rests in the subjection of government to a public opinion whose mandates are certain to be destructive of the order. Implicit in that proposition is the assumption that mass opinion in the long run tends toward positions incompatible with the demands of the health of the order and that mass opinion tends to pull governments into harmony with those positions. Thus, we have the picture of a mass opinion animated by greed and by a disregard for the rights of man. Politicians must, the conclusion is, sooner or later adopt that view and in the process ultimately create a dictatorship of a majority dedicated to the reduction of all men to a drab equality, an action to be maintained only by a destruction of freedom. Or the argument is that governments accountable to democratic masses invariably tend to take the easy route, to dodge the hard decisions, to avoid at moments of crisis demands for the sacrifices by the populace necessary for the maintenance of the system. Governments, by their subjection to mass opinion, lose decisiveness and are bereft of the will to act, a condition creative of special dangers for the democracy that exists in a hostile international environment. All these consequences flow inevitably from the interaction between leadership and mass opinion as cliques of leaders seek power and, in so doing, are compelled to appeal to mass opinions that contain within themselves the seeds of national destruction. By a kind of Gresham's law, those leadership cliques with a wisdom greater than that of mass opinion either perish or embrace the follies of the mass.[7]

What can we say about this melancholy hypothesis? For a certainty, there are democracies and democracies. Perhaps in some situations the hypothesis fits the facts, but our analyses of the American scene caution us against easy acceptance of so glib a theory of the dynamics of democratic self-destruction. We have pictured public opinion as the product of an interaction between political influentials and the mass of the people, an interaction that may produce alterations in mass opinion. In the course of time that interaction may also alter the modal position of the influentials as a novel doctrine asserted by one sector of the influentials gains acceptance among the masses. Mass opinion is not self-generating; in the main, it is a response to the cues, the proposals, and the visions propagated by the political activists.

If this conception of the formation of opinion has validity, democracies decay, if they do, not because of the cupidity of the masses, but because of the stupidity and self-seeking of leadership echelons. Politicians often make of the public a scapegoat for their own shortcomings; their actions, they say, are a necessity for survival given the state of public opinion. Yet that opinion itself results from the preachings of the influentials, of this generation and of several past generations.

Moreover, even if mass opinion assumes forms incompatible with the national interest, the articulation between government and mass opinion is so loose that politicians enjoy a considerable range of discretion within which to exercise prudence and good sense. Our explorations into the nature and form of mass opinion leave no doubt that its directives tend toward generality rather than specificity. Even on broad issues on which opinion becomes fairly well crystallized room may remain for choice among a variety of specific actions. Furthermore, translation of opinion into actions of electoral punishment or reward is a tortuous and uncertain procedure. The predictability of

[7] An argument to the effect of this paragraph but in a far more sophisticated form is put in Walter Lippmann: *The Public Philosophy* (Boston: Little, Brown; 1955), especially ch. 3–5. See the perceptive comment on Lippmann's analysis in David B. Truman: "The American System in Crisis," *Political Science Quarterly*, LXXIV (1959), 481–97.

electoral response to a particular action remains so uncertain that the avoidance of a sensible decision because it will lose votes is usually the work of a man whose anxieties outweigh his capacities of prediction.

The argument amounts essentially to the position that the masses do not corrupt themselves; if they are corrupt, they have been corrupted. If this hypothesis has a substantial strain of validity, the critical element for the health of a democratic order consists in the beliefs, standards, and competence of those who constitute the influentials, the opinion-leaders, the political activists in the order. That group, as has been made plain, refuses to define itself with great clarity in the American system; yet analysis after analysis points to its existence. If a democracy tends toward indecision, decay, and disaster, the responsibility rests here, not in the mass of the people.[8]

[8] This analysis and its implications should be pondered well by those young gentlemen in whose education the Republic has invested considerable sums.

APPENDIXES

THROUGHOUT the text several sets of issue questions put in opinion surveys have been relied upon heavily; indices constructed from responses to survey questions have also frequently been used. For convenience the texts of the issue propositions are presented at this point, along with explanations of the construction of the principal indices employed.

1 · Issue Questions in the 1956 Campaign Survey

The chief indicators of opinions employed in this book consist of responses of a national sample to a series of issue propositions put by the Survey Research Center in its 1956 pre-election interviews with the respondents in a national sample. The part of the interview schedule containing these propositions was as follows:

> Around election time people talk about different things that our government in Washington is doing or should be doing. Now I would like to talk to you about some of the things that our government *might* do. Of course different things are important to different people, so we don't expect everyone to have an opinion about all of these.
>
> 12. I would like you to look at this card as I read each question and tell me how you feel about the question. If you don't have an opinion, just tell me that; if you do have an opinion, choose one of the other answers.

12a. "The government ought to cut taxes even if it means putting off some important things that need to be done."

Now, would you say you have an opinion on this or not?

Yes   No

(IF "NO," GO ON TO Q. 12b)

(IF "YES"): Do you agree that the government *should* do this or do you think the government should *not* do it?

1. Agree strongly; government definitely should
2. Agree but not very strongly
3. Not sure; it depends
4. Disagree but not very strongly
5. Disagree strongly; government definitely should not
6. Don't know

(On the schedule this list of alternatives was repeated for each issue proposition.)

12b. "The government in Washington ought to see to it that everybody who wants to work can find a job."

12c. "This country would be better off if we just stayed home and did not concern ourselves with problems in other parts of the world."

12d. "The government ought to help people get doctors and hospital care at low cost."

12e. "The United States should give economic help to the poorer countries of the world even if they can't pay for it."

12f. "If Negroes *are not* getting fair treatment in jobs and housing, the government in Washington should see to it that they do."

12g. The government ought to see to it that big business corporations don't have much say about how the government is run."

12h. "The best way for this country to deal with Russia and Communist China is to act just as tough as they do."

12i. "If cities and towns around the country need help to build more schools, the government in Washington ought to give them the money they need."

12j. "The United States should keep soldiers overseas where they can help countries that are against communism."

12k. "The government should leave things like electric power and housing for private businessmen to handle."

12l. "The government ought to see to it that labor unions don't have much say about how the government is run."

12m. "The United States should be willing to go more than half-way in being friendly with the other countries of the world."

12n. "The government ought to fire any government worker who is accused of being a communist even though they can't prove it."

12o. "The United States should give help to foreign countries even if they are not as much against communism as we are."

12p. "The government in Washington should stay out of the question of whether white and colored children go to the same school."

2 · Scales on Liberalism and on Internationalism

The responses on some of the policy propositions included in the 1956 Survey Research Center survey took such a form that the respondents could be ranked on two Guttman scales. One of these scales was constructed from responses to propositions on domestic issues and is usually referred to in the text as a "liberalism" scale. The items constituting the scale were the following:

"If cities and towns around the country need help to build more schools, the government in Washington ought to give them the money they need."

"If Negroes *are not* getting fair treatment in jobs and housing, the government in Washington should see to it that they do."

"The government in Washington ought to see to it that everybody who wants to work can find a job."

"The government ought to help people get doctors and hospital care at low cost."

"The government should leave things like electric power and housing for private businessmen to handle."

Persons who fall in the scale type at the liberal end would take the position currently regarded as "liberal" on each of the five items. At the opposite end of the scale those persons are placed who express the "conservative" position on each of the five items. It should not be supposed that the scale ranks persons along an abstract liberal-conservative continuum; yet it certainly differentiates those persons disposed to take the "liberal" position on this particular set of questions from those most dedicated to the "conservative" position.

The second scale consisted of four items relating to foreign policy and is usually referred to in the text as a measure of "internationalism." The items composing this scale were as follows:

> "This country would be better off if we just stayed home and did not concern ourselves with problems in other parts of the world."

> "The United States should give economic help to the poorer countries of the world even if they can't pay for it."

> "The United States should keep soldiers overseas where they can help countries that are against communism."

> "The United States should give help to foreign countries even if they are not as much against communism as we are."

Placement of persons along the scale composed of these items permits a rough differentiation according to willingness to tolerate or support involvement abroad on the kinds of matters covered by the scale items. Persons who take the "internationalist" position on all the items differ in outlook from those who take the contrary view.

Construction of the scales and the assignment of respondents to positions on the scales was the work of Warren E. Miller, of the Survey Research Center, a redoubtable technician in these matters. For a discussion of the scales, see Angus Campbell *et al.: The American Voter* (New York: Wiley, 1960), pp. 194–8.

3 · 1952 Policy Questions

Fairly frequent use has been made of responses to several issue questions asked by the Survey Research Center of a national sample in its study of the 1952 presidential campaign. The text of the questions most often used is as follows:

> Now, I want to ask you how you feel about some of the issues that people are talking about these days. For example—

> 21. Some people think the national government should do more in trying to deal with such problems as unemployment, education, housing, and so on. Others think that the government is already doing too much. On the whole, would you say that what the government has done has been about right, too much, or not enough?

23. Have you heard anything about the Taft-Hartley Law?
23a. (If has heard) How do you feel about it? Do you think it's all right as it is, do you think it should be changed in any way, or don't you have any feelings about it?
23b. (1) (If should be changed) Do you think the law should be changed just a little, changed quite a bit, or do you think it should be *completely* repealed? (How is that?)

24. Some people think that since the end of the last world war this country has gone too far in concerning itself with problems in other parts of the world. How do you feel about this?

25. Some people feel that it was our government's fault that China went Communist, others say there was nothing that we could do to stop it. How do you feel about this?

26. Do you think we did the right thing in getting into the fighting in Korea two years ago, or should we have stayed out?

For the complete schedule used in the 1952 SRC campaign study, see Angus Campbell, Gerald Gurin, and Warren E. Miller: *The Voter Decides* (Evanston: Row, Peterson; 1954), pp. 215–27.

4 · Miscellaneous Indexes

Uses of the index of issue familiarity, an index of political involvement, an index of political participation, and a measure of the sense of political efficacy recur in the text. The questions on which these indices were based and the manner of their construction are indicated below.

Index of Issue Familiarity. Each respondent in the Survey Research Center's 1956 presidential election survey was placed on an index of issue familiarity. The index ranked persons according to their willingness to express an opinion on the sixteen issue propositions, reproduced in Appendix I, and according to their willingness to express a judgment on government performance with respect to the issues. For each of the sixteen issue propositions the interview schedule also included a question such as the following:

> On the question of the government seeing to it that everybody who wants to work can find a job, is the government going too far, doing less than it should, or doing just about right?

> Haven't heard what the government is doing
> Definitely too far
> A little too far

About right
A little less than it should
A lot less than it should
Don't know

This question was asked only of those who had earlier in the interview expressed an opinion on the related issue proposition. A person who expressed an opinion on the issue proposition and also had a judgment on government performance with respect to the issue was regarded as "familiar" with the question. The data permitted the placement of individuals on an index from 0 to 16, depending upon the number of issues with which they showed familiarity as defined. In the tables in this book the points on the index were consolidated into four categories: those familiar with fourteen to sixteen issues; those familiar with eleven to thirteen issues; those familiar with eight to ten issues; and those familiar with seven issues or less. These categories constituted, in the order listed, the following percentages of the total sample: 31, 25, 19, and 25.

Political Involvement. The measure of political involvement is in form a measure of concern about the particular presidential campaign but probably also taps a more general psychological concern about politics. It rests on responses to two questions. Respondents were asked in the early warm-up phase of the pre-election interview: "Generally speaking, would you say that you personally care a great deal which party wins the presidential election this fall or that you don't care very much which party wins?" Replies to this question were coded on a five-point scale from least to most "care" about the election outcome. Another question was: "Some people don't pay much attention to the political campaigns. How about you, would you say that you have been very much interested, somewhat interested, or not much interested in following the political campaigns so far this year?" By combination of the responses to these two questions individuals were ranked on an index of political involvement.

Participation Index. The responses to a series of post-election inquiries in the 1952 and 1956 Survey Research Center surveys form the basis for an index of political participation which has been frequently used throughout the text. Respondents were asked whether they had voted and also were asked the following questions:

> I have a list of some of the things that people do that help a party or a candidate win an election. I wonder if you could tell

me whether you did any of these things during the last election campaign.

17a. Did you talk to any people and try to show them why they should vote for one of the parties or candidates?

17b. Did you give any money or buy tickets or anything to help the campaign for one of the parties or candidates?

17c. Did you go to any political meetings, rallies, dinners, or things like that?

17d. Did you do any other work for one of the parties or candidates?

17e. Do you belong to any political club or organization?

17f. Did you wear a campaign button or put a campaign sticker on your car?

In the construction of the index of participation those persons who voted and participated in at least one of the additional ways touched by this series of questions were ranked high; another category consisted of those persons who only voted; another small class consisted of persons who had failed to vote but participated in at least one of the ways indicated by the above list of questions; the low category consisted of persons who neither voted nor participated in any other way in the campaign. In some of the tables in the text the small class of persons who failed to vote but participated in other ways is excluded and the other categories are designated as high, medium, and low participators.

Political Efficacy. A rough measure of variations in the strength of the sense of political efficacy among respondents was constructed from expressions of agreement or disagreement with the following statements.

I don't think public officials care much what people like me think.

The way people vote is the main thing that decides how things are run in this country.

Voting is the only way people like me can have any say about how the government runs things.

People like me don't have any say about what the government does.

Sometimes politics and government seems so complicated that a person like me can't really understand what's going on.

Agreement with the second item and disagreement with the first, third, fourth, and fifth items were treated as efficacious responses. The items were interspersed in the schedule with other statements included for other purposes. The responses were grouped into five types. Variations in the sense of political efficacy, so measured, had a positive relationship with variations in political participation. For a detailed discussion of the concept of the sense of political efficacy, see Angus Campbell, Gerald Gurin, Warren E. Miller: *The Voter Decides* (Evanston: Row, Peterson; 1954), pp. 187–94.

The second of the list of items above was not used in the 1956 survey. In the 1952 analysis the efficacy items formed a Guttman scale; in the 1956 analysis the responses to the items were combined into a simple cumulative index to rank the respondents. Hence the 1952 and 1956 efficacy measures are not exactly comparable.

INDEX

activists, *see* political activists

Adler, K. P., 365

advertisers: in electronic media, 386; influence on press, 381

advertising agencies, and program content, 386

age, and opinion on welfare policy, 255

Air Force, public relations activities, 417

Alexander, A., 317n

Allard, Winston, 493n

Allport, F. H., 8n, 28n, 172n, 295

Almond, Gabriel, 16, 44, 46, 47, 106n, 395n

Alpert, Harry, 422n

America First Committee, 35

American Broadcasting Company, affiliated stations, 375n

American Farm Bureau Federation, 430, 504, 524

American Institute of Public Opinion: poll on AAA, 450; admis-

American Institute (*continued*) sion of Hawaii to statehood, 32; aliens on relief, 43n; America's postwar role, 106; Bricker amendment, 82, 84; CIO, 521n; conscription, 422; conservatism, 343n; "country liked best," 43n; court reorganization, 279; daylight saving, 115; Dean Acheson, 246; entry into World War I, 277; gasoline rationing, 426; group interests of parties, 434; holidays, 115; "influence," 45n; knowledge of House of Representatives, 494–5; labor vote, 523; League of Nations, 278; lotteries, 104n; meaning of liberal, 281n; military conscription, 277; old-age pensions, 30; presidential vote in union households, 523; prohibition, 115; public expenditures, 429–30; religion, 294n;

A NOTE ON THE TYPE

THE TEXT of this book was set on the Linotype in JANSON, a re-cutting made direct from the type cast from matrices long thought to have been made by Anton Janson, a Dutchman who was a practising type-founder in Leipzig during the years 1668–1687. However, it has been conclusively demonstrated that these types are actually the work of Nicholas Kis (1650–1702) a Hungarian who learned his trade most probably from the master Dutch type-founder Dirk Voskens. The type is an excellent example of the influential and sturdy Dutch types that prevailed in England prior to the development by William Caslon of his own incomparable designs, which he evolved from these Dutch faces. The Dutch in their turn had been influenced by Claude Garamond in France. The general tone of Janson, however, is darker than Garamond and has a sturdiness and substance quite different from its predecessors.

Composed, printed, and bound by
Kingsport Press, Inc., Kingsport, Tennessee.
Paper manufactured by
S. D. Warren Co., Boston.
Typography and binding design by
VINCENT TORRE